# Barcelona

**timeout.com/barcelona**

**Published by Time Out Guides Ltd,** a wholly owned subsidiary of Time Out Group Ltd.
Time Out and the Time Out logo are trademarks of Time Out Group Ltd.


Previous editions 1996, 1998, 2000, 2001, 2002, 2003, 2004, 2005, 2006.

10 9 8 7 6 5 4 3 2 1

**This edition first published in Great Britain in 2007 by Ebury Publishing**
Ebury Publishing is a division of The Random House Group Ltd,
20 Vauxhall Bridge Road, London SW1V 2SA

**Random House Australia Pty Limited** 20 Alfred Street, Milsons Point, Sydney, New South Wales 2061, Australia
**Random House New Zealand Limited** 18 Poland Road, Glenfield, Auckland 10, New Zealand
**Random House South Africa (Pty) Limited** Isle of Houghton, Corner Boundary Road & Carse O'Gowrie, Houghton 2198, South Africa

Random House UK Limited Reg. No. 954009

**Distributed in USA by Publishers Group West**
1700 Fourth Street, Berkeley, California 94710

**Distributed in Canada by Publishers Group Canada**
250A Carlton Street, Toronto, Ontario M5A 2L1

For further distribution details, see www.timeout.com

ISBN 10: 1-84670-004-3
ISBN 13: 9781846700040

A CIP catalogue record for this book is available from the British Library

Colour reprographics by Wyndeham Icon, 3 & 4 Maverton Road, London E3 2JE

Printed and bound in Germany by Appl

Papers used by Ebury Publishing are natural, recyclable products made from wood grown in sustainable forests

**Palau de la Música Catalana**. *See p101.*

**Time Out Guides Limited**
**Universal House**
**251 Tottenham Court Road**
**London W1T 7AB**
**Tel + 44 (0)20 7813 3000**
**Fax + 44 (0)20 7813 6001**
**Email guides@timeout.com**
**www.timeout.com**

## Editorial

**Editor (Barcelona)** Sally Davies
**Editor (London)** Claire Boobbyer
**Listings Editors** Alex Phillips, Roberto Rama, Dylan Simanowitz
**Proofreader** Sylvia Tombesi-Walton
**Indexer** Sam Le Quesne

**Editorial/Managing Director** Peter Fiennes
**Series Editor** Ruth Jarvis
**Deputy Series Editor** Lesley McCave
**Financial Director** Gareth Garner
**Guides Co-ordinator** Holly Pick
**Accountant** Kemi Olufuwa

## Design

**Art Director** Scott Moore
**Art Editor** Pinelope Kourmouzoglou
**Senior Designer** Josephine Spencer
**Graphic Designer** Henry Elphick
**Digital Imaging** Simon Foster
**Ad Make-up** Jenni Prichard

## Picture Desk

**Picture Editor** Jael Marschner
**Deputy Picture Editor** Tracey Kerrigan
**Picture Researcher** Helen McFarland

## Advertising

**Sales Director** Mark Phillips
**International Sales Manager** Ross Canadé
**International Sales Executive** Simon Davies
**Advertising Sales** (Barcelona) Creative Media Group
**Advertising Assistant** Kate Staddon

## Marketing

**Group Marketing Director** John Luck
**Marketing Manager** Yvonne Poon
**Marketing & Publicity Manager, US** Rosella Albanese

## Production

**Group Production Director** Mark Lamond
**Production Manager** Brendan McKeown
**Production Coordinator** Caroline Bradford

## Time Out Group

**Chairman** Tony Elliott
**Financial Director** Richard Waterlow
**TO Magazine Ltd MD** David Pepper
**Group General Manager/Director** Nichola Coulthard
**Managing Director, Time Out International** Cathy Runciman
**TO Communications Ltd MD** David Pepper
**Group Art Director** John Oakey
**Group IT Director** Simon Chappell

## Contributors

**Introduction** Claire Boobbyer. **In the Detail series** Sally Davies. **History** Nick Rider, Sally Davies (*Living the lingua franca* Stephen Burgen). **Barcelona Today** William Truini (*Fine print* Sally Davies). **Architecture** Nick Rider, Sally Davies (*21st-century pride* Stephen Burgen). **Separated But Not Divorced** Stephen Burgen (*Flying the flag* Nadia Feddo). **Where to Stay** Annie Bennett (*Spa sensation* Tara Stevens). **Sightseeing** Sally Davies, Nadia Feddo, Nick Mead, John O'Donovan (*Catalan Columbus conundrum* Jonathan Bennett; *Chronicle of a life foretold* Michael Kessler). **Restaurants** Sally Davies. **Cafés, Tapas & Bars** Sally Davies; *additional reviews* Kirsten Foster. **Shops & Services** Kirsten Foster. **Festivals & Events** Nadia Feddo (*Rave rival* Patrick Welch). **Children** Nadia Feddo. **Film** Jonathan Bennett (*Barcelona woos Bollywood* Nadia Feddo). **Galleries** Alex Phillips. **Gay & Lesbian** Dylan Simanowitz. **Music & Nightlife** Michael Kessler, Patrick Welch (*Midweek mayhem* Sally Davies). **Performing Arts** *Classical Music & Opera* Dani Campi (*Classical Catalans* Nadia Feddo); *Theatre & Dance* Stephen Burgen. **Sport & Fitness** Dani Campi (*Champion of the World* Michael Kessler). **Trips Out of Town** Sally Davies, Tara Stevens (*Chick flit* Alex Johnson). **Directory** Alex Phillips (*Lost and found* William Truini).

**Maps** john@jsgraphics.co.uk.

**Photography by** Natalie Pecht, except: page 12 Archivo Iconografico,S.A./Corbis; pages 16, 46, 48 Godofoto; page 19 Aisa; page 22 Palacio del Senado, Madrid, Spain, Index/The Bridgeman Art Library; page 26 STF/AFP/Getty Images; pages 59, 115, 157, 158, 165 Olivia Rutherford; page 262 Miquel Bargalló – Tony Coll; page 266 AFP/Getty Images; page 270 Rex Features; page 294 Superstock.

The following images were provided by the featured establishments/artists: pages 217, 240, 281.

**The Editors would like to thank** Edoardo Albert, Lluis Bosch, Lorena Martínez, John O'Donovan, Montse Planas, Montse Pozo, Gustavo Sânchez, Alena Widows, Jorge Berdiñas, David Rodríguez and Lesley McCave.

# Contents

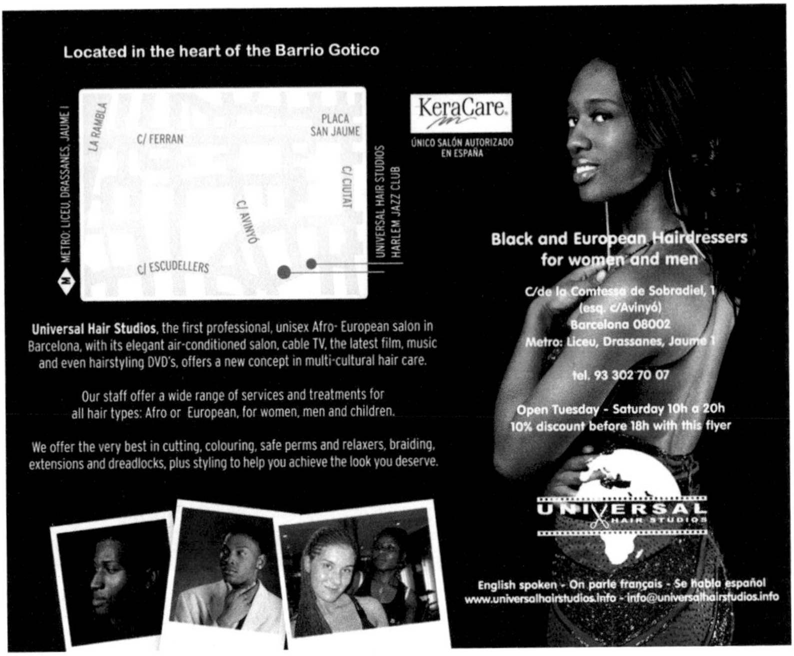
Located in the heart of the Barrio Gotico
METRO: LICEU, DRASSANES, JAUME I
LA RAMBLA
C/ FERRAN
PLACA SAN JAUME
C/ CIUTAT
C/ AVINYÓ
C/ ESCUDELLERS
UNIVERSAL HAIR STUDIOS
HARLEM JAZZ CLUB
KeraCare
ÚNICO SALÓN AUTORIZADO EN ESPAÑA
Universal Hair Studios, the first professional, unisex Afro- European salon in Barcelona, with its elegant air-conditioned salon, cable TV, the latest film, music and even hairstyling DVD's, offers a new concept in multi-cultural hair care.
Our staff offer a wide range of services and treatments for all hair types: Afro or European, for women, men and children.
We offer the very best in cutting, colouring, safe perms and relaxers, braiding, extensions and dreadlocks, plus styling to help you achieve the look you deserve.
Black and European Hairdressers for women and men
C/de la Comtessa de Sobradiel, 1
(esq. c/Avinyó)
Barcelona 08002
Metro: Liceu, Drassanes, Jaume 1
tel. 93 302 70 07
Open Tuesday - Saturday 10h a 20h
10% discount before 18h with this flyer
UNIVERSAL HAIR STUDIOS
English spoken - On parle français - Se habla español
www.universalhairstudios.info - info@universalhairstudios.info

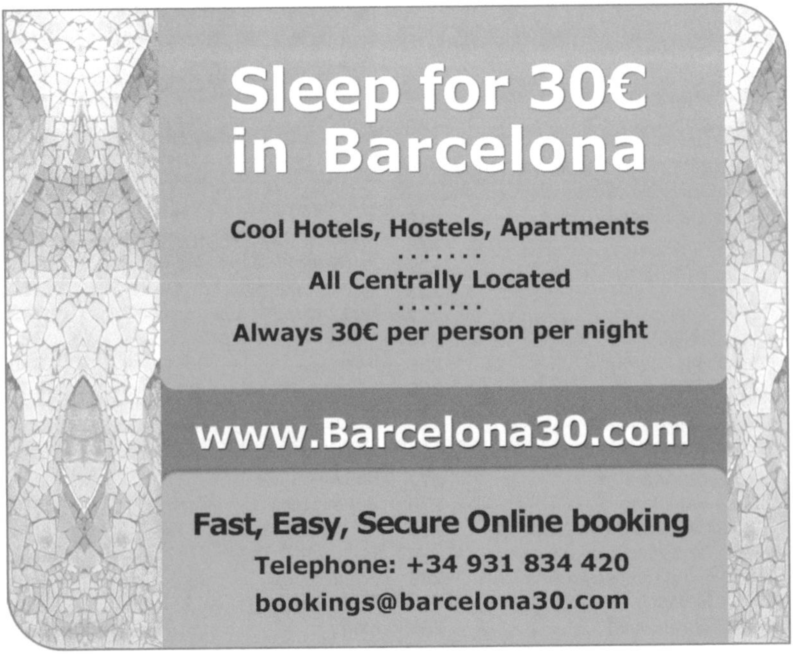
Sleep for 30€ in Barcelona
Cool Hotels, Hostels, Apartments
All Centrally Located
Always 30€ per person per night
www.Barcelona30.com
Fast, Easy, Secure Online booking
Telephone: +34 931 834 420
bookings@barcelona30.com

# Introduction



Barcelona has something that, she knows, no other city has got. She's beautiful, sassy, cultured, suntanned and proud. She's decorated with quirky and handsome buildings; her streets are stuffed full of foraged food; she teases with her fine shops and is playful with her annual calendar of festivities. And this stylish city, displaying magnificently towards the Mediterranean, knows how to keep on top of her game.

Barcelona flirts with those that will keep her pretty. She knows that the Gothic structures and the Modernista architectural flights of fantasy attract visitors to spend nine million euro a day on tourism, but she may wonder how to attract visitors back or how to lure those drawn by the competition elsewhere in Europe.

Thus, in a nod to the success of French president Mitterrand's *grands projets* in Paris, the city woos international architects who fall for her charms and can't wait to adorn her with bricks and mortar, glass and water, in stunning style.

In the last few years Barcelona has been bejewelled and fêted by her faithful countryman Ricardo Bofill, who has designed the Hotel Vela, a sail-shaped luxury hotel; Pere Puig, who is building a luxury ten-storey hotel, and Josep Mias who is behind a new market in the Barceloneta area with a wavy, sea-green roof fitted with state-of-the-art solar panels. Lord Richard Rogers might well have won the 2007 Stirling Prize for Architecture with his space-age Madrid Barajas airport terminal, but he knows Barcelona is the queen of urban revival. His partnership is involved in a facelift of the Las Arenas bullring in Montjuïc that will see it emerge as a futuristic shopping and leisure centre this year. Not to be outdone, American Frank Gehry and Brit Zaha Hadid are queueing up to make their mark. Gehry's second Barcelona project is the redevelopment of a derelict neighbourhood, La Sagrera, for the arrival of the high-speed Madrid–Barcelona–France train link, which could see five twisting towers soar out of the cityscape; Hadid will build a new university campus.

But there is also appeal in recycling. As well as the bullring project, several old structures have been converted into hotels – a restored palace, a tobacco company headquarters, a newspaper office and a former hospital. All now house beds and books, baths and bars.

Barcelona is appreciative of small decoration too. In this edition of the guide, the 'In the detail' series highlights the micro – a letterbox, an orphans' turnstile, a mural. It was inspired by an idea of the Ajuntament, *El Periódico* newspaper and the municipal TV channel. They asked *barcelonins* to choose their favourite features of the city and post their suggestions in five special letterboxes around town; the favourites were featured in a book, *Petits Paisatges de Barcelona*. It is this spirit of pride, commonality and acknowledgement of importance that has embedded the city with more than 1,000 years of attitude. And it is thanks to this attitude that Barcelona has taken great strides in 2006 in the political tug of war it plays as it tries to win absolute Catalan nationhood status from the taurine Spanish government.

## ABOUT TIME OUT CITY GUIDES

This is the tenth edition of *Time Out Barcelona*, one of an expanding series of Time Out guides produced by the people behind the successful listings magazines in London, New York, Chicago, Mumbai and Dubai. Our guides are all written by resident experts who have striven to provide you with all the most up-to-date information you'll need to explore the city or read up on its background, whether you're a local or a first-time visitor.

## THE LIE OF THE LAND

We have divided the city into areas – simplified, for convenience, from the full complexity of Barcelona's geography – and the relevant area name is given with each venue listed in this guide. We've also included addresses, phone numbers, and websites. Wherever possible, a map reference is provided for venues listed; the maps can be found at the back of the book.

## ESSENTIAL INFORMATION

For all the practical information you might need for visiting Barcelona – including visa and customs information, details of local transport, a listing of emergency numbers, information on local weather and a selection of useful websites – turn to the Directory at the back of this guide. It begins on page 303.

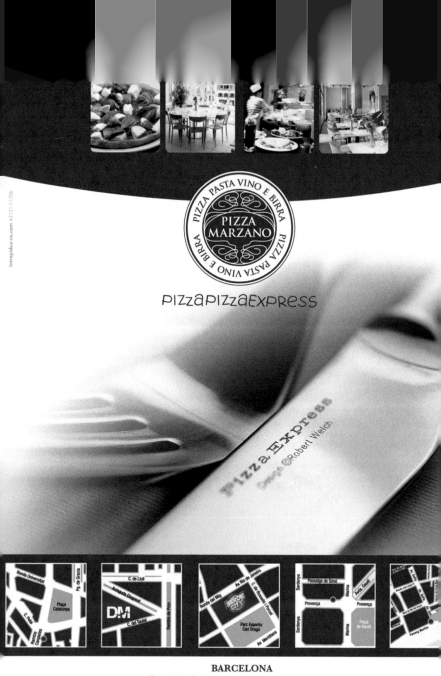

## THE LOWDOWN ON THE LISTINGS

We have tried to make this book as easy to use as possible. Addresses, phone numbers, bus information, opening times and admission prices are all included in the listings. However, businesses can change their arrangements at any time. Before you go out of your way, we'd strongly advise you to phone ahead to check particulars. While every effort has been made to ensure the accuracy of the information contained in this guide, the publishers cannot accept responsibility for any errors it may contain.

## LANGUAGE

Barcelona is a bilingual city; street signs, tourist information and menus can be in either Catalan or Spanish, and this is reflected in the guide. We have tried to use whichever is more commonly used or appropriate in each case.

## PRICES AND PAYMENT

We have listed prices in euro (€) throughout, and we have noted where venues accept the following credit cards: American Express (AmEx), Diners Club (DC), MasterCard (MC) and Visa (V). Some will also accept travellers' cheques, and/or other cards such as Carte Blanche. Wherever possible we have factored in the sales tax (*IVA*), which many restaurants and hotels leave out of their advertised rates.

The prices we've listed in this guide should be treated as guidelines, not gospel. If prices vary wildly from those we've quoted, ask whether there's a good reason. If not, go elsewhere. Then please let us know. We aim to give the best and most up-to-date advice, so we want to know if you've been badly treated or overcharged.

## TELEPHONE NUMBERS

It is necessary to dial provincial area codes with all the numbers in Spain, even for local calls. Hence all normal Barcelona numbers begin 93, whether you're calling from inside or outside the city. From abroad, you must dial 34 (the international dialling code for Spain) followed by the number given in this book – which includes the initial 93. For more information on telephones and codes, see p320.

## MAPS

The map section includes a map of the entire region for planning trips out of town and maps of the local rail and metro networks, some overviews of the greater Barcelona area and its neighbourhoods; detailed street maps of the Eixample, the Raval, Gràcia and other districts, and a large-scale map of the Old City with a comprehensive street index. The maps start on page 335, and pinpoint specific locations of hotels (❶), restaurants (❶) and cafés and bars (❶).

## LET US KNOW WHAT YOU THINK

We hope you enjoy *Time Out Barcelona*, and we'd like to know what you think of it. We welcome tips for places that you consider we should include in future editions and we do take note of your criticism of our choices. You can email us at guides@timeout.com.

## Advertisers

We would like to stress that no establishment has been included in this guide because it has advertised in any of our publications and no payment of any kind has influenced any review. The opinions given in this book are those of Time Out writers and entirely independent.

There is an online version of this book, along with guides to over 100 international cities, at **www.timeout.com**.

# In Context



## Features



**Pavelló Mies van der Rohe**. *See p120.*

An 18th-century depiction of Barcelona harbour.

# History

## City of fighters, survivors and nationalists.

As city histories go, Barcelona's has been far from smooth. Economic disaster has followed boom as embattled times have followed peaceful ones, partly thanks to Catalonia's precarious fortunes as a political entity – sometimes an independent, powerful nation and, indeed, once a world power; sometimes an embattled subdivision of a larger entity. While cultural, political and social diversity flourish in today's Barcelona, it has not always been that way. For long periods of its history, the city was the victim of attempts by governments in Madrid to absorb Catalonia within a unified Spanish state. Under several leaders, notably Philip V in the 17th century and Franco in the 20th century, these attempts resulted in a policy aimed at stamping out any vestige of Catalan culture or independence. However, the region always re-emerged stronger, more vibrant and with a heightened desire to show the world its distinctive character, both socially as well as culturally.

### IN THE BEGINNING

The Romans founded Barcelona in about 15 BC on the Mons Taber, a small hill between two streams that provided a good view of the Mediterranean and which today is crowned by a cathedral. At the time, the plain around it was sparsely inhabited by the Laetani, an agrarian Iberian people who produced grain and honey, and gathered oysters. Then called Barcino, the town was smaller than Tarraco (Tarragona), which was the capital of the Roman province of Hispania Citerior, but it had the only harbour between there and Narbonne.

Like virtually every other Roman new town in Europe, Barcino was originally a fortified rectangle with a crossroads at its centre (which is where the Plaça Sant Jaume is today). It was also a decidedly unimportant provincial town, but the rich plain provided it with a produce garden, and the sea nearby gave it an incipient maritime trade. It acquired a Jewish community soon after its foundation and became associated with Christian martyrs, most particularly Santa

Eulàlia, Barcelona's first patron saint. Eulàlia was supposedly executed at the end of the third century via a series of revolting tortures that included being rolled naked in a sealed barrel full of glass shards down the alley now called Baixada ('Descent') de Santa Eulàlia.

The people of Barcino accepted Christianity in 312, together with the rest of the Roman empire, which by then was under growing threat of invasion. In response, the town's rough defences were replaced with massive stone walls in the fourth century, many sections of which can still be seen today. It was these ramparts that ensured Barcelona's continuity, making the stronghold desirable to later warlords.

Nonetheless, defences like these could not prevent the empire's disintegration. In 415 Barcelona, as it became known, briefly became capital of the kingdom of the Visigoths, under their chieftain Ataülf. They soon moved on southwards to extend their control over the whole of the Iberian peninsula, and for the next 400 years the town was a neglected backwater. The Muslims swept across the peninsula after 711, crushing Goth resistance; they made little attempt to settle Catalonia, but much of the Christian population retreated into the Pyrenees, the first Catalan heartland.

Then, at the end of the eighth century, the Franks drove south, against the Muslims, from across the mountains. In 801 Charlemagne's son, Louis the Pious, took Barcelona and made it a bastion of the Marca Hispanica (Spanish March), which was the southern buffer of his father's empire. This gave Catalonia a trans-Pyrenean influence entirely different from that of the other Christian states in Spain; equally, it is for this reason that the closest relative of the Catalan language is Provençal, not Castilian.

When the Frankish princes returned to their main business further north, loyal counts were left behind to rule sections of the Catalan lands. At the end of the ninth century Count Guifré el Pilós (Wilfred 'the Hairy') managed to gain control over several of these Catalan counties from his base in Ripoll. By uniting them under his rule, he laid the basis for a future Catalan state, founding the dynasty of the Counts of Barcelona, which reigned in an unbroken line until 1410. His successors made Barcelona their capital, thereby setting the seal on the city's future.

As a founding patriarch, Wilfred is the stuff of legends, not least of which is that he was the creator of the Catalan flag. The story goes that he was fighting the Saracens alongside his lord, the Frankish emperor, when he was severely wounded. In recognition of Wilfred's heroism, the emperor dipped his fingers into his friend's blood and ran them down the count's golden shield; thus, the Quatre Barres, four bars of red on a yellow background, also known as La Senyera. Recorded facts make this story highly unlikely, but whatever its origins, the four-stripe symbol was first recorded on the tomb of Count Ramon Berenguer II from 1082, making it the oldest national flag in Europe. What is not known is exactly in what way Wilfred was so notably hairy.

**'Catalonia was one of the first areas in Europe to use its vernacular language, as well as Latin, in written form and as a language of culture.'**

In 985, a century after Wilfred, a Muslim army attacked and sacked Barcelona. The hirsute count's great-grandson, Count Borrell II, requested aid from his theoretical feudal lord, the Frankish king. He received no reply, and so repudiated all Frankish sovereignty over Catalonia. From then on, although the name was not yet in use, Catalonia was effectively independent, and the Counts of Barcelona were free to forge its destiny.

### CONFIDENT GROWTH

In the first century of the new millennium, Catalonia was consolidated as a political entity, and entered an age of cultural richness. This was the great era of Catalan Romanesque art, with the building of the magnificent monasteries and the churches of northern Catalonia, such as Sant Pere de Rodes near Figueres, and the painting of the glorious murals now housed in the Museu Nacional on Montjuïc. There was also a flowering of scholarship, reflecting Catalan contacts with northern Europe and with Islamic and Carolingian cultures. In Barcelona, shipbuilding and trade in grain and wine grew, and a new trade developed in textiles. The city expanded both inside its old Roman walls and outside them, with *vilanoves* (new towns) appearing at Sant Pere and La Ribera.

Catalonia also gained more territory from the Muslims to the south, beyond the Penedès, and – either through marriage or with Arab booty – in what is now southern France. The most significant marriage, however, occurred in 1137, when Ramon Berenguer IV (1131-62) wed Petronella, who was heir to the throne of Aragon. In the long term, the marriage bound Catalonia into Iberia. The uniting of the two dynasties created a powerful entity known

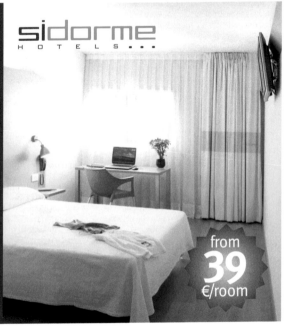

as the Crown of Aragon: each element retained its separate institutions, and was ruled by monarchs known as the count-kings. Since Aragon was already a kingdom, it was given precedence, and its name was often used to refer to the state, but the language used in the court was Catalan and the centre of government remained in Barcelona.

Ramon Berenguer IV also extended Catalan territory to its current frontiers in the Ebro valley. At the beginning of the next century, however, the dynasty lost virtually all its land north of the Pyrenees to France, when Count-King Pere I 'the Catholic' was killed at the Battle of Muret in 1213. This proved a blessing. In future years, the Catalan-Aragonese state became oriented towards the Mediterranean and the south, and was able to embark on two centuries of imperialism that would be equalled in vigour only by Barcelona's burgeoning commercial enterprise.

## EMPIRE BUILDING

Pere I's successor was the most expansionist of the count-kings. Jaume I 'the Conqueror' (1213-76) abandoned any idea of further adventures in Provence and joined the campaign against the Muslims to the south, taking Mallorca in 1229, Ibiza in 1235 and, at greater cost, Valencia in 1238 (he made the latter another separate kingdom, the third part of the Crown of Aragon). Barcelona became the centre of an empire that spanned across the Mediterranean.

The city grew tremendously. In the middle of the 13th century, Jaume I ordered the building of a second wall along the line of the Rambla and roughly encircling the area between there and the modern Parc de la Ciutadella, thus bringing La Ribera and the other *vilanoves* within the city. In 1274 he also gave Barcelona a form of representative self-government: the Consell de Cent, a council of 100 chosen citizens, an institution that would last for more than 400 years. In Catalonia as a whole, royal powers were strictly limited by a parliament, the Corts, with a permanent standing committee known as the Generalitat.

The count-kings commanded a powerful fleet and a mercenary army centred on the Almogàvers, irregular warriors who had been hardened in the endless battles against the Muslims on the Catalan frontier. The Almogàvers were themselves feared equally by Christians and Muslims, as they travelled the Mediterranean conquering, plundering and enslaving in the name of God and the Crown of Aragon.

In 1282 Pere II 'the Great' sent his armies into Sicily; Catalan domination over the island would last for nearly 150 years. The Catalan empire reached its greatest strength under Jaume II 'the Just' (1291-1327). Corsica (1323) and Sardinia (1324) were added to the Crown of Aragon, although the latter would never submit to Catalan rule and would from then on be a constant focus of revolt.

## **In the detail** Mount Tàber millstone

In 15 BC Roman soldiers established a colony on a small hill called the Mons Taber, which later became the settlement of Barcino. Medieval Barcelona and all subsequent buildings in the Barri Gòtic were constructed on top of the site; over the last century many a local resident has set out to remodel a bathroom and turned up a lump of ancient masonry.

The highest point of the Mons Taber was the space still marked by a large millstone, now set into the pavement outside the **Centre Excursionista de Catalunya** at C/Paradis 10; the building also contains the **Temple Romà d'Augusti** (*see p94*), with its four Corinthian columns. This would have been the focus, and highest building, within the complex of the Roman forum that once stood here. A small brass plaque above the millstone indicates that it sits 16.9 metres (55 feet) above sea level.

**Wilfred the Hairy** breaths his last. *See p13.*

## THE GOLDEN AGE

The Crown of Aragon was often at war with Arab rulers, but its capital flourished through commerce with every part of the Mediterranean, both Christian and Muslim. Catalan ships also sailed into the Atlantic, to England and Flanders, their ventures actively supported by the count-kings and burghers of Barcelona and regulated by the first-ever code of maritime law, known as the *Llibre del Consolat de Mar* (written in 1258-72). By the late 13th century around 130 consulates ringed the Mediterranean, all engaged in a complex system of trade.

Not surprisingly, this age of power and prestige was also the great era of building in medieval Barcelona. The count-kings' imperial conquests may have been ephemeral, but their talent for permanence in building can still be seen today. Between 1290 and 1340, the construction of most of Barcelona's best-known Gothic buildings was initiated. Religious edifices such as the cathedral, Santa Maria del Mar and Santa Maria del Pi were matched by civil buildings such as the Saló de Tinell and the Llotja, the old market and the stock exchange. As a result, Barcelona contains the most important collection of historic Gothic civil architecture anywhere in Europe.

The ships of the Catalan navy were built in the monumental Drassanes (shipyards), begun by Pere II and completed under Pere III, in 1378. In 1359 Pere III also built the third, final city wall along the line of the modern Paral·lel, Ronda Sant Pau and Ronda Sant Antoni. This gave the Old City of Barcelona its definitive shape. La Ribera, 'the waterfront', was the centre of trade and industry in the 14th century city. Just inland, the Carrer Montcada was where newly enriched merchants displayed their wealth in opulent Gothic palaces. All around were the workers of the various craft guilds, grouped together in their own streets.

The Catalan Golden Age was also an era of cultural greatness. Catalonia was one of the first areas in Europe to use its vernacular language, as well as Latin, in written form and as a language of culture.

The oldest written texts in Catalan are the Homílies d'Organyà, 12th-century translations from the Bible. The court and the aristocracy seem to have attained an unusual level of literacy very early: Jaume I even wrote an autobiography, the *Llibre dels Feits*, or 'Book of Deeds', in which he recounted his achievements and conquests.

Incipient Catalan literature was given a vital thrust by Ramon Llull (1235-1316). After a debauched youth, he experienced a series of religious visions and became the first man in post-Roman Europe to write philosophy in a vernacular language. Steeped in Arabic and Hebrew writings, Llull brought together

Christian, Islamic, Jewish and classical ideas, and wrote a vast amount on other subjects too, from theories of chivalry to poetry and visionary tales, in doing so effectively creating Catalan as a literary language. Catalan translations were undertaken from Greek and Latin. Chroniclers such as Ramon Muntaner recorded the exploits of count-kings and Almogàvers; in 1490, in the twilight of the Golden Age, the Valencian Joanot Martorell published *Tirant lo Blanc*, a bawdy adventure widely considered the first European novel.

## REVOLT AND COLLAPSE

The extraordinary prosperity of the medieval period did not last. The count-kings had overextended Barcelona's resources, and overinvested in far-off ports. By 1400 the effort to maintain their conquests by force, especially Sardinia, had exhausted the spirit and the coffers of the Catalan imperialist drive. The Black Death, which arrived in the 1340s, also had a devastating impact on Catalonia, intensifying the bitterness of social conflicts between the aristocracy, the merchants, the peasants and the urban poor.

In 1410 Martí I 'the Humane' died without an heir, bringing to an end the line of counts of Barcelona, unbroken since Wilfred 'the Hairy'. The Crown of Aragon was passed to a member of a Castilian noble family, the Trastámaras: Fernando de Antequera (1410-16). In the 1460s the effects of war and catastrophic famine led to a sudden collapse into violent and destructive civil war and peasant revolt. The population was depleted to such an extent that Barcelona would not regain the numbers it had had in 1400 (40,000) until the 18th century.

In 1469 an important union for Spain initiated a woeful period in Barcelona's history; dubbed by some Catalan historians the *Decadència*, it eventually led to the end of Catalonia as a separate entity. In that year, Ferdinand of Aragon (1479-1516) married Isabella of Castile (1476-1504), thereby uniting the different Spanish kingdoms, even though they would retain their separate institutions for another two centuries.

## EAST OF EDEN

As Catalonia's fortunes had declined, so those of Castile to the west had risen. In 1492 Granada, the last Muslim foothold in Spain, was conquered; Isabella decreed the expulsion of all Jews from Castile and Aragon; and, most famously, Columbus discovered America.

It was Castile's seafaring orientation towards the Atlantic, as opposed to the Mediterranean, that confirmed Catalonia's decline. The discovery of the New World was a disaster for Catalan commerce: trade shifted decisively away from the Mediterranean, and Catalans were barred from participating in the exploitation of the new empire until the 1770s. The weight of Castile within the monarchy was increased, and it soon became the clear seat of government.

In 1516 the Spanish crown passed to the House of Habsburg, in the shape of Ferdinand and Isabella's grandson, Holy Roman Emperor Charles V. His son, Philip II of Spain, established Madrid as the capital of all his dominions in 1561. Catalonia was managed by viceroys, and the power of its institutions was increasingly restricted, with a down-at-heel aristocracy and a meagre cultural life.

## GRIM REAPERS

While Castilian Spain went through its Golden Century, Catalonia was left on the margins. However, worse was to come in the following century with the two national revolts, both heroic defeats that have since acquired a role in central Catalan mythology.

The problem for the Spanish monarchy was that Castile was an absolute monarchy and thus could be taxed at will, but in the former Aragonese territories, and especially Catalonia, royal authority kept coming up against a mass of local rights and privileges. As the Habsburgs' empire became entrenched in wars and expenses that not even American gold could meet, the Count-Duke of Olivares, the formidable great minister of King Philip IV (1621-65), resolved to extract more money and troops from the non-Castilian dominions of the Crown. The Catalans, however, felt they were taxed enough already.

In 1640 a mass of peasants, later dubbed Els Segadors (the Reapers), gathered on the Rambla in Barcelona, outside the Porta Ferrissa (Iron Gate) in the second wall. The peasants rioted against royal authority, surged into the city and murdered the viceroy, the Marquès de Santa Coloma. This began the general uprising known as the Guerra dels Segadors, or the 'Reapers' War'. The authorities of the Generalitat, led by its president Pau Claris, were fearful of the violence of the poor; lacking the confidence to declare Catalonia independent, they appealed for protection from Louis XIII of France. French armies, however, were unable to defend Catalonia adequately, and in 1652 a destitute Barcelona capitulated to the equally exhausted army of Philip IV. In 1659 France and Spain made peace with a treaty that gave the Catalan territory of Roussillon, around Perpignan, to France. After the revolt, Philip IV and his ministers were magnanimous, allowing the Catalans to retain what was left of their institutions despite their disloyalty.

## THE REIGN IN SPAIN

Fifty years later came the second of the great national rebellions, this one being the War of the Spanish Succession. In 1700 Charles II of Spain died without an heir, and Castile accepted the grandson of Louis XIV of France, Philip of Anjou, as King Philip V of Spain (1700-46). However, the alternative candidate, Archduke Charles of Austria, promised that he would restore the traditional rights of the former Aragonese territories, and won their allegiance as a result. He also had the support, in his fight against France, of Britain, Holland and Austria.

But Catalonia had backed the wrong horse. In 1713 Britain and the Dutch made a separate peace with France and withdrew their aid, leaving the Catalans stranded, with no possibility of victory. After a 13-month siege in which every citizen was called to arms, Barcelona fell to the French and Spanish armies on 11 September 1714. The most heroic defeat of all, the date marked the most decisive political reverse in Barcelona's history, and is now commemorated as Catalan National Day, the Diada. Some of Barcelona's resisters were buried next to the church of Santa Maria del Mar in the Born, in the Fossar de les Moreres (Mulberry Graveyard), now a memorial.

In 1715 Philip V issued his decree of Nova Planta, abolishing all the remaining separate institutions of the Crown of Aragon and so, in effect, creating 'Spain' as a single, unitary state. Large-scale 'Castilianisation' of the country was initiated, and Castilian replaced the Catalan language in all official documents. In Barcelona, extra measures were taken to keep the city under control. The crumbling medieval walls and the castle on Montjuïc were refurbished with new ramparts, and a massive new citadel was built on the eastern side of the Old City, where the Parc de la Ciutadella is today. To make space, thousands were expelled from La Ribera and forcibly rehoused in the Barceloneta, Barcelona's first-ever planned housing scheme, with its barrack-like street plan unmistakably provided by French military engineers. The citadel became the most hated symbol of the city's subordination.

## URBAN RENAISSANCE

Politically subjugated and without a significant native ruling class, Catalonia nevertheless revived in the 18th century. Shipping picked up, and Barcelona started a booming export trade to the New World in wines and spirits from Catalan vineyards, and textiles, wool and silk. In 1780 a merchant called Erasme de Gómina opened Barcelona's first true factory, a hand-powered weaving mill in C/Riera Alta with 800 workers. In the next decade, Catalan trade with Spanish America quadrupled; Barcelona's population had grown from 30,000 in 1720 to around 100,000 by the end of the 18th century.

The prosperity was reflected in a new wave of building in the city. Neo-classical mansions appeared, notably on C/Ample and La Rambla, but the greatest transformation was La Rambla itself. Until the 1770s it had been a dusty, dry riverbed where country people came to sell their produce, lined on the Raval side mostly with giant religious houses and on the other with Jaume I's second wall. In 1775 the captain-general, the Marqués de la Mina, embarked on an ambitious scheme to demolish the wall and turn the Rambla into a paved promenade. Beyond the Rambla, the previously semi-rural Raval was swiftly becoming densely populated.

Barcelona's expansion was briefly slowed by the French invasion of 1808. Napoleon sought to appeal to Catalans by offering them national recognition within his empire, but was met with curiously little response. After six years of turmoil, Barcelona's growing business class resumed its many projects in 1814, with the restoration of the Bourbon monarchy in the shape of Ferdinand VII (1808-33).

## GETTING UP STEAM

Ferdinand VII attempted to reinstate the absolute monarchy of his youth and reimpose his authority over Spain's American colonies, but he failed. On his death he was succeeded by his three-year-old daughter Isabella II (1833-68), but the throne was also claimed by his brother Carlos, who was backed by the country's most reactionary sectors.

To defend Isabella's rights, the regent, Ferdinand's widow Queen María Cristina, was obliged to seek the support of liberals, and so granted a very limited form of constitution. Thus began Spain's Carlist Wars, which had a powerful impact in conservative rural Catalonia, where Don Carlos's faction won a considerable following, in part because of its support for traditional local rights and customs.

While this struggle went on, a liberal-minded local administration in Barcelona, freed from subordination to the military, was able to engage in city planning, opening up the soon-to-be fashionable C/Ferran and Plaça Sant Jaume in the 1820s and later adding the Plaça Reial. A change came in 1836, when the government in Madrid decreed the Desamortización (or the 'disentailment') of Spain's monasteries. In Barcelona, where convents and religious houses still took up great sections of the Raval and the Rambla, a huge area was freed for development. The Rambla took on the appearance it roughly retains today, while the Raval filled up with tenements and textile mills several storeys high.

In 1832 the first steam-driven factory in Spain was built on C/Tallers, sparking resistance from hand-spinners and weavers. Most of the city's factories were still relatively small, however, and the Catalan manufacturers were aware that they were at a disadvantage in competing with the industries of Britain and other countries to the north. Complicating matters further, they didn't even have the city to themselves. Not only did the anti-industrial Carlists threaten from the countryside, but Barcelona soon became a centre of radical ideas. Its people were notably rebellious, and liberal, republican, free-thinking and even utopian socialist groups proliferated between sporadic bursts of repression. (In 1842 a liberal revolt, the Jamancia, took over Barcelona, and barricades went up around the city. This would be the last occasion on which Barcelona was bombarded from the castle on Montjuïc, as the army struggled to regain control.)

**'The 1888 Exhibition left Barcelona with huge debts, a new look and lots of reasons to believe in itself as a paradigm of progress.'**

By this time, the Catalan language had been relegated to secondary status, spoken in every street but rarely written or used in cultured discourse. Then, in 1833, Bonaventura Carles Aribau published his *Oda a la Pàtria*, a romantic eulogy in Catalan of the country, its language and its past. The poem had an extraordinary impact and is still traditionally credited with initiating the Renaixença ('rebirth') of Catalan heritage and culture. The year 1848 was a high point for Barcelona and Catalonia, with the inauguration of the first railway in Spain, from Barcelona to Mataró, and the opening of the Liceu opera house.

### SETTING AN EIXAMPLE

The optimism of Barcelona's new middle class was counterpointed by two persistent obstacles: the weakness of the Spanish economy as a whole, and the instability of their own society, which was reflected in atrocious labour relations. No consideration was given to the manpower behind the industrial surge: the underpaid, overworked men, women and children who lived in appalling conditions in high-rise slums within the cramped city. In 1855 the first general strike took place in Barcelona. Inaugurating a long cycle of conflict, the captain-general, Zapatero, refused to permit any workers' organisations to function, and bloodily suppressed all resistance.

**Ramon Llull**. *See p16.*

One response to the city's problems that had almost universal support in Barcelona was the demolition of the city walls, which had imposed a stifling restriction on its growth. For years, however, the Spanish state refused to relinquish its hold on the city. To find space, larger factories were established in villages around Barcelona, such as Sants and Poblenou, and in 1854 permission finally came for the demolition of the citadel and the walls. The work began with enthusiastic popular participation, crowds of volunteers joining in at weekends. Barcelona at last broke out of the space it had occupied since the 14th century and spread outwards into its new *eixample* (extension), to a controversial new plan by Ildefons Cerdà.

In 1868 Isabella II, once a symbol of liberalism, was overthrown by a progressive revolt. During the six years of upheaval that followed, power in Madrid would be held by the provisional government, a constitutional monarchy under an Italian prince and later a federal republic. However, workers were free to organise; in 1868 Giuseppe Fanelli brought the first anarchist ideas, and two years later, the first Spanish workers' congress took place in

## **Walk on** Roman remains

**Duration**: 45 minutes.

The Roman settlement of Barcino has had an unappreciated impact on the two millennia of life that followed its beginnings. Many of Barcelona's most familiar streets – C/Hospital, even Passeig de Gràcia – follow the line of Roman roads, and the best way to get an idea of the Roman town is to walk the line of its walls. Along the way sit all kinds of Roman remains, poking out from where they were reused or constructed over by medieval builders and those who followed them.

A good place to start a walk is at **C/Paradís**, between the cathedral and Plaça Sant Jaume, where a round millstone is set into the paving to mark what was believed to be the precise centre of the Mons Taber (*see p15* **In the detail**). It's here that you'll find the remains of the **Temple Romà d'Augusti** (*see p94*). Where C/Paradís meets the Plaça Sant Jaume was where Barcino's two main thoroughfares once met; the road on the left, **C/Llibreteria**, began life as the **Cardus Maximus**, the main road to Rome. Just off this road is the Plaça del Rei and the extraordinary **Museu d'Història de la Ciutat**, below which is the largest underground excavation of a Roman site in Europe.

Rejoining C/Llibreteria, turn left at **C/Tapineria** to reach **Plaça Ramon Berenguer el Gran** and the largest surviving stretch of ancient wall, incorporated into the medieval Palau Reial. Continue along Tapineria, where you'll find many sections of Roman building, to **Avda de la Catedral**. The massive twin-drum gate on C/Bisbe, while often retouched, has not changed in its basic shape, at least at the base, since it was the main gate of the Roman town. To its left you can see fragments of an aqueduct, and at its front Joan Brossa's bronze letters, spelling out 'Barcino'. If you take a detour up C/Capellans to **C/Duran i Bas**, you can see another four arches of an aqueduct; heading left and straight over the Avda Portal de l'Àngel is the Roman necropolis (*photo left*) in **Plaça Vila de Madrid**, with the tombs clearly

Barcelona. The radical forces were divided between many squabbling factions, while the established classes of society felt increasingly threatened and called for the restoration of order. The Republic proclaimed in 1873 was unable to establish its authority, and succumbed to a military coup less than a year later.

### THE MIDAS TOUCH

In 1874 the Bourbon dynasty, in the person of Alfonso XII, son of Isabella II, was restored to the Spanish throne. Workers' organisations were again suppressed. The middle classes, however, felt their confidence renewed. The 1870s saw a frenzied boom in stock speculation, known as the *febre d'or* (gold fever), and the real take-off of building in the Eixample. From the 1880s Modernisme became the preferred style of the new district, the perfect expression for the confidence and impetus of the industrial class. The first modern Catalanist political movement was founded by Valentí Almirall.

Barcelona felt it needed to show the world all that it had achieved, and that it was more than just a 'second city'. In 1885 a promoter named Eugenio Serrano de Casanova proposed to the city council the holding of an international exhibition, such as had been held successfully in London, Paris and Vienna. Serrano was a highly dubious character who eventually made off with large amounts of public funds, but by the time this became clear, the city fathers had fully committed themselves to the event.

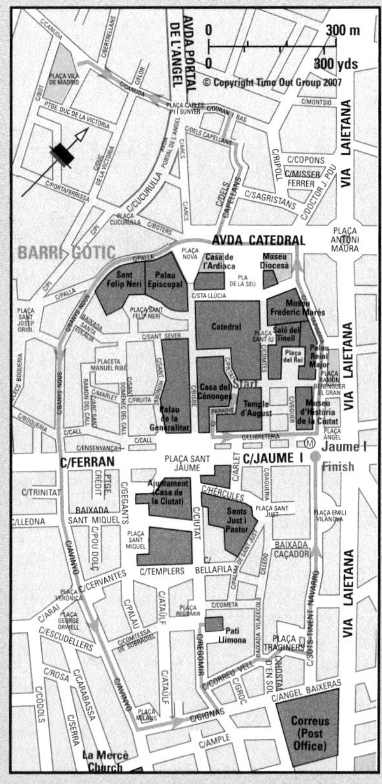


visible. In accordance with Roman custom, these had to be outside the city walls.

Returning to the cathedral, turn right into **C/Palla.** A little way along sits a large chunk of Roman wall, only discovered in the 1980s when a building was demolished. C/Palla runs into **C/Banys Nous**; at No.16 sits a centre for disabled children, inside which is a piece of wall with a relief of legs and feet (phone ahead for a viewing time; 93 318 14 81). At No.4 is **La Granja** (*see p173*), a lovely old café with yet another stretch of Roman wall at the back; beyond this is the junction with **C/Call**, the other end of the *cardus*, and so the opposite side of the Roman town from Llibreteria-Tapineria. The staff of the clothes wholesalers at C/Call 1 are also used to people wandering in to examine their piece of Roman tower. Carry on across C/Ferran and down **C/Avinyó**, the next continuation of the perimeter. Two sides of the cave-like dining room at the back of **El Gallo Kiriko**, the Pakistani restaurant at No.19, are actually formed by portions of the Roman wall.

From **C/Milans**, turn left on to **C/Gignás**. Near the junction with **C/Regomir** are remains of the fourth sea gate of the town, which would have faced the beach, and the Roman shipyard. Take a detour up C/Regomir to visit one of the most important relics of Barcino, the **Pati Llimona** (*see p90*); then, continue walking up **C/Correu Vell**, where there are more fragments of wall, to reach one of the most impressive relics of Roman Barcelona in the small, shady **Plaça Traginers**: a Roman tower and one corner of the ancient wall, in a remarkable state of preservation despite having had a medieval house built on top of it. Finally, turn up **C/Sots-Tinent Navarro**, which boasts a massive stretch of Roman rampart, to end the walk at Plaça de l'Àngel.

The Universal Exhibition of 1888 was used as a pretext for the final conversion of the Ciutadella into a park. Giant efforts had to be made to get everything ready in time, a feat that led the mayor, Francesc Rius i Taulet, to exclaim that 'the Catalan people are the yankees of Europe'. The first of Barcelona's three great efforts to demonstrate its status to the world, the 1888 Exhibition signified the consecration of the Modernista style, as well as the end of provincial, dowdy Barcelona and its establishment as a modern-day city on the international map.

## THE CITY OF THE NEW CENTURY

The 1888 Exhibition left Barcelona with huge debts, a new look and lots of reasons to believe in itself as a paradigm of progress. The Catalan Renaixença continued, and acquired a more political tone. In 1892 the Bases de Manresa, a draft plan for Catalan autonomy, were drawn up. Middle-class opinion gradually became more sympathetic to political Catalanism.

A truly decisive moment came in 1898, when the underlying weakness of the Spanish state was made plain over the superficial prosperity of the first years of the Bourbon restoration. It was then that Spain was forced into a short war with the United States, in which it lost its remaining empire in Cuba, the Philippines and Puerto Rico. Industrialists were horrified at losing the lucrative Cuban market, and despaired of the ability of the state ever to reform itself. Many swung behind a conservative nationalist

Ferdinand and Isabella. See p17.

movement: the Lliga Regionalista (Regionalist League), founded in 1901 and led by Enric Prat de la Riba and the politician-financier Francesc Cambó, promised both national revival and modern, efficient government.

At the same time, however, Barcelona continued to grow, fuelling Catalanist optimism. In 1897 the city officially incorporated most of the surrounding smaller communities, reaching a population of over half a million, and in 1907 it initiated the 'internal reform' of the Old City by creating the Via Laietana, which cut right through it.

Catalan letters were thriving. The Institut d'Estudis Catalans (Institute of Catalan Studies) was founded in 1906, and Pompeu Fabra set out to create the first Catalan dictionary. Above all, Barcelona had a vibrant artistic community, centred on Modernisme, which consisted of great architects and established painters such as Rusiñol and Casas, but also the many penniless bohemians who gathered round them, among them a young Picasso.

The bohemians were drawn to the increasingly wild nightlife of the Raval, where cabarets, bars and brothels multiplied at the end of the 19th century. Located around the cabarets, though, were the very poorest of the working classes, for whom conditions had only continued to decline; Barcelona had some of the worst cases of overcrowding and the highest mortality rates in Europe. Local philanthropists called for something to be done, but Barcelona was more associated with revolutionary politics and violence than with peaceful social reform. Rebellion among the working classes pre-dated the arrival of anarchism; in the 19th century the Roman Catholic Church was the frequent target of the mobs, protesting against its collusion with the authorities and the control it exercised over the day-to-day life of the poorer classes.

In 1893 more than 20 people were killed in a series of anarchist terrorist attacks, which included the notorious throwing of a bomb into the wealthy audience at the Liceu. The perpetrators acted alone, but the authorities seized the opportunity to round up the usual suspects for questioning – mainly local anarchists and radicals. Several of them, known as the 'Martyrs of Montjuïc', were later tortured and executed in the castle above the city. One retaliation came in 1906, when a Catalan anarchist tried to kill King Alfonso XIII on his wedding day.

Anarchism was still only in a fledgling stage among workers in the 1900s. However, rebellious attitudes, along with growing republican sentiment and a fierce hatred of the Roman Catholic Church, united the underclasses and led them to take to the barricades. The Setmana Tràgica (Tragic Week) of 1909 began as a protest against the conscription of troops for the colonial war in Morocco, but degenerated into a general riot, with the destruction of churches by excited mobs. Suspected culprits were summarily executed, as was the anarchist educationalist Francesc Ferrer, who was accused of 'moral responsibility' even though he wasn't even in Barcelona at the time.

These events dented the optimism of the Catalanists of the Lliga. However, in 1914 they secured from Madrid the Mancomunitat, or administrative union, of the four Catalan provinces, the first joint government of any kind in Catalonia in 200 years. Its first president was Prat de la Riba, who would be succeeded on his death in 1917 by the architect Puig i Cadafalch (*see p48* **Flying the flag**). However, the Lliga's plans for an orderly Catalonia were to be obstructed by a further surge in social tensions.

### CHAMPAGNE AND SOCIALISTS

Spain's neutral status during World War I gave a huge boost to the Spanish, and especially Catalan, economy. Exports soared as Catalonia's manufacturers made millions supplying uniforms to the French army. Barcelona's industry was at last able to diversify from textiles into engineering, chemicals and other more modern sectors.

Barcelona also became a place of refuge for anyone in Europe who wanted to avoid the war. Its international refugee community included artists Sonia and Robert Delaunay, Francis Picabia, Marie Laurencin and Albert Gleizes, but the city was also a bolt-hole for all kinds of low-life from around Europe. The Raval area was soon dubbed the Barrio Chino (Chinatown), identifying it as an area of sin and perdition.

Some of the regular patrons of the lavish new cabarets were industrialists; many of the war profits were spent immediately in conspicuous consumption. The war also set off massive inflation, driving people from rural Spain into the big cities. Barcelona doubled in size in 20 years to become the largest city in Spain, and also the fulcrum of Spanish politics. Workers' wages, meanwhile, had lost half their real value.

The chief channel of protest in Barcelona was the anarchist workers' union, the Confederación Nacional del Trabajo (CNT), constituted in 1910, which gained half a million members in Catalonia by 1919. The CNT and the socialist Union General de Trabajadores (UGT) launched a joint general strike in 1917, roughly co-ordinated with a campaign by the Lliga and other liberal politicians for political reform. However, the politicians soon withdrew at the prospect of serious social unrest. Inflation continued to intensify, and in 1919 Barcelona was paralysed for more than two months by a CNT general strike over union recognition. Employers refused to recognise the CNT, and the most intransigent among them hired gunmen to get rid of union leaders. Union activists replied in kind, and virtual guerrilla warfare developed between the CNT, the employers and the state. More than 800 people were killed on the city's streets over five years.

In 1923, in response both to the chaos in the city and a crisis in the war in Morocco, the captain-general of Barcelona, Miguel Primo de Rivera, staged a coup and established a military dictatorship under King Alfonso XIII. The CNT was already exhausted, and it was suppressed. Conservative Catalanists, longing for an end to disorder and the revolutionary threat, initially supported the coup, but were rewarded by the abolition of the Mancomunitat and a vindictive campaign by the Primo regime against the Catalan language and national symbols.

This, however, achieved the opposite of the desired effect, helping to radicalise and popularise Catalan nationalism. After the terrible struggles of the previous years, the 1920s were actually a time of notable prosperity for many in Barcelona, as some of the wealth recently accumulated filtered through the economy. It was also, though, a highly politicised society, in which new magazines and forums for discussion – despite the restrictions of the dictatorship – found a ready audience.

A prime motor of Barcelona's prosperity in the 1920s was the International Exhibition of 1929, the second of the city's great showcase events. It had been proposed by Cambó and Catalan business groups, but Primo de Rivera saw that it could also serve as a propaganda event for his regime. A huge number of public projects were undertaken in association with the main event, including the post office in Via Laietana, the Estació de França and Barcelona's first metro line, from Plaça Catalunya to Plaça d'Espanya. Thousands of migrant workers came from southern Spain to build them, many living in decrepit housing or shanty towns on the city fringes. By 1930 Barcelona was very different from the place it had been in 1910; it contained more than a million people, and its urban sprawl had crossed into neighbouring towns such as Hospitalet and Santa Coloma.

For the Exhibition itself, Montjuïc and Plaça d'Espanya were comprehensively redeveloped, with grand halls by Puig i Cadafalch and other local architects in the style of the Catalan neo-classical movement Noucentisme, a backward-looking reaction to the excesses of Modernisme. They contrasted strikingly, though, with the German pavilion by Ludwig Mies van der Rohe (the Pavelló Barcelona), which emphatically announced the trend towards rationalism.

### THE REPUBLIC SUPPRESSED

Despite the Exhibition's success, Primo de Rivera resigned in January 1930, exhausted. The king appointed another soldier, General

Berenguer, as prime minister, with the mission of restoring stability. The dictatorship, though, had fatally discredited the old regime, and a protest movement spread across Catalonia against the monarchy. In early 1931 Berenguer called local elections as a first step towards a restoration of constitutional rule. The outcome was a complete surprise, for republicans were elected in all of Spain's cities. Ecstatic crowds poured into the streets, and Alfonso XIII abdicated. The Second Spanish Republic was proclaimed on 14 April 1931.

The Republic arrived amid real euphoria, especially in Catalonia, where it was associated with hopes for both social change and national reaffirmation. The clear winner of the elections in the country had been the Esquerra Republicana, a leftist Catalanist group led by Francesc Macià. A raffish, elderly figure, Macià was one of the first politicians in Spain to win genuine affection from ordinary people. He declared Catalonia to be an independent republic within an Iberian federation of states, but later agreed to accept autonomy within the Spanish Republic.

The Generalitat was re-established as a government that would, potentially, acquire wide powers. All aspects of Catalan culture were then in expansion, and a popular press in Catalan achieved a wide readership. Barcelona was also a small but notable centre of the avant-garde. Miró and Dalí had already made their mark in painting; under the Republic, the Amics de l'Art Nou (ADLAN, Friends of New Art) group worked to promote contemporary art, while the GATCPAC architectural collective sought to work with the new authorities to bring rationalist architecture to Barcelona.

## Living the lingua franca

Catalonia has always been a place of passage. If you don't want to clamber over the Pyrenees, it's always been the easiest place to cross what is now the Franco-Spanish frontier. The Romans came through on their way south, making their capital at Tarraco (Tarragona), as did the Goths. Then the Moors came by on their push into France, and so too did Charlemagne's Franks when they drove the Moors back south of the River Ebro. Girona and Barcelona also had established Jewish populations by the 1st century AD. All these peoples got mixed into the recipe for what by the year 1000 had become Catalonia.

After that there was little significant immigration for a millennium until, after the Civil War, the impoverished Spanish peasantry fled the south and west for the cities of Madrid, Bilbao and Barcelona. Today, more than 40 per cent of Catalans are Spanish immigrants. Because these Spaniards arrived during a period when the Catalan language had been suppressed by the Franco regime, they had no way of learning it even if they wanted to. Furthermore, as immigrants everywhere gravitate towards their own kind, they tended to congregate in the new districts of Barcelona that were built to accommodate them, as well as in Tarragona and the Maresme, the stretch of coast north of Barcelona. Many of these areas still have a more Spanish than Catalan flavour. As the language is at the very core of what it is to be Catalan, the arrival of millions of Spanish speakers under a regime hostile to all things Catalan posed a real threat to the nation.

Many of those who arrived in the 1950s and 1960s never did learn to speak Catalan, or not well, but their children did. Since the restoration of democracy and Catalan autonomy in 1979, all schooling is carried out in Catalan and so it is virtually impossible to grow up not speaking it. With the exception of Hebrew, few minority languages can boast such a spectacular comeback.

The new wave of immigration that has brought some three million people to Spain since 2000 has pushed the Catalan population from six to seven million in the space of five years. While this has been a shock for Spain as a whole, as the country had experienced virtually no immigration for more than 1,000 years, the language issue makes it all the more unsettling for Catalonia. Probably a majority of these immigrants are already bilingual, as many of the Latin Americans speak Spanish and an indigenous language, the Pakistanis Urdu and English, and the Moroccans Arabic and French, so picking up Catalan presents less of a challenge to them than it might to, say, an English person. On the other hand, many of the non-Latinos will consider their time more usefully spent learning Spanish, which has some 500 million speakers, rather than Catalan, with around 10 million. In any case, as no immigrants speak Catalan, this has put enormous strain on the educational system,

In Madrid, the Republic's first government was a coalition of republicans and socialists led by Manuel Azaña, its overriding goal to modernise Spanish society through liberal-democratic reforms. However, as social tensions intensified, the coalition collapsed, and a conservative republican party, with support from the traditional Spanish right, secured power shortly after new elections in 1933. For Catalonia, the prospect of a return to right-wing rule prompted fears that it would immediately abrogate the Generalitat's hard-won powers. On 6 October 1934, while a general strike was launched against the central government in Asturias and some other parts of Spain, Lluís Companys, leader of the Generalitat since Macià's death the previous year, declared Catalonia independent. The 'uprising', however, turned out to be something of a farce: the Generalitat had no means of resisting the army, and the new 'Catalan Republic' was rapidly suppressed. The Generalitat was thus suspended and its leaders were imprisoned.

Over the following year, fascism seemed to become a real threat for the left, as political positions became polarised. Then, in February 1936, elections were won by the Popular Front of the left across the country. The Generalitat was reinstated, and in Catalonia the next few months were peaceful. In the rest of Spain, though, tensions were close to bursting point; right-wing politicians, refusing to accept the loss of power, talked openly of the need for the military to intervene. In July 1929 the stadium on Montjuïc was to be the site of the Popular Olympics, a leftist alternative to the Olympics of that year in Nazi Germany. On 18 July, the day of the Games' inauguration, army

as resources are diverted towards teaching newcomers the language of instruction.

Spain has not faced the challenge of integrating a non-Christian population since the Moors invaded in 711, and among the regions with the highest number of Muslim immigrants (principally Moroccans, sub-Saharan Africans and Pakistanis) is Catalonia. At a time when militantly traditionalist Islam is in the ascendant, this may prove a more disruptive process than it was in Britain or France 30 years ago, and Catalonia is having to face the fact that there's a lot more to integration than teaching everyone to speak Catalan. Real efforts are being made to forge cross-cultural links via government-sponsored initiatives or through cultural activities hosted by centres such as the innovative Centre de Cultura Contemporània de Barcelona (CCCB; *see p107*). Having been a bicultural, bilingual society, Catalonia is now getting into step with the rest of multicultural, multilingual Europe. History suggests that both the society and the language can rise to the challenge.

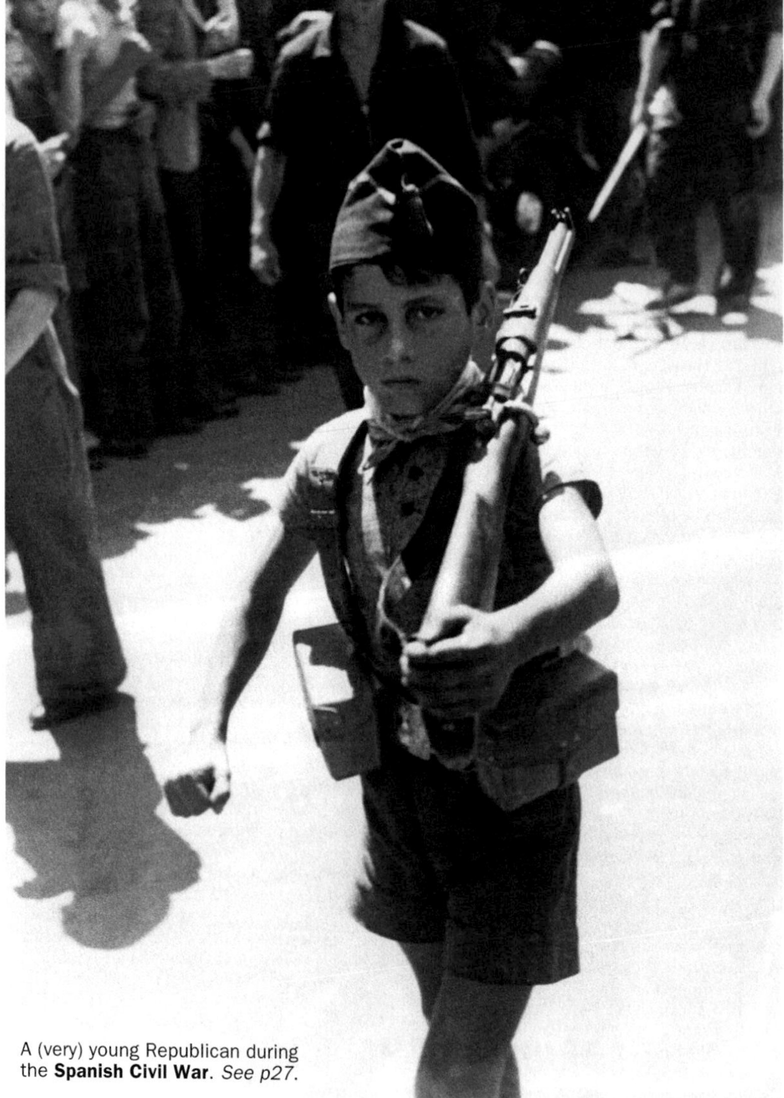

A (very) young Republican during the **Spanish Civil War**. *See p27.*

generals launched a coup against the Republic and its left-wing governments, expecting no resistance.

## UP IN ARMS

In Barcelona, militants from the unions and leftist parties, on alert for weeks, suddenly poured into the streets to oppose the troops in fierce fighting. Over the course of 19 July, the military were gradually worn down, and they finally surrendered in the Hotel Colón on Plaça Catalunya (by the corner with Passeig de Gràcia, the site of which is now occupied by the Radio Nacional de España building). Opinions have always differed as to who could claim most credit for this remarkable popular victory: workers' militants have claimed it was the 'people in arms' who defeated the army, while others stress the importance of the police remaining loyal to the Generalitat throughout the struggle. A likely answer is that they actually encouraged each other.

Tension released, the city was taken over by the revolution. People's militias of the CNT, different Marxist parties and other left-wing factions marched off to Aragon, led by streetfighters such as the anarchists Durruti and García Oliver, to continue the battle. The army rising had failed in Spain's major cities but won footholds in Castile, Aragon and the south, although in the heady atmosphere of Barcelona in July 1936 it was often assumed that their resistance could not last long, and that the people's victory was near inevitable.

Far from the front, Barcelona was the chief centre of the revolution in republican Spain, the only truly proletarian city. Its middle class avoided the streets, where, as George Orwell recorded in his *Homage to Catalonia*, everyone you saw wore workers' clothing. Barcelona became a magnet for leftists from around the world, drawing writers André Malraux, Ernest Hemingway and Octavio Paz. All kinds of industries and public services were collectivised, including cinemas, the phone system and food distribution. Ad hoc 'control patrols' of the revolutionary militias roamed the streets supposedly checking for suspected right-wing agents and sometimes carrying out summary executions, a practice that was condemned by many leftist leaders.

The alliance between the different left-wing groups was unstable and riddled with tensions, though. The communists, who had some extra leverage because the Soviet Union was the only country prepared to give the Spanish Republic arms, demanded the integration of these loosely organised militias into a conventional army under a strong central authority. The following months saw continual political infighting between the discontented CNT, the radical Marxist party Partit Obrer d'Unificació Marxista (POUM) and the communists. Co-operation broke down totally in May 1937, when republican and communist troops seized the telephone building in Plaça Catalunya (on the corner of Portal de l'Àngel) from a CNT committee, sparking off the confused war-within-the-civil-war witnessed by Orwell from the roof of the Teatre Poliorama. A temporary agreement was patched up, but shortly afterwards the POUM was banned, and the CNT excluded from power. A new republican central government was formed under Dr Juan Negrín, a socialist allied to the communists.

After that, the war gradually became more of a conventional conflict. This did little, however, to improve the Republic's position, for the nationalists under General Francisco Franco and their German and Italian allies had been continually gaining ground throughout it all. Madrid was under siege, and the capital of the Republic was moved to Valencia, and then to Barcelona, in November 1937.

Catalonia received thousands of refugees, as food shortages and the lack of armaments ground down morale. Barcelona also had the sad distinction of being the first major city in Europe to be subjected to sustained intensive bombing – to an extent that has rarely been appreciated – with heavy raids throughout 1938, especially by Italian bombers based in Mallorca. The Basque Country and Asturias had already fallen to Franco, and in March 1938 his troops reached the Mediterranean near Castellón, cutting the main republican zone in two. The Republic had one last throw of the dice, in the Battle of the Ebro in the summer of 1938, when for months the Popular Army struggled to retake control of the river. After that, the Republic was exhausted. Barcelona fell to the Francoist army on 26 January 1939. Half a million refugees fled to France, to be interned in barbed-wire camps along the beaches.

## THE FRANCO YEARS

In Catalonia, the Franco regime was iron-fisted and especially vengeful. Thousands of Catalan republicans and leftists were executed, among them Generalitat president Lluís Companys; exile and deportation were the fate of thousands more. Publishing, teaching and any other public cultural expression in Catalan, including even speaking it in the street, were prohibited, and every Catalanist monument in the city was dismantled. All independent political activity was suspended, and the entire political and cultural development of the country during the previous century and a half was brought to a drastic and abrupt halt.

The epic nature of the Spanish Civil War is known worldwide; more present in the collective memory of Barcelona, though, is the long *posguerra* or post-war period, which lasted for nearly two decades after 1939. During those years, the city was impoverished, and, as a result, food and electricity were rationed; Barcelona would not regain its prior standard of living until the mid 1950s. Nevertheless, migrants in flight from the still more brutal poverty of the south started to flow into the city, occupying precarious shanty towns around Montjuïc and other areas in the outskirts. Reconstruction work on the nearly 2,000 buildings destroyed by bombing was slow, and the regime built little during its first few years other than monumental showpieces and the vulgarly ornate basilica on top of Tibidabo, which was said to have been erected to expiate Barcelona's 'sinful' role during the war.

Some underground political movements were able to operate: the anarchist Sabaté brothers carried on their own small-scale urban guerrilla campaign, and 1951 saw the last gasp of the pre-war labour movement in a general tram strike. Some Catalan high culture was tolerated, and the young Antoni Tàpies held his first exhibition in 1949. For many people, though, the only remaining focus of any collective excitement was Barcelona football club, which took on an extraordinary importance at this time, above all in its twice-yearly meetings with the 'team of the regime', Real Madrid.

As a fascist survivor, the Franco regime was subject to a UN embargo after World War II. Years of international isolation and attempted self-sufficiency came to an end in 1953, when the USA and the Vatican saw to it that this anti-communist state was at least partially re-admitted to the western fold. Even a limited opening to the outside world meant that foreign money finally began to enter the country, and the regime relaxed some control over its population. In 1959 the Plan de Estabilización ('Stabilisation Plan'), drawn up by Catholic technocrats of the Opus Dei, brought Spain definitively within the western economy, throwing its doors wide open to tourism and foreign investment. After years of austerity, tourist income at last brought the Europe-wide 1960s boom to Spain and set off change at an extraordinarily fast pace.

**'New freedoms – in culture, sexuality and work – were explored, and newly released energies expressed in a multitude of ways.'**

Two years earlier, in 1957, José María de Porcioles was appointed mayor of Barcelona, a post he would retain until 1973. Porcioles has since been regarded as the personification of the damage that was inflicted on the city by the Franco regime during its 1960s boom; he was also accused of covering Barcelona with drab high-rises and road schemes without any concern for the city's character. Sadly, many very valuable historic buildings, such as the grand cafés of the Plaça Catalunya, were torn down to make way for terribly bland modern business blocks, and minimal attention was paid to collective amenities.

After the years of repression and the years of development, 1966 marked the beginning of what became known as *tardofranquisme*, 'late Francoism'. Having made its opening to the outside world, the regime was losing its grip, and labour, youth and student movements began to emerge from beneath the shroud of repression. Nevertheless, the Franco regime never hesitated to show its strength. Strikes and demonstrations were dealt with savagely, and just months before the dictator's death, the last person to be executed in Spain by the traditional method of the garrotte, a Catalan anarchist named Puig Antich, went to his death in Barcelona. In 1973, however, Franco's closest follower, Admiral Carrero Blanco, was killed by a bomb planted by the Basque terrorist group ETA, leaving no one to guard over the core values of the regime. Change was in the air.

## GENERALISIMO TO GENERALITAT

When Franco died on 20 November 1975, the people of Barcelona celebrated; by evening, there was not a bottle of cava left in the city. But no one knew quite what would happen next. The Bourbon monarchy was restored under King Juan Carlos, but his intentions were not clear. In 1976 he charged a little-known Francoist bureaucrat, Adolfo Suárez, prime minister, with the task of leading the country to democracy.

The first years of Spain's 'transition' were difficult. Nationalist and other demonstrations continued to be repressed by the police with considerable brutality, and far-right groups threatened less open violence. However, political parties were legalised, and June 1977 saw the first democratic elections since 1936. They were won across Spain by Suárez's own new party, the Union de Centro Democratico (UCD), and in Catalonia by a mixture of socialists, communists and nationalists.

It was, again, not clear how Suárez expected to deal with the huge demands of Catalonia, but shortly after the elections he surprised everyone by going to visit the president of the Generalitat in exile, veteran pre-Civil War politician Josep Tarradellas. His office was the only institution of the old Republic to be so recognised, perhaps because Suárez astutely identified in the old man a fellow conservative. Tarradellas was invited to return as provisional president of a restored Generalitat, and he arrived amid huge crowds in October 1977.

The following year, the first free council elections since 1936 were held in Barcelona. They were won by the Socialist Party, with Narcís Serra appointed as mayor. The Socialist Party has retained control of the council ever since. In 1980 elections to the restored Generalitat were won by Jordi Pujol and his party, Convergència i Unió, which held power for the next 23 years.

## CITY OF DESIGN

Inseparable from the restoration of democracy was a complete change in the city's atmosphere after 1975. New freedoms – in culture, sexuality and work – were explored, and newly released energies expressed in a multitude of ways. Barcelona soon began to look different too, as the inherent dowdiness of the Franco years was

# Key events

**c15 BC** Barcino founded by Roman soldiers.
**cAD 350** Roman stone city walls built.
**415** Barcelona briefly capital of the Visigoths.
**719** Muslims attack and seize Barcelona.
**801** Barcelona taken by the Franks.
**985** Muslims sack Barcelona; Count Borrell II renounces Frankish sovereignty.
**1035-76** Count Ramon Berenguer I of Barcelona extends his possessions into southern France.
**1137** Count Ramon Berenguer IV marries Petronella of Aragon, uniting the two states in the Crown of Aragon.
**1213** Pere I is killed and virtually all his lands north of the Pyrenees are seized by France.
**1229** Jaume I conquers Mallorca, then Ibiza (1235) and Valencia (1238); second city wall built in Barcelona.
**1274** Consell de Cent, municipal government of Barcelona, established.
**1282** Pere II conquers Sicily.
**1298** Gothic cathedral begun. Population of city c40,000.
**1323-4** Conquest of Corsica and Sardinia.
**1347-8** Black Death cuts population by half.
**1462-72** Catalan civil war.
**1479** Ferdinand II inherits Crown of Aragon, and with his wife Isabella unites the Spanish kingdoms.
**1492** Final expulsion of Jews, and discovery of America.
**1522** Catalans refused permission to trade in America.
**1640** Catalan national revolt, the Guerra dels Segadors.
**1652** Barcelona falls to Spanish army.
**1702** War of Spanish Succession begins.
**1714** Barcelona falls to Franco-Spanish army after siege.
**1715** Nova Planta decree abolishes Catalan institutions; new ramparts and citadel built around Barcelona. Population 33,000.
**1808-13** French occupation.
**1814** Restoration of Ferdinand VII.
**1833** Aribau publishes *Oda a la Pàtria*, beginning of Catalan cultural renaissance. Carlist wars begin.
**1836-7** Dissolution of Barcelona monasteries.
**1842-4** Barcelona bombarded for the last time from Montjuïc, to quell Jamancia revolt.
**1854** Demolition of Barcelona city walls.
**1855** First general strike is violently suppressed.
**1859** Cerdà plan for the Eixample approved.
**1868** September: revolution overthrows Isabella II. November: first anarchist meetings held in Barcelona.
**1873** First Spanish Republic.
**1874** Bourbon monarchy restored under Alfonso XII.
**1882** Work begins on the Sagrada Família.
**1888** Barcelona Universal Exhibition.
**1899** FC Barcelona founded; electric trams introduced to the city.
**1900** Population of Barcelona 537,354.
**1909** Setmana Tràgica, anti-church and anti-army riots.
**1910** CNT anarchist workers' union founded.
**1921** First Barcelona Metro line opened.
**1923** Primo de Rivera establishes dictatorship in Spain.
**1929** Barcelona International Exhibition.
**1930** Population 1,005,565. Fall of Primo de Rivera.
**1931** 14 April: Second Spanish Republic.
**1934** October: Generalitat attempts revolt against new right-wing government in Madrid, and is then suspended.
**1936** February: Popular Front wins Spanish elections; Catalan Generalitat restored.
19 July: military uprising against left-wing government is defeated in Barcelona.
**1937** May: fighting within the republican camp in Barcelona.
**1939** 26 January: Barcelona taken by Franco's army.
**1959** Stabilisation Plan opens up the Spanish economy.
**1975** 20 November: Franco dies.
**1977** First democratic general elections in Spain since 1936; provisional Catalan Generalitat re-established.
**1978** First democratic local elections in Barcelona won by Socialists.
**1980** Generalitat fully re-established under Jordi Pujol.
**1982** Pasqual Maragall becomes mayor.
**1992** Olympics Games held in Barcelona.
**1996** Partido Popular wins Spanish elections.
**1997** Joan Clos replaces Maragall as mayor.
**2000** Partido Popular wins absolute majority in the Madrid parliament.
**2003** Coalition of left-wing parties wins control of Generalitat.
**2004** PSOE (Socialist Party) wins the Spanish elections.
**2006** Mayor Clos resigns, becoming Spanish minister of industry, commerce and tourism.

swept away by a new Catalan style for the new Catalonia: postmodern, high-tech, punkish, comic strip, minimalist and tautly fashionable. For a time, street culture was highly politicised, but simultaneously it was also increasingly hedonistic. In the 1980s design mania struck the city, a product of unbottled energies and the rebirth of Barcelona's artistic, artisan and architectural traditions.

This emphasis on a slick, fresh style first began underground, but it was soon taken up by public authorities and, above all, the Ajuntament, as a part of its drive to reverse the policies of the regime. The highly educated technocrats in the socialist city administration began, slowly at first, to 'recover' the city from its neglected state, and in doing so enlisted the elite of the Catalan intellectual and artistic community in their support. No one epitomises this more than Oriol Bohigas, the architect and writer who was long the city's head of culture and chief planner. A programme of urban renewal was initiated, beginning with the open spaces, public art and low-level initiatives, such as the campaign in which hundreds of historic façades were given an overdue facelift.

This ambitious, emphatically modern approach to urban problems acquired much greater focus after Barcelona's bid to host the 1992 Olympic Games was accepted, in 1986. Far more than just a sports event, the Games were to be Barcelona's third great effort to cast aside suggestions of second-city status and show the world its wares. The exhibitions of 1888 and 1929 had seen developments in the Ciutadella and on and around Montjuïc; the Olympics provided an opening for work on a citywide scale. Taking advantage of the public and private investment the Games would attract, Barcelona planned an all-new orientation of itself towards the sea, in a programme of urban renovation of a scope unseen in Europe since the years of reconstruction after World War II.

Inseparable from all this was Pasqual Maragall, mayor of Barcelona from 1982 to 1997, a tireless 'Mr Barcelona' who appeared in every possible forum to expound his vision of the role of cities, and intervened personally to set the guidelines for projects or secure the participation of major international architects. In the process, Barcelona, a byword for modern blight only a few years before, was turned into a reference point in urban affairs. Maragall also established a personal popularity well beyond that of his Catalan Socialist Party (PSC).

## ENDGAMES

The Games were finally held in July and August 1992 and universally hailed as an outstanding success. Barcelona and Catalonia rode out Spain's post-1992 recession better than any other part of the country. The Ajuntament announced still more large-scale projects, such as the old Port and the Raval. Pasqual Maragall, however, was to stand down amid general surprise in 1997, after winning a fifth term. He was succeeded as mayor by his then little-known deputy, Joan Clos, who remained in post until his resignation in August 2006. Maragall, meanwhile, sought to work his electoral magic beyond the city limits by becoming the socialist candidate for president of the Generalitat in the 1999 elections. He would not succeed for a few years yet, however, as once again Pujol was to triumph, thanks in no small part to his several years of successful horse-trading with the then minority PP central government.

In 2001 Pujol finally announced, two years in advance, that he would not be standing for another term, and named his then deputy, Artur Mas, as his chosen successor. When new regional elections finally came round on 16 November 2003, though, the results defied all predictions. Maragall, media front-runner for months, seemed once again to have been disappointed, as the PSC won a few more votes than Convergència, but also gained fewer seats in the Catalan parliament. For a short while it appeared Mas had triumphed, until it became clear that the real winners of the night, taking seats off both the 'majors', were previously fringe left-wing parties: the 'eco-communists' of the ICV and, above all, Esquerra Republicana (ERC). The ERC is directly descended from the old Esquerra of the 1930s, and it all but doubled its vote, so that in some areas as much as one-fifth of voters supported a party that, at least theoretically, is in favour of total or partial Catalan independence, and that rejects the Spanish monarchy.

A month of wrangling followed, until it was announced that the PSC had agreed to form a left-wing coalition with the ERC and ICV, bringing Convergència's apparently eternal hold on local power to an end. Maragall would finally get the Generalitat, but only in return for a commitment to push strongly for a new Autonomy Statute. In this he was mostly successful (*see pp46-49*), but after a series of political gaffes was pressured into agreeing to step down for the elections in November 2006. What is still not clear at the time of writing is whether his proposed successor, José Montilla – known as Pepe – has the requisite charisma to carry off the crown (the Catalan press photographers joke that he is never snapped smiling), and whether, as some fear, his Andalucían roots will turn the nationalists among the voters against him.

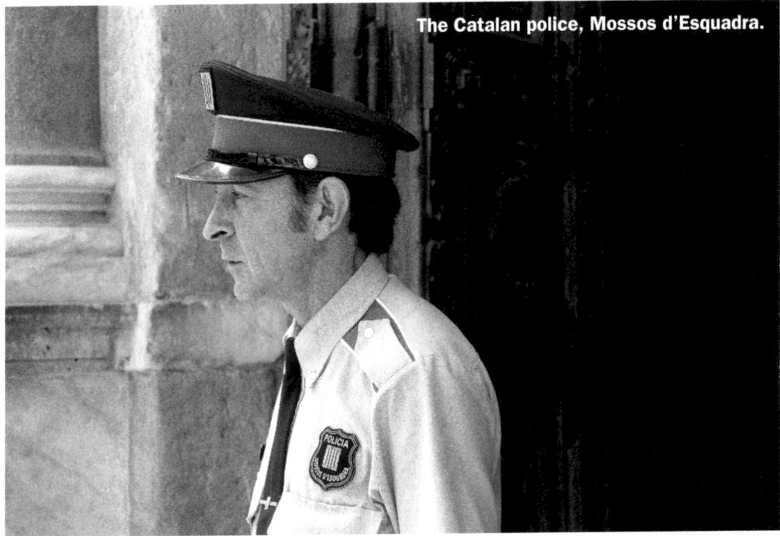
The Catalan police, Mossos d'Esquadra.

# Barcelona Today

## City on the verge of civil outrage.

A year ago, alarm bells began sounding over at city hall. In a town governed by socialists, one might be forgiven for thinking the unease was over rampant property speculation, uncontrolled rent hikes, racial discrimination or a decline in services. But no, the bells were ringing for another reason: the city was dirty. And not just literally dirty, but sullied in its social fabric. Prostitutes brazenly plied their trade in public, hordes of unruly youths staged drinking parties in the streets and graffiti was everywhere.

The upstanding citizens of Barcelona were outraged, or, to be more accurate, outrage was voiced by the conservative local media, the same ones who had painted this picture in the first place. Something had to be done. To nip this uncouth new Barcelona in the bud, the man who was then ostensibly in charge of matters, the image-driven, but basically unimaginative mayor Joan Clos put his well-clad socialist foot down. In early 2006, he implemented what are known as the *incivisme* laws, municipal ordinances aimed to control uncivil behaviour.

These new laws range from clearly specified infractions, such as urinating in the street, vandalism, illegal street trading or offering or requesting sexual services in public, to more vague crimes involving the improper use of public space, or attacks on a person's dignity. The fines vary according to the degree and type of infraction, but are by no means trifling: taking a leak on a street corner or buying a beer from an illegal street vendor can now cost you a hefty €750 (*see p33* **Fine print**).

Despite all the media hype about the city's untidiness, however, many local residents have raised their eyebrows at the new laws. What these residents know is that Barcelona, or at least its old heart, has always been dirty, in every sense of the word.

In fact, for most of the 20th century, an invisible moral wall stood between the sordid but lively Old City and the proper but boring new city.

Many Eixample residents never ventured below Plaça Catalunya, altogether avoiding what they viewed as the depravity of the city centre, while those on the other side of the fence claimed it was precisely the laid-back, 'live and let live' atmosphere of the old city that gave it its unique air. It was only with the massive rise of tourism towards the end of the 20th century that this situation began to change.

**'For a city increasingly dependent on tourism as its main source of revenue, it's only logical that it should care about its image.'**

So if the dirt has always been there, what are the new laws really about? For starters, municipal elections will be held in 2007. And while the socialists haven't lost their grip on Barcelona since democracy's return in the late 1970s, their popularity under Clos dwindled after the tepid reception of the Universal Forum of Cultures in 2004. That thinly disguised real-estate venture (which cost a cool €3 billion) furthered a general perception that he, and the rest of the municipal socialists, had lost touch with the people. Clos, at any rate, has found an honourable exit from his job as mayor, having accepted Spanish prime minister Zapatero's invitation to become the Spanish minister of industry, commerce and tourism. His hand-picked heir for the post of mayor is a respected but relatively unknown fellow socialist, Jordi Hereu. As Barcelona's new mayor, Hereu will face municipal elections in May 2007.

Keeping conservative challengers at bay may be one reason for the city crackdown à la Giuliani. The other reason is simple: image. For a city increasingly dependent on tourism as its main source of revenue (tourists spend upwards to nine million euro a day in Barcelona), it's only logical that it should care about its image. What's a bit of local disgruntlement over City Hall's heavy-handedness compared to putting at risk the city's shiny international reputation?

## RESEARCH RESURGENCE

To be fair, a concerted effort is also being made to move beyond image promotion and actually retool the city for the 21st century, with the aim of attracting longer-term professional residents. The much-publicised high-tech park in Poble Nou, 22@, can now boast big names like General Electric, while a brand-new, state-of-the-art biomedical research centre has opened in the Barceloneta. Shaped like a gigantic biological cell, this €100-million venture (known as the PRBB after its initials in Catalan) will house some 80 international research teams. Located conveniently beside the Hospital del Mar, the research centre has, among other features, a 3,000 square metre (9,842 square feet) space for rearing mice and zebra fish for experimentation.

## CIVIL REVIVAL

As for who is actually enforcing the new laws, Clos has had the help of the freshly installed Mossos d'Esquadra ('Squadron Lads'), the Catalan police force that, since November of 2005, has taken on full duties within Barcelona. This predominantly youthful force can now be seen zipping purposefully about the city, filling in the void left by the departing, less-than-welcome Spanish national police. Despite their visibility, however, it's yet to be seen whether the Mossos will do a better job staying on top of petty street crime and bag-snatching, which, are the work of an altogether more devious crew than the otherwise innocent individuals targeted by the new *incivisme* laws.

The Mossos has arrived on the scene just as the city has achieved, in the form of a new city charter, its greatest level of political autonomy in more than 60 years. Approved after 25 years of bickering between the various municipal, autonomous and national governments, the charter gives the city more control over its finances, local justice and policing, along with other matters. On a national level, the city charter's counterpart is the Catalan Estatut (the reform bill of the Catalan Statute of Autonomy), a significant recent step in transforming Catalonia's status within Spain (*see pp46-50*).

## HEADING TO THE POLLS

Generalitat president Pasqual Maragall, who rose to international fame as Barcelona's Olympic mayor, has earned his place in the history books after his successful steering of the new Estatut to fruition. Despite his achievement, however, the Catalan president failed to maintain the support of his own party, the Partit dels Socialistes de Catalunya (PSC), or the other members of the three-party alliance that helped him govern. One reason for this lack of support may stem from the so-called *Maragalladas* he is prone to uttering. These are brusque, off-the-cuff remarks utterly lacking in political tact.

After announcing he would not run again for office, Maragall set the date for Catalan elections at 1 November 2006, leaving the field to his political heir in the PSC, José Montilla, Zapatero's former minister of industry. With the fracturing of the socialists and the other leftist parties of Maragall's three-party government, notably with the distancing of the Catalan nationalists Esquerra Republicana (ERC) led by attention-grabbing firebrand Josep Carod-Rovira, the stage is set for an

## Fine print

Barcelona has produced a raft of new curious laws. There can be few other cities in the world that have made it a criminal offence, for example, to be 'tempted... by tricksters'. In essence, if you spot a con man and decide to do business with him regardless, you are liable to lose not only your shirt, but up to €3,000 in fines.

This is one of several, often seemingly impenetrable, new by-laws introduced in 2006 to counteract '*incivisme*' in the city, and are attracting ridicule and opprobrium in equal measure. The category hitting the headlines has been prostitution, with the offering or accepting of sexual services being outlawed where it is likely to impede public use of a street or space (this, naturally, is open to a thousand interpretations), but there are several others likely to affect the unwitting tourist.

Take, for example, the *Time Out* reader who, enjoying a quiet beer on the beach with his girlfriend, was approached by a couple of policemen and fined €70. His crime was not causing a disturbance, or even drinking alcohol in public, it was drinking alcohol from a can in a public place. Consumption of alcohol in a public space (apart from pavement bars or café tables) is forbidden where 'this may cause a nuisance' and where it comes 'in a bottle or can'. Fines can reach an impressive €1,500.

Spitting, defecating and urinating in the street attract penalties of up to €300, whereas spray-painting a wall, sleeping on a public bench, handing out leaflets or flyposting could see you fined €120-€3,000, and skateboarding, rollerskating or cycling over street furniture from €750 to €3,000.

Most egregious penalty, though, must surely go to that imposed on anyone using shampoo in a beach shower. The fine for this is €1,500. The justification is even more irrational: 'For reasons of hygiene, the use of soaps or other personal hygiene products is forbidden.'

electoral showdown between the PSC socialists and the conservative Catalan nationalists of Convergència i Unió (CiU). The political rumour mill has it that the two opposing parties will make an unlikely alliance after the elections.

Whatever the outcome, a good deal of credit for the success of the Estatut and Catalonia's now freer hand to manage its own affairs must be given to Spanish prime minister José Luis Rodríguez Zapatero. The socialist prime minister has so far managed to turn his stunning political upset of the right-wing Partido Popular (PP) in 2004 into a fruitful and much-admired term, albeit much to the chagrin of the right. Part of the right's vexation with Zapatero lies in the fact that he was voted into office three days after a horrific train bombing by Islamic fundamentalists. The PP essentially threw the election by making a hideous miscalculation shortly after the bombing, deliberately misleading the populace by attempting to blame ETA for the tragedy, apparently in order to deflect further criticism of the PP's pro-Iraq War stance. Unlike many politicians, Zapatero has remained true to his word once in office: he promptly pulled Spanish troops out of Iraq, passed legislature allowing same-sex marriages (*see p240* **Wedding Belles**), and ushered through the Catalan Estatut. Under his government, ETA has even announced a permanent ceasefire.

All of this has the PP foaming at the mouth, to the extent of causing one army general to threaten an invasion of Catalonia if the Estatut were to go ahead. The general, needless to say, was immediately removed from his command, but the PP has continued to be relentless in its verbal attacks.

## HAIR-RAISING HOUSING HIKES

Sit down with any *barceloní* for more than five minutes, and the conversation will soon turn to the price of flats and the difficulty of buying one. The cost of a half-decent flat within central Barcelona has risen more than 60 per cent in the last few years. Rents aren't far behind, more than doubling in less than a decade and putting them beyond the reach of most young couples on the lookout for independence. Many are opting to move to the peripheries: the urban sprawl of the huge satellite town L'Hospitalet, for example, or the bucolic calm of La Floresta, only 20 minutes by train from Plaça Catalunya.

The new bête noire of Barcelona's residents is '*el especulador*': the real-estate entrepreneur who buys entire buildings in the centre of town, empties them of their unprofitable, rent-paying long-term residents, as often as not through relentless harassment known locally as 'mobbing', and sells them at an exorbitant sum, often to people from outside Spain who'll pay an inflated asking price. Support for the old local tradition of squatting has taken on a new resonance, and is now seen as cheerleading a rare poke in the eye for the ambitious property developers.

Still, while life in the centre of Barcelona has changed substantially over the last few years, it's arguably changed less than in comparable European cities, or at least for the moment. Thanks to a certain measure of intervention by the city council – rent-protected flats in the centre for young people in any major new development (though not enough, scream detractors), a moratorium on the granting of licences for larger shops – this has remained a city with a centre in which people actually want to live. If only they could afford it.

## MULTICULTURAL MELANGE

In the 1960s Barcelona's population swelled by nearly 50 per cent, as hundreds of thousands of immigrants arrived from the poorer areas of Spain to work in the city's booming industries. Locals looked down on these new arrivals; the offensive epithet *charnego* (derived from *nocharnego*, or 'someone who wanders the street at night') was invented to describe them. An ethnic class system sprang up, dividing Catalans from the Spaniards who poured their drinks, drove their taxis and worked in their factories. The children of these immigrants now make up a substantial proportion of the population and are themselves Catalans. Increasingly confident of their role within a new Catalan society, they're at the forefront of a cultural scene where *mestizaje*, the Spanish word for ethnic mix, is the new cool. It's a trend typified by the wildly popular rumba-flamenco-hip-hop fusion bands such as Ojos de Brujo or Manu Chao, heard everywhere.

Similarly, the Raval, still an economically depressed area filled with North African and Pakistani immigrants, is now the coolest part of town. It has even spawned its own CD: *The Raval Sessions*, a compilation of local acts that mixes North African rhythms and fast Spanish lyrics. However, multiculturalism is a concept that sometimes sits uneasily in a small country that's intensely proud of its local traditions and has spent centuries defending them from the Spanish big brother next door. Some *catalanistes* are concerned that after the huge strides made since the end of the dictatorship, the promotion of Catalan as Barcelona's official language is in danger of taking a step back.

Immigrant populations have more than trebled in three years in fringe areas of the city such as Nou Barris and Sant Martí. By far the biggest group to arrive over the last few years are Ecuadoreans, closely followed by other Latin Americans, as well as North Africans, Pakistanis and Filipinos. Most use Spanish as their lingua franca; while subsidised Catalan lessons are available from the regional government, those entering the low-wage service industry argue, not without good reason, that they don't need to learn the more obscure language, and would rather spend their time trying to earn money. Their offspring, on the other hand, won't have a choice in the matter: all public schooling is carried out in Catalan.

Meanwhile, the municipal government continues with its efforts to keep the city's 'quality of life' rankings among the highest in Europe. A considerable number of squats and semi-legal cultural associations that doubled as alternative, late-night hangouts have been shut down. More comical have been attempts to stop buskers who aren't very good: buskers now need to audition for a licence, and to book pitches in the Old City.

On the world stage, the city hasn't lost any of its appeal. It was recently the highlight of two major exhibitions in New York. Barcelona has apparently mastered the art of mixing urban spaces with private money, and hosting big-scale events that help cover the costs of construction. It's what former mayor Joan Clos calls 'a successful city operating in a free market'. It remains to be seen, however, if this balancing act between keeping neighbourhoods vital and accommodating big business can be maintained indefinitely, or whether, in fact, the scales have already begun to tip too far in favour of the latter. At any rate, such issues will surely play their part in the municipal elections in early 2007.

Sant Pau del Camp. *See p36.*

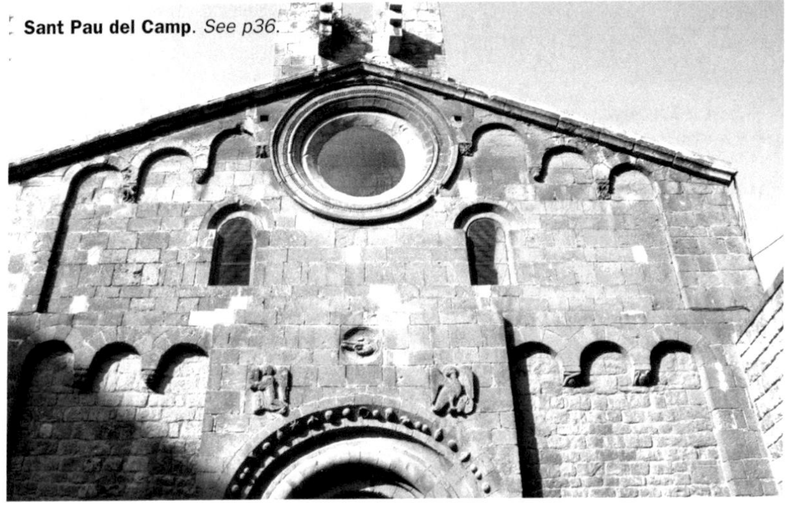

# Architecture

2,000 years of city chic.

A major 2006 exhibition on new Spanish architecture at New York's MoMA caused no little pride in the country of its focus. It was, however, to kick-start a heated debate over Barcelona's architectural prowess. Criticism came from two directions: on the one hand, it was claimed that Barcelona is becoming an urban-design theme park, its chronic housing shortage being glossed over while millions of euro are spent on big-name architects and flashy landmark buildings; and on the other hand, that this would be all very well if the architects in question were at least local.

There are more than 5,000 trained architects in Barcelona – a remarkable figure, given an overall population of 1.5 million – and yet, with the notable exception of the late Enric Miralles, recent big names to be commissioned are all from elsewhere: Jean Nouvel, Zaha Hadid, Herzog and de Meuron and Barcelona stalwart Lord Rogers (Richard Rogers). This sits uneasily with many of those who take pride in the use of grand architectural projects as a means of expressing a local identity, and yet Spain has looked beyond its borders for artistic and architectural talent since Moorish times. Where Catalonia particularly succeeds, since Gaudí's day and even earlier, is in having the vision and courage to commission new buildings that at the time have seemed ambitious and, often, outlandish.

Architecture is sometimes regarded as Catalonia's greatest contribution to the history of art. Indeed, there are few cities in the world that boast as many examples of architectural flair as Barcelona; no fewer than nine of its buildings have now been designated as UNESCO World Heritage sites (*see p124* **And the winner is...**). Catalan craftsmen have been famed since the Middle Ages for their use of fine materials and skilled finishings, and Catalan architects have been both artists and innovators: traditional Catalan brick vaulting techniques were the basis of visionary structural innovations that allowed later architects to span larger spaces and build higher structures. Contemporary Catalan architects have inherited the international prestige of their forebears; the work of artists such as Ricardo Bofill, Oriol Bohigas or Enric Miralles can be seen in a number of major cities around the world.

Unlike many European cities, Barcelona has never rested on its architectural laurels or tried to preserve its old buildings as relics.

## Don't miss Modernisme

**Fàbrica Casaramona**
Puig's former textile mill is a prime example of Modernista industrial building. *See p42.*

**Hospital de Sant Pau**
One of the most successful examples of the application of Modernista style and vivid decoration to a practical purpose. *See p42.*

**Hotel España**
Domènech i Montaner designed the bar, Eusebi Arnau the curvaceous fireplace, and the main dining room is adorned with water-nymph murals by Ramon Casas. *See p65.*

**Manzana de la Discòrdia**
Gaudí's utterly original Casa Batlló, Puig i Cadafalch's cautious, medievalist Casa Ametller and the lush curves of Domènech i Montaner's Casa Lleó Morera. *See p42.*

**Museu Nacional d'Art de Catalunya**
Painting by Rusiñol, Casas and Nonell, and decorative art including the spectacular wood furniture of Gaspar Homar. *See p45.*

**Museu de Zoologia**
Domènech i Montaner's 'Castle of Three Dragons' sums up the fairy-tale side of Modernisme, but was also highly innovative in its use of iron, glass and brick. *See p42.*

**Palau de la Música Catalana**
Domènech i Montaner's extraordinary concert hall is the epitome of Modernisme; the explosion in tile, sculpture and glass makes any event here special. *See p42.*

**Palau Güell**
Beyond the quite striking features of the structure itself is a wonderful Gaudí interior. *See p41.*

**Park Güell**
An incomplete, tantalising vision of Gaudí's ideal world. *See p42.*

**La Pedrera**
A fine contrast to the Sagrada Família: Gaudí's most successful combination of imagination and radical architectural innovation. *See p42.*

**Sagrada Família**
Modernisme's most eccentric, ambitious monument. *See p41.*

Contemporary buildings are often daringly constructed alongside or even within old ones, and a mix of old and new is a prime characteristic of some of the most successful recent projects seen in Barcelona, which all goes to create a thoroughly modern city firmly rooted in its architectural heritage. The importance of architecture is also reflected in public attitudes: Barcelona's citizens take a keen interest in their buildings. A range of architectural guides, some in English, is available and informative leaflets on building styles are also provided (in English) at tourist offices (*see p321*).

### ROMAN TO GOTHIC

The Roman citadel of Barcino was founded on the hill of Mons Taber, just behind the cathedral, which to this day remains the religious and civic heart of the city. It left an important legacy in the fourth-century city wall, fragments of which are visible at many points around the Old City. Barcelona's next occupiers, the Visigoths, left little, although a trio of fine Visigothic churches survives in nearby Terrassa. When the Catalan state began to form under the counts of Barcelona from the ninth century, its dominant architecture was massive, simple Romanesque. In the Pyrenean valleys, there are hundreds of fine Romanesque buildings, notably at **Sant Pere de Rodes**, **Ripoll**, **Sant Joan de les Abadesses** and **Besalú**. There is, however, little in Barcelona.

On the right-hand side of the cathedral, if you are looking at the main façade, is the 13th-century **chapel of Santa Llúcia**, which is incorporated into the later building; tucked away near Plaça Catalunya is the **church of Santa Anna**; and in La Ribera sits the **Capella d'en Marcús**, a tiny travellers' chapel. The city's greatest Romanesque monument, however, is the beautifully plain 12th-century church and cloister of **Sant Pau del Camp**, built as part of a larger monastery.

By the 13th century Barcelona was the capital of a trading empire, and was growing rapidly. The settlements – called *ravals* or *vilanoves* – that had sprung up outside the Roman walls were brought within the city by the building of Jaume I's second set of walls, which extended west to the Rambla. This commercial growth and political eminence formed the background to the great flowering of Catalan Gothic, which saw the construction of many of the city's most important civic and religious buildings. The **cathedral** was begun in 1298, in place of an 11th-century building. Work began on the **Ajuntament** (Casa de la Ciutat) and **Palau de la Generalitat** – later subject to extensive alteration – in 1372 and 1403 respectively. Major additions were made to the **Palau Reial** of the Catalan-Aragonese kings, especially the **Saló del Tinell** of 1359-62. The great hall of the **Llotja** (Stock Exchange) was finished in 1380-92. Many of Barcelona's finest buildings were built or completed in these years, in the midst of the crisis that followed the Black Death.

Catalan Gothic has characteristics that distinguish it from northern, classic Gothic. It is simpler, and gives more prominence to solid, plain walls between towers and columns, rather than the empty spaces between intricate flying buttresses that were trademarks of the great French cathedrals. This means that the Catalan buildings appear much more massive. In façades, as much emphasis is given to horizontals as to verticals; octagonal towers end in cornices and flat roofs, not spires. Decorative intricacies are mainly confined to windows, portals, arches and gargoyles. Many churches have no aisles but only a single nave, the classic example of this being the beautiful **Santa Maria del Pi** in Plaça del Pi, built between 1322 and 1453. This style has, ever since, provided the historic benchmark for Catalan architecture. It is simple and robust, yet elegant and practical. Innovative, sophisticated techniques were developed: the use of transverse arches supporting timber roofs allowed the spanning of great halls uninterrupted by columns, a system used in the **Saló del Tinell**. Designed by Pere III's court architect Guillem Carbonell, it has some of the largest pure masonry arches in Europe, the elegance and sheer scale of which give the space tremendous splendour. The **Drassanes**, built from 1378 as the royal shipyards (and now the **Museu Marítim**), is really just a very beautiful shed, but its enormous parallel aisles make this one of the most imposing spaces in the city.

La Ribera, the Vilanova del Mar, was the commercial centre of the city, and gained the magnificent masterpiece of Catalan Gothic, **Santa Maria del Mar**, built in 1329-84. Its superb proportions are based on a series of squares imposed on one another, with three aisles of almost equal height. The interior is quite staggering in its austerity.

The architecture of medieval Barcelona, at least that of its noble and merchant residences, can be seen at its best along **Carrer Montcada**, next to Santa Maria. Built by the city's merchant elite at the height of its confidence and wealth, this line of buildings conforms to a very Mediterranean style of urban palace and makes maximum use of space. A plain exterior faces the street, with heavy doors opening into an imposing patio, on one side of which a grand external staircase leads to the main rooms on the first floor (*planta noble*), which often have elegant open loggias.

## MARKING TIME

By the beginning of the 16th century, political and economic decline meant that there were far fewer patrons for new buildings in the city. A good deal was built in the next 300 years, but rarely in any distinctively Catalan style; as a result, these structures have often been disregarded. In the 1550s the **Palau del Lloctinent** was built for the royal viceroys on one side of Plaça del Rei, while in 1596 the present main façade was added to the **Generalitat**, in an Italian Renaissance style.

The Church also built lavishly around this time. Of the baroque convents and churches along La Rambla, the **Betlem** (1680-1729), at the corner of C/Carme, is the most important survivor. Later baroque churches include **Sant Felip Neri** (1721-52) and **La Mercè** (1765-75). Another addition, after the siege of Barcelona in 1714, was new military architecture, since the

**Santa Maria del Mar.**

city was encased in ramparts and fortresses. Examples remaining include the **Castell de Montjuïc**, the buildings in the **Ciutadella**, and the **Barceloneta**.

A more positive 18th-century alteration was the conversion of La Rambla into a paved promenade, a project that began in 1775 with the demolition of Jaume I's second wall. Neo-classical palaces were built alongside: **La Virreina** and the **Palau Moja** (at the corner of C/Portaferrisa) both date from the 1770s. Also from that time, but in a less classical style, is the **Gremial dels Velers** (Candlemakers' Guild) at Via Laietana 50, with its two-coloured stucco decoration.

However, it wasn't until the closure of the monasteries in the 1820s and '30s that major rebuilding on the Rambla could begin. Most of the first constructions that replaced them were still in international, neo-classical styles. The site that is now the **Mercat de la Boqueria** was first remodelled in 1836-40 as Plaça Sant Josep to a design by Francesc Daniel Molina, based on the English Regency style of John Nash. That project is buried beneath the 1870s market building, but its Doric colonnade can still be detected. Molina also designed the **Plaça Reial**, begun in 1848. Other fine examples from the same era are the colonnaded **Porxos d'en Xifré**, blocks built in 1836 opposite the Llotja on Passeig Isabel II, by the Port Vell.

## BIRTH OF THE MODERN CITY

In the 1850s Barcelona was able to expand physically, with the demolition of the walls, and psychologically, with economic expansion and the cultural reawakening of the Catalan Renaixença. And, from the off, one could see in operation one of the characteristics of modern Barcelona: audacious planning. The city would eventually spread outwards and be connected up to Gràcia and other outlying towns through the great grid of the **Eixample**, designed by **Ildefons Cerdà** (1815-75). An engineer by trade, Cerdà was a radical influenced by utopian socialist ideas, and concerned with the poor condition of workers' housing in the Old City.

With its love of straight lines and grids, Cerdà's plan was closely related to visionary rationalist ideas of its time, as was the idea of placing two of its main avenues along a geographic parallel and a meridian. Cerdà's central aim was to alleviate overpopulation while encouraging social equality by using quadrangular blocks of a standard size, with strict building controls to ensure they were built only on two sides, to a limited height, and with a garden. Each district would be of 20 blocks, with all community necessities. In the event, however, this idealised use of space was rarely achieved, private developers regarding Cerdà's restrictions as pointless interference. Buildings

The 'garden of warriors' on the roof of **La Pedrera**. *See p42.*

## 21st-century pride

The Museum of Modern Art in New York recently mounted an exhibition in celebration of modern Spanish architecture in which Catalan architects such as Enric Miralles figured prominently. Meanwhile, the Barcelona city authorities, ever on the lookout for Paris-style *grands projets* appear to have embarked on a policy of giving what little land is left in the city over to big-name architects to erect signature buildings; this, in spite of worsening housing shortage. So far, what most of these buildings have in common is that they are very tall.

Up until the 1992 Olympic Games, Barcelona was a low-rise city, and the only tower was the brutally ugly Edifici Colom in Drassanes, erected in 1970. Then the city's own version of the Twin Towers went up on the seafront next to Frank Gehry's giant bronze fish, and since then there has barely been an architect of world renown that has not left their hallmark on the city', from Sir Norman Foster's communication tower on the Collserola all the way to Santiago Calatrava's elegant white 'needle' on Montjuïc. The biggest impact on the skyline has come from Jean Nouvel's 144-metre (472-foot) Torre Agbar (photo above) in Glòries. Nouvel says, somewhat improbably, that the tower echoes the mountains of Montserrat, but the rather more prosaic locals invariably refer to it either as 'the suppository' or 'the vibrator'. Nouvel has already begun work on a new project, a park down the road from his tower in Poblenou, the former mill district known as 'little Manchester'.

Beyond Poblenou, where Diagonal meets the sea, the 2004 Forum of International Cultures gave the green light to build a number of new towers, including the Hotel Princess by the Catalan practice Tusquets Díaz, while closer to town the late Enric Miralles's sleekly beautiful Torre Gas Natural now rises up from the Passeig Marítim. Lord Rogers, still in the process of transforming the old bullring in Plaça Espanya into a shopping centre, has since completed the 105-metre (345-foot) Hotel Hesperia, complete with a domed, top-flight restaurant, in Hospitalet, a depressed and overcrowded Barcelona suburb. It will soon have Dominic Perrault's 120-metre (393-foot) Habitat Sky for company.

Frank Gehry was never going to be satisfied with a mere fish, and has been entrusted with the redevelopment of a derelict part of Sagrera in readiness for the arrival of the high-speed train that will link Barcelona with Madrid and France. The proposed five twisting towers, dominated by the 148-metre (486-foot) Edifici Núvia Sagrera, is already being dubbed 'Barcelona's Guggenheim'. Not to be outdone, Zaha Hadid is to build the new university campus close to the Besòs river, a structure composed of an irregular spiral of 12 superimposed layers that is large but not excessively tall. In spite of all this reaching for the sky, God will still be able to lord it over Mammon when the central tower of Gaudí's Sagrada Familia is completed in, they say, 2017. At 170 metres (528 feet), it will be taller than any of the city's current skyscrapers.

exceeded planned heights, and all the blocks from Plaça Catalunya to the Diagonal were enclosed. Even the planned gardens failed to withstand the onslaught of construction.

However, the development of the Eixample did see the refinement of a specific type of building: the apartment block, with giant flats on the *principal* floor (first above the ground), often with large glassed-in galleries for the drawing room, and small flats above. In time, the interplay between the Eixample's straight lines and the disorderly tangle of the older city became an essential part of the city's identity.

## MODERNISME

Art nouveau was the leading influence in the decorative arts in Europe and the US between 1890 and 1914. In Barcelona, its influence merged with the cultural and political movement of the Catalan Renaixença to produce what became known as Modernisme (used here in Catalan to avoid confusion with 'modernism' in English, which refers to 20th-century functional styles).

For all of Catalonia's traditions in building and the arts, no style is as synonymous with it as Modernisme. This is in part due to the huge modern popularity of its most famous proponent, Gaudí, and to its mix of decoration, eccentric unpredictability, dedicated craftsmanship and practicality. Modernisme can also be seen as matching certain archetypes of Catalan character, as a passionately nationalist expression that made use of Catalan traditions of design and craftwork. Artists strove to revalue the best of Catalan art, showing interest in the Romanesque and Gothic of the Catalan Golden Age; Domènech i Montaner, for example, combined iron-frame construction with distinctive brick Catalan styles from the Middle Ages, regarding them as an 'expression of the Catalan earth'.

All art nouveau had a tendency to look at both the past and future, combining a love of decoration with new industrial techniques and materials; so it was in Catalonia. Even as they constructed a nostalgic vision of the Catalan motherland, Modernista architects plunged into experiments with new technology. Encouraged by wealthy patrons, they designed works made of iron and glass, introduced electricity, water and gas piping to building plans, were the first to tile bathroom and kitchen walls, made a point of allowing extensive natural light and fresh air into all rooms, and toyed with the most advanced, revolutionary expressionism.

Catalan Modernista creativity was at its peak from 1888 to 1908. The Eixample is the style's display case, with the greatest concentration of art nouveau in Europe, but Modernista buildings can be found in innumerable other locations: in streets behind the Avda Paral·lel and villas on Tibidabo, in shop interiors and dark hallways, in country town halls and in the cava cellars of the Penedès.

International interest in Gaudí often eclipses the fact that there were many other remarkable architects and designers working at that time. Indeed, Modernisme was much more than an architectural style: the movement also included painters such as **Ramon Casas**, **Santiago Rusiñol** and **Isidre Nonell**, sculptors such as **Josep Llimona**, **Miquel Blay** and **Eusebi Arnau**, and furniture-makers like the superb Mallorcan **Gaspar Homar**. Much more than any other form of art nouveau, it extended into literature, thought and music, marking a whole generation of Catalan writers, poets, composers and philosophers. Although it was in architecture that it found its most splendid expression, Modernisme was an artistic movement in the fullest sense of the word, and, in Catalonia, it took on a nationalistic element.

Seen as the genius of the Modernista movement, **Antoni Gaudí i Cornet** was really a one-off, an unclassifiable figure. His work was a product of the social and cultural context of the time, but also of his own unique perception of the world, together with a deep patriotic devotion to anything Catalan.

Gaudí worked first as assistant to Josep Fontseré in the 1870s on the building of the **Parc de la Ciutadella**; the gates and fountain are attributed to him. Around the same time he also designed the lamp-posts in the **Plaça Reial**, but his first major commission was for **Casa Vicens** in Gràcia, built between 1883 and 1888. An orientalist fantasy, the building is structurally quite conventional, but Gaudí's controlled use of surface material already stands out in the neo-Moorish decoration, multicoloured tiling and superbly elaborate ironwork on the gates. Gaudí's **Col·legi de les Teresianes** convent school (1888-9) is more restrained, but the clarity and fluidity of the building, with its simple finishes and use of light, is very appealing.

In 1878 Gaudí met Eusebi Güell, heir to one of the largest industrial fortunes in Catalonia. The pair shared ideas on religion, philanthropy and the socially redemptive role of architecture, and Gaudí produced several buildings for Güell. Among them were **Palau Güell** (1886-8), an impressive, historicist building that established his reputation, and the crypt at **Colònia Güell** outside Barcelona, one of his most structurally experimental and surprising buildings.

In 1883 Gaudí, a profoundly religious conservative Catholic, became involved in the design of the **Sagrada Família**, begun the previous year. Part of his obsession with the building came from a belief that it would help redeem Barcelona from the sins of secularism and the modern era. From 1908 until his death in 1926 Gaudí worked on no other projects.

The Sagrada Família became the testing ground for Gaudí's ideas on structure and form, although he would live to see the completion of only the crypt, apse and Nativity façade, with its representation of 30 species of plants. As his work matured, he abandoned historicism and developed free-flowing, sinuous expressionist forms. His boyhood interest in nature began to take over from more architectural references, and what had previously provided external decorative motifs became the inspiration for the actual structure of his buildings.

In his greatest years, Gaudí combined other commissions with his cathedral; **La Pedrera**, which he begun in 1905, was his most complete project. The building has an aquatic feel about it: the balconies resemble seaweed, and the undulating façade is reminiscent of the sea, or rocks washed by it. Interior patios are in blues and greens, and the roof resembles an imaginary landscape inhabited by mysterious figures. The **Casa Batlló**, on the other side of Passeig de Gràcia, was an existing building that Gaudí remodelled in 1905-7; the roof looks like a reptilian creature perched high above the street. The symbolism of the façade is the source of endless speculation. Some link it to the myth of St George and the dragon; others maintain it is a celebration of carnival, with its harlequin-hat roof, wrought-iron balcony 'masks' and cascading, confetti-like tiles. This last element was an essential contribution of Josep Maria Jujol, who many believe was even more skilled than his master as a mosaicist.

Gaudí's fascination with natural forms found full expression in the **Park Güell** (1900-14), where he blurred the distinction between natural and artificial forms in a series of colonnades winding up the hill. These paths lead up to the large central terrace projecting over a hall; a forest of distorted Doric columns planned as the marketplace for Güell's proposed 'garden city'. The terrace benches are covered in some of the finest examples of *trencadís* (broken mosaic work), again mostly by Jujol.

Modernista architecture received a vital, decisive boost around the turn of the 19th century from the **Universal Exhibition of 1888**. The most important buildings for the show were planned by the famed **Lluís Domènech i Montaner** (1850-1923), who was then far more prominent than Gaudí as a propagandist for Modernisme in all its forms, and much more of a classic Modernista architect. Domènech was one of the first Modernista architects to develop the idea of the 'total work', working closely with large teams of craftsmen and designers on every aspect of a building. Not in vain was he dubbed 'the great orchestra conductor' by his many admirers.

Most of the Exhibition buildings no longer exist, but one that does is the **Castell dels Tres Dragons** in the Ciutadella park, designed as the Exhibition restaurant and now the **Museu de Zoologia**. It already demonstrated many key features of Modernista style: the use of structural ironwork allowed greater freedom in the creation of openings, arches and windows; and plain brick, instead of the stucco usually applied to most buildings, was used in an exuberantly decorative manner.

Domènech's greatest creations are the **Hospital de Sant Pau**, built as small 'pavilions' within a garden to avoid the usual effect of a monolithic hospital, and the fabulous **Palau de la Música Catalana**, an extraordinary display of outrageous decoration. He also left quite a few impressive constructions in Reus, near Tarragona, notably the ornate mansions **Casa Navàs** and **Casa Rull**, as well as the spectacular pavilions of the **Institut Pere Mata**, a psychiatric hospital and forerunner of the Hospital de Sant Pau.

Third in the trio of leading Modernista architects was **Josep Puig i Cadafalch** (1867-1957), who showed a neo-Gothic influence in such buildings as the **Casa de les Punxes** (or the 'House of Spikes', officially the **Casa Terrades**) in the Diagonal, combined with many traditional Catalan touches. Nearby on Passeig de Sant Joan, at No.108, is another of his masterpieces: the **Casa Macaya**, its inner courtyard inspired by the medieval palaces of C/Montcada. Puig was responsible for some of the best industrial architecture of the time, an area in which Modernisme excelled: the Fundació La Caixa's cultural centre recently moved from Casa Macaya to another of Puig i Cadafalch's striking creations, the **Fàbrica Casaramona** at Montjuïc, built as a textile mill; outside Barcelona he designed the extraordinary **Caves Codorniu** wine cellars. His best-known work, however, is the **Casa Amatller**, between Domènech's **Casa Lleó Morera** and Gaudí's **Casa Batlló** in the **Manzana de la Discòrdia**.

The style caught on with extraordinary vigour all over Catalonia, and some of the most engaging architects are not very well known internationally. Impressive apartment blocks and mansions were built in the Eixample by **Joan Rubió i Bellver** (Casa Golferichs, Gran Via 491), **Salvador Valeri** (Casa Comalat, Avda Diagonal 442) and **Josep Vilaseca**. North of Barcelona is La Garriga, where **MJ Raspall** built exuberant summer houses for the rich and fashionable families of the time; there are also some dainty Modernista residences in

Palau de la Música Catalana. See p42.

coast towns, such as Canet and Arenys de Mar. Some of the finest Modernista industrial architecture is in Terrassa, designed by the municipal architect **Lluís Moncunill** (1868-1931), while another local architect, **Cèsar Martinell**, built co-operative cellars that are true 'wine cathedrals' in Falset, Gandesa and many other towns in southern Catalonia.

## THE 20TH CENTURY

By the 1910s Modernisme had become too extreme for the Barcelona middle classes; Gaudí's later buildings, indeed, were met with derision. The new 'proper' style for Catalan architecture was **Noucentisme**, which stressed the importance of classical proportions. However, it failed to produce anything of much note: the main buildings that survive are those of the 1929 Exhibition, Barcelona's next 'big event' that served as the excuse for the bizarre, neo-baroque **Palau Nacional**. The Exhibition also brought the city one of the most important buildings of the century: Ludwig Mies van der Rohe's German Pavilion, the **Pavelló Barcelona**, rebuilt near its original location in 1986. Its impact at the time was extraordinary; even today, it seems modern in its challenge to the conventional ideas of space.

Mies van der Rohe had a strong influence on the main new trend in Catalan architecture of the 1930s, which, reacting against Modernisme and nearly all earlier Catalan styles, was quite emphatically functionalist. Its leading figures were **Josep Lluís Sert** and the **GATCPAC** collective (Group of Catalan Architects and Technicians for the Progress of Contemporary Architecture), who struggled to introduce the ideas of Le Corbusier and of the International Style to local developers. Under the Republic, Sert built a sanatorium off C/Tallers and the **Casa Bloc**, a workers' housing project at Passeig Torres i Bages 91-105 in Sant Andreu. In collaboration with Le Corbusier, GATCPAC also produced a plan for the radical redesign of the whole of Barcelona as a 'functional city', the **Pla Macià** of 1933-4; drawings for the scheme present a Barcelona that looks more like a Soviet-era new town in Siberia, and few regret that it never got off the drawing board. In 1937 Sert also built the Spanish Republic's pavilion for that year's Paris Exhibition, since rebuilt in Barcelona as the **Pavelló de la República** in the Vall d'Hebron. His finest work, however, came much later in the shape of the **Fundació Joan Miró**, built in the 1970s after he had spent many years in exile in the United States.

Mies van der Rohe's German Pavilion, **Pavelló Barcelona**. *See p43.*

## BARCELONA'S NEW STYLE

The Franco years had an enormous impact on the city. As the economy expanded at breakneck pace in the 1960s, Barcelona received an influx of migrants, in a context of property speculation and minimal planning controls; the city became ringed by a chaotic mass of high-rise suburbs. Another legacy of the era are some ostentatiously tall office blocks, especially on the Diagonal and around Plaça Francesc Macià.

When an all-new democratic city administration took over the reins of Barcelona at the end of the 1970s, there was a lot to be done. A generation of Catalan architects had been chafing at Francoist restrictions for years. However, the tone set early on, above all by Barcelona's chief planner Oriol Bohigas – who has continued to design individual buildings as part of the MBM partnership with Josep Martorell and David Mackay – was one of 'architectural realism', with a powerful combination of imagination and practicality.

Budgets were limited, so resources initially were to be concentrated not on buildings but on the gaps between them: public spaces, a string of fresh, modern parks and squares, many of which were to incorporate original artwork. From this beginning, Barcelona placed itself at the forefront of international urban design.

Barcelona's renewal programme took on a far more ambitious shape with the award of the 1992 Olympics, helped by a booming economy in the late 1980s. The third and most spectacular of the city's great events, the Barcelona Games were intended to be stylish and innovative, but most of all they were designed to provide a focus for a sweeping renovation of the city, with emblematic new buildings and infrastructure projects linked by clear strategic planning.

The three main Olympic sites – **Vila Olímpica**, **Montjuïc** and **Vall d'Hebron** – are quite different. The Vila Olímpica had the most comprehensive masterplan: drawn up by Bohigas and MBM themselves, it sought to extend Cerdà's grid down to the seafront. The main project on Montjuïc was to be the transformation of the 1929 stadium, but there is also Arata Isozaki's **Palau Sant Jordi** and its space-frame roof. Vall d'Hebron is the least successful of the three sites, but Esteve Bonell's **Velòdrom** is one of the finest (and earliest) of the sports buildings, built in 1984 before the Olympic bid had even succeeded.

Not content with all the projects completed by 1992, the city continued to expand through the '90s. Post-1992, the main focus of activity shifted to the **Raval** and the **Port Vell** (old port), and then more recently to the Diagonal Mar area in the north of the city. Many of the striking buildings here are by local architects, among them Helio Piñón and Albert Viaplana. Their work combines fluid, elegant lines with a strikingly modern use of materials, from the controversial 1983 **Plaça dels Països Catalans** through transformations of historic buildings such as the Casa de la Caritat, now the **Centre de Cultura Contemporània**, and all-new projects like **Maremàgnum** in the port.

Other important contributions in the post-Olympic remodelling of Barcelona were made by foreign architects: notable examples include Richard Meier's bold white **MACBA** and Norman Foster's **Torre de Collserola** on Tibidabo, which has become an emblem for Barcelona's skyline. Recently, two venerable buildings have been extensively remodelled in the service of the city's residents: the last stage of Gae Aulenti's interior redesign of the **Palau Nacional** on Montjuïc has been finished after 14 years to create the expanded **Museu Nacional d'Art de Catalunya**, and the **CosmoCaixa** building in Tibidabo, which again converts a 19th-century hospice into a spectacular exhibition space, this time as home to the new science museum. Also undergoing a major facelift, after decades lying as an abandoned shell, the Mudéjar-style arches of Las Arenas bullring are being converted by Lord Rogers into a big and futuristic shopping and leisure centre due to open in 2007.

In the 21st century, architectural projects are increasingly circumscribed by commercial imperatives, sometimes causing tensions between the traditions of Barcelona urban architecture, the needs of a city of this size and the globalisation of commerce. The huge changes to the cityscape linked to the Fòrum Universal de les Cultures 2004 are a case in point. The area at the mouth of the Besòs river, near where Avda Diagonal meets the sea, was transformed for the occasion, most notably by the construction of a triangular building, the **Edifici Fòrum**, designed by Herzog and de Meuron of Tate Modern fame. Nearby, Enric Miralles created a fiercely modern and rather soulless park, the **Parc Diagonal Mar**.

Whether this fourth stage in the re-imagining of the city can be linked to those outbursts of Barcelona's architectural creativity in the service of urban planning is debatable. While the value of many of these buildings is unquestionable, some see the dark hand of big business behind the latest developments and dismiss the new expansions connected to the Fòrum as more about making money than art. On the other hand, others defend this new, pragmatic approach to remodelling the city as another example of Barcelona's 1,000-year-old capacity to reinvent itself in the search to create a city that is both beautiful to look at and comfortable to live in.

The heroic defeat of Barcelona on 11 September 1714

# Separated But Not Divorced

Catalonia insists, Spain resists.

Catalonia is a nation. This was the opening phrase of the draft Statute of Autonomy agreed by the Catalan parliament in 2005 and presented for approval by Madrid. Oh no it's not came the reply, to paraphrase the Spanish parliament's wordy amendment.

It may seem odd to demand that nationhood be acknowledged in writing at a time when globalisation is blurring nationality, but this represents just the latest chapter in Catalonia's long assertion of its separateness. The region's claim to nationhood may stand on shaky ground as even in its most glorious heyday it was in coalition with the crown of Aragon, but its insistence on a separate identity does not. Historically and temperamentally, it is closer to France than Spain, and linguistically Catalan's closest relative is not Spanish but Provençal.

The story of Catalonia's role within and without Spain is well covered in the chapter on history; here – the Catalan and Spanish parliaments having agreed a new Statute of Autonomy in 2006 – we focus on the often contradictory struggle around the issues of autonomy and independence.

Catalonia and its national aspirations have been comprehensively stamped upon by centralist Spanish forces on three main occasions: with the fall of Barcelona to the forces of Felipe V in 1714, the dictatorships of Primo de Rivera (1923-30) and that of Franco (1939-75). As a result there is a common belief among Catalans, from separatists to the most mildly nationalist, that the nation is in constant jeopardy and that, as they are fond of putting it, 'Catalan identity is hanging by a thread'.

To outsiders, Catalans often appear stuck in the past, on what was and what might have been, but this is because, in terms of cultural repression, the past is never far enough behind.

The modern history of Catalan autonomy begins with the 1914 Mancomunitat (Commonwealth), which brought together the four Catalan provinces under a degree of self-government, the first taste of self-rule in 200 years. The Mancomunitat, an administrative body whose greatest achievements were in education and the boost it gave to Catalan press and publishing, had the character of a pre-state institution, both an echo of the pre-1714 Generalitat and a foreshadowing of its reincarnation in the 1930s. Its cultural emphasis was reflected in the fact that its second leader was Josep Puig i Cadafalch, the Modernista architect (*see p48* **Flying the flag**). The Mancomunitat was suppressed by Primo de Rivera in 1925, but buying Catalan books and newspapers continued as a form of passive resistance under the dictator, rather as supporting Barça did under Franco.

The triumph of republican parties across Spain in the 1931 elections was mirrored by

## The labyrinth of passion

In November 2003 José Luis Rodríguez Zapatero, leader of the then opposition Socialist Party, said in Barcelona: 'I will support the reform of the Statute of Catalonia that the Catalan parliament approves.' Like withdrawing Spanish troops from Iraq, this was a campaign promise he didn't expect to have to fulfil as at the time he was a long shot and all the polls pointed to the right-wing Partido Popular winning a third term. But then came the train bombs on 11 March 2004. The PP's cynical attempt to pin them on ETA backfired and an outraged and insulted electorate handed Zapatero the country. True to his word, he backed the Estatut (statute), but it was not in his gift to stop the Madrid parliament from amending (emasculating, some would say) the text approved by the Catalan parliament. It was in the interests of both Zapatero and all the Catalan parties to reach an agreement, and in the eyes of many this was achieved more through political expediency than on points of principle. Both Barcelona and Madrid manoeuvred to marginalise the separatist Esquerra Republicana (ERC), which was thrown into such a state of confusion that it moved from calling on its supporters to vote Yes, then No, then to spoil their ballots. In any event, ERC was forced out of the tripartite government and the Estatut was approved by referendum on 18 June 2006 with 74% in favour and 20% against, with a turnout of 49.5%. Fewer than 6% followed the ERC line and handed in blank or spoiled ballots.

The most contentious issue in the version Catalonia presented to the Spanish parliament was the blunt, opening sentence: 'Catalonia is a nation.' There was no way that any Spanish government was going to let that through, and the question of nationhood was shunted into the preamble and recast as follows: 'The Parliament of Catalonia, in line with the feelings and desires of the citizens of Catalonia, has defined Catalonia as a nation in a great majority.' This scarcely amounts to a declaration of independence.

The other sticking point was, inevitably, language. Under the 1979 statute, Catalan and Spanish are recognised as co-official languages, and all citizens have the right to express themselves in either. In the new document 'the right' is altered to 'the right and the duty' to understand both languages. As this runs counter to the Spanish constitution and international charters on human rights, it is clearly unenforceable. However, it is another attempt to entrench Catalan as the lingua franca at a time when there is a resurgence in demand for children to be at least partly schooled in Spanish, which parents have a right to demand.

Given that the statute is unlikely to be revised for a generation, to the outsider, Catalonia seems to have gained little aside from a few more percentage points in the amount of taxation they can hang on to before handing over the rest to Madrid and a bit more leeway to negotiate on its own behalf with Brussels. But, as then President Pasqual Maragall remarked at the start of the negotiations, the key arguments would be about the names of things, not their substance. What matters is that this statute has brought Catalonia more, not less, than before, even if it falls far short of what they wanted. Madrid refuses to recognise Catalonia as a nation but is willing to concede that Catalans think it is. In symbolic terms, this is a victory. Catalans have grown accustomed to attrition; you could even say they have developed a taste for it.

## Flying the flag

After Gaudí and Domènech i Montaner, the third most important Catalan architect of the 19th century was Josep Puig i Cadafalch (1867-1956). Deeply Catalan, Puig (pictured) was greatly concerned that 'architecture must bear testimony to the spirit of the people'. His strong, regionalist sentiments were also apparent away from the drawing board: he was president of the Mancomunitat (the semi-autonomous government of Catalonia) from 1917 to 1923 and also headed the Institute of Catalan Studies for 14 years. Keen to embrace the bygone days of Catalan independence, he was deeply involved in the Jocs Florals, a poetry contest dating from the Middle Ages, which he saw as a vehicle for promoting the Catalan language, as well as Catalan culture and politics.

Although Puig disliked the term Modernista, his buildings are generally grouped in that category and include the lavishly decorated Palau Baró de Quadras (Avda Diagonal 373), and the red-brick Fábrica Casaramona (now the CaixaForum, *see p117*). Perhaps in reaction to the contemporary vogue for neo-Arabic architecture, Puig chose to emphasise Catalonia's northern-ness by incorporating strong northern European elements into two of his most famous works: the Casa Amatller on the Passeig de Gràcia, which has a stepped Flemish pediment (*see p123*), and the Casa de les Punxes ('House of Spikes'), 416-420 Avda Diagonal, which resembles a Bavarian castle, although Puig could not resist adding a plaque of Saint George, with the legend 'Holy Patron of Catalonia, give us back our liberty.'

Puig used his political clout to exhort architectural contracts from the city council, including plans for the urbanisation of Montjuïc. The 1929 World Exhibition was the catalyst for much of the work and Puig designed the central showpiece of the Quatre Barres (Four Columns). Built in 1919, the 18-metre (60-foot) high columns stood in front of where the 'magic fountain' now plays to the crowds and represented the four stripes of the Catalan flag. They were demolished in 1928 by the Spanish dictator Primo de Rivera for being too symbolic of Catalan independence.

As the flap over the controversial new statute stokes the fires of regional identity, the city council is planning the requisite piece of accompanying public statuary. Puig's *Quatre Barres* should fit the bill perfectly. The idea was to reinstate the columns in 2007 to mark the 50th anniversary of Puig i Cadafalch's death (a slight tweaking of the figures as he actually died on 23 December 1956), but dragging bureaucratic feet means this is unlikely to happen in time.

the victory of Esquerra Republicana under Francesc Macià in Catalonia. When the Second Spanish Republic was declared on 14 April, 1931, Macià matched it by declaring Catalonia an independent republic, but this was soon watered down to an autonomous region. Under the 1932 Statute of Autonomy, the Generalitat was revived with considerable power in the fields of civil law and administration, and Catalan language acquired co-official status. But even in those heady days, with revolution in the air, the Spanish republicans trimmed back the powers claimed for the Generalitat.

In 1934, with a new and distinctly anti-Catalan government installed in Madrid, Lluís Companys, president of the Generalitat, declared Catalonia a state within the Spanish federal republic and called for a general strike. It was a mistake. There was no uprising, and Madrid took the opportunity to suppress the Generalitat once more. Companys's republic had lasted ten hours.

The Generalitat was re-established under Companys in 1936, but then the Civil War broke out and it was clear from the outset that one of the objectives of the officers behind the nationalist rebellion was to overthrow the autonomous Catalan government which offended their idea of a unified Spain. When Barcelona fell, Companys fled to France but, at Franco's behest, the Nazis tracked him down in Brittany and he was brought back to Barcelona, where he was executed on Montjuïc on 15 October 1940.

While Franco's repression in terms of imprisonment and execution of his enemies was perhaps as ferocious in other areas, notably Andalucía and Castilla-León, he had a particular loathing for all things Catalan and systematically crushed all of Catalonia's political and cultural institutions, at the same time criminalising the language. Catalan autonomy was a dead letter until he himself died in 1975, opening the way for the restoration of democracy.

**'Catalans want recognition that they are a people apart.'**

In 1977 a provisional Generalitat was installed by decree, and Josep Tarradellas, the Catalan president in exile, returned to Barcelona. The Spanish government began drawing up a new constitution for a federal state of 17 autonomous regions, which included the recognition of three 'historic nationalities': Catalans, Basques and Galicians. Once again the Catalans drew up a statute, and Madrid started trimming it back. Catalan language was granted only co-official status, so while it was obligatory to understand Spanish, the same didn't apply to Catalan, something the Catalans have sought to remedy in the latest statute. While they gained more powers over education, and therefore the use of Catalan, than in 1932, in terms of judicial powers and public order, they ended up with less in 1979 than in 1932. Neither in 1979 nor in 2006 did they manage to get an equivalent of the Basques' *concierto económico*, under which the Basques collect the taxes and hand over a slice to Madrid.

Nevertheless, the 1979 statute was approved by referendum, although with a turnout of only 59.6 per cent. In his 23 years as president, however, Jordi Pujol shrewdly used his Convergència i Unió party to prop up coalition governments in Madrid in return for more concessions for Catalonia. His successor, Artur Mas, helped to smooth the passage of the 2006 statute by agreeing, if need be, (by common consent, if not by his own admission) to support a future minority Socialist government in exchange for prime minister Zapatero easing the statute through the Spanish parliament.

So, what do the Catalans want? Ask a Spaniard, and they'll say they want too much, or they don't know what they want and even if they did know, if they got it, they would still complain. A growing minority want true independence, up, according to creditable polls, from 29 per cent in 1996 to 36 per cent in 2005. However, more than 45 per cent oppose independence, while the 'don't knows' hover around the 15 per cent mark. Given that at least half the population have close Spanish family ties, plus the surge of immigrants from outside Spain who have no Catalan nationalist agenda, separatism seems likely to remain a minority cause. What most Catalans want is simply recognition that they are a people apart, different, in a country where nearly everyone's sense of belonging is based on their province, their *pueblo*, their *barrio* and – in the case of Catalonia – their language. No one mistakes a Scotsman for an Englishman and, fundamentally, that's what Catalans want: recognition. Whenever Barça play a team from England, someone is there with a banner that reads: 'Catalonia is not Spain'. You can't imagine a Scot holding up a banner with the words 'Scotland is not England'. Aye, there's the rub. The Scots have, largely, lost their language but kept their identity, while the Catalans have asserted their language. Meanwhile the world remains unconvinced they are not just Spaniards who speak funny.

The ass, symbol of Catalan nationhood.

# Where to Stay



## Features



**Hostal Goya**. *See p75.*

# Where to Stay

Lots of luxury and a *hostal* revolution.



New hotels have been springing up over the last few years, and the trend shows no sign of slowing down. While this has certainly made it easier to find accommodation in a city with year-round high occupancy, unfortunately, most new places are at least four-star standard, when there is a real dearth of more modest hotels that offer fewer frills but provide all the facilities most travellers need.

The upside of this glut of top-end accommodation is that hotels are continually revising their rates according to demand and, at off-peak times, when there are fewer business travellers, offer rooms at heavily reduced prices. Be sure to check online for preferential rates. The downside is that Barcelona hosts a mind-boggling number of trade fairs and conferences every year, which can bring in up to 50,000 visitors at a time, all looking for the best possible deal. At these times, some hoteliers double or even triple their rates.

There is now quite a good range of boutique hotels, but again, they are mostly at the upper end of the scale. If you look hard enough, however, there is plenty of charm at the budget end too, as many *hostales* are situated in fabulous old buildings with elaborate doorways, grand staircases and beautiful tiled floors. A new generation of hoteliers is transforming old-fashioned, gloomy *hostales* into bright, friendly establishments with en-suite bathrooms, internet access and other 21st-century essentials.

Booking in advance is strongly advised, at least in those places where it's possible: many of the cheaper hotels won't accept reservations. Hotels often require you to guarantee your booking with credit-card details or a deposit; whether or not you've provided either, it's always worth calling a few days before your arrival to reconfirm the booking (get it in writing if you can; many readers have reported problems) and to check the cancellation policy. Often you will lose at least the first night.

To be sure of getting a room with natural light or a view, ask for an outside room (*habitació/habitación exterior*), which will usually face the street. Many of Barcelona's buildings are built around a central patio or airshaft, and the inside rooms (*habitació/habitación interior*) around them can be quite gloomy, albeit quieter. However, in some cases, these inward-facing rooms look on to large, open-air patios or gardens, which have the benefit of being quiet and having a view.

Hotels of two-star quality and more (listed under Expensive and Mid-range) have air-conditioning as standard. Air-con is increasingly common even in no-frills places, however, and around half the *hostales* in the Budget listings are equipped with it.

The law now prohibits smoking in communal areas in hotels. As a result, some hotels have banned smoking altogether, and many have the majority of floors/rooms as non-smoking.

Theft is a problem in some places, especially in lower-end establishments, but occasionally also in luxury ones. If you're sleeping cheap, you might want to travel with a padlock to lock your door, or at least lock up your bags. As a rule of thumb, check to see if youth-hostel rooms have lockers if you're sharing with other people. Use hotel safes where possible.

> ❶ Green numbers given in this chapter correspond to the location of each hotel as marked on the street maps. *See pp337-45.*

### STAR RATINGS AND PRICES

Accommodation in Catalonia is divided into two official categories: hotels (H) and *pensiones* (P). To be a hotel (star-rated one to five), a place must have en-suite bathrooms in every room. Ratings are based on physical attributes rather than levels of service; often the only difference between a three- and a four-star hotel is the presence of a meeting room. *Pensiones*, usually cheaper and often family-run, are star-rated one or two, and are not required to have en-suite bathrooms (though many do). Some *pensiones* are called *hostales*, but, confusingly, are not youth hostels; those are known as *albergues*.

For a double room, expect to pay €50-€75 for a budget *pensión*, €80-€180 for a mid-range spot and from €200 to more than €500 for a top-of-the-range hotel. However, prices can vary considerably depending on the time of year; always check for special deals. All bills are subject to seven per cent *IVA* (value added tax) on top of the basic price; this is not normally included in the advertised rate, but we have factored it into the prices we have given. Breakfast is not included unless stated.

## Booking agencies

### Barcelona Hotel Association

*Via Laietana 47, 1º, 2ª, Barri Gòtic (93 301 62 40/ fax 93 301 42 92/www.barcelonahotels.es). Metro Urquinaona.* **Open** 9am-6pm Mon-Fri. **Map** p344 D3.

The website of this hoteliers' organisation lists 350 hotels and apartments in all categories, and there are also special offers and last-minute rates. Credit card details must usually be given to make a reservation online, but accounts are not debited until you check out. Reservations cannot be made in the office, although information can be provided here.

### Barcelona On-Line

*Gran Via de les Corts Catalanes 662, Eixample (93 343 79 93/fax 93 317 11 55/www.barcelona-on-line.es). Metro Passeig de Gràcia.* **Open** 9am-7pm Mon-Fri; 9am-2pm Sat. **Map** p342 G8.

This is a highly professional agency where you can book hostel, hotel rooms and private apartments online, on the phone or at the above office. Staff are multilingual and the service is free, but, depending on the hotel, there can be a fee if you cancel less than 48 hours before arrival. You'll also need to make a prepayment for apartment reservations.

### Viajes Iberia

*Plaça de Sants 12, Eixample (93 431 90 00/902 11 62 21/fax 93 432 00 53/www.viajesiberia.com). Metro Plaça de Sants.* **Open** 9.30am-7.30pm Mon-Fri; 9.30am-1.30pm Sat. **Credit** AmEx, DC, MC, V. **Map** p337 A7.

This agency can book a room at many of Barcelona's hotels and some *pensiones*. The reservation fee varies, and you will need to pay a deposit.

**Other locations**: throughout the city.

## Barri Gòtic & La Rambla

La Rambla is flanked by hotels ranging from no-frills to luxury, but the totally touristy environment – not to mention the noise – may prove a bit much for some people. The medieval labyrinth of the Gòtic conceals cheaper alternatives, but bear in mind that old buildings can sometimes be grotty rather than charming. Some rooms do not get much light, and taxis cannot get down the narrower streets.

## Expensive

### H10 Racó del Pi

*C/Pi 7 (93 342 61 90/fax 93 342 61 91/www.h10hotels.es). Metro Liceu.* **Rates** €160.50-€214 single; €187.25-€256.80 double. **Credit** AmEx, DC, MC, V. **Map** p344 C4 ❶

Part of the H10 chain, the Racó del Pi offers spacious rooms with parquet floors, handsome terracotta-tiled bathrooms and an elegant glass conservatory on the ground floor. It can be a bargain out of season. Check the website for details.

*Bar. Disabled-adapted room. Internet (dataport, shared terminal, wireless in rooms). Non-smoking rooms (8). TV.*

**Other locations**: H10 Catalunya Plaza, Plaça Catalunya 7, Eixample (93 317 71 71); and throughout the city.

### H1898

*La Rambla 109 (93 552 95 52/fax 93 552 95 50/ www.nnhotels.es). Metro Catalunya or Liceu.* **Rates** €160.50-€481.50 single/double; €1,284-€2,033 suite. **Credit** AmEx, DC, MC, V. **Map** p344 B3 ❷

A dapper new luxury hotel in a splendid 19th-century building – famously the former Philippine

## The best Hotels

### For never leaving the premises

With its own hip club, spa and roof terrace with views of Gaudí's La Pedrera, there is more than enough to keep you amused from morning till night at the **Hotel Omm** (*see p69*). Uptown at the **Gran Hotel La Florida** (*see p77*), you can gaze across Barcelona from the stainless-steel pool rather than actually tramp around the city, then recover with a cocktail in the chill-out zone surrounded by hundreds of candles.

### For feeling like a local

Mix with real *barcelonins* by staying slightly outside the centre at the **Petit Hotel** (*see p77*), **Hostal H.M.B.** (*see p76*), the **Hotel Nuevo Triunfo** (*see p67*) or the **Hostal Poblenou** (*see p67*), and get a taste of neighbourhood life rather than tourist traps.

### For popping out to the shops

From the **Prestige Paseo de Gràcia** (*see p73*), the **Hotel Majestic** (*see p69*) or the **Hotel Condes de Barcelona** (*see p69*) you can just clatter down the stairs in your stilettos to the upmarket boutiques along the Passeig de Gràcia, while the **Hostal Lausanne** (*see p57*) or the **Hotel Petit Palace Opera Garden** (*see p55*) are handier for the more high-street vibe of Portal de l'Àngel and C/Portaferrissa.

### For delusions of grandeur

As you sweep through the arched entrance and up the grand staircase, you'll feel as snooty as the nobility who once inhabited the building where the **Pensión Hostal Mari-Luz** (*see p57*) is housed, while around the corner, the no-frills **Pensió Alamar** (*see p57*) was part of the palace belonging to the Countess of Sobradiel.

Tobacco Company headquarters – right on La Rambla. Rooms are subject to Henley Regatta-type colour schemes; one floor is all perky green-and-white stripes, another is red and white, and so on. The more expensive rooms have generously sized wooden-decked terraces, while some of the suites have private plunge pools.
*Bar (2). Business centre. Disabled-adapted rooms (6). Gym. Internet (wireless). Non-smoking hotel. Parking (€21.40/day). Pool (outdoor/indoor). Restaurant. Room service. Spa. TV (pay movies).*

### Hotel Colón

*Avda Catedral 7 (93 301 14 04/fax 93 317 29 15/ www.hotelcolon.es). Metro Jaume I.* **Rates** €144.45-€171.20 single; €197.95-€246.10 double; €321-€374.50 suite. **Credit** AmEx, DC, MC, V. **Map** p344 D4 ❸
If you have had it up to here with minimalism, stay at this stalwart of the Barcelona hotel scene and sink into a chintzy armchair that actually looks like a chair rather than an artwork. With thick carpets and walls bedecked in bright floral prints, the Colón is all about making guests feel comfortable. The great location, on the square in front of the cathedral, is best enjoyed in the rooms that overlook the magnificent Gothic edifice, some of which have balconies.
*Bar. Internet (dataport, wireless). Restaurant. Room service. TV (pay movies).*
**Other locations**: Hotel Regencia Colón, C/Sacristans 13, Barri Gòtic (93 318 98 58).

### Hotel Le Meridien Barcelona

*La Rambla 111 (93 318 62 00/fax 93 301 77 76/ www.barcelona.lemeridien.com). Metro Liceu.* **Rates** €428-€481.50 single/double; €588.50-€2,140 suite. **Credit** AmEx, DC, MC, V. **Map** p344 B3 ❹
Le Meridien is a great place for spotting celebrities, attracted by the lure of its ultra-luxurious suites. The hotel has revamped its genteel image with wood floors and leather furnishings, along with Egyptian cotton bedlinen, rain showers and plasma-screen TVs. Despite its size (it has 233 rooms), it manages to retain an air of intimacy thanks to its helpful, friendly staff. All rooms are soundproofed, and the best look out over La Rambla.
*Bar. Disabled-adapted rooms (4). Fitness centre. Internet (high-speed). Non-smoking floors (4). Parking (€20-€25/day). Restaurant. Room service. TV.*

### Hotel Neri

*C/Sant Sever 5 (93 304 06 55/fax 93 304 03 37/ www.hotelneri.com). Metro Jaume I.* **Rates** €278.20-€347.75 single/double; €379.85-€470.80 suite. **Credit** AmEx, DC, MC, V. **Map** p345 C5 ❺
A sumptuous, sensual boutique hotel, located in a former 18th-century palace, that has clearly been designed with a view to the ultimate romantic weekend. The lobby, which teams flagstone floors and wooden beams with funky designer fixtures, red velvet and lashings of gold leaf, gives a taste of what's to come in the 22 rooms, where neutral tones, natural materials and rustic finishes (untreated wood and unpolished marble) stand in stylishly orchestrated contrast with bolts of lavish satins and velvets, sharp design and high-tech perks (hi-fis, plasma-screen TVs).
*Bar. Disabled-adapted room. Internet (wireless). Non-smoking rooms (10). Restaurant. Room service. TV (pay movies).*

### Hotel Petit Palace Opera Garden

*C/Boqueria 10 (93 302 00 92/fax 93 302 15 66/ www.hthoteles.com). Metro Liceu.* **Rates** €128.40-€294.25 single/double; €144.45-€310.30 triple; €160.50-€342.40 quadruple. **Credit** AmEx, DC, MC, V. **Map** p345 B5 ❻
A private mansion was completely gutted to create this new minimalist haven on a busy shopping street just off La Rambla. The 61 rooms are white and futuristic, with a different zingy colour on each floor and opera scores printed on the walls above the beds. Lamps and chairs lend a swinging '60s air, so pack your kinky boots and groovy flares to enjoy your stay to the full. Some bathrooms have massage showers, others jacuzzi baths. Only breakfast is served in the chic dining room. The best thing, perhaps, is the secret garden at the back: a real luxury in this densely packed area.
*Bar. Disabled-adapted rooms (2). Internet (wireless). Non-smoking hotel. Room service. TV.*

## Mid-range

### Duc de la Victòria

*C/Duc de la Victòria 15 (93 270 34 10/fax 93 412 77 47/www.nh-hotels.com). Metro Catalunya.* **Rates** €105.95-€150.90 single/double. **Credit** AmEx, DC, MC, V. **Map** p344 C3/4 ❼
The trusty NH chain has high standards of comfort and service, and this good-value downtown branch is no exception. The 156 rooms, with blue-and-beige colour scheme, may be unexciting, but the superior quality beds ensure you get a good night's sleep. A stone's throw from La Rambla, with lots of bars, restaurants and shops nearby.
*Disabled-adapted rooms (4). Internet (dataport). Non-smoking floors (4). Restaurant (lunch only). Room service. TV (pay movies).*

### Hostal Jardí

*Plaça Sant Josep Oriol 1 (93 301 59 00/fax 93 342 57 33). Metro Liceu.* **Rates** €70-€86 single; €86-€96 double. **Credit** AmEx, DC, MC, V. **Map** p345 B5 ❽
A victim of its own success, the Jardí now requires you to book three months in advance. There is a rather institutional feel about both rooms and lobby, but the location is excellent, overlooking a pretty square in the Barri Gòtic. It is only really worth staying here if you get one of the best rooms with a balcony from which to enjoy the view. Apart from the frugal furnishings, some rooms are dark, but all have en-suite bathrooms, and the place is sparkling clean.
*Non-smoking hotel. TV.*

### Hotel Oriente

*La Rambla 45 (93 302 25 58/fax 93 412 38 19/ www.husa.es). Metro Liceu.* **Rates** €79.90-€147.65 single; €107-€179.75 double; €169.15-€200.10 triple. **Credit** AmEx, DC, MC, V. **Map** p345 A6 ⑨

It was Barcelona's first-ever 'grand hotel' in 1842, but the Oriente had been getting increasingly shabby until a recent renovation that has brightened things up considerably. All bedrooms now have pale wood floors, minimalist design and sleek electrical gadgetry, in striking contrast to the ritzy ballroom and dining room. Sadly, no amount of renovation can do away with the noise from La Rambla; it is highly recommended that light sleepers ask for a room at the back of the hotel, or pack earplugs.

*Bar (Mar-Oct only). TV.*

## Budget

### Hostal Fontanella

*Via Laietana 71, 2° (tel/fax 93 317 59 43/ www.hostalfontanella.com). Metro Urquinaona.* **Rates** €37.45-€44.94 single; €56.71-€75.97 double; €89.88-€106.36 triple. **Credit** AmEx, DC, MC, V. **Map** p344 D2 ⑩

The splendid Modernista lift lends a somewhat unjustified aura of grandeur to this 11-room *hostal,* where Laura Ashley devotees will feel totally at home amid the chintz, lace and dried flowers. The downside of the Fontanella's central location – on the thoroughfare bordering the Born, the Barri Gòtic and the Eixample – is that outward-facing rooms are abuzz with the sound of busy traffic. However, it's a clean and comfortable place to stay, and double-glazing has recently been installed.

*TV.*

### Hostal Lausanne

*Portal de l'Àngel 24, 1° 1ª (tel/fax 93 302 11 39/ www.hostallausanne.com). Metro Catalunya.* **Rates** €30-€35 single; €50-€65 double; €65-€95 triple. **No credit cards. Map** p344 C3 ⑪

Situated on one of downtown's busiest shopping streets, this *hostal* occupies the first floor of an impressive building. Unlike some *hostales,* which can be poky, the place feels spacious, with light pouring in from both ends of the building. Of the 17 basic rooms, four have en-suite bathrooms and some have balconies. It may be a bit dated, but it's a friendly and safe place, with a fun backpacker vibe. The street is as quiet at night as it is busy during the day.

*Internet (shared service). TV room.*

### Hostal Noya

*La Rambla 133, 1° (93 301 48 31). Metro Catalunya.* **Rates** €20-€25 single; €36-€42 double. **No credit cards. Map** p344 B2/3 ⑫

Cheap and cheerful, the Noya is run by the smiling, helpful Feli, who is always on hand to welcome you as you get your breath back after lugging your bags up three flights of stairs. Rooms are basic to say the least, but some have balconies looking out on to La Rambla and there are handsome old tiles on the floor. The lone bathroom is weathered and worn, and it can get busy since it's shared between 12 rooms (there is a separate WC), but all bedrooms do have their own washbasins.

**Other locations**: Pensión Bienestar, C/Quintana 3, Barri Gòtic (93 318 72 83).

### Hostal Rembrandt

*C/Portaferrissa 23, pral 1ª (tel/fax 93 318 10 11/ www.hostalrembrandt.com). Metro Liceu.* **Rates** €25-€35 single; €40-€55 double; €60-€90 triple. **Credit** MC, V. **Map** p344 C4 ⑬

A charming 28-room *hostal*: fairly stylish (for the price) with lots of wood panelling, soft lighting and a lift. An added bonus is the pretty interior courtyard, which makes for a pleasant chill-out zone/eating area. Rooms out front can be a little noisy, but the passing stream of humanity means you will never be bored. The same people also rent out apartments on nearby C/Canuda (€60-€100 for two people.

### Hotel Toledano

*La Rambla 138, 4° (93 301 08 72/fax 93 412 31 42/ www.hoteltoledano.com). Metro Catalunya.* **Rates** €37.45-€41.75 single; €56.70-€68.48 double; €86.70 triple; €96.30 quadruple. **Credit** AmEx, DC, MC, V. **Map** p344 B3 ⑭

All 17 rooms in this kitsch hotel are spotless and some have air-conditioning, but whether you end up with acres of space or just up from a broom cupboard is a lottery. Some rooms have balconies overlooking La Rambla, while others provide a glimpse of the cathedral. Service is friendly, and – unusually for this category – there is free wireless internet in the rooms as well as shared terminals. A book-exchange system is another nice touch. There are 11 more basic rooms in the *pensión* upstairs (same number). Booking is essential.

*Internet (shared terminal, wireless). TV room.*

### Pensió Alamar

*C/Comtessa de Sobradiel 1, 1° 2ª (93 302 50 12/ www.pensioalamar.com). Metro Jaume I or Liceu.* **Rates** €20-€25 single; €36-€45 double. **Credit** AmEx, DC, MC, V. **Map** p345 C6 ⑮

Eight of the basic, yet tasteful, rooms at this family-run *hostal* have plant-filled balconies overlooking the street in the heart of the Barri Gòtic. Beds are new and excellent quality, with crisp cotton sheets, and windows are double-glazed to keep noise to a minimum. The downside is the 12 rooms share two bathrooms. There are good discounts for longer stays, and larger rooms for families. Single travellers are made very welcome, with no supplement for occupying a double room. Guests can make their own meals in a well-equipped kitchen and do their laundry. More suitable for those looking for a quiet, homely atmosphere than clubbers.

### Pensión Hostal Mari-Luz

*C/Palau 4 (tel/fax 93 317 34 63/www.pensionmariluz.com). Metro Jaume I or Liceu.* **Rates** €35-€51 double; €16-€20/person 4-6-person rooms. **Credit** AmEx, DC, MC, V. **Map** p345 C6 ⑯

The spectacular views and infinity pool at the **Grand Hotel Central**.

The entrance and staircase of this 18th-century stone building are certainly imposing, but the downside is that you have to climb several flights of stairs to reach the Mari-Luz. The effort is well worth it, however, for the smiling service and homey atmosphere. Stripped wood doors and old floor tiles add character to the 15 otherwise-plain but quiet rooms, some of which face a plant-filled inner courtyard. There are dorms as well as double and triple rooms (No.4 and No.6 have good en-suite bathrooms). Renovation work due to be completed in early 2007 will improve facilities but threatens to do away with the original tiled floors.
**Other locations**: Pensión Fernando, C/Ferran 31, Barri Gòtic (93 301 79 93).

### Residencia Victòria

*C/Comtal 9, 1° 1ª (93 318 07 60/93 317 45 97/ victoria@atriumhotels.com). Metro Catalunya.*
**Rates** €26 single; €39-€42 double; €55 triple.
**Credit** MC, V. **Map** p344 C3 ⑰
This spacious and peaceful *pensión* is located on the second floor (no lift). Rooms are basic, clean and light, all with sinks but no en-suite bathrooms. Extras include communal cooking and washing facilities, and a cute outdoor terrace. Friendly service keeps people coming back, so book in advance.
*TV room.*

## Born & Sant Pere

New hotels are cropping up in revamped old buildings in these medieval areas. Now an established cool zone, with restaurants, bars and boutiques livening up its tiny lanes, the Born is also next to one of the city's finest parks.

## Expensive

### Grand Hotel Central

*Via Laietana 30 (93 295 79 00/fax 93 268 12 15/www.grandhotelcentral.com). Metro Jaume I.*
**Rates** €173.34-€362.20 single/double; €469.73-€614.18 suite. **Credit** AmEx, DC, MC, V.
**Map** p345 D5 ⑱
The Grand Hotel Central is another of the recent wave of Barcelona hotels to adhere to the unwritten but tyrannical design protocol that grey is the new black. The Central's shadowy, Hitchcockian corridors open up on to sleekly appointed rooms that come with flat-screen TVs, DVD players and Molton Brown toiletries. But the real charm of the hotel lies up above, on its roof. Here you can sip a cocktail and admire the fabulous views while floating comfortably in the vertiginous infinity pool.
*Bar. Business centre. Disabled-adapted rooms (4). Gym. Internet (wireless). Non-smoking floors (4). Parking (€25/day). Pool (outdoor). Restaurant. Room service. TV.*

## Mid-range

### Banys Orientals

*C/Argenteria 37 (93 268 84 60/fax 93 268 84 61/www.hotelbanysorientals.com). Metro Jaume I.*
**Rates** €85.60 single; €101.70 double; €133.75-€176.55 suite. **Credit** AmEx, DC, MC, V.
**Map** p345 D6 ⑲
Opened in 2002 to great acclaim, Banys Orientals remains one of the best deals to be found in Barcelona. It exudes cool, from its location at the heart of the Born to the deeply stylish shades-of-grey

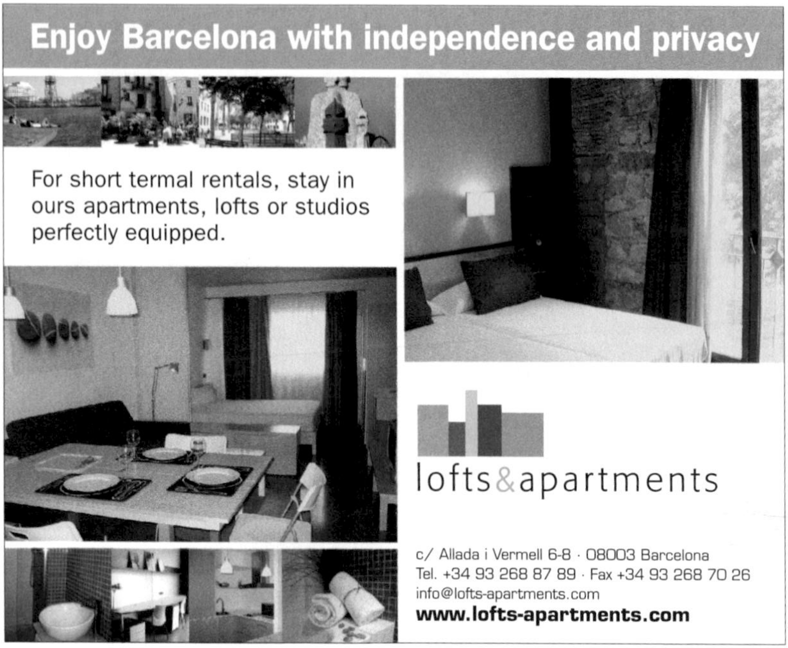
Enjoy Barcelona with independence and privacy
For short termal rentals, stay in ours apartments, lofts or studios perfectly equipped.
lofts&apartments
c/ Allada i Vermell 6-8 · 08003 Barcelona
Tel. +34 93 268 87 89 · Fax +34 93 268 70 26
info@lofts-apartments.com
www.lofts-apartments.com

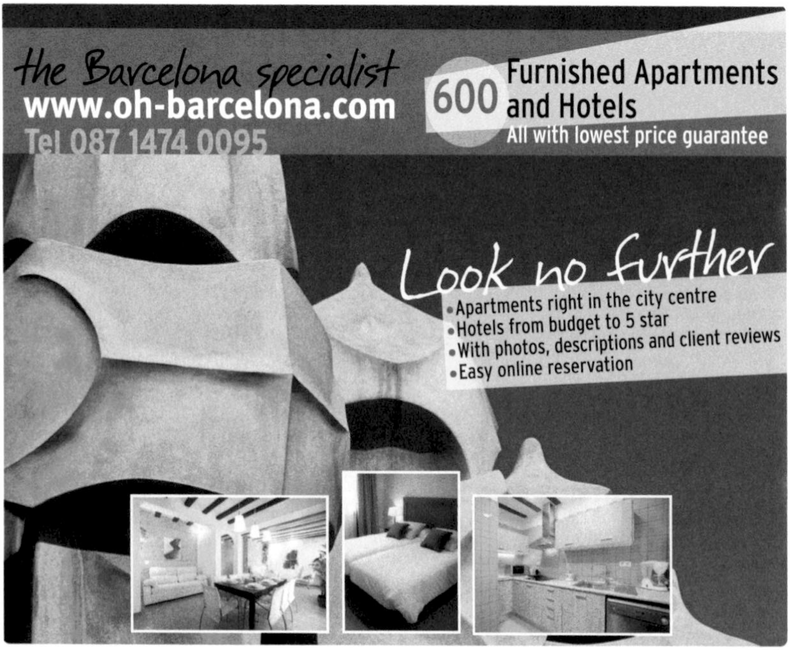
the Barcelona specialist
www.oh-barcelona.com
Tel 087 1474 0095
600 Furnished Apartments and Hotels
All with lowest price guarantee
Look no further
• Apartments right in the city centre
• Hotels from budget to 5 star
• With photos, descriptions and client reviews
• Easy online reservation

# Apartment advice

Renting a flat (for agencies *see p53*) can be a great way of experiencing the city, but it pays to do your research. Most short-stay apartments are in the Old Town – in the Barri Gòtic, Raval, Born or Barceloneta. While handy for most sights and nightlife, many buildings in these areas date back at least a couple of hundred years, so it is crucial to find out what condition they are in. A lot of places have been tastefully restored, retaining original features such as wooden beams, open-brick walls and tiled floors. But, it still pays to check what the entrance and staircase are like, as some are decidedly unsavoury. Check the street it is on, as some of the lanes in the Old City can be very quiet at night. Just because an area has been dubbed as trendy does not make it totally safe.

A more common problem, however, is noise. With such a density of population, and open windows from spring to autumn, features such as soundproofing and air-conditioning are worth taking into account.

If, on the other hand, partying late into the night is on the cards, it might be an idea to mention this upfront, so an agency can look instead for suitable accommodation away from quiet neighbourhoods.

Holiday apartments are often designed to sleep numerous people in the smallest feasible space. If you are planning to be out all day and most of the night, this could suit and save quite a sum compared to a hotel. In Barceloneta in particular, flats tend to be tiny, but this is not necessarily a problem if they have been well converted, and the proximity to the beach is a big advantage in summer.

Going self-catering allows for the opportunity to actually buy edibles at Barcelona's fabulous food markets. As well as the famous Boqueria on La Rambla, there is the recently revamped Santa Caterina in the Born, which is distinctly upmarket and houses a hip tapas bar and restaurant too. Barceloneta's market is currently being improved, but there is a temporary version to keep its residents going, in the meantime. Staying in the Raval means alternating between the Boqueria and the more down-to-earth Sant Antoni, where there is rarely a tourist in sight.

minimalism of its rooms, and nice touches such as complimentary mineral water place on the landings. The main debit in its style book is the smallish size of some of the double rooms. Plans to create a luxurious new service by tapping into the eponymous thermal baths that lie underneath the hotel are in the proverbial pipeline.
*Disabled-adapted room. Internet (high-speed). Restaurant. TV.*

### Chic&basic

*C/Princesa 50 (93 295 46 52/fax 93 295 46 53/ www.chicandbasic.com.) Metro Arc de Triomf or Jaume I.* **Rates** €107-€214 double. **Credit** AmEx, DC, MC, V. **Map** p345 F5 ⑳

With a name like this, you know what to expect. So, if you like gleaming white contrasted with a bit of sleek black and a space-age theatrical vibe, you'll love Chic&basic. If you've ever dreamed of entering your room through a shimmering curtain of transparent plastic twirls, as if you were walking into a waterfall, this is definitely the place for you. The building retains its original grand staircase, now furnished with oversized chairs and sofas, and on the ground floor is the fashionable White Bar (what else?). A chill-out room contains practicalities such as tea- and coffee-making facilities, a fridge and a microwave, as well as black sofas and pouffes.
*Bar. Disabled-adapted room. Gym. Internet (wireless). Non-smoking hotel. Restaurant. TV.*

### Ciutat Barcelona

*C/Princesa 35 (93 269 74 75/fax 93 269 74 76/ www.ciutathotels.com.) Metro Jaume I.* **Rates** (incl breakfast) €80.25-€133.75 single; €123.05-€181.90 double; €149.80-€203.30 suite. **Credit** AmEx, DC, MC, V. **Map** p345 E5 ㉑

Specify your preference for a red, blue or green room when booking at this hotel, which opened in 2006 and is big on colour coordination – even the plastic cups in the chic bathrooms match the colour scheme. Retro shapes prevail in the stylish furnishings and decoration, disguising the fact that rooms are rather small. Up on the roof there is a great terrace with a small pool, and the Colors restaurant on the ground floor is popular with non-guests.
*Bar. Disabled-adapted rooms (4). Internet (high-speed). Non-smoking floors (4). Pool (outdoor). Restaurant. Room service. TV (cable).*

## Budget

### Hostal Orleans

*Avda Marquès de l'Argentera 13, 1° (93 319 73 82/ fax 93 319 22 19/www.hostalorleans.com). Metro Barceloneta.* **Rates** €25-€30 single; €51-€55 double; €65-€70 triple; €80 quadruple. **Credit** AmEx, DC, MC, V. **Map** p345 F7 ㉒

It may look a bit grungy from the street, but the Orleans is surprisingly luxurious for a *hostal*, with comfortable, refurbished rooms and en-suite

bathrooms that would not look out of place several categories up the hotel scale. Spacious quadruple rooms are a steal for groups. It's a good location for Born nightlife and is right by França station, where the airport trains arrive and depart.
*TV.*

### Pensió 2000

*C/Sant Pere Més Alt 6, 1° (93 310 74 66/fax 93 319 42 52/www.pension2000.com). Metro Urquinaona.* **Rates** €40.65-€50.40 single; €48.20-€70.50 double; €20 3rd person; €17 4th person. **Credit** AmEx, MC, V. **Map** p344 D3 ㉓
Friendly owners Manuela and Orlando run one of Barcelona's most endearing and best-value *pensiones* in a charming old building opposite the Palau de la Música. Only two of its six bright and airy rooms are en suite, but the communal facilities are truly sparkling, and there are outdoor breakfast tables. With tall windows, buttercup-yellow walls and a lounge peppered with books and toys, it's a cheery sunbeam of a place, with a warm, relaxed atmosphere. The large rooms also make it a good bet for holidaying families.

## Raval

The Raval is the edgy neighbour of the Barri Gòtic, but recent regeneration means it's also the coolest *barri* for bars and restaurants, with a lively multicultural vibe.

## Expensive

### Casa Camper

*C/Elisabets 11 (93 342 62 80 /fax 93 342 75 63/ www.casacamper.com). Metro Catalunya.* **Rates** (incl breakfast & snack) €196.88-€230.05 single; €214-€251.45 double; €235.40-€273.95 suite. **Credit** AmEx, DC, MC, V. **Map** p344 A3 ㉔
Devised by the Mallorcan footwear giant, this is a holistic concept-fest of a boutique hotel where Mediterranean simplicity meets contemporary cool. The funky style was devised by leading designer Ferran Amat, and you get a pair of plastic Camper clogs to shuffle around in. You get more than a room for your money, as across the corridor is your own personal lounge, complete with an extra TV and a hammock. There is nothing as naff as a minibar, but you can help yourself to free snacks and refreshments in the café whenever the fancy takes you. Specially designed bicycles are available for rent at €17.40/4hrs or €23.20/day. **Photos** *p64.*
*Business centre. Disabled-adapted room. Internet (wireless). Non-smoking hotel. TV (pay movies, DVD).*

### Hotel Ambassador

*C/Pintor Fortuny 13 (93 342 61 80/fax 93 302 79 77/www.rivolihotels.com). Metro Catalunya.* **Rates** €146.60-€248.25 single; €288.90-€352.05 double; €479.35-€801.45 suite. **Credit** AmEx, DC, MC, V. **Map** p344 B3 ㉕
The four-star Ambassador has been refurbished, and now boasts a heady blend of water features, gold paint and smoked glass, a glittering colossus of a chandelier and a free-standing Modernista bar that dominates the lounge area. Rooms are straightforward with no scary designer features, and there's also a pool and a jacuzzi on the rooftop.
*Bar. Disabled-adapted rooms (4). Gym. Internet (dataport: some rooms, shared terminal). Non-smoking floor. Parking (€17.70/day). Pool (outdoor). Restaurant. Room service. TV (pay movies).*

## Mid-range

### Abba Rambla Hotel

*C/Rambla del Raval 4 (93 505 54 00/fax 93 505 54 01/www.abbahoteles.com). Metro Liceu or Sant Antoni.* **Rates** €96.30-€117.70 single; €102.75-€124.15 double. **Credit** AmEx, MC, V. **Map** p342 E10 ㉖
Overlooking the Rambla del Raval, an open space flanked by bars and restaurants, the Abba Rambla is a comfortable and friendly base for nightlife and sightseeing, although rooms are a bit bland. More stylish are the ground-floor lounge and breakfast bar, where you eat perched on high stools.
*Disabled-adapted room. Internet (shared & wireless throughout hotel). Non-smoking rooms (11).*

### Hostal Gat Raval

*C/Joaquín Costa 44, 2° (93 481 66 70/fax 93 342 66 97/www.gataccommodation.com). Metro Universitat.* **Rates** €44.95 single; €71.70-€80.25 double. **Credit** AmEx, MC, V. **Map** p342 E9 ㉗
Gat Raval embodies everything that 21st-century budget accommodation should be: smart, clean and funky, with bright, sunshiny rooms each of which boasts a work by a local artist. Some rooms have balconies while others have views of the MACBA. The only downsides are that nearly all the bathrooms are communal (though they are very clean) and there is no lift.
*Internet (pay terminal). TV.*

### Hostal Gat Xino

*C/Hospital 155 (93 324 88 33/fax 93 324 88 34/ www.gataccommodation.com). Metro Sant Antoni.* **Rates** (incl breakfast) €56.70-€67.40 single; €79.20-€96.30 double; €128.40 4-person suite. **Credit** AmEx, MC, V. **Map** p342 E10 ㉘
The 'Gats' are pioneers of a new way to stay: inexpensive, modern places that combine the polish of a classy boutique hotel with the practicality and price of a B&B. This is the second one to open, and it has a bright, breezy breakfast room complete with apple-green polka-dot walls, a wood-decked patio and a roof terrace with black beanbags on which to chill out. There's more bright green to be found in the bedrooms (all of which are en suite), with good-quality beds, crisp white linen, flat-screen TVs and backlit panels of Raval scenes. The best rooms have small terraces of their own.
*Internet (pay terminal, wireless in rooms), TV.*

**Casa Camper**. *See p63.*

### Hostal-Residencia Ramos

*C/Hospital 36 (93 302 07 23/fax 93 302 04 30/ www.hostalramos.com). Metro Liceu.* **Rates** €30-€40 single; €60-€72 double; €85-€95 triple. **Credit** MC, V. **Map** p345 A5 (29)

This family-run *hostal* offers one of the best deals in the Raval. There's no air-conditioning, but plenty of windows and balconies keep it cool – if you can stand the street noise. Rooms (all en suite) are basic and vary in size, but are light and airy. The best have balconies looking on to the *plaça*, where there is usually a mix of the Raval's multicultural communities and newer, super-cool inhabitants to keep you amused.

*TV.*

### Hotel España

*C/Sant Pau 9-11 (93 318 17 58/fax 93 317 11 34/ www.hotelespanya.com). Metro Liceu.* **Rates** (incl breakfast) €53.50-€70.62 single; €85.60-€144.45 double; €115.35-€176.55 triple. **Credit** AmEx, DC, MC, V. **Map** p345 A5 (30)

The lower floors at this Modernista landmark were designed by Domènech i Montaner in 1902. The main restaurant is decorated with floral tiling and elaborate woodwork, while the larger dining room beyond it features dreamy murals of mermaids by Ramon Casas, and the bar boasts a sculpted marble fireplace. After all this grandeur, the bedrooms are unexciting but have been considerably improved in recent years. All are en suite, and the nicest ones open on to a bright interior patio.

*Disabled-adapted rooms (2). Restaurant. TV.*

### Hotel Mesón Castilla

*C/Valldonzella 5 (93 318 21 82/fax 93 412 40 20/ www.mesoncastilla.com). Metro Universitat.* **Rates** (incl breakfast) €112.35 single; €139.10-€155.15 double; €181.90 triple; €214 quadruple. **Credit** AmEx, DC, MC, V. **Map** p344 A2 (31)

If you want a change from contemporary design, check into this chocolate-box hotel, which opened in 1952. Before then, it was a private house belonging to an aristocratic Catalan family. Public areas are full of antiques and curious artworks, while the rooms are all different and decorated with hand-painted furniture from Olot in northern Catalunya, with tiled floors. The best have tranquil terraces, with a delightful plant-packed one off the breakfast room.

*Parking (€20/day). TV.*

### Hotel Principal

*C/Junta de Comerç 8 (93 318 89 74/fax 93 412 08 19/www.hotelprincipal.es). Metro Liceu.* **Rates** €70-€130 single; €75-€170 double. **Credit** AmEx, DC, MC, V. **Map** p345 A5 (32)

Although officially only a two-star hotel, after an impressive revamp, the family-run Principal offers rooms of a four-star standard, with flat-screen TVs, original artworks and marble bathrooms, some with massage showers. Guests can relax on loungers on the roof, where there is also a suite with a private terrace. The buffet breakfast is served in a pleasant, light room. Unless you hit a peak period when rates rise, it is very good value for money.

*Disabled-adapted rooms (3). Internet (pay wireless, shared terminal). Non-smoking floors (2). TV.*

### Hotel Sant Agustí

*Plaça Sant Agustí 3 (93 318 16 58/fax 93 317 29 28/www.hotelsa.com). Metro Liceu.* **Rates** (incl breakfast) €96.30-€112.35 single; €107-€149.80 double; €139.10-€186.20 triple. **Credit** AmEx, DC, MC, V. **Map** p345 A5 (33)

With its sandstone walls and huge, arched windows looking on to the *plaça*, not to mention the pink-marble lobby filled with forest-green furniture, this imposing hotel is the oldest in Barcelona. Housed in the former convent of St Augustine, it was converted into a hotel in 1840. Rooms are spacious and comfortable, but there's no soundproofing. Good buffet breakfast.

*Bar. Disabled-adapted rooms (2). Internet (shared terminal). Restaurant (dinner only). TV.*

## Budget

### Hostal La Palmera

*C/Jerusalem 30 (93 317 09 97/fax 93 342 41 36/ hostallapalmera@terra.es). Metro Liceu.* **Rates** (incl breakfast) €32.10-€37.50 single; €53.50-€58.85 double. **Credit** MC, V. **Map** p344 A4 (34)

With a great location behind La Boqueria market, this well-run, basic *hostal* is a short stagger from some of Raval's funkiest bars, but is surprisingly quiet at night. The decor is unremarkable, but the rooms are light, airy and spotless, most have en-suite bathrooms and some have balconies overlooking the market. What more do you need?

**Other locations**: Hostal Bertolin, C/Carme 116, 1º, Raval (93 329 06 47/reservations 93 317 09 97).

### Hosteria Grau

*C/Ramelleres 27 (93 301 81 35/fax 93 317 68 25/ www.hostalgrau.com). Metro Catalunya.* **Rates** €35.30 single; €74.90-€90.95 double; €99.50-€107 triple; €80.25-€171.20 apartment. **Credit** AmEx, DC, MC, V. **Map** p344 B2 (35)

This charming, family-run *hostal* oozes character, with a tiled spiral staircase and fabulous 1970s-style communal areas, including a funky café next door. The open fireplace is a luxury if you visit in the winter. Rooms are basic, comfortable and fairly quiet. There are also some apartments available on the top floor. A popular choice, so book well in advance.

*Bar. Internet (pay terminal). TV room.*

## Barceloneta & the Ports

Hotels are springing up along Barcelona's waterfront, particularly in the stretch between the Hotel Arts and the Forum, north of the city centre. These are mostly four-stars aimed at business travellers, so rates fall at weekends and during holiday periods. Staying in this area is a good idea if you want to spend more time on the beach than sightseeing.

## Expensive

### Hotel Arts

*C/Marina 19-21 (93 221 10 00/fax 93 221 10 70/ www.ritzcarlton.com). Metro Ciutadella-Vila Olímpica.* **Rates** €390-€813 double; €508-€1,926 suite; €1,284-€2,568 apartment; €10,700 royal suite. **Credit** AmEx, DC, MC, V. **Map** p343 K12 36

The 44-storey, Ritz-Carlton-run Arts has redesigned all its rooms, and continues to score top marks for unfailingly exemplary service. Bang & Olufsen CD players, interactive TV, sea and city views and a 'Club' floor for VIPs are just some of the hedonistic perks that await the hotel's guests. The avant-garde flower arrangements make the lobby a pleasant place to hang out rather than just pass through. Outdoors, the beachfront pool overlooks Frank Gehry's bronze fish sculpture, and there is a range of bars and restaurants to cater to your every whim. The spectacular duplex apartments have round-the-clock butlers and chef services, while the luxurious Six Senses Spa on floors 42 and 43 has fabulous views and is open to non-guests. In summer, parents can leave children at the kids' club.

*Bar. Business centre. Disabled-adapted rooms (4). Gym. Internet (high-speed, wireless). Non-smoking floors (20). Parking (€37.50/day). Pool (outdoor). Restaurants (4). Room service. Spa. TV and DVD.*

### Hotel Duquesa de Cardona

*Passeig Colom 12 (93 268 90 90/fax 93 268 29 31/ www.hduquesadecardona.com). Metro Drassanes or Jaume I.* **Rates** €208 single; €181.90-€299.60 double; €305-€369.20 suite. **Credit** AmEx, DC, MC, V. **Map** p345 C7 37

This elegantly restored 16th-century palace retains lots of its original palatial features and is furnished with natural materials – wood, leather, silk and stone – that are complemented by a soft colour scheme that reflects the paintwork. The cosy bedrooms make it the ideal hotel for a romantic stay, particularly the deluxe rooms and junior suites on the higher floors that have views out across the harbour. The beach is a ten-minute walk away, but guests can sunbathe on the decked roof terrace and then cool off afterwards in the mosaic-tiled plunge pool. The arcaded hotel restaurant serves a menu of modern Catalan dishes.

*Business centre. Disabled-adapted room. Internet (high-speed). Non-smoking floors (3). Pool (outdoor). Restaurant. Room service. TV.*

### Hotel Medinaceli

*Plaça del Duc de Medinaceli 8 (93 481 77 25/fax 93 481 77 27/www.gargallo-hotels.com). Metro Drassanes.* **Rates** €199 single; €238.60 double. **Credit** AmEx, DC, MC, V. **Map** p345 B8 38

The 44 rooms in this restored palace near the harbour, which opened in 2006, are done out in soothing rusty shades, and some have views over the dusty square, with palm trees and fountain, where Pedro Almodóvar filmed scenes in *Todo Sobre Mi Madre*. Some of the bathrooms have jacuzzi baths, while others come with massage showers. Repro versions of the sofa Dalí created inspired by Mae West's lips decorate the lobby, while anyone with an urge to emulate Posh and Becks's wedding can pose to their heart's content on the crimson velvet thrones in the first-floor courtyard.

*Bar. Disabled-adapted rooms (2). Internet (wireless). Non-smoking hotel. TV.*

## Budget

### Hostal Poblenou

*C/Taulat 30, pral (tel/fax 93 221 26 01/ www.hostalpoblenou.com). Metro Poble Nou.* **Rates** (incl breakfast) €53.50 single; €74.90 double. **Credit** MC, V.

Poblenou is a delightful *hostal* in an elegant restored building that offers a lot more than you would expect for the money. The five rooms are all light and airy, with their own bathrooms, and breakfast is served on a sunny terrace. There is wireless internet as well as a shared terminal, and guests can help themselves to tea, coffee and mineral water at no extra cost. The owner, Mercedes, is on hand to provide any help or information you might need during your stay. Situated a few minutes' walk from the beach in the characterful Poblenou neighbourhood, this hotel is a good way to get an authentic experience away from the tourist hordes.

*Internet (shared terminal, wireless). Non-smoking rooms (2). TV.*

# Montjuïc & Poble Sec

Away from the concentration of tourists but within reasonable walking distance of La Rambla, Poble Sec is a proper neighbourhood, squashed in between Montjuïc mountain and the Avda Paral·lel. It is a good choice if you are planning on visiting some of the museums and attractions on Montjuïc, and also if your interests lie rather with the bars and restaurants of the Raval.

## Mid-range

### Hotel Nuevo Triunfo

*C/Cabanes 34 (93 442 59 33/fax 93 443 21 10/ www.hotelnuevotriunfo.net). Metro Paral·lel.* **Rates** €73 single; €103 double. **Credit** MC, V. **Map** p342 E11 39

With 40 fresh, bright and spotless rooms the Hotel Nuevo Triunfo is located in a peaceful street at the foot of Montjuïc. Rooms are bland but comfortable enough, and the four most desirable – two of which are singles – counteract the austerity of the sparse, modern fittings with their charming plant-filled terraces. A good place to try when more central places are full.

*Disabled-adapted room. Internet (pay terminal). TV.*

## Budget

### Hostal BCN Port

*Avda Paral·lel 15, entl (93 324 95 00/fax 93 324 93 53/www.hostalbcnport.com). Metro Drassanes or Paral·lel.* **Rates** €59.35-€84.55 single; €84.55-€95.25 double; €98.45-€109.15 triple; €117.70-€133.75 quadruple. **Credit** MC, V. **Map** p342 E12 40

A smart new *hostal* near the ferry port, the BCN Port has rooms that are furnished in a chic contemporary style with not a hint of the kitsch decor prevalent in more traditional budget places. All the 19 rooms have en-suite bathrooms, as well as TVs and air-conditioning. Handy for La Rambla and Montjuïc, as well as the waterfront. Check the website for last-minute discounts.

*Internet (wireless). Non-smoking rooms (8). TV.*

# Eixample

Uptown and upmarket, the broad avenues forming the vast grid of streets of the Eixample district contain dozens of architectural gems, interspersed with boutiques and bars. As well as some of Barcelona's most fashionable hotels, there are some great budget options hidden away in Modernista buildings too.

## Expensive

### Hotel Axel

*C/Aribau 33 (93 323 93 93/fax 93 323 93 94/ www.axelhotels.com). Metro Universitat.* **Rates** €96.30-€140.20 single; €164.50-€209.70 double; €298.55-€343.50 suite. **Credit** AmEx, DC, MC, V. **Map** p342 F8 41

Housed in a Modernista building, with multi-coloured tiles in the lobby and bright rooms with bleached floors, the Axel is a cornerstone of the Gaixample, as the area around the hotel is known. The good-looking (of course) staff sport T-shirts with the logo 'heterofriendly', and certainly everyone is made welcome at this funky boutique hotel. King-size beds with 30cm mattresses come as standard, as does free mineral water from fridges in the corridors. 'Superior' rooms have stained-glass gallery balconies and hydro-massage bathtubs. The Sky Bar on the rooftop is where it all happens, with a little pool, jacuzzi, sun deck, sauna and steam room. Non-guests are welcome to frequent the bar and roof terrace, where club nights are held, so there is always a bit of a buzz going on.

*Bar. Business centre. Disabled-adapted rooms (2). Gym. Internet (wireless).Non-smoking hotel. Pool (outdoor). Restaurant. Room service. Sauna. TV.*

### Hotel Catalonia Ramblas

*C/Pelai 28 (93 316 84 00/fax 93 316 84 01/ www.hoteles-catalonia.es). Metro Catalunya.* **Rates** €171.20-€235.40 single; €203.30-€267.50 double; €470.80-€535 suite. **Credit** AmEx, DC, MC, V. **Map** p344 B1 42

**Hotel Granados 83**. *See p69.*

The former building of *La Vanguardia* newspaper has been so thoroughly revamped for its new role as a hotel that little more than the pretty green-and-white Modernista façade remains of the original structure, which was designed in 1903 by Josep Majó Ribas. Wood laminate is used throughout the lobby, corridors and rooms, giving the place a rather wardrobey feel, apart from on the vast open space of the ground floor. A staircase at the rear takes you out to a pleasant pool and sun deck, which, along with the handy location and the excellent service typical of this chain, makes this new hotel a good practical option, despite the blandness of the decor.

*Bar (2). Business centre. Disabled-adapted rooms (4). Gym. Internet (wireless). Non-smoking floors (8). Pool (outdoor). Restaurants (2). Room service. Spa. TV (cable).*

### Hotel Claris

*C/Pau Claris 150 (93 487 62 62/fax 93 215 79 70/ www.derbyhotels.es). Metro Passeig de Gràcia.* **Rates** €192.60-€460.10 single/double; €516.80 suite; €627-€1,043.30 duplex. **Credit** AmEx, DC, MC, V. **Map** p338 G7 43

Antiques and contemporary design merge together behind the neo-classical exterior of the Claris, which contains the largest private collection of Egyptian art in Spain. Some bedrooms are on the small side, while others are duplex, but all have Chesterfield sofas and plenty of art. Warhol prints liven up the fashionable East 47 restaurant. The rooftop pool is just about big enough to swim in, with plenty of loungers, and a cocktail bar and DJ.

*Business centre. Gym. Internet (wireless). Non-smoking floors (4). Parking (€20/day). Pool (outdoor). Restaurants. Room service. TV.*

### Hotel Condes de Barcelona

*Passeig de Gràcia 73-75 (93 445 00 00/fax 93 445 32 32/www.condesdebarcelona.com). Metro Passeig de Gràcia.* **Rates** €190.35-€365.80 single/double; €508.30 suite. **Credit** AmEx, DC, MC, V. **Map** p338 G7 (44)

Renowned for its good service, the family-owned Condes is made up of two buildings that face each other on C/Mallorca at the intersection of Passeig de Gràcia. The building on the north side occupies a 19th-century palace and has a plunge pool on the roof, where the terrace offers evening dining and jazz. In the newer building, rooms on the seventh floor have terraces and a bird's-eye view of La Pedrera. Lodgings range from comfortable standard rooms to themed suites that boast extras such as jacuzzis. Both offer 'romantic weekend' packages, including champagne, theatre tickets, gourmet lunch boxes and airport transfers.

*Bar. Disabled-adapted rooms (2). Gym. Internet (dataport, web TV, wireless). Non-smoking floors (3). Parking (€16.60/day). Pool (outdoor). Restaurant. Room service. TV (music, pay movies).*

### Hotel Cram

*C/Aribau 54 (93 216 77 00/fax 93 216 77 07/www.hotelcram.com). Metro Universitat.* **Rates** (incl breakfast) €145.50-€246.10 single; €162.65-€278.20 double; €256.80-€438.70 suite. **Credit** AmEx, DC, MC, V. **Map** p342 F8 (45)

A pretty corner building dating back to 1892, with a salmon-pink façade, now has a startling contemporary interior. The subtly-lit red-and-black lobby makes you feel you are entering a nightclub, and indeed, there is the now-inevitable chill-out lounge with oversized cushions in tones of burnished gold and burgundy on the ground floor. Most of the 67 rooms have balconies, while suites have private sun decks. Some rooms have semicircular shower booths, others jacuzzi tubs. Breakfast is served on the roof terrace, where there is a black-tiled small pool and bar. The first floor houses Michelin-starred restaurant Gaig (*see p165*).

*Bar (2). Disabled-adapted rooms (2). Internet (wireless). Non-smoking floors (5). Parking (€16.05/day). Pool (outdoor). Restaurant. Room service. TV.*

### Hotel Granados 83

*C/Enric Granados 83 (93 492 96 70/fax 93 492 96 90/www.derbyhotels.es). Metro Diagonal.* **Rates** €96.30-€214 single; €107-€375.50 double; €176-€856 duplex/triplex. **Credit** AmEx, DC, MC, V. **Map** p338 F7 (46)

The original ironwork structure of this handsome former hospital, built in the 19th century, lends a rather unexpected New York industrial feel to the Granados 83, which opened in 2006. In the gallery district, on one of the most chic streets in the Eixample, this is a smart, rather than showy, place in which to stay. Part of the Derby group, which is always big on artworks, it has a Buddhist and Hindu vibe, with somewhat Japanesey decor in the restaurant and garden. The 77 rooms, with brickwork walls, include duplex and triplex versions, some with their own terraces and plunge pools. For those mere mortals inhabiting the standard rooms, there is a rooftop pool and sun deck. Check the website for some good-value packages. **Photo** *p68.*

*Bar (2). Business centre. Disabled-adapted rooms (2). Internet (high-speed). Non-smoking floors (4). Parking (€17.15/day). Pool (outdoor). Restaurant. Room service. TV.*

### Hotel Jazz

*C/Pelai 3 (93 552 96 96/fax 93 552 96 97/www.nnhotels.es). Metro Catalunya.* **Rates** €139.10-€203.30 single; €160.50-€224.70 double; €176.55-€278.20 triple; €321 suite. **Credit** AmEx, DC, MC, V. **Map** p344 A1 (47)

Rooms at the Hotel Jazz are super-stylish in calming tones of, naturally, grey, beige and black, softened with parquet floors and spiced up with dapper pin-stripe cushions and splashes of funky colour. The beds are larger than usual for hotels, and the bathrooms feature cool, polished black tiles. A rooftop pool and sun deck top things off.

*Bar. Business centre. Disabled-adapted rooms (4). Internet (high-speed, wireless). Non-smoking hotel. Pool (outdoor). TV.*

**Other locations**: Hotel Barcelona, Universal Avda Paral·lel 76-78, Poble Sec (93 567 74 47); and throughout the city.

### Hotel Majestic

*Passeig de Gràcia 68 (93 488 17 17/fax 93 488 18 80/www.hotelmajestic.es). Metro Passeig de Gràcia.* **Rates** €312-€417.50 single/double; €535-€810 suite; €1,600-€3,900 apartment. **Credit** AmEx, DC, MC, V. **Map** p338 G7 (48)

The Majestic has long been one of Barcelona's grandest hotels. Behind a neo-classical façade lies a panoply of perks, such as a service that allows you to print a selection of the day's newspapers from all over the world from the comfort of the lobby. Its crowning achievement is the ninth floor, which boasts an apartment and a sumptuous Sagrada Família Suite with a private, outdoor jacuzzi. Non-guests can enjoy the high life in the rooftop pool and gym, which offer wonderful views out over the city while you sweat or swim. Rooms are suitably opulent, decorated with classical flair. The Drolma restaurant is one of the finest in the city.

*Bars (2). Business centre. Disabled-adapted rooms (4). Gym. Internet (wireless). Non-smoking floors (6). Parking (€23.50/day). Pool (outdoor). Restaurant. Room service. TV (pay movies).*

### Hotel Omm

*C/Rosselló 265 (93 445 40 00/fax 93 445 40 04/www.hotelomm.es). Metro Diagonal.* **Rates** €215-€374.50 single/double; €428-€481.50 junior suite; €535-€802.50 suite. **Credit** AmEx, DC, MC, V. **Map** p338 G6 (49)

silver
APARTHOTEL
barcelona
Situated in a shopping and CENTRAL area, It's close to Barcelona's historical centre
Tube: FONTANA
Double from 72€/night
www.hotelsilver.com
Bretón de los Herreros,26 08012 BCN
Phone: +34 932189100 Fax: +34 934161447
reservations@hotelsilver.com

King's Flat
Great apartments
Central location
Great prices
Personal Service
Queen's Flat
Stay in the
Authentic Barcelona
web
www.casaLauren.com
email
lauren@casaLauren.com
Casa Lauren .com

Barcelonaforrent apartments
www.barcelonaforrent.com +34 93 457 9329
Rent for days, weeks or months
Apartments for both business
and leisure in Barcelona
www.barcelonaforrent.com
Tel. +34 93 457 9329

# Spa sensation

Come the 21st century, no city hoping to cut it as a city-slickers' weekend break is likely to succeed without the addition of some serious pamperville attractions.

In the last five years Barcelona has gone from a desert to an oasis of sensory treats for those looking to slough off the years and last Christmas's pudding, or simply recover from the effects of a jet-setting lifestyle. Happily, though, spa treatment is no longer the exclusive domain of those with a hefty bank account. Alongside the sexy spas of the swankiest hotels, the city has now opened the doors of cheaper, more accessible day spas.

While the city's super-duper spas are undoubtedly fabulous, Barcelona is adopting a New York-style outlook. This means that while nail spas and holes in the wall offering ten-minute back rubs are still a rarity, it's now possible to duck into a spa store for a lunchtime pick-me-up. Adjacent to the Hotel Avenida Palace, **Sinequantum** (Gran Via de les Corts Catalanes 605, 93 302 58 57,www.sinequantum.com) looks like a hairdressers, and is a hairdressers, save for one crucial difference: the treatment rooms at the back. Pearly-white decor and soothing Tibetan tunes offer cocoon-like peace after the frenetic pace of shopping on Passeig de Gràcia. The spa offers a full range, from chocolate slimming treatments to revitalising mint massage and vitamin C and oxygen facial treatments.

Further uptown, **Spa Aqua Diagonal** (Gran de Gràcia, 93 238 4160, www.aquaurbanspa.com) is a dedicated water-therapy centre with whirlpools, pebble-floored jet showers and hydro-massage all designed to detox, de-stress and decellulite. In addition, you can also indulge in various luxury packages, including anti-ageing wine therapy; the Dead Sea Voyage – a renovating cleanse with Vichy water massage and a chocolate-and-spice face and body treatment. All good enough to eat.

If you've money to burn, chill out at the Hotel Arts's **Six Senses Spa** (*see p67*). Perched high above the city, on the 43rd floor of the skyscraper, it offers dazzling views of the big blue from its black-marble, his 'n' hers wet rooms, complete with jacuzzi, fiendishly hot Finnish sauna and eye-watering 'ice shower' for a seriously stimulating scrub down. Luxury treatments based on organic lotions and potions include hot stones and four-handed massages, while the post-pamper lounges are havens of calm, with ginger tea and magazines to complement yet more stunning views.

With equally breathtaking views, the **Gran Hotel La Florida** (*see p77*) is for those who luxuriate in a little isolation. The L-shaped, indoor-outdoor steel infinity pool is reason enough for a visit, but there's also a supremely appointed Turkish bath and a stack of high-class beauty treatments.

The much-anticipated **Spaciomm** at the Hotel Omm (*see p69; photo above*) is finally open, with Zen-like natural decor in wood, stone, iron and coconut matting. Specialist treatments include a Tibetan facial to cure headaches, and shiatsu or reflexogy for pre-menstrual tension.

Then there's the **Metropolitan Spa** in Richard Rogers' newly opened Hesperia Tower (Gran Via, 08 L'Hospitalet, www.hesperiahoteles.com). It's the biggest in town and is geared towards those who seek beauty on the inside as well as the out. As well as offering personal training and an Olympic-sized swimming pool, it has state-of-the-art aqua spa circuits, including Turkish baths, while the beauty spa specialises in stimulating mud facials and detoxifying seaweed body wraps. Just say aah...

Feng shui goes space age at the drop-dead cool Omm. Don't even think of passing through the doors, let alone crossing the lobby, in anything less than this season's most coveted outfit. Bedrooms are soothingly stylish, with lacquer screens and every gadget imaginable. Get a corner room with a window seat and spend all day watching the urban scene unfold below, before heading down to the Spaciomm spa for a Japanese massage to unblock those chakras, or maybe a session in the Pilates studio (provided you have the right workout kit, obviously). Up on the roof, the plunge pool offers fabulous views of Gaudí's landmark buildings. *See p165* for Moo, the hotel restaurant. **Photo** *p74*.
*Bar. Disabled-adapted rooms (2). Internet (high-speed, wireless). Non-smoking floors (4). Pool (outdoor). Restaurant. Room service. TV.*

### Hotel Pulitzer

*C/Bergara 8 (93 481 67 67/fax 93 481 64 64/ www.hotelpulitzer.es). Metro Catalunya.* **Rates** €144-€225.60 single; €161.60-€320.90 double. **Credit** AmEx, DC, MC, V. **Map** p344 B2 50
Just off Plaça de Catalunya, the Pulitzer has become a popular place to meet before a night out. A discreet façade reveals an impressive lobby that's stuffed with comfortable white leather sofas, a reading area overflowing with glossy picture books and a swanky bar and restaurant. The rooftop terrace is a fabulous spot for a cocktail, with squishy loungers, scented candles and tropical plants, and views across the city. The rooms themselves are not terribly spacious, but they are sumptuously decorated with cool elephant-grey marble, fat fluffy pillows and kinky leather trim. For a bit of pampering or some rigorous exercise, guests have free use of the nearby Holmes Place gym.
*Bar. Disabled-adapted rooms (5). Internet (dataport). Non-smoking floors (4). Restaurant. Room service. TV.*

### Prestige Paseo de Gràcia

*Passeig de Gràcia 62 (93 272 41 80/fax 93 272 41 81/www.prestigehotels.com). Metro Passeig de Gràcia.* **Rates** €245-€333 single/double; €465-€526.50 junior suite. **Credit** AmEx, DC, MC, V. **Map** p338 G7 51
Perfectly situated for just about everything, this sublime boutique hotel was created by architect Josep Juanpere, who took a 1930s building and revamped it with funky oriental-inspired minimalist design and Japanese gardens. The rooms are equipped with Bang & Olufsen plasma-screen TVs, intelligent lighting systems, free minibars and even umbrellas. Outside their rooms, the hotel's guests hang out in the cool Zeroom lounge-bar-library, where expert concierges (of the funky rather than fusty variety) are constantly on hand to help you get the most out of your stay in Barcelona. If you can't bear to leave it all behind, you can even buy a copy of one of the designer fixtures (all are on sale) to take home.
*Bar. Disabled-adapted room. Internet (dataport, wireless). Room service. TV.*
**Other locations**: Prestige Congress, Pedrosa B 9-11, Hospitalet de Llobregat (93 267 18 00).

## Mid-range

### Hostal d'Uxelles

*Gran Via de les Corts Catalanes 688, pral (93 265 25 60/fax 93 232 85 67/www.hotelduxelles.com). Metro Tetuán.* **Rates** €69.55-€82.40 single; €89.90-€102.75 double; €112.35-€126.25 triple; €155.50-€180.20 quadruple. **Credit** AmEx, MC, V. **Map** p343 H8 52
A pretty, tastefully decorated *hostal*, with very friendly staff, which is a delightful place to stay and a bargain to boot. What more could you want? The angels above reception are a hint of what's to come: Modernista tiles, cream walls with gilt-framed mirrors, antique furnishings and bright, Andaluz-tiled bathrooms (all en suite). Pastel colours rule, and drapes hang romantically above the bedsteads. The best rooms have plant-filled balconies with tables and chairs, where you can have breakfast.
*Room service. TV.*
**Other locations**: Hostal d'Uxelles, 2 Gran Via de les Corts Catalanes 667, entl 2ª (93 265 25 60).

### Hostal Palacios

*Rambla de Catalunya 27, 1º (93 301 30 79/ fax 93 301 37 92/www.hostalpalacios.com). Metro Catalunya.* **Rates** €58.85-€71.70 single; €81-€101.65 double; €107-€126.30 triple; €160.50 suite. **Credit** AmEx, DC, MC, V. **Map** p342 F8 53
Situated in a sumptuous Modernista building, the 11 rooms at the Palacios are well equipped and decorated in a tasteful classical style, more typical of a four-star hotel, with good bathrooms, air-con, digital TV and internet connection. Rates may seem high for an *hostal*, but the standard of the rooms (particularly the larger ones), together with the location, make the Palacios good value for money.
*Internet (wireless). TV.*

### Hotel Astoria

*C/París 203 (93 209 83 11/fax 93 202 30 08/ www.derbyhotels.es). Metro Diagonal.* **Rates** €85.60-€160.50 single; €156.95-€248.25 double; €251.75 suite. **Credit** AmEx, DC, MC, V. **Map** p338 F6 54
With its art deco restaurant and dramatic lobby with a domed, stuccoed ceiling adorned with frescoes of dolphins, the Astoria successfully combines classic charm with designer features. The 117 rooms have been stylishly revamped, though vintage features have been preserved. The bar, with its marble floors, chandeliers and Chesterfield sofas, is the perfect setting for a pre-dinner cocktail, and there is a sauna and rooftop swimming pool too.
*Bar. Gym. Internet (dataport, wireless). Non-smoking hotel except outside terrace. Parking (€21.40/day). Pool (outdoor). Restaurant (lunch only). Room service. TV.*

### Hotel Constanza

*C/Bruc 33 (93 270 19 10/fax 93 317 40 24/ www.hotelconstanza.com). Metro Urquinaona.* **Rates** €107-€128.40 single; €128.40-€158.60 double; triple a supplement of €30 per person; €160.50-€195.20 apartments (2 persons, €30 for each extra person). **Credit** AmEx, MC, V. **Map** p344 E1 55

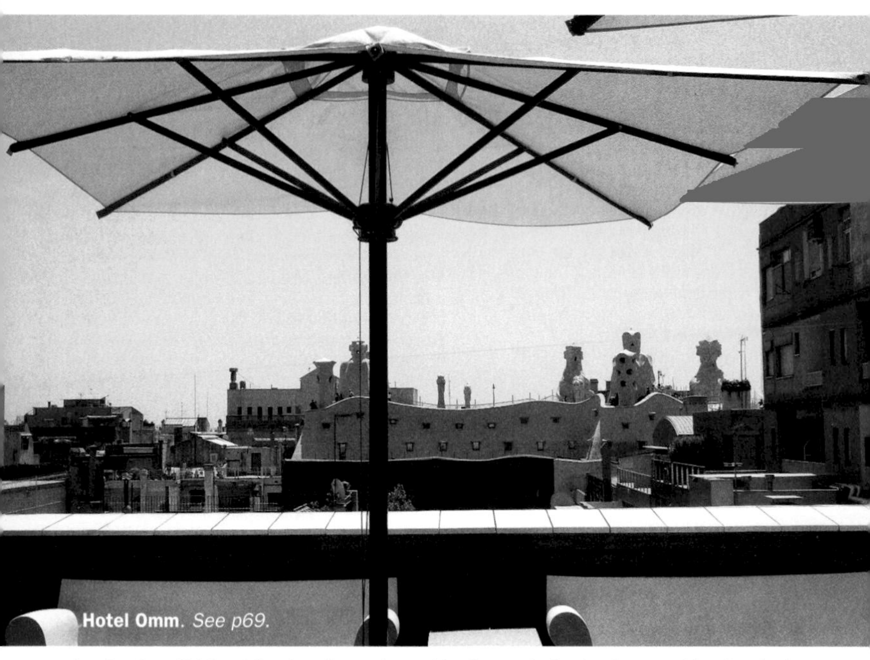
Hotel Omm. See p69.

A seriously stylish hotel that doesn't cost the earth? In Barcelona? You may find that combination unlikely, but it is happily true in the case of Hotel Constanza. The lobby of the hotel looks a bit like the chill-out lounge of an exclusive nightclub, with box, white sofas, lots of dark wood and Japanese silk screens painted with giant white lilies separating the breakfast room from the main area. Upstairs, wine-coloured corridors lead to sumptuous bedrooms with dark wood and leather furnishings, huge pillows and quality cotton sheets. Those at the back are quietest, and some of them have their own private terraces. Renovations are due to be completed in spring 2007, following temporary closure in December, to increase the number of rooms from 20 to 60. There are also seven apartments in tones of white, cream and camel, which are ideal for families.
*Internet (dataport). Non-smoking hotel. TV.*

### Market Hotel

*Passatge Sant Antoni Abat 10 (93 325 12 05/fax 93 424 29 65/www.markethotel.com.es). Metro Sant Antoni.* **Rates** (incl breakfast) €80.25 single; €94.15-€112.35 double; €128.40 suite. **Credit** AmEx, MC, V. **Map** p342 D9 56
The people who brought us the wildly successful Quinze Nits chain of restaurants apply their low-budget, hi-design approach to this new hotel, single-handedly filling €60-€100 accommodation gap in the process. The monochrome rooms, though not huge, are comfortable and stylish for the price and downstairs is a handsome and keenly priced restaurant typical of the group. The noisy arrival at dawn of the stallholders of the nearby Mercat Sant Antoni is the only real drawback.
*Disabled-adapted rooms (2). Internet (wireless). Restaurant. TV.*

### the5rooms

*C/Pau Claris 72 (93 342 78 80/fax 93 342 78 81/ www.thefiverooms.com). Metro Catalunya or Urquinaona.* **Rates** (incl breakfast) €133.75-€176.55 double. **Credit** MC, V. **Map** p344 D1 57
An unusual but very welcome addition to the Barcelona hotel scene, the5rooms is a chic and comfortable B&B in a handsome building, where the delightful Jessica Delgado makes every effort to make guests feel at home. Books and magazines are dotted around the stylish sitting areas and bedrooms, and breakfast is served at any time of day. No questions asked. Jessica is also a useful source of information on the city.
*Internet (wireless). Restaurant. Room service. TV.*

## Budget

### Hostal Central Barcelona

*C/Diputació 346, pral 2ª (93 245 19 81/fax 93 270 07 54/www.hostalcentralbarcelona.com). Metro Tetuán.* **Rates** €32.10-€42.80 single; €61-€68.50 double; €96.30 triple; €28-€38/person 4-6-person suite. **Credit** DC, MC, V. **Map** p343 J8 58

Lodging at the Central, spread across two floors of an old Modernista building, is like staying in a rambling flat rather than at a *hostal*. Rooms have kept their original tiling and high ceilings, but they are kitted out with air-conditioning and double glazing, keeping out the roar of the traffic. Most have en-suite facilities, but the modern glass-brick cubicles in some eat up bedroom space. Walls painted in a wide palette, from duck-egg blue to daffodil yellow, jolly things up. Clean and friendly, this is a bargain for budget travellers and is a metro ride away from most sights.
*Non-smoking hotel.*

### Hostal Centro

*C/Balmes 83, 1° 2ª (93 323 30 88/fax 93 452 34 04/ www.hostal-centro.net). Metro Passeig de Gràcia.* **Rates** €25-€45 single; €45-€65 double; €65-€85 triple. **Credit** MC, V. **Map** p338 F7 59

Housed in a Modernista building with a lift and original tiled floors, most rooms at this *hostal* are surprisingly spacious, with en-suite bathrooms (cheaper rooms have shared bathroom). The best have views out on to C/Balmes or the patio at the rear. With internet access and hot and cold drinks' machines, this is a basic, but practical, place to stay, close to many of the main sights but a block away from the tourist beat.
*Internet (wireless).*

### Hostal Eden

*C/Balmes 55, pral 1ª (93 454 66 20/fax 93 452 66 21/www.hostaleden.net). Metro Passeig de Gràcia.* **Rates** €35-€48.15 single; €55-€69 double; €80.25 triple; €90.95 quadruple. **Credit** AmEx, MC, V. **Map** p338 F8 60

Located on three floors of a Modernista building, this warm and relaxed *hostal* with friendly, helpful staff offers free internet access and has a sunny patio with a shower for you to cool off. The best rooms have marble bathrooms with corner baths, and Nos.114 and 115, at the rear, are quiet and have large windows overlooking the patio. Room 103 is dark but good-sized and quirky, with a sprawling bathroom behind sliding doors.
*Internet (2 shared terminals). TV.*

### Hostal Girona

*C/Girona 24, 1° 1ª (tel/fax 93 265 02 59/ www.hostalgirona.com). Metro Urquinaona.* **Rates** €32.10-€44.95 single; €66.35-€69.65 double. **Credit** DC, MC, V. **Map** p344 F1 61

This gem of a *hostal* is filled with antiques, chandeliers and oriental rugs. The rooms may be on the simple side, but they all have charm and to spare, with tall windows, pretty paintwork (gilt detail on the ceiling roses) and tiled floors. It's worth splashing out on rooms in the refurbished wing, with en-suite bathrooms, although the rooms in the older wing are good too, and some have en-suite showers. Brighter, outward-facing rooms have small balconies overlooking C/Girona or bigger balconies on to a huge and quiet patio. Gorgeous and good value.
*TV.*

### Hostal Goya

*C/Pau Claris 74, 1° (93 302 25 65/fax 93 412 04 35/ www.hostalgoya.com). Metro Urquinaona.* **Rates** €40.65-€62.50 single; €72.75-€96.30 double. **Credit** MC, V. **Map** p344 D1 62

Why can't all *hostales* be like this? Located in a typical Eixample building with fabulous tiled floors, the bedrooms are done out in chocolates and creams, with comfy beds, chunky duvets and cushions; the bathrooms are equally luxurious. The best rooms either give out on to the street or the terrace at the back. The Goya is excellent value for money and a real gem of a place to stay. What's more, guests leaving the city in the evening after a busy final few hours sightseeing can still use a bathroom to shower and change before they go. That's service. **Photo** *p77.*
*TV room.*

### Hostal San Remo

*C/Ausiàs Marc 19, 1° 2ª (93 302 19 89/ www.hostalsanremo.com). Metro Urquinaona.* **Rates** €36-€42 single; €58-€62 double. **Credit** MC, V. **Map** p344 E2 63

Staying in this bright, neat and peaceful apartment feels a bit like staying with an amenable relative. The friendly owner Rosa and her fluffy white dog live on site and take good care of their guests. All seven of the rooms are equipped with air-conditioning, blue-and- white striped bedspreads and modern wooden furniture; five out of seven have en-suite bathrooms, and most of them have a little balcony and double glazing. A good place to stay.
*TV.*

### Residencia Australia

*Ronda Universitat 11, 4° 1ª (93 317 41 77/ fax 93 317 07 01/www.residenciaustralia.com). Metro Universitat.* **Rates** €28-€33 single; €49.55-€79 double; €12-€20 extra bed. **Credit** MC, V. **Map** p344 B1 64

Maria, the owner of Residencia Australia, fled Franco's Spain to Australia in the 1950s and only returned after the Generalissimo's death to carry on the family business and open this small, friendly, home-from-home *pensión*. There are just four cute rooms (one en suite); all are cosy, clean and simply furnished. There's a minimum two-night stay. The family also has two apartments nearby that can be booked if rooms are full.
*Internet (shared terminal). TV (some rooms).*

## Gràcia

One of Barcelona's most charismatic *barris*, Gràcia is just off the beaten tourist track, which only adds to its allure. Its narrow streets and leafy squares have a villagey feel to them, but there are also plenty of decent restaurants, shops and nightlife available. What's more, for those wanting sanctuary from the tourist hordes but easy access to Barcelona's attractions, it's only a five- to ten-minute metro ride to the centre.

## Expensive

### Casa Fuster

*Passeig de Gràcia 132 (93 255 30 00/fax 93 255 30 02/www.hotelcasafuster.com). Metro Diagonal.* **Rates** €410.90-€434.40 single/double; €500.75-€596 deluxe; €858 junior suite; €1,431-€2,003 suite. **Credit** AmEx, DC, MC, V. **Map** p338 G6 65

At the upper end of the city's most distinguished boulevard, the Casa Fuster's top-notch installations make for a luxurious stay; but the hotel's cachet ultimately resides in its history. Designed by the illustrious Modernista architect Lluís Domènech i Montaner (of Palau de la Música fame) as a family home for the aristocratic Fuster family, it has regained its former glory as a swanky hotel with both art nouveau and art deco features. The 96 opulent rooms have original architectural details, along with flat-screen TVs and remote-controlled lighting. Suites have king-size beds and wrought-iron balconies. The bathrooms have period tiling alongside hydro-massage bathtubs and power showers. The curving crimson sofas in the splendid Café Viennese, with huge windows on to the Passeig de Gràcia, are perfect for recovering from a few hours' retail therapy.

*Bar. Business centre. Disabled-adapted rooms (5). Gym. Internet (high-speed).Non-smoking floors (3). Pool (outdoor). Restaurant. Room service. TV (pay movies).*

## Mid-range

### Hotel Confort

*Travessera de Gràcia 72 (93 238 68 28/fax 93 238 73 29/www.mediumhoteles.com). Metro Diagonal or Fontana.* **Rates** €90.95-€160.50 single; €96.30-€192.60 double. **Credit** AmEx, DC, MC, V. **Map** p338 F5 66

The Confort is light-years ahead of other two-star establishments, with 36 simple, but smart, modern bedrooms with curvy, light, wood furnishings and gleaming marble bathrooms. All the rooms get lots of light, thanks to several interior patios. There's a bright dining room and lounge, with a large leafy terrace that makes a lovely setting for a sunny summer breakfast or a cool drink on a balmy night. Although the hotel is just off the tourist track, most sights are withing walking distance and there are plenty of restaurants in the vicinity.

*Disabled-adapted room. Internet (dataport, pay terminal). TV.*

**Other locations**: Hotel Monegal, C/Pelai 62, Eixample (93 302 65 66); and throughout the city.

## Budget

### Hostal H.M.B.

*C/Bonavista 21, 1º (93 368 20 13/fax 93 368 19 96/www.hostalhmb.com). Metro Diagonal.* **Rates** €42.80-€48.15 single; €64.20-€85.60 double; €107-€128.40 quadruple. **Credit** MC, V. **Map** p338 G6 67

An excellent addition to the budget hotel scene, the H.M.B. opened in 2006 and feels crisp, clean and airy. Situated on the first floor with a lift, it has 12 rooms, which have high ceilings and are decorated in tones of blue and green with wood floors, flat-screen TVs and good lighting. All have private marble bathrooms with good showers. Bright contemporary artwork adorns the lobby and corridors.

*Internet (wireless). Non-smoking hotel. TV.*

# Sants

Although the Plaça d'Espanya and the Parc Joan Miró have their charms, the only reason to stay in Sants is to catch an early train. Rates here drop at weekends and other off-peak business seasons. It's a ten- to 15-minute metro ride to town.

## Expensive

### B-Hotel

*Gran Via 389-391 (93 552 95 00/fax 93 552 95 01/www.nnhotels.com). Metro Espanya.* **Rates** €117.70-€214 single; €149.80-€267.50 double. **Credit** AmEx, DC, MC, V. **Map** p341 C8 68

Designed by leading contemporary architect Alfredo Arribas in 2005, B-Hotel is yet another chic, minimalist place to stay, with much use of charcoal grey in the 84 comfortable rooms. Although a couple of miles from La Rambla, it is close to Montjuïc, where several major museums are situated. It is across the street from the Fira exhibition arenas, and has good access to the airport. As well as the main bar, there is a wine cellar for dedicated tasting and quaffing.

*Bar. Business centre. Disabled-adapted rooms (3). Internet (wireless). No-smoking hotel. Parking (€26.75/day). Pool (outdoor). Room service. Spa. TV.*

## Budget

### Hostal Sofía

*Avda Roma 1-3, entl (93 419 50 40/fax 93 430 69 43/www.perso.wanadoo.es/hostalsofia). Metro Sants Estació.* **Rates** €35 single; €40-€60 double; €50-€60 triple. **Credit** DC, MC, V. **Map** p341 C7 69

The 17 basic rooms of Hostal Sofía, situated just across the busy roundabout from the city's main station, are a very sound budget option if an early train or quick stopover forces you to spend the night in the city. Some rooms have en-suite bathrooms. As the *hostal* is on the first floor and traffic is fierce, outward-facing rooms are usually very noisy.

*TV (some rooms).*

# Zona Alta

Perhaps not ideal for a first visit to Barcelona, but staying in the city's more uptown neighbourhoods is not a bad idea if you've

Hostal Goya. See p75.

done the tourist trail on your previous trips. In the Zona Alta you'll get a taste of what Barcelona life is like in a chic residential area with some excellent restaurants (*see p171*).

## Expensive

### Gran Hotel La Florida

*Carretera de Vallvidrera al Tibidabo 83-93 (93 259 30 00/fax 93 259 30 01/www.hotellaflorida.com).* **Rates** €331.70-€428 single/double; €660-€830 junior suite; €1,075-€1,605 suite. **Credit** AmEx, DC, MC, V.

From 1925 to the 1950s, this was Barcelona's grandest hotel, frequented by royalty and film stars. It has lavish suites designed by artists including Rebecca Horn, private terraces and gardens, a five-star restaurant, a summer outdoor nightclub, and a luxury spa. Perched on Tibidabo, La Florida offers bracing walks in the hills and breathtaking 360-degree views, which culminate in a jaw-dropping infinity pool (with a heated indoor part for winter dips). It calls itself an 'urban resort' and is indeed a good choice if you want to relax in opulent style and spend most evenings in the hotel. Bear in mind that getting a cab from town at night can be tricky: there's a free shuttle service but it only runs until 8pm in summer and earlier in winter (though this may change). Check the website for discounts.

*Bar. Business centre. Disabled-adapted rooms (2). Gym. Internet (high-speed, wireless). Non-smoking floor. Parking (€19.30/day). Pool (outdoor/indoor). Restaurant. Room service. Spa. TV (pay movies).*

## Mid-range

### Petit Hotel

*C/Laforja 67, 1° 2ª (93 202 36 63/fax 93 202 34 95/ www.petit-hotel.net). FGC Muntaner.* **Rates** €68.50-€73.85 single; €81.30-€101.65 double; €107 triple; €128.40 quadruple. **Credit** MC, V. **Map** p338 E5 70

This charming and convivial B&B has four neat, fresh-feeling bedrooms set around the comfortable and softly lit lounge. Although only two of the rooms are en suite, the others have large, immaculate modern bathrooms located just outside. The owners, Rosa and Leo, are always happy to chat to guests and provide insider information on the city. Breakfast, which is better than in many hotels, is served 8.30am-1.30pm. Located in the smart neighbourhood of Sant Gervasi, close to Diagonal and with good restaurants and nightlife nearby. Apartments are also available.

*Internet (pay terminal). TV.*

## Apartment hotels

### Citadines

*La Rambla 122, Barri Gòtic (93 270 11 11/fax 93 412 74 21/www.citadines.com). Metro Catalunya.* **Rates** €136-€180 1-2-person studio; €210-€260 1-4-person apartment; €20-€30 cleaning. **Credit** AmEx, DC, MC, V. **Map** p344 B3 71

A gleaming apartment block in a prime location on La Rambla, Citadines offers 115 smartly renovated studios and 16 one-bedroom apartments (all sleep four). Reliable, rather than exciting, it's ideal for longer business trips, groups or families, in an extremely handy location. One weekly clean is included in the price; there's an option to pay extra for the daily cleaning service. Breakfast (€13) is served in a cafeteria on the first floor, which looks out over La Rambla.

*Disabled-adapted rooms (4). Parking (€21/day). TV.*

### Hispanos Siete Suiza

*C/Sicilia 255, Eixample (93 208 20 51/fax 93 208 20 52/www.hispanos7suiza.com. Metro Sagrada Família.* **Rates** (apartments, incl breakfast) €133.75-€197.75 1-2 people; €165.85-€230 3 people; €198-€262.15 4 people; €481.50 up to 6 people. **Credit** AmEx, DC, MC, V. **Map** p339 J7 72

Looking for something different? Lovers of vintage automobiles will get a real kick out of the Hispanos Siete Suiza, named after the seven lovingly restored pre-war motors that take up much of the lobby here. The 19 elegant and spacious apartments each have a kitchen and sitting area decked out with parquet floors, a terrace and two bedrooms. Decor is classical and inoffensive, with no designer trickery. All profits go to the cancer research foundation that runs the hotel. The complex also has a good restaurant called La Cupola. (Rates rise considerably during holidays.)

*Bar. Disabled-adapted room. Internet (dataport). Parking (€15/day). Restaurant. Room service. TV.*

Alberg Mare de Déu de Montserrat.

## Apartment & room rentals

Short-term room and apartment rental is a rapidly expanding market. People who have visited the city several times, or want to spend longer than a few days, are increasingly opting for self-catering accommodation rather than hotels. Some companies rent out their own apartments, while others act as intermediaries between apartment owners and visitors, taking a cut of the rents. *See also p61* **Apartment advice**.

When renting, it pays to use a little common sense. Check the small print (payment methods, deposits, cancellation fees, etc) and exactly what is included (cleaning, towels and so on) before booking. Note that apartments offered for rental tend to be very small.

In addition to the companies listed below, the following offer apartments: www.inside-bcn.com, www.barcelonaliving.com, www.oh-barcelona.com, www.rentaflatinbarcelona.com, www.friendlyrentals.com, www.1st-barcelona.com, www.rentthesun.com, www.apartmentsbcn.net, www.flatsbydays.com, and the gay-operated www.outlet4spain.com. In addition, www.habitservei.com can also help to find rooms in shared flats.

### Barcelona-Home

*C/Viladomat 89-95 Ent. 3 (93 423 34 73/fax 93 423 34 73/www.barcelona-home.com).* **Open** 10am-2pm, 3.30-7pm Mon-Fri. **Rates** vary. **No credit cards. Map** p341 D9.

A reputable company staffed by knowledgeable young people, Barcelona-Home aims to sort out accommodation problems and provide other services including guided tours, airport transfers, language courses and whatever else clients might need. Apartment rental prices are surprisingly reasonable considering the level of service, and the website is a great starting point for information on Barcelona.

### Loquo

*www.loquo.com.*

The holiday rentals section of this website has listings by individuals rather than companies, often at lower rates than agencies. People use the site to advertise their flats if they are going away on holiday and want to sublet, for example, although most are more formal arrangements. Bear in mind that postings can accentuate the positive and omit the less desirable aspects of a property, so be sure to double-check details.

## Youth hostels

For reliable student and youth services, and agencies and websites that can take telephone and online reservations for hostels and apartments, see *p320* **Study**.

### Alberg Mare de Déu de Montserrat

*Passeig de la Mare de Déu del Coll 41-51, Gràcia (93 210 51 51/fax 93 210 07 98/www.tujuca.com). Metro Vallcarca.* **Open** *Reception* 8am-3pm, 4.30-11pm daily. **Rates** (incl breakfast) €15.40-€19 under-25s; €18.80-€22.55 over-25s; €2/per person/stay sheets. **Credit** DC, MC, V.

Located in a magnificent building north of the centre, this hostel boasts an architectural edge over the average, with many original features, including Modernista tilework, whimsical plaster carvings and stained-glass windows, not to mention the beautiful gardens. Over the years, it has served as a private mansion, hospital and orphanage. IYHF cards are not obligatory (available here for €5), but beds cost €2 extra without one.
*Disabled-adapted room. Internet (pay terminals). Kitchen. Laundry facilities. Non-smoking hostel. Parking (free).Restaurant. TV room.*

### Barcelona Mar Youth Hostel

*C/Sant Pau 80, Raval (93 324 85 30/fax 93 324 85 31/www.barcelonamar.com). Metro Paral·lel.*
**Open** 24hrs daily. **Rates** (incl breakfast) €16-€23; €2.50 per person/stay sheets. **Credit** AmEx, DC, MC, V. **Map** p342 E11 73
The no-nonsense Barcelona Mar Youth Hostel, with its pleasant communal areas, sparkling washrooms and handy on-site facilities is cheap as chips. There are no individual rooms, only dorms neatly stacked with bunk beds, but in a token nod to privacy, there are areas that can be cordoned off by drapes.
*Bicycle rental. Disabled-adapted room. Internet. Laundry. Lockers (free). Non-smoking hostel. TV room.*

### Center Ramblas Youth Hostel

*C/Hospital 63, Raval (93 412 40 69/fax 93 317 17 04/www.center-ramblas.com). Metro Liceu.*
**Open** 24hrs daily. **Rates** (incl breakfast) €15.40-€18.80 under-25s; €19-€22.55 over-25s, €2-€3 per person/stay sheets & towels. **No credit cards.** **Map** p344 A4 74
This super-friendly hostel has 201 beds in all, in dorms that sleep three to ten. Facilities include free internet access, a communal fridge, microwave, safes and individual lockers for each guest, It's a good place to meet up and make friends with other young travellers, but beds sell out fast, so reserve your space at least two weeks in advance.
*Disabled-adapted room. Internet (shared terminal). Lockers (free). Non-smoking hostel. TV room.*

### Centric Point

*Passeig de Gràcia 33, Eixample (93 215 65 38/ fax 93 246 15 52/www.centricpointhostel.com/ www.equity-point.com). Metro Passeig de Gràcia.*
**Open** 24hrs daily. **Rates** (incl breakfast) €17-€25 per person dormitory; €35-€50 per person twins; single use €80. €2 per person/night sheets/ blankets/towels. **Credit** DC, MC, V. **Map** p338 G8 75
The newest addition to the Equity Point group goes considerably upmarket, with more than 400 beds in an impressive Modernista building in one of the swankiest locations in the city. There are doubles and dorms, mostly with en-suite facilities. There is also free internet access and satellite TV, as well as complimentary breakfast. Lots of information on Barcelona is available, and you can book lots of tours.
*Disabled-adapted rooms (2). Internet (wireless). Lockers (free). Non-smoking hostel. TV room.*

### Gothic Point

*C/Vigatans 5, Born (93 268 78 08/fax 93 310 77 55/www.gothicpoint.com). Metro Jaume I.*
**Open** 24hrs daily. **Rates** (incl breakfast) €17-€25 per person; €2 per person/night sheets/blankets/ towels. **Credit** DC, MC, V. **Map** p345 D6 76
Belonging to the same group as Centric Point above, this friendly hostel has a faintly Asian feel familiar to anyone who's done the backpacker route thanks to paper lanterns and wall murals, no doubt. Dorms (six to 14 beds) are a bit cramped, and although an undersheet and pillowcase are provided, anything else must be rented. There are washing machines and dryers, a microwave and fridge. Beach bums might prefer to stay at Sea Point on the seafront.
*Disabled-adapted room. Internet (shared terminal). Lockers (€1.20). Non-smoking hostel. TV room.*
**Other locations**: Sea Point, Plaça del Mar 1-4, Barceloneta (93 224 70 75/www.seapointhostel.com); La Ciutat Albergue Residencia, Alegre de Dalt 66, Zona Alta (93 213 03 00/http://laciutat.nnhotels.es).

### Itaca Alberg-Hostel

*C/Ripoll 21, Barri Gòtic (93 301 97 51/ www.itacahostel.com). Metro Catalunya or Urquinaona.* **Open** *Reception* 7am-4am daily. **Rates** (incl sheets) €18-€22 dormitory; €50-€55 twin. **Credit** MC, V. **Map** p344 D4 77
Although right in the centre of the city, this is a laid-back place where you can recharge your batteries in peace. On a quiet street a stone's throw from the cathedral, it has a homely atmosphere that is highlighted by its swirling murals, squishy sofas and lobby music, all conspiring to give it a homely atmosphere; there's also a communal kitchen, a breakfast room and shelves of books and games. Its 33 beds are in five cheerful and airy dorms, all with balconies. The bathrooms are clean.
*Dining room. Internet (pay terminal). Kitchen. Lockers (free). Non-smoking hostel.*

## Campsites

For more information on campsites, get the *Catalunya Campings* or the *Campsites Close to Barcelona* books from tourist offices or bookshops, or log on to www.campingtotal.org or www.barcelonaturisme.com.

### Camping Masnou

*Carretera N2, km 633, El Masnou, Outer Limits (tel/fax 93 555 15 03).* **Open** *Reception* Oct-May 9am-noon, 3-7pm daily. June-Sept 8am-10pm daily. *Campsite* 7am-11.30pm daily. **Rates** €5.50/person; €4.50 1-10s; free under-1s; €5.50 car/caravan; €5 electricity. **Credit** MC, V.

### Tres Estrellas

*Carretera C-31, km 186.2, Gavà (93 633 06 37/fax 93 633 15 25/www.camping3estrellas.com).* **Open** *Reception* mid Mar-mid Oct 9am-9pm daily. *Campsite* 24hrs daily. Closed mid Oct-mid Mar. **Rates** €5.50-€6.59/person; €4.10-€4.40 3-10s; free under-3s; €7.10-€7.50 car/caravan; €4.60 electricity. **Credit** MC, V.

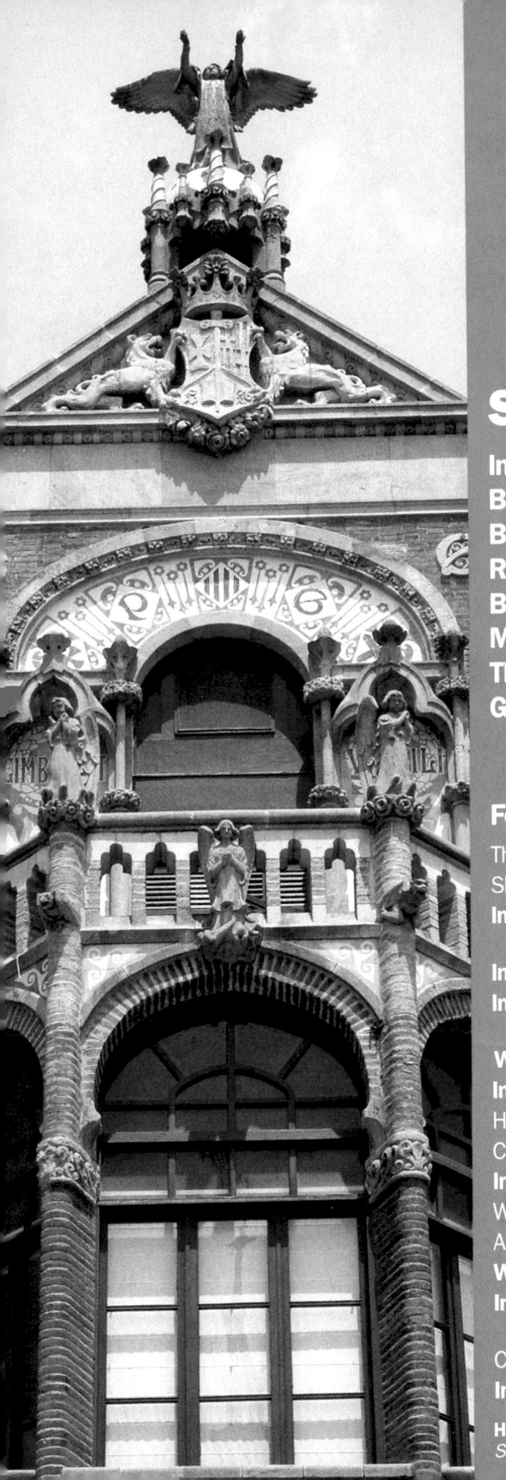

# Sightseeing



## Features



**Hospital de la Santa Creu I Sant Pau.** *See p125.*

# Introduction

More than the heart of the city.

Visitors at Park Güell. *See p132.*

The evocative beauty of the Old City is so alluring that many visitors remain willing captives to its labyrinthine streets, entranced by the atmosphere and wealth of ancient buildings. It's a shame to miss out on the rest of the city, however; the architecural glories of the Eixample, the hills of Montjuïc and Tibidabo, and the new Forum district, which has emerged bright and bold from the ashes of a post-industrial wasteland.

Cutting straight through the Old City are La Rambla and Via Laietana. **La Rambla**, once a seasonal riverbed that formed the western limit of the 13th-century city, is now a tree-lined boulevard dividing the **Barri Gòtic** from the **Raval**. It is best strolled on a quiet Sunday morning, before it sells its soul to the tacky commercialism of living statues, souvenir shops and prostitutes. **Via Laietana**, driven through a century ago amid howls of protest from conservationists, is the boundary between the Barri Gòtic and **Sant Pere** and the achingly trendy **Born**. On a slight hill between these two thoroughfares is the **Plaça Sant Jaume**, the heart of the city ever since it was the centre of the Roman fort from which Barcelona grew. Now it is home to two bastions of government, the **Ajuntament** (City Hall) and the **Generalitat** (the regional government).

With the demolition of the medieval walls in 1854, the open fields beyond the choleric city were a blank canvas for planners, architects and sculptors. The **Eixample** (literally, the 'expansion'), with its gridiron layout, is a showcase for the greatest works of Modernisme, including the **Sagrada Família**, **La Pedrera** and the **Hospital Sant Pau**. When the only traffic was the horse and cart, these whimsical flights of architectural fancy must have been still more impressive; nowadays the Eixample can be noisy and polluted, as almost every road carries four lanes of traffic. Beyond lies the **Park Güell**, with Gaudí's emblematic dragon, and *barris* such as **Gràcia**, **Sants** and **Sarrià**, once independent towns that were swallowed up into the city.

Despite dramatic improvements in the last couple of years, there is still a problem of bag snatching from the unwary. Compared to London or New York, this isn't a violent city at all, but it can be inconvenient to see someone running off with a bag containing your wordly goods. Don't go out dripping with gold, and beware of ladies selling posies and men who want to help clean bird shit off your shoulder.

### GETTING AROUND

The Old City is compact and can be crossed on foot in about 20 minutes. A fun and eco-friendly way to get around (and to head to the beach) is to hire a **Trixi** rickshaw (www.trixi.com), usually decked out to advertise shops. Running 11am-8pm, April to November, and costing €10 per half-hour, they can be hailed on the street, or by calling 93 310 13 79. The public transport system serves every part of the city and is cheap and efficient. *See also p319* **Bussing it**.

## Discount schemes

As well as the schemes described below, a ticket on the **Bus Turístic** (*see p85*) also includes a book of coupons valid for admittance to many of the city's museums and attractions.

### Articket

The Articket (€20) gives free entry to seven major museums and art galleries (one visit allowed to each venue over a period of six months): **Fundació Miró** (*see p118*), **MACBA** (*see p107*), the **MNAC** (*see p119*), **La Pedrera** (*see p127*), the **Fundació Tàpies** (*see p125*), the **CCCB** (*see p107*) and the **Museu Picasso** (*see p99*). The ticket is available from each of the participating venues, as well as at tourist offices (*see p323*), on the internet via Tel-entrada or www.barcelonaturisme.com and at branches of Caixa Catalunya.

### Barcelona Card

**Rates** *2 days* €23; €19 concessions. *3 days* €28; €24 concessions. *4 days* €31; €26 concessions. *5 days* €34; €30 concessions.

This pass allows two to five days of unlimited transport on the metro and buses, as well as discounts on the airport bus and cable cars, and reduced entry to a wide variety of museums and attractions, along with discounts at dozens of restaurants, bars and shops. The Barcelona Card is sold at the airport, tourist offices (*see p323*), **L'Aquàrium** (*see p224*), **Casa Batlló** (*see p124*), the **Monument a Colom** (*see p111*), Estació de Sants railway station, Estació Nord bus station, at branches of **El Corte Inglés** (*see p189*) and on the tourist office website (www.barcelonaturisme.com).

### Ruta del Modernisme

*902 076 621/www.rutadelmodernisme.com.*
**Rates** €12; €7 concessions.

Not so much a route as a guidebook to 115 Modernista buildings both in Barcelona and 13 other Catalan towns, and one that ties in with the small red circles you can see set into pavements. It's available at the Plaça Catalunya tourist office (*see p323*), the **Hospital Sant Pau** (*see p125*) and the **Pavellons Güell** (*see p137*), and contains vouchers entitling discounts of between 15% and 50% on entry to the buildings (valid for one year). There's a suggested one-day itinerary, a list of the 30 most important Modernista buildings, and one of the most beautiful old shops. Profits go towards conservation of the buildings.

### Ruta del Disseny

*www.rutadisseny.com.*

Again, not a route, but a guide to the city's 100 best-designed buildings, as chosen by experts such as Oriol Bohigas and Javier Mariscal. It's divided into four categories: drink, food, shopping and architecture, and also has nine well-chosen itineraries. The guidebook (containing a map) is available at bookshops, the Plaça Catalunya tourist office (*see p323*) and the **Hospital Sant Pau** (*see p125*) or there is a comprehensive website.



## Tours

### By bike

#### Barcelona by Bicycle

*Un Cotxe Menys, C/Esparteria 3, Born (93 268 21 05/www.bicicletabarcelona.com). Metro Barceloneta.* **Open** 10am-7pm Mon-Sat; 10am-2pm Sun (call ahead for bike hire outside these times). **Tours** *Jan, Feb* 11am daily. *Mar-Dec* 11am, 4.30pm Mon, Wed, Fri; 11am, 7.30pm Tue, Thur, Sat; 11am Sun. **Rates** *Tours* €22 incl guide & bike rental. *Hire* €5 1hr; €11 half-day; €15 1 day; €70 1wk. **No credit cards**. **Map** p345 E7.

Individuals or small groups simply meet in Plaça Sant Jaume for a three-hour English-speaking tour. Booking is required for a tailor-made tour, and the meeting point for that is C/Esparteria 3. Bike hire is also available.

#### Fat Tire Bike Tours

*C/Escudellers 48 (93 301 36 12/www.fattire biketours.com). Metro Drassanes.* **Tours** *Mar-mid Apr* 12.30pm daily. *Mid Apr-Sep* 11.30am, 4.30pm, 7pm daily. *Sept-mid Dec* 12.30pm daily. **Rates** *Tours* €22. *Hire* €4 1hr; €7 3hrs; €10 6hrs.
**No credit cards**. **Map** p345 C6.

Booking isn't necessary, although there are discounts for pre-arranged groups. Tours meet in Plaça Sant Jaume and last over four hours, taking in the Old City, Sagrada Família, Ciutadella park and the beach.

### By bus

#### Barcelona Tours

*93 317 64 54/www.barcelonatours.es.* **Tours** . *Nov-May* 9am-8pm daily; approx every 15-20mins; *June-Oct* 9am-8pm daily; approx every 8-10mins. **Tickets** *1 day* €19; €12 concessions. *2 days* €23; €15 concessions. Free under-4s. Available on board bus.
**No credit cards**.

A decent recorded commentary on the sights, via headphones, and fewer passengers are the advantages to these bright orange buses. The disadvantages are that tours are not as frequent as those of rival Bus Turístic, and there are no discounts offered to attractions. In the Old City a logical place to start

Most reliable scooters at the best prices in town!
Bajada de San Miguel 6 ~ 08006 Barcelona
Metro station; <L3>Liceu or <L4>Jaume I
tel(24h): +(34)600 370 343 fax: +(34)93 30 21 204
www.barcelonamoto.com ~ info@barcelonamoto.com
20€ per day*
ubject to availability. Price does not include VAT
rent a scooter
and discover the fun, live Barcelona like locals do. Explore all the hidden parts of the city. Save money on taxis and stop sweating in metros.
rent a scooter
BARCELONAMOTO.com
600 370 343
LEAD
SCOOTER & ELECTRIC BIKE RENTAL
BARCELONAMOTO

is outside the Hard Rock Café in Plaça Catalunya. It takes around three hours to cover the large tour circuit which includes La Pedrera, Sagrada Família, Park Güell and Nou Camp.

### Bus Turístic

**Tours** *Apr-Oct* 9am-9pm daily; approx every 6-10 mins. *Nov-Mar* 9am-7pm daily; approx every 30 mins. **Tickets** 1 day €18; €11 concessions. 2 days €22; €14 concessions. Free under-4s. Available from tourist offices or on board bus. **No credit cards.**

Bus Turístic (white and blue, with colourful images of the sights) runs two circular routes, both passing through Plaça Catalunya: the northern (red) route passes La Pedrera, Sagrada Família, Park Güell, the tram stop to Tibidabo and Pedralbes; the southern (blue) route takes in Montjuïc, Port Vell, Vila Olímpica and the Barri Gòtic. Both are one-way. Ticket holders get discount vouchers for a range of attractions.

## On foot

The **Travel Bar** (C/Boqueria 27, 93 342 52 52) organises pub/club crawls on Tuesday, Thursday and Saturday at 9.30pm for €15.

### Barcelona Walking Tours

*807 117 222/www.barcelonaturisme.com.* **Tours** (English) *Gothic* 10am daily. *Picasso* 10.30am Tue-Sun. *Modernisme* 6pm Fri-Sun. *Gourmet* 11am Fri, Sat **Tickets** *Gothic, Modernisme* €9; €3 concessions. *Picasso, Gourmet* (reservations essential) €11; €5 concessions. **No credit cards.** **Map** p344 C2.

Run by the city council, these popular walking tours now have four itineraries. The Gourmet tour includes 13 stops in the city's emblematic cafés, food shops and markets. The Gothic tour concentrates on the history and buildings of the Old City, while the Picasso visits the artist's haunts and ends with a visit to the Picasso Museum (entry is included in the price). The Modernisme tour is a circuit of the 'Golden Square' in the Eixample, taking in Gaudí's Casa Batlló and La Pedrera. Tours take around 90mins to 2hrs, excluding the museum trip. All tours start in the underground tourist office in Plaça Catalunya.

### My Favourite Things

*Mobile 637 265 405/www.myft.net.*

Outings (€26) that include peeks into the hidden nooks of the city, sailing trips along the seafront, and salsa or flamenco lessons. Phone or log on for details.

### Saboroso

*Mobile 667 770 492/www.saboroso.com.*

Clued-up and charming British food-lovers offer tailor-made gastronomic tours of Barcelona, as well as trips to vineyards in the Penedès and the Priorat.



# Three days in Barcelona

You could, of course, eschew the sights altogether and follow our **walks** on *p20, p102* and *p128*. Or you could hop on either of the **tourist buses** (*see p83*) and let the sights come to you. But if you must fill two photo albums when you get home, here's how.

**DAY ONE**

Start with a stroll down **La Rambla**. Cut into the **Plaça Reial**, admire Gaudí's lamp-posts and from there head to the heart of the **Barri Gòtic** and the **cathedral**. Crossing the Via Laietana takes you to the **Palau de la Música Catalana**, with its fantastic façade. From here head down into the Born proper, and perhaps tuck into some lunchtime tapas outside the majestic **Santa Maria del Mar**. From here it's a skip and a hop to the **Museu Picasso**. If you've any energy left, wander down to the **Port Vell**, **Barceloneta** and the **beach**, with its seafront restaurants.

**DAY TWO**

Head up the **Passeig de Gràcia** to admire the masterpieces of the **Manzana de la Discòrdia**. Further up is Gaudí's **La Pedrera**, with its Modernista apartment and strange and beautiful roofscape. You'll have to backtrack slightly to catch a direct metro to Gaudí's most legendary work, the **Sagrada Família**. The Avda Gaudí has several good places for you to grab a *bocadillo*, after which you could drop into the stunning **Hospital Sant Pau**. From here hop in a cab (or on a tourist bus) to the beautiful colours of Gaudí's **Park Güell**. The 24 bus will get you back in time for dinner.

**DAY THREE**

Venture into the Raval to see the **MACBA** and the nearby **CCCB**. Walk to the Ronda Sant Antoni to take a 55 bus up to **Montjuïc** and the **Fundació Miró**, which is also a good spot for lunch. From here you can walk to the **Olympic stadium** and then to the nearby **Jardí Botànic** for leafy tranquillity and spectacular views. Walk back past the Fundació Miró to get to the **cable car** at Miramar, which will take you on a vertiginous ride to the **Port Vell** and the myriad seafood restaurants along Passeig Joan de Borbó.

# Barri Gòtic

The shock of the old.

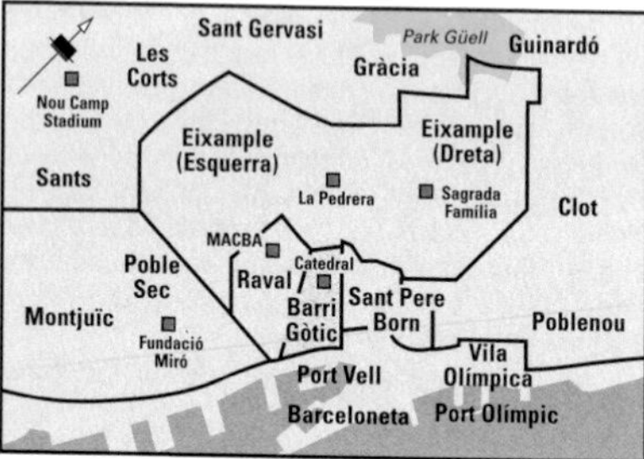


## Maps pp344-345

An almost perfectly preserved medieval time capsule, the Gothic Quarter is an unmissable part of town for any visitor. Here, history is written in stone as Roman ruins rub shoulders with medieval palaces and great Gothic buildings, all set amid a tangle of narrow streets that have now been largely pedestrianised.

For the last 2,000 years, the heart of the city has been Plaça Sant Jaume, set on the gentle hill of Mons Taber where the Roman 'acropolis' once stood. At the crossroads of the streets of C/Call, C/Bisbe and C/Ciutat, dominating the forum, was the **Temple of Augustus**, four columns of which can still be seen (*see p94*) in C/Pietat. The square now contains the municipal government (**Ajuntament**; *see p89*) and Catalan regional government (**Palau de la Generalitat**; *see p94*) buildings, which stand opposite each other. They have not always done so: the square was only opened up in 1824, when a church was demolished. Soon after, the stolid neo-classical façade was added to the Ajuntament.

The façade of the Generalitat (1598-1602), on the other hand, is one of the few Renaissance buildings in the city. This architectural dearth can be explained by a terrible series of wars that lasted from about 1460 to 1715. The greater part of both buildings, however, was built in the early 15th century. Both buildings' original main entrances – that of the Generalitat (1416-18) being particularly fine – open on to what was once the *decumanus maximus* at the side.

On this street is one of the most photographed features of the Barri Gòtic, the neo-Gothic **Pont dels Sospirs** (Bridge of Sighs) across C/Bisbe from the Generalitat. It's a pastiche from 1928, when the idea of the locale as a 'Gothic Quarter' took off. Other alterations from the same period include the decorations on the **Casa dels Canonges** (a former set of canons' residences, and now Generalitat offices), on the other side of the bridge. A little further down C/Bisbe is the Plaça Garriga i Bachs, with Josep Llimona's bronze monument to the martyrs of 1809, dedicated to the *barcelonins* who rose up against Napoleon and were executed.

In C/Santa Llúcia, in front of the cathedral, is **Casa de l'Ardiaca** (*see p96* **In the detail**); originally a 15th-century residence for the archdeacon (*ardiaca*), it has a superb tiled patio. The huge square at the foot of the steps leading up to the cathedral is **Plaça Nova**, which houses an antiques market every Thursday (*see p207*) and is a traditional venue for festivals, music concerts and *sardana* dancing (*see p216*). At ground level, on the south-east corner of the square is ***Barcino***, a visual poem by Joan Brossa installed in 1994, referring to the ancient name for Barcelona, which was supposedly named by the Carthaginians after Hannibal's father, Hamil Barca. Directly above is the **Roman aqueduct**; the final archway of the city's two aqueducts dating from the 1st century AD is preserved inside the tower that defended the north-eastern side of the gate; one of these has been externally rebuilt. Fast forward two millennia to the opposite side of Plaça Nova, dominated by one of the first high rise blocks in the city, the **Col·legi d'Arquitectes** (Architects' Association). It's mainly of interest for its graffiti-style sand-blasted triptych of Catalan folk scenes, designed by Picasso while in self-imposed exile in the 1950s and executed by Norwegian artist Carl Nesjar. Behind its atypical style is a story that when Picasso heard that Miró was also being considered, he responded dismissively that he could easily 'do a Miró'. The middle section depicts the *gegants* (giant figures who lead processions at popular festivals) and figures holding palm branches; the left-hand section (on C/dels Arcs) symbolises the joy of life, while the right-hand section (on C/dels Capellans) depicts the Catalan flag. There are also two interior friezes depicting a *sardana* dance and a wall of arches.

In front of the cathedral, on the right as you come out, is the **Museu Diocesà** (*see p91*), housing religious art; around the side of the cathedral, meanwhile, is the little-visited but fascinating **Museu Frederic Marès** (*see p93*).

Further along is the 16th-century **Palau del Lloctinent** (Palace of the Lieutenant, or, here, 'Viceroy'); currently undergoing restoration, it once housed the archive of the Crown of Aragon. It was also the local headquarters for the Spanish Inquisition, from where the unfortunates were carted off to the Passeig del Born to be burnt. The building was once part of the former royal palace (**Palau Reial**), and has another exit to the medieval palace square, the well-preserved **Plaça del Rei**. The complex houses the **Museu d'Història de la Ciutat** (*see p93*) and includes some of Barcelona's most historically important buildings: the Escher-esque 16th-century five-storey watchtower (**Mirador del Rei Martí**) and the **Capella de Santa Àgata**, which houses the very stone where the breasts of Saint Agatha were allegedly laid when the Romans chopped them off in Catania. Parts of the palace are said to date back to the tenth century, and there have been many remarkable additions to it since, notably the 14th-century **Saló del Tinell**, a medieval banqueting hall that is a definitive work of Catalan Gothic. It is here that Ferdinand and Isabella are said to have received Columbus on his return from America.

The narrow streets centred on C/Call once housed a rich Jewish ghetto (*call*). At the corner of C/Sant Domènec del Call and C/Marlet is the medieval **synagogue**, now restored and open to the public (*see p94*). At C/Marlet No.1 is a 12th-century inscription from a long-demolished house. Hebrew inscriptions can be seen on stones in the eastern wall of the **Plaça Sant Iu**, across from the cathedral, and at ankle level in the south-west corner of the Plaça del Rei.

Near the centre of the *call* is the beautiful little **Plaça Sant Felip Neri** and its fine baroque church, whose damaged façade is the result of an Italian bombing raid during the Civil War. More than 200 people were killed, many of them refugee children on a Sunday outing. This square is another 20th-century invention; the shoemakers' guild building (now housing the **Museu del Calçat**, *see p90*) was moved here in 1943 to make way for the Avda de la Catedral, while the nearby tinkers' guild was moved earlier last century, when Via Laietana was driven through the district. Close by are the attractive **Plaça del Pi** and **Plaça Sant Josep Oriol**, where there are great pavement bars and artisanal weekend markets. The squares are separated by **Santa Maria del Pi**, one of Barcelona's most distinguished Gothic churches, with a magnificent rose window and spacious single nave. Opposite is the 17th-century neo-classical retailers' guild-hall, with its colourful 18th-century sgraffiti.



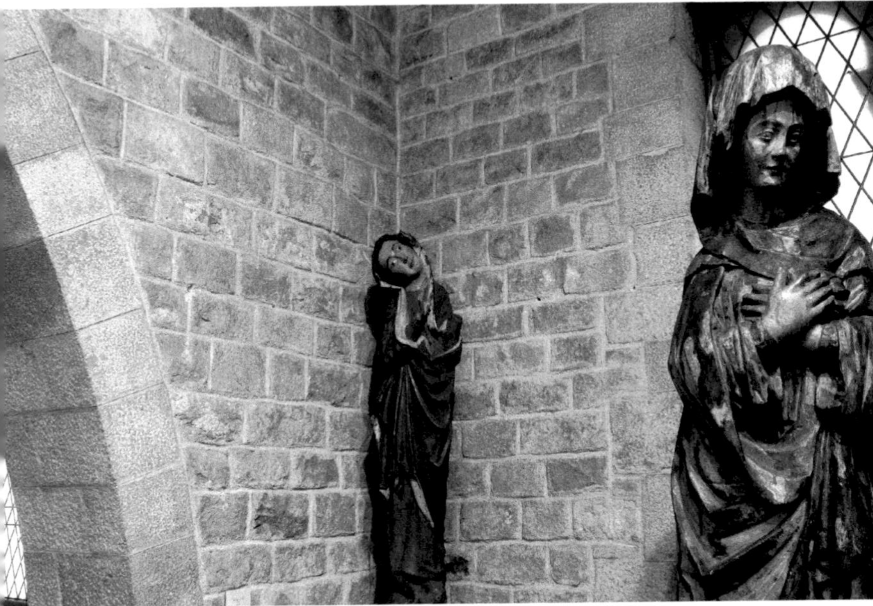

In a niche of its own: **Museu Frederic Marès**. *See p93*.

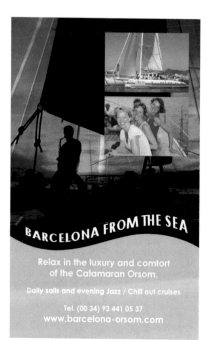

Despite the expansion of Barcelona into the Eixample, the old centre has remained a hub of cultural, social and political life. In C/Montsió, a narrow street off Portal de l'Àngel, is the **Els Quatre Gats** café (*see p173*), legendary haunt of Picasso and other artists and bohemians, in a wonderful Modernista building designed by Puig i Cadafalch. Between C/Portaferrissa and Plaça del Pi is **C/Petritxol**, one of the most charming streets of the Barri Gòtic, known for its traditional *granges* offering coffee and cakes, and also housing the **Sala Parés** (*see p234*), the city's oldest art gallery; Rusiñol, Casas and the young Picasso all exhibited here. On the other side of C/Portaferrissa, heading up C/Bot, is the newly done-up **Plaça Vila de Madrid**, where there are the excavated remains of a Roman necropolis and a rare expanse of city-centre grass. Between here and the Plaça Catalunya is the marvellous little Romanesque **Església de Santa Anna**, begun in 1141 and containing an exquisite 14th-century cloister.

Back on the seaward side of the Barri Gòtic, if you walk from Plaça Sant Jaume up C/Ciutat, to the left of the Ajuntament, and turn down the narrow alley of C/Hércules, you'll come to **Plaça Sant Just**, a fascinating old square with a recently restored Gothic water fountain from 1367, and the **Església de Sants Just i Pastor**, built in the 14th century on the site of a chapel founded by Charlemagne's son Louis the Pious, and now looking rather unloved inside.

The once-wealthy area between here and the port became more run-down throughout the 20th century. It has a different atmosphere from the northern part of the Barri Gòtic: shabbier and with less prosperous shops. The city authorities made huge efforts to change this, particularly in the 1990s, when new squares were opened up: **Plaça George Orwell** on C/Escudellers, known as the 'Plaça del Trippy' by the youthful crowd that hangs out there and the subject of much heated debate when CCTV was recently introduced (the irony of which was lost on no one), and **Plaça Joaquim Xirau**, off La Rambla. Another tactic was the siting of parts of the Universitat Pompeu Fabra on the lower Rambla. Just above is the area's heart: **Plaça Reial**, known for its bars, cheap backpacker hostels and rather scuzzy atmosphere at night. It's still a popular spot for a drink or an outdoor meal (provided you don't mind the odd drunk and are prepared to keep an eye on your bags). An addition from the 1840s, the *plaça* has the **Tres Gràcies** fountain in the centre and **lamp-posts** designed by the young Gaudí. It's the only work he ever did for the city council.

The grand porticoes of some of the buildings around the **Església de La Mercè**, once the merchants' mansions, stand as testament to the former wealth of the area before the building of the Eixample. The **Plaça de la Mercè** itself was only created in 1982, with the destruction of the houses that used to stand here; the 19th-century fountain was moved here from the port. There is also a dwindling number of lively *tascas* (small traditional tapas bars) on C/Mercè. Beyond C/Ample and the Mercè, you emerge from narrow alleys or the pretty **Plaça Duc de Medinaceli** on to the **Passeig de Colom**, where a few shipping offices and ships' chandlers still recall the atmosphere of decades gone by. Monolithic on Passeig de Colom is the **Capitanía General**, the army headquarters, whose façade has the dubious distinction of being the one construction in Barcelona that is directly attributable to the dictatorship of Primo de Rivera.

## Ajuntament (City Hall)

*Plaça Sant Jaume (93 402 70 00/special visits 93 402 73 64/www.bcn.es). Metro Jaume I or Liceu.* **Open** *Office* 8.30am-2.30pm Mon-Fri. *Visits* 10am-1.30pm Sun. **Admission** free. **Map** p345 C6.

Around the left-hand corner of the city hall's rather dull 18th-century neo-classical façade is the old entrance in the wonderfully flamboyant 15th-century Catalan Gothic façade. Inside, the centre-piece and oldest part, is the famous Saló de Cent, where the Consell de Cent (Council of One Hundred)

Pretty **Plaça Sant Felip Neri**. *See p87.*

Sightseeing

Plaça Reial. See p89.

ruled the city between 1372 and 1714. The Saló de Cròniques is filled with Josep Maria Sert's immense black-and-gold mural (1928), depicting the early 14th-century Catalan campaign in Byzantium and Greece under the command of Roger de Flor. Full of art and sculptures by the great Catalan masters from Clarà to Subirachs, the interior of the city hall is open for guided tours (in different languages) on Sundays.

### Catedral

*Pla de la Seu (93 342 82 60/www.catedralbcn.org). Metro Jaume I.* **Open** *Combined ticket* 1.30-4.30pm daily. *Church* 8am-12.45pm, 5-7.30pm Mon-Fri; 8am-12.45pm, 5-6pm Sat; 8-9am, 5-6pm Sun. *Cloister* 9am-12.30pm, 5-7pm daily. *Museum* 10am-1pm, 5.15-7pm daily. **Admission** *Combined ticket* €4. *Church & cloister* free. *Museum* €1. *Lift to roof* €2. *Choir* €1.80. **No credit cards**. **Map** p345 C5/D5.

The present-day cathedral (Santa Església Catedral Basílica de Barcelona) is the third church to stand on this site. The first was a three-naved basilica that was destroyed by Al-Mansur in 985, the remains of which can be seen in the Museu d'Història de la Ciutat (*see p93*); of the second Romanesque building, only two doors and the chapel of Santa Llúcia to the right of the main façade remain. Construction on the Gothic cathedral began in 1298 but went at a pace that makes the Sagrada Família project look snappy; the work on the neo-Gothic façade remained unfinished until the end of the 19th century, being completed by the architects Josep Oriol Mestres and August Font i Carreras, who took inspiration from a 15th-century drawing by Mestre Carlí. It is a cavernous and slightly forbidding place, but contains many images, paintings and sculptures and an intricately carved choir built in the 1390s. The cathedral museum, which is in the 17th-century chapterhouse, displays paintings and sculptures, including works by Gothic masters Jaume Huguet, Bernat Martorell and Bartolomé Bermejo. Santa Eulàlia, patron saint of Barcelona, lies in the dramatically lit crypt in an alabaster tomb carved with scenes from her martyrdom. To one side, there's a lift to the roof; take it for a magnificent view of the Old City. The glorious light-filled cloister is famous for its fierce geese (*see p96* **In the detail**) and half-erased floor engravings, marking which guild paid for which side chapel: scissors for the tailors, shoes for the cobblers and so on. A combined ticket (*visita especial*) has a special timetable intended to keep tourists and worshippers from bothering one another. During the afternoons, ticketholders have the run of the cloister, church, choir and lift, and can enter some chapels and take photos (normally prohibited).

### Centre Civic Pati Llimona

*C/Regomir 3 (93 268 47 00). Metro Jaume I.* **Open** 9am-2pm, 4.30-8.30pm Mon-Fri; 10am-2pm, 4-8pm Sat. **Exhibitions** 9am-2pm, 4.30-10pm Mon-Fri; 10am-2pm, 4-8pm Sat. Closed Aug. **Admission** free. **Map** p345 C6.

Centre Civic Pati Llimona incorporates part of a round tower that dates from the first Roman settlement with later Roman baths and a 15th-century residence. The excavated foundations of the tower are visible from behind glass from the street. The building is now used as a civic centre and is open to the public, staging frequent photography exhibitions.

### Museu del Calçat (Shoe Museum)

*Plaça Sant Felip Neri 5 (93 301 45 33). Metro Jaume I.* **Open** 11am-2pm Tue-Sun. **Admission** €2.50; free under-7s. **No credit cards**. **Map** p345 C5.

Housed in what was once part of the medieval shoemakers' guild, this quirky little footwear museum details the cobbler's craft from Roman sandals to '70s platform boots. The earlier examples are reproductions, while those from the 17th century to the present day are originals, including swagged musketeers' boots and delicately hand-painted 18th-century party shoes. There is also a section devoted to celebrity footwear, including shoes belonging to cellist Pau Casals and the first Catalan boot to reach the summit of Everest, worn by Carles Vallès in 1985. Another highlight is the enormous pair of shoes made for the statue of Columbus (*see p111*), which are, according to Guinness, the biggest in the world.

### Museu Diocesà

*Avda de la Catedral 4 (93 315 22 13). Metro Jaume I.*
**Open** 10am-2pm, 5-8pm Tue-Sat; 11am-2pm Sun.
**Admission** €6; €3 concessions; free under-7s.
**Credit** (shop only) MC, V. **Map** p344 D4.

A hotchpotch of religious art punctuated with exhibitions on unrelated themes, Barcelona's Diocesan Museum is worth a visit for a gander at its 14th-century alabaster virgins, altarpieces by Bernat Martorell and wonderful Romanesque murals. The building itself is also interesting, and includes the Pia Almoina, a former almshouse, stuck on to a Renaissance canon's residence, which in turn was built inside a Roman tower.



## Shadow of the Wind

They're calling it Barcelona's *Da Vinci Code*, a sprawling thriller with phenomenal international success, endorsed by readers as unlikely as German vice chancellor Joschka Fischer, who declared 'You'll drop everything and read the whole night through.' Like Dan Brown's book, however, *Shadow of the Wind* attracts almost as much scepticism as enthusiasm, with its clunky narrative contrivances, its mostly hackneyed characterisation and its endless expository dialogue. Rarely does a character speak without doing so 'heavy-heartedly', 'sadly', 'with tears in his eyes' or 'smiling'.

Wearying though all this becomes, there's no denying that at the heart of Carlos Ruiz Zafón's book lies a ripping good yarn, enhanced by some atmospheric description of a cowed and fearful post-war Barcelona. The story takes a young Daniel Sempere on a quest to hunt down Julián Carax, the author of an obsolete novel, *Shadow of the Wind*, the remaining copies of which a mysterious figure is hunting down and burning, with Daniel's copy next in his sights. On this mission, Daniel meets a host of characters from all walks of society, in gloomy Gothic hospices, palatial uptown apartments and any number of Barcelona locations in between.

Keen readers will start in C/Arc del Teatre, under an archway off La Rambla and home to the Cemetery of Forgotten Books, where Daniel first comes across Carax's novel. Or, perhaps in C/Santa Anna, on the other side of La Rambla, where Daniel and his father lived 'a stone's throw from the church square'. Running almost parallel is C/Canuda, where Daniel meets Gustavo Barceló in the Ateneo library – still standing and with a delightful café on the first floor. South from here is the Plaça Reial, home to the unobtainable Clara Barceló, although more often than not she and Daniel would end up in a milk bar on C/Petrixol – almost certainly the Granja Dulcinea at No.2, still serving hot chocolate with whipped cream. Just east of here is the Plaça Felip Neri, where Julian's would-be lover Nuria Monfort would sit and read.

No true fan of the book, however, could resist a trip uptown to visit the creaking mansion where Julian's true love and nemesis Penélope meets her tragic end. The 'Frare Blanc' is now the restaurant Asador de Aranda, at Avda Tibidabo 31, a Modernista confection of a place, best known for its milk-fed lamb roasted in a wood oven. Best known until now, that is.

BARCELONA MODERNISME ROUT

# New Guided Visits !!

Domènech i Montaner's **Hospital de Sant P**
Daily visits in English at 10'15 and 12'15 am

Domènech i Montaner's **Palau Montaner**
Visits in English every Saturday at 10'30 am

...and **Gaudí's Pavellons Güell**
Friday through Monday at 10'15 and 12'15 am

**More information at 933 177 652 and www.rutadelmodernisme.com**

 Ajuntament de Barcelona

 Institut del Paisatge Urbà i la Qualitat de Vida

### Museu Frederic Marès

*Plaça Sant Iu 5-6 (93 310 58 00/www.museumares.bcn.es). Metro Jaume I.* **Open** 10am-7pm Tue-Sat; 10am-3pm Sun. **Admission** €3; €1.50 concessions; free under-16s. Free 3-7pm Wed, 1st Sun of mth. **Guided tours** noon Sun. **Credit** (shop only) AmEx, MC, V. **Map** p345 D5.

Barcelona's most celebrated pack rat, Frederic Marès (1893-1991) managed to fill a whole palace with his obsessive hoardings after he cut a deal with the Ajuntament: he would donate his extraordinary collections to the city, if, in return, the city would find an appropriate building in which to house both them and him.

The result is one of the city's most eclectic museums, where the kaleidoscope of objects reflects Marès' wide-ranging interests in travel and sculpture and also his indulgently tolerated kleptomania as he 'borrowed' many items from his wealthy friends.

The ground floor of the museum contains an array of Romanesque crucifixes, virgins and saints, while the first floor takes sculpture right up to the 20th century. The basement contains the remains from ecclesiastical buildings that date back to Roman times: capitals, tombs, gargoyles, stone window frames and entire church portals, exquisitely carved. On the second floor is the Gentleman's Room, which is stuffed to the gunwales with walking sticks, key fobs, smoking equipment, matchboxes and opera glasses, while the charming Ladies' Room contains more feminine items such as fans, sewing scissors, nutcrackers and perfume flasks. Also on the second floor is a room devoted to photography, and Marès's study and library, now filled with sculptures (many of them his own). Note: the museum used to close floors down on different days of the week. All floors are now open. Tickets are valid for two days (not necessarily consecutive). **Photo** *p87.*

### Museu d'Història de la Ciutat

*Plaça del Rei 1 (93 315 11 11/www.museuhistoria.bcn.es). Metro Jaume I.* **Open** *June-Sept* 10am-8pm Tue-Sat; 10am-3pm Sun. *Oct-May* 10am-2pm, 4-8pm Tue-Sat; 10am-3pm Sun. **Guided tours** by appointment. **Admission** *Permanent exhibitions* €4; €2.50 concessions; free under-16s. *Temporary exhibitions* varies. *Both* free 4-8pm 1st Sat of mth. **No credit cards. Map** p345 D5.

The City History Museum had a chance beginning. Stretching from the Plaça del Rei to the cathedral are 4,000sq m of subterranean Roman excavations, including streets, villas and storage vats for oil and wine, which were discovered by accident in the late 1920s when a whole swathe of the Gothic Quarter was upended to make way for the central avenue of Via Laietana. The excavations continued until 1960; today, the underground labyrinth is accessed via the

## In the detail
## Casa de l'Ardiaca's letterbox

The House of the Archdeacon (*see p86*), which nowadays hosts the city's historical and photographic archives, was built on 12th-century foundations in the 14th and 15th centuries, and used as the archdeacon's residence for a relatively short time before falling into disrepair for many decades. At the end of the 19th century it was bought and overhauled, becoming the home of the Lawyers' Association. As part of the renovations, Modernista architect Lluis Domènech i Montaner was drafted in to spruce up the façade; most notably he provided it with its charming marble letterbox.

The meaning of the tortoise and swifts that decorate the postal opening is open to much interpretation, but may have been a reflection on the speed of the postal service as opposed to the expectations of its customers, or it may have referred to the legal system (as evidenced by the sword, shield and scales of justice). In this version, the swifts again refer to the wants of the clients (in this case, those filing lawsuits) with the tortoise representing the law's delay, while the ivy leaves were believed to refer to the endless bureaucratic hurdles standing in the way of the legal process.

**Bruno Quadros** building. *See p95.*

Casa Padellàs, a merchant's palace dating from 1498, which was laboriously moved from its original location in C/Mercaders for the construction of Via Laietana. Admission allows access to the Capella de Santa Àgata – with its 15th-century altarpiece by Jaume Huguet, one of the greatest Catalan painters in medieval times – and the Saló del Tinell, at least when there's no temporary exhibition. This majestic room (1370) began life as the seat of the Catalan parliament and was converted in the 18th century into a baroque church, which was dismantled in 1934. The Rei Martí watchtower is still closed to the public while it awaits reinforcement. Tickets for the museum are also valid for the monastery at Pedralbes (*see p137*) and the Museu Verdaguer (*see p136*).

### Palau de la Generalitat

*Plaça Sant Jaume (93 402 46 17/www.gencat.net). Metro Jaume I or Liceu.* **Guided tours** every 30mins 10.30am-1.30pm 2nd & 4th Sun of mth; also 9.30am-1pm, 4-7pm Mon, Fri by appointment. **Admission** free. **Map** p345 C5.

Like the Ajuntament, the Palau de la Generalitat has a Gothic side entrance that opens out on to C/Bisbe, with a beautiful relief of St George (Sant Jordi), patron saint of Catalonia, made by Pere Johan in 1418. Inside the building, the finest features are the first-floor Pati de Tarongers ('Orange Tree Patio'), which was to become the model for many patios in Barcelona, and the magnificent chapel of Sant Jordi of 1432-4, which is the masterpiece of Catalan architect Marc Safont. The Generalitat is traditionally open to the public on Sant Jordi (St George's Day, 23 April), when its patios are spectacularly decorated with red roses. But be aware that queues are huge. It normally also opens on 11 September (Catalan National Day) and 24 September (La Mercè).

### Sinagoga Shlomo Ben Adret

*C/Marlet 5 (93 317 07 90/www.calldebarcelona.org). Metro Jaume I or Liceu.* **Open** 11am-6pm Mon-Fri; 11am-3pm Sat-Sun. **Admission** €2. **Map** p345 C5.

It's only in the last few years that historians have come to agree that the small basement in the building at C/Marlet No.5 was the synagogue of the main *call*. The front of the building, slightly skewing the street, fulfils religious requirements by which the façade has to face Jerusalem; the two windows at knee height allow light to enter from that direction.

### Temple Romà d'Augusti

*C/Paradís 10 (93 315 11 11). Metro Jaume I.* **Open** 10am-8pm Tue-Sun. **Admission** free. **Map** p345 D5.

The largest single Roman relic in the city is housed in the Centre Excursionista de Catalunya (a hiking club): four fluted Corinthian columns that formed the rear corner of the Temple of Augustus, built in the first century BC as the hub of the town's forum. Opening hours can vary, so it's wise to call ahead before making a special trip.

## La Rambla

This mile-long boulevard is one of the most famous promenades in the world. The identikit souvenir shops, pickpockets and surging crowds of tourists have driven away many of the locals who used to come here to play chess or have political debates, but despite a fall in fortunes, it remains the first port of call for visitors to the city. The multitude of human statues, fortune-tellers, card sharps, puppeteers, dancers and musicians might be infuriating to anyone late for work, but for those with a seat at a pavement café, it's not far short of pure theatre. Be warned that pickpockets are not the only thieves operating here – unless you are happy to pay €15 for a stein of diluted cola you should avoid the terrace bars and restaurants along the Ramblas.

The name derives from *ramla*, an Arabic word for sand; originally, this was a seasonal riverbed, running along the western edge of the 13th-century city. From the Middle Ages to the baroque era, many churches and convents were built along here, some of which have given their names to sections of it: as one descends from Plaça Catalunya, it is successively called Rambla de Canaletes, Rambla dels Estudis (or dels Ocells), Rambla de Sant Josep (or de les Flors), Rambla dels Caputxins and Rambla de Santa Mònica. For this reason, many people refer to it in the plural, as Les Rambles.

La Rambla also served as the meeting ground for city and country dwellers, for on the far side of these church buildings lay the still scarcely built-up Raval, 'the city outside the walls', and rural Catalonia. At the **fountain** on the corner with C/Portaferrissa, colourful tiles depict the city gateway that once stood here (*porta ferrissa* means 'iron gate'). The space by the gates became a natural marketplace; from these beginnings sprang **La Boqueria** (*see p208*), now the largest market in Europe.

La Rambla took on its recognisable present form between approximately 1770 and 1860. The second city wall came down in 1775, and La Rambla was paved and turned into a boulevard. But the avenue only acquired its definitive shape after the closure of the monasteries in the 1830s, which made swathes of land available for new building. No longer on the city's edge, La Rambla became a wide path through Barcelona's heart.

As well as having five names, La Rambla is divided into territories. The first part – at the top, by Plaça Catalunya – has long belonged, by unwritten agreement, to groups of men perpetually engaged in a *tertulia*, a classic Iberian half-conversation, half-argument about anything from politics to football. The Font de Canaletes drinking fountain is beside them; if you drink from it, goes the legend, you'll return to Barcelona. Here too is where Barça fans converge in order to celebrate their increasingly frequent triumphs.

Next comes perhaps the best-loved section of the boulevard, which is known as **Rambla de les Flors** because of its line of magnificent flower stalls, which are open into the night. To the right is the **Palau de la Virreina** exhibition and cultural information centre (*see p96*), and the superb Boqueria market. A little further is the **Pla de l'Os** (or **Pla de la Boqueria**), which is the centrepoint of La Rambla, with a pavement **mosaic** created in 1976 by Joan Miró. On the left, where more streets run off into the Barri Gòtic, is the extraordinary **Bruno Quadros** building (1883), with umbrellas on the wall and a Chinese dragon protruding over the street.

The lower half of La Rambla is initially more restrained, flowing between the sober façade of the **Liceu** opera house (*see p261*) and the more fin-de-siècle (architecturally and atmospherically) **Cafè de l'Opera** (*see p173*), which is Barcelona's second most famous café after the Zurich. The modernisation of the Liceu metro stop has had this area behind fences and green netting for the best part of a year, but the project should be completed by early 2007. On the right is C/Nou de la Rambla (where you'll find Gaudí's neo-Gothic **Palau Güell**, which is closed to the public until 2007; *see p109*); the promenade then widens into the **Rambla de Santa Mònica**. The area has long been popular among prostitutes; clean-up efforts have reduced their visibility and renovations (including the 1980s addition of an arts centre, the **Centre d'Art Santa Mònica**) have done much to dilute the seediness of the area, but single males walking at night can expect

**La Rambla**. *See p94.*

Sightseeing

to be approached. Across the street are the unintentionally hilarious **Museu de Cera** (Wax Museum; *see p225*) and, at weekends, many stalls selling bric-a-brac and craftwork. Then it's just a short skip to the port, and the **Monument a Colom** Columbus column (*see p111*).

### Centre d'Art Santa Mònica

*La Rambla 7 (93 316 28 10/www.cultura.gencat.net/casm). Metro Drassanes.* **Open** 11am-8pm Tue-Sat; 11am-3pm Sun. **Admission** usually free. **Map** p345 A7.

The cloister and tower of the convent of Santa Mònica (1626) were turned into this exhibition space in 1988, with recent alterations allowing for more space. Each year there are around 20 shows from local and international artists and photographers.

### Museu de l'Eròtica

*La Rambla 96 bis (93 318 98 65/www.erotica-museum.com). Metro Liceu.* **Open** *June-Sept* 10am-10pm daily. *Oct-May* 10am-9pm daily. **Admission** €7.50; €6.50 concessions. **Credit** AmEx, MC, V. **Map** p344 B4.

Mostly visited by stags and hens in search of a cheap thrill, the Erotic Museum is anything but. Expect plenty of filler in the form of airbrushed paintings of the maidens-and-serpents school, with the odd fascinating item such as studded chastity belts or a Victorian walking stick topped with an ivory vagina; some genuine rarities include Japanese drawings, 19th-century engravings by German Peter Fendi and compelling photos of brothels in Barcelona's Barrio Chino in the decadent 1930s. Other curiosities include S&M apparatus and simulated erotic phone lines illustrating the 'sensuality of the voice', but the Eròtica is something of an embarrassment for a district with such connoisseurship of the bawdy.

### Palau de la Virreina

*La Rambla 99 (93 301 77 75/www.bcn.es/cultura). Metro Liceu.* **Open** 11am-2pm, 4-8pm Tue-Sat; 11am-3pm Sun. **Admission** €3; €1.50 concessions; free under-16s. **No credit cards. Map** p344 B4.

This classical palace, with baroque features, takes its name from the widow of an unpopular former viceroy of Peru, who commissioned it and lived in it after its completion in the 1770s. The Virreina houses the city cultural department and has information on events and shows but also boasts strong programming in its two distinct exhibition spaces. Upstairs is dedicated to one-off exhibitions, with the smaller downstairs gallery focused on historical and contemporary photography.

## In the detail The cathedral geese

The gaggle of clanking geese in the cathedral cloister has been there since the 15th century, but no one seems able to agree on its significance. Perhaps the most popular version pertains to Santa Eulàlia, patron saint of Barcelona, who is buried in the cathedral's crypt. The daughter of an aristocractic family in Sarrià, she was known for her charitable works and her fearlessness. The legend goes that, during the final persecution of Diocletian in 303, the young Eulàlia went to see the governor of Barcelona, Dacian, to take issue with him over his cruelty to the Christian community. Dacian was so enraged with the temerity of this 13-year-old upstart that he sentenced her to as many gruesome punishments as she had years. Among them: her flesh was torn with hooks; she was lashed; she was put inside a barrel filled with broken glass and nails and rolled down a slope (today, the Baixada de Santa Eulàlia, behind the cathedral); she was placed in a box with hungry fleas; her wounds were sprinkled with boiling oil; finally, she was nailed to a cross in what is now the Plaça del Pedró in the Raval. The 13 geese are said to represent Eulàlia's age and her punishments.

Only slightly more prosaically, the geese may well be a homage to the Roman origins of the site, in reference to the sacred geese who guarded the Capitol (and indeed were responsible for its salvation during the attempted attack by the Gauls). In fact, Barcelona's geese are Roman geese, distinguished by the tufts on their heads.

# Born & Sant Pere

Where chapels meet shoe shops.

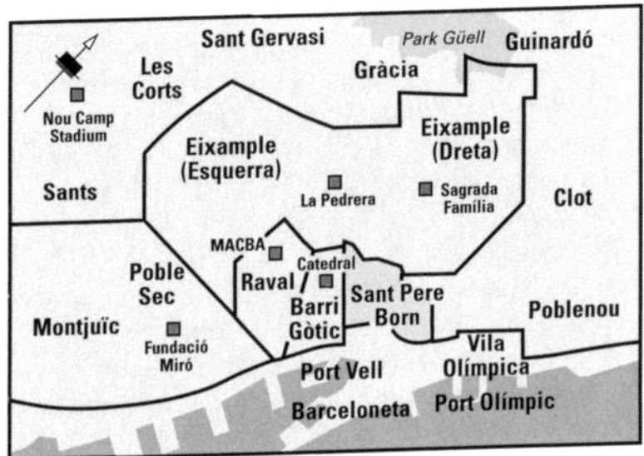


## Maps pp344-345

The Born has been the commercial hub of Barcelona since medieval times, but these days it trades in designer duds and haircuts rather than fish and vegetables. The food stores clustered around the old market have become fashionable bars and restaurants, full of the chattering dotcommers, graphic designers and photographers who now populate the area. Not quite as impeccably groomed, but catching up fast, is the neighbouring district of Sant Pere. With its dazzling new Santa Caterina market and freshly designed boulevards, it is gradually regaining some of the glory it enjoyed during the Golden Age, when it was a favourite residential area of the city's merchant elite.

Both districts together are still sometimes referred to as La Ribera ('the waterfront'), a name that recalls the time before permanent quays were built, when the shoreline reached much further inland and the area was contained within a 13th-century wall.

From the north-east, the grand gateway to the area is the **Arc de Triomf**, an imposing, red-brick arch built by Josep Vilaseca as the entrance for the 1888 Universal Exhibition. On the west side, the Josep Reynés sculptures adorning the arch represent Barcelona hosting visitors to the Exhibition, while the Josep Llimona sculptures on the east side depict prizes being awarded to the Exhibition's most outstanding contributors.

The Ribera is demarcated to the east by the **Parc de la Ciutadella** (*see p102*), and to the west by Via Laietana, both products of historic acts of urban vandalism. The first came after the 1714 siege, when the victors, acting on the orders of Philip V, destroyed 1,000 houses, hospitals and monasteries to construct the fortress of the Ciutadella (citadel). The second occurred when the Via Laietana was struck through the district in 1907, in line with the theory of 'ventilating' unsanitary city districts by driving wide avenues through them; it is now a traffic-choked canyon. In 2007 work will start on turning over some of Via Laietana's car lanes to pedestrians to add some much-needed atmosphere.

Within La Ribera, Sant Pere and the Born are divided by C/Princesa – also made more pedestrian-friendly in 2006 – running between the Parc de la Ciutadella and the **Plaça de l'Àngel** (once called the Plaça del Blat, or 'wheat square'), the former commercial and popular heart of the city where all grain was traded. The area north of C/Princesa is centred around the monastery of **Sant Pere de les Puelles**, which still stands, if greatly altered, in Plaça de Sant Pere. For centuries this was Barcelona's main centre of textile production; to this day, streets such as Sant Pere Més Baix and Sant Pere Més Alt contain many textile wholesalers and retailers.

The area may be medieval in origin, but its finest monument is one of the most extraordinary works of Modernisme – the

**Museu Picasso**. *See p99.*

**Palau de la Música Catalana** (*see p101*), facing C/Sant Pere Més Alt. Less noticed on the same street is a curious feature, the **Passatge de les Manufactures**, a 19th-century arcade between C/Sant Pere Més Alt and C/Ortigosa.

Sant Pere is currently undergoing dramatic renovation, with the gradual opening up of a continuation of the Avda Francesc Cambó, which now swings around to meet with C/Allada-Vermell, a wide street that was formed when a block was demolished in 1994. The district's market, **Mercat de Santa Caterina**, is one of Barcelona's oldest, and has been rebuilt to a design by the late Enric Miralles (who also famously designed the Scottish Parliament); remains of the medieval **Convent de Santa Caterina** are shown below glass at one end. Another convent located nearby is the **Convent de Sant Agustí**, which is now a civic centre, on C/Comerç. The entrance contains *Deuce Coop*, a magical 'light sculpture' by James Turrell, which was commissioned by the Ajuntament in the 1980s and is turned on after dark.

Where C/Carders meets C/Montcada is the Placeta d'en Marcús, with a small chapel, the 12th-century **Capella d'en Marcús**, built as part of an inn. It was founded by Bernat Marcús, who is said to have organised Europe's first postal service, the *correus volants* ('flying runners'). This chapel, then outside the city wall, was where his riders set off from for the north, and it also provided a refuge for them and other travellers who arrived after the city gates had closed for the night.

From this tiny square, **C/Montcada**, one of the unmissable streets of old Barcelona, leads into the Born. The street takes its name from the Montcada dynasty, who served the counts of Barcelona for generations, finally becoming the leading power in the land in the mid 11th century. A medieval Fifth Avenue, it is lined with a succession of medieval merchants' mansions, the greatest of which house a variety of museums, including the **Museu Tèxtil** (*see p101*), the **Museu Barbier-Mueller** of pre-Columbian art and, above all, the **Museu Picasso** (for both, *see p99*). In 1148 land ceded to Guillem Ramon de Montcada became the site for the construction of this street, where the opulence of the many merchant-princes of the time is still very visible. The streets nearby were filled with workshops supplying anything the inhabitants needed, and these trades are commemorated in the names of many of the streets.

## **In the detail** Ciutadella's mammoth

After the destruction of Philip V's hated citadel (*see p102*), Ciutadella Park was overhauled for the Universal Exhibition of 1888, a grand and influential affair that threw Barcelona into the international spotlight after years in the doldrums. Once it was over, however, it was felt that the purpose of the park should reach beyond the merely ludic, and a scheme was proposed to turn the whole site into something more educational. The idea, put forward by geologist and writer Norbert Font i Sagué, was to build 12 scale models of prehistoric species.

The first was the giant mammoth – five by three and a half metres – and made out of reinforced concrete. It was loved by the people of Barcelona from the moment it was unveiled; its trunk still forms an endlessly fascinating climbing frame for kids, a century after its creation in 1906. Sadly it was never joined by the other 11 planned creatures; Font died young in 1910 and his sketches for models of dinosaurs were never used.

Other parts of the plan to turn the park into a place of learning were eventually to come to fruition, however, and Ciutadella Park still houses the zoo and museums of geology and zoology (now known collectively as the Museu de Ciències Naturals de la Ciutadella, *see p99*).

'Born' originally meant 'joust' or 'list', and in the Middle Ages, and for many centuries thereafter, the neighbourhood's main artery, the **Passeig del Born**, was the centre for the city's festivals, processions, tournaments, carnivals and the burning of heretics by the Inquisition. At one end of the square is the old **Born market**, which is a magnificent 1870s wrought-iron structure and used to be Barcelona's main wholesale food market. It closed in the 1970s, and the market was transferred elsewhere. Plans to turn the structure into a library were thwarted by the discovery of perfectly preserved medieval remains. The foundations of buildings razed by Philip V's troops were found to contain hundreds of objects, some domestic and some, like rusty bombs, suggesting the traumas of the period. A viewing platform, with useful diagrams and notes, has been erected on C/Fusina and ultimately the remains will be incorporated into a cultural centre and museum, although progress seems painfully slow.

On the small side street of C/Fusina next to the market, the Metrònom, a recently closed-down art gallery, has a handsome Modernista interior with stained-glass skylights and iron columns. It still opens every winter to host an experimental music festival.

At the other end of the Passeig from the market stands the greatest of all Catalan Gothic buildings, the spectacular basilica of **Santa Maria del Mar** (*see p103*). On one side of it, a funnel-shaped red-brick square was opened in 1989 on the site where it is believed the last defenders of the city were executed after Barcelona fell to the Spanish army in 1714. Called the **Fossar de les Moreres** ('Mulberry Graveyard'), the square is inscribed with patriotic poetry, and nationalist demonstrations converge here every year on Catalan National Day, 11 September. The 'eternal flame' sculpture is a more recent, and less popular, addition.

From here, narrow streets lead to the **Plaça de les Olles**, or the grand **Pla del Palau** and another symbol of La Ribera, **La Llotja** (the 'exchange'). Its neo-classical outer shell was added in the 18th century, but its core is a superb 1380's Gothic hall, sadly closed to the public, save for occasional functions organised through the Chamber of Commerce. Until the exchange moved to the Passeig de Gràcia in 1994, this was the oldest continuously functioning stock exchange in Europe.

## Museu Barbier-Mueller d'Art Precolombí

*C/Montcada 14 (93 310 45 16/www.barbier-mueller.ch). Metro Jaume I.* **Open** 11am-7pm Tue-Fri; 10am-7pm Sat; 10am-3pm Sun. **Admission** €3; €1.50 concessions; free under-16s. Free 1st Sun of mth. **Credit** (shop only) AmEx, MC, V. **Map** p345 E6.

Located in the 15th-century Palau Nadal, this world-class collection of pre-Columbian art was ceded to Barcelona in 1996 by the Barbier-Mueller Museum in Geneva. The Barcelona holdings focus solely on the Americas, representing most of the styles from the ancient cultures of Meso-America, Andean America and the Amazon region. Dramatically spotlit in black rooms, the frequently changing selection of masks, textiles, jewellery and sculpture includes pieces dating from as far back as the second millennium BC running to the early 16th century (showing just how loosely the term 'pre-Columbian' can be used).

## Museu de Ciències Naturals de la Ciutadella

*Passeig Picasso, Parc de la Ciutadella (93 319 69 12/www.bcn.es/museuciencies). Metro Arc de Triomf.* **Open** 10am-2pm Tue, Wed, Fri-Sun; 10am-6pm Thur. **Admission** *All exhibitions & Jardí Botànic* €4.20; €2.70 concessions. *Museums only* €3.50; €2 concessions. *Temporary exhibitions* €3.50; €2 concessions. Free under-12s. Free 1st Sun of mth. **No credit cards. Map** p343 H11.

Now more than 125 years old, the Natural History Museum comprises the zoology and geology museums in the Parc de la Ciutadella. Both suffer from old-school presentation: dusty glass cases that are filled with moth-eaten stuffed animals and serried rows of rocks. However, the zoology museum is redeemed by its location in the Castell dels Tres Dragons, which was built by Domènech i Montaner as the café-restaurant for the 1888 Universal Exhibition, and by its interesting temporary exhibitions. For children aged three to 12, Dragó, DRAGONET offers a series of free activities with hands-on exploration of the animal world. The geology part, housed in the Museu Martorell, is for aficionados only, with a dry display of minerals, painstakingly classified, alongside explanations of geological phenomena found in Catalonia. More interesting is the selection from the museum's collection of 300,000 fossils, many found locally. A combined ticket also grants entrance to the Jardí Botànic on Montjuïc (*see p118*).

## Museu Picasso

*C/Montcada 15-23 (93 319 63 10/www.museupicasso.bcn.es). Metro Jaume I.* **Open** (last ticket 30mins before closing) 10am-8pm Tue-Sun. **Admission** *Permanent collection only* €6; €4 concessions. *With temporary exhibition* €8.50; €5.50 concessions; free under-16s. Free (museum only) 1st Sun of mth. **Credit** (shop only) AmEx, MC, V. **Map** p345 E6.

When it opened in 1963, the museum dedicated to Barcelona's favourite adopted son was housed in the Palau Aguilar; the permanent collection of some 3,500 pieces now spreads across five adjoining palaces, two of which are devoted to temporary exhibitions.

By no means an overview of the artist's work, the Museu Picasso – the city's most visited museum – is rather a record of the vital formative years that the young Picasso spent nearby at La Llotja art school (where his father taught), and later hanging

Barcelona City Break
Hotels
Apartments
Youth hostels
Transfers
Guided tours
Bike tours
Helicopter tours
Walking tours
Sailing trips
Cooking lessons
FC Barcelona
F1 Grand Prix
BARCELONA
ON-LINE
www.barcelona-on-line.es
Bookings: +34 93 343 79 93
email: tobook@barcelona-on-line.es
Gran Via de les Corts Catalanes, 662, 1er 1ra
08010 - Barcelona

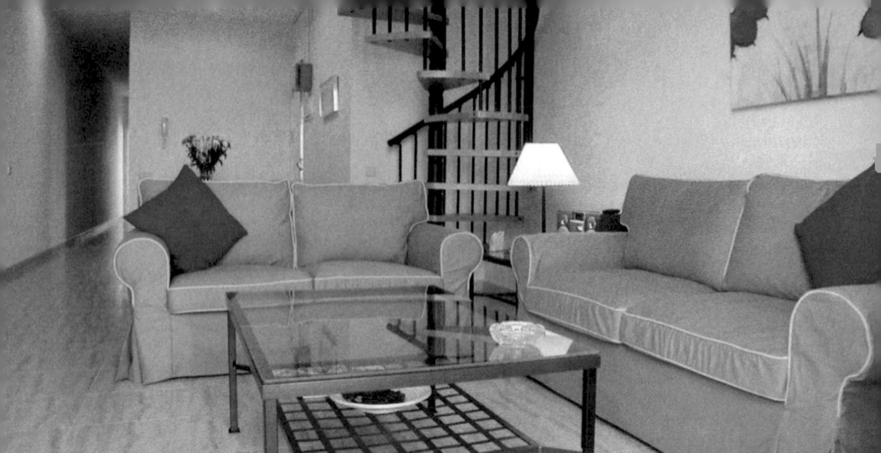

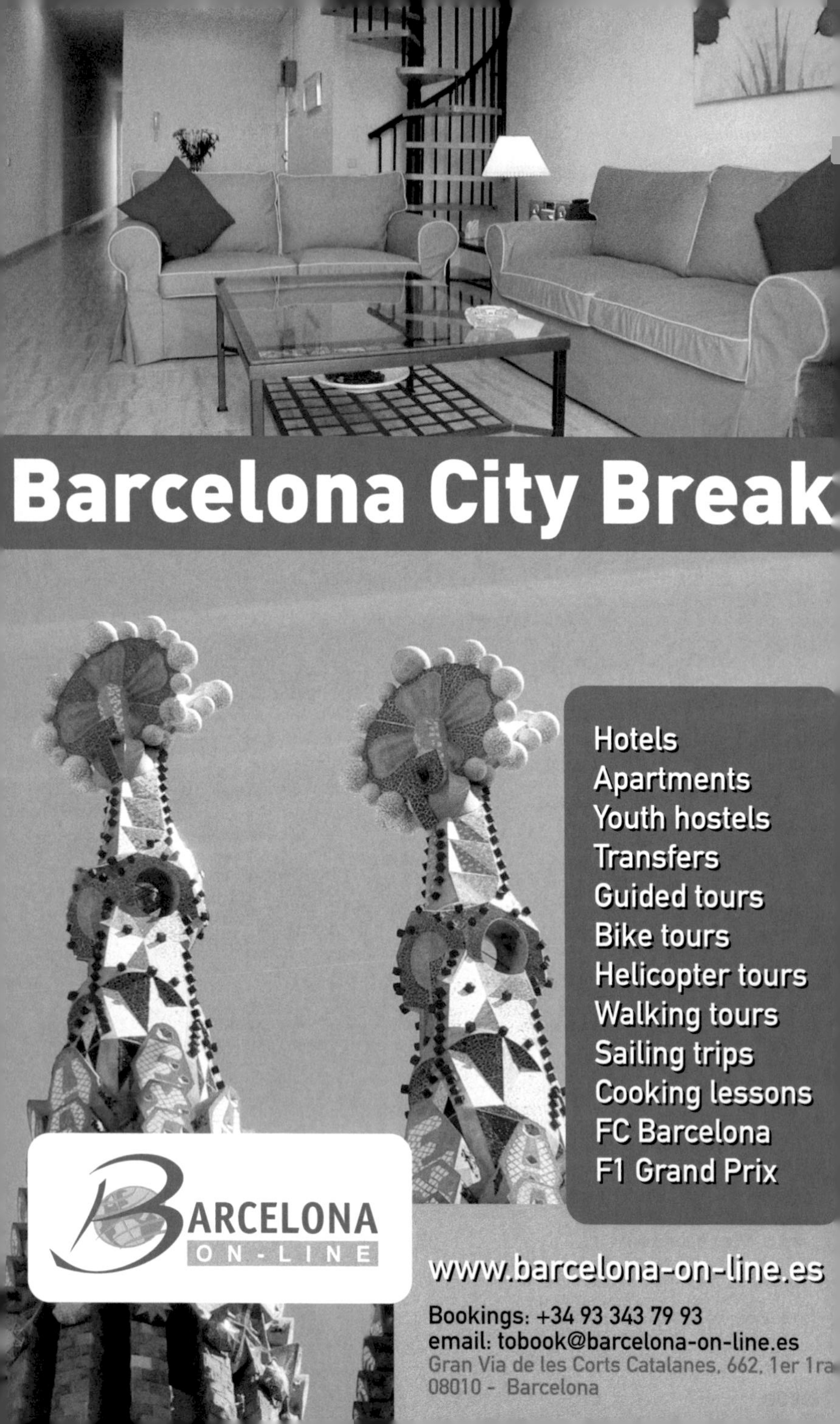

out with Catalonia's fin-de-siècle avant-garde. Those looking for hits like *Les Demoiselles d'Avignon* (1907) and the first Cubist paintings from the time (many of them done in Catalonia), as well as his collage and sculpture, will be disappointed. The founding of the museum is down to a key figure in Picasso's life, his friend and secretary Jaume Sabartés, who donated his own collection for the purpose. Tribute is paid with a room dedicated to Picasso's portraits of him (best known is the Blue Period painting of Sabartés wearing a white ruff), and Sabartés's own doodlings. The seamless presentation of Picasso's development from 1890 to 1904, from deft pre-adolescent portraits to sketchy landscapes to the intense innovations of his Blue Period, is unbeatable, then it leaps to a gallery of mature Cubist paintings from 1917. The pièce de résistance is the complete series of 58 canvases based on Velázquez's famous *Las Meninas*, donated by Picasso himself after the death of Sabartés, and now stretching through the Great Hall. The display later ends with linocuts, engravings and a wonderful collection of ceramics that were donated by Picasso's widow. **Photo** *p97.*

## Museu Tèxtil

*C/Montcada 12 (93 319 76 03/www.museutextil.bcn.es). Metro Jaume I.* **Open** 10am-6pm Tue-Sat; 10am-3pm Sun. **Admission** *Combined admission with Museu de les Arts Decoratives & Museu de Ceràmica* €3.50; €2 concessions; free under-16s. Free 1st Sun of mth. **Credit** (shop only) AmEx, DC, MC, V. **Map** p345 E6.

Housed in two adjoining palaces, the extensive Textile Museum is divided into three main sections: textiles, liturgical vestments, tapestry and rugs; clothing and accessories; and the city's lace and embroidery collection. The permanent exhibition provides a chronological tour of this branch of the history of art and technology, from its oldest piece, a man's Coptic tunic from a 7th-century tomb, through to Karl Lagerfeld. Among curiosities, such as the world's largest collection of kid's skin gloves or an 18th-century bridal gown in black figured silk, the real highlight is the historic fashion collection – from baroque to 20th-century – that Manuel Rocamora donated in the 1960s; this is one of the finest of its type anywhere. Recent important donations include more than 100 pieces by Spanish designer Cristóbal Balenciaga, who is famous for the 1958 baby-doll dress and pillbox hat. The museum shop is a great place to pick up presents, and there's a wonderful café outside in the courtyard. At an unspecified date in the future, the museum is to move to the new Museu de Disseny (Design Museum) in the Plaça de les Glòries.

## Museu de la Xocolata

*C/Comerç 36 (93 268 78 78/www.museuxocolata.com). Metro Jaume I.* **Open** 10am-7pm Mon, Wed-Sat; 10am-3pm Sun. **Admission** €3.80; €3.30 concessions; free under-7s. **Credit** MC, V. **Map** p345 F5.

The best-smelling museum in town draws chocoholics of all ages to its collection of *mones* (chocolate sculptures); made by Barcelona's master *pastissers* for the annual Easter competition, the *mones* range from multicoloured models of Gaudí's Casa Batlló to extravagant scenes of Don Quixote tilting at windmills or *Ben-Hur*. Inevitably, this is not a collection that ages well: photos have replaced most of the older sculptures, and those that are not in glass cases bear the ravages of hands-on appreciation from the museum's smaller visitors. A brief history of chocolate is pepped up with audio-visual displays and the odd touch-screen computer, but the busiest area is the glass-fronted cookery workshop, with classes for all ages and levels. That, and the irresistible chocolate shop.

## Palau de la Música Catalana

*C/Sant Francesc de Paula 2 (93 295 72 00/www.palaumusica.org). Metro Urquinaona.* **Open** *Box office* 10am-9pm Mon-Sat. *Guided tours* 9.30am-3pm daily. **Admission** €8; €7 concessions. **Credit** (minimum €20) MC, V. **Map** p344 D3.

Possibly the most extreme expression of Modernista architecture ever built, the façade of Domènech i Montaner's concert hall, with its bare brick, busts and mosaic friezes representing Catalan musical traditions and composers, is impressive enough, but it is surpassed by the building's staggering interior. Making up for its famously poor acoustics, decoration erupts everywhere: the ceiling centrepiece is of multicoloured stained glass; 18 half-mosaic, half-relief figures representing the musical Muses appear out of the back of the stage; and on one side, massive Wagnerian valkyries ride out to accompany a bust of Beethoven. By the 1980s, the Palau was bursting under the pressure of the musical activity going on inside it, and an extension and renovation project by

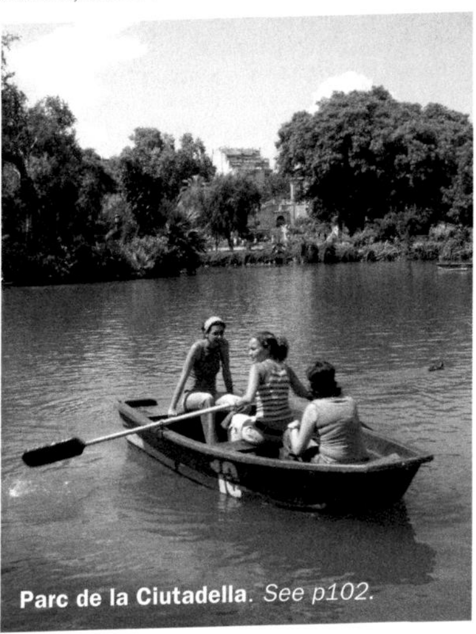

Parc de la Ciutadella. *See p102.*

# **Walk on** Medieval trading

**Duration**: 45 minutes.
From **Plaça de l'Àngel**, site of the Plaça del Blat, the grain market, cross Via Laietana to **C/Bòria**, a name that probably means 'outskirts' or 'suburbs', since it was outside the original city. C/Bòria continues into the evocative little **Plaça de la Llana**, the old centre of wool (*llana*) trading in the city, which is now an animated meeting place for the Dominican Republic community. Alleys to the left were associated with food trades: **C/Mercaders** ('traders', probably in grain), **C/Oli** ('olive oil') just off it, and **C/Semoleres**, where semolina was made. To the right on Bòria is **C/Pou de la Cadena** ('well with a chain'), a reminder that water was essential for textile working.

After Plaça de la Llana, the Roman road's name becomes **C/Corders** ('rope-makers') and then **C/Carders** ('carders' or combers of wool). Where the name changes there is a tiny square, Placeta Marcús, with an even smaller Romanesque chapel, the **Capella d'en Marcús**, built in the early 12th century.

If you carry on a little way along C/Carders (keeping an eye out for pickpockets and bag-snatchers, who tend to favour this area), you arrive at the **Plaça Sant Agustí Vell**, where the architecture can be dated as far back as the Middle Ages. Just off it, **C/Basses de Sant Pere** leads away to the left, where you'll find a 14th-century house.

Retrace your steps down C/Carders, then turn left into **C/Blanqueria** ('bleaching'). Here wool was washed before being spun. At **C/Assaonadors** ('tanners'), turn right. At the end of this street, behind the Marcús chapel, is a statue of John the Baptist, patron saint of the tanners' guild.

Now you are at the top of **C/Montcada**, one of Barcelona's great museum centres and a beautiful street in itself. The first of the line of medieval merchants' palaces you reach after crossing C/Princesa is the **Palau Berenguer d'Aguilar**, home of the **Museu Picasso**, which has also taken over four more palaces. Opposite is one of the finest and largest palaces, the **Palau dels Marquesos de Llió**, now the **Museu Tèxtil**, with a fine café. Further down to the right is the milliners' street, **C/Sombrerers**; opposite it is Barcelona's narrowest street, **C/Mosques** ('flies'), not even wide enough for an adult to lie across, and now closed off with an iron gate because too many people were pissing in it at night. C/Montcada ends at **Passeig del Born**, a hub of the city's trading for 400 years.

Oscar Tusquets that spanned more than 20 years involved the demolition of the ugly church next door to make way for the extension of the façade, a subterranean concert hall and a new entrance. Rather than try and compete with the exisiting façade, the new part has subtler, organic motifs.

Guided tours are available in English, Catalan or Spanish every 30 minutes or so. Be sure to ask questions, particularly if there's something you really want to know – the guides are very knowledgeable, but unless drawn out by customers they tend to concentrate mainly on the triumphs of the renovation. If you have a chance, a preferable way to see the hall is by catching a concert (*see p261*).

### Parc de la Ciutadella

*Passeig Picasso (no phone). Metro Arc de Triomf or Barceloneta.* **Open** 10am-sunset daily. **Map** p343 H11/J11.

Named after the hated Bourbon citadel – the largest in Europe – that occupied this site from 1716 to 1869, this elegant park came into being after the anti-Bourbon revolution of 1868, when General Prim announced that the area could be reclaimed for public use. The garrison fort was gleefully pulled down and pleasure gardens built to host the 1888 Universal Exhibition; Domènech i Montaner's Castell de Tres Dragons at the entrance served as the cafeteria, while the Arc de Triomf to the north formed the main entrance. Prim is honoured with an equestrian statue at the southern end.

Although half the land is taken up by the city zoo, the park is still surprisingly extensive and contains a host of attractions, including the Natural History Museum, a boating lake and more than 30 pieces of imaginative statuary. The giant mammoth statue (*see p98* **In the detail**), which can be found at the far side of the boating lake, is a huge hit with kids, as is the trio of prancing deer by the zoo that is dedicated to Walt Disney. Beside the lake, which has recently been renovated, is the *Cascade*, an ornamental fountain topped with Aurora's chariot on which the young Gaudí worked as assistant to Josep Fontseré, the architect of the park. On the old parade ground in the middle of a small pond is one of the most striking sculptures of Catalan Modernisme: *El Desconsol* (Grief) by Josep Llimona. Not to be missed are Fontseré's slatted wooden *Umbracle* (literally, 'shade house'), which provides a pocket of tropical forest within the city, and the elegant *Hivernacle*

Turn left, and on the left is **C/Flassaders** ('blanket makers'), and to the right **C/Rec**, the old irrigation canal. Go down Rec to turn right into **C/Esparteria**, where *espart* (hemp) was woven. Turnings off it include **C/Calders**, where smelting furnaces were found, and **C/Formatgeria**, where one would have gone for cheese. After that is **C/Vidrieria**, where glass was stored and sold. Esparteria runs into C/Ases, which crosses **C/Malcuinat** ('badly cooked'). Turn left into **C/Espaseria** ('sword-making') to emerge out of ancient alleys on to the open space of Pla del Palau. Turn right, and then right again into **C/Canvis Vells** ('old exchange'). There's a tiny street to the left, **C/Panses**, that has an archway above it, with an ancient stone carving of a face over the second floor. This face indicated the location of a legalised brothel.

At the end of Canvis Vells is **Plaça Santa Maria** and the parish church, **Santa Maria del Mar**. On the left-hand side is **C/Abaixadors** ('unloaders'), where porters used to unload their goods; from the square, **C/Argenteria** ('silverware') will lead back to Plaça de l'Àngel.

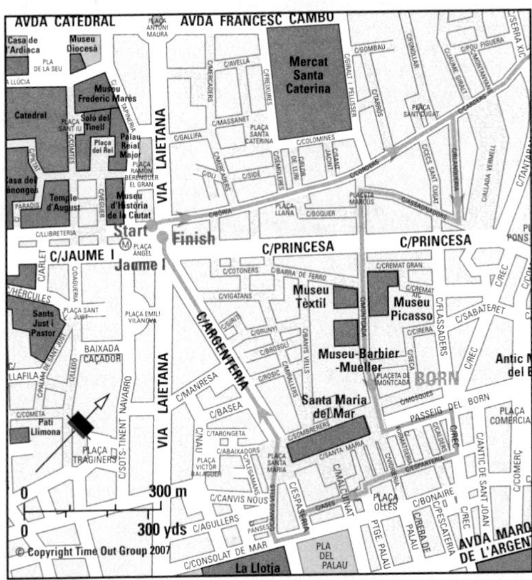


('winter garden') designed by Josep Amargós in 1884, an excellent example of the iron and glass architecture of the Eiffel Tower period. Outside, on the Passeig Picasso, is Antoni Tàpies's *A Picasso*, which is a giant Cubist monument to the artist. **Photo** *p101*.

## Sala Montcada

*C/Montcada 14 (93 310 06 99/www.fundacio.lacaixa.es/salamontcada). Metro Jaume I.* **Open** 10am-8pm daily. **Admission** free. **Map** p345 E6.

This is a diminutive contemporary arts outpost of the CaixaForum (*see p117*), and is equally groundbreaking in its own right. Each year three different curators develop excellent mixed programmes of Spanish and international artists.

## Santa Maria del Mar

*Plaça de Santa Maria (93 310 23 90). Metro Jaume I.* **Open** 9am-1.30pm, 4.30-8pm Mon-Sat; 10am-1.30pm, 4.30-8pm Sun. **Admission** free. **Map** p345 E6.

Possibly the most perfect surviving example of the Catalan Gothic style, this graceful basilica stands out for its characteristic horizontal lines, large bare surfaces, square buttresses and flat-topped octagonal towers. Its superb unity of style is down to the fact that it was built relatively quickly, with construction taking just 55 years (1329-1384). Named after Mary in her role as patroness of sailors, it was built on the site of a small church known as Santa Maria del Arenys (sand), for its position close to the sea. In the broad, single-nave interior, two rows of perfectly proportioned columns soar up to fan vaults, creating an atmosphere of space around the light-flooded altar. There's also superb stained glass, especially the great 15th-century rose window above the main door. The original window, built only slightly earlier, fell down during an earthquake, killing 25 people and injuring dozens more.

It's perhaps thanks to the group of anti-clerical anarchists who set this magnificent church ablaze for 11 days in 1936 that its superb features can be appreciated – without the wooden baroque altar and chapel furniture that clutter so many Spanish churches, the simplicity of its lines can emerge. The incongruous modern window at the other end was a 1997 addition, belatedly celebrating the Olympics. On Saturdays the basilica is in great demand for weddings, and its unbeatable acoustics make it a popular venue for music concerts; particularly stirring are the requiem mass at Easter and Handel's Messiah at Christmas.

# Raval

Mean streets.

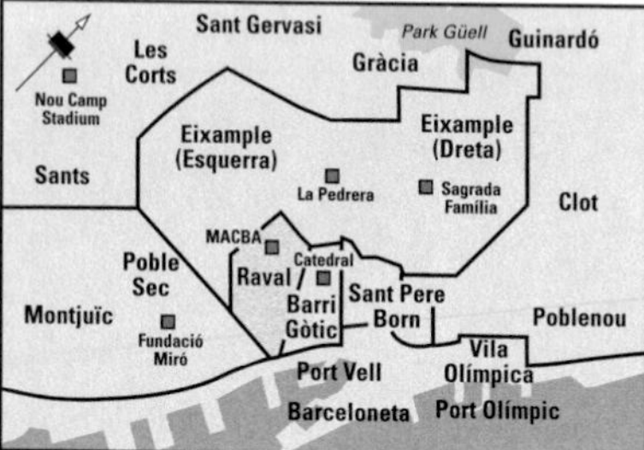


**Map p342**

One of the most notorious neighbourhoods in Barcelona, the Raval has Jean Genet as its poster child: a thieving 1920s rent boy who revelled in the intoxicating mix of absinthe bars, seedy theatres, brothels, anarchist groups and doss-houses. Although the old red-light district still retains its traditional population of prostitutes, transsexuals, drug addicts and poor labourers, it has become more notorious of late as an immigrant ghetto. In 2006 more than half the *barri*'s residents were from outside Spain, the vast majority being from Pakistan and Ecuador; the Raval is one of the most ethnically diverse places in Europe; shop signs are in a babel of languages and advertise everything from halal meat to Bollywood videos and cheap phonecalls home to South America. The incoming population is also very young – it is estimated that 70 per cent are under 35 years old – and the Raval's growing popularity with western foreigners, students and artists is transforming this tough working-class area into an urban playground of cafés, skateboard ramps, fashion shops and art galleries.

Although the area has been gentrified almost beyond recognition with new boulevards and art museums, it is still a pickpocketing hotspot. Visitors need to take care when exploring the Raval, particularly after dark in the area down towards the port; that said, as long as you exercise the usual precautions such as staying off badly lit side-streets and not conspicuously flaunting your new digital camera, the area makes for an exhilarating wander.

Ever on the margins, Raval (*arrabal* in Spanish) is a generic word adapted from the Arabic *ar-rabad*, meaning 'outside the walls'. When a defensive wall was built down the north side of La Rambla in the 13th century, the area now sandwiched between Avda Paral·lel and La Rambla was a sparsely populated green belt of garden plots. Overthe centuries, the land was to absorb the functional spillover from the city in the form of monasteries, churches, religious hospitals, prisons and virtually any noxious industry that citizens didn't want on their doorstep. When industrialisation arrived in the 18th century, this area became Barcelona's working-class district.

This was also the area of town where the most land was available; more emerged after liberal governments had dissolved the monasteries in 1836, and early industries, mainly the textile mills, mushroomed. Some of the bleak buildings known as *cases-fàbriques* (residential factories) can still be seen here; among them is the **Can Ricart** textile factory on C/Sant Oleguer, now converted into a swimming pool and sports centre that opened to the public in July 2006, and connects to the existing sports centre on C/Sant Pau.

Workers lived in crowded slums devoid of ventilation or running water, and malnutrition, TB, scrofula and typhus kept the average life expectancy to 40 years. It's no coincidence that the city's sanatoriums, orphanages and hospitals were based here. Then known to most people as the Quinto, or 'Fifth District', the area was also where the underclasses forged the centre of revolutionary Barcelona, a breeding ground for anarchists and other radicals. Innumerable riots and revolts began here; entire streets became no-go areas after dark.

Heroin's arrival in the late 1970s caused extra problems; the semi-tolerated petty criminality became more threatening and affected the tourist trade. Spurred on by the approaching 1992 Olympics, the authorities made a clean sweep of the Lower Raval. Whole blocks with associations to drugs or prostitution were demolished, and many of the displaced families were transferred to housing estates on the edge of town, out of sight and out of mind.

A sports centre, a new police station and office blocks were constructed, and some streets were pedestrianised. But the most dramatic plan was to create a '*Raval obert al cel*' ('Raval open to the sky'), the most tangible result of which is the sweeping, palm-lined Rambla del Raval. Completed in 2000, it's a continuation of the Avda Drassanes, an earlier attempt to open up the Raval in the 1960s. Nearly five blocks vanished in its wake, and more fell, some very grudgingly indeed, to provide land for the current grand project: **L'Illa de la Rambla del Raval** (also known as the Illa Robador), a mega-complex halfway up the new *rambla* that will contain a hotel, offices, protected housing, shops and the Filmoteca. Construction began in 2004; the underground parking and some of the housing is now complete – the first residents occupied the apartments in July 2006, and work has now begun on the star of the show, a luxury ten-storey hotel owned by the Barceló chain and designed by Pere Puig that should provide the area with a glittering new landmark.

Efforts to bring life to the *rambla* include licences for new clubs and bars, Botero's deliciously bulging *Gat* (Cat) sculpture and an ethnic weekend street market. The market's multicultural nature reflects the number of immigrants living in the Raval, originally attracted by the lower cost of housing. The facelift has raised the prices, though, and as the immigrants, often young men sleeping ten to a room, are squeezed out, a wealthier community of arty western expats and university students has moved in, scattering the area with galleries, boutiques and cafés. C/Doctor Dou is now packed with galleries, C/Ferlandina is packed with boho cafés, and the old industrial spaces along C/Riereta now serve as studios to more than 40 artists.

## Upper Raval

The Upper Raval is rapidly shedding its association with the louche Lower Raval to become one of the city centre's hippest areas; in recent years, a plethora of late-night bars, galleries and restaurants has cropped up, and the addition of the four-star Casa Camper design hotel has sealed its reputation as the new Born. The very smartest streets are in the north-west of the neighbourhood, between C/Carme and Plaça Catalunya, and they are sometimes known as the Eixample of the Raval.

From La Rambla, signposts for MACBA carefully guide visitors along the gentrified 'tourist corridors' of C/Tallers and C/Bonsuccès to a bourgeois bohemian's playground of cafés, galleries and boutiques. The epicentre of the Upper Raval is the Plaça dels Àngels, where the 16th-century **Convent dels Àngels** houses both the **FAD** design institute and a gigantic almshouse, the **Casa de la Caritat**, converted into a cultural complex housing the **MACBA** (*see p107*) and the **CCCB** (*see p107*). When the clean, high-culture MACBA opened in 1995, it seemed to embody everything the Raval was not, and it was initially mocked as an isolated and isolating social experiment. But, over the years, the square has become unofficial home to the city's skateboarders and surrounding streets have filled with restaurants and boutiques. In 2006, after seven years of building work, the university faculties of philosophy, geography and history finally opened opposite the entrance to the CCCB, and the thousands of students who now flock here are changing the character of the place.

Below here C/Hospital and C/Carme meet at the Plaça Pedró, where the tiny Romanesque chapel (and ex-lepers' hospital) of **Sant Llàtzer** sits. From La Rambla, the area is accessed along either street or through the **Boqueria** market, itself the site of the Sant Josep monastery until the sale of church lands led to its destruction in the 1830s. Behind the Boqueria is the **Antic Hospital de la Santa Creu** (*see p107*), which took in the city's sick from the 15th century until 1926; it now houses Catalonia's main library and the headquarters of the Institute of Catalan Studies; and **La Capella**, an attractive exhibition space. C/Carme is capped at the Rambla end by the 18th-century **Església de Betlem** (Bethlehem) with its serpentine pillars and geometrically patterned façade. Its name features on many shop signs nearby; older residents still refer to this part of the Raval as Betlem.



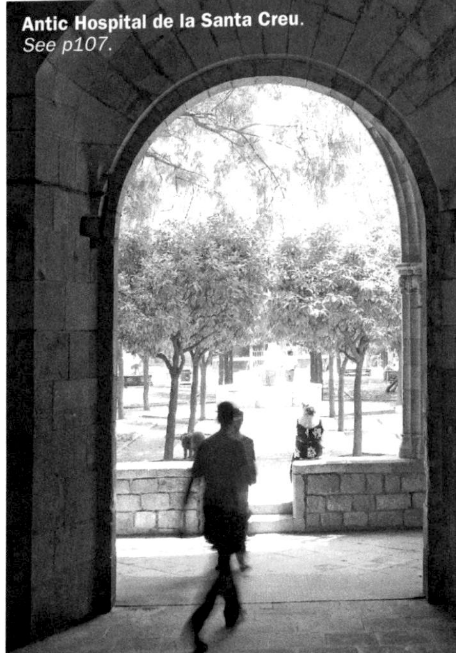
**Antic Hospital de la Santa Creu.** *See p107.*

## In the detail Orphans' Turnstile

A coat of arms, a slot for alms and a small circular wooden framed door, now cemented in place, are all that remains of the façade of the Casa de la Misericòrdia at C/Ramalleres 17, on the Plaça Vicenç Martorell. Founded as a hospice in 1583, this was later to become the Casa Provincial de Maternitat i Expòsits (Maternity and Abandoned Children's Home), run by nuns.

From 1853 to 1931 the wooden turnstile (popularly, though not completely accurately, known as the 'orphans' turnstile') was a way to leave a very young child anonymously in the nuns' care. The infant would be placed on the revolving surface, a screen would close behind it and the nuns would hang a label round his or her neck stating the date of entry. Little, if anything, was ever known of these children's previous lives.



### Antic Hospital de la Santa Creu & La Capella

*C/Carme 47-C/Hospital 56 (no phone). Metro Liceu.* **Open** 9am-8pm Mon-Fri; 9am-2pm Sat. *La Capella* (93 442 71 71) noon-2pm, 4-8pm Tue-Sat; 11am-2pm Sun. **Admission** free. **Map** p344 A4.

This is one of Europe's earliest medical centres. There was a hospital on this site as early as 1024, but in the 15th century it expanded to centralise all the city's hospitals and sanatoriums (with the exception of the Santa Margarida leper colony, which remained outside the city walls). By the 1920s it was hopelessly overstretched, and its medical facilities were moved uptown to the Hospital Sant Pau. One of the last patients was Gaudí, who died here in 1926; it was also here that Picasso painted one of his first important pictures, *Dead Woman* (1903).

The buildings remain some of the most majestic in the city, combining a 15th-century Gothic core with baroque and classical additions. They're now given over to cultural institutions, among them the Massana Arts School, Catalonia's main library (and the second largest in Spain), the Institute of Catalan Studies and the Royal Academy of Medicine. Highlights include a neo-classical lecture theatre complete with revolving marble dissection table (open 10am-2pm Mon-Fri), and the entrance hall of the Casa de Convalescència, tiled with lovely baroque ceramic murals telling the story of Sant Pau (St Paul); one features an artery-squirting decapitation scene. La Capella, the hospital chapel, was rescued from a sad fate as a warehouse and sensitively converted to an exhibition space for contemporary art. The beautifully shady colonnaded courtyard is a popular spot for reading or eating lunch.

### CCCB (Centre de Cultura Contemporània de Barcelona)

*C/Montalegre 5 (93 306 41 00/www.cccb.org). Metro Catalunya.* **Open** *Mid June-mid Sept* 11am-8pm Tue-Sat; 11am-3pm Sun. *Mid Sept-mid June* 11am-2pm, 4-8pm Tue, Thur, Fri; 11am-8pm Wed, Sat; 11am-7pm Sun. **Admission** *1 exhibition* €4.40; €3.30 concessions & Wed. *2 exhibitions* €6; €5.50 concessions & Wed. Free under-16s. **Credit** MC, V. **Map** p344 A2.

Spain's largest cultural centre was opened in 1994 at the Casa de la Caritat, a former workhouse, built in 1802 on the site of a medieval monastery. The massive façade and part of the courtyard remain from the original building; the rest was rebuilt in dramatic contrast, all tilting glass and steel, by architects Piñón and Viaplana, known for the Maremàgnum shopping centre (*see p190*). As a centre for contemporary culture, the CCCB tends to pick up whatever falls through the cracks elsewhere: a slew of film cycles and multimedia presentations, and various flamenco, literary, music and dance festivals (*see pp216-223* Festivals & Events). The CCCB's exhibitions tend to favour production values over content, but there are occasional gems.

### MACBA (Museu d'Art Contemporani de Barcelona)

*Plaça dels Àngels 1 (93 412 08 10/www.macba.es). Metro Catalunya.* **Open** *June-Sept* 11am-8pm Mon, Wed-Fri; 10am-8pm Sat; 10am-3pm Sun. *Oct-May* 11am-7.30pm Mon, Wed-Fri; 10am-8pm Sat; 10am-3pm Sun. **Guided tours** (Catalan/Spanish) 6pm Wed, Sat; noon Sun. **Admission** *Museum* €7.50; €6 concessions. *Temporary exhibitions* €4; €3 concessions. **Credit** MC, V. **Map** p344 A2.

# Hanging out

If an Englishman's house is his castle, then an urban Spaniard's balcony is his garden. It's also his garage, toolshed, laundry and dog kennel. A look skywards will reveal anything from pet canaries to bicycles, ladders and mini marijuana farms squeezed into these tiny spaces, which are often the only extra storage space available in the cramped flats of districts like the Raval and the Barceloneta.

Small though they are, balconies play their part in Barcelona's traditions. On the night before Dia dels Reis (Three Kings' Day) on 6 January, children leave out a pair of their shoes and some bread and water for the camels, in the hope that Gaspar and his gang will pass in the night and drop off the booty on the balcony. After the blessing of the palms for Palm Sunday the long woven fronds are traditionally taken home and threaded between the railings of the balcony, where they remain for the whole year to ward off evil. On Sant Jordi (23 April) and other days of national pride such as the Dia de Catalunya (11 September), the red and yellow striped *senyera* flag is hung out on display. Equally, when Barça FC has a big match – and particularly if they trounce Madrid, many balconies are decorated with scarves, flags and anything else in the blue and purple team colours. Those whose balconies line the route of the *correfocs* (fire runs) are traditionally begged by the runners to throw down water to put out the dragon's flames and devils' fireworks although this practice has been discouraged in recent years because of the danger of wet explosives.

Being a public-private space, balcony etiquette can be a thorny issue: officially, there is a €120 fine for hanging washing from the balcony if the building has an alternative space such as a roof terrace or interior gallery. In practice, this means that older areas like the Raval are festooned with wet washing, while nobody would dream of doing such a thing in the snooty (and sooty) Eixample. Other balcony crimes include overwatering plants that then drip on to pedestrians' heads below, locking out barking dogs and not taking appropriate measures to avoid dropped clothes pegs, cigarette butts and even falling masonry (responsible for several deaths in recent years).

No work of art inside the MACBA can quite live up to the wow factor of Richard Meier's cool iceberg of a museum set in the vast skateboarder plains of the Plaça dels Àngels. Even some of the best sculptures are on the outside: *La Ola* (The Wave) a curving bronze behemoth by Jorge Oteiza, and the monochrome mural *Barcelona*, by Eduardo Chillida. Since it opened in 1995, the place has fattened up its holdings considerably, but the shows are often heavily political in concept and occasionally radical to the point of inaccessibility. If you can't or won't see the socio-political implications of, say, a roomful of beach balls, the MACBA may leave you cold.

The exhibits cover the last 50 years or so; although there's no permanent collection as such, some of these works are usually on display. The earlier pieces are strong on artists such as Antonio Saura and Tàpies (of whom director Manuel Borja Villel is an ardent fan), who were members of the Dau-al-Set, a group of radical writers and painters, much influenced by Miró, who kickstarted the Catalan art movement after the post-Civil War years of cultural apathy. Jean Dubuffet, and Basque sculptors Jorge Oteiza and Eduardo Chillida also feature. Works from the last 40 years are more global, with the likes of Joseph Beuys, Jean-Michel Basquiat, AR Penck and photographer Jeff Wall; the contemporary Spanish collection includes Catalan painting (Ferran García Sevilla, Miquel Barceló) and sculpture (Sergi Aguilar, Susana Solano). Every Thursday from July to September, the MACBA stays open until midnight (€3 after 8pm) and offers guided tours of the exhibitions (at 8.30pm and 10pm) and concerts in the first-floor terrace bar.

## Lower Raval

The lower half of the Raval, from C/Hospital downwards, is generally referred to as the Barrio Chino (translated into Catalan as 'Barri

Xino' or simply 'el Xino'). The nickname was coined in the 1920s by a journalist comparing the neighbourhood to San Francisco's Chinatown, and referred to its underworld feel rather than to any Chinese population. In those days, drifters filled the bars and there were cheap hostels along streets such as Nou de la Rambla, alongside high-class cabarets and brothels for the rich and cheap porn pits for the poor. A glimpse of the old sleaze can still be found in bars such as Bar Pastís and Marsella (also known as the 'absinthe bar', *see p180*). A small and appropriately seedy square is named after Jean Genet, whose novel *The Thief's Journal* (1949) describes his days as a Xino rent boy and beggar in the 1920s and '30s. For more insight into the area read André Pieyre de Mandiargues' *The Margin* (1967) and Raval-born Manuel Vázquez Montalbán's series of detective books. Other examinations of the neighbourhood include Joan Colom's internationally acclaimed series of Xino photographs taken in the late 1950s, José Luís Guerín's hard-hitting film *Work in Progress* (2001) and the music of Manu Chao.

Just beneath C/Hospital in the Plaça Sant Agustí lies one of the Raval's more arresting pieces of architecture, the unfinished 18th-century **Església de Sant Agustí** (No.2, 93 318 62 31, mass Mon-Fri 7pm; noon, 1pm & 7pm Sat, noon, 1pm, 6pm & 7pm Sun). The stone beams and jags protruding from its left flank (on C/Arc de Sant Agustí) and the undecorated sections of the baroque façade show how suddenly work stopped when funding ran out. Inside, the Capella de Santa Rita is packed out on her feast day, 22 May; Rita is the patron saint of lost causes and it is to her that the unhappy and unrequited bring their red roses to be blessed.

C/Nou de la Rambla, the area's main street, is home to Gaudí's first major project: **Palau Güell** (*see below*). Nearby, in C/Sant Pau, is a Modernista landmark, Domènech i Montaner's **Hotel España**, and at the end of the same street sits the Romanesque church of **Sant Pau del Camp** (*see below*). Iberian remains dating to 200 BC have been found next to the building, marking it as one of the oldest parts of the city. At the lower end of the area were the **Drassanes** (shipyards), now home to the **Museu Marítim** (*see p112*). Along the Avda Paral·lel side of this Gothic building lies the only large remaining section of Barcelona's 14th-century city wall.

## Palau Güell

*C/Nou de la Rambla 3 (93 317 39 74). Metro Drassanes or Liceu.* **Guided tours** 10am-1pm, 4-6.30pm Mon-Sat. **Map** p345 A6.

The Palau Güell is due to reopen in spring 2007, having undergone two years of major structural renovation. A fortress-like edifice shoehorned into a narrow six-storey sliver, it has the distinction of being the then 34-year-old Gaudí's first major commission, begun in 1886, for textile baron Eusebi Güell, the man who was to become his most important patron. Both men were passionate Catalan nationalists and Catholics; these two themes reverberate throughout the mansion, from the stripes of the Catalan flag on the façade to the stained-glass windows featuring historical Catalan heroes in the family parlour. The overall feeling is so sombre and gloomy that Antonioni used the house as a setting for his 1977 film *The Passenger*, and it is little wonder that the family favoured their more comfortable residence up in Pedralbes. The guided tour starts in the subterranean stables, where Gaudí's trademark parabolic brick arches form an exotic canopy of stone palm fronds on the ceiling; the curious pine cobblestones at the entrance are to deaden the noise of the horses' hooves. On the next floor, the visitor's vestibule has ornate mudéjar carved ceilings from which the Güells could snoop on their arriving guests through the jalousie trellis-work; at the heart of the house lies the spectacular six-storey hall complete with musicians' galleries and topped with a dome covered in cobalt honeycomb tiles; it even features a bizarre fold-out chapel of hammered copper complete with organ and retractable kneelers. The tour continues upstairs through the chilly stone bedrooms and the surprisingly modern-looking ceramic bathroom. The antidote to this dark and gnomish palace lies on its roof terrace, decorated with a breathtaking rainbow forest of 20 mosaic-covered chimneys; the central spire is topped with a wrought-iron weather vane in the shape of a bat, a legendary guardian of Catalan heroes and part of Jaume I's coat of arms. On the white chimney at the end nearest the Ramblas, look out for a hologram of Cobi, Javier Mariscal's 1992 Olympic mascot, which was added when the chimney was restored.

## Sant Pau del Camp

*C/Sant Pau 101 (93 441 00 01). Metro Paral·lel.* **Open** *Visits* noon-1pm, 7.30-8.30pm Mon-Fri. *Mass* 8pm Sat; noon Sun. **Admission** €1. **Map** p342 E11.

The name, St Paul in the Field, reflects a time when the Raval was still countryside. Archaeologists date the construction of this little Romanesque church back 1,000 years; indeed, the date carved on the church's most prestigious headstone – that of Count Guifré II Borell, son of Wilfred the Hairy and inheritor of all Barcelona and Girona – is AD 912.

The church's impressive façade includes sculptures of fantastical flora and fauna along with human grotesques. The tiny cloister is another highlight with its extraordinary Visigoth capitals, triple-lobed arches and central fountain. Restored after stints as a school in 1842, an army barracks from 1855 to 1890 and a bombsite in the Civil War, it remains remarkably intact.

# Barceloneta & the Ports

It's a shore thing.

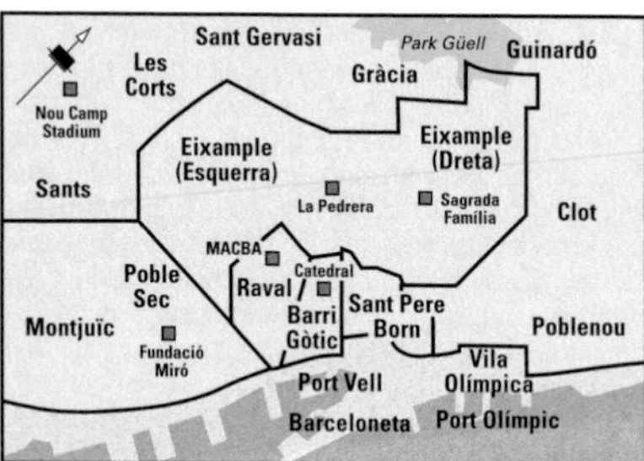


**Maps pp342-343**

## Port Vell

A pre-Olympic Games stroll down the Ramblas did not end with a view of yachts, the Maremàgnum shopping centre and a palm-fringed boulevard. Instead, pedestrians were greeted by the huge metal crates of Barcelona's container port, empty warehouses, a roaring motorway and railroad yards, making it a run-down area crawling with thieves, prostitutes and all manner of lowlifes. Turning Barcelona around to face the sea was one of the most drastic urban renewal projects the city has ever undertaken, and the area – rechristened Port Vell ('Old Port') – has changed beyond recognition, attracting more than 18 million visitors a year. The clean-up has extended to the whole seven kilometres (four miles) of city seashore, which is now a virtually continuous strip of modern construction bristling with new docks, marinas, hotels, cruise ships and ferry harbours and leisure areas such as Diagonal Mar ending out at the **Fòrum** (*see p140*), with its giant swimming area. New shoreline projects include Ricardo Bofill's Nova Bocana harbour development, where work is starting in early 2007 on a new maritime esplanade, leisure complex and sail-shaped luxury hotel. Unless environmentalists succeed in their fight to save the coastline, work is also due to start on a new maritime zoo next to the Fòrum to provide more space for the dolphins and other aquatic animals currently living in the city zoo.

Barcelona has always had a natural harbour, sheltered by the protective mass of the mountain of Montjuïc, but the first wharves were not built until the Middle Ages, when Barcelona was on its way to being the dominant power in the western Mediterranean. The immense Drassanes Reials (Royal Shipyards) are among the world's finest surviving pieces of civilian Gothic architecture; they now house the **Museu Marítim** (*see p112*) and bear witness to the sovereignty of the Catalan navy as the city became a military centre and the hub of trading routes between Africa and the rest of Europe. The city's power was dealt a blow when Christopher Columbus sailed west and found what he thought was the East; soon the Atlantic became the important trade route and Barcelona went into recession. Prosperity returned in the 19th century, when the city became the base for the Spanish industrial revolution.

Despite putting the city out of business, Columbus was commemorated in 1888 with the **Monument a Colom** (*see p111*), a statue inspired by Nelson's Column, complete with eight majestic lions. Consistent with the great discoverer's errant sense of direction, his pointing finger is not directed west to the Americas, but eastwards, to Mallorca. He might turn out to have the last laugh, however, if Spanish DNA investigations can back claims that he came from Genova in Mallorca rather than Genoa in Italy (*see p112* **Columbus Catalan conundrum**). A cynic might suggest that he is pointing in bemusement at the **World Trade Center**, a ship-shaped construction built on a jetty and housing offices, a five-star hotel and a tower for the **Transbordador Aeri** cable car (*see p113*). Or he could be pointing at the **Moll d'Espanya** ('wharf of Spain'), an artificial island linked to land by the undulating Rambla de Mar footbridge housing the **Maremàgnum** shopping mall (*see p190*), an **IMAX** cinema (*see p230*) and **L'Aquàrium** (*see p224*).

Take a lift through the centre of Columbus's column to check out the view from the top, or jump aboard the cable car (*transbordador aeri*). Below, both the **catamaran** and the **Golondrinas** pleasure boats (for both, *see p111*) begin their excursions out to sea. To the right, beyond the busy ferry and cruise ports, is the grandly named **Porta d'Europa**, the longest drawbridge in Europe, which curtains off the vast container port. Big as it is, plans are underway to enlarge the container port by diverting the mouth of the River Llobregat a mile or so to the south, doubling the present port area in size by 2050. Andreu Alfaro's enormous ***Onas*** (Waves) greatly cheers up the gridlocked roundabout of Plaça de la Carbonera, where a grim basin of coal commemorates where the steamboats once refuelled.

To the left of Columbus is the refurbished **Moll de la Fusta** ('Wood Wharf') boulevard, built after the city sea walls were demolished in 1878. The wooden pergolas, one of which is topped by Javier Mariscal's popular fibreglass ***Gamba*** (Prawn), are all that remain of some ill-fated restaurants and clubs, while traffic noise and congestion has been greatly reduced by passing the coastal motorway underneath the boulevard. Just over the grassy slopes is the ***Ictineo II***, a replica of the submarine created by Narcis Monturiol – the world's first submarine according to the Catalans – launched from Barcelona port in 1862. Roy Lichtenstein's ***Barcelona Head*** signposts the marina, with more than 450 moorings for leisure boats, and the **Palau de Mar**, a converted warehouse filled with seafood restaurants and the **Museu d'Història de Catalunya** (*see below*).

## Catamaran Orsom

*Portal de la Pau, Port de Barcelona (93 441 05 37/ www.barcelona-orsom.com). Metro Drassanes.* **Sailings** (approx 1hr 20mins) *Mar-Oct* noon-8pm, 3-4 sailings daily. **Tickets** €12/€14.50; €6-€9.50 concessions. **No credit cards**. **Map** p342 F12.

Departing from the jetty just by the Monument a Colom, this 23m (75ft) catamaran is the largest in Barcelona; it chugs up to 80 seafarers round the Nova Bocana harbour area, before unfurling its sails and peacefully gliding across the bay. There are 8pm jazz cruises from June to September or, if you don't want to fight for the trampoline sun deck, the catamaran can also be chartered for private trips.

## Las Golondrinas

*Moll de Drassanes (93 442 31 06/www.las golondrinas.com). Metro Drassanes.* **Sailings** *Drassanes to breakwater & return* (35mins) Jan-Mar, Nov, Dec 11am-2pm Mon-Fri; 11.45am-7pm Sat, Sun. Apr-June, Oct 11am-6pm Mon-Fri; 11.45am-7pm Sat, Sun. July-Sept 11.45am-7.30pm daily. **Tickets** €4; €2 concessions; free under-4s. *Drassanes to Port Fòrum & return* (1hr 30mins) Jan-Mar, Nov, Dec 11.30am, 1.30pm Mon-Fri; 11.30am, 1.30pm, 4.30pm Sat, Sun. Apr-June, Oct 11.30am, 1.30pm, 4.30pm Mon-Fri; 11.30am, 1.30pm, 4.30pm, 6.30pm Sat, Sun. July-Sept 11.30am, 1.30pm, 4.30pm, 6.30pm, 8.30pm daily. **Tickets** €9.70; €4.10-€6.80 concessions; free under-4s. **Credit** MC, V. **Map** p342 F12.

For more than 115 years the 'swallow boats' have chugged around the harbour, giving passengers a bosun's-eye view of Barcelona's rapidly changing seascape out as far as the Port Fòrum. The fleet is made up of three double-decker pleasure boats and two glass-bottomed catamarans, moored next to the Orsom catamaran (*see above*). Boats leave around every 40 minutes for the shorter trip.

## Monument a Colom

*Plaça Portal de la Pau (93 302 52 24). Metro Drassanes.* **Open** 9am-8.30pm daily. **Admission** €2.30; €1.50 concessions; free under-4s. **No credit cards. Map** p342 F12.

Located where the Ramblas meets the port, the Columbus monument was designed for the Universal Exhibition of 1888. It's hard to believe from ground level, but Colom himself is actually 7m (23ft) high; his famous white barnet comes courtesy of the city pigeons. A tiny lift takes you up inside the column to a circular bay for a panoramic view of the city and port. Claustrophobes and vertigo sufferers should stay away; the slight sway can be unnerving.

## Museu d'Història de Catalunya

*Plaça Pau Vila 3 (93 225 47 00/www.mhcat.net). Metro Barceloneta.* **Open** 10am-7pm Tue, Thur-Sat; 10am-8pm Wed; 10am-2.30pm Sun. **Admission** €3; €2.10 concessions; free under-7s. Free to all 1st Sun of mth. **Credit** (shop only) MC, V. **Map** p342 G12/F12.

Now celebrating its tenth anniversary, the Catalan History Museum spans the Paleolithic era right up to Jordi Pujol's proclamation as president of the Generalitat in 1980 and offers a virtual chronology

Barceloneta beach. See p113.

Sightseeing

## Columbus Catalan conundrum

The race is on to find genetic proof to confirm an 80-year-old theory that the man who arrived in the Americas probably took some *pan con tomate* and *butifarra* with him, and maybe even danced a *sardana* in celebration on that distant Caribbean shore.

No one knows for sure where Christopher Columbus came from – possibly, it is argued, because Columbus was a Jew and a pirate, neither of which were very popular in the 15th century, so he disguised his past and reinvented himself as the world's first transatlantic cruiser. The theory that he was Catalan was first raised as long ago as 1927, by Peruvian scholar Luis Ulloa y Cisneros, former director of the Lima National Library. It was denounced shortly afterwards by another Peruvian scholar, in favour of the traditional theory that he was Genoese. Since then the argument has smouldered on. Needless to say, few people are very interested in Columbus's Catalan roots, with the exception of a small group of Catalan academics, who seem to spend a lot of their time promoting their own research and denigrating the work of their (mostly Catalan) colleagues.

The theory that Columbus was Catalan is based on various hypotheses, which, like most hypotheses, are reasonable or far-fetched, depending on your perspective and/or nationality. These include the spelling of his name in official documents, the fact that he had a Catalan style of handwriting, that he claimed to have served as a corsair for the short-lived Catalan king Renat d'Anjou in his civil war against Joan II, that he had lots of Catalan friends, and took lots of Catalans with him on his second voyage. All very inconclusive.

But now, with modern DNA analysis, technology has been brought in to add weight to the argument. Catalan and Mallorcan men with the surname Colom or Colón have been tested to see if their DNA matches that of Columbus; men in Genoa with the surname Colombo are also being tested. The idea is that if there is a match with Columbus's genes in either of these two groups, it will conclusively prove he was from the same area. Although to a sceptic it might just prove that Columbus, or a close descendant, managed to father rather more illegitimate offspring than the average 15th-century playboy. It had been hoped that results would be known in time for the 500th anniversary of the explorer's death, on 20 May 1506. Unfortunately, the Genoese samples were inexplicably delayed, so that at the time of writing, no conclusive findings have been announced. But it is fitting that no one really knows the origins of a discoverer who didn't really know where he was going, and when he got there, didn't really know what he had found.

of the region's past revealed through two floors of text, photos, film, animated models and reproductions of everything from a medieval shoemaker's shop to a 1960s bar. Hands-on activities such as trying to lift a knight's armour or irrigating lettuces with a Moorish water wheel add a little pzazz to the rather dry early history; to exit the exhibition, visitors walk over a huge 3D map of Catalonia. Every section has a decent introduction in English, but the reception desk will lend a copy of the in-depth English-language museum guide free of charge. The excellent temporary exhibitions, often collections of photos and posters, typically examine recent aspects of regional history. The museum occupies a stylishly converted 19th-century port warehouse, and the views from the rooftop café terrace are unbeatable.

### Museu Marítim

*Avda de les Drassanes (93 342 99 20/www.museumaritimbarcelona.com). Metro Drassanes.*
**Open** 10am-8pm daily. **Admission** €6.40; €3 concessions; free under-7s. Temporary exhibitions vary. Combined ticket with Las Golondrinas (35mins) €8.30; €4.40-€6.10 concessions; free under-4s. **Credit** MC, V. **Map** p342 F12.

A full-scale replica of Don Juan de Austria's royal galley is the mainstay of the collection at the Museu Marítim, complete with a ghostly crew of galley slaves projected on to the rowing banks. The original ship was built in these very same shipyards, one of the finest examples of civil Gothic architecture in Spain and a monument to Barcelona's importance in Mediterranean naval history. With the aid of an audio guide, the maps, nautical instruments, multimedia displays and models show you how shipbuilding and navigation techniques have developed over the years. Admission also covers the Santa Eulàlia schooner docked in the Moll de la Fusta.

### Transbordador Aeri

*Torre de Sant Sebastià, Barceloneta (93 441 48 20). Metro Barceloneta.* **Open** *Mid June-mid Sept* 10.45am-7.15pm daily. *Mid Sept-mid June* 10.30am-5.45pm daily. **Tickets** €9 single; €12.50 return; free under-3s. **No credit cards. Map** p342 E12/F13/G13.
Designed as part of the 1929 Expo, these rather battered old cable cars run between the Sant Sebastià tower at the very far end of Passeig Joan de Borbó to the Jaume I tower in front of the World Trade Center; the final leg ends at the Miramar lookout point on Montjuïc. The towers are accessed by lifts.

## Barceloneta

Once a working-class neighbourhood dependent on fishing and heavy industry, this triangular spit of land is now a prime slice of seafront real estate where many of the famously tiny apartments are being converted into short-stay holiday flats. But Barceloneta has not completely lost its charm; the interior of this cramped and chaotic neighbourhood (hidden behind the restaurant-lined boulevard of Passeig Joan de Borbó) is a real slice of old Barcelona.

Barceloneta had a turbulent birth. When the old maritime *barri* of La Ribera was demolished in 1714 to make way for the citadel (*see p102*), thousands were left homeless. It was not until 1753 that the new district of Barceloneta was created; the homeless refugees had had to make do with makeshift slums on the beach for nearly 40 years. Military engineer Prosper Verboom maximised the potential of the triangle of reclaimed marshland with narrow rows of cheap worker housing set around a parade ground (now the market square). The two-storey houses became home to fishermen, sailors and dock workers, and soon became so overcrowded that they were split in half and later quartered. These famous *quarts de casa* typically measured no more than 30 square metres (323 square feet), had no running water until the 1960s and often held families of ten or so. Most were later built up to six or more levels, but even today, three-tier bunk beds are not uncommon, and in the summer months the street becomes an extended living room.

Since the beach clean-up, Barceloneta has enjoyed a much higher profile, and current redevelopment includes university housing and Enric Miralles's towering Gas Natural headquarters, which is covered in mirrored glass. In the heart of the neighbourhood is the new **market** designed by Josep Mias; scheduled to be open by early 2007, it features a wavy sea-green roof fitted with 180 solar panels and incorporates recycled materials from the original 1884 structure. The area has also been the beneficiary of a staggering amount of sculpture, particularly around the Port Vell. Lothar Baumgarten's ***Rosa dels Vents*** (Wind Rose; *see p114* **In the detail**) has the names of Catalan sea winds embedded in the pavement, and, at the other end of Passeig Joan de Borbó is Juan Muñoz's disturbing sculpture of five caged figures known as ***Una habitació on sempre plou*** (A Room Where it Always Rains). Behind it is the city's popular municipal **swimming pool** (*see p274*) newly marked by the soaring figures of Alfredo Lanz's ***Homenatge a la Natació*** (Homage to Swimming) to mark the 2003 World Swimming Championships held in Barcelona. Monuments within the quarter include the 18th-century church of **Sant Miquel del Port**, with a muscular sculpture of the Archangel Michael on the façade and the ***Font de Carmen Amaya*** at the sea end of C/Sant Carles, a fountain dedicated to the famous gypsy flamenco dancer who was born in 1913 in the squalid beach settlement of Somorrostro.

Nearby, the Port still preserves a small fishing area with the clock tower that gives its name to the wharf – Moll del Rellotge ('Clock Wharf'). Further down, the road leads to the Nova Bocana development, which should be finished by 2010. The complex will combine leisure and cultural facilities with offices and industry and will be dominated by Ricardo Bofill's Hotel Vela, a sail-shaped luxury hotel. If you head left at the end of Passeig Joan de Borbó, you'll reach Barceloneta beach and Rebecca Horn's tower of rusty cubes, ***Estel Ferit*** (Wounded Star), which pays homage to the much-missed beach shacks. The Passeig Marítim esplanade runs north from here, and is a popular hangout for in-line skaters, locals walking off their Sunday paella and outpatients from the enviably positioned Hospital del Mar. At its far end are Frank Gehry's shimmering copper ***Fish***, the new U-shaped biomedical research park fronted by the pleasant wooden-decked Plaça Charles Darwin and the twin skyscrapers of the Hotel Arts (*see p65*) and the Torre Mapfre, which form an imposing gateway to the Port Olímpic.

## Beaches

Now crowded with sunbathers, it's hard to believe that Barcelona's beaches were once a filthy Hell's Bathroom of slimy rocks, sewage, heavy industry and warehouses. Barceloneta was the only sandy part, but any usable parts of the narrow grey beach were clogged with private swimming baths and beach shacks (*xiringuitos*) that served seafood on trestle tables set up on

# In the detail
## *Wind Rose*

As part of the city's move to beautify itself – and particularly the port area – in time for the 1992 Olympic Games, a group of sculptures was commissioned by Catalan curator Gloria Moure and became known as *Configuracions Urbanes*. One of the best loved of these is Lothar Baumgarten's *Wind Rose*, which sprawls up the portside Passeig Joan de Borbó.

Best viewed from above, it has a perfect vantage point in the Museu d'Història de Catalunya (*see p111*). Take the lift to the top floor, where a practically unknown café boasts the biggest terrace and some of the best views in all of Barcelona. From here you can scrutinise the pavement below and you'll see giant cast-iron letters forming words stretching in all directions. These are the names of the various Catalan winds – *tramuntana, llevant, xaloc, migjorn, ponent, garbí, mestral* and *gregal* – the letters being positioned according to the direction from which the winds blow.

the sand. Once the 1992 Olympics opened Barcelona's eyes to the commercial potential of its shoreline, the beaches were swiftly cleared and filled with tons of golden sand, imported palm trees and landscaped promenades.

However, the beaches have become a victim of their own popularity, and keeping them clean is something of a Sisyphean task for the city council. Dubbed the Bay of Pigs by the papers, the most central area was so dirty that in 2005 the nightly patrols collected over 4,000 cubic metres of rubbish, which included more than 1.5 million cigarette butts. The massive clean-up campaign includes doubling the number of beachfront toilets, adding new bins, and endless posters and loudspeaker announcements reminding people to pick up their rubbish.

The beach furthest south is **Platja de Sant Sebastià**, right in front of the swimming pools, popular with nudists and anyone willing to swap an uninspiring background of industrial rubble for a bit more space. Next is **Platja de Sant Miquel**, which gets insanely crowded in the summer months; it's a slightly grubby version of Ibiza, with plenty of thongs and piercings on display, and *xiringuitos* pumping out house music. **Platja de Barceloneta** provides a sandy porch for restaurants and nightclubs; the covered walkway is home to tables where old men play dominoes, and it also houses the new beach centre – its small beach library lends out books, magazines and papers (some in English) in July and August. After the Port Olímpic and just down from the Ciutadella-Vila Olímpica metro station, **Platja de Nova Icària** is much broader, with plenty of space for volleyball and beach tennis, while **Platja de Bogatell** boasts the hippest *xiringuito* with torches and loungers out at night from May to October. Further north, **Platja de Mar Bella** is all about sport, with the sailing and water-sports club Base Nàutica and a popular half-pipe for skateboarders and BMXers behind. The more remote beaches of **Nova Mar Bella** and the new **Llevant** have rather unexotic backdrops of high-rise residential blocks and are generally fairly quiet.

## Vila Olímpica

The land lying further up the coast was once an area of thriving industry, but by the 1980s it had fallen into disuse and presented the perfect blank slate for a team of 30 prize-winning architects to design the model neighbourhood of the Olympic Village for the games in 1992. Based on Cerdà's Eixample grid, it provided accommodation for 15,000 athletes, parks, a cinema, four beaches and a leisure marina.

The lack of cafés and shops, however, leaves it devoid of Mediterranean charm. Most social activity takes place in the Port Olímpic, home to sailboats, restaurants, a large casino and a waterfront strip of cheesy nightclubs. Wide empty boulevards lend themselves to large-scale sculpture, including a jagged pergola on Avda Icària by Enric Miralles and Carme Pinós, in memory of the ripped-up railway tracks, and Antoni Llena's abstract *David i Goliat* in the Parc de les Cascades.

# Montjuïc

Where the grass is greener.

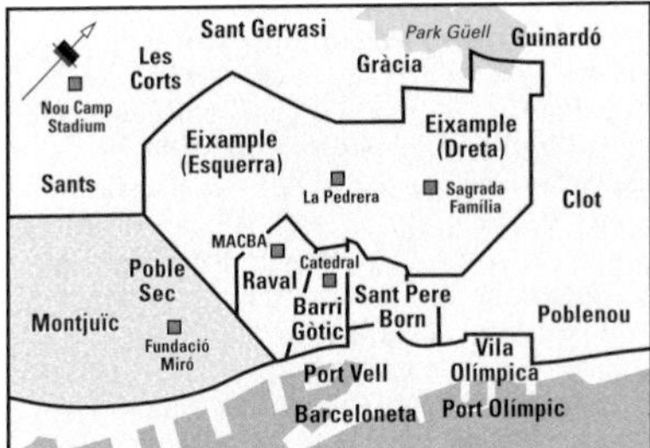


**Maps pp341-p342**

In a city with as few parks as Barcelona, the hills of Montjuïc offer a precious escape from the urban hustle with pleasure gardens, spectacular views and all manner of museums and galleries. Santiago Calatrava's Olympic 'needle' and other buildings from the 1992 games are scattered over the landward side, while facing the sea are a lighthouse and an enormous cemetery. Yet, despite all the attractions, the difficulty of accessing Montjuïc means that its green spaces are greatly underused by local citizens; plans to convert it into the 'Central Park' of Barcelona involve opening up access from the neighbourhood of Poble Sec with broad boulevards and escalators leading up to Avinguda Miramar; as a temporary boost, the Ajuntament has already launched a new Montjuïc bus service (*see p118*).

The mists of time obscure the etymology of Montjuïc, but an educated guess is that 'juïc' comes from the old Catalan word meaning Jewish. It was here that the medieval Jewish community buried their dead; some of the excavated headstones are now kept in the **Museu Militar** (*see p119*).

Other headstones with Hebraic inscriptions can be seen in the walls of the 16th-century Palau de Lloctinent, just to the east of the cathedral; following the expulsion of all Jews from Spain by Ferdinand and Isabella in 1492, the cemetery was plundered and the stone reused. The sea-facing side of the mountain still houses a huge cemetery today, the **Cementiri del Sud-Oest** (*see p117*).

The 17th-century fortress, the **Castell de Montjuïc**, was rebuilt in its current form after Philip V's troops broke the siege of Barcelona in 1714. From its vantage point overlooking the city, the central government was able to impose its will on the unruly populace until the death of Franco. From here, in 1842, the city was bombed to repress an uprising against the government's policies. And in this fortress many Republicans were executed after the Civil War, including Generalitat president Lluís Companys, who was killed in 1940, victim No.2,761 of Franco's firing squads in Catalonia. However, the new Socialist government ceded formal ownership of the castle to the city of Barcelona in 2004, and approved a law that allows for the pardon of Civil War victims.

The 1929 Exhibition was the first attempt to turn the hill into a leisure area. Then, in the 1940s, thousands of immigrant workers from the rest of Spain settled on the hill. Some squatted in precarious shacks, while others rented brick and plaster sheds laid out along improvised streets that covered the hillside, then virtually treeless. These *barraques* thrived until the last few stragglers moved out in the 1970s, although the area still attracts intermittent waves of illegal tent and hut

**Castell de Montjuïc and Museu Militar.** *See p119.*

dwellers. Energetic visitors can follow the same steep routes these residents once took home, straight up C/Nou de la Rambla or C/Margarit in Poble Sec; the stairway at the top leaves you just a short distance from the **Fundació Joan Miró** (*see p118*) and the Olympic stadium area.

The long axis from **Plaça d'Espanya** is still the most popular access to the park, with the climb now eased by a sequence of open-air escalators. In the centre of Plaça d'Espanya itself is a monument designed by Josep Maria Jujol (who created the wrought-iron balconies on La Pedrera), with representations of the rivers Ebre, Tagus and Guadalquivir. Where Paral·lel meets Plaça d'Espanya is **Las Arenas**, the old neighourhood bullring. The last bull met its fate here in the 1970s and until 2003 the bullring lay derelict. The ubiquitous Lord Rogers is currently overseeing the mammoth transformation project, to be completed in 2007, which will turn the ring into a circular leisure complex while restoring the existing neo-Mudéjar façade. The vision encompasses a 'piazza in the sky', a giant roof terrace that will allow for alfresco events and offer panoramic views over Barcelona.

On the other side of the square, two Venetian-style towers announce the beginning of the **Fira**, the trade-show area, with pavilions from 1929 and newer buildings used for conventions and congresses. To the left is the Palau d'Esports, recently converted into the **Barcelona Teatre Musical** (*see p264*) hosting large-scale musical theatre. Further up, the rebuilt **Pavelló Mies van der Rohe** *(see p120)*, a modernist classic, contrasts sharply with the neo-classical structures nearby. Across the street, Puig i Cadafalch's Modernista factory has been converted into the excellent **CaixaForum** cultural centre (*see p117*). Further up the hill is the bizarre **Poble Espanyol** (*see p120*), a model village also designed in 1929 especially to showcase Spanish crafts and architecture.

Presiding over it all is the bombastic **Palau Nacional**, originally built as a 'temporary exhibition' for the Expo, and now home to the **Museu Nacional d'Art de Catalunya** (*see p118*), housing Catalan art from the last millennium and recently reopened after a lengthy refurbishment. At night, the entire setting is illuminated by a water-and-light spectacular, the **Font Màgica** (*see p117*), still operating with its complex original mechanisms. Other nearby buildings erected for the 1929 Expo have been converted into the **Museu d'Arqueologia de Catalunya** (*see p119*) and the **Ciutat del Teatre** (theatre city) complex. From the same period are the nearby **Teatre Grec** (Greek theatre), used for summer concerts during the Grec Festival, and the beautifully restored **Jardins Laribal**, designed by French landscape architect JCN Forestier. At the top of this garden is the **Font del Gat** information centre. The **Museu Etnològic** (*see p119*), a typical 1970s construction, sits just below it.

If walking isn't your thing, another way up the hill is via the **funicular railway**, integrated with the city's metro system, leaving from the Paral·lel station. The **Telefèric** cable car, which usually links this station to the **castle**, is being extended down to the port and is due to open in spring 2007. A more circuitous way up is by the **Transbordador Aeri** cable car across the harbour to **Miramar**, a peaceful spot with unmatchable views across the city that has been somewhat taken over by the new five-star **Gran Hotel Miramar**, which opened in August 2006.

Montjuïc's **Anella Olímpica** (Olympic Ring) is a convergence of diverse constructions all laid out for the 1992 Olympic Games. The **Estadi Olímpic** (home to the city's 'second' football team, Espanyol, until they moved to Cornellà in 2006), although entirely new, was built within the façade of a 1929 stadium by a design team led by Federico Correa and Alfonso Milà. The horse sculptures are copies of the originals by Pau Gargallo. Next to it is the most original and attractive of the Olympic facilities, Arata Isozaki's **Palau Sant Jordi** indoor arena, its undulating façade evoking Gaudí, and its high-tech interior featuring a transparent roof. Only 15 years after the Olympics, these two buildings are already falling into disrepair and undergoing a ten-million euro renovation in 2007. In the hard, white *plaça* in front rises Santiago Calatrava's remarkable, Brancusi-inspired **communications tower**.

Across the square is the city's best swimming pool, the **Piscines Bernat Picornell** (*see also p274*), while further down is the INEFC physical education institute, by architect Ricardo Bofill. Walk across the road and you look over a cliff on to a rugby pitch and an equestrian area, where children can take pony rides. The cliff itself is a favourite hangout for rock-climbers.

The many parks and gardens include the **Jardins Mossèn Costa i Llobera** (*see p118*), which abound in tropical plants, but particularly cacti, just below Miramar, on the steep flank nearest the port. Not far above are the **Jardins del Mirador**, from where there is a spectacular view over the harbour. These gardens are also the starting point for a new path for pedestrians and cyclists, running precariously below the castle and leading to a magical outdoor café, **La Caseta del Migdia** (*see p181*). One of the newest parks is the nearby **Jardins de Joan Brossa**, featuring humorous, hands-on contraptions where children can manipulate water courses and practise creative adventure sports. Walk down towards the funicular station and you will reach the enchanting **Jardins Cinto Verdaguer**, fresh from a €1.5-million makeover, with ponds filled with lotus flowers and water lilies.

All these gardens play an adjunct role to the creative biospheres of the **Jardí Botànic**, just above the Olympic stadium, exquisitely designed and finally maturing into an important scientific collection (*see p118*).

## CaixaForum

*Casaramona, Avda Marquès de Comillas 6-8 (93 476 86 00/www.fundacio.lacaixa.es). Metro Espanya.* **Open** 10am-8pm Tue-Sun. **Admission** free. **Credit** (shop only) AmEx, DC, MC, V. **Map** p341 B9.

One of the masterpieces of industrial modernism, this former red-brick yarns and textiles factory was designed by Puig i Cadafalch in 1911. It spent most of the last century in a sorry state, acting briefly as a police barracks and then falling into dereliction. Fundació La Caixa, the charitable arm of Catalonia's largest savings bank, bought it and rebuilt it. The original brick structure was supported, while the ground below was excavated to house a strikingly modern entrance plaza by Arata Isozaki, a Sol LeWitt mural, a 350-seat auditorium, bookshop and library. In addition to the smaller permanent contemporary art collection, upstairs there are three impressive spaces for temporary exhibitions – often among the most interesting in the city.

## Cementiri del Sud-Oest

*C/Mare de Déu de Port 54-58 (93 484 17 00). Bus 38.* **Open** 8am-6pm daily. **Admission** free.

Designed by Leandro Albareda in 1880, this enormous necropolis, perched at the side of the motorway out of town, serves as a daily reminder to commuters of their own mortality. It has housed the city's dead since 1883, originally placing them in four sections: one for Catholics, one for Protestants, one for non-Christians and a fourth for aborted foetuses. It now stretches over the entire south-west corner of the mountain, with family tombs stacked five or six storeys high. Many, especially those belonging to the gypsy community, are a riot of colour and flowers. The Fossar de la Pedrera memorial park remembers those fallen from the International Brigades and the Catalan martyrs from the Civil War. There is also a Holocaust memorial and a mausoleum to former Generalitat president Lluís Companys. The cemetery is much visited, especially on All Saints' Day, when the roads are clogged with cars. In 2007, modernisation and expansion of the facilities should be underway providing more parking space, flower stalls, a new entrance, and rehousing the city collection of funeral carriages (*see p127*).

## Font Màgica de Montjuïc

*Plaça d'Espanya (93 316 10 00/www.bcn.es/fonts). Metro Espanya.* **Fountain** *May-Sept* 8-11.30pm Thur-Sun; music every 30mins 9.30pm-midnight. *Oct-Apr* 7-9pm Fri, Sat; music every 30mins 7-9pm. **Map** p341 B9.

Still using its original art deco waterworks, the 'magic fountain' works its wonders with 3,600 pieces of tubing and more than 4,500 light bulbs. Summer evenings after nightfall see the multiple founts swell and dance to anything from soft rock to the 1812 Overture, and, of course, Freddie Mercury and Montserrat Caballé's Barcelona, showing off its kaleidoscope of pastel colours, while searchlights play in a giant fan pattern over the palace dome. In July 2006 a new piece was inaugurated with the fountain choreographed to El Moldava by Czech composer Bedrich Smetana, a piece inspired by the life-giving properties of water.

**Fundació Joan Miró**. *See p118.*

### Fundació Joan Miró

*Parc de Montjuïc (93 329 19 08/www.bcn.fjmiro.es). Metro Paral·lel then Funicular de Montjuïc/61 bus.* **Open** *July-Sept* 10am-8pm Tue, Wed, Fri, Sat; 10am-9.30pm Thur; 10am-2.30pm Sun. *Oct-June* 10am-7pm Tue, Wed, Fri, Sat; 10am-9.30pm Thur; 10am-2.30pm Sun. **Guided tours** 11.30pm Sat, Sun. **Admission** *All exhibitions* €7.50; €5 concessions. *Temporary exhibitions* €4; €3 concessions; free under-14s. **Credit** MC, V. **Map** p341 C11.

Josep Lluís Sert, who spent the years of the Franco dictatorship as dean of architecture at Harvard University, designed one of the world's great museum buildings on his return. Approachable, light and airy, these white walls and arches house a collection of more than 225 paintings, 150 sculptures and all of Miró's graphic work, plus some 5,000 drawings. The permanent collection, highlighting Miró's trademark use of primary colours and simplified organic forms symbolising stars, the moon, birds and women, occupies the second half of the space. On the way to the sculpture gallery is Alexander Calder's reconstructed *Mercury Fountain*, originally seen at the Spanish Republic's Pavilion at the 1937 Paris Fair. In other works, Miró is shown as a cubist (*Street in Pedralbes*, 1917), naïve (*Portrait of a Young Girl*, 1919) and surrealist (*Man and Woman in Front of a Pile of Excrement*, 1935). In the upper galleries, large, black-outlined paintings from Miró's final period precede a room of works with political themes. **Photo** *p117.*

**Museu Etnològic.** *See p119.*

Temporary shows vary wildly in content and quality, but at best can match the appeal of the permanent exhibition. The Espai 13 in the basement features young contemporary artists. Outside is a pleasant sculpture garden with fine work by some contemporary Catalan artists.

### Galeria Olímpica

*Estadi Olímpic, Parc de Montjuïc (93 426 06 60/ www.fundaciobarcelonaolimpica.es). Metro Espanya/ bus all routes to Plaça d'Espanya.* **Open** *Apr-Sept* 10am-2pm, 4-7pm Mon-Fri. *Oct-Mar* (by appointment) 10am-1pm, 4-6pm Mon-Fri. **Admission** €2.70; €2.40-€1.50 concessions. **Credit** AmEx, MC, V. **Map** p341 B11.

Of fairly limited interest, this is a hotchpotch of imagery and paraphernalia commemorating the 1992 Olympics, including costumes from the opening ceremony and the ubiquitous mascot Cobi.

### Jardí Botànic

*C/Doctor Font i Quer (93 426 49 35/www.jardi-botanic.bcn.es). Metro Espanya.* **Open** *Apr-June, Sept* 10am-5pm Mon-Fri; 10am-8pm Sat, Sun. *July, Aug* 10am-8pm daily. *Oct-Mar* 10am-5pm daily. **Admission** €3; €1.50 concessions; free under-16s. Free last Sun of mth. **No credit cards. Map** p341 B11/12.

After the original 1930s botanical garden was disturbed by the construction for the Olympics, the only solution was to build an entirely new replacement. This opened in 1999, housing plants from seven global regions with a climate similar to that of the Western Mediterranean. Everything about the futuristic design, from the angular concrete pathways to the raw sheet steel banking (and even the design of the bins), is the complete antithesis of the more naturalistic, gardens of England. It is meticulously kept, with all plants being tagged in Latin, Catalan, Spanish and English along with their date of planting, and has the added advantage of wonderful views across the city. There is a small space housing occasional temporary exhibitions and free audio guides to lead visitors through the gardens.

### Jardins Mossèn Costa i Llobera

*Ctra de Miramar 1. Metro Drassanes or Paral·lel.* **Open** 10am-sunset daily. **Admission** free. **Map** p341 D12.

The port side of Montjuïc is protected from the cold north wind, creating a microclimate two degrees centigrade warmer than the rest of the city, which is perfect for 800 species of the world's cactus. It is said to be the most complete collection of its type in Europe. Along with the botanic curiosities, there is a vast Josep Viladomat bronze of a young girl making lace.

### Linea Montjuïc Turistic

*Torres Venecianas, Plaça d'Espanya (934 15 60 20). Metro Espanya.* **Open** *June-Sept* 10am-10pm daily. *Oct-May* 10am-10pm daily. **Frequency** Every 40mins. **Tickets** *Day pass* €3, €2 concessions. **No credit cards. Map** p341 B9.

The bus stops at the main attractions, including Fundació Joan Miró, the castle and the Olympic pool. The winter schedule may vary as the timetable has yet to be confirmed.

### Museu d'Arqueologia de Catalunya

*Passeig de Santa Madrona 39-41 (93 423 21 49/56 01/www.mac.es). Metro Poble Sec.* **Open** 9.30am-7pm Tue-Sat; 10am-2.30pm Sun. **Admission** €2.40; €1.68 concessions; free under-16s. **Credit** (shop only) MC, V. **Map** p341 C10.

The time frame for this archaeology collection starts with the Palaeolithic period, and there are relics of Greek, Punic, Roman and Visigoth colonisers, up to the early Middle Ages. A massive Roman sarcophagus is carved with scenes of the rape of Persephone (Proserpina), and an immense statue of Aesculapius, the god of medicine, towers over one room. A few galleries are dedicated to the Mallorcan Talayotic cave culture, and there is a very good display on the Iberians, the pre-Hellenic, pre-Roman inhabitants of south-eastern Spain. An Iberian skull with a nail driven through it effectively demonstrates a typical method of execution from that time. The display ends with the marvellous, jewel-studded headpiece of a Visigoth king. One of the best-loved pieces, inevitably, is an alarmingly erect Priapus, found during building work in Sants in 1848 and kept under wraps 'for moral reasons' until 1986.

### Museu Etnològic

*Passeig de Santa Madrona s/n (93 424 68 07/ www.museuetnologic.bcn.es). Metro Poble Sec.* **Open** *Late June-late Sept* noon-8pm Tue-Sat; 11am-3pm Sun. *Late Sept-late June* 10am-7pm Tue, Thur; 10am-2pm Wed, Fri-Sun. **Admission** €3; €1.50 concessions; free under-16s, over-65s. **No credit cards**. **Map** p341 B10.

Recently spruced up and expanded, the ethnology museum houses a vast collection of items, from Australian Aboriginal boomerangs to rugs and jewellery from Afghanistan, although by far the most comprehensive collections are from Catalonia. Of the displays upstairs, most outstanding are the Moroccan, Japanese and Philippine exhibits, though there are also some interesting pre-Columbian finds. Of the attempts to arrange the pieces in thematically interesting ways, 'Taboo' transpires to be a rather limp look at nudity in different cultures; more successful is 'Sacred' a run through the world of religious rituals. Temporary exhibitions incude the fruits of a two-year study of contemporary Gyspy culture in Catalonia (until July 2007). **Photo** *p118*.

### Museu Militar

*Castell de Montjuïc, Ctra de Montjuïc 66 (93 329 86 13). Metro Paral·lel then funicular & cable car.* **Open** *Apr-Oct* 9.30am-8pm Tue-Sun. *Nov-Mar* 9.30am-5pm Tue-Fri; 9.30am-8pm Sat, Sun. **Admission** €2.50; €1-€1.25 concessions; free under-7s. **No credit cards**. **Map** p341 B10.

Appropriately housed in one wing of the old hilltop fortress, the Military Museum is a grim slice of local history. The fortress was used to bombard rather than protect Barcelona in past conflicts, and as a prison and place of execution, the castle has strong repressive associations. The exhibits here include armour, swords, lances, muskets (beautiful Moroccan *moukhala*), rifles and pistols. Other highlights include 23,000 lead soldiers representing a Spanish division of the 1920s. Oddly, a display of Jewish tombstones from the mountain's desecrated medieval cemetery is the only direct reminder of death within its thick walls. If the Spanish government cedes the castle to the city of Barcelona, there are plans to turn part of the building into a centre for peace studies (*see p120* **War then peace?**) **Photo** *p115*.

### MNAC (Museu Nacional d'Art de Catalunya)

*Palau Nacional, Parc de Montjuïc (93 622 03 76/www.mnac.es). Metro Espanya.* **Open** 10am-7pm Tue-Sat; 10am-2.30pm Sun. **Admission** *Permanent exhibitions* €8.50; €6 concessions. *Temporary exhibitions* €3-€5. Free under-7s and 1st Thur of mth. **Credit** MC, V. **Map** p341 B10.

'One museum, a thousand years of art' is the slogan of the National Museum of Catalan Art, and the stunning collection provides a dizzying overview of Catalan art from the 12th to the 20th centuries. Newly renovated, the museum now has a whole extra floor to absorb the holdings of the section of the Thyssen-Bornemisza collection that was previously kept in the convent in Pedralbes, along with the mainly Modernista holdings from the former Museum of Modern Art in Ciutadella park, a fine photography section, coins and the bequest of Francesc Cambó, founder of the autonomist Lliga Regionalista, a regionalist conservative party.

The highlight of the museum, however, is still the Romanesque collection. As art historians realised that scores of solitary tenth-century churches in the Pyrenees were falling into ruin – and with them were going extraordinary Romanesque mural paintings that had served to instruct doubting villagers in the basics of the faith – the laborious task was begun of removing murals intact from church apses. The display here features 21 mural sections in loose chronological order. One highlight is the tremendous *Crist de Taüll*, from the 12th-century church of Sant Climent de Taüll. Even 'graffiti' scratchings (probably by monks) of animals, crosses and labyrinths have been preserved.

The Gothic collection is also excellent and starts with some late 13th-century frescoes that were discovered in 1961 and 1997, when two palaces in the city were being renovated. There are carvings and paintings from local churches, including works of the indisputable Catalan masters of the Golden Age, Bernat Martorell and Jaume Huguet. The highlight of the Thyssen collection is Fra Angelico's *Madonna of Humility* (c1430s), while the Cambó bequest contains some stunning Old Masters – works by Titian, Rubens and El Greco among them. Also unmissable is the Modernista collection, which includes the original mural of *Ramon Casas and Pere Romeu on a Tandem* (1897), which decorated Els Quatre Gats. The rich collection of decorative arts includes original furniture from Modernista houses such as the Casa Amatller and Gaudí's Casa Batlló.

### Pavelló Mies van der Rohe

*Avda Marquès de Comillas (93 423 40 16/ www.miesbcn.com). Metro Espanya.* **Open** 10am-8pm daily. **Admission** €3.50; €2 concessions; free under-18s. **Credit** (shop only) MC, V. **Map** p341 B9.

Mies van der Rohe built the Pavelló Alemany (German Pavilion) for the 1929 Universal Exhibition not as a gallery, but as a simple reception space, sparsely furnished by his trademark 'Barcelona Chair'. The pavilion was a founding monument of modern rationalist architecture, with its flowing floor plan and a revolutionary use of materials. Though the original pavilion was demolished afterthe exhibition, a fine replica was built on the same site in 1986, the simplicity of its design setting off the warm tones of the marble and expressive Georg Kolbe sculpture in the pond.

### Poble Espanyol

*Avda Marquès de Comillas (93 325 78 66/ www.poble-espanyol.com). Metro Espanya.* **Open** 9am-8pm Mon; 9am-2am Tue-Thur; 9am-4am Fri, Sat; 9am-midnight Sun. **Admission** €7.50; €5.50 concessions; €15 family ticket; free under-7s. **Credit** AmEx, MC, V. **Map** p341 A9/B9.

Built for the 1929 Universal Exhibition, this mock Spanish Village is a minimally cheesy architectural theme park with reproductions of traditional buildings from every region in Spain. The cylindrical towers at the entrance are copied from the walled city of Ávila and lead on to a typical Castilian main square from which visitors can explore a tiny white-

## War then peace?

Dominating Barcelona's skyline from its hilltop perch, Montjuïc castle is a military fortress rather than a turreted Cinderella fantasy, and its past is no prettier than its appearance. A star-shaped pentagon with enormous moats and bastions, it was initially built as a fort in the 17th century, but the castle was turned against the city when it was used to bombard the Catalans into submission in 1842 and also as a prison, torture centre and execution site for political dissidents during the dictatorship. As a potent symbol of repression, its owner-ship is a loaded issue: the castle (part of which is now the Museu Militar, *see p119*) was partially ceded to Barcelona by Franco in 1960, but the ongoing fight for its complete handover has recently become a political hot potato.

Prime minister José Luis Zapatero promised the restitution of the castle to the city in June 2004 and negotiations were going smoothly until the very last minute in February 2006, when José Bono, the Spanish Minister of Defence, imposed three conditions: the presence of a military detachment, the maintenance of some military antennae and, most gallingly, to keep the castle's Spanish flag flying alongside the Catalan flag because 'Montjuïc is Spanish territory'.

Barcelona flatly rejected this proposal, but the situation was saved from stalemate when Bono announced his resignation in April 2006. Barely able to conceal its glee, the Barcelona town council was confident the deal would soon be in the bag, although negotiations have yet to reach a final agreement at the time of writing. One possible plan floated for the castle's future is to counter its unsavoury history by turning it into an institution devoted to peace studies; Zapatero has already promised a homage to Lluís Companys, president of the Generalitat, who was executed at the castle in 1940, in the form of a tombstone engraved with his final words: 'Peace, justice and love.'

Most visitors to the castle go for its spectacular views over Barcelona, and the parkland surrounding the castle has been extensively relandscaped to make the area more accessible. If you don't mind an uphill walk, the most impressive way to reach the castle is by the port-crossing cable car.

Inside, the military museum is little visited by tourists, despite having got rid of its gift shop selling unsavoury fascist paraphernalia and stashing away its Franco statue (the last in the city). The museum collection itself is excellent: ancient armour, broadswords and muskets share the immense space with displays of rare pistols, early automatic weapons and military paintings. The castle's long hall features some 23,000 lead pieces depiciting a full 1920s Spanish battalion in marching formation, while in room 19 there is a miniature model of the military display in Madrid for the proclamation of Juan Carlos I as king in 1975. A strangely incongruous sight among these displays of Spanish military might is the room of medieval Jewish tombstones from the former cemetery site, a quiet reminder that the days of 'peace, justice and love' have been few and far between.

Poble Espanyol. *See p120.*

washed street from Arcos de la Frontera in Andalusia, then on to the 16th-century House of Chains from Toledo, and so on. There are numerous bars and restaurants, a flamenco *tablao* and more than 60 shops selling Spanish crafts although prices are not especially cheap. Outside, street performers recreate bits of Catalan and Spanish folklore; there are children's shows and The Barcelona Experience, an audio-visual presentation (available in English). The Poble is unmistakably aimed at tourists, but it has been working to raise its cultural profile, as with the Fundació Fran Daurel collection of contemporary art, hosting music festivals such as B-estival (*see p220*) and the recent opening of a quality gallery of Iberian arts and crafts.

### Telefèric de Montjuïc

*Estació Funicular, Avda Miramar (93 443 08 59/ www.tmb.net). Metro Paral·lel then funicular.* **Open** 9am-10pm daily. **Admission** €1.20. **No credit cards**. **Map** p341 C11/D11.
The Telefèric, with its four-person cable cars, is closed for renovations until spring 2007, after which it will extend down to the port. In the meantime there is a replacement bus service (11am-7.15pm daily, every 15mins), running from the funicular to the castle.

## Poble Sec & Paral·lel

**Poble Sec**, the name of the neighbourhood between Montjuïc and the Avda Paral·lel, means 'dry village', which is explained by the fact that it was 1894 before the thousands of poor workers who lived on the flanks of the hill celebrated the installation of the area's first water fountain (which is still standing in C/Margarit).

The name Avda Paral·lel derives from the fact that it coincides exactly with 41° 44' latitude north, one of Ildefons Cerdà's more eccentric conceits. The avenue was the prime centre of Barcelona nightlife in the first half of the 20th century, and was full of theatres, nightclubs and music halls. A statue on the corner with C/Nou de la Rambla commemorates Raquel Meller, a legendary star of the street who went on to equal celebrity around the world. She now stands outside Barcelona's notorious live-porn venue, the Bagdad. Apart from this, most of the area' cabarets have disappeared, although there are still theatres and cinemas along the Paral·lel. A real end of an era came in 1997, when El Molino, the most celebrated of the avenue's traditional, vulgar old music halls, suddenly shut up shop. It seemed to symbolise the change that had come to the neighbourhood – now the Poble Sec's main cultural space is the starkly modern **Ciutat de Teatre** theatre complex (*see p266*).

Today, Poble Sec is a friendly, working-class area of quiet, relaxed streets and leafy squares. On the stretch of the Paral·lel opposite the city walls, three tall chimneys stand amid modern office blocks. They are all that remains of the Anglo-Canadian-owned power station known locally as *La Canadença* ('The Canadian'). This was the centre of the city's largest general strike, in 1919. Beside the chimneys an open space has been created and dubbed the **Parc de les Tres Xemeneies** (Park of the Three Chimneys).

Towards the Paral·lel are some distinguished Modernista buildings, which local legend has maintained were built for *artistas* from the nude cabarets by their rich sugar daddies. At C/Tapioles 12 is a beautiful, narrow wooden Modernista door with particularly lovely writhing ironwork, while at C/Elkano 4 is La Casa de les Rajoles, which is known for its peculiar mosaic façade.

### Refugi Antiaeri del Poble Sec

*C/Nou de la Rambla 175 (93 319 02 22). Metro Paral·lel.* **Open** (guided tour & by appointment only) 11am 1st Sat of mth. *Call to book* 10am-2pm, 4-6pm Mon, Tue, Tue, Thur, Fri. **Admission** €3.20; free under-7s. **Meeting place** Biblioteca Francesc Boix, C/Blai 34. **No credit cards**. **Map** p341 D11.
About 1,500 Barcelona civilians were killed during the air bombings of the Civil War, a fact that the government long silenced. As Poble Sec particularly suffered the effects of bombing, a large air-raid shelter was built partially into the mountain at the top of C/Nou de la Rambla; this is one of some 1,200 in the entire city. Now converted into a museum, it is worth a visit. The guided tour takes 90 minutes.

# The Eixample

True grid.

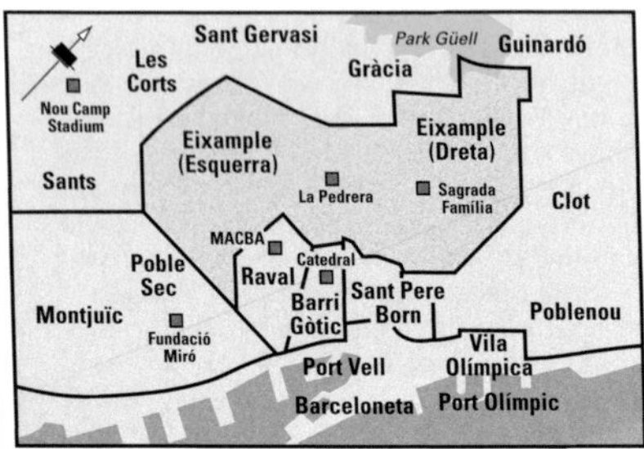


Sightseeing

## Maps pp338-341

In contrast to the narrow alleyways and winding streets that characterise much of Barcelona, the vast, grid-patterned Eixample ('enlargement') almost seems out of character with the rest of the city. It's no surprise then that the Eixample was a late 19th-century extension to Barcelona but has now become home to some of the city's most elegant buildings, swankiest shops and some of its most well-heeled residents. The grid system can leave visitors somewhat confused from one road to the next, so it's useful to take the plush bisecting avenue of **Passeig de Gràcia** as a reference point. Incorporating some of the city's classiest boutiques, it's the showpiece of the **Quadrat D'Or** (Golden District) – a square mile between C/Muntaner and C/Roger de Flor that contains 150 protected buildings, many of them Modernista gems.

The Eixample was Europe's first expansive work of urban planning, necessitated by the chronic overcrowding of old Barcelona which, by the 1850s, had become rife with cholera and crime, hemmed in by its much-hated city walls. It was eventually decided the walls must come down, whereupon the Ajuntament held a competition to build an ambitious urban zone in the open land outside them. It was won by municipal architect Antoni Rovira i Trias, whose popular fan-shaped design can be seen at the foot of the statue of him in the Gràcia *plaça* that bears his name. The Madrid government, however, vetoed the plan, instead choosing the work of social idealist Ildefons Cerdà, a military engineer.

Cerdà's plan, reflecting the rationalist mindset of the era, was for a grid of uniform blocks to stretch from Montjuïc to the Besòs river, criss-crossed by two diagonal highways, Avda Diagonal and Avda de la Meridiana, and meeting at Plaça de les Glòries, which was to become the hub of the modernised city. The ideas were utopian: each block was to be built on only two sides and be no more than two or three storeys high; the remainder of the space was to contain gardens, their leafy extremes joining at the crossroads and forming a quarter of a bigger park. Of course, when it came to the practical business of filling the grid (which never became as extensive as planned), many of the engineer's plans were ignored by developers. A concrete orchard of gardenless, fortress-like, six or seven-storey blocks grew up instead.

Fortunately, the period of construction coincided with Barcelona's golden age of architecture: the city's bourgeoisie employed Gaudí, Puig i Cadafalch, Domènech i Montaner and the like to build them ever more daring townhouses in an orgy of avant-garde one-upmanship. The result is extraordinary but can be tricky to negotiate on foot; the lack of open spaces and similarity of many streets can leave you somewhat confused. The city council, meanwhile, is attempting to make the area more liveable: in 1985 the ProEixample was set up to reclaim some of the courtyards proposed in Cerdà's plans so that everybody living in the area should be able to find an open space within 200 metres (650 feet) of their home. Two of the better examples are the palm-fringed mini-beach around the **Torre de les Aigües** water tower (C/Llúria 56) (*see p227*) and the patio at **Passatge Permanyer** (C/Pau Claris 120).

The overland railway that once ran down C/Balmes has traditionally been the dividing line of the neighbourhood. Either side of this, the fashionable **Dreta** ('Right') contains the most distinguished Modernista architecture, the main museums and the shopping avenues. The **Esquerra** ('Left'), meanwhile, was built slightly later; it contains some great markets and some less well-known Modernista sights.

## The Dreta

Trees, ceramic benches and idle ramblers make the **Passeig de Gràcia** feel like a calmer Champs-Elysées; this is one of the most pleasant walks in the city. From Plaça Catalunya, you can stroll all the way up the grand street, which, at the point it meets

The shimmering **Casa Batlló**. *See p124.*

Diagonal, joins straight on to **Gran de Gràcia** which leads you straight through the heart of Gràcia. The Eixample's central artery is notable for its magnificent wrought-iron **lamp-posts** by Pere Falqués and for its **pavement**, hexagonal slabs decorated with intertwining nautilus shells and starfish. First designed for the patio of Gaudí's **Casa Batlló** (*see p124*), they were repeated in his aquatic-looking apartment block **La Pedrera** (*see p127*) before covering the whole boulevard.

The Passeig de Gràcia has always been the Eixample's most desirable address, and it's where you'll find Modernisme's most flamboyant townhouses. For a primer, head to the block known as **Manzana de Discòrdia**, which boasts buildings designed by the era's three great architects. Its name is a pun on *manzana,* which in Spanish means both 'block' and 'apple', and alludes to the fatal choice of Paris when judging which of a group of divine beauties would win the golden Apple of Discord.

If the volume of camera-toting admirers is anything to go by, the fairest of these Modernista lovelies is undoubtedly Gaudí's **Casa Batlló**, permanently illuminated by flashbulbs. The runners-up are Domènech i Montaner's **Casa Lleó Morera**, a decadently melting wedding cake of a building (partially defaced during the architecturally delinquent Franco era) on the corner of C/Consell de Cent at No.35, and Puig i Cadafalch's **Casa Amatller** (No.41). Built for a chocolate baron, the latter has a stepped Flemish pediment covered in shiny ceramics and looking good enough to eat, along with a gallery of medieval grotesques sculpted by Eusebi Arnau.

Other buildings on the Passeig de Gràcia hit parade also impress. The **Casa Casas** (No.96) was once home to Ramon Casas, one of the city's greatest painters, and now houses design emporium Vinçon. The first floor of the building has a Modernista interior; there's also a patio overlooking La Pedrera's rear façade. In addition, Enric Sagnier's neo-Gothic **Cases Pons i Pascual** (Nos.2-4) is worth a look, while the **Casa Vídua Marfà** (No.66) has one of the most breathtakingly sumptuous entrance halls in the Eixample.

The other great building of the Modernisme movement is, of course, the towering mass of the **Sagrada Família** (*see p128*). Whether you love it or hate it (and George Orwell called it 'one of the most hideous buildings in the world'), it has become the city's emblem and sine qua non of Barcelona tourist itineraries. A less famous masterpiece in the shape of Domènech i Montaner's **Hospital de la Santa Creu i Sant Pau** (*see p125*) bookends the northerly extreme of the Avda Gaudí. A few blocks further south, there's more welcome space in the **Parc de l'Estació del Nord** and, on C/Marina, one of Barcelona's weirdest museums, the macabre **Museu de Carrosses Fúnebres** (*see p127*).

The streets above the Diagonal boast some striking Modernista buildings, such as Puig i Cadafalch's 1901 **Palau Macaya** at Passeig de Sant Joan 108. Other buildings of interest include the tiled **Mercat de la Concepció** on C/Aragó, designed by Rovira i Trias, and the fairy-tale castle-esque **Casa de les Punxes** designed yet again by the prolific Joan Puig i Cadafalch. Moving down C/Roger de Llúria, you pass the **Casa Thomas** and the **Palau Montaner**, both designed by Lluis Domenech i Montaner, and on reaching C/Casp, you arrive at one of Gaudí's lesser-known works, the **Casa Calvet**. Over to the right is the egg-topped **Plaça de Braus Monumental**, but the city's

# And the winner is...

It's a dream come true for the tourist office. In July 2005 the city's UNESCO gongs almost doubled: Barcelona, which already boasts more World Heritage Sites than Paris or Florence, was declared to have nine sites of 'outstanding cultural importance to the common heritage of humankind'.

Inevitably, the hand of Antoni Gaudí was behind most of these and, indeed, all of the recent additions. Those buildings to be added are the emblematic dragon-like **Casa Batlló** (*see p124*); the undervisited **Casa Viçens** townhouse (*see p132*) in Gràcia; the crypt and Nativity Façade of the **Sagrada Família** (*see p128*) and the extraordinary crypt of the **Colònia Güell** in Santa Coloma de Cervelló (*see p109*). These join the architectural pantheon that already includes three Gaudí creations – **La Pedrera** apartment block (*see p127; photo right*), the neo-Gothic **Palau Güell** (*see p109*) in the Raval and the fantastical **Park Güell** (*see p132*) in Gràcia.

Gaudí is not the only architect whose work has been recognised by the committee as 'to represent a masterpiece of human creative genius', however, and his Modernista contemporary, Lluis Domènech i Montaner is recognised for two stunning buildings too: the colourfully decorated **Palau de la Música Catalana** (*see p101*) in the Born, and what must surely be the world's most beautiful hospital, the **Hospital de la Santa Creu i Sant Pau** (*see p125*).

last active bullring is now mainly frequented by tour buses from the Costa Brava; out of season, it hosts tatty travelling circuses. Not far from the bullring, at C/Lepant 150, are the ultra-modern premises of **L'Auditori de Barcelona**, where all major classical concerts are held (*see p260*). Back towards the bullring and just off the main drag is what is considered to be Modernisme's first ever building, designed by Domènech i Montaner, now housing the **Fundació Antoni Tàpies** (*see p125*). The area is rich in museums: over the other side is the **Museu Egipci de Barcelona** (*see p127*), next door to the eclectic collection in the **Fundació Francisco Godia** (*see p125*).

## Casa Àsia

*Avda Diagonal 373 (93 238 73 37/www.casaasia.es). Metro Diagonal.* **Open** 10am-8pm Mon-Sat; 10am-2pm Sun **Admission** free. **Map** p338 G6.

This much-needed Asian contribution to Barcelona's cultural scene is located in another of modernist architect Puig i Cadafalch's creations, the Palau Baró de Quadras. The Casa Àsia cultural centre acts as both an exhibition space and ambassador for all things in Asia and the Asian Pacific. Recent exhibits include rare documentary films and photos on the anniversary of Hiroshima and Tarun Chopras's photo exposition on life in urban India. It also features an oriental café on the ground floor and an excellent multimedia library on the fourth floor that offers visitors the opportunity to hire CDs, DVDs and books on presentation of their passport or ID card. Forthcoming events for 2007 include a series of critical readings on Krishnamurti, courses on Japanese culture and even Chinese astrology. *See also p232* **Barcelona woos Bollywood**.

## Casa Batlló

*Passeig de Gràcia 43 (93 216 03 06/www.casabatllo.es). Metro Passeig de Gràcia.* **Open** 9am-8pm daily. **Admission** €16.50; €13.20 concessions; free under-7s. **Credit** V. **Map** p338 G8.

For many the Casa Batlló, sitting in the same block as masterworks by his two closest rivals, Puig i Cadafalch and Domènech i Montaner, is the most telling example of Gaudí's pre-eminence over his Modernista contemporaries. Opinions differ on what the building's remarkable façade represents, most particularly its polychrome shimmering walls, its sinister skeletal balconies and its hump-backed scaley roof. Some say it's the spirit of carnival, others a Costa Brava cove. However, the most popular theory, which takes into account the architect's deeply patriotic feelings, is that it depicts Sant Jordi and the dragon: the idea being that the cross on top is the knight's lance, the roof is the back of the beast, and the balconies below are the skulls and bones of its hapless victims.

The building was constructed for textile tycoon Josep Batlló between 1902 and 1906, and the chance to explore the interior (at a cost) offers the best opportunity of understanding how Gaudí, sometimes considered the lord of the bombastic and overblown, was really the master of tiny details, from the ingenious ventilation in the doors to the amazing natural light reflecting off the azure walls of the inner courtyard and the way in which the brass window handles are curved so as to fit precisely the shape of a hand. An apartment within has now opened to the public, and, more recently, access has been granted to the attic and roof terrace: the whitewashed arched rooms of the top floor, originally used for washing and hanging clothes, are among the master's most atmospheric spaces. **Photo** *p123*.

### Fundació Antoni Tàpies

*C/Aragó 255 (93 487 03 15/www.fundaciotapies.org). Metro Passeig de Gràcia.* **Open** 10am-8pm Tue-Sun. **Admission** €4.20; €2.10 concessions; free under-16s. **Credit** (over €6) MC, V. **Map** p338 G8.

Antoni Tàpies, Barcelona's most celebrated living artist, set up the Tàpies Foundation in this, the former Montaner i Simon publishing house, in 1984, dedicating it to the study and appreciation of contemporary art. It is now a cultural centre and museum dedicated to the work and life of the man himself, with temporary exhibitions, symposiums, lectures, films and lecture sessions. Tàpies promptly crowned the building with a glorious tangle of aluminium piping and ragged metal netting (*Núvol i Cadira*, or *Cloud and Chair*), which was a typically contentious act by an artist whose work, a selection of which is on permanent display on the top floor of the gallery, has caused controversy since he burst on the scene in the 1960s. 'Give the organic its rights,' he proclaimed, and thus devoted his time to making the seemingly insignificant significant, using materials such as mud, string, rags and cardboard to build his rarely pretty but always striking works. The building remains one of the earliest examples of modernism and was the first building in the Eixample to integrate industrial typology by combining exposed brick and iron. 2007 starts with a new exhibition focusing on social- and political-themed posters designed by Tàpies, including those published in resistance to Franco's dictatorship.

### Fundació Francisco Godia

*C/València 284 pral (93 272 31 80/www.fundacionfgodia.org). Metro Passeig de Gràcia.* **Open** 10am-8pm Mon, Wed-Sun. Closed Aug. **Admission** €4.50; €2.10 concessions; free under-5s. **Credit** (shop only) MC, V. **Map** p338 G7.

Godia's first love was motor racing: he was a Formula 1 driver for Maserati in the 1950s. His second love, though, was art, which explains how, since 1999, this private museum has come to house an interesting selection of medieval religious art, historic Spanish ceramics and modern painting. Exhibits date all the way from the 12th century and are largely medieval sculptures and paintings. Highlights include Alejo de Vahía's medieval *Pietà* and a baroque masterpiece by Lucio Giordano, along with some outstanding Romanesque sculptures and 19th-century oil paintings by Joaquín Sorolla and Ramon Casas. The modern collection has works by Miró, Julio González, Tàpies and Manolo Hugué. The beginning of 2007 sees the conclusion of an exhibition of previously unseen artwork from the Middle Ages up until the First Renaissance, including medieval ceramics and religious iconography.

### Hospital de la Santa Creu i Sant Pau

*C/Sant Antoni Maria Claret 167 (93 291 90 00/www.santpau.es). Metro Hospital de Sant Pau.* **Map** p339 L5/L6.

White-coated doctors mingle with recovering patients and camera-wielding tourists in the green and pleasant grounds of Domènech i Montaner's 'garden city' of a hospital, a collection of pavilions abundantly adorned with the medieval flourishes that characterise the architect's style. The hospital, now a UNESCO World Heritage Site, is composed of 18 pavilions and connected by an underground tunnel system spreading over nine blocks in the north-east corner of the Eixample. It is set at a 45° angle from the rest of Ildefons Cerdà's grid system,

Hospital de la Santa Creu i Sant Pau.

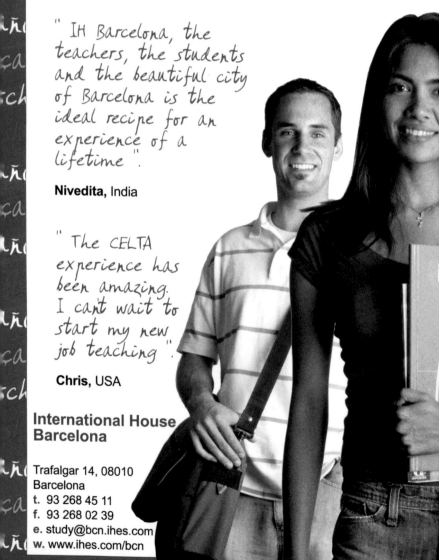

so that it catches more sun: Domènech i Montaner built the hospital very much with its patients in mind, convinced that aesthetic harmony and pleasant surroundings were good for the health. Unfortunately, the old buildings don't entirely suit the exigencies of modern medicine: by 2006 much of the patient care will be phased out and moved to the Nou Sant Pau, which is a recently inaugurated white monstrosity of a building on the north side of the hospital grounds, leaving the old complex to be used mainly for educational and research purposes.

The public enjoy free access to the grounds, and guided tours (€5) are held daily between 10.15am and 1.15pm. Call 902 076 621 or consult www.rutadelmodernisme.com to check which languages are offered at which times.

### Museu de Carrosses Fúnebres

*C/Sancho de Avila 2 (93 484 17 10). Metro Marina.* **Open** 10am-1pm, 4-6pm Mon-Fri; 10am-1pm Sat, Sun (wknds call to check). **Admission** free. **Map** p343 K10.

Finding this, still surely the most obscure and macabre museum in Barcelona, hasn't got any easier. You'll need to ask at the reception desk of the Ajuntament's funeral service and, eventually, a security guard will take you down to a perfectly silent and splendidly shuddersome basement housing the world's biggest collection of funeral carriages and hearses dating from the 18th century through to the 1950s. There are ornate baroque carriages and more functional Landaus and Berlins, and a rather wonderful '50s silver Buick. The white carriages were designed for children and virgins, and there's a windowless black-velour mourning carriage for the forlorn mistress. The vehicles are manned by ghoulish dummies dressed in period gear whose eyes follow you around the room, making you glad of that security guard.

### Museu Egipci de Barcelona

*C/València 284 (93 488 01 88/www.fundclos.com). Metro Passeig de Gràcia.* **Open** 10am-8pm Mon-Sat; 10am-2pm Sun. **Admission** *Museum* €6; €5 concessions; free under-5s. **Credit** AmEx, MC, V. **Map** p338 G7.

Two floors of this museum showcase a well-chosen collection spanning 3,000 years of Nile-drenched culture. Exhibits include religious statuary, such as the massive baboon heads used to decorate temples, everyday copper mirrors or alabaster headrests, and oddly moving infant sarcophagi. Outstanding pieces include some painstakingly matched fragments from the Sixth Dynasty Tomb of Iny, a bronze statuette of the goddess Osiris breastfeeding her son Horus, and mummified cats, baby crocodiles and falcons. Another highlight is a 5,000-year-old bed, which still looks comfortable enough to sleep in. On Friday and Saturday nights, there are dramatic reconstructions of popular themes, such as the mummification ritual or the life of Cleopatra, for which reservations are essential. The museum is owned by renowned Egyptologist Jordi Clos, and entrance is waived for guests staying at the Hotel Claris, also owned by Clos. If you go on Fridays at 5pm, there are free guided tours of the museum by English-speaking guides.

### Museu del Perfum

*Passeig de Gràcia 39 (93 216 01 21/www.museodelperfume.com). Metro Passeig de Gràcia.* **Open** 10.30am-1.30pm, 4.30-8pm Mon-Fri; 10.30am-2pm Sat. **Admission** €5; €3 concessions. **Map** p338 G8.

In the back room of the Regia perfumery sits this collection of nearly 5,000 scent bottles, cosmetic flasks and related objects. The collection is divided into two parts. One shows all manner of unguent vases and essence jars in chronological order, from a tube of black eye make-up from predynastic Egypt to Edwardian atomisers and a prized double-flask pouch that belonged to Marie Antoinette. The second section exhibits perfumery brands such as Guerlain and Dior; some are in rare bottles, among them a garish Dalí creation for Schiaparelli and a set of rather disturbing golliwog flasks by Vigny Paris. The museum's most recent addition includes a collection of 19th-century perfume powder bottles and boxes.

### Parc de l'Estació del Nord

*C/Nàpols (no phone). Metro Arc de Triomf.* **Open** 10am-sunset daily. **Admission** free. **Map** p343 J10/K10.

Otherwise known as Parc Sol i Ombra (meaning 'Sun and Shadow'), this slightly shabby space is perked up by the three pieces of art in glazed blue ceramic by New York sculptor Beverley Pepper. Along with a pair of incongruous white stone entrance walls, *Espiral Arbrat* (*Tree Spiral*) is a spiral bench set under the cool shade of lime-flower trees and *Cel Caigut* (*Fallen Sky*) is a 7m-(23ft-) high ridge rising from the grass, while the tiles recall Gaudí's *trencadís* smashed-tile technique.

### La Pedrera (Casa Milà)

*Passeig de Gràcia 92-C/Provença 261-5 (902 400 973/www.caixacatalunya.es). Metro Diagonal.* **Open** 10am-8pm daily. **Admission** €8; €4.50 concessions; free under-12s. **Guided tours** (in English) 4pm Mon-Fri. **Credit** MC, V. **Map** p338 G7.

The last secular building designed by Antoni Gaudí, the Casa Milà (popularly known as La Pedrera, 'the stone quarry') has no straight lines and is a stupendous and daring feat of architecture, the culmination of the architect's experimental attempts to recreate natural forms with bricks and mortar (not to mention ceramics and even smashed-up cava bottles). Now a UNESCO World Heritage Site, it looks like it might have been washed up on the shore, its marine feel complemented by Jujol's tangled balconies, doors of twisted kelp ribbon, sea-foamy ceilings and interior patios as blue as a mermaid's cave. When it was completed in 1912, it was so far ahead of its time that the woman who financed it as her dream home, Roser Segimon, became the laughing stock of the city – hence the ugly 'stone quarry' tag. Its rippling

# **Walk on** Modernisme

**Duration**: 1 hour 30 minutes.
The tour begins with the splendid **Casa Comalat** by Valeri i Pupurull, which has the unusual distinction of two façades. The front (Avda Diagonal 442) has 12 voluptuously curvy stone balconies complete with wrought-iron railings, while the more radical back façade (C/Còrsega 316) is a colourful harlequin effect with curiously bulging green-shuttered balconies. Almost opposite on Avda Diagonal is Puig i Cadafalch's sombre **Palau Baró de Quadras**, now home to the **Casa Àsia** exhibition space (*see p124*), and his **Casa Terrades** (Nos.416-20), known colloquially as La Casa de les Punxes ('House of Spikes') for its spiky turrets and gables. Look out for the individual entrances and staircases built for each of the family's three daughters.

Turn down C/Girona and right on C/Mallorca to see Barenys i Gambús's fantasy **Casa Dolors Xiró** at No.302, followed by two Domènech i Montaner masterpieces: the **Casa Josep Thomas** (No.291) and the **Palau Ramón de Montaner** (No.278), which now houses offices.Double back a few steps and turn downhill on to C/Roger de Llúria. On the corner at No.80 is Fossas i Martinez's spike-topped **Casa Villanueva** and, just opposite at No.82, striking columns of stained-glass windows decorate Granell i Manresa's **Casa Jaume Forn**. Just a few steps further down C/Roger de Llúria at No.85, the **Queviures Murrià** grocery retains original decoration by painter Ramon Casas and, on the right at No.74, is the lovely stained glass and floral decoration of the **Farmàcia Argelaguet**, one of many Modernista pharmacies in the area.

Retrace your steps up to the corner again, and turn right on to C/València. Continue for three blocks, and at No.339 is a stunning corner building by Gallissà i Soqué: the **Casa Manuel Llopis i Bofill**. The façade is a blend of red brick and white sgraffito by Josep Maria Jujol, while the neo-Mudéjar turrets, ceramics and keyhole shapes take their inspiration from the Alhambra in Granada.

Backtrack a block and turn left on C/Girona. At No.86 is the **Casa Isabel Pomar**, Rubió i Bellver's eccentric sliver of a building that squeezes in a neo-Gothic pinnacle, lively red brickwork and a staggered gallery window on the first floor. This contrasts with the spacious feel of Viñolas I Llosas's **Casa Jacinta Ruiz** (No.54). Glass galleries are a characteristic feature of Modernista houses, but here the jutting windows form the pivot for the design and give a three-dimensional effect. Further down, turn right on Gran Via, to another

façade, bereft of straight lines, led local painter Santiago Rusiñol to quip that a snake would be a better pet than a dog for the inhabitants of the building. But, La Pedrera has become one of Barcelona's best-loved buildings, and is adored by architects for its extraordinary structure: it is supported entirely by pillars, without a single master wall, allowing the vast asymmetrical windows of the façade to invite in great swathes of natural light.

There are three exhibition spaces. The first-floor art gallery hosts free exhibitions of eminent artists, while upstairs is dedicated to a finer appreciation of Antoni Gaudí: you can visit a reconstructed Modernista flat on the fourth floor, with a sumptuous bedroom suite by Gaspar Homar, while the attic, framed by parabolic arches worthy of a Gothic cathedral, holds a museum dedicated to an insightful overview of Gaudí's career.

Informative titbit-filled guided tours in English are run daily at 4pm. Best of all is the chance to stroll on the roof of the building amid its *trencadís*-covered ventilation shafts: their heads are shaped like the helmets of medieval knights, which led the poet Pere Gimferrer to dub the spot 'the garden of warriors'.

### Sagrada Família

*C/Mallorca 401 (93 207 30 31/www.sagradafamilia.org). Metro Sagrada Família.* **Open** *Mar-Sept* 9am-8pm daily. *Oct-Feb* 9am-6pm daily. **Admission** €8; €5 concessions; €3 7-10 years; free under-6s. Lift to spires €2. **Credit** (shop only) MC, V. **Map** p339 K7.

The Temple Expiatori de la Sagrada Família manages to be both Europe's most fascinating building site and Barcelona's most emblematic creation. At times breathtaking, at other times grotesque, it deserves the hubbub of superlatives that float around it, though not all are positive. George Orwell berated the 1930s anarchists for 'showing bad taste by not blowing it up'. They did, however, manage to set fire to Gaudí's intricate plans and models for the building, which was his final project before his death. Ongoing work is a matter of some conjecture and controversy, with the finishing date expected to be somewhere within the region of 25-30 years. It was hoped the masterpiece would be completed in 2026 to coincide with the 100th anniversary of Gaudí's death, although this now seems unlikely. This is, however, somewhat of an improvement on the prognosis in the 1900s, when construction was expected to last

extravagant Modernista pharmacy, **Farmàcia Vilardell** (No.650), and Salvat i Espasa's elegant **Casa Ramon Oller** (No.658).

From there, turn left down C/Pau Claris and left again on to C/Casp. At No.22, **Casa Llorenç Camprubí**, Ruiz i Casamitjana's intricate stonework is a delight, but the real treasure lies a little further along at No.48. Gaudí's **Casa Calvet** may look somewhat conventional, but closer study reveals characteristic touches: the columns framing the door and gallery allude to the bobbins used in the owner's textile factory, while the wrought iron depicts a mass of funghi surrounded by stone flowers. The corbel underneath the gallery interweaves the Catalan coat of arms with Calvet's initial 'C'.

Turn right down C/Girona on to C/Ausiàs Marc, one of the most notable streets of the Quadrat d'Or. At Nos.37-39 are the **Cases Tomàs Roger** by prominent Modernista architect Enric Sagnier, combining graceful arches with beautifully restored sgraffito. At No.31 is the **Farmàcia Nordbeck**, with la dark wood and stained-glass exterior. The last stop before reaching Plaça Urquinaona is the **Casa Manuel Felip** (No.20), designed by a little-known architect, Fernández i Janot, with sumptuous stonework and slender galleries connecting the first two floors.

several hundred years; advanced computer technology is now being used to shape each intricately designed block of stone offsite to speed up the process. Nevertheless, the church's first mass has been put back a year and is now scheduled for Sant Josep's day (19 March) 2008, 126 years after its foundation stone was laid.

Gaudí, who is said to have once joked 'My client is not in a hurry', is buried beneath the nave; he dedicated more than 40 years to the project, the last 14 exclusively. Many consider the crypt, the apse and the Nativity façade, which were completed in his lifetime, as the most beautiful elements of the church. The latter, facing C/Marina, looks at first glance as though some careless giant has poured candlewax over a Gothic cathedral, but closer inspection shows every protuberance to be an intricate sculpture of flora, fauna or human figure, combining to form an astonishingly moving stone tapestry depicting scenes from Christ's life. The other completed façade, the Passion, which faces C/Sardenya, is more austere, with vast diagonal columns in the shape of bones and haunting sculptures by Josep Maria Subirachs. Japanese sculptor Etsuro Sotoo has chosen to adhere more faithfully to Gaudí's intentions, and has fashioned six more modest musicians at the rear of the temple, as well as the exuberantly coloured bowls of fruit to the left of the Nativity façade.

An estimated five million tourists visit the Sagrada Família each year, more than two and a half million of them paying the entrance fee. A combination of ticket revenues and charitable donations exclusively fund the continued construction of the project. A ticket allows you to wander through the interior of the church, a marvellous forest of vast columns laid out in the style of the great Gothic cathedrals, with a multi-aisled central nave crossed by a transept. The central columns are fashioned of porphyry, perhaps the only natural element capable of supporting the church's projected great dome; destined to rise 170m (558ft), this will make the Sagrada Família once again the highest building in the city. There is also a range of tours available in several different languages.

An admission ticket also gives visitors access to the museum in the basement, offering insight into the history of the construction, original models for sculptural work and the chance to watch sculptors working at their plaster-cast models through a large window. But

## In the detail *Balconies of Barcelona*

As part of the city council's campaign to beautify Barcelona in preparation for 1992's Olympic Games, it was decided to camouflage some of its unsightly party walls. One of the most spectacular projects, undertaken by French cooperative La Cité de la Creation, is *Balcons de Barcelona*, on the corner of Plaça de la Hispanitat with C/Enamorats. A stunning 450sq m (19,380sq ft) trompe l'oeil painting of balconies spread over six floors, from which a galaxy of Catalan luminaries and famous former Barcelona residents look out over the square.

Columbus is up on the terrace, above Modernista artist Santiago Rusiñol on the fifth. On the third floor are poet Joan Maragall, inventor of the submarine Narcís Monturiol, and anarchist and radical educator Francesc Ferrer; while clustered on the second floor are former presidents of the Generalitat Francesc Macià, Lluís Companys and Josep Tarradellas, next to Gaudí, and the creator of the Eixample, Ildefons Cerdà.

The next storey down holds a potpourri of talent, from artists Joan Miró and Picasso to cellist Pau Casals, flamenco singer Carmen Amaya and poet Jacint Verdaguer. Music-hall star Raquel Meller stands alongside novelist Mercè Rodoreda on the ground floor.

the highlight of any trip is a vertiginous hike up one of the towers (you can also take a lift), which affords unprecedented views through archers' windows.

## The Esquerra

The left side of the Eixample was always a lot less fashionable than the right, and eventually became the setting for the sort of city services the bourgeoisie didn't want ruining the upmarket tone of their new neighbourhood. A huge slaughterhouse was built at the eastern edge of the area (and was only knocked down in 1979, when it was replaced by the **Parc Joan Miró** *see below*). Also here is the busy **Hospital Clínic**, an ugly, functional building that covers two blocks between C/Corsega and C/Provença; on C/Entença, a little further out, was the grim, star-shaped **La Model** prison. It has been relocated out of town and replaced by subsidised houses and offices. The huge **Escola Industrial** on C/Comte d'Urgell, formerly a Can Batlló textile factory, was redesigned in 1909 as a centre to teach workers the methods used in the burgeoning textile industry. The nearby Avda de Sarrià is home to **FilmoTeca** (*see p229*) at No.33, an arthouse cinema subsidised by the local government that shows everything from re-runs of Alfred Hitchcock movies to Led Zeppelin concerts. A programme with the screening schedule for the month is available at the entrance.

Not all the civic buildings are so grim. The central **Universitat de Barcelona** building on Plaça Universitat, completed in 1872, is an elegant construction with a pleasant cloister-like garden. Two markets bustle with locals rather than tourists: the **Ninot**, by the hospital, and **Sant Antoni**, on the edge of the Raval, which turns into a second-hand book market on Sunday mornings. The Esquerra also contains a number of Modernista jewels, such as the **Casa Boada** (C/Enric Granados 106) and the **Casa Golferichs** (Gran Via 191), built in 1901 by Joan Rubio i Bellver, one of Gaudí's main collaborators. Beyond the hospital, the Esquerra leads to **Plaça Francesc Macià**, centre of the city's business district and a gateway to the Zona Alta.

### Parc Joan Miró (Parc de l'Escorxador)

*C/Tarragona (no phone). Metro Espanya or Tarragona.* **Open** 10am-sunset daily. **Map** p341 C8.

The demolition of the old slaughterhouse provided much-needed parkland, although there's little greenery here. The rows of stubby palms and grim cement lakes are dominated by a library and Miró's towering phallic sculpture *Dona i Ocell* (*Woman and Bird*).

# Gràcia & Other Districts

Fierce identities and facelifts.

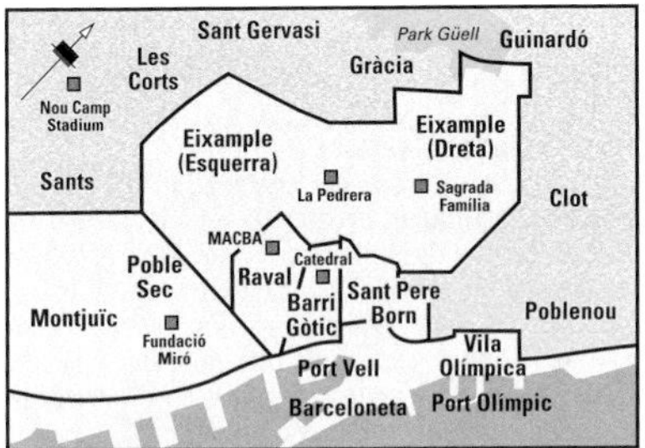


## Maps pp338-339

It's hard to imagine that little more than 100 years ago, Gràcia was still a town in its own right, proudly and distinctly separate from the increasing urban sprawl of Barcelona. The construction of the Eixample in 1850, however, soon encroached on to the open fields between the Old City and Gràcia and, by 1897, Barcelona had pretty much swallowed up the fiercely independent conurbation. Gràcia's nominal independence was rendered pretty much irrelevant and amid howls of protest from its populace, the town was annexed. Since then, dissent has been a recurring feature in Gràcia's history: streets boast names such as Llibertat, Revolució and Fraternitat, and for the 64 years preceding the Civil War, there was a satirical political magazine called *La Campana de Gràcia*, named after the famous bell in Plaça Rius i Taulet.

The political activity came from the effects of rapid industrial expansion. This was a mere village in 1821, centred around the 17th-century convent of Santa Maria de Gràcia, with just 2,608 inhabitants. By the time of annexation, however, the population had risen to 61,935, making it the ninth largest town in Spain and a hotbed of Catalanism, republicanism and anarchism. Today, few vestiges of radicalism remain: sure, the *okupa* squatter movement inhabits a relatively high number of buildings in the area, but private property developers and the local council have been waging a campaign to dislodge them with increasing success. Nevertheless, it's still not uncommon to see the odd anarchist protest in a *plaça* while you sup on a *café con leche*, and some bars still arrange political gatherings and documentary screenings. The local **Verdi** and **Verdi Park** cinemas (*see p230*) sometimes get involved with a selection of politically charged and socially conscious films (and all in their original languages).

Nowadays, the *barri* is a favourite hangout of the city's bohemians. There are many workshops and studios here and the numerous small, unpretentious bars are often frequented by artists, designers and students. However, Gràcia really comes into its own for a few days in mid August, when its famous *festa major* grips the entire city (*see p221*). Residents spend months in advance preparing startlingly original home-made street decorations, and all of Barcelona converges on the tiny *barri* to party. Open-air meals are laid on for the residents of Gràcia, bands are dotted on every street, films are screened in *plaças* and bars, while old-timers sing along to *habaneros* (shanties) and resident squatters pogo to punk bands. Of Gràcia's many squares, **Plaça de la Virreina** is perhaps the most

Gaudí's **Casa Vicens**. *See p132.*

Sightseeing

relaxing spot, silvered by the chairs and tables of bar terraces, and overlooked by Sant Joan church. **Plaça del Sol** is busier: home to half a dozen bars and restaurants, it's the main focus of the drinking crowd and the anarchist contingent. Other favourites include **Plaça Rius i Taulet**, dominated by a 33-metre (108-foot) bell tower; the leafy **Plaça Rovira** (with a bronze statue of the neighbourhood's pensive planner, Antoni Rovira i Trias, sitting on a bench, his rejected plan for the Eixample at his feet); the rather rougher **Plaça del Diamant**, which was the setting for the Mercè Rodoreda novel *The Time of the Doves* (and with a peculiar sculpture to prove as much; *see p134* **Chronicle of a life retold**); and **Plaça John Lennon**, where the Beatles singer is remembered with a huge model of the *Give Peace a Chance* single.

Much of Gràcia was built in the heyday of Modernisme, something evident in the splendid main drag, C/Gran de Gràcia. Many of the buildings are rich in nature-inspired curves and fancy façades, but the finest example is Lluís Domènech i Montaner's **Casa Fuster** at No.2, recently reopened as a luxury hotel (*see p76*). Gaudí's disciple Francesc Berenguer was responsible for much of the civic architecture, most notably the **Mercat de la Llibertat** (Barcelona's oldest covered market and still proudly adorned with Gràcia's old coat of arms) and the old **Casa de la Vila** (Town Hall) in Plaça Rius i Taulet.

However, the district's most overwhelming Modernista gem is one of Gaudí's earliest and most fascinating works, the **Casa Vicens** (*see p41*) of 1883-8, hidden away in C/Carolines. The building is a private residence and thus not open to visitors, but the castellated red brickwork and colourful tiled exterior with Indian and Mudéjar influences should not be missed; notice, too, the spiky wrought-iron leaves on the gates. And one of Gaudí's last works, the stunning **Park Güell** (*see below*), is a walk away, across the busy Travessera de Dalt and up the hill. It's well worth the effort (there are even escalators at certain points): not only for the architecture, but also for the magnificent view of Barcelona and the sea.

While Gràcia may have lost its independence, its small and winding streets have lost none of their charm, and this often overlooked area is one of the most rewarding to explore and escape from the hustle and bustle of the city.

### Fundació Foto Colectània

*C/Julián Romea 6, D2 (93 217 16 26/ www.colectania.es). FGC Gràcia.* **Open** 11am-2pm, 5-8.30pm Mon-Fri. **Admission** free. **Map** p338 F5.

This private foundation is dedicated to the promotion of photography and collections of major Spanish and Portuguese photographers from the 1950s. It also has an extensive library of Spanish and Portuguese photography books, including out-of-print ones.

### Park Güell

*C/Olot (Casa-Museu Gaudí 93 219 38 11). Metro Lesseps/bus 24, 25.* **Open** *Park* 10am-sunset daily. *Museum* Apr-Sept 10am-7.45pm daily. Oct-Mar 10am-5.45pm daily. **Admission** *Park* free. *Museum* €4; €3 concessions; free under-9s. **Credit** (shop only) MC, V. **Map** p339 H2/H3/J2/J3.

Gaudí's brief for this spectacular project was to emulate the English garden cities so admired by his patron Eusebi Güell (hence the spelling of 'park'): to lay out a self-contained suburb for the wealthy, but also to design the public areas. The original plan was for the plots to be sold off and the properties themselves subsequently designed by other architects. The idea never took off – perhaps because it was too far from the city, perhaps because it was too radical – and the Güell family donated the park to the city in 1922.

It is a real fairy-tale place; the fantastical exuberance of Gaudí's imagination is breathtaking. The visitor was previously welcomed by two life-sized mechanical gazelles – a typically bizarre religious reference by Gaudí to medieval Hebrew love poetry – although these were unfortunately destroyed in the Civil War. The two gatehouses that do still remain were based on designs the architect made earlier for the opera *Hansel and Gretel*, one of them featuring a red and white mushroom for a roof. From here, walk up a splendid staircase flanked by multicoloured battlements, past the iconic mosaic lizard sculpture, to what would have been the marketplace. Here, 100 palm-shaped pillars hold up a roof, reminiscent of the hypostyle hall at Luxor. On top of this structure is the esplanade, a circular concourse surrounded by undulating benches in the form of a sea-serpent decorated with shattered tiles – a technique called *trencadís*, which was actually perfected by Gaudí's overshadowed but talented assistant Josep Maria Jujol. Like all Gaudí works, these seats are by no means a case of design over function; they are as comfortable as park benches come, and no wonder – it's thought that Gaudí used the mould of a woman's buttocks to achieve the curvature of the bench surface.

The park itself, now a UNESCO World Heritage Site, is magical, with twisted stone columns supporting curving colonnades or merging with the natural structure of the hillside. The park's peak is marked by a large cross and offers an amazing panorama of Barcelona and the sea. Gaudí lived for a time in one of the two houses built on the site (which was, in fact, designed by his student Berenguer). It's since become the Casa-Museu Gaudí; guided tours, some in English, are given. The best way to get to the park is on the 24 bus; if you go via Lesseps metro, be prepared for a steep uphill walk. **Photos** *p133*.

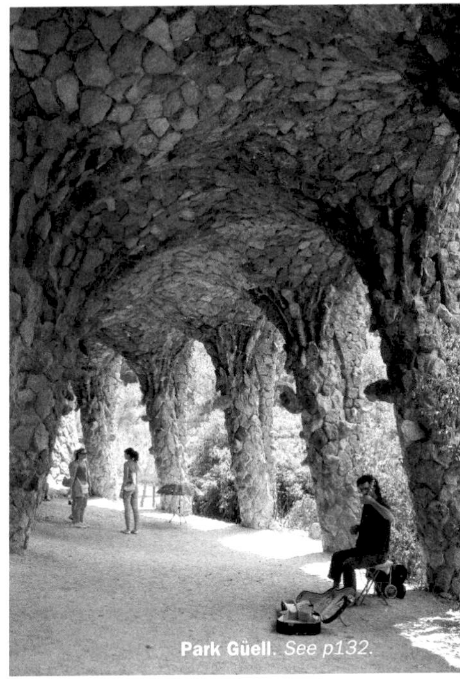

**Park Güell**. *See p132.*

## Sants

For many arriving by bus or train, Estació de Sants is their first uninspiring sight of Barcelona. Most take one look at the forbidding **Plaça dels Països Catalans**, which looks like it was designed with skateboard tricks in mind, and get the hell out of the area. Over the next few years, however, the station is set for a long-overdue facelift as the new high-speed Barcelona-France train terminal is built (due to be finished in 2008). Still, there's no avoiding the fact that Sants (meaning 'Saints') is not exactly the most picturesque part of town – and be warned, the station is particularly popular among the city's bag-snatchers – but for those with time to spare, it's worth a few hours' investigation for historic, if not aesthetic, reasons. Mid August is one of the better times to visit as, immediately following the *festa major de Gràcia*, Sants launches its own, albeit lower-key, version, and the *barri* sheds its drab industrial coat in favour of street parties, decorations and music.

Sants was originally built to service those who arrived after the town gates had shut at



## Chronicle of a life retold

In 1962 the Catalan writer Mercè Rodoreda was just beginning to gain prominence as a budding novelist. The Spanish Civil War and its repression of the Catalan language saw Rodoreda go into exile, and it was 20 years before she finally produced the book many knew she was capable of writing. *La Plaça del Diamant* (inexplicably translated in English as *The Time of The Doves*) was published in 1962, when Rodoreda was 53, and has since become the most revered of all Catalan novels.

Mirroring much of Rodoreda's own life, *La Plaça del Diamant* is the story of a young woman, Natalia, who, without the guidance of a mother, narrates through internal monologues the trials and tribulations of her life set against the outbreak of the Civil War and its aftermath. (It's at a dance in Plaça Diamant that Natalia meets her first husband). It's a langorous, perceptive and almost fantastical read that has since been adapted for the stage, screen and televison. It also put Plaça Diamant on the map.

Today, a statue by Xavier Medina-Campeny titled *La Colometa*, Natalia's nickname in the novel, stands in the square. But the book, which Gabriel García Márquez describes as the greatest post-war Spanish novel, has most certainly embedded the *plaça* with a deep and lasting cultural heritage of its own.

Gràcia has always been a hotbed of anarchist agitation and anti-authoritarianism. If there's a crustier modern-day symbol of that rebellion, then for many young anarchists, socialists, Catalan nationalists and squatters it would be Plaça Diamant. Some years ago the square marched out of its membership of the La Federació de Festa Major and it has been the centre for the alternative fiesta ever since. During the fiestas the square becomes the focal point of every wannabe punk, heavy metal rock band and left-wing Catalan singer-songwriters shouting it out to the establishment.

During the last weekend in January, Plaça Diamant, along with Plaça Virreina and Plaça Rius i Taulet, hosts the Mallorcan festival of Sant Antoni, which celebrates the traditional agricultural harvest with *foguerons* (bonfires) and fire-spitting devils. After the noise dies down, hundreds of people descend on the square to eat Mallorcan products, throw a *butifarra* (Catalan sausage) on the fire and generally make merry.

2006 marked a turning point for Plaça Diamant – a major renovation included the planting of new trees and the addition of more benches, a kids' play area, a replica fountain and extra lighting; it also saw the official opening of the bomb shelter built in 1939 against Franco's raids. The work was long overdue; for many years it was arguably the ugliest and most run-down of Gràcia's numerous squares. Even *La Colometa* was touched up – she's got a spanking new perch to rest on. Rodoreda would have approved.

9pm, with inns and blacksmiths there to cater for latecomers. In the 19th century, though, it became the industrial motor of the city. Giant textile factories such as the **Vapor Vell** (which is now a library), **Parc de l'Espanya Industrial** (now a futuristic park; *see below*), and **Can Batlló** (still a workplace) helped create the bourgeois wealth that the likes of Eusebi Güell spent on the Modernista dream homes that still grace more salubrious areas of the city. The inequality did not go unnoticed. The *barri* has been a hotbed of industrial action: the first general strike in Catalonia broke out here in 1856, only to be violently put down by the infamous General Zapatero (known as the 'Tiger of Catalonia'). The left-wing nationalist ERC party, which now shares power in the Generalitat, was also founded here in 1931, at C/Cros 9.

Most routes of interest start and end at the hub of the *barri*, **Plaça de Sants**, in the middle of C/Sants high street, where Jorge Castillo's *Ciclista* statue is also to be found. Also worth checking out are the showy Modernista buildings at Nos.12, 130, 145 and 151, all designed by local architect Modest Feu.

Opera fans may also be interested in visiting one of Sant's oldest streets, the tiny commercial thoroughfare of C/Galileu, where tenor José Carreras was born at No.1 in 1946. And, just off C/de Sants is C/Sant Medir, the starting point for the *barri*'s **Festa de Sant Medir**, held in mid March every year, where local representatives canter around in horse-drawn carriages throwing caramel sweets to children.

Returning back to Plaça de Sants and taking C/Olzinelles, you'll find the quaint Plaça Bonet i Mixi and the **Parroquia de Santa Maria del Sants** church, from which it is believed the *barri* got its name. This is the focal point for locals around Easter, when Semana Santa (Holy Week) grips Spain. Following C/Sants in the direction of Montjuïc, the road name suddenly changes to C/Creu Coberta, an old Roman road once known as the Cami d'Espanya, 'the road to Spain'. Following C/Creu Coberta further, you'll find the large, lively and colourful **Mercat d'Hostafrancs**, where there's also a stop for the tourist bus. Further along still is C/Sant Roc, where you will find the Modernista-inspired **Església de l'Angel Custodi**. The road finally ends at the huge roundabout of **Plaça d'Espanya**, nestled at the foot of Montjuïc and home to the city's main exhibition centre, **La Fira**. The huge circular arena here is the old **Las Arenas bullring**, which is slowly being transformed into a commercial shopping centre to a plan by Richard Rogers Partnership and Alonso Balaguer.

### Parc de l'Espanya Industrial

*Passeig de Antoni (no phone). Metro Sants-Estació.* **Open** 10am-sunset daily. **Map** p341 B7.

In the 1970s the owners of the old textile factory announced their intention to use the land to build blocks of flats. The neighbourhood, though, put its collective foot down and insisted on a park, which was eventually built in 1985. The result is a puzzling space, designed by Basque Luis Peña Ganchegui, with ten watchtowers overlooking a boating lake with a statue of Neptune in the middle, flanked by a stretch of mud used mainly for walking dogs. By the entrance kids can climb over Andrés Nagel's *Drac*, a massive and sinister black dragon sculpture.

## Les Corts

Row after row of apartment blocks now obscure any trace of the rustic origins of Les Corts (literally, 'cowsheds' or 'pigsties'), as the village itself was swallowed up by Barcelona in the late 19th century. But search and you will find **Plaça de la Concòrdia**, a quiet square dominated by a 40-metre (131-foot) bell tower. This is an anachronistic oasis housing the civic centre **Can Deu**, formerly a farmhouse and now home to a great bar that hosts jazz acts every other Thursday. The area is much better known, though, for what happens every other weekend, when tens of thousands pour in to watch FC Barcelona, whose **Nou Camp** (*see below*) takes up much of the west of the *barri*. At night, the area is the haunt of transvestite prostitutes and their kerb-crawling clients.

### Nou Camp – FC Barcelona

*Avda Arístides Maillol, access 9, Les Corts (93 496 36 00/08/www.fcbarcelona.com). Metro Collblanc or Palau Reial.* **Open** 10am-6.30pm Mon-Sat; 10am-2pm Sun. **Admission** €5.30; €3.70 concessions; free under-5s. *Guided tour* €9.50; €6.60 concessions. **Credit** (shop only) MC, V. **Map** p337 A3/4.

The Nou Camp, where FC Barcelona has played since 1957, is one of football's great stadiums, a vast cauldron of a ground that holds 98,000 spectators. That's a lot of noise when the team is doing well, and an awful lot of silence when it isn't. If you can't get there on match day (and you can usually pick up tickets if you try) but love the team, it's worth visiting the club museum. The excellent guided tour of the stadium takes you through the players' tunnel to the dugouts and then, via the away team's changing room, on to the President's box, where there is a replica of the European Cup, which the team won at Wembley in 1992. The club museum commemorates those glory years, making much of the days when the likes of Kubala, Cruyff, Maradona, Koeman and Lineker trod the hallowed turf, with pictures, video clips and souvenirs spanning the century that has passed since the Swiss business executive Johan Gamper first founded the club. *See also p270.*

## Tibidabo & Collserola

During the devil's temptation of Christ, he took Jesus to the top of a mountain and offered him all before him, with the words '*tibi dabo*' (Latin for 'To thee I will give'). This gave rise to the name of the dominant peak of the Collserola massif, with its sweeping views of the whole of the Barcelona conurbation stretching out to the sea: quite a tempting offer, given the present-day price of the city's real estate. The ugly, neo-Gothic **Sagrat Cor** temple crowning the peak has become one of the city's most recognisable landmarks; it's clearly visible for miles around. At weekends, thousands of people head to the top of the hill in order to whoop and scream at the **funfair** (*see p226*). Nowadays the only one in Barcelona, it's been running since 1921 and has changed little since: the rides are creaky and old-fashioned, but very quaint. More recent additions to it include a marionette show and the first freefall ride in Spain, where visitors are dropped 38 metres (125 feet) in 2.8 seconds. Within the funfair is also the **Museu d'Autòmats**, a fine collection of fairground coin-operated machines from the early 1900s.

Getting up to the top on the clanking old **Tramvia Blau** (Blue Tram; *see p139*) and then the **funicular railway** (*see below*) is part of the fun; between the two is Plaça Doctor Andreu, a great place for an alfresco drink. For the best view of the city, either take a lift up Norman Foster's communications tower, the **Torre de Collserola** (*see below*), or up to the *mirador* at the feet of Christ atop the Sagrat Cor.

The vast **Parc de Collserola** is more a series of forested hills than a park; its shady paths through holm oaks and pines open out to spectacular views. It's most easily reached by FGC train on the Terrassa-Sabadell line from Plaça Catalunya or Passeig de Gràcia, getting off at **Baixador de Vallvidrera** station. A ten-minute walk from the station up into the woods (there's an information board just outside the station) will take you to the **Vil·la Joana**, an old *masia* covered in bougainvillea and containing the **Museu Verdaguer** (93 204 78 05, open 10am-2pm, 4-8pm Tue-Sat, 10am-3pm Sun, admission €3, free 1st Sat of mth) dedicated to 19th-century Catalan poet Jacint Verdaguer, who used this as his summer home. Just beyond the Vil·la Joana is the park's **information centre** (93 280 35 52, open 10am-4pm daily), which has basic maps for free and more detailed maps for sale. Most of the information is in Catalan, but staff are helpful.

**Monestir de Pedralbes.** *See p137.*

### Funicular de Tibidabo

*Plaça Doctor Andreu to Plaça Tibidabo (93 211 79 42). FGC Avda Tibidabo then Tramvia Blau.* **Open** As funfair (*see p226*), but starting 30mins earlier. **Tickets** *Single* €2; €1.50 concessions. *Return* €3; €2 concessions. **No credit cards**.

This art deco vehicle offers occasional glimpses of the city below as it winds through the pine forests up to the summit. The service has been running since 1901, but only according to a complicated timetable. If it's not running, take the FGC line from Plaça de Catalunya to Peu del Funicular, get the funicular up to Vallvidrera Superior, and then catch the 111 bus to Tibidabo (a process not half as complicated as it sounds). Alternatively, it's nearly an hour's (mostly pleasant) hike up from Plaça Doctor Andreu for those who are feeling energetic.

### Torre de Collserola

*Ctra de Vallvidrera al Tibidabo (93 406 93 54/ www.torredecollserola.com). FGC Peu Funicular then funicular.* **Open** *Apr-June, Sept* 11am-2.30pm, 3.30-7pm Wed-Fri; 11am-7pm Sat, Sun. *July, Aug* 11am-2.30pm, 3.30-8pm Mon-Fri; 11am-8pm Sat, Sun. *Oct-Mar* 11am-2.30pm, 3.30-6pm Mon-Fri; 11am-6pm Sat, Sun. **Admission** €5; €4 concessions; free under-4s. **Credit** AmEx, MC, V.

Just five minutes' walk from the Sagrat Cor is its main rival and Barcelona's most visible landmark, Lord Foster's communications tower, built in 1992 to transmit images of the Olympics around the world. Visible from just about everywhere in the city and always flashing at night, the tower is loved and hated in equal measure. Those who don't suffer from vertigo attest to the stunning views of Barcelona and the Mediterranean from the top.

## Zona Alta

**Zona Alta** (the 'upper zone', or 'uptown') is the name given collectively to a series of smart neighbourhoods including **Sant Gervasi**, **Sarrià**, **Pedralbes** and **Putxet** that stretch out across the lower reaches of the Collserola hills. The handful of tourist sights found here include the **Palau Reial**, with its gardens and museums, the **Museu de Ceràmica** and **Museu de les Arts Decoratives** (*see p138*), the **CosmoCaixa** science museum (*see below*) and the remarkable **Pedralbes Monastery** (*see below*), which is still well worth a visit despite the fact that its selection of religious paintings from the **Thyssen-Bornemisza collection** has been moved to the revamped Museu Nacional d'Art de Catalunya (MNAC; *see p119*). The centre of Sarrià and the streets of old Pedralbes around the monastery retain a flavour of the sleepy country towns these once were.

For many downtown residents, the Zona Alta is a favourite place to relax in the parks and gardens that wind into the hills. At the end of Avda Diagonal, next to the functional Zona Universitària (university district), is the **Jardins de Cervantes**, with its 11,000 rose bushes, the striking *Dos Rombs* (Two Rhombuses) sculpture by Andreu Alfaro and, during the week, legions of picnicking students. From the park, a turn back along the Diagonal towards Plaça Maria Cristina and Plaça Francesc Macià will take you to Barcelona's main business and shopping district. Here is the small **Turó Parc**, a semi-formal garden good for writing postcards amid inspirational plaques of poetry. The **Jardins de la Tamarita**, at the foot of Avda Tibidabo, is a pleasant dog-free oasis with a playground, while further up at the top of the tramline is the little-known **Parc de la Font de Racó**, full of shady pine and eucalyptus trees. A fair walk to the north-east, an old quarry has been converted into a swimming pool, the **Parc de la Creueta del Coll** (*see p138*).

Gaudí fans are rewarded by a trip up to the **Pavellons de la Finca Güell** at Avda Pedralbes 15; its extraordinary and rather frightening wrought-iron gate features a dragon into whose gaping mouth the foolhardy can fit their heads. Once inside the gardens, via the main gate on Avda Diagonal, make sure to look out for a delightful fountain designed by the master himself. Across near Putxet is Gaudí's relatively sober **Col·legi de les Teresianes** (C/Ganduxer 85-105), while up towards Tibidabo, just off Plaça Bonanova, rises his remarkable Gothic-influenced **Torre Figueres** or **Bellesguard**.

### CosmoCaixa

*C/Teodor Roviralta 47-51 (93 212 60 50/www.fundacio.lacaixa.es). Bus 60/FGC Avda Tibidabo then Tramvia Blau (see p139).* **Open** 10am-8pm Tue-Sun. **Admission** €3; €2 concessions; free under-3s. *Planetarium* €2; €1.50 concessions; free under-3s. **Credit** AmEx, DC, MC, V.

The long-awaited revamp of the Fundació La Caixa's science museum and planetarium, to create the biggest in Europe, has been only partially successful. First off, its size is somewhat misleading: apart from a couple of new (and, admittedly, important) spaces – the Flooded Forest, a reproduction of a corner of Amazonia complete with flora and fauna, and the Geological Wall – the collection has not been proportionally expanded to fit the new building. A glass-enclosed spiral ramp runs down an impressive six floors, but actually represents quite a long walk to reach the main collection five floors down.

It is here that temporary exhibitions are housed too. From here, it's on to the Matter Room, which covers 'inert', 'living', 'intelligent' and then 'civilised' matter: in other words, natural history. However, for all the fanfare made by the museum about taking exhibits out of glass cases and making scientific theories accessible, many of the displays still look very dated. Written explanations are often impenetrable, containing phrases such as 'time is macroscopically irreversible', and making complex those concepts that previously seemed simple.

On the plus side, the installations for children are excellent: the Bubble Planetarium pleases kids aged three to eight, and the wonderful Clik (ages three to six) and Flash (seven to nine) introduce children to science through games. Toca Toca! ('Touch Touch') educates children on which animals and plants are safe and which to avoid. One of the real highlights, for both kids and adults, is the hugely entertaining sound telescope outside on the Plaça de la Ciència.

Upcoming exhibitions for 2007 include a foray into biodiversity and the Música, Más Música exhibition, which looks at the links between science and music. The museum also recently opened the Planeta Tierra section in collaboration with the European Space Agency, which looks at environmental preservation projects funded by the La Caixa Foundation and features lots of interesting interactive videos.

### Monestir de Pedralbes

*Baixada del Monestir 9 (93 203 92 82). FGC Reina Elisenda.* **Open** 10am-2pm Tue-Sun. **Admission** €4; €2.50 concessions; free under-12s. Free 1st Sun of mth. **Credit** (shop only) AmEx, DC, MC, V.

In 1326 the widowed Queen Elisenda of Montcada used her inheritance to buy this land and build a convent for the Poor Clare order of nuns, which she soon joined. The result is a jewel of Gothic architecture with an understated single-nave church with fine stained-glass windows and a beautiful three-storey 14th-century cloister. The place was out of bounds to the general public until 1983, when the nuns, a closed order, opened it up as a museum in the mornings (when they escape to a nearby annexe).

The site offers a fascinating insight into life in a medieval convent, taking you through its kitchens, pharmacy and refectory, with its huge vaulted ceiling. To one side is the tiny chapel of Sant Miquel, with murals dating to 1343 by Ferrer Bassa, a Catalan painter and student of Giotto. In the former dormitory next to the cloister is a selection of objects belonging to the nuns. Among them are illuminated books, furniture and items reflecting the artistic and religious life of the community. **Photo** *p136.*

### Museu de Ceràmica & Museu de les Arts Decoratives

*Palau Reial de Pedralbes, Avda Diagonal 686 (93 280 16 21/www.museuceramica.bcn.es/ www.museuartsdecoratives.bcn.es). Metro Palau Reial.* **Open** 10am-6pm Tue-Sat; 10am-3pm Sun. **Admission** *Combined admission with Museu Tèxtil* €3.50; €2 concessions; free under-16s. Free 1st Sun of mth. **No credit cards. Map** p337 A2.

These two collections – accessible, along with the Textile Museum (*see p101*), on the same ticket – are housed in the august Palau Reial; originally designed for the family of Eusebi Güell, Gaudí's patron, it was later used as a royal palace but was reclaimed as public property when the Spanish Republic was declared in 1931. The Museum of Decorative Arts is informative and fun, and looks at the different styles informing the design of artefacts in Europe since the Middle Ages, from Romanesque to art deco and beyond. A second section is devoted to post-war Catalan design of objects as diverse as urinals and man-sized inflatable pens.

The Ceramics Museum is equally fascinating, showing how Moorish ceramic techniques from the 13th century were developed after the Reconquista with the addition of colours (especially blue and yellow) in centres such as Manises (in Valencia) and Barcelona. Two 18th-century murals are of sociological interest: one, *La Xocolatada*, shows the bourgeoisie at a garden party, while the other, by the same artist, depicts the working classes at a bullfight in the Plaza Mayor in Madrid. Upstairs is a section showing 20th-century ceramics, including a room dedicated to Miró and Picasso. The two museums, along with the Textile Museum and several smaller collections, are to be merged in the future in a Museu de Disseny (Design Museum) as part of the cultural overhaul of the Plaça de les Glòries.

### Parc de la Creueta del Coll

*C/Mare de Déu del Coll (no phone). Metro Penitents.* **Open** 10am-sunset daily. **Admission** free.

Created from a quarry in 1987 by Josep Matorell and David Mackay, the team that went on to design the Vila Olímpica, this park boasts a sizeable swimming pool complete with a 'desert island' and a sculpture by Eduardo Chillida: a 50-ton lump of curly granite suspended on cables, called *In Praise of Water*. Three people were injured by it in 1998 when the cables snapped: make sure you view from a safe distance.

## **In the detail** Meridian Arc

When Ildefons Cerdà conceived his plan for the Eixample (*see p122*), the area known as Glòries was to be its focus. Nowadays it's little more than a traffic hub; a convoluted spaghetti junction surrounded by charmless high-rise blocks. The council has, however, made attempts to spruce it up and restore its importance in recent years, with the addition of cultural centres such as the Teatre Nacional de Catalunya (*see p265*) and L'Auditori (*see p260*) and architectural projects such as Jean Nouvel's Torre Agbar (*see p139*). In the middle of the roundabout, below the level of the traffic, is the Plaça de les Glories, a small, scruffy park, undistinguished but for the **Arc del Meridià**.

This iron sculpture commemorates the study carried out by Jean-Baptiste Delambre and Pierre-Françoise Méchain, with the aid of Catalan scientists, in the creation of the metric system at the end of the 18th century. The pair spent six years measuring the Paris meridian between Dunkirk and Barcelona, from which they calculated the circumference of the earth and defined the metre as one 40-millionth of that.

The sculpture is built to scale (40 metres/131 feet) and represents the orography – hills, mountains and valleys – of the line between here and Dunkirk. In theory it sits along the meridian itself, although this has been hard to prove.

### Tramvia Blau

*Avda Tibidabo (Plaça Kennedy) to Plaça Doctor Andreu (93 318 70 74/www.tramvia.org/tramviablau). FGC Avda Tibidabo.* **Open** *Mid June-mid Sept* 10am-8pm daily. *Mid Sept-mid June* 10am-6pm Sat. **Frequency** 20mins. **Tickets** €2.10 single; €3.10 return. **No credit cards.**

*Barcelonins* and tourists have been clanking 1,225m (4,000ft) up Avda Tibidabo in the 'blue trams' since 1902. In the winter months, when the tram only operates on weekends, a rather more prosaic bus takes you up (or you can walk it in 15 minutes).

## Poblenou & beyond

**Poblenou** has been many things in its time: a farming community, a fishing port, the site of heavy industry factories and a trendy post-industrial suburb. Now it's also a burgeoning technology and business district, snappily tagged 22@. Many of the factories around here closed down in the 1960s; these days, buildings that have not already been torn down or converted into office blocks are used as schools, civic centres, workshops, art studios, open spaces or, increasingly, coveted lofts.

The main drag, the pedestrianised **Rambla de Poblenou**, dating from 1886, is a much better place for a relaxing stroll than its busy central counterpart, and gives this still-villagey area a heart. Meanwhile, a bone's throw away, the city's oldest and most atmospheric cemetery, the **Cementiri de l'Est**, shows that most *barcelonins* spend their death as they did their life: cooped up in large high-rise blocks. Some were able to afford roomier tombs, many of which were built at the height of the romantic-Gothic craze at the turn of the 19th century. A leaflet or larger guide (€15) sold at the entrance suggests a route around 30 of the more interesting monuments.

Nearby, **Plaça de les Glòries** finally seems ready to fulfil its destiny. The creator of the Eixample, Ildefons Cerdà, hoped that the square would become the new centre of the city, believing his grid-pattern blocks would spread much further north than they did and shift the emphasis of the city from west to east. Instead, it became little more than a glorified roundabout on the way out of town. Nowadays, it's best-known for its huge commercial shopping complex and the bustling market **Mercat de las Encants** (open Mon, Wed, Fri, Sat from 8.30am), which has everything from kitchen sinks to dodgy DVDs. From here, a wide and relatively quiet stretch of Diagonal is filled with joggers, cyclists and in-line skaters as it leads towards the sea.

Now, with the hugely phallic **Torre Agbar** to landmark the area from afar, the *plaça* has

Funky **Pont de Calatrava**. *See p140.*

also become the gateway to Diagonal Mar and the new commercial and leisure area on the shoreline, known as the Fòrum, after the event in 2004 for which it was created. The tower, designed by French architect Jean Nouvel and owned by the Catalan water board, has been a bold and controversial project. A concrete skyscraper with a domed head and a glass façade, it's not unlike London's famed Gherkin. Nouvel says it's been designed to reflect the Catalan mentality: the concrete represents stability and severity; the glass, openness and transparency. At 144 metres (472 feet), it's Barcelona's third highest building (behind the two Olympic towers) and contains no fewer than 4,400 multiform windows. Remarkably, it has no air-conditioning: the windows let the breeze do the job. Nouvel claims Gaudí as the inspiration for the multicoloured skin – it has 4,000 LED lights that change colour at night – of a building that has already polarised public opinion and come to dominate the district.

One breath of fresh air in the rather stagnant area north of here is the **Parc del Clot**. Just beyond it is the **Plaça de Valentí Almirall**, with the old town hall of Sant Martí and a 17th-century building that used to be the Hospital de Sant Joan de Malta somewhat at odds with the buildings that have mushroomed around them.

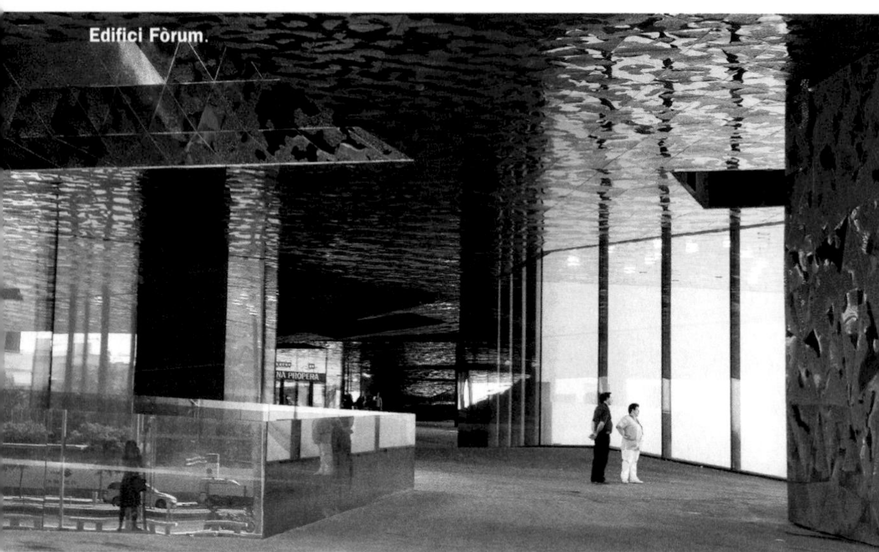

Edifici Fòrum.

Further north, up C/Sagrera, the entrance to a former giant truck factory now leads to the charming **Parc de la Pegaso**. The area also has a fine piece of recent architecture, the supremely elegant **Pont de Calatrava** bridge. Designed by Santiago Calatrava, it links to Poblenou via C/Bac de Roda.

## Diagonal Mar

Many detractors of the **Fòrum** (*see below*), which was the six-month cultural symposium that was held in 2004, felt that its real purpose was to regenerate this post-industrial wasteland. Certainly, a large element of its legacy are the enormous conference halls and hotels that it is hoped will eventually draw many wealthy business clients into the city, together with a scarcely believable increase in real-estate values. More recently, the Fòrum has benefited the city's youth, with its wide-open spaces providing an excellent venue for two of the Barcelona's biggest music festivals, Primavera Sound (*see p219*) and Summercase (*see p220*).

If you're approaching from the city, the first sign of this resurgent *barri* is **Parc de Diagonal Mar**, containing an angular lake decorated with scores of curling aluminium tubes and vast Gaudían flowerpots. Designed by the late Enric Miralles (he of Scottish Parliament fame), the park may not be to most *barcelonins*' taste, but the local seagull population has found it to be an excellent roosting spot. Just over the road from here is the Diagonal Mar shopping centre, a still woefully undervisited three-storey mall of high-street chains, cinemas and the grand Hotel Princesa, a triangular skyscraper designed by architect, designer, artist and local hero Oscar Tusquets.

The **Edifici Fòrum**, a striking blue triangular construction by Herzog and de Meuron (responsible for London's Tate Modern), is the centrepiece of the €3-billion redevelopment. The remainder of the money was spent on the solar panels, marina, new beach and the **Illa Pangea**, an island 60 metres (197 feet) from the shore, reachable only by swimming. It's all a far cry from the local residential neighbourhood, **Sant Adrià de Besòs**, a poor district of tower blocks that includes the notorious La Mina neighbourhood, a hotbed of drug-related crime. It's hoped that the new development will help regenerate the area, best known for its Feria de Abril celebrations in April (*see p218*), the Andalucían community's version of the more famous annual celebrations in Seville. There's also a fine *festa major* in **Badalona**, just up the coast, in May, in which a large effigy of a devil is burned on the beach in a shower of fireworks.

## Horta & around

Horta, which is to the far west of the blue metro line, is a picturesque little village that remains aloof from the city that swallowed it up in 1904. Originally a collection of farms (its name means 'market garden'), the *barri* is still peppered with old farmhouses, such as **Can Mariner** on C/Horta, dating back to 1050, and the medieval **Can Cortada** at the end of C/Campoamor, which is now a huge restaurant located in beautiful grounds. An abundant water supply also made Horta the place where much of the city's laundry was done: a whole community of *bugaderes* (washerwomen) lived and worked in lovely C/Aiguafreda, where you can still see their wells and open-air stone washtubs.

To the south, joined to Gràcia by Avda Mare de Déu de Montserrat, the steep-sided neighbourhood of **Guinardó**, with its steps and escalators, consists mainly of two big parks. **Parc del Guinardó**, a huge space designed in 1917 (making it Barcelona's third oldest park) full of eucalyptus and cypress trees, is a relaxing place to escape. The smaller **Parc de les Aigües** shelters the neo-Arabic **Casa de les Altures** from 1890, Barcelona's most eccentrically beautiful council building.

The **Vall d'Hebron** is a leafy area located just above Horta in the Collserola foothills. Here, formerly private estates have been put to public use; among them are the chateau-like **Palauet de les Heures**, now a university building. The area was one of the city's four major venues for the Olympics and is rich in sporting facilities, including public football pitches, tennis courts, and cycling and archery facilities at the **Velòdrom**. It's also the home to one of Barcelona's major concert venues. Around these environs there are several striking examples of street sculpture, including Claes Oldenburg's *Matches* and Joan Brossa's *Visual Poem* (in the shape of the letter 'A'). The area also conceals the rationalist **Pavelló de la República** (*see p43*) and the zany **Parc del Laberint** (*see below*), dating back to 1791 and surrounded by a modern park. More modern still is the **Ciutat Sanitària**, Catalonia's largest hospital; a good proportion of *barcelonins* first saw the light of day here.

### Parc del Laberint

*C/Germans Desvalls, Passeig Vall d'Hebron (no phone). Metro Mundet.* **Open** 10am-sunset daily. **Admission** €2; €1.20 concessions Mon, Tue, Thur-Sat; free under-6s, over-65s. Free Wed, Sun.

In 1791 the Desvalls family, owners of this marvellously leafy estate, hired Italian architect Domenico Begutti to design scenic gardens set around a cypress maze, with a romantic stream and a waterfall. The mansion may be gone (replaced with a 19th-century Arabic-influenced building), but the gardens are remarkably intact, shaded in the summer by oaks, laurels and an ancient sequoia. Best of all, the maze, an ingenious puzzle that still intrigues those brave enough to try it, is also still in use. Nearby stone tables provide a handy picnic site. On paying days, last entry is one hour before sunset.

### Pavelló de la República

*Avda Cardenal Vidal y Barraquer (93 428 54 57). Metro Montbau.* **Open** 9am-8pm Mon-Fri. **Admission** free.

This functionalist building houses a university library specialising in materials from the Civil War and the clandestine republican movement that operated during Franco's dictatorship. It was built in 1992 as a facsimile of the emblematic rationalist pavilion of the Spanish Republic designed by Josep Lluís Sert for the Paris Exhibition in 1937 and later to hold Picasso's *Guernica*. It makes an interesting juxtaposition to Oldenburg's pop art *Matches* over the road.

## The outer limits

**L'Hospitalet de Llobregat** lies beyond Sants, completely integrated within the city's transport system but nevertheless a distinct municipality, with its own sense of separateness. The area also boasts a rich cultural life, with good productions at the **Teatre Joventut** (C/Joventut 10, 93 448 12 10) and excellent art exhibitions at the **Tecla Sala Centre Cultural** (*see below*).

**Sant Andreu** is another vast residential district in the north-east of the city, and was once a major industrial zone. Apart from the Gaudí-designed floor mosaic in the **Sant Pacià church** on C/Monges, there's little reason to venture here, unless you have an historical interest in Josep Lluís Sert's rationalist **Casa Bloc**, which were originally workers' residences from the brief republican era.

The name of **Nou Barris**, on the other side of the Avda Meridiana, translates as 'nine neighbourhoods', but the area is actually a collection of 11 former hamlets. The council has compensated for the area's poor housing (many tower blocks were built in the area in the 1950s and have fallen into disrepair) with the construction of public facilities such as the **Can Dragó**, a sports centre incorporating the biggest swimming pool in the city, and **Parc Central**. The district is centred on the roundabout at Plaça Llucmajor, which also holds Josep Viladomat's bold *La República*, a female nude holding aloft a sprig of laurel as a symbol of freedom. The renovation of the nearby **Seu de Nou Barris** town hall has brightened up an area that badly needed it, although it's not quite a tourist draw yet.

### Tecla Sala Centre Cultural

*Avda Josep Tarradellas 44, Hospitalet de Llobregat (93 338 57 71/www.l-h.es/ccteclasala). Metro La Torrassa.* **Open** 11am-2pm, 5-8pm Tue-Sat; 11am-2pm Sun. **Admission** free.

Tecla Sala is an old textile factory now housing a number of cultural concerns, including a vast library and this excellent gallery, which exhibits an eclectic mixture of national and international artists.

Taxidermista...
Taxidermista...
Cafè Restaurant
Plaça Reial, 8
08002 Barcelona

# Eat, Drink, Shop



## Features



**Vila Viniteca**. *See p206.*

# Restaurants

What we are about to receive.

**Shunka**, famous for its filling portions. *See p147.*

It's been a tumultuous couple of decades in Iberian kitchens. The first Spanish food revolution came in the 1980s with a group of enlightened Basque chefs who had the audacity to steal some of the stars and the limelight from their French counterparts. The second is happening now, this time with Catalonia as its powerhouse. Once again, the catalyst for change has been a chef, this time Ferran Adrià and his legendary restaurant **El Bulli** (*see p171*) on the Costa Brava.

While Adrià's kitchens have spawned many notable alumni, such as Carles Abellan at **Comerç 24** (*see p150*) and Jordi Ruiz at **Neri Restaurante** (*see p147*), the trickledown effect of his global success (in April 2006 El Bulli was voted 'Best Restaurant in the World' by over 500 international critics) has also had a huge impact on the gastronomy of the region. Not only is cookery the new rock 'n' roll among young Spaniards, but suddenly gourmet pilgrims from the States, Japan and Australia are showing up with the express intention of splashing some cash in restaurants.

This has led to an increase in overall quality, but also to a rash of new and excellent dining options, among them **Cinc Sentits** (*see p165*), **Lasarte** (*see p168*) and **Oleum** (*see p163*). Other welcome new additions, albeit of a less rarefied nature, include the wonderfully homely **Tapioles 53** (*see p164*), excellent Asian food at **Wushu** (*see p163*) or just a really good pizza at **Ravalo** (*see p160*). Generally, though, local resistance to spices and the difficulty of sourcing key ingredients make it hard to find good Indian, Chinese or Italian food. Middle

Eastern and Japanese restaurants have been rather more successful, along with a growing number of Latin American places. Most ethnic variety is found in Gràcia.

### WHAT HAPPENS WHEN

Lunch starts around 2pm and goes on until roughly 3.30pm or 4pm; dinner is served from about 9pm until 11.30pm or midnight. Some restaurants open earlier in the evening, but arriving before 9.30pm or 10pm generally means you'll be dining alone or in the company of foreign tourists. Reserving a table is generally a good idea at weekends, and also on Monday lunchtimes, when few restaurants are open. Many also close for lengthy holidays, including about a week over Easter, two or three weeks in August or early September, and often the first week in January. We have listed closures of more than a week where possible.

### PRICES AND PAYMENT

Eating out in Barcelona is not as cheap as it used to be, but low mark-ups on wines keep the cost relatively reasonable for northern Europeans and Americans. All but the most upmarket restaurants are required by law to serve an economical fixed-price *menú del día* (*menú* is not to be confused with the menu, which is *la carta*) at lunchtime; this usually consists of a starter, main course, dessert, bread and something to drink. The idea is to provide cheaper meals for the workers, but while it can be a real bargain, it is not by any means a taster menu or a showcase for the chef's greatest hits; rather, they're a healthier version of what in other countries might amount to a snatched lunchtime sandwich.

Laws governing the issue of prices are routinely flouted, but, legally, menus must declare if the seven per cent *IVA* (VAT) is included in prices or not (it rarely is), and also if there is a cover charge (generally expressed as a charge for bread). Catalans, and the Spanish in general, tend to tip very little, but tourists let their conscience decide.

## Barri Gòtic

## Catalan

### Cafè de l'Acadèmia

*C/Lledó 1 (93 319 82 53). Metro Jaume I.* **Open** 9am-noon, 1.30-5pm, 8.45pm-1am Mon-Fri. Closed 3wks Aug. **Main courses** €11.80-€17.15. *Set lunch* €8.50-€12. **Credit** AmEx, DC, MC, V. **Map** p345 D6 ❶

Enjoy a power breakfast among the suits from the nearby town hall, bask in the sunshine over lunch at one of the tables outside on the evocative little Plaça Sant Just, or take a date for an alfresco candle-lit dinner. The regular menu of creative Catalan classics offers superb value and has had no need to change direction over the years, so you can expect to find home-made pasta (try shrimp and garlic), creamy risotto with foie, guinea fowl with a tiny tarte tatin and lots of duck.

### Can Culleretes

*C/Quintana 5 (93 317 30 22). Metro Liceu.* **Open** 1.30-4pm, 9-11pm Tue-Sat; 1.30-4pm Sun. Closed July. **Main courses** €6-€11. *Set lunch* €12-€15. **Credit** MC, V. **Map** p345 B5 ❷

The rambling dining rooms at the 'house of teaspoons' have been packing 'em in since 1786 and show no signs of slowing. The secret to this restaurant's longevity is a straightforward one: honest, hearty cooking and decent wine served at the lowest possible prices. Under huge oil paintings and a thousand signed black-and-white photos, diners munch sticky boar stew, tender pork with prunes and dates, goose with apples, partridge escabeche and superbly fresh seafood.

### Mercè Vins

*C/Amargós 1 (93 302 60 56). Metro Urquinaona.* **Open** 8am-5pm Mon-Fri. *Set lunch* €8.80 Mon-Fri. **Credit** V. **Map** p344 D3 ❸

In the morning this cosy restaurant, with its green beams, buttercup walls and fresh flowers, functions as a breakfast bar, before moving on to serve a set

## The best Restaurants

**For crustacea**

**Cal Pep** (*see p155*); **Mundial Bar** (*see p156*); **La Paradeta** (*see p156*); most places in **Barceloneta** (*see pp161-3*).

**For ethnic eats**

**Himali** (*see p170*); **Matsuri** (*see p148*); **San Kil** (*see p170*); **Thai Café** (*see p156*); **Wushu** (*see p153*).

**For budget bites**

**Can Culleretes** (*see p145*); **Elisabets** (*see p157*); **Les Quinze Nits** (*see p149*).

**For a bit of glam**

**Neri Restaurante** (*see p147*); **Noti** (*see p169*); **Moo** (*see p165*).

**For sunny terraces**

**Agua** (*see p161*); **Bestial** (*see p161*); **Cafè de l'Acadèmia** (*see p145*); **Els Pescadors** (*see p171*); **La Venta** (*see p171*).

**For serious dining**

**Alkimia** (*see p165*); **Cinc Sentits** (*see p165*); **Gaig** (*see p165*); **Lasarte** (*see p168*); **Saüc** (*see p168*).

lunch, while on Friday nights it dishes up *pica-pica* plates of ham and cheese, with generous rounds of bread rubbed with tomato. The standard of cooking on the lunch deals can vary a bit, but occasionally a pumpkin soup or inventive salad might appear, along with sausages with garlicky sautéed potatoes. Dessert regulars are flat, sweet *coca* bread with a glass of muscatel, chocolate flan or figgy pudding.

### Neri Restaurante

*C/Sant Sever 5 (93 304 06 55/www.hotelneri.com). Metro Jaume I.* **Open** 1.30-3.30pm, 8.30-11pm daily. **Main courses** €26.75-€31.60. **Credit** AmEx, DC, MC, V. **Map** p345 C5 ❹

These days, any Barcelona restaurant worth its *fleur de sel* has an alumnus of enfant terrible Ferran Adrià heading up its kitchens, and the Neri is no exception. Jordi Ruiz has eschewed the wilder excesses of molecular gastronomy, however, and cooks with a quiet assurance in tune with the sombre Gothic arches, crushed velvet and earthy tones of his dining room, creating a perfect, tiny lamb Wellington to start; cannelloni formed with artichoke petals and stuffed with wild mushrooms, or a fillet of hake on creamed parsnip with apricots and haricot beans.

### Pitarra

*C/Avinyó 56 (93 301 16 47/www.pitarra.com). Metro Liceu.* **Open** 1-4pm, 8.30-11pm Mon-Sat. Closed Aug. **Main courses** €9.60-€20.30. *Set lunch* €10.50 Mon-Sat. **Credit** MC, V. **Map** p345 C7 ❺

Once home to the Catalan playwright Frederic 'Pitarra' Soler and his watchmaking uncle, this smart, bright, traditional restaurant is still a shrine to the art of horology, as well as a virtual museum of poems, photographs and drawings presented to the author by the Catalan great and good. Classic dishes include partridge casserole, pheasant in a creamy cava sauce and langoustines with wild mushrooms; the desserts are not quite so accomplished.

### Els Quatre Gats

*C/Montsió 3 (93 302 41 40/www.4gats.com). Metro Catalunya.* **Open** 1pm-1am daily. **Main courses** €14-€22. *Set lunch* €12.80 Mon-Fri, €22.50 Sat. **Credit** AmEx, DC, MC, V. **Map** p344 C3 ❻

This Modernista classic, designed by Puig i Cadafalch and once frequented by Picasso and various other luminaries of the period, nowadays caters mainly to tourists. The inevitable consequences include higher prices, so-so food and, worst of all, house musicians. It's still dazzling in its design, however, so to avoid the worst excesses of touristification, come at lunchtime for a reasonably priced and respectably varied *menú* and spare yourself 'Bésame Mucho' in the process.

## Chilean

### Xeroga

*C/Parc 1 (93 412 62 75). Metro Drassanes.* **Open** 1-5pm, 8pm-midnight daily. **Main courses** €6-€13.50. **Credit** MC, V. **Map** p345 B8 ❼

Under the same ownership as the El Paraguayo restaurant (*see p148*) next door, Xeroga is the Chilean arm, slightly cheaper and slightly shabbier, but sharing the same good-natured South American vibe, its walls hung with bright oil paintings, a gold-stitched sombrero and a cracked and burnished guitar. On offer are various empanadas (*pino* is the classic – meat, olives, egg and raisin), ceviche, *mariscal* (shellfish and hake in a fish broth) and *bife a lo pobre* – a trucker's breakfast of thin steak, two fried eggs and a stack of chips.

## Indian

### Goa

*C/Ample 46 (93 310 15 22). Metro Jaume I.* **Open** 1-5pm, 7pm-midnight daily. **Main courses** €6.50-€12. *Set lunch* €7.30 Mon-Fri. **Credit** AmEx, DC, MC, V. **Map** p345 C7 ❽

Under new ownership, Goa has had a tangerine-and-fuschia facelift which goes some way towards softening its cavernous nature. If you're from Brick Lane, Bradford or Bangalore, it maybe isn't for you, but otherwise it's pretty good by local Indian restaurant standards. The pilau rice is underwhelming, but naan comes fresh and piping hot, the rogan josh and chicken jalfrezi will warm the cockles of your heart and veggie accompaniments such as aloo palak are especially tasty.

## Japanese

### Shunka

*C/Sagristans 5 (93 412 49 91). Metro Jaume I.* **Open** 1.30-3.30pm, 8.30-11.30pm Tue-Fri; 2-4pm, 8.30-11.30pm Sat, Sun. Closed Aug & ten days at Christmas. **Main courses** €12.90-€22.50. *Set lunch* €14.50 Tue-Fri. **Credit** AmEx, DC, MC, V. **Map** p344 D4 ❾

Increasingly compromised by its own success, Shunka is still one of the better Japanese restaurants in town, and a favourite haunt of superchef Ferran Adrià. Reserve a table for the sumo-sized set lunch of rich miso soup, a leafy salad topped with salmon and punchy vinegar and teriyaki dressing, followed by vegetable and shrimp tempura and six pieces of maki and extremely good nigiri-zushi. The best seats are in front of the performing chefs. **Photo** *p144.*

### Tokyo

*C/Comtal 20 (93 317 61 80). Metro Catalunya.* **Open** 1.30-4pm, 8-11pm Mon-Sat. **Main courses** €13.90-€22.50. *Set lunch* €14.90 Mon-Thur. **Credit** MC, V. **Map** p344 D3 ❿

Resist the suggestion that is no *menú*, for this is the way to eat here. A zingy little salad is followed by a mountain of prawn and vegetable tempura and a platter of maki rolls, nigiri and a bowl of miso soup. It's a simple, cosy space that's been cleverly divided with slatted wooden partitions, with a reassuring Japanese presence. On the à la carte menu, the speciality is edomae (hand-rolled nigiri-zushi), but the

# Get over it

Spanish restaurants get a bad press from the rest of the world, and some, perhaps, deserve it. Many more, however, are guilty of nothing more than following the local customs. It's worth knowing what these are in advance.

The oft-heard complaint of the northern tourist regarding the lack of vegetables fails to take into account that these are served first, in order that the meat may be better appreciated. Ironically, this then gives rise to another complaint, when a mere plate of vegetables is presented as a starter. 'My water wasn't chilled!' is another, but Spaniards often prefer water at room temperature.

When the food arrives, if one person hasn't ordered a starter, it's considered polite to bring their main course to the table with other diners' starters. As in France, there is no stigma attached to leaving the cutlery to be used for a second course. Side plates for bread, meanwhile, or finger bowls with shellfish, are virtually unknown in all but the smartest restaurants (scented wipes are considered less messy). And so the list goes on.

This is not to say that every last foible of Spanish kitchens can be defended, of course, and why the ping of a microwave is greeted with anticipation rather than horror is one mystery that remains unsolved.



meat and veg sukiyaki, which is cooked at your table, is also good. Check out Javier Mariscal's grateful signed drawing of Cobi (the Olympic mascot) dressed as a Japanese chef.

## Mediterranean

### El Gran Café

*C/Avinyó 9 (93 318 79 86). Metro Liceu.* **Open** 1-4.30pm, 7.30pm-midnight daily. **Main courses** €11.80-€20.35. *Set lunch* €12.85 Mon-Fri. **Credit** AmEx, DC, MC, V. **Map** p345 C6 ⓫

Fluted columns, bronze cavorting nymphs, suspended globe lamps and wood panelling successfully replicate a classic Parisian vibe, as do those cornerstones of brasserie cuisine: onion soup, duck magret, tarte tatin and – even – crêpes Suzette. The imaginative Catalan dishes spliced into the menu also work, but what is less convincing is the waiters' need to sport headphones and other assorted gadgetry, and a distinctly non-Gallic attitude towards the hastily assembled set lunch.

### El Salón

*C/Hostal d'en Sol 6-8 (93 315 21 59). Metro Jaume I.* **Open** 1.30-4pm, 8.30-11.30pm Mon-Sat. **Main courses** €10.70-€15.50. *Set lunch* €7.50 Mon-Sat. **Credit** MC, V. **Map** p345 D7 ⓬

Under new ownership, El Salón remains as welcoming as ever and has retained its faintly bohemian style. Prices have come down a notch, and the dishes have become a little simpler – creamed carrot soup, lamb brochettes, tuna with ginger and brown rice, *botifarra* and beans, and ice-cream made with Galician Arzoa-Ulloa cheese to finish – but this remains one of the more charming places to eat in the Barri Gòtic.

### Taxidermista

*Plaça Reial 8 (93 412 45 36). Metro Liceu.* **Open** 1.30-4pm, 8.30pm-12.30am Tue-Sun. Closed 3wks Jan. **Main courses** €8.85-€19.80. *Set lunch* €9.20 Tue-Fri. **Credit** AmEx, DC, MC, V. **Map** p345 B6 ⓭

When this was a taxidermist's, Dalí famously ordered 200,000 ants, a tiger, a lion and a rhinoceros – the latter wheeled into the Plaça Reial so that the artist could be photographed sitting on top. Those who leave here stuffed nowadays are generally tourists, though, unusually, this hasn't affected standards, which remain reasonably high. À la carte offerings include foie gras with quince jelly; langoustine ravioli with seafood sauce; steak tartare; and some slightly misjudged fusion elements, such as wok-fried spaghetti with vegetables. The lunch *menú* is excellent, with two- or three-course deals.

## Pan-Asian

### Matsuri

*Plaça Regomir 1 (93 268 15 35). Metro Jaume I.* **Open** 1.30-3.30pm, 8.30-11.30pm Mon-Fri; 8.30pm-midnight Sat. **Main courses** €7.35-€16.10. **Credit** MC, V. **Map** p345 C6 ⓮

Matsuri is more convincing than most of the city's Asian restaurants, with a perfectly executed look – trickling fountain, dark shades of terracotta and amber, wooden carvings and wall-hung candles – saved from cliché by the thoroughly occidental lounge soundtrack. Reasonably priced tom yam soup, sushi, pad Thai and other South-east Asian favourites top the list, while less predictable choices include a zingy mango and prawn salad dressed with lime and chilli, and a rich, earthy red curry with chicken and aubergine.

## Paraguayan

### El Paraguayo

*C/Parc 1 (93 302 14 41). Metro Drassanes.* **Open** 1-4pm, 8pm-midnight daily. **Main courses** €12.85-€25.70. **Credit** AmEx, DC, MC, V. **Map** p345 B8 ⓯

Pleasures are exclusively carnal at this warm, wood-panelled little steakhouse, brightened with Colombian paintings of buxom madams and their dapper admirers. The cuts of beef are unusual and complicated to translate, but to try a range of *vacío, entraña, bife de cuadril, churrasco* and so on, the lunchtime tasting menu isn't a bad idea at €15 (and it will serve two people), while the €33 T-bone feeds up to four. Baked potatoes are the standard side dish, but beyond that, El Paraguayo is, like most South American restaurants, an unwitting pioneer of the Atkins Diet.

## Peruvian

### Peimong

*C/Templers 6-10 (93 318 28 73). Metro Jaume I.* **Open** 1-4pm, 8-11.30pm Tue-Sat; 1-4pm Sun. **Main courses** €6.60-€10.80. **Credit** DC, MC, V. **Map** p345 C6 ⑯

With its tapestries of Macchu Pichu and plastic flowers, Peimong wins no prizes for design, but it makes up for its rather unforgiving and overlit interior with some tasty little South American dishes. Start with a Pisco Sour and a dish of big fat yucca chips, or maybe some stuffed corn tamales, and then move on to ceviche, *pato en aji* (a hunk of duck with a spicy sauce and rice) or the satisfying *lomo saltado* – pork fried with onions, tomatoes and coriander.

## Pizzeria

### La Verònica

*C/Avinyó 30 (93 412 11 22). Metro Liceu.* **Open** *Sept-July* 7pm-1am Mon-Thur; 7pm-1.30am Fri; 12.30pm-1.30am Sat, Sun. *Aug* 7.30pm-1am Mon-Thur; 7.30pm-1.30am Fri; 1.30-7.30pm Sat, Sun. Closed 2wks Feb. **Main courses** €7.50-€13.90. **Credit** MC, V. **Map** p345 C6 ⑰

La Verònica's shortcomings (its huge popularity among young foreigners, the minuscule spacing between tables) are all but hidden by night, when candles add a cosy glow to the red, orange and yellow paintwork. Its pizzas are crisp, thin and healthy, and come with such toppings as smoked salmon, or apple, gorgonzola and mozzarella. Salads include the Nabocondensor, a colourful tumble of parsnip, cucumber and apple, and there is a short but reliable wine list. Terrace tables on the Plaça George Orwell carry a 10% surcharge.

## Spanish

### Mesón Jesús

*C/Cecs de la Boqueria 4 (93 317 46 98). Metro Jaume I or Liceu.* **Open** 1-4pm, 8-11pm Mon-Fri. Closed Aug-early Sept. **Main courses** €5.80-€18. *Set lunch* €9.50 Mon-Fri. *Set dinner* €15 Mon-Fri. **Credit** MC, V. **Map** p345 B5 ⑱

The feel is authentic Castilian, with gingham tablecloths, oak barrels, cartwheels and pitchforks hung around the walls, while the waitresses are incessantly cheerful with a largely non-Spanish-speaking clientele, and especially obliging when it comes to children. The menu is limited and never changes, but the dishes are reliably good and inexpensive to boot – try the sautéed green beans with ham to start, then the superb grilled prawns or a tasty fish stew.

**La Strada**. *See p153.*

### Les Quinze Nits

*Plaça Reial 6 (93 317 30 75). Metro Liceu.* **Open** 1-3.45pm, 8.30-11.30pm daily. **Main courses** €5.35-€10. *Set lunch* €7.70 Mon-Fri. **Credit** AmEx, MC, V. **Map** p345 B6 ⑲

Top of many tourists' dining agenda, with a queue stretching halfway across the Plaça Reial, the Quinze Nits (and its many other incarnations across town) manages all this with distinctly so-so food. The secret? Combining fast-food speed and prices with striking spaces, smart table linen and soft lighting. Diners get to feel special, eat local dishes and come away with nary a dent in their wallets. Order simply – soups, salads, grilled fish – and a reasonable meal can still be had. Queues tend to be shorter at the other branches.

**Other locations**: La Dolça Herminia, C/Magdalenes 27 (93 317 06 76); La Fonda, C/Escudellers 10 (93 301 75 15), and throughout the city.

## Born & Sant Pere

### Catalan

#### Comerç 24

*C/Comerç 24 (93 319 21 02/www.comerc24.com). Metro Arc de Triomf.* **Open** 1.30-3.30pm, 8.30pm-midnight Mon-Sat. **Main courses (tapas)** €7.40-€15. **Credit** MC, V. **Map** p344 F4 ⑳

One of the acknowledged masters of Catalan new wave cuisine, Carles Abellan was, unsurprisingly, a disciple of Ferran Adrià in the kitchens of El Bulli (*see p171*). But nowadays he ploughs his own, highly successful furrow in this urbane and sexy restaurant. A selection of tiny playful dishes (described as 'tapas') changes seasonally but might include a 'Kinder egg' (lined with truffle); tuna sashimi and seaweed on a wafer-thin pizza crust; a fun take on the *bikini* (a cheese and ham toastie); or a densely flavoured fish *suquet*. Order a selection in the shape of the *menú festival* to understand Catalonia's food revolution a little better.

### Cuban

#### Habana Vieja

*C/Banys Vells 2 (93 268 25 04). Metro Jaume I.* **Open** 1.30-3.30pm, 8.30-11.30pm Mon-Sat. **Main courses** €8.60-€12.90. **Credit** AmEx, DC, MC, V. **Map** p345 E6 ㉑

A tiny, laid-back Cuban restaurant, with plenty of *son* and rumba to get the evening going. The sharp taste of limes in the mojitos and caipirinhas complements the love-it-or-hate-it parade of Havana cuisine, which involves lots of meat, stodge and frying pans. Rice and beans accompany tender *ropa vieja* (shredded chilli beef), or there is fried yucca with *mojo cubano* (garlic sauce) and banana or *malanga* (a taro-like root vegetable) fritters with fresh guava for dessert. The prices seem high, but portions are big enough to share.

### Global

#### Cuines Santa Caterina

*Mercat Santa Caterina, Avda Francesc Cambó (93 268 99 18). Metro Jaume I.* **Open** 1-4pm, 8-11.15pm Mon-Wed, Sun; 1-4pm, 8pm-12.15am Thur-Sat. **Main courses** €7.50-€12.50. **Credit** AmEx, DC, MC, V. **Map** p344 E4 ㉒

It's not quite as dazzling as it was when it opened in 2005, with higher prices and a slightly more lax attitude to quality control, but CSC still has its charms. The menu holds a little of everything you fancy, from langoustine tempura to a baked spud with cheese and *sobrassada* sausage, with an excellent chocolate tart or red-fruit millefeuille to finish. The rice, flour, crates of veg and so on arrayed along the vast windows, coupled with the well-made olive wood furniture, give everything a pleasantly honest, Mediterranean feel.

# A matter of taste

**This little piggy**

...went to market, along with the lamb and the calf, and so did their tongues (*llengues*), testicles (*turmes*), trotters (*peus*), brains (*cervellets*), snouts (*morros*), ears (*orelles*), tripe (*tripa*), cheeks (*galtes*), sweetbreads (*lletonets*) and bellies (*ventres*).

**Rabbit face**

Don't be surprised when a tiny jawbone, complete with teeth, fetches up in your rabbit casserole. This dates back to the days when rabbit was sold by the wriggling sackful and unscrupulous traders might sneak in the odd cat. Thumper's gnashers are put into the pot to reassure you that you didn't get the one with the whiskers. Which brings us to...

**Roast cat**

OK, it's been a good couple of hundred years since anyone has eaten *gat rostit* round here, but should you wish to try one of Europe's earliest recipes, Coleman Andrew's fabulous *Catalan Cuisine* tells you how and advises you to discard the brains. It is said they have the power to make men crazy.

***Kokotxas***

A Basque speciality, *kokotxas* are membranes found in the throats of cod and hake, with an elusive gelatinous texture, like licking a snail trail. Generally served with garlic and parsley, they are an expensive and rare delicacy. Long may they remain so.

**Vichy Catalan**

Ask for sparkling water in Barcelona and you will generally get Vichy Catalan. Laden with minerals, it has a metallic tang, but its slight saltiness does grow on you. Should it not grow on you, it is at least good for you. Or tastes like it is.

**Sea cucumbers**

In fact the *espardenya* tastes just like very pricey squid, but its lifestyle choices are harder to swallow. It self-eviscerates when panicked, apparently, and according to the *Oxford Companion to Food*, it houses small fishes in its anus, which survive by 'nibbling at the host's gonads'. *Bon appétit.*

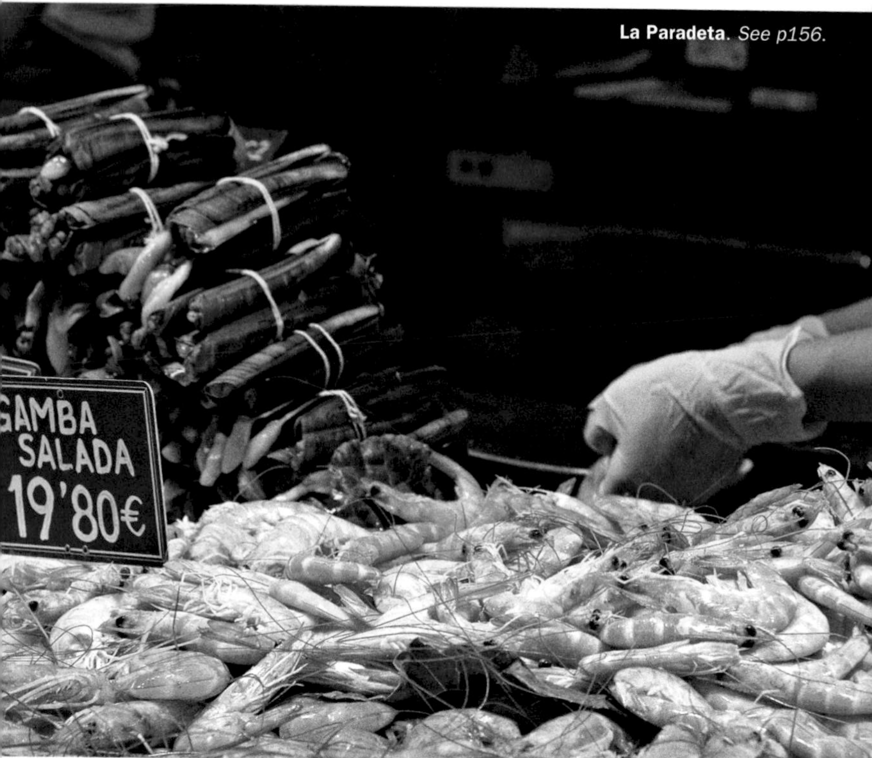


**La Paradeta**. *See p156.*

**Hofmann**

*C/Argenteria 74-78 (93 319 58 89/www.hofmann-bcn.com). Metro Jaume I.* **Open** 1.30-3.15pm, 9-11.15pm Mon-Fri. Closed Aug. **Main courses** €21.40-€42.80. *Set lunch* €33.20. **Credit** AmEx, DC, MC, V. **Map** p345 E6 ㉓

Said to be the best cookery school in the world after the Cordon Bleu, Hofmann puts its pupils to good use in its top-class restaurant. A succession of small dining rooms includes a bright atrium, and another decorated in deep reds, orange and green – adorned with plants and dramatic flower arrangements. The affordable lunch *menú* might start with a truffle salad, followed by bream in bacon or carré of lamb with mustard sauce, but, as with the à la carte menu, the puddings are really the high point here. Artful constructions such as a jam jar and lid made of sugar and filled with red fruit, or a tarte tatin in a spun-sugar 'cage', are as delicious as they are clever.

**Re-Pla**

*C/Montcada 2 (93 268 30 03). Metro Jaume I.* **Open** 1.30-4pm, 8.30pm-midnight daily. **Main courses** €8-€20. **Credit** DC, MC, V. **Map** p345 E5 ㉔

A casually hip but nonetheless welcoming restaurant serving Asian-Mediterranean fusion. The wildly varied menu might include anything from a sushi platter to ostrich with green asparagus, honey and grilled mango slices. Veggie options are clearly marked, and desserts are rich and creative. For once, the lighting is wonderfully romantic and the sleek artwork easy on the eye, though some may feel uncomfortable with the sort of waiters who pull up a chair while recounting the day's specials.

**Other locations**: Pla, C/Bellafila 7, Barri Gòtic (93 412 65 52).

## Indian

**Kama**

*C/Rec 69 (93 268 10 29). Metro Barceloneta.* **Open** 7.30pm-3am Mon, Sun; 1pm-3am Tue-Sat. **Main courses** €10-€13. **Credit** MC, V. **Map** p345 F7 ㉕

The default spiciness setting for Kama's mostly Indian food is mild (in deference to the Catalan palate), but if owner Ketan hears a British accent, he'll ask if you'd like the heat turned up a little. Once you've factored in rice and naan, the prices can seem

a little steep for a Ruby, but you're paying for the Barcelona Treatment: moody lighting; a hot-pink neon bar area; banquette seating; a covetable Kama Sutra frieze and ethno-chill-out on the sound system. Happy-hour cocktails are available 6-8pm.

## Italian

### La Strada

*C/Pescateria 6 (93 268 27 11). Metro Barceloneta.* **Open** 1.30-3.30pm Mon; 1.30-3.30pm, 9-11.30pm Tue-Fri; 9-11.30pm Sat. **Main courses** €11-€16. *Set lunch* €10 Mon-Fri. **Credit** MC, V. **Map** p345 E7 ㉖

This peaceful little spot decorated in pale autumnal shades is hidden down an easily missed sidestreet off Avda Marquès de l'Argentera. Its fixed lunch comprises simple Italian food made with high-quality ingredients: *bruschetta pomodori*; *farfalle al pesto*; salmon trout with garlic, chives and toasted almonds; and lemon zabaglione. The set dinner is more of a tasting menu, with samplers of six of the chef's recommended dishes – as well as home-made gnocchi and pasta are less predictable offerings such as carpaccio of venison with redcurrants. **Photo** *p149.*

## French

### La Cua Curta

*C/Carassa s/n (93 310 00 15). Metro Jaume I.* **Open** 8.30pm-midnight Tue-Sun. **Main courses** €4.40-€12. **Credit** MC, V. **Map** p345 E6 ㉗

Having tired of mullets and swingers' bars, the retro-obsessed of Barcelona have turned their attention to the quietly thriving fondue restaurants. Yes, it's hip to dip once again, but *Abigail's Party* this is not: quaintly Gallic, with its etched mirrors and lacy embroidered lampshades, La Cua Curta is a refined affair, where only the menus glued to record sleeves evoke anything but the 1920s. Start with a generous salad before tackling one of the dozen variations on the emmenthal and gruyère theme, and stay off the water if you intend to digest the cheese.

## Malaysian

### Bunga Raya

*C/Assaonadors 7 (93 319 31 69). Metro Jaume I.* **Open** 8pm-midnight Tue-Sun. **Main courses** €5.50-€8. **No credit cards**. **Map** p345 E5 ㉘

The 'Hibiscus Flower' beautifully (and almost certainly unwittingly) evokes a genuine Malaysian restaurant, with its slightly musty and forgotten air, its faded tourist-board posters and its dusty bamboo panelling. It has a faithful local following for the excellent-value taster menu (€12.95), consisting of a pile of coconut rice accompanied by beef rendang, fried peanuts with coconut shavings, spicy pineapple, marinated beansprout salad, chicken and beef satay, and a bowl of chicken curry. Other good dishes include curried anchovies and a really tasty tom yam soup.

## Mexican

### Itztli

*C/Mirallers 7 (93 319 68 75/www.itztli.es). Metro Barceloneta or Jaume I.* **Open** noon-11pm Tue-Sun. **Main courses** £3.25-€3.85. **No credit cards Map** p345 E6 ㉙

Fortify yourself in the interminable queue for the Picasso Museum with a takeaway chicken burrito from this nearby Mexican snack bar. Keenly priced around the €3.50 mark, burritos also come with beef, chili con carne or veg, as do tacos. Also on offer are quesadillas, wraps, nachos and salads, and there's a good range of Mexican beers, tinned goods and fiery chilli sauces for sale.

## Pan-Asian

### Wushu

*C/Colomines 2 (93 310 73 13/www.wushu-restaurant.com). Metro Jaume I.* **Open** noon-midnight Tue-Sat; noon-4pm Sun. **Main courses** €8-€9.90. *Set lunch* €9.90 Tue-Fri. **Credit** MC, V. **Map** p345 E5 ㉚

Within a month of Wushu's opening in summer 2006, its six tables were some of the Born's most sought after. The formula is hard to beat: superb Asian wok cooking (pad Thai, *lo mein* and the only *laksa* to be found in Barcelona) courtesy of Australian chef Bradley Ainsworth; charming service; generous portions; and low prices. In fact, it's only thanks to the all-day opening that you can count on getting a seat at all.

## Pizzeria

### Pizza Paco

*C/Allada-Vermell 11 (mobile 670 338 992). Metro Arc de Triomf.* **Open** 6pm-midnight Mon-Fri; 1pm-midnight Sat, Sun. **Main courses** €7. **No credit cards. Map** p345 F5 ㉛

Spawned from the improbably successful hole-in-the-wall bar opposite, Casa Paco, this one aims to provide the ballast. In fact, it functions better as a bar than a pizza restaurant (though the pizzas are really pretty good), and you'll struggle to get your order heard over the general hubbub (and The Strokes). One to incorporate into a night on the tiles, rather than an evening's outing in itself.

## Seafood

### Cal Pep

*Plaça de les Olles 8 (93 310 79 61/www.calpep.com). Metro Barceloneta.* **Open** 8-11.45pm Mon; 1.30-4pm, 8-11.45pm Tue-Sat. Closed Aug. **Main courses** €8.55-€19.25. **Credit** AmEx, DC, MC, V. **Map** p345 E7 ㉜

As much tapas bar as restaurant, Cal Pep is always packed: get here early for the coveted seats at the front. There is a cosy dining room at the back, but it's a shame to miss the show. The affable Pep will take the order steering the neophytes towards the *trifásico* – a mélange of fried whitebait, squid rings

# Catalan dishes

Many dishes apparently from other cuisines – risotto, *canelons*, ravioli – are as entrenched in the Catalan culinary tradition as any other. Two names borrowed from the French, which frequently appear on Catalan menus, are *foie* (as opposed to *fetge/higado* or foie gras), which has come to mean hare, duck or goose liver prepared with liqueur, salt and sugar; and *coulant* – rather like a small soufflé, but melting in the centre.

***a la llauna*** literally 'in the tin' – baked on a metal tray with garlic, tomato, paprika and wine

***all i oli*** garlic crushed with olive oil to form a mayonnaise-like texture, similar to aïoli

***amanida catalana***/*ensalada catalana* mixed salad with a selection of cold meats

***arròs negre***/*arroz negro* 'black rice', seafood rice cooked in squid ink

***botifarra***/*butifarra* Catalan sausage. Variants include *botifarra negre* (blood sausage) and *blanca* (mixed with egg)

***botifarra amb mongetes***/*butifarra con judías* sausage with haricot beans

***calçots*** a variety of large spring onion, available only from December to spring, and eaten char-grilled, with *romesco* sauce

***carn d'olla*** traditional Christmas dish of various meats stewed with *escudella*, then served separately

***conill amb cargols***/*conejo con caracoles* rabbit with snails

***crema catalana*** custard dessert with burned sugar topping, similar to crème brûlée

***escalivada***/*escalibada* grilled and peeled peppers, onions and aubergine

***escudella*** winter stew of meat and vegetables

***espinacs a la catalana***/*espinacas a la catalana* spinach fried in olive oil with garlic, raisins and pine nuts

***esqueixada*** summer salad of marinated salt cod with onions, olives and tomato

***fideuà***/*fideuá* paella made with vermicelli instead of rice

***mar i muntanya*** a traditional Catalan combination of meat and seafood, such as lobster and chicken in the same dish

***mel i mató*** curd cheese with honey

***pa amb tomàquet***/*pan con tomate* bread prepared with tomato, oil and salt

***picada*** a mix of nuts, garlic, parsley, bread, chicken liver and little chilli peppers, which is often used to enrich and thicken dishes

***romesco*** a spicy sauce from the coast south of Barcelona, made with crushed almonds and hazelnuts, tomatoes, oil and a special type of red pepper (*nyora*)

***samfaina*** a mix of onion, garlic, aubergine and red and green peppers (similar to ratatouille)

***sarsuela***/*zarzuela* fish and seafood stew

***sípia amb mandonguilles***/*sepia con albóndigas* cuttlefish with meatballs

***suquet de peix***/*suquet de pescado* fish and potato soup

***torrades***/*tostadas* toasted *pa amb tomàquet*

***xató*** salad containing tuna, anchovies and cod, with a *romesco*-type sauce and shrimp. Other favourites are the exquisite little *tallarines* (wedge clams), and *botifarra* sausage with beans. Then, squeeze in four shot glasses of foam – coconut with rum, coffee, *crema catalana* and lemon.

### Mundial Bar

*Plaça Sant Agustí Vell 1 (93 319 90 56). Metro Arc de Triomf or Jaume I.* **Open** 1-4pm, 8.30-11.30pm Tue-Sat; noon-3.30pm Sun. Closed Aug. **Main courses** €5.35-€21.40. **Credit** MC, V. **Map** p344 F4 (33)
Since 1925 this venerable family establishment has been dishing up no-frills platters of seafood, cheeses and the odd slice of cured meat. Colourful tiles and a marble trough of a bar add charm to the rather basic decor, but it's not as cheap as it looks. People come for the steaming piles of fresh razor clams, shrimp, oysters, fiddler crabs and the like, but there's also plenty of tinned produce, so check the bar displays to see exactly which is which.

### La Paradeta

*C/Comercial 7 (93 268 19 39). Metro Arc de Triomf or Jaume I.* **Open** 8-11.30pm Tue-Fri; 1-4pm, 8pm-midnight Sat; 1-4pm Sun. **Main courses** €6-€20. **No credit cards**. **Map** p345 F6 (34)
Superb seafood, served refectory-style. Choose from glistening mounds of clams, mussels, squid, spider crabs and whatever else the boats have brought in, let them know how you'd like it cooked (grilled, steamed or *a la marinera*), pick a sauce (Marie Rose, spicy local *romesco*, *all i oli* or onion), buy a drink and wait for your number to be called. A great – and cheap – experience for anyone not too grand to clear their own plate. **Photos** *p152 and p153.*

## Thai

### Thai Café

*C/Comerç 27 (93 268 39 59). Metro Jaume I.* **Open** 12.30-4pm, 8pm-midnight Mon-Thur; 8pm-1am Fri, Sat. **Main courses** €8.60-€15.70. *Set lunch* €13.40 Mon-Fri. **Credit** AmEx, MC, V. **Map** p345 F7 (35)
Aromatic *tom kha gai* soup, fishcakes, pad Thai and tangy chicken with chilli and holy basil in a pop-art package: hot-pink and lime-green candy stripes along the wall, pre-club electronica and ergonomically moulded white chairs where amused-looking media types gesture with chopsticks and cigarettes. In an effort to boost the lunch scene, the restaurant has recently introduced a quick-fix massage service – for an extra €4 you can get a 15-minute back rub before you eat.

# Raval

## Catalan

### Drassanes

*Museu Marítim, Avda Drassanes (93 317 52 56). Metro Drassanes.* **Open** 1-4pm Mon, Tue; 1-4pm, 9pm-midnight Wed-Sat. **Main courses** €9.65-€17.65. *Set lunch* €10.35 Mon-Fri; €16.50 Sat. **Credit** DC, MC, V. **Map** p345 A8 (36)
Drassanes is dwarfed by the lofty 14th-century arches of the former shipyard, now housing the Maritime Museum. The restaurant fills up at lunchtime with office workers enjoying a generally

**Ravalo**. *See p160.*

good-value set menu. The quality of the food varies, but at its best, it is unbeatable, with Catalan classics such as *botifarra* sausage with wild mushrooms appearing alongside grilled fish and pasta. Going à la carte, the dishes traverse the globe, from wok-fried prawns and vegetables on yakisoba noodles, to duck magret with sour apple sauce or Thai curry.

### Elisabets

*C/Elisabets 2-4 (93 317 58 26). Metro Catalunya.* **Open** 7am-11pm Mon-Sat. Closed 3wks Aug. **Set lunch** €8.50 Mon-Fri. **Set dinner** €11-€13 Fri. **No credit cards. Map** p344 B3 37

Also open in the mornings for breakfast, and late night for drinking at the bar, Elisabets maintains a sociable local feel, despite the recent gentrification of its street. Dinner, served only on Fridays, is actually a selection of tapas, and otherwise only the set lunch or myriad *bocadillos* are served. The lunch deal is terrific value, however, with osso buco, vegetable and chickpea stew, baked cod with garlic and parsley, and roast pork knuckle all making regular appearances on the menu.

## Filipino

### Fil Manila

*C/Ramelleres 3 (93 318 64 87). Metro Catalunya.* **Open** 11am-midnight daily. Closed Tue Nov-Feb. **Main courses** €4.90-€14. **Credit** Amex, DC, MC, V. **Map** p344 B3 38

Unpretentious and undervisited, Fil Manila may just have the longest menu of any restaurant in Barcelona. Malay, Chinese and Spanish influences all contribute to the classic flavours of sour fish soup, *pancit* (noodles), chicken and pork adobo, fried *lumpia* (crispy vegetable or meat rolls) or a *halo-halo* dessert of fruits, crushed ice and milk. The bamboo-lined decor doesn't try too hard to be exotic, and the faithful patronage of local Filipinos augurs well for the food's authenticity.

## Global

### Dos Trece

*C/Carme 40 (93 301 73 06). Metro Liceu.* **Open** 9pm-midnight Mon, Sun; 2-4pm, 9pm-midnight Tue-Sat. **Main courses** €7-€10.20. *Set lunch* €10.30 Tue-Sat. **Credit** AmEx, DC, MC, V. **Map** p344 A4 39

Is it a bar? Is it a restaurant? Is it a nightclub? Where's my salad? Dos Trece caters to everyone from hangover victims, with brunch on Sunday, to musos and their friends, with occasional, though increasingly rare, jam sessions. Apart from a little fusion confusion (Thai curry with nachos; Cajun chicken with mash; curried sausage with baked apple; and all manner of things with yucca chips) the food's not half bad for the price, but the service could look a little livelier.

### FoodBall

*C/Elisabets 9 (93 270 13 63). Metro Catalunya.* **Open** noon-11pm daily. **Main courses** €1.95-€2.95/ball. *Set meal* €4.99-€8.99. **Credit** MC, V. **Map** p344 A3 40

Camper shoes joined forces with Marti Guixé, the Catalan food designer, to create this very bizarre catering concept. First off, the food is presented in,

A taste of Léon in Barcelona: **Las Fernández**. *See p160.*

yes, balls. Spherical patties of rice holding chicken, mushrooms, seaweed and tofu, or dense globes of carob and dates. Then there's the space – tiered concrete strewn with raffia pads and facing a TV screen where goldfish glide and waves crash on the shore, while earnest murals extol the virtues of ethnic diversity and organic food ('Revolution begins in the vegetable patch'). Payment with cowrie shells must surely be just around the corner.

### El Pati

*C/Montalegre 7 (93 318 65 04). Metro Catalunya.* **Open** 9am-5pm Mon-Fri. Closed Aug. **Set lunch** €10.30. **Credit** Amex, MC, V. **Map** p344 A2 41

The charm of this café comes from its situation in the Pati Manning, an arcaded 18th-century patio decorated with colourful tiling and sgraffiti. The lunch deal is a good option, where €10.30 gets you spinach ravioli with courgette sauce, followed by layers of pork and aubergine slices in a balsamic vinegar reduction, or roast chicken with fat wedge chips, a drink and a dessert. Outside lunch hours, croissants, sandwiches and so on are served.

### Zarabanda

*C/Ferlandina 55 (mobile 653 169 539). Metro Sant Antoni.* **Open** 7.30pm-midnight daily. Closed 2wks Aug. **Main courses** €6.50-€9.50. **No credit cards**. **Map** p342 E9 42

Probably the only place in town to have a shared bowl of nachos as a signature dish, Zarabanda attracts a fair few students looking for somewhere more comfortable than a bar but cheaper than a restaurant. Its cosy vibe is nudged along with low lighting, creative paintwork and the much sought-after space on the one, battered, sofa; the food is decent and good value, particularly the salads and crêpes. Occasional flamenco, jazz and even electro take over the tiny stage.

## Mediterranean

### Biblioteca

*C/Junta de Comerç 28 (93 412 62 21). Metro Liceu.* **Open** 1-4pm, 8.30-11.30pm Tue-Sat. Closed Aug 2wks. **Main courses** €9.50-€15.70. *Set lunch* €10.30 Tue-Fri. **Credit** AmEx, MC, V. **Map** p345 A5 43

A very Zen-like space with beige minimalist decor, Biblioteca is all about food. Food and books about food, that is. From Bocuse to Bourdain, they are all for sale, and their various influences collide in some occasionally sublime cooking. Beetroot gazpacho with live clams and quail's egg is a dense riot of flavour, and endive salad with poached egg and *romesco* wafers superb. Mains aren't quite as head-spinning, but they are accomplished nevertheless. The set lunch offers more basic fare of pasta dishes and creative salads, and there's an excellent wine list.

### Pla dels Àngels

*C/Ferlandina 23 (93 329 40 47). Metro Universitat.* **Open** 1.30-4pm, 9-11.30pm Mon-Thur, Sun; 1.30-4pm, 9pm-midnight Fri, Sat. **Main courses** €4.65-€7.45. *Set lunch* €6.40 Mon-Fri. **Credit** DC, MC, V. **Map** p342 F9 44

Beautifully designed, in keeping with its position opposite the MACBA, Pla dels Àngels is a riot of colour and chimera, something that also translates to its menu (glued to a wine bottle, no less). A range of salads might include mango, yoghurt and mint oil, or radicchio, serrano ham and roast peppers, followed by a short list of pasta and gnocchi and a cou-

Eat, Drink, Shop

Oleum. *See p163.*

ple of meat dishes. 'Delirium tremens' is a rich chocolate fantasy. The cheap-as-chips set lunch includes two courses and a glass of wine.

### Silenus

*C/Àngels 8 (93 302 26 80). Metro Liceu.* **Open** 1.30-4pm, 8.30-11.30pm Mon-Thur; 1.30-4pm, 8.30pm-midnight Fri, Sat. **Main courses** €12.85-€22.50. *Set lunch* €12 Mon-Fri; €16 Sat. **Credit** AmEx, DC, MC, V. **Map** p344 A3 ❺
Run by arty types for arty types, Silenus works hard to maintain its air of scuffed elegance, with carefully chipped and stained walls on which the ghost of a clock is projected and the faded leaves of a book float up on high. The food, too, is artistically presented (although the omnipresence of poppy seeds becomes quite funny by the time you start picking them from your ice-cream), and never more so than with the lunchtime tasting menu. This allows a tiny portion of everything on the menu, from French onion soup to a flavoursome haricot-bean stew and entrecôte with mashed potatoes.

## Pizzeria

### Ravalo

*Plaça Emili Vendrell 1 (93 442 01 00). Metro Sant Antoni.* **Open** 8pm-midnight Tue-Sun. **Main courses** €7.50-€10.70. **Credit** MC, V. **Map** p342 E10 ❻
Perfect for fans of the thin and the crispy, Ravalo's table-dwarfing pizzas take some beating, thanks to flour (and a chef) imported from Naples. Most pizzas, like the Sienna, come with the cornerstone toppings you'd expect – in this case *mozzarella di bufala*, speck, cherry tomatoes and rocket – but less familiar offerings include the Pizza Soufflé, which comes filled with ham, mushrooms and an eggy mousse (better than it sounds, really). The restaurant's terrace overlooking a quiet square is open year-round. **Photos** *p156 and p157.*

## Spanish

### Las Fernández

*C/Carretas 11 (93 443 20 43). Metro Paral·lel.* **Open** 9pm-2am Tue-Sun. **Main courses** €6.45-€8.55. **Credit** DC, MC, V. **Map** p342 E10 ❼
An inviting entrance, pillar-box red, is a beacon of cheer on one of Barcelona's less salubrious streets. Inside, the three Fernández sisters have created a bright and unpretentious bar-restaurant that specialises in wine and food from their native León. Alongside *cecina* (dried venison), gammon and sausages from the region are lighter, Mediterranean dishes and generous salads; smoked salmon with mustard and dill; pasta filled with wild mushrooms; and sardines with a citrus escabeche. **Photo** *p159.*

## Vegetarian

### Juicy Jones

*C/Hospital 74 (93 443 90 82). Metro Liceu.* **Open** noon-11pm daily. **Main courses** €3.25-€6.25. **No credit cards. Map** p342 F10 ❽
A new branch of this riotously colourful, vegan restaurant that is oriented towards backpackers, with an endless and inventive list of juices, salads and filled baguettes. While tts heart is in the right place, it's staffed, it would seem, by slightly clueless language-exchange students; this is not somewhere you can expect a speedy lunch. Bring a book.
**Other locations**: C/Cardenas 7 (93 302 43 20).

### Organic

*C/Junta de Comerç 11 (93 301 09 02). Metro Liceu.* **Open** 12.30am-midnight daily. **Main courses** €8.20-€11.50. *Set lunch* €9 Mon-Fri; €12 Sat, Sun. **Credit** AmEx, DC, MC, V. **Map** p345 A5 ❾
The last word in refectory chic, Organic is better designed and lighter in spirit (its motto: 'Don't panic, it's organic!') than the vast majority of the city's vegetarian restaurants. The friendly and attentive staff will usher you inside, seat you and give you a rundown on meal options: an all-you-can-eat salad bar, a combined salad bar and main course, or the full whammy – salad, soup, main course and dessert. Listen for the bell and collect your plate when ready. Beware the little extras (such as drinks), which hitch up the prices a fair bit.

### Sésamo

*C/Sant Antoni Abat 52 (93 441 64 11). Metro Sant Antoni.* **Open** 1-3.30pm Mon; 1-3.30pm, 8.30-11.30pm Wed-Sat; 8.30-11.30pm Sun. **Main courses** €10-€13. *Set lunch* (approx) €8.80 Mon-Fri; €10 Sat. **Credit** MC, V. **Map** p342 E10 50

Another veggie restaurant not taking itself too seriously (yoga adverts, but no whale song), Sésamo offers a creative bunch of dishes served in a cosy, buzzing back room. Salad with risotto and a drink is a bargain at just €6.50, or you could try cucumber rolls stuffed with smoked tofu and mashed pine nuts; crunchy polenta with baked pumpkin, gorgonzola and radicchio; or spicy curry served in popadom baskets with dahl and wild rice. There is also a selection of Japanese tapas.

## Barceloneta & the Ports

## Global

### Somorrostro

*C/Sant Carles 11 (93 225 00 10). Metro Barceloneta.* **Open** 7-11.30pm Mon, Thur-Sun. **Main courses** €4.60-€20.35 **Credit** DC, MC, V. **Map** p343 H13 51

Named after the shanty town of Andalucian immigrants that once stood nearby on the beach, Somorrostro is a refreshingly non-fishy, non-traditional restaurant for these parts. Its bare-bricked walls and red-and-black decor attract a young, buzzy crowd, attended to by permanently confused waiters. The food ranges from cucumber, tomato and yoghurt soup with home-made bread, to an unexpectedly successful tandoori duck magret.

## Italian

### Bestial

*C/Ramón Trias Fargas 2-4 (93 224 04 07). Metro Barceloneta.* **Open** 1-4pm, 8-11.30pm Mon-Thur; 1.30-5pm, 8.30pm-12.30am Fri, Sat. **Main courses** €9.65-€19.25. *Set lunch* €15 Mon-Fri. **Credit** AmEx, DC, MC, V. **Map** p343 K13 52

Its tiered wooden decking and ancient olive trees making it the most elegant restaurant on this stretch of beach, Bestial is a peerless spot for alfresco seaside dining. The interior design manages to match the splendour of the exterior, with black-clad waiters sashaying along sleek runways holding their trays high. At weekends, coloured lights play over the tables as a DJ takes to the decks. The food is modern Italian: dainty mini-pizzas, rocket salads with Parma ham and a lightly poached egg, tuna with black olive risotto and all the puddings you'd expect to find – panna cotta, tiramisu and limoncello sorbet.

## Mediterranean

### Agua

*Passeig Marítim 30 (93 225 12 72/www.aguadeltragaluz.com). Metro Barceloneta/bus 45, 57, 59, 157.* **Open** 1-3.45pm, 8.30-11.30pm Mon-Thur,

**Tapioles 53**, a cosy setting for accomplished food. *See p164.*

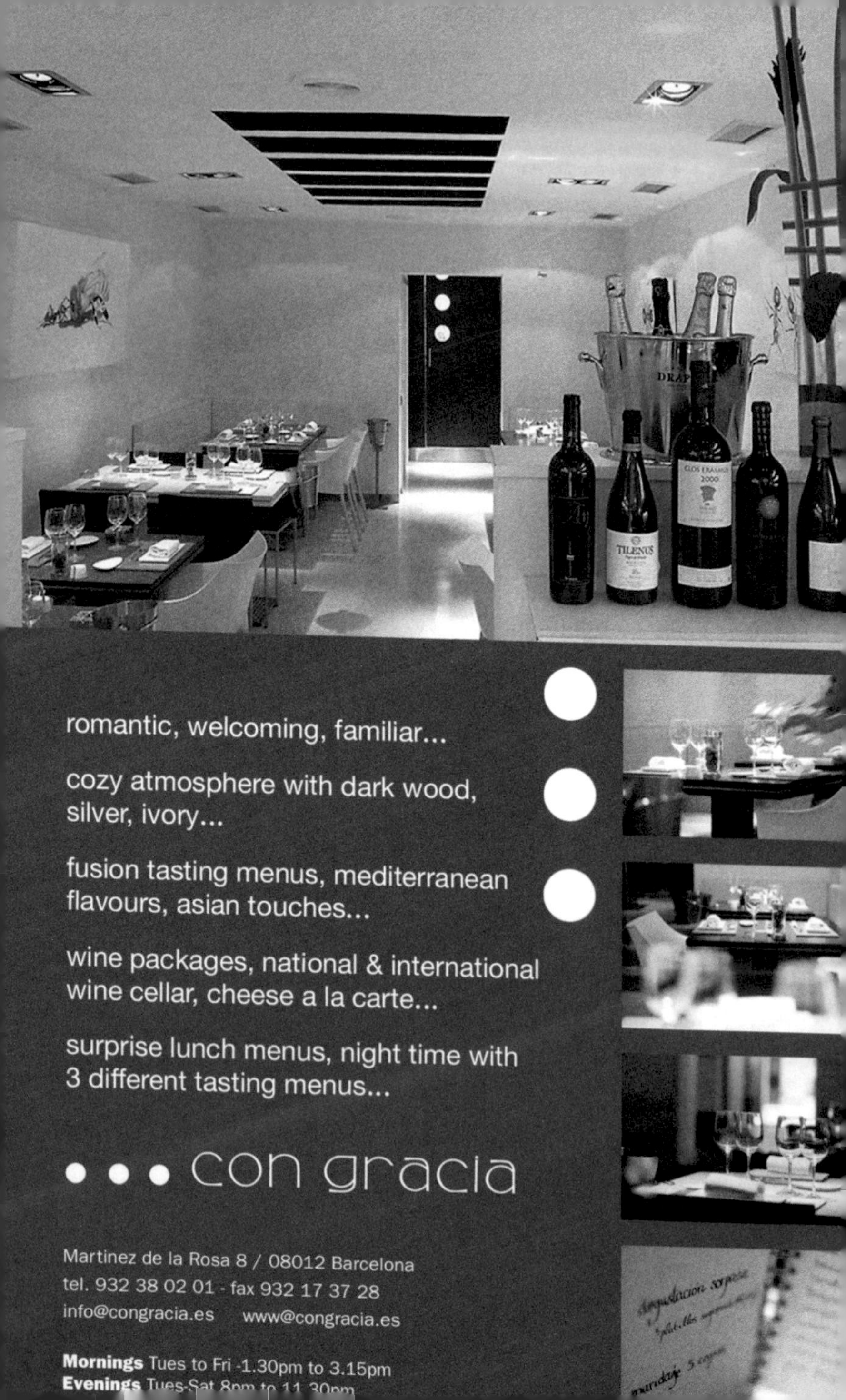
romantic, welcoming, familiar...
cozy atmosphere with dark wood, silver, ivory...
fusion tasting menus, mediterranean flavours, asian touches...
wine packages, national & international wine cellar, cheese a la carte...
surprise lunch menus, night time with 3 different tasting menus...
• • • con gracia
Martinez de la Rosa 8 / 08012 Barcelona
tel. 932 38 02 01 - fax 932 17 37 28
info@congracia.es www@congracia.es
Mornings Tues to Fri -1.30pm to 3.15pm
Evenings Tues-Sat 8pm to 11.30pm

Sun; 1-4.30pm, 8pm-12.30am Fri, Sat. **Main courses** €8.60-€17.15. **Credit** AmEx, DC, MC, V. **Map** p343 J13 53
One of the freshest, most relaxed places to eat in the city, with a large terrace smack on the beach and an animated sunny interior. The menu rarely changes, but regulars never tire of the competently executed monkfish tail with *sofregit*, the risotto with partridge, and fresh pasta with juicy little prawns. Scrummy puddings include marron glacé mousse and sour apple sorbet. The wine mark-up is quite high for such reasonably priced food; a couple of notable exceptions are white Creu de Lavit or red Añares.

## Seafood

### Can Ramonet

*C/Maquinista 17 (93 319 30 64). Metro Barceloneta.* **Open** 10.30am-4pm, 8pm-midnight Mon-Sat; 10.30am-4pm Sun. Closed 2wks Jan, 2wks Aug. **Main courses** €14-€32. **Credit** AmEx, DC, MC, V. **Map** p343 H12 54
A classic among Barceloneta's seafood restaurants, this quaint, rose-coloured space with two quiet terraces is mostly overlooked by tourists, being deep in the heart of the neighbourhood. Consequently, it suffers none of the drop in standards of some of those paella joints on nearby Passeig Joan de Borbó. Spectacular displays of fresh seafood show what's on offer that day, but it's also worth sampling the velvety fish soup and the generous paellas.

### Can Solé

*C/Sant Carles 4 (93 221 50 12). Metro Barceloneta.* **Open** 1.30-4pm, 8-11pm Tue-Thur; 1.30-4pm, 8.30-11pm Fri, Sat; 1.30-4pm Sun. Closed 2wks Aug. **Main courses** €14.55-€28.25. **Credit** AmEx, DC, MC, V. **Map** p342 H13 55
One of Barceloneta's most traditional seafood restaurants, where for over a century portly, jovial waiters have been charming moneyed regulars. Over the years many of these have added to the framed photos, sketches and paintings that line the sky-blue walls. What continues to lure them is the freshest shellfish (share a plate of *chipirones* in onion and garlic, Cantabrian anchovies or red shrimp to start) and fillets of wild turbot, lobster stews and sticky paellas. Beware the steeply priced extras (coffee, cover).

### Set Portes

*Passeig Isabel II 14 (93 319 30 33/www.7portes.com). Metro Barceloneta.* **Open** 1pm-1am daily. **Main courses** €10.20-€36.40. **Credit** AmEx, DC, MC, V. **Map** p345 E7 56
The eponymous seven doors open on to as many dining salons, all kitted out in elegant 19th-century decor. Long-aproned waiters bring regional dishes, served in enormous portions, including a stewy fish zarzuela with half a lobster, a different paella daily (shellfish, for example, or rabbit and snails), and a wide array of fresh seafood or heavier dishes such as herbed black-bean stew with pork sausage, and *orujo* sorbet to finish. Reservations are available only for certain tables (two to three days in advance is recommended); without one, get there early or expect a long wait outside.

### El Suquet de l'Almirall

*Passeig Joan de Borbó 65 (93 221 62 33). Metro Barceloneta.* **Open** 1-4pm, 9-11pm Tue-Sat; 1-4pm Sun. Closed 2wks Aug. **Main courses** €17.15-€34.25. **Credit** MC, V. **Map** p342 G13 57
One of the famous beachfront *chiringuitos* that was moved and refurbished in time for the '92 Olympics, El Suquet remains a friendly family concern despite the smart decor and mid-scale business lunchers. Fishy favourites range from *xató* salad to *arròs negre* and include a variety of set menus, such as the 'blind' selection of tapas, a gargantuan taster menu and, most popular, the *pica-pica*, which includes roast red peppers with anchovies, a bowl of steamed cockles and clams, and a heap of *fideuà* with lobster.

# Montjuïc & Poble Sec

## Catalan

### La Font del Gat

*Passeig Santa Madrona 28 (93 289 04 04). Funicular Parc Montjuïc/bus 55.* **Open** 1-4pm Tue-Sun. Closed 3 wks Aug. **Set lunch** €10.70-€21.40. **Credit** MC, V. **Map** p341 B11 58
A welcome watering hole perched high on Montjuïc between the Miró and ethnological museums. This small and informal-looking restaurant, has a surprisingly sophisticated menu: ravioli with truffles and wild mushrooms, for example, or foie gras with Modena caramel. However, most come for the set lunch: start with scrambled egg with Catalan sausage and peppers or a salad, follow it with baked cod or chicken with pine nuts and basil, and finish with fruit or a simple dessert. Tables outside attract a surcharge.

### Oleum

*Palau Nacional (93 289 06 79). Metro Espanya.* **Open** 1-4pm Tue-Sun. **Main courses** €17.10-€28. **Credit** AmEx, DC, MC, V. **Map** p341 B10 59
That the MNAC's new restaurant is to be considered a serious contender in Barcelona's dining scene is indicated by the two Antoni Tàpies canvases flanking – and almost outdoing – the stunning view across the city. Dishes run the gamut from scallops on squid-ink noodles with lime foam to suckling pig with an onion tarte tatin, or St Peter's fish poached in a fennel broth. Despite one or two teething troubles (distracted service and a couple of deliquescent foams), your average museum caff this is not. **Photo** *p160.*

## Global

### La Soleá

*Plaça del Sortidor 14 (93 441 01 24). Metro Poble Sec.* **Open** noon-midnight Tue-Sat; noon-4pm Sun. **Main courses** €6.50-€11. **No credit cards**. **Map** p341 D11 60

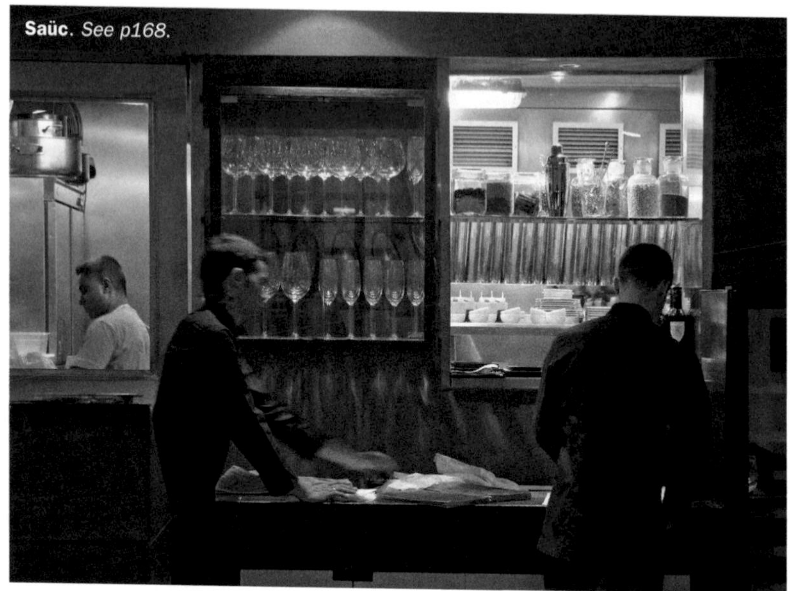
Saüc. *See p168.*



From the name to the sprawling terrace and the cheerful waiters to the orange-and-yellow decor, everything about La Soleá radiates sunshine. There's barely a continent that hasn't been visited on the menu, which holds houmous, tabouleh and goat's-cheese salad alongside juicy burgers served with roquefort or mushrooms, smoky tandoori chicken, Mexican tacos, vegetable samosas and slabs of Argentine beef. For all its international appeal, however, the location in a quiet Poble Sec square makes this a firmly local restaurant, buzzing with kids, dogs and the greeting cries of neighbours, with prices to match.

## Italian

### La Bella Napoli

*C/Margarit 12 (93 442 50 56). Metro Paral·lel.* **Open** 8.30pm-midnight Mon, Tue; 1.30-4pm, 8.30pm-midnight Wed-Sun. **Main courses** €8-€25.70. **Credit** DC, MC, V. **Map** p341 D10 61

La Bella Napoli's once-legendary queues (which would snake out of the door) are thankfully a thing of the past thanks to a major renovation and the addition of a new and spacious bare-bricked dining room. Welcoming Neapolitan waiters, in nifty red T-shirts to match the red gingham tablecloths, can talk you through the long, long list of antipasti and pasta dishes, while you can't go wrong with the crispy baked pizzas, such as the Sofia Loren, with provolone, basil, bresaola, cherry tomatoes, rocket and parmesan. Beer is Moretti and the wine list is all-Italian.

### Xemei

*Passeig de la Exposició 85 (93 553 5140). Metro Poble Sec.* **Open** 1-3pm, 9.30pm-midnight Mon, Wed-Sun. **Main courses** €12-€18. **Credit** MC, V. **Map** p341 C10 62

Heartwarming Venetian country cooking, from home-made pasta to peppered ribbons of liver and onions with fried polenta. The *cicchetti* is a great way to start: a plate of antipasti involving fresh anchovies, figs with pecorino and *sarda in saor* (sardines marinated in vinegar and onions), while peach crostata makes for an indulgent finish. When the weather allows, book a pavement table; the dining room can get a little cramped and noisy.

## Mediterranean

### Tapioles 53

*C/Tapioles 53 (93 329 22 38/www.tapioles53.com). Metro Paral·lel or Poble Sec.* **Open** 9-11.30pm Tue-Sat. **Set menu** €34-€54. **Map** p341 D11 63

Eating at Tapioles 53 is just like eating at a friend's house; if, that is, you have any friends who cook this well with a canny eye for seductive lighting. Tucked down a residential Poble Sec side street, behind a doorbell and slatted blinds, it's the brainchild of Australian chef Sarah Stothart, who wanted to create a cosy atmosphere with accomplished but unpretentious food – fabulous home-made bread with wild mushroom soup; boeuf bourguignon; fresh pasta with baby broad beans and artichokes; rose-water rice pudding with pomegranate, or ginger and mascarpone cheesecake.

The freshest produce is bought daily, and Sarah cooks according to demand, so it helps to book ahead. **Photo** *p161.*

## Eixample

### Catalan

#### Alkimia

*C/Indústria 79 (93 207 61 15). Metro Joanic or Sagrada Família.* **Open** 1.30-3.30pm, 8.30-11pm Mon-Fri. Closed 2wks Aug. **Main courses** €20.35-€38.50. **Credit** DC, MC, V. **Map** p339 J6 64

It came as no surprise to Alkimia's regulars when it was awarded a Michelin star (as a consequence of which, reservations are now all but essential). A great way to explore is to sample the gourmet menu, which offers four savoury courses, including complex dishes that play with Spanish classics – for instance, liquid *pa amb tomàquet* with suet sausage, wild rice with crayfish, strips of tuna on a bed of foamed mustard – and a couple of desserts. An excellent wine cellar adds to the experience.

#### Casa Calvet

*C/Casp 48 (93 412 40 12). Metro Urquinaona.* **Open** 1-3.30pm, 8.30-11pm Mon-Sat. Closed 2 wks Aug. **Main courses** €24.20-€34.15. **Credit** AmEx, DC, MC, V. **Map** p344 E1 65

The loafer's guide to sightseeing would surely have Casa Calvet at the top of the list: a place where you can sample stellar cuisine and appreciate the master of Modernisme at the same time. One of Gaudí's more understated buildings from the outside, Casa Calvet has an interior full of glorious detail in the carpentry, stained glass and tiles. The food is up to par, with surprising combinations almost always hitting the mark: squab with puréed pumpkin, risotto of duck confit and truffle with yoghurt ice-cream, and smoked foie gras with mango sauce. The puddings are supremely good, particularly the pine-nut tart with foamed *crema catalana*, and the cheeseboard contains some unexpected finds.

#### Cinc Sentits

*C/Aribau 58 (93 323 94 90/www.cincsentits.com). Metro Passeig de Gràcia or Universitat.* **Open** 1.30-3.30pm Mon; 1.30-3.30pm, 8.30-11.15pm Tue-Sat. **Main courses** €17.15-€25.70. **Credit** AmEx, MC, V. **Map** p338 F7 66

Run by Catalan-Canadian siblings, the 'Five Senses' is the most reasonably priced of Barcelona's top-end restaurants, and should be on everyone's dining agenda. Talented chef Jordi Artal shows respect for the classics (melt-in-the-mouth suckling pig with apple compôte, for instance, or Catalan flat coca bread with foie gras and crispy leeks), while adding a very personal touch in dishes such as lamb cutlets with a crust of porcini dust. To finish, be sure to save room for the artisanal Catalan cheese pairings or the 'five textures of lemon'. Reservations are generally essential at night; try to visit at lunch if you're after a more peaceful experience.

#### Gaig

*Hotel Cram, C/Aragó 214 (93 429 10 17/www.restaurantgaig.com). Metro Passeig de Gràcia.* **Open** 9-11pm Mon; 1.30-3.30pm, 9-11pm Tue-Sat. **Main courses** €26.75-€37.45. **Credit** AmEx, DC, MC, V. **Map** p338 F8 67

Sadly displaced from its long-term (for over 130 years, in fact) home in Horta after structural problems, Gaig has lost none of its shine in the process. Carles Gaig's cooking never fails to thrill. From the crayfish tempura amuse-gueule, served with a dip of creamed leek salted with a piece of pancetta, through to a shot glass holding layers of tangy lemon syrup, *crema catalana* mousse, caramel ice-cream and topped with burned sugar (to be eaten by plunging the spoon all the way down), every dish is as surprising and perfectly composed as the last. If you treat yourself to one top-class restaurant while in Barcelona, let it be this one.

#### Moo

*C/Rosselló 265 (93 445 40 00/www.hotelomm.es). Metro Diagonal.* **Open** 1.30-4pm, 8.30-11pm Mon-Sat. **Main courses** (half portions) €16.05-€24 **Taster menu** €80, €112. **Credit** AmEx, DC, MC, V. **Map** p338 G6 68

Indulge at **Lasarte**. *See p168.*

Eat, Drink, Shop

# Menu glossary

## Essential terminology

| Catalan | Spanish | |
|---|---|---|
| ***una cullera*** | *una cuchara* | a spoon |
| ***una forquilla*** | *un tenedor* | a fork |
| ***un ganivet*** | *un cuchillo* | a knife |
| ***una ampolla de*** | *una botella de* | a bottle of |
| ***una altra*** | *otra* | another (one) |
| ***més*** | *más* | more |
| ***pa*** | *pan* | bread |
| ***oli d'oliva*** | *aceite de oliva* | olive oil |
| ***sal i pebre*** | *sal y pimienta* | salt and pepper |
| ***amanida*** | *ensalada* | salad |
| ***truita*** | *tortilla* | omelette |
| (note: ***truita*** can also mean 'trout') | | |
| ***la nota*** | *la cuenta* | the bill |
| ***un cendrer*** | *un cenicero* | an ashtray |
| ***vi negre/ rosat/blanc*** | *vino tinto/ rosado/ blanco* | red/rosé/ white wine |
| ***bon profit*** | *Aproveche* | Enjoy your meal |
| ***sóc*** | *soy* | I'm a... |
| ***vegetarià/ana*** | *vegetariano/a* | vegetarian |
| ***diabètic/a*** | *diabético/a* | diabetic |

## Cooking terms

| | | |
|---|---|---|
| ***a la brasa*** | *a la brasa* | char-grilled |
| ***a la graella/ planxa*** | *a la plancha* | grilled on a hot metal plate |
| ***a la romana*** | *a la romana* | fried in batter |
| ***al forn*** | *al horno* | baked |
| ***al vapor*** | *al vapor* | steamed |
| ***fregit*** | *frito* | fried |
| ***rostit*** | *asado* | roast |
| ***ben fet*** | *bien hecho* | well done |
| ***a punt*** | *medio hecho* | medium |
| ***poc fet*** | *poco hecho* | rare |

## *Carn i aviram/Carne y aves/* Meat & poultry

| | | |
|---|---|---|
| ***ànec*** | *pato* | duck |
| ***bou*** | *buey* | beef |
| ***cabrit*** | *cabrito* | kid |
| ***colomí*** | *pichón* | pigeon |
| ***conill*** | *conejo* | rabbit |
| ***embotits*** | *embotidos* | cold cuts |
| ***fetge*** | *higado* | liver |
| ***gall dindi*** | *pavo* | turkey |
| ***garrí*** | *cochinillo* | suckling pig |
| ***guatlla*** | *codorniz* | quail |
| ***llebre*** | *liebre* | hare |
| ***llengua*** | *lengua* | tongue |
| ***llom*** | *lomo* | loin (usually pork) |
| ***oca*** | *oca* | goose |
| ***ous*** | *huevos* | eggs |
| ***perdiu*** | *perdiz* | partridge |
| ***pernil (serrà)*** | *jamón serrano* | dry-cured ham |
| ***pernil dolç*** | *jamón york* | cooked ham |
| ***peus de porc*** | *manos de cerdo* | pigs' trotters |
| ***pintada*** | *gallina de Guinea* | guinea fowl |
| ***pollastre*** | *pollo* | chicken |
| ***porc*** | *cerdo* | pork |
| ***porc senglar*** | *jabalí* | wild boar |
| ***vedella*** | *ternera* | veal |
| ***xai/be*** | *cordero* | lamb |

## *Peix i marisc/Pescado y mariscos/*Fish & seafood

| | | |
|---|---|---|
| ***anxoves*** | *anchoas* | anchovies |
| ***bacallà*** | *bacalao* | salt cod |
| ***besuc*** | *besugo* | sea bream |

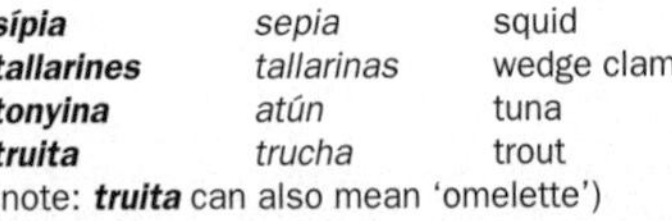

| | | |
|---|---|---|
| ***caballa*** | *verat* | mackerel |
| ***calamarsos*** | *calamares* | squid |
| ***cloïsses*** | *almejas* | clams |
| ***cranc*** | *cangrejo* | crab |
| ***escamarlans*** | *cigalas* | crayfish |
| ***escopinyes*** | *berberechos* | cockles |
| ***espardenyes*** | *espardeñas* | sea cucumbers |
| ***gambes*** | *gambas* | prawns |
| ***llagosta*** | *langosta* | spiny lobster |
| ***llagostins*** | *langostinos* | langoustines |
| ***llamàntol*** | *bogavante* | lobster |
| ***llenguado*** | *lenguado* | sole |
| ***llobarro*** | *lubina* | sea bass |
| ***lluç*** | *merluza* | hake |
| ***moll*** | *salmonete* | red mullet |
| ***musclos*** | *mejillones* | mussels |
| ***navalles*** | *navajas* | razor clams |
| ***percebes*** | *percebes* | barnacles |
| ***pop*** | *pulpo* | octopus |
| ***rap*** | *rape* | monkfish |
| ***rèmol*** | *rodaballo* | turbot |
| ***salmó*** | *salmón* | salmon |
| ***sardines*** | *sardinas* | sardines |

| | | |
|---|---|---|
| ***sípia*** | *sepia* | squid |
| ***tallarines*** | *tallarinas* | wedge clams |
| ***tonyina*** | *atún* | tuna |
| ***truita*** | *trucha* | trout |

(note: ***truita*** can also mean 'omelette')

## Verdures/Legumbres/Vegetables

| | | |
|---|---|---|
| ***albergínia*** | *berenjena* | aubergine |
| ***all*** | *ajo* | garlic |
| ***alvocat*** | *aguacate* | avocado |
| ***bolets*** | *setas* | wild mushrooms |
| ***carbassos*** | *calabacines* | courgette |
| ***carxofes*** | *alcahofas* | artichokes |
| ***ceba*** | *cebolla* | onion |
| ***cigrons*** | *garbanzos* | chickpeas |
| ***col*** | *col* | cabbage |
| ***enciam*** | *lechuga* | lettuce |
| ***endivies*** | *endivias* | chicory |
| ***espinacs*** | *espinacas* | spinach |
| ***mongetes blanques*** | *judías blancas* | haricot beans |
| ***mongetes verdes*** | *judías verdes* | French beans |
| ***pastanagues*** | *zanahorias* | carrot |
| ***patates*** | *patatas* | potatoes |
| ***pebrots*** | *pimientos* | peppers |
| ***pèsols*** | *guisantes* | peas |
| ***porros*** | *puerros* | leek |
| ***tomàquets*** | *tomates* | tomatoes |
| ***xampinyons*** | *champiñones* | mushrooms |

## Postres/Postres/Desserts

| | | |
|---|---|---|
| ***flam*** | *flan* | crème caramel |
| ***formatge*** | *queso* | cheese |
| ***gelat*** | *helado* | ice-cream |
| ***música*** | *música* | dried fruit and nuts, served with muscatel |
| ***pastís*** | *pastel* | cake |
| ***tarta*** | *tarta* | tart |

## Fruïta/Fruta/Fruit

| | | |
|---|---|---|
| ***figues*** | *higos* | figs |
| ***gerds*** | *frambuesas* | raspberries |
| ***maduixes*** | *fresas* | strawberries |
| ***pera*** | *pera* | pear |
| ***pinya*** | *piña* | pineapple |
| ***plàtan*** | *plátano* | banana |
| ***poma*** | *manzana* | apple |
| ***préssec*** | *melocotón* | peach |
| ***prunes*** | *ciruelas* | plums |
| ***raïm*** | *uvas* | grapes |
| ***taronja*** | *naranja* | orange |

As desirable as the rooms at the Hotel Omm (*see p69*) are the tables in its fine restaurant, Moo. Superbly inventive cooking is overseen by renowned Catalan chef Joan Roca – from El Celler de Can Roca (*see p290*) in Girona – and designed as half portions, the better to experience the full range, from sea bass with lemongrass to exquisite suckling pig with a sharp Granny Smith purée. Particular wines (from a list of 500) are suggested to go with every course, and many dishes are even built around them: finish, for example, with 'Sauternes', the wine's bouquet perfectly rendered in mango ice-cream, saffron custard and grapefruit jelly. To top it all off nicely, service is truly exemplary.

### Saüc

*Ptge Lluis Pellicer 12 (93 321 01 89). Metro Hospital-Clinic.* **Open** 1.30-3.30pm, 8.30-10.30pm Tue-Sat. **Main courses** €25-€30. *Set lunch* €25. **Credit** AmEx, MC, V. **Map** p338 E6 ⓺⓽

Book early for one of the coveted tables at Saüc ('elderberry'), particularly for lunch. The €20 set-lunch deal, including water and coffee, is one of Barcelona's classiest, with dishes ranging from accomplished Catalan comfort food in the shape of spicy Mallorcan *sobrassada* sausage with potatoes and poached egg to more sophisticated fare such as cod with apple aïoli, cherry tomatoes and spinach. The extras – excellent bread, a shot glass of pepper and potato soup with pancetta as an aperitif, home-made petits fours – are also an unexpected touch in a *menú del día*. **Photo** *p164.*

### Toc

*C/Girona 59 (93 488 11 48/www.tocbcn.com). Metro Girona.* **Open** 1.30-3.30pm, 8.30-11.30pm Mon-Fri; 8.30-11.30pm Sat. **Main courses** €16-€20.35. *Set lunch* €29. **Credit** AmEx, MC, V. **Map** p343 H8 ⓻⓪

Minimalist to the point of clinical, Toc nonetheless offers a menu that is all heart and colour. Old Catalan favourites such as *esqueixada* (salt cod salad) and *cap i pota* (calves' head stew) are revived with pzazz alongside squab and truffled pâté or chilled beetroot gazpacho. Look out for the green-tea fruitcake with pears in red wine to finish, and a well-thought-out wine list that contains some excellent local bottles at low mark-ups.

### Windsor

*C/Còrsega 286 (93 415 84 83). Metro Diagonal.* **Open** 1-4pm, 8.30-11pm Mon-Fri; 8.30-11pm Sat. Closed Aug. **Main courses** €20.30-€22.40. **Credit** AmEx, DC, MC, V. **Map** p338 F6 ⓻⓵

Let down slightly by a smart but drab dining room and a preponderance of British and American businessmen, Windsor nevertheless serves some of the most creative and uplifting food around. Start with an amuse-gueule of a tomato reduction with pistachio; warm up with wild mushroom cannelloni in truffle sauce or a divine foie gras on thin slices of fruitcake; and peak with a dense, earthy dish of cod on black lentils followed by a foamed *crema catalana*. Then come down to earth with the bill.

**La Parra**. *See p171.*

## French

### Ty-Bihan

*Ptge Lluis Pellicer 13 (93 410 90 02). Metro Hospital Clínic.* **Open** 1.30-3.30pm Mon; 1.30-3.30pm, 8.30-11.30pm Tue-Fri; 8.30-11.30pm Sat. **Main courses** €6.95-€9.65. *Set lunch* €10.70 Mon-Fri. **Credit** V. **Map** p338 E6 ⓻⓶

Functioning both as a crêperie and a Breton cultural centre, Ty-Bihan has chosen a smart, spacious look over wheat sheaves and pitchforks. A long list of sweet and savoury galettes (crêpes that are made with buckwheat flour) is followed up with scrumptious little blinis – try them smothered in strawberry jam and cream – and crêpes suzettes served in a pool of flaming Grand Marnier. The Petite menu will take care of *les enfants*, while a bowl or two of Breton cider takes care of the grown-ups.

## Mediterranean

### Lasarte

*Hotel Condes de Barcelona, C/Mallorca 259 (93 445 32 42/www.restaurantlasarte.com). Metro Passeig de Gràcia.* **Open** 1.30-3.30pm, 8.30-11pm Mon-Fri. Closed Aug. **Mains** €31-€39.60. **Credit** AmEx, DC, MC, V. **Map** p338 G7 ⓻⓷

Triple-Michelin-starred San Sebastián chef Martin Berasategui has now established a culinary outpost over here, overseeing a menu that incorporates many of his signature dishes. One of the most spectacular of these is the layered terrine of foie gras, smoked eel and caramelised apple, while other

dishes of note include a succulent pigeon breast with a foie gras prepared from its own liver, or roast sea bass with hot citrus vinaigrette and creamed 'marrowbone' of cauliflower. Puddings range from superbly refreshing – apple 'ravioli' in a mint and lime jus with coconut ice-cream and rum granita – to impossibly indulgent: a rich bread and butter pudding with coffee ice-cream and plum compôte. **Photo** *p165*.

### Noti

*C/Roger de Llúria 35 (93 342 66 73/www.noti-universal.com). Metro Passeig de Gràcia or Urquinaona.* **Open** 1.30-4pm, 8.30pm-midnight Mon-Fri; 8.30pm-midnight Sat. **Main courses** €10.70-€31. *Set lunch* €20.55 Mon-Fri. **Credit** AmEx, DC, MC, V. **Map** p342 G8 74

At the very cutting edge of the vanguard, Noti is at once wildly glamorous and deadly serious about its food. Centrally positioned tables surrounded by reflective glass and gold panelling make celebrity-spotting unavoidable, but other reasons for coming here include a rich and aromatic fish soup with velvety rouille; lobster carpaccio with crispy seaweed; smoky hunks of seared tuna; and a succulent lamb brochette with spiced couscous and spring vegetables. Modern jazz gives way to house as the night progresses, and the restaurant becomes a bar for the city's most gorgeous.

### Tragaluz

*Ptge de la Concepció 5 (93 487 01 96/www.grupotragaluz.com). Metro Diagonal.* **Open** 1.30-4pm, 8.30pm-midnight Mon-Wed, Sun; 1.30-4pm, 8.30pm-12.30am Thur-Sat. **Main courses** €8.60-€26.75. *Set lunch* €21.40 Mon-Fri. **Credit** AmEx, DC, MC, V. **Map** p338 G7 75

The stylish flagship for this extraordinarily successful restaurant group (which includes Agua and Bestial, *for both see p161*) has weathered the city's culinary revolution well and is still covering new ground in Mediterranean creativity. Prices have risen a bit recently, and the wine mark-up is hard to swallow, but there's no faulting tuna tataki with a cardamom wafer and a dollop of ratatouille-like *pisto*; monkfish tail in a sweet tomato *sofrito* with black olive oil; or juicy braised oxtail with cabbage. Finish your meal with cherry consommé or a thin tart of white-and-dark chocolate.

## Gràcia

### Catalan

### Octubre

*C/Julián Romea 18 (93 218 25 18). Metro Diagonal/FGC Gràcia.* **Open** 1.30-3.30pm, 9-11pm Mon-Fri; 9-11pm Sat. Closed Aug. **Main courses** €8-€12. **Credit** V. **Map** p338 F5 76

Time stands still in this quiet little spot, with its quaint old-fashioned decor, swathes of lace and brown table linen. Time often stands still, in fact, between placing an order and receiving any food, but this is all part of Octubre's sleepy charm. Also contributing to its appeal is a roll-call of reasonably priced, mainly Catalan dishes. Beef in mustard sauce is excellent, and the wild mushroom risotto, while not outstanding, is fine for the reasonable price. The puddings also vary a fair bit, but Octubre is more about atmosphere than anything else.

## Iraqi

### Mesopotamia

*C/Verdi 65 (93 237 15 63). Metro Fontana.* **Open** 8.30pm-midnight Tue-Sat. Closed 2wks Apr. **Main courses** €12.75. *Set dinner* €24.75. **No credit cards. Map** p339 H4 77

The policy at Barcelona's only Iraqi restaurant is to have everything on the menu at the same price, so that the cost won't hold anybody back from ordering what they want. The menu is based on Arab 'staff of life' foods, such as yoghurt and rice. Best value is the enormous taster menu, which includes great Lebanese wines, a variety of dips for your *riqaq* bread, bulgur wheat with aromatic roast meats and vegetables, sticky baklava and Arabic teas. Also good are the potato croquettes stuffed with minced meat, almonds and dried fruit.

## Japanese

### Shojiro

*C/Ros de Olano 11 (93 415 65 48). Metro Fontana.* **Open** 1.30-3.30pm Mon; 1.30-3.30pm, 9-11.30pm Tue-Sat. Closed 2wks Apr, 2wks Aug. **Main courses** *Set lunch* €15.75 (all incl). *Set dinner* €46 (only food). **Credit** MC, V. **Map** p338 G5 78

A curious but successful mix of Catalan and Japanese applies to the decor as much as the food, with original mosaic flooring and dark-green paintwork setting off a clean feng-shuied look. There are only set meals (water, wine, coffee and tax are all included in lunch), starting with an *amuse-bouche*, then offering sushi with strips of nori, sticky rice and salad, or courgette soup with pancetta as a starter, then salmon teriyaki or spring-chicken confit with a potato dauphinois as mains. Puddings might include a wonderfully refreshing own-made apple ice-cream.

## Korean

### San Kil

*C/Legalitat 22 (93 284 41 79). Metro Fontana or Joanic.* **Open** 12.30-4pm, 8.30pm-midnight Mon-Sat. Closed 2wks Aug. **Main courses** €8-€14. **Credit** MC, V. **Map** p339 J4 79

If you've never eaten Korean food before, it pays to gen up before you head to this bright and spartan restaurant. *Panch'an* is the ideal starter: four little dishes containing vegetable appetisers, one of which will be tangy *kimch'i* (fermented cabbage with chilli). Then try mouth-watering *pulgogi* – beef served sizzling at the table and eaten rolled into lettuce leaves – and maybe *pibimbap* – rice with vegetables (and occasionally meat) topped with a fried egg. Just as you're finishing up with a shot of *soju* rice wine, the Korean telly sparks up, and it's time to move on.

## Mexican

### Cantina Machito

*C/Torrijos 47 (93 217 34 14). Metro Fontana or Joanic.* **Open** 1-4pm, 7pm-12.30am daily. **Main courses** €7.30-€13.40. **Credit** MC, V. **Map** p339 H5 80

One of life's perpetual mysteries is whether Mexican desserts are any good or not, given that no one has ever had room for one. Here, for example, 'your starter for ten' takes on a whole new meaning, with the tasty but unfinishable *orden de tacos*, while mains largely comprise of *enmoladas* or enchiladas the size of wine bottles, beached next to a sea of thick mole sauce. Talking of wine, the mark-up on Raimat is almost negligible here, while for beer fans there's Coronita or dark, malty Negra Modelo. The tequila shots and Margaritas go without saying.

## Nepalese

### Himali

*C/Milà i Fontanals 68 (93 285 15 68). Metro Joanic.* **Open** noon-4pm, 8pm-midnight Tue-Sun. **Main courses** €6.45-€11.50. *Set lunch* €7.75. **Credit** AmEx, MC, V. **Map** p339 H6 81

Cocking a snook at the many mediocre Indian restaurants around, Barcelona's first Nepalese eaterie has become a real hit. Faced with an alien and impenetrable menu, you might be tempted by the set meals but they are not always the best option: be sure to press the waiters for recommendations or try *mugliaco kukhura* (barbecued butter chicken in creamy tomato sauce) or *khasi masala tarkari* (baked spicy lamb). Meat cooked in the tandoori oven (*txulo*) is also worth a try, and there are plenty of vegetarian options.

## Pizzeria

### La Tarantella

*C/Fraternitat 37 (93 284 98 57). Metro Fontana.* **Open** 8.30pm-midnight Tue; 1.30-4pm, 8.30pm-midnight Wed-Sun. **Main courses** €7.50-€12.85. *Set lunch* €9.45. **Credit** MC, V. **Map** p338 H6 82

Forge through the unpromising, brightly lit tunnel of a bar to a cosy, low-ceilinged backroom warmed with yellow paintwork, beams and oil paintings. Here you can dine on decent budget Italian grub – salads, fresh pasta and a long list of pizzas. Toppings are generous, rather too much so at times, and the house pizza, for example, comes slathered in mozzarella, ham, mushrooms and onion, while the Extremeño is a mountain of mozzarella, chorizo and egg.

## Seafood

### Botafumeiro

*C/Gran de Gràcia 81 (93 218 42 30). Metro Fontana.* **Open** 1pm-1am daily. **Main courses** €16-€32.10. **Credit** AmEx, DC, MC, V. **Map** p338 G5 83

Love it or hate it (and the size, the racket and the overwhelmingly *arriviste* diners mean no one leaves undecided), there's no denying Botafumeiro's success, and its dozens of tables are rarely empty for long. The speciality here is seafood in every shape and form, which is served with military precision by the fleet of nautically clad waiters. The turbot with clams is excellent and, at the other end of the scale, cod with chickpeas is not half bad either. Non-fish-eaters have a reasonable choice of typically Galician numbers to choose from, including a rich *caldo gallego* (a delicious cabbage and pork broth) and *lacón con grelos* (boiled gammon with turnip tops). Try it for yourself to see which side of the fence you fall on.

## Spanish

### Envalira

*Plaça del Sol 13 (93 218 58 13). Metro Fontana.* **Open** 1.30-4pm, 9pm-midnight Tue-Sat; 1.30-5pm Sun. Closed Aug. **Main courses** €9.60-€18. **Credit** MC, V. **Map** p338 G5 ⓸④

Old-school Spain lives on as penguin-suited waiters solemnly hand out brown PVC menus at plastic teak-effect tables under painfully austere lighting. But it's all worth it for the food: as traditionally brown as the drab decor, it runs the full gamut of hefty Iberian classics. Start your meal with fish soups or lentils and go on to paellas, roast meats and seafood stews, followed by serious, own-made *crema catalana* or *tarta de Santiago*. Arrive early for the leather banquettes at the front.

# Other districts

## Catalan

### Can Travi Nou

*C/Jorge Manrique, Horta (93 428 03 01). Metro Horta or Montbau.* **Open** 1.30-4pm, 8.30-11pm Mon-Sat; 1.30-4pm Sun. **Main courses** €12.85-€25.70. **Credit** AmEx, DC, MC, V.

An ancient rambling farmhouse clad in electric violet bougainvillea and perched high above the city, Can Travi Nou offers wonderfully rustic dining rooms with roaring log fires in winter, while in summer the action moves out to a covered terrace in a bosky, candlelit garden. The food is usually fine – hearty, filling, traditional Catalan cuisine – though it's a little expensive for what it is, and suffers from the sheer volume being churned out of the kitchen. Puddings are better and served with a *porrón* (a glass jug with a drinking spout) of muscatel. But the Can Travi Nou experience is really all about location, location, location.

### La Parra

*C/Joanot Martorell 3, Sants (93 332 51 34). Metro Hostafrancs.* **Open** 8.30am-12.30pm Tue-Fri; 2-4.30pm, 8.30pm-12.30am Sat; 2-4.30pm Sun. Closed Aug. **Main courses** €6-€21. **Credit** MC, V. **Map** p341 B7 ⑧⑤

A converted 19th-century coaching inn with a shady vine-covered terrace. The open wood grill sizzles with various parts of goat, pig, rabbit and cow, as well as a few more off-piste items such as deer and even foal. Huge, oozing steaks are slapped on to wooden boards and accompanied by baked potatoes, calçots, grilled vegetables and *all i oli*, with jugs of local wines from the giant barrels. **Photos** *p168 and p169.*

### Els Pescadors

*Plaça Prim 1, Poblenou (93 225 20 18/www.elspescadors.com). Metro Poblenou.* **Open** 1-3.45pm, 8.30pm-midnight daily. **Main courses** €15-€34.20. **Credit** AmEx, DC, MC, V.

In a forgotten, almost rustic square of the newly hip Poblenou *barrio* lies this first-rate fish restaurant, with tables under the canopy formed by two huge and ancient *ombú* trees. Suspend your disbelief with the crunchy sardine skeletons that arrive as an aperitif (trust us, they're delicious), and move on to tasty fried *chipirones*, followed by cod and pepper paella or creamy rice with prawns and smoked cheese. Creative desserts include the likes of strawberry gelatine 'spaghetti' in a citric soup, and the waiters are exceptionally professional and friendly.

### La Venta

*Plaça Doctor Andreu (93 212 64 55). FGC Avda Tibidabo, then Tramvia Blau.* **Open** 1.30-3.15pm, 9-11.15pm Mon-Sat. **Main courses** €10.20-€21.25. **Credit** AmEx, DC, MC, V.

La Venta's Moorish-influenced interior plays second fiddle to the terrace for every season: shaded by day and uncovered by night in summer, sealed and warmed with a wood-burning stove in winter. Complex starters include lentil and spider crab salad; sea urchins au gratin (a must); and langoustine ravioli, filled with leek and foie mousse. Simpler, but high-quality mains run from rack of lamb to delicate monkfish in filo pastry with pesto.

# Out of town

### El Bulli

*Cala Montjoi (972 15 04 57/www.elbulli.com). By train to Figueres, then bus to Roses, then taxi.* **Open** *Apr-June* 8-10pm Wed-Sat; 1-2.30pm, 8-10pm Sun. *July-Sept* 7.30-10pm daily. Closed Oct-Mar. **Set dinner** €177. **Credit** AmEx, DC, MC, V.

Darling of the Sunday papers, El Bulli is possibly the most talked-about restaurant in the world today; thus it merits a mention here, despite its location up on the Costa Brava. There is only a *degustación*, and diners must arrive by 8.30pm if they are to finish the 30 or so courses by midnight. Dinner is an extraordinary experience, occasionally exalted and frequently frustrating: diners are cossetted guinea pigs, their reactions scanned by the maître d' and the great Ferran Adrià himself. Raw quail's yolk in caramelised gold leaf; sautéed rabbit brains with a truffled cigar of veal marrowbone; edible clingfilm peppered with trout's eggs – every dish is as much food for the mind as the stomach.

# Cafés, Tapas & Bars

The art of drinking.

From the fiercely lit, zinc-countered old men's social clubs to ersatz Maghrebi lounges with sofas and hookahs, the proliferation of bars in Barcelona – many of which are open all day and most of the night – says more about the Spaniards' love of social ritual than their love of alcohol. The Spanish do not drink to get drunk, and find it amusing when foreigners stand to leave a bar and drain their glass on the way out: a Spaniard will leave his half-full in the same circumstances.

Drinking, here, is not an end in itself, but simply a way to oil the wheels of reflection or conversation; starting, perhaps, with a thoughtful shot of *anis* with a morning coffee and ending with *la penúltima*, the final drink of the night with friends (*última* is never uttered, and to do so would be bad luck), with all manner of snifters in between.

### BEER BEFORE WINE

If you ask for a *caña*, you'll be given a small draught beer; a *jarra* is closer to a pint. Ask for a *cerveza*, meanwhile, and you'll be given a bottle. Damm beer is ubiquitous in Catalonia, with Estrella, a strong lager, the most popular variety. Damm also produces an even stronger lager (Voll Damm) and a dark one (Bock Damm). Shandy (*clara*) is popular, untainted by the stigma it has in the UK.

Among wines, Rioja is well known, but there are many excellent wines from other regions in the north of Spain, such as the Penedès in Catalonia, Navarra or El Duero. Most wine drunk here is red (*negre/tinto*), but Galicia produces good whites too, including a slightly sparkling and very refreshing wine called *vino turbio*. Of course, Catalonia has its many cavas, running from *semi-sec* (which is 'half-dry', but actually pretty sweet) to *brut nature* (very dry).

### CAFFEINE KICKS

Spanish coffee is very strong and generally excellent. The three basic types are *cafè sol/café solo* (in Catalan, also known simply as '*café*'), a small strong black coffee; *tallat/cortado*, the same but with a little milk; and *cafè amb llet/café con leche*, the same with more milk. Cappuccino has yet to catch on; whipped cream as a substitute for foam is not unheard of. Then there's *café americano* (a tall black coffee diluted with more water) and spiked coffee: a *carajillo*, which is a short, black coffee with a liberal dash of brandy. If you want another type of liqueur, you have to specify, such as *carajillo de ron* (rum) or *carajillo de whisky*. A *trifásico* is a *carajillo* with a layer of milk. Decaffeinated coffee (*descafeinado*) is widely available, but specify for it *de máquina* (from the machine) unless you want Nescafé. Decaff is popular and very good.

Tea, on the other hand, is pretty poor. If you can't live without it, ask for cold milk on the side ('*leche fría aparte*') or run the risk of getting a glass of hot milk and a teabag. Basic herbal teas, such as chamomile (*manzanilla*), limeflower (*tila*) and mint (*menta*), are common.

### ETIQUETTE

Except in busy bars, or when sitting outside, you won't usually be required to pay until you leave. If you have trouble attracting a waiter's attention, a loud but polite '*oiga*' or, in Catalan, '*escolti*' is acceptable. On the vexed question of throwing detritus on the floor (cigarette ends, paper napkins, olive pits and so on), it's safest to keep an eye on what the locals are doing.

## The best Cafés

### For brunch

**Bodega Manolo** (*see p186*); **Milk** (*see p173*) and **La Nena** (*see p186*).

### For tapas

**El Bitxo** (*see p175*); **Cervesería Catalana** (*see p184*); **La Cova Fumada** (*see p181*); **Mam i Teca** (*see p179*) and **Quimet i Quimet** (*see p183*).

### For ice-cream

*See p179* **The Italian job**.

### For authenticity

**Bar Celta** (*see p173*); **Granja M Viader** (*see p178*); **Marsella** (*see p180*) and **El Portalón** (*see p174*).

### For dizzying views

**La Caseta del Migdia** (*see p183*); **Merbeyé** (*see p187*) and **La Miranda del Museu** (*see p181*).

Eat, Drink, Shop

# Barri Gòtic

## Cafés

### Arc Café

*C/Carabassa 19 (93 302 52 04). Metro Drassanes or Jaume I.* **Open** noon-1.30am Mon-Thur, Sun; noon-2am Fri, Sat. **Credit** AmEx, DC, MC, V. **Map** p345 C7 ❶

A sunny and convivial café popular with expats: it's a veritable Babel of languages. The winning strategy is in predicting exactly what the foreigners might be missing, from a Thai curry (properly spicy) on Thursdays and Fridays to a slice of cheesecake in the afternoons. Sadly, though, the eggs 'n' bacon brunches are a thing of the past and the café now opens only at noon.

### Café de l'Opera

*La Rambla 74 (93 317 75 85). Metro Liceu.* **Open** 8.30am-2.15am Mon-Thur, Sun; 8.30am-2.45am Fri, Sat. **No credit cards. Map** p345 B5 ❷

The last oasis of old-style class on the increasingly commercial Rambla, Café de l'Opera has bags of fin-de-siècle charm and attentive bow-tied waiters to dish out coffee, *ensaimadas* (Mallorcan spiralled pastries, dusted with sugar) and a small selection of tapas. Its situation means that nowadays it sees a largely tourist clientele, but few venture upstairs, which is where peace is to be found.

### Čaj Chai

*C/Sant Domènec del Call 12 (mobile 610 334 712). Metro Jaume I.* **Open** 3-10pm daily. **No credit cards. Map** p345 C5 ❸

One for serious drinkers of the brown stuff, Čaj Chai is based on a Prague tearoom. Here, serenity reigns and First Flush Darjeeling is approached with the reverence afforded to a Château d'Yquem. A range of leaves comes with tasting notes describing, not only the origins, but suggestions for maximum enjoyment. Baklava and home-made cakes are on hand to aid contemplation further.

### La Clandestina

*Baixada Viladecols 2 (93 319 05 33). Metro Jaume I.* **Open** 10am-10pm Mon-Thur, Sun; 10am-midnight Fri, Sat. Closed 2wks Aug. **No credit cards. Map** p345 D6 ❹

Turn in at the sign of the hanging kettle for a mellow, New Age teahouse serving breakfasts, home-made cakes and a huge range of interesting teas – including masala chai, lotus flower, or cherry and redcurrant – along with an impressive array of fresh fruit juices and lassis for those wanting a cold refreshment. The trapeze hanging from the ceiling is occasionally swung into action.

### La Granja

*C/Banys Nous 4 (93 302 69 75). Metro Liceu.* **Open** *June-Sept* 9.30am-2pm, 5-9pm Mon-Sat. *Oct-May* 9.30am-2pm, 5-9pm Mon-Sat; 5-10pm Sun. **No credit cards. Map** p345 C5 ❺

There are a number of these old *granjes* (milk bars, often specialising in hot chocolate) around town, but this is one of the loveliest, with handsome antique fittings and its very own section of Roman wall at the back. You can stand your spoon in the chocolate, which won't be to all tastes. However, the spicy version with chilli or the mocha espresso will set you up for a hard day's shopping.

### Milk

*C/Gignas 21 (93 268 09 22/www.milkbarcelona.com). Metro Jaume I.* **Open** 6.30pm-3am Mon-Sat; noon-3am Sun. **Credit** AmEx, DC, MC, V. **Map** p345 D7 ❻

Milk's candlelit, low-key baroque look, charming service and cheap prices make it ideal for that first date, and music covering the laid-back gamut from Al Green to Hotel Costes can only oil the wheels. Cocktails are a speciality, as is good solid home-made bistro grub from Caesar salad to fish and chips. A good Sunday brunch includes fruit smoothies, fry-ups and pancakes.

### Els Quatre Gats

*C/Montsió 3 bis (93 302 41 40/www.4gats.com). Metro Catalunya.* **Open** 8am-2am daily. **Credit** AmEx, DC, MC, V. **Map** p344 C3 ❽

Housed in a gorgeous building designed in 1897 by Puig i Cadafalch, Els Quatre Gats was once the popular hangout of the city's finest artists, including Pablo Picasso, who held his first exhibition here, and Modernistes Santiago Rusiñol and Ramon Casas, who painted pictures for the place. The food served in the adjoining restaurant could be better, but the setting certainly couldn't.

### Schilling

*C/Ferran 23 (93 317 67 87). Metro Liceu.* **Open** *Sept-July* 10am-3am Mon-Sat; noon-2.30am Sun. *Aug* 5pm-3am daily. **Credit** (over €10) AmEx, DC, MC, V. **Map** p345 B5 ❾

Schilling's airy, smart interior and position smack in the centre of the Old City make it Barcelona's meeting place par excellence (not to mention the city's number one spot for budding travel writers to scribble in their journals), but the aloofness of the staff can become tiring.

## Tapas

### Bar Celta

*C/Mercè 16 (93 315 00 06). Metro Drassanes.* **Open** noon-midnight Tue-Sun. **Credit** AmEx, MC, V. **Map** p345 C7 ❿

No-frills, noisy, brightly lit and not recommended for anyone feeling a bit rough, Bar Celta is nonetheless one of the more authentic experiences to be had in the Gòtic. A Galician tapas bar, it specialises in food from the region, such as *lacón con grelos* (boiled gammon with turnip tops) and good seafood – try the steamed *navajas* (razor clams) or the *pulpo* (octupus) – and crisp Albariño wine served in traditional white ceramic bowls.

Eat, Drink, Shop

**Bubó**. *See p175.*

### Bar Pinotxo

*La Boqueria 466-467, La Rambla 89 (93 317 17 31). Metro Liceu.* **Open** 6am-4.30pm Mon-Sat. Closed 3wks Aug. **No credit cards. Map** p344 B4 ⓫

Just inside the entrance, to the right, of the Boqueria, is this essential market bar, run by Juanito, one of the city's best-loved figures. It's popular witih ravenous night owls on their way home and lunchtime foodies in the know. Tapas are available, along with excellent daily specials such as tuna casserole or scrambled eggs with clams.

### Onofre

*C/Magdalenes 19 (93 317 69 37/www.onofre.net). Metro Urquinaona.* **Open** 10am-4pm, 8pm-12.30am Mon-Thur; noon-4pm, 8pm-1am Fri, Sat. Closed Aug. **Credit** DC, MC, V. **Map** p344 D3 ⓬

A reasonably priced wine bar and tapas restaurant, specialising in cured meats, hams and artesanal cheeses from around the country (while the wines, unusually for a Spanish tapas bar, come from all over the globe). Dishes include a superb goat's cheese salad with anchovies and a tasty cod carpaccio. The bar's diminutive size and stone floors mean it can get noisy when full.

### El Portalón

*C/Banys Nous 20 (93 302 11 87). Metro Liceu.* **Open** 9am-midnight Mon-Sat. Closed Aug. **Credit** MC, V. **Map** p345 C5 ⓭

A rare pocket of authenticity in the increasingly touristy Barri Gòtic, this traditional tapas bar is located in what were once medieval stables, and it doesn't seem to worry too much about inheriting the ancient dust. The tapas list is extensive, but the *torrades* are good too: toasted bread topped with red peppers and anchovy, cheese, ham or whatever takes your fancy. These are washed down with house wine from terracotta jugs.

### Taller de Tapas

*Plaça Sant Josep Oriol 9 (93 301 80 20). Metro Liceu.* **Open** noon-midnight Mon-Thur, Sun; noon-1am Fri, Sat. **Credit** AmEx, DC, MC, V. **Map** p345 B5 ⓮

The more successful the two branches of this tourist-oriented tapas bar become, the more frequently quality control is inclined to dip. At its best, though, it's an easy, multilingual environment, with plentiful outdoor seating at both of its branches, in which to try tapas from razor clams to locally picked wild

mushrooms. At busy periods, however, the service can be hurried and unhelpful, with dishes prepared in haste and orders confused, so it pays to avoid the lunchtime and evening rush hours.
**Other locations**: C/Argenteria 51, Born (93 268 85 59).

### La Vinateria del Call

*C/Sant Domènec del Call 9 (93 302 60 92). Metro Jaume I or Liceu.* **Open** 8.30pm-1am Mon-Sat; 8.30pm-midnight Sun. **Credit** AmEx, DC, MC, V. **Map** p345 C5 ⓯
La Vinateria's narrow entrance, furnished with dark wood and dusty bottles, has something of the Dickensian tavern about it, but once inside there's an eclectic music selection, from flamenco to rai, and lively multilingual staff. The wine list and range of hams and cheeses are outstanding; try the *cecina de ciervo* – wafer-thin slices of cured venison – and finish with home-made fig ice-cream.

## Bars

### Bar Bodega Teo

*C/Ataulf 18 (93 315 11 59). Metro Drassanes or Jaume I.* **Open** 9.30am-3pm, 5pm-2am Mon-Thur; 9.30am-3pm, 5pm-3am Fri, Sat. **Credit** AmEx, MC, V. **Map** p345 C7 ⓰
The split personality of BBT means that mornings see it filling with ancient locals, who've been coming to this old bodega since 1951 to fill their jugs and bottles with wine from huge oak barrels. Night-times hold a different proposition altogether, with young foreigners and *barcelonins* sipping Moscow Mules amid the eclectic decor – fairy lights, futuristic insect lamps, a backlit panel of an expressive mandarin duck – and a blaze of stargazer lilies on the bar. An affairsy snug is curtained off at the back.

### Ginger

*C/Palma de Sant Just 1 (93 310 53 09). Metro Jaume I.* **Open** 7pm-2.30am Tue-Thur; 7pm-3am Fri, Sat. Closed 2wks Aug. **Credit** MC, V. **Map** p345 D6 ⓱
Ginger manages to be all things to all punters: swish cocktail bar; purveyor of fine tapas and excellent wines, and, above all, a superbly relaxed place to chat and listen to music. The foreigner quotient has risen in recent years, it's true, but it would be short-sighted to dismiss this little gem of Barcelona nightlife for that.

### Kiosko de la Cazalla

*C/Arc del Teatre (93 301 50 56). Metro Drassanes.* **Open** 10am-2am Tue, Wed, Sun; 10am-3am Thur-Sat. **No credit cards**. **Map** p345 A7 ⓲
Recently reopened after seven years boarded up, this emblematic hole-in-the-wall bar set into the arch at the entrance of C/Arc del Teatre was for most of the last century a firm favourite of bullfighters and flamenco dancers, prostitutes and sailors. Little has changed since it first raised its hatch in 1912, and the tipple of choice is still the *cazalla*, an aniseedy firewater to warm the cockles.

# Born & Sant Pere

## Cafés

### La Báscula

*C/Flassaders 30 (93 319 98 66). Metro Jaume I.* **Open** 1-11.30pm Tue-Sat. **No credit cards**. **Map** p345 E6 ⓳
Under threat from the demolition demons at City Hall (sign the petition near the till), this former chocolate factory is a real find, with excellent vegetarian food and a deceptively large dining room situated out back. An impressively encyclopaedic list of drinks runs from chai to Glühwein, taking in cocktails, milkshakes, smoothies and iced tea, and the pasta and cakes are as good as you'll find anywhere.

### Bocamel

*C/Comerç 8 (93 268 72 44/www.bocamel.com). Metro Arc de Triomf.* **Open** *Sept-July* 8.30am-8.30pm Mon-Fri; 8.30am-3pm, 5-8.30pm Sat; 8.30am-3pm Sun. *Aug* 8.30am-4pm Mon-Wed; 8.30am-8pm Thur, Fri; 8.30am-3pm Sat, Sun. **Credit** MC, V. **Map** p345 F4 ⓴
It's the mouthwatering, home-made chocolate bonbons, Sachertorte, petits fours and brownies that bring most customers through the door, but Bocamel is also worth knowing about for its breakfast pastries and a short but sweet lunch menu. Needless to say, it's a good idea to hold out for pudding.

### Bubó

*C/Caputxes 10, Plaça Santa Maria (93 268 72 24/www.bubo.ws). Metro Jaume I.* **Open** 3-10pm Mon; 10am-10pm Tue, Wed, Sun; 10am-11pm Thur; 10am-1am Fri, Sat. **Credit** AmEx, MC, V. **Map** p345 E7 ㉑
Be a hit at any dinner party with a box of Bubó's exquisitely sculpted petits fours or make afternoon tea fashionable again with a tray of its colourful fruit sablés, brandy snaps or dreamily rich Sachertorte. Or just sit in a window seat and gorge yourself silly.
**Photos** *p174*.

### Tèxtil Cafè

*C/Montcada 12 (93 268 25 98). Metro Jaume I.* **Open** 10am-midnight Tue-Thur, Sun; 10am-2am Fri, Sat. **Credit** MC, V. **Map** p345 E6 ㉒
Perfectly placed for C/Montcada museum-goers, and with a graceful 14th-century courtyard, Tèxtil Cafè is an elegant place in which to enjoy a coffee in the shade, or under gas heaters in winter, with decent breakfast and lunch menus to boot. For music lovers, there's a DJ on Wednesday and Sunday evenings, followed, on Sunday, by live jazz, although this attracts a €5 supplement.

## Tapas

### El Bitxo

*C/Verdaguer i Callis 9 (93 268 17 08). Metro Urquinaona.* **Open** 1-4pm, 7pm-midnight Mon-Thur, Sun; 1-4pm, 7pm-1am Fri, Sat. **No credit cards**. **Map** p344 D3 ㉓

PASEO JOAN DE BORBO 22 BARCELONETA
THE BAR ON THE WAY TO THE BEACH
THE FASTNET
932953005 IRISH PUB
LIVE FOOTBALL BIG SCREEN
GREAT FOOD ~ FRIENDLY SERVICE

This area is not blessed with decent watering holes; a surprising fact, given the presence of the Palau de la Música and its concert-going crowds. Now the balance is finally being redressed with this small, lively tapas bar specialising in excellent cheese and charcuterie from the small Catalan village of Oix. Kick off the evening with a Power Vermut (made up of red vermouth, Picon, gin and Angostura bitters) and end it with a bottle of the gutsy house red.

### Euskal Etxea

*Placeta Montcada 1-3 (93 310 21 85). Metro Jaume I.* **Open** *Bar* 6.30-11.30pm Mon; 11.30am-4pm, 6.30-11.30pm Tue-Sat. *Restaurant* 8.30-11.30pm Mon; 1.30-4pm, 8.30-11.30pm Tue-Sat. Closed 1wk Dec-Jan. **Credit** AmEx, MC, V. **Map** p345 E6 ㉔

A Basque cultural centre and *pintxo* bar. Help yourself to dainty *jamón serrano* croissants, chicken tempura with saffron mayonnaise, melted provolone with mango and crispy ham, or a mini-brochette of pork, but hang on to the toothpicks spearing each one: they'll be counted and charged for at the end.

### Mosquito

*C/Carders 46 (93 268 75 69/www.mosquitotapas.com). Metro Arc de Triomf or Jaume I.* **Open** 1pm-1am Tue-Thur, Sun; 1pm-3am Fri, Sat. **Credit** MC, V. **Map** p345 F5 ㉕

Don't be put off. The announced 'exotic tapas' are not another lame attempt to sex up fried calamares by way of tower presentation and yucca chips, but tiny versions of good to excellent dishes from the Indian subcontinent and elsewhere in Asia. Food ranges from chicken tikka to Thai omelettes and masala dosas and daisy-fresh sashimi.

## Bars

### L'Antic Teatre

*C/Verdaguer i Callis 12 (93 315 23 54). Metro Urquinaona.* **Open** noon-11pm daily. **No credit cards. Map** p344 E4 ㉖

A slightly madcap theatre run by a slightly madcap crew has, as its most fabulous feature (unless you count a bloke who uses his own blood to make black pudding on stage), a hidden garden dotted with tables cloaked in fruity vinyl and reverberating to the sound of young-enough-to-know-better hippies. These days you must be a member (€3) to drink.

### Casa Paco

*C/Allada Vermell 10 (no phone). Metro Arc de Triomf or Jaume I.* **Open** *Apr-Sept* 9am-2am Mon-Thur, Sun; 9am-3am Fri, Sat; *Oct-Mar* 6pm-2am Tue-Thur, Sun; 6pm-3am Fri, Sat. **No credit cards. Map** p345 F5 ㉗

It sounds like an old man's bar and looks like an old man's bar, but this scruffy, yet amiable, hole-in-the-wall has been *the* underground hit of recent years, thanks largely to occasional visits from Barcelona's DJ-in-chief, Christian Vogel. Other contributing and crucial factors include a sprawling terrace and the biggest V&Ts in the known world.

El Bitxo. *See p175.*

### Espai Barroc

*C/Montcada 20 (93 310 06 73). Metro Jaume I.* **Open** 8pm-2am Tue-Sat; 6-10pm Sun. **Admission** €7 incl 1 drink Mon-Wed, Fri-Sun; €20 incl 1 drink Thur. **Credit** MC, V. **Map** p345 E6 ㉘

A sombre-hued riot of baroque excess, with hundreds of flickering candles lighting up oil paintings, tapestries, sculptures, flowers and bowls of fruit, to the accompaniment of Handel, Brahms and live opera on Thursdays. The location is also great: deep within the 17th-century Palau Dalmases, with tables outside in summer. Expensive and undeniably elitist, but utterly unique.

### Gimlet

*C/Rec 24 (93 310 10 27). Metro Barceloneta or Jaume I.* **Open** 10pm-3am daily. **No credit cards. Map** p345 F6 ㉙

This subdued little wood-panelled cocktail bar has an Edward Hopper feel on quiet nights. The long mahogany counter has been burnished by the same well-clad elbows and patrolled by the same laconic barman for many years, and Gimlet is considered something of a classic, though the measures can be a little too ladylike for modern tastes.

### Mudanzas

*C/Vidrieria 15 (93 319 11 37). Metro Barceloneta or Jaume I.* **Open** *Sept-July* 10am-2.30am Mon-Thur, Sun; 10am-3am Fri, Sat. *Aug* 5pm-2.30am Mon-Thur, Sun; 5.30pm-3am Fri, Sat. **Credit** MC, V. **Map** p345 E6 ㉚

Eternally popular with all ages and nationalities, Mudanzas has a beguiling, old-fashioned look, with marble-topped tables, a black and white tiled floor and a jumble of well-thumbed newspapers. Be warned: it gets very smoky in the winter months, though some relief is to be had at the upstairs tables.

### Va de Vi

*C/Banys Vells 16 (93 319 29 00). Metro Jaume I.* **Open** 6pm-1am Mon-Wed, Sun; 6pm-2am Thur; 6pm-3am Fri, Sat. **Credit** MC, V. **Map** p345 E6 ㉛

Opened a few years ago by a former sommelier, artist and sculptor, this Gothic-style wine bar looks like it's been around forever. There are more than 1,000 wines on the list, many available in a *cata* (small tasting measure) – at a price. The usual Spanish selections are accompanied by wines from the New World and elsewhere.

### La Vinya del Senyor

*Plaça Santa Maria 5 (93 310 33 79). Metro Barceloneta or Jaume I.* **Open** noon-1am Mon-Thur; noon-2am Fri, Sat; noon-midnight Sun. **Credit** AmEx, DC, MC, V. **Map** p345 E7 ㉜

Another classic wine bar, this one has an unmatchable position right in front of Santa Maria del Mar. With high-quality tapas and so many excellent wines on its list (the selection changes every two weeks), it is, however, a crime to do as most tourists do and take up its terrace tables just for the view.

### El Xampanyet

*C/Montcada 22 (93 319 70 03). Metro Jaume I.* **Open** noon-4pm, 7-11.30pm Tue-Sat; noon-4pm Sun. Closed Aug. **Credit** MC, V. **Map** p345 E6 ㉝

The eponymous poor man's champagne is actually a fruity and drinkable sparkling white, served in old-fashioned saucer glasses and best accompanied by the house tapa, a little plateful of delicious fresh anchovies from Cantábria. Run by the same family since the 1930s, El Xampanyet is lined with coloured tiles, barrels and antique curios, and with a handful of marble tables.

## Raval

## Cafés

### Baraka

*C/Valldonzella 25 (93 304 10 61). Metro Universitat.* **Open** 11am-10.30pm Mon-Fri; 4-10.30pm Sat. **Credit** AmEx, MC, V. **Map** p342 F9 ㉞

At the back of a beautiful old building converted into a health-food shop is this cosy little bar, where everything from the wine and beer to the milk used in the fair-trade coffee, is organic and cheap – not a common combination. Should anything ail you, staff will make up an appropriate medicinal tea from the shop's stock of more than 100 herbs.

### Bar Fidel

*C/Ferlandina 24 (93 317 71 04). Metro Sant Antoni.* **Open** 8pm-2am Mon-Thur, Sun; 8pm-2.30am Fri, Sat. **No credit cards. Map** p342 E9 ㉟

There are no Mojitos or cigars and no sign of the bearded one, but Bar Fidel is popular, particularly among students, for its legendary *bocadillos* (filled baguettes). The basic ingredients – though there are 100 permutations – are cured Canary Islands ham, chicken and pork. There are veggie options too.

### Bar Kasparo

*Plaça Vicenç Martorell 4 (93 302 20 72). Metro Catalunya.* **Open** *May-Aug* 9am-midnight daily. *Sept-Apr* 9am-10pm daily. Closed mid Dec-mid Jan. **No credit cards. Map** p344 B2 ㊱

The favourite bar of Barcelona's beleaguered parents, Australian-run Bar Kasparo has outdoor seating (only) overlooking a playground on a quiet, traffic-free square. As well as sandwiches and tapas, there is a daily-changing selection of dishes from around the globe, soups and salads, and the kitchen stays open all day.

### Bar Mendizábal

*C/Junta de Comerç 2 (no phone). Metro Liceu.* **Open** *June-Oct* 10am-1am daily. *Nov-May* 10am-midnight daily. **No credit cards. Map** p344 A4 ㊲

An emblematic Raval bar, its multicoloured tiles a feature in thousands of holiday snaps, Mendizábal has been around for decades but is really little more than a pavement stall. On offer are myriad fruit juices, *bocadillos* and, in winter, soup, served to tables across the road in the tiny square opposite.

### Buenas Migas

*Plaça Bonsuccés 6 (93 318 37 08). Metro Liceu.* **Open** *June-Sept* 10am-midnight Mon-Thur, Sun; 10am-1am Fri, Sat. *Oct-May* 10am-11pm Mon-Thur, Sun; 10am-midnight Fri, Sat. **Credit** MC, V. **Map** p344 B3 ㊳

'Good Crumbs' (from a phrase meaning 'to get on with someone'), is a ferociously wholesome kind of place, all gingham and pine and chewy spinach tart. The speciality is tasty focaccia with various toppings, along with the usual high-fibre, low-fun cakes you expect to find in a vegetarian café. This branch has several tables outside.

**Other locations**: Baixada de Santa Clara 2, off Plaça del Rei, Barri Gòtic (93 319 13 80); Passeig de Gràcia 120, Eixample (93 238 55 49).

### Granja M Viader

*C/Xuclà 4-6 (93 318 34 86). Metro Liceu.* **Open** 5-8.45pm Mon; 9am-1.45pm, 5-8.45pm Tue-Sat. Closed 3wks Aug. **Credit** AmEx, MC, V. **Map** p344 B3 ㊴

The chocolate milk drink Cacaolat was invented in this old *granja* in 1931, and it is still on offer, along with strawberry and banana milkshakes, *orxata* (tiger nut milk) and hot chocolate. It's an evocative, charming place with century-old fittings and enamel adverts, but the waiters refuse to be hurried.

### Iposa

*C/Floristes de la Rambla 14 (93 318 60 86). Metro Liceu.* **Open** *Sept-July* 1pm-2.30am Mon-Sat. *Aug* 7pm-2.30am Mon-Sat. Closed 2wks Dec-Jan. **Credit** MC, V. **Map** p344 A4 ㊵

At lunch and dinner, Iposa functions almost exclusively as a restaurant, serving a handful of simple and low-priced dishes. The rest of the time it makes

Eat, Drink, Shop

# The Italian job

It is a truth universally acknowledged that if it's ice-cream you're after, you should look to the sign of the red, white and green flag. Even the Catalans, often somewhat reluctant to admit to the culinary superiority of other nations, will travel across town to queue for authentic Italian *gelati*.

One of the most recent *gelaterias* to open, **Gelaaati!** (C/Llibreteria 7, Barri Gòtic, 93 310 50 45) was rammed within a month, and with good reason. All flavours are made freshly on the premises every day, using natural ingredients – no colourings, no preservatives. Especially good are the hazelnut, pistachio and raspberry, but more unusual flavours include soya bean, celery and avocado. Nearby is the more established **Gelateria Pagliotta** (C/Jaume I 15, 93 310 53 24), another to use only seasonal, natural ingredients and in the hands of the fourth generation of an ice-cream-making family. The specialities here include sorbets, frozen yoghurts and ice-cream for diabetics.

Up in the north of the Eixample, **Cremeria Toscana** (*photo left*, C/Muntaner 161, 93 539 38 25, closed Mon) is a charming little ice-cream parlour, where around 20 different flavours are made daily, from tangy mandarin to impossibly creamy coconut. *I dopocena* ('after dinner') are miniature gourmet sundaes, mixing parmesan and pear flavours; mascarpone and tiramisu; chocolate and pistachio; or liquorice and mint. Beyond here, in a leafy square in Gràcia, is the **Gelateria Caffetteria Italiana** (Plaça Revolució 2, 93 210 2339, closed Mon, Tue & Nov-Feb), run by an Italian mother-and-daughter team and famous for its dark chocolate flavour – of which it runs out every night.

Like pizza, football and gesticulation, however, making ice-cream is one of many habits stolen from the Italians by the Argentines and then bettered. **Fratello** (Passeig Joan de Borbó 15, 93 221 48 39), the Barcelona arm of a Buenos Aires-based chain, is one of the best. Handily located on the main drag up to the beach, its *helado* is freshly made on the premises every day in a dazzling array of flavours: try the butterscotch-like *dulce de leche* or zingy zabaglione.

for a cosy, vaguely bohemian bar with chilled-out music, decent art exhibited on its walls and coveted tables outside on a quiet, traffic-free square.

### Madame Jasmine

*Rambla del Raval 22 (no phone). Metro Liceu.*
**Open** 10am-2.30am Tue-Fri, Sun; 10am-3am Fri, Sat. **No credit cards**. **Map** p342 E10 41

Kitted out like a slightly bizarre and crumbling theatre set, Madame Jasmine sports silver spray-painted geckos, oriental lamps and feather boas amid its beams and retro '70s tiling. Its generous salads and heaped *bocadillos* are named after historical Raval characters and local street names.

## Tapas

### Mam i Teca

*C/Lluna 4 (93 441 33 35). Metro Sant Antoni.*
**Open** (*kitchen*) 1-4pm; 8.30pm-midnight Mon, Wed-Fri, Sun; 8.30pm-midnight Sat. Closed 2wks Aug. **Credit** AmEx, MC, V. **Map** p342 E10 42

A bright little tapas restaurant with only three tables, so it pays to reserve. All the usual tapas, from anchovies to cured meats, are rigorously sourced, and complemented by superb daily specials such as organic *botifarra*, pork confit and asparagus with shrimp. The bar (which is also open afternoons) is worth mentioning for a superior vodka and tonic.

La Cova Fumada. See p181.



### Els Tres Tombs

*Ronda Sant Antoni 2 (93 443 41 11). Metro Sant Antoni.* **Open** 6am-2am daily. **No credit cards.** **Map** p342 E10 43

Not, perhaps, the most inspired tapas bar in town, with its overcooked *patatas bravas*, sweaty Manchego and vile loos, but still a long-time favourite for its pavement terrace and proximity to the Sunday morning book market. The *tres tombs* in question are nothing more ghoulish than the 'three turns' of the area performed by a procession of men on horseback during the Festa dels Tres Tombs in January.

## Bars

### 23 Robador

*C/Robador 23 (mobile 667 267 034). Metro Liceu.* **Open** 8pm-2am Tue-Thur, Sun; 8pm-3am Fri, Sat. **No credit cards.** **Map** p345 A5 44

Inside this stone-walled and smoke-filled lounge, Raval denizens dig the jazz jam on Wednesdays, the flamenco on Sundays and, in between times, a DJ who plays a genre-defying range of music that might include Joy Division and DJ Shadow on the same night. A manga-style mural painted on the back wall by one of Barna's many graffiti artists adds to the underground appeal.

### Boadas

*C/Tallers 1 (93 318 95 92). Metro Catalunya.* **Open** *Sept-June* noon-2am Mon-Thur; noon-3am Fri, Sat. *July, Aug* noon-3pm, 6pm-2am Mon-Thur; noon-3pm, 6pm-3am Fri, Sat. **No credit cards.** **Map** p344 B3 45

Set up in 1933 by Miguel Boadas, born to Catalan parents in Havana (where he became the first barman at the legendary La Floridita), this classic cocktail bar has changed little since Hemingway used to come here. In a move to deter the hordes of rubbernecking tourists, there is now a dress code.

### Cafè de les Delicies

*Rambla del Raval 47 (93 441 57 14). Metro Liceu.* **Open** 6pm-2am Mon, Tue, Thur, Sun; 6pm-3am Fri, Sat. Closed 3wks Aug. **No credit cards.** **Map** p342 E10 46

David Soul! Boney M! Olivia Newton-John! The functioning 1970s jukebox is reason enough to visit this cosy little bar, even without the excellent G&Ts, the chess, the variety of teas, the terrace and the shelves of books for browsing. A coveted alcove with a sofa, low armchairs and magazines is opened at busy times, or there is a quiet dining room at the back.

### London Bar

*C/Nou de la Rambla 34 (93 318 52 61). Metro Liceu.* **Open** 6.30pm-3.30am daily. **Credit** AmEx, MC, V. **Map** p345 A6 47

The only thing familiar to Londoners will be the punters; otherwise, the Modernista woodwork and smoky, yellowing charm is 100% Barcelona. A little stage at the back has seen it all over the last century, from circus to cabaret, but is now mostly used for jazz, blues and the gentler end of pub rock.

### Marsella

*C/Sant Pau 65 (93 442 72 63). Metro Liceu.* **Open** 10pm-2.30am Mon-Thur; 10pm-3am Fri, Sat. **No credit cards.** **Map** p342 E/F11 48

Marsella was opened in 1820 by a native of Marseilles, who may have changed the course of Barcelona's artistic endeavour by introducing absinthe, still a mainstay of the bar's delights. Untapped 100-year-old bottles of the stuff sit in glass cabinets alongside old mirrors and William Morris curtains, probably covered in the same dust kicked up by Picasso and Gaudí.

### The Quiet Man

*C/Marqués de Barberà 11 (93 412 12 19). Metro Liceu.* **Open** 6pm-3am daily. **No credit cards.** **Map** p345 A6 49

One of the original and best of the city's many Oirish pubs, the Quiet Man's a peaceful place with wooden floors and stalls that eschews the beautiful game

for occasional poetry readings and pool tournaments on its two back-room tables. There is Guinness (properly pulled) and Murphy's, and you're as likely to find Catalans here as you are to see homesick expats and holidaymakers.

### Spiritual Café

*Museu Marítim, Avda Drassanes (mobile 677 634 031). Metro Drassanes.* **Open** *May-Sept* 9pm-3am Wed-Sun. **Credit** MC, V. **Map** p345 A7 ⑩

Deliciously different: a late-night alfresco lounge bar that fills the patio of the Maritime Museum in summer with chilled sounds and zephyrs of incense. Low, round tables scrawled with Arabic script and lit with candles float on a sea of rugs and cushions, while a team of student waiters offers massages, acrobatics, juggling, Tibetan chants and poetry.

# Barceloneta & the Ports

## Cafés

### Daguiri

*C/Grau i Torras 59, corner of C/Almirall Aixada (93 221 51 09). Metro Barceloneta.* **Open** *June-Oct* 11am-2am Mon-Fri, Sun; 10am-1am Sat. *Nov-May* 11am-2am Mon, Thur-Sun. **Credit** (minimum €8) DC, MC, V. **Map** p343 H13 ⑪

Daguiri works hard not to become a one-trick seaside summer terrace, with a raft of measures aimed squarely at foreign residents. Wi-Fi connections, a language exchange, Murphy's, Guinness and a stack of newspapers from around the world feature among them. Throughout the day, there's cheesy garlic bread, delectable filled ciabatta, tapas, dolmades and dips, and home-made chocolate or carrot cake.

### La Miranda del Museu

*Museu d'Història de Catalunya, Plaça Pau Vila 3 (93 225 50 07). Metro Barceloneta.* **Open** 10am-7pm Tue, Wed; 10am-7pm, 9-11pm Thur-Sat; 10am-4pm Sun. **Credit** MC, V. **Map** p345 E8 ⑫

Don't go spreading this about, but there's a secret rooftop café with terrific views, cheap and reasonable set lunches (along with coffee and pastries at breakfast time) and a vast terrace, sitting right at the edge of the marina, perched high above the humdrum tourist traps. Walk into the Catalan History Museum and take the lift to the top floor. You don't need to buy a ticket to the museum.

### La Piadina

*C/Meer 48 (mobile 660 806 172). Metro Barceloneta.* **Open** 1-10pm Tue-Sun. **No credit cards. Map** p343 H13 ⑬

A *piadina* is a warmed Italian wrap, made using something akin to a large pitta. Fillings here come in 30 different permutations on the basic tomato, mozzarella, ham, rocket and mushroom theme. La Piadina is a comfortable little place with newspapers and makeshift sofas, and it really exists to provide superior takeaway snacks to beach-goers. To find it, turn inland at Rebecca Horn's tower of rusting cubes on the beach.

## Tapas

### Bar Colombo

*C/Escar 4 (93 225 02 00). Metro Barceloneta.* **Open** noon-3am daily. Closed 2wks Jan-Feb. **No credit cards. Map** p342 G13 ⑭

Deck-shod yachties and moneyed locals stroll by all day, oblivious to this unassuming little bar and its sunny terrace overlooking the port. In fact, nobody seems to notice it; odd, given its fantastic location and generous portions of *patatas bravas*. The only drawback is the nerve-jangling techno that occasionally fetches up on the stereo.

### Can Paixano

*C/Reina Cristina 7 (93 310 08 39/www.canpaixano.com). Metro Barceloneta.* **Open** 9am-10.30pm Mon-Sat. Closed 3wks Aug-Sept. **No credit cards. Map** p345 E8 ⑮

It's impossible to talk, get your order heard or move your elbows, and yet the 'Champagne Bar', as it's invariably known, has a global following. Its narrow, smoky confines are always mobbed with Catalans and adventurous tourists making the most of the dirt-cheap house cava and sausage *bocadillos* (you can't buy a bottle without buying a couple as ballast). A must.

### La Cova Fumada

*C/Baluard 56 (93 221 40 61). Metro Barceloneta.* **Open** 8.30am-3.30pm Mon-Wed; 8.30am-3.30pm, 6-8.30pm Thur, Fri; 8.30am-1.30pm Sat. Closed Aug. **No credit cards. Map** p343 H13 ⑯

This cramped little bodega is said to be the birthplace of the potato *bomba*, served with a chilli sauce. Here, when they say spicy, they mean it. Especially tasty are the chickpeas with *morcilla* (black pudding), roast artichokes and marinated sardines. Its huge following of lunching workers means it can be hard to get a table after 1pm.

Eat, Drink, Shop

## Fishhh!

For 11 kinds of oysters and an encyclopedic selection of French Champagnes, Catalan *cavas*, and white wines from across Spain (all served by the glass), this sleek, dazzling new dining spot in the L'Illa Diagonal is becoming one of the city's favourite semi-clandestine seafood emporiums. Lluís Genaro, whose family has provided Barcelona's leading restaurateurs with peerless seafood for generations (the Genaro fish dealership is in the Boqueria), and his consort, CUINASIA mastermind Anette Abstoss, have finally launched their own gastronomic destination. Fresh shellfish and tuna; mussels steamed in beer with fried potatoes; *calamari* cooked in batter; grilled *dorado* and lubina...whatever Lluís detects, from your bearing and demeanour, that you may need on any given day will make a quick shopping trip to L'Illa into an event. You can also buy fish to take home, linger at one of the slender white tables, or slide into a booth and try some of the Mediterranean's finest fare. You're in good hands here.

*Comercial Centre L´illa Avenida, Diagonal 557, Local 1-46, Barcelona 08029 Ⓜ Maria Cristina*
*Tel. 93 444 1139 fishdiagonal@yahoo.es*

**LES CORTS**

### El Vaso de Oro

*C/Balboa 6 (93 319 30 98). Metro Barceloneta.* **Open** 9am-midnight daily. Closed Sept. **No credit cards**. **Map** p343 H12 57

The enormous popularity of this long, narrow cruise-ship style bar tells you everything you need to know about the tapas, but it also means that he who hesitates is lost when it comes to ordering. Elbow yourself out a space and demand, loudly, *chorizitos*, *patatas bravas*, *solomillo* (cubed steak) or *atún* (tuna, which here comes spicy).

## Bars

The loud, tacky bars lining the Port Olímpic draw a mixture of drunken stag parties staring at the go-go girls and curious locals staring at the drunken stag parties.

### Luz de Gas – Port Vell

*Opposite the Palau de Mar, Moll del Dipòsit (93 484 23 26). Metro Barceloneta or Jaume I.* **Open** *Apr-Oct* noon-3am daily. Closed mid Nov-mid Mar. **Credit** AmEx, DC, MC, V. **Map** p345 E8 58

It's cheesy, but this boat/bar also has its romantic moments. By day, bask in the sun with a beer on the upper deck, or rest in the shade below. With nightfall, candles are brought out, wine is uncorked and, if you can blot out the Lionel Richie, it's everything a holiday bar should be.

# Montjuïc & Poble Sec

## Cafés

### Fundació Joan Miró

*Parc de Montjuïc (93 329 07 68). Metro Paral·lel then Funicular de Montjuïc.* **Open** *July-Sept* 10am-7.30pm Tue-Sat; 10am-2.30pm Sun. *Oct-June* 10am-6.30pm Tue-Sat; 10am-2.30pm Sun. **Credit** MC, V. **Map** p341 C11 59

Inside the Miró museum is this pleasant restaurant and café; the former overlooks the sculpture garden, while the latter has tables outside in a grassy courtyard dotted with Miró's pieces. The sandwiches made with 'Arab bread' are expensive but huge; there are also pasta dishes and daily specials.

## Tapas

### Quimet i Quimet

*C/Poeta Cabanyes 25 (93 442 31 42). Metro Paral·lel.* **Open** noon-4pm, 7-10.30pm Mon-Fri; noon-4pm Sat. Closed Aug. **Credit** MC, V. **Map** p341 D11 60

Packed to the rafters with dusty bottles of wine, this classic but minuscule bar makes up for in tapas what it lacks in space. The specialities are preserved clams, cockles, mussels and so on, which are not to all tastes, but the *montaditos*, sculpted tapas served on bread, are spectacular. Try salmon sashimi with cream cheese, honey and soy, or cod, passata and black olive pâté. The bar is now no-smoking.

## Bars

### La Caseta del Migdia

*Mirador del Migdia, Passeig del Migdia s/n (mobile 617 956 572). Bus 55 or bus Parc de Montjuïc/funicular de Montjuïc then 10min walk. Follow signs to Mirador de Montjuïc.* **Open** *June-Sept* 8pm-2.30am Thur, Fri; 11am-2.30am Sat; 11am-1am Sun. *Oct-May* 10am-6pm Sat, Sun. **No credit cards**. **Map** p341 A12 61

Follow the Camí del Mar footpath around Montjuïc castle to find one of the few vantage points from which to watch the sun set. Completely alfresco, high up in a clearing among the pines, this is a magical space, scattered with deckchairs, hammocks and candlelit tables. DJs spinning funk, rare groove and lounge alternate surreally with a faltering string quartet; food is pizza and other munchies.

# Eixample

## Cafés

### Bauma

*C/Roger de Llúria 124 (93 459 05 66). Metro Diagonal.* **Open** 8am-midnight Mon-Fri, Sun. Closed 3wks Aug. **Credit** AmEx, DC, MC, V. **Map** p338 G6 62

Bauma is an old-style café-bar that's perfect for lazy Sunday mornings, with its battered leather seats, ceiling fans and an incongruous soundtrack of acid jazz. Along with well-priced, substantial dishes such as baked cod and wild boar stew, there's an impressive list of tapas and sandwiches.

### Café Berlin

*C/Muntaner 240-242 (93 200 65 42). Metro Diagonal.* **Open** *Sept-July* 10am-2am Mon-Wed; 10am-3am Thur-Sat. *Aug* 5.30pm-2am Mon-Wed; 5.30pm-3am Thur-Sat. **Credit** V. **Map** p338 E5 63

Downstairs in the basement, low sofas fill with amorous couples, while upstairs all is sleek and light, with brushed steel, dark leather and a Klimtesque mural. A rack of newspapers and plenty of sunlight make Berlin popular for coffee or snacks all day; as well as tapas, there are pasta dishes, *bocadillos* and cheesecake, but beware the 20% surcharge for pavement tables.

### Dolso

*C/València 227 (93 487 59 64). Metro Passeig de Gràcia.* **Open** 9am-10.30pm Mon; 9am-11.30pm Tue-Thur; 9am-1am Fri; 11am-1am Sat. **Credit** AmEx, DC, MC, V. **Map** p338 F7 64

Heaven on earth for the sweet of tooth, Dolso calls itself a 'pudding café', where even the retro-baroque wallpaper is chocolate-coloured. Desserts run from refreshingly light (a 'gin and tonic' rendered in clear jelly, lemon sorbet, candied peel and juniper berries) to wickedly indulgent (chocolate fondant with sherry reduction and passion fruit sorbet). A short range of sandwiches and topped ciabatta keeps the spoilsports happy.

The **Cervesería Catalana** is popular for its tapas as well as its beer.

### La Paninoteca Cremoni

*C/Rosselló 112 (93 451 03 79). Metro Hospital Clínic.* **Open** 9.30am-5pm, 7.30pm-midnight Mon-Fri; 1-5pm, 8.30pm-midnight Sat. Closed 3wks Aug. **Credit** AmEx, DC, MC, V. **Map** p338 E7 65

Named after the 19th-century inventor of the celebrated Italian sandwich, this is a sunny spot, with a white-painted rustic look enlivened by a huge photograph of Siena. Neither the owners nor the ingredients can make much claim to Italian provenance, but nonetheless panini such as the *siciliano* – olive bread, mozzarella, aubergine, tomato and basil – make a wonderful change from endless *bocadillos de jamón.*

## Tapas

### Bar Mut

*C/Pau Claris 192 (93 217 43 38). Metro Diagonal.* **Open** 8.30am-midnight Mon-Fri; 10.30am-midnight Sat; noon-5pm, 8.30pm-midnight Sun. **Credit** AmEx, DC, MC, V. **Map** p338 G6 66

There's more than a soupçon of the *16ème arrondissement* in this smart, traditional bar; well-heeled Catalans, BCBG to the core, chatter loudly and dine on excellent, well-sourced tapas – foie gras, wild sea bass and *espardenyes* (sea cucumbers). The wine selection is similarly upmarket, and the bottles are displayed so seductively behind plate glass that you may find yourself drinking and spending rather more than you bargained for.

### La Bodegueta

*Rambla de Catalunya 100 (93 215 48 94). Metro Diagonal.* **Open** 8am-2am Mon-Sat; 6.30pm-1am Sun. Closed 2wks Aug. **No credit cards. Map** p338 G7 67

Resisting the rise of the surrounding area, this former wine *bodega* is unreconstructed, dusty and welcoming, supplying students, businessmen and everyone in between with reasonably priced wine, vermouth on tap and prime-quality tapas amid the delicate patterns of century-old tiling. In summer, there are tables outside on the almost-pedestrianised Rambla de Catalunya.

### Cervesería Catalana

*C/Mallorca 236 (93 216 03 68). Metro Passeig de Gràcia.* **Open** 8am-1.30am Mon-Fri; 9am-1.30am Sat, Sun. **Credit** AmEx, DC, MC, V. **Map** p338 F7 68

The 'Catalan Beerhouse' lives up to its name with a winning selection of brews from around the world, but the real reason to come is the tapas. A vast array is yours for the pointing; only hot *montaditos*, such as bacon, cheese and dates, have to be ordered from the kitchen. Arrive early for a seat at the bar, and even earlier to sit at one of the pavement tables.

### Inopia

*C/Tamarit 104 (93 424 52 31). Metro Poble Sec.* **Open** 7pm-midnight Mon-Fri; 1-3.30pm, 7pm-midnight Sat. Closed Aug. **Credit** MC, V. **Map** p341 D9 69

Being brother (and pastry chef) to infamous chef Ferran Adrià has been both a curse and a blessing for Albert Adrià. On the one hand, his traditional tapas bar has been rammed since it opened in spring 2006; on the other, its old-school look and approach has disappointed those expecting El Bulli-style culinary fireworks. If classic tapas – *patatas bravas*, Russian salad, croquettes, tripe and so on – are to your liking, however, Inopia does them as well as anywhere.

## Bars

### La Barcelonina de Vins i Esperits

*C/València 304 (93 215 70 83). Metro Passeig de Gràcia.* **Open** *Sept-June* 6pm-2am Mon-Fri; 7.30pm-2am Sat; 8pm-1am Sun. *July, Aug* 6pm-2am Mon-Fri; 7.30pm-2am Sat. **Credit** V. **Map** p338 G7 ⑩70
With its hundreds of bottles sitting behind chicken wire and its bright lighting a dentist's delight, La Barcelonina is that rare thing: an unpretentious wine bar. Oenophiles and local workers rub shoulders at the bar, poring over a long wine list that includes some excellent cavas, and preparing for the night ahead with a handful of tapas or a salad.

### Dry Martini

*C/Aribau 162-166 (93 217 50 72). FGC Provença.* **Open** 1pm-2.30am Mon-Thur; 1pm-3am Fri; 6.30pm-3am Sat; 6pm-2.30am Sun. **Credit** AmEx, DC, MC, V. **Map** p338 F6 71
This is a shrine to the eponymous cocktail, honoured in Martini-related artwork and served in a hundred forms. All the trappings of a traditional cocktail bar are here – bow-tied staff, leather banquettes, drinking antiques and wooden cabinets displaying a century's worth of bottles – but the stuffiness is absent: music owes more to trip hop than middle-aged crowd-pleasers, and the barmen welcome all comers.

# Gràcia

## Cafés

### Flash Flash

*C/Granada del Penedès 25 (93 237 09 90). FGC Gràcia.* **Open** 1.30pm-1.30am daily. **Credit** AmEx, DC, MC, V. **Map** p338 F5 72
Opened in 1970, this bar was a design sensation in its day, with its white leatherette banquettes and walls imprinted with silhouettes of a life-size frolicking, Twiggy-like model. They call it a *tortilleria*, with 60 or so tortilla variations, alongside a list of kid-friendly dishes and adult-friendly cocktails.

### Salambó

*C/Torrijos 51 (93 218 69 66). Metro Fontana or Joanic.* **Open** noon-1am Mon-Thur, Sun; noon-3am Fri, Sat. **Credit** MC, V. **Map** p339 H5 73
The time-honoured meeting place for Verdi cinemagoers, Salambó is a large and ever-so-slightly staid split-level café that serves coffee, teas and filled ciabatta to the *barri*'s more conservative element. At night, those who are planning to eat are given preference when it comes to bagging a table.

# Golden delicious

According to legend, Jaume I, surveying his new Valencian lands after his victory over the Moors in 1238, stopped to quench his thirst when he saw a young Arab girl carrying a jug of creamy-looking liquid. He took a gulp, exclaimed '*Això es or, xata*' ('That is gold, girl'), and so *orxata* (*horchata* in Spanish) was born.

The drink in question was a kind of dairy-free milk made with ground-up *chufas* (tiger nuts). The *chufa* is actually a small tuber, growing underground and mainly cultivated in Valencia, where it has its own *denominación de origen* and regulatory body. *Orxata* is made by soaking the *chufas* and adding sugar and, occasionally, lemon or orange zest. Though the drink's spiritual home is still Valencia, it's found all over Barcelona, though few places make it fresh. The *ne plus ultra* of Barcelona's *orxata* bars is the ancient family concern **Sirvent** (C/Parlament 56, 93 441 27 20), between the Raval and Poble Sec. Here people will queue into the early hours for a paper cup of the grey stuff, served under unremitting strip lighting and with no concessions to modern decor. Sirvent's ice-creams are also excellent, as is its range of nougat-like *turrones* in winter.

Eat, Drink, Shop

## Tapas

### Bodega Manolo

*C/Torrent de les Flors 101 (93 284 43 77). Metro Joanic.* **Open** 9.30am-7pm Tue, Wed; 9.30am-1am Thur, Fri; 12.30-4.30pm, 8.30pm-1am Sat; 10.30am-3pm Sun. Closed Aug. **No credit cards**. **Map** p339 H4 74

Another old family bodega with a faded, peeling charm (though under renovation at the time of writing), barrels on the wall and rows of dusty bottles, Manolo specialises not only in wine, but in classy food: try the foie gras with port and apple. At the other end of the scale, and also with its place, comes the 'Destroyer': egg, bacon, sausage and chips.

### Sureny

*Plaça de la Revolució 17 (93 213 75 56). Metro Fontana or Joanic.* **Open** 8.30pm-midnight Tue-Thur; 8.30pm-1am Fri, Sat; 1-3.30pm, 8pm-midnight Sun. Closed last wk Sept, 1st wk Oct, 2nd wk Apr. **Credit** MC, V. **Map** p339 H5 75

A well-kept gastronomic secret, Sureny boasts superb gourmet tapas and waiters who know what they're talking about. As well as the usual run-of-the-mill tortilla 'n' calamares fare, look out for tuna marinated in ginger and soy sauce, partridge and venison when in season, and a sublime duck foie gras with redcurrant sauce.

## Bars

### Bo!

*Plaça Rius i Taulet 11 (93 368 35 29). Metro Fontana.* **Open** 10am-1am Mon-Thur; 10am-2.30am Fri-Sun. **Credit** MC, V. **Map** p338 G5 76

Decent tapas, creative sandwiches and generous portions, plus plenty of terrace tables, make this a favourite spot in one of Gràcia's most emblematic, lively squares. If Bo!'s seats are taken, you'll do nearly as well on one of neighbouring bar Amelie's chairs.

### Casa Quimet

*Rambla de Prat 9 (93 217 53 27). Metro Fontana.* **Open** 6.30pm-2am Mon-Thur,-Sun. Closed Aug. **No credit cards**. **Map** p338 G5 77

Yellowing jazz posters cover every inch of wall-space, dozens of ancient guitars hang from the ceiling and a succession of ticking clocks compete to be heard over the voice of Billie Holiday at Casa Quimet. This other-worldly 'Guitar Bar' (as the place is invariably known to locals) occasionally springs to life with an impromptu jam session but, most of the time, it's a perfect study in melancholy.

### La Nena

*C/de Ramón y Cajal 36 (93 285 14 76). Gràcia (93 285 1476). Metro Fontana or Joanic.* **Open** *Oct-July* 9am-10pm daily. *Aug, Sept* 9am-2pm, 4-10pm daily. Closed 3wks Aug. **No credit cards**. **Map** p338 H5 78

Casa Quimet.

Samsara.



An oasis at breakfast time, La Nena (the little girl) is as cutesy as its name suggests, and the sweetness carries over into the menu: home-made cakes, biscuits, freshly whipped cream, ice-creams, and chocolate are what this little girl is made of. But the more health-minded can take refuge in farm-bought yoghurts, a wide range of mueslis, and freshly made juices from orange to papaya.

### Noise i Art

*C/Topazi 26 (93 217 50 01). Metro Fontana.*
**Open** 6pm-2.30am Tue-Thur, Sun; 7pm-3am Fri, Sat. Closed 2wks end Aug, 1st wk Sept. **No credit cards**. **Map** p338 H4 79
It's known locally as the 'IKEA Bar' which, though some of the plastic fittings do look strangely familiar, doesn't really do justice to the colourful, pop art interior. A chilled and convivial atmosphere is occasionally livened up with a flamenco session, and all the usual Gràcia staples, such as houmous and tabbouleh, are served along with various salads and pasta dishes. Mostly, though, this is a great place to sit and shoot the breeze.

### Puku Café

*C/Guilleries 10 (93 368 25 73). Metro Fontana.*
**Open** 7pm-1.30am Mon-Wed; 7pm-2pm Thur; 7pm-3am Fri, Sat. Closed 1st 2wks Aug. **Credit** AmEx, DC, MC, V. **Map** p338 H5 80
Puku Café has two very different vibes going on. During the week it's a colourful meeting place, where the casually hip hang out over a bottle of wine and maybe some cactus and lime ice-cream. At weekends, however, there's a transformation: the amber walls and deep orange columns prop up a younger, scruffier crowd, nodding along to some of the city's best DJs spinning a varied playlist based around electropop.

### Samsara

*C/Terol 6 (93 285 36 88). Metro Fontana or Joanic.*
**Open** *June-Sept* 8.30pm-2am Mon-Thur; 8.30pm-3am Fri, Sat. *Oct-May* 1.30-4pm, 8.30pm-2am Mon-Thur; 1.30-4pm, 8.30pm-3am Fri; 8.30pm-3am Sat. **Credit** MC, V. **Map** p339 H5 81
A combination of Moroccan-themed decor and intelligent cooking, Samsara has built up quite a following among Gràcia foodies. Its tapas are diminutive but don't want for flavour or imagination: try monkfish ceviche with mango, or watermelon gazpacho with basil oil. Photos line the walls, and a DJ plays lounge and the smoothest of house later in the week.

# Tibidabo

## Bars

### Merbeyé

*Plaça Doctor Andreu, Tibidabo (93 417 92 79). FGC Avda Tibidabo then Tramvia Blau/bus 60.*
**Open** noon-2.30am Mon-Thur; noon-3.30am Fri, Sat; noon-2am Sun. **Credit** MC, V.
Merbeyé is a cocktail bar that comes straight from central casting: moodily lit, plush with red velvet and hung with prints of jazz maestros. In summer there's also a peaceful, stylish terrace for alfresco fun. The clientele runs from shabby gentility to flashy Barça players and their bling-encrusted wives.

# Shops & Services

Seek and you shall find.

Sea views and shops aplenty at **Maremàgnum**. *See p190.*



Catalonia's position as a great seafaring nation and the quality of its local products – from silverware to olive oil – have meant Barcelona has always been a hub for happy shoppers. Nowadays, this is a city where many shops still have their original ornate 150-year-old façades, or have been in the same hands for four generations, offering a great contrast to today's homogenous high streets. Of course, much of Barcelona is now given over to Zaras and Mangos, but at least these are local stores. And the fact that you now have to seek out the store that roasts its own nuts in a century-old oven, and the workshop that has made carnival costumes since the 1900s just makes browsing through Barcelona's bustling modern-meets-medieval streets all the more of a treasure hunt.

Most shops don't open until 10am and then close for lunch from 2pm to around 5pm. In a move that may seem like financial suicide, many small shops also close on Saturday afternoons and all day Monday. Large shops and chains, however, soldier through until 8pm, an hour later on Saturdays. The regulations governing Sunday and holiday opening hours are fiendishly complicated. Generally speaking, however, restaurants, bakeries, flower stalls, convenience stores and shops in tourist zones such as La Rambla or Maremàgnum can open seven days a week, and nearly all stores open on the four Sundays before Christmas.

The rate of sales tax (IVA) depends on the type of product: it's currently seven per cent on food and 16 per cent on most other items. In any of the 700 or so shops that display a Tax-Free Shopping sticker on their door, non-EU residents can request a Tax-Free Cheque on purchases of more than €90.15. Before leaving the EU, these must be stamped at customs (at Barcelona airport, this is located in Terminal A by the Arrivals gate) and can immediately be reclaimed in cash at La Caixa bank.

Returning goods, even when they are faulty, can be difficult in all but the largest stores. However, all shops are required to provide a complaints book (ask for an *hoja de reclamación*). The mere act of asking for it sometimes does the trick, but, if not, take your receipt and copy of the complaint form to the local consumer information office, OMIC (Ronda Sant Pau 43-45, Raval, 93 402 78 41, www.omic.bcn.es, open 9am-1pm Mon-Fri).

Note that if you're paying by credit card, you usually have to show photographic ID, such as a passport or driving licence. Bargain-hunters should note that sales (*rebaixes/rebajas*) begin after the retail orgy of Christmas and Epiphany, running from 6 January to mid February, and again during July and August.

## One-stop shopping

### Barcelona Glòries

*Avda Diagonal 208, Eixample (93 486 04 04/ www.lesglories.com). Metro Glòries.* **Open** *Shops* 10am-10pm Mon-Sat. **Credit** varies. **Map** p343 L8.

Since opening in 1995, this mall, office and leisure centre has become the focus of local life. There's a seven-screen cinema (films are mostly dubbed into Spanish) and more than 220 shops, including a Carrefour supermarket, an H&M, a Mango and a Disney Store, facing on to a large, café-filled square decorated with jets of coloured water. Family-oriented attractions include a free pram-lending service, play areas and entertainment such as bouncy castles and trampolines. As a leisure zone, Glòries stays open until 1am.

### El Corte Inglés

*Plaça Catalunya 14, Eixample (93 306 38 00/ www.elcorteingles.es). Metro Catalunya.* **Open** 10am-10pm Mon-Sat. **Credit** AmEx, DC, MC, V. **Map** p344 C2.

El Corte Inglés flagship store (shaped like a cruise liner) is a dominant landmark in Plaça Catalunya. It flies in the face of Barcelona's retail traditions – goods are relatively easy to return, and the staff are generally helpful when you want assistance, and unobtrusive when you don't. Visitors are catered for with store directories in other languages and a translation service. The Plaça Catalunya branch is the place for toiletries and cosmetics, clothes and accessories and homewares. It also houses a well-stocked but pricey supermarket and gourmet food store, plus services ranging from key cutting to currency exchange. The Portal de l'Àngel branch stocks music, books, stationery and sports gear from trainers to training bikes.

**Other locations**: Portal de l'Àngel 19-21, Plaça Catalunya (93 306 38 00); Avda Diagonal 471-473, Eixample (93 493 48 00); Avda Diagonal 617, Eixample (93 366 71 00); L'Illa (sports clothing only), Avda Diagonal 545, Eixample (93 363 80 90).

### Diagonal Mar

*Avda Diagonal 3, Poblenou (902 530 300/www. diagonalmar.com). Metro El Maresme-Forum.* **Open** *Shops* 10am-10pm Mon-Sat. *Food court & entertainment* 10am-midnight Mon-Thur; 10am-2am Fri, Sat; 11am-midnight Sun. **Credit** varies.

This three-level mall has an airy marine theme and a sea-facing roof terrace filled with cafés and restaurants of the fast-food variety. As business is a little slow (except at the giant Alcampo supermarket), it's a good queue-free option. Other anchors include El Corte Inglés, Zara, Mango and FNAC. There's also a bowling alley, regular exhibitions, concerts and children's entertainment every Sunday at 12.30pm.

### FNAC

*El Triangle, Plaça Catalunya 4, Eixample (93 344 18 00/www.fnac.es). Metro Catalunya.* **Open** 10am-10pm Mon-Sat. *Newsstand* 10am-10pm daily. **Credit** AmEx, MC, V. **Map** p344 B2.

This French multimedia superstore supplies info and entertainment on all possible formats. The ground floor has an eclectic and comprehensive selection of magazines, plus national and local papers. Take your purchase to read in the small café on the same floor, then buy the tickets for the gig you've just read about at the ticket desk next to the café. Pick up the photos you've just had processed and compare them to the professional versions on the walls around you, before going to listen to the

## The best Shops

### For Sunday browsing

**Maremàgnum** (*see p190*); **Art Escudellers** (*see p206*) and **Book and Coin market** (*see p208*).

### For party tricks, trinkets and *tragos*

**El Rei de la Màgia** (*see p211*); **Cereria Mas** (*see p211*) and **Vila Viniteca** (*see p206*).

### For dressing like a local

**La Manual Alpargatera** (*see p199*); **Rafa Teja Atelier** (*see p201*) and **Sombreria Obach** (*see p213*).

### For eating like a local

**Planelles Donat** (*see p203*); **La Botifarreria de Santa Maria** (*see p202*) and **Casa Gispert** (*see p202*).

### For sparkle-loving magpies

**Hipotesi** (*see p201*); **L'Arca de l'Àvia** (*see p190*) and **Arlequí Mascares** (*see p211*).

### For platinum card holders

**Bagués** (*see p200*); **Bulevard dels Antiquaris** (*see p190*) and **Jean-Pierre Bua** (*see p195*).

### For cheap and street chic

**Produit National Brut** (*see p200*), **Czar** (*see p199*) and **Freya** (*see p200*).

### For the big night out (and morning after)

**Sephora** (*see p207*); **Le Boudoir** (*see p197*), and **Herboristeria del Rei** (*see p211*).

photographer speak in the auditorium around the corner. On your way out, get cash from the cashpoint to pay for the holiday you're going to book in its travel agency. And that's all on the ground floor. Above this there are two floors of CDs, DVDs, computer software, hardware and peripherals, hi-fis, still and video cameras, MP3 players, home cinema systems and books in various languages.
**Other locations**: Diagonal Mar, Avda Diagonal 3, Poblenou (93 502 99 00); L'Illa, Avda Diagonal 545-557, Eixample (93 444 59 00).

### L'Illa

*Avda Diagonal 545-557, Eixample (93 444 00 00/ www.lilla.com). Metro Maria Cristina.* **Open** 10am-9.30pm Mon-Sat. *Supermarket* 9.30am-9.30pm Mon-Sat. **Credit** varies. **Map** p337 C4.
This monolithic mall's design is based on the idea of a skyscraper lying on its side, and you will also feel like collapsing if you try and explore it all at once. It features all the usual fashion favourites but has a good range of Catalan brands such as Camper, Custo and Antonio Miró. It has been gaining a good reputation lately for its food offerings, with specialist gourmet food stalls and interesting eateries such as sushi and oyster bars.

### Maremàgnum

*Moll d'Espanya, Port Vell (93 225 81 00/www.maremagnum.es). Metro Drassanes.* **Open** 10am-10pm daily. **Credit** varies. **Map** p342 F12/13.
When Viaplana and Piñon's black-mirrored shopping centre opened in 1995, it was *the* place to hang out. After years of declining popularity, it has been spruced up, has ditched most of the bars and discos and taken a step upmarket with shops such as Xocoa (for great chocolate), Calvin Klein and Parisian accessories from boudoirish Lollipops. High-street staples are all present (Mango, H&M, Women's Secret) and the ground floor focuses on the family market, with sweets, children's clothes and a Barça shop. There's also a tapas bar and restaurants. **Photo** *p188.*

## Antiques

A long-standing antiques market is held outside the cathedral every Thursday (*see p207*), and dealers set up stands at **Port Vell** at weekends. **C/Palla** is the main focus for antiques in the Barri Gòtic; however, they're of variable quality. Dazzlingly expensive antiques can be found on **C/Consell de Cent** in the Eixample, and the more affordable around **C/Dos de Maig**, near Els Encants flea market (*see p208*).

### L'Arca de l'Àvia

*C/Banys Nous 20, Barri Gòtic (93 302 15 98/ www.larcadelavia.com). Metro Liceu.* **Open** 10am-2pm, 5-8pm Mon-Fri; 11am-2pm Sat. **Credit** AmEx, DC, MC, V. **Map** p345 C5.
The costume designer for the film *Titanic* came to this vintage clothes emporium for inspiration. The 'Grandmother's Ark' is a treasure trove of delicate lacy things from the era when a lady wouldn't think of leaving the house without a collection of fine-edged hankies to drop in a suitor's path. The silk *camisetas de suerte* make a fine gift for any newborn, or treat yourself to a fringed shawl, exquisite fan or some flouncy white underthings.

### Bulevard dels Antiquaris

*Passeig de Gràcia 55, Eixample (93 215 44 99/ www.bulevarddelsantiquaris.com). Metro Passeig de Gràcia.* **Open** *Oct-June* 10.30am-1.30pm, 4.30-8.30pm Mon-Sat. *July-Sept* 10am-1.30pm, 4.30-8.30pm Mon-Fri. **Credit** AmEx, MC, V. **Map** p338 G7.
One of the most convenient and safest places to shop for antiques in Barcelona (experts inspect every object for authenticity). Miró and Tapies fans can buy limited-edition prints of works by these local artists at March (No.42). Check out the style of ethnic art that influenced the likes of Miró at Raquel Montagut (No.11), where you can pick up a Nigerian funeral urn if that's just what your hallway is missing. Collectors will love the antique playthings at Tric Trac (No.43) and Govary's (No.54).

### Novecento

*Passeig de Gracia 75, Eixample (93 215 1183). Metro Passeig de Gràcia.* **Open** 10am-2pm, 4-8.30pm Mon-Fri; 10am-2pm, 5-8pm Sat. Closed 3wks Aug. **Credit** AmEx, V. **Map** p338 G7.
If you had a very rich, very old great-grandma; this might be what her jewellery box would look like: tumbling strings of raw amber, fiery precious stones set into crosses, delicate cameos on gossamer ribbons. Novecento's windows read like a jewellery museum. It's not all diamond chokers, though. Some pretty costume pieces can be picked up for tens, rather than thousands, of euro.

## Bookshops

Museum shops are often the best bet for books on art, photography, film, architecture and design. A glut of shops specialising in comics, film and other visual art forms can be found in the Arc de Triomf area. In other areas, **Kowasa** (C/Mallorca 235, Eixample, 93 215 80 58, www.kowasa.com) is worth a look for photography enthusiasts. For books on Catalonia, head to the **Palau Robert** shop (*see p323*) or the **Llibreria de la Generalitat** (La Rambla 118, Barri Gòtic, 93 302 64 62); the old-fashioned and proudly nationalistic **Llibreria Quera** (C/Petritxol 2, Barri Gòtic, 93 318 07 43) has plenty of maps, and literature on outdoor pursuits in the region. Don't expect friendly help if you go in speaking Spanish; if you don't speak Catalan, stick to English.

### Casa del Llibre

*C/Passeig de Gràcia 62, Eixample (93 272 34 80/ www.casadellibro.com). Metro Passeig de Gràcia.* **Open** 9.30am-9.30pm Mon-Sat. **Credit** AmEx, DC, MC, V. **Map** p338 G7.

Part of a well-established Spanish chain, this general bookstore offers a diverse assortment of titles that includes some English-language fiction. Glossy, Barcelona-themed coffee-table tomes with good gift potential sit by the front right-hand entrance.

### La Central

*C /Mallorca 237, Eixample (93 487 50 18/www.la central.com). Metro Diagonal/FGC Provença.* **Open** 9.30am-9.30pm Mon-Fri; 10am-9pm Sat. **Credit** AmEx, DC, MC, V. **Map** p338 F7.

La Central is a serious bookshop with a seriously good selection of new books in English. It has a good website (though with only basic pages in English) with news, reviews and an online shop. To prove just how serious they take literature, the staff never, ever, smile. Don't take it personally. The branch in the MACBA is, unsurprisingly, focused on art and design.

**Other locations**: C/Elisabets 6, Raval (93 317 02 93); Plaça del Àngels 1, Raval (no phone).

## Specialist

### Altaïr

*Gran Via de les Corts Catalanes 616, Eixample (93 342 71 71/www.altair.es). Metro Universitat.* **Open** 10am-2pm, 4.30-8.30pm Mon-Fri; 10am-3pm, 4-8.30pm Sat. **Credit** AmEx, DC, MC, V. **Map** p342 F8.

Every aspect of travel is covered in this, the largest travel bookshop in Europe. You can pick up guides to free eating in Barcelona, academic tomes on geolinguistics, handbooks on successful outdoor sex, and CDs of tribal music. Of course, all the less arcane publications are here too: maps for hikers, travel guidebooks, multilingual dictionaries, travel diaries and notebooks and select equipment such as money belts and mosquito nets.

### BCN Books

*C/Roger de Llúria 118, Eixample (93 457 76 92). Metro Passeig de Gràcia.* **Open** *July, Aug* 10am-8pm Mon-Fri. *Sept-June* 10am-8pm Mon-Fri; 10am-2pm Sat. **Credit** MC, V. **Map** p338 G/H7.

This well-stocked English-language bookstore has a wide range of learning and teaching materials for all ages. There's also a decent selection of contemporary and classic fiction, a good kids' section, some travel guides and plenty of dictionaries.

**Other locations**: C/Rosselló 24, Eixample (93 476 33 43); C/Amigó 81, Eixample (93 200 79 53).

### Freaks

*C/Ali Bei 10, Eixample (93 265 80 05/www.libfreaks.com). Metro Arc de Triomf.* **Open** 10am-2pm, 5-9pm Mon-Sat. **Credit** DC, MC, V. **Map** p343 H9.

Books, comics and films, with an unparalleled range of off-the-wall reading matter, are sold at Freaks. DVDs and videos run from arthouse to martial arts, via oddball animation, gore and porn. There are also film books, a clued-up selection of comics and graphic novels, and an eclectic assortment of art, design, illustration and photography books: this is the place to get that Barbie doll catalogue you never knew you wanted.

### Hibernian Books

*C/Montseny 17, Gràcia (93 217 47 96/www.hibernian-books.com). Metro Fontana.* **Open** *Sept-July* 4-8.30pm Mon; 10.30am-8.30pm Tue-Sat. *Aug* 11am-2pm, 5-8.30pm Mon-Sat. **No credit cards. Map** p338 G5.

Hibernian Books feels like a proper British second-hand bookshop, with a pleasantly dusty intellectual air that's not undermined by the shelfloads of Danielle Steele and Jilly Cooper, left by visitors offloading their beach reads before heading home. There are books here for all tastes – from beautifully bound early editions to classic Penguin paperbacks, biographies, manuals, cookbooks, poetry and plays – in all more than 30,000 titles. If you want to get rid of your Jeffrey Archer, you can swap for something from their stock.

# Children

## Clothes

One floor of the Plaça Catalunya branch of **El Corte Inglés** is devoted to kids, while **Galeries Maldà** (C/Portaferrissa 22, no phone, Barri Gòtic) is a small shopping centre with plenty of kids' shops. Larger branches of **Zara** (*see p195*) have decent clothes sections.

### Chicco

*Ronda Sant Pere 5, Eixample (93 301 49 76/www.chicco.es). Metro Catalunya.* **Open** 10am-8.30pm Mon-Fri; 10am-9pm Sat. **Credit** AmEx, DC, MC, V. **Map** p344 D2.

The market leader in Spain, this colourful store has every conceivable baby-care item, from dummies and high chairs to bottle-warmers and travel cots. Its clothes and shoes are practical and well designed, and made for kids up to eight. There's also lingerie for the pre- and post-natal mother.

### Menuts

*C/Santa Anna 37, Barri Gòtic (93 301 90 83). Metro Catalunya.* **Open** 5-8pm Mon; 10.30am-1.30pm, 5-8pm Tue-Fri; 11am-8.30pm Sat. Closed 2wks Aug. **Credit** AmEx, MC, V. **Map** p344 C3.

Handmade baby and toddler outfits in traditional styles: smocked tops, matinée jackets, crocheted hats and very cute booties. The tiniest sizes are for dolls.

### Monkey Biz

*C/Balmes 114, Eixample (93 272 27 08/www.monkey-biz.com). Metro Diagonal/FGC Provença.* **Open** 10.30am-8.30pm Mon-Sat. **Credit** AmEx, MC, V. **Map** p338 F6.

The Monkey Biz monkeys have been busy collecting the coolest clothes and accessories from around the world: cute cotton Mikihouse togs from Japan and Naturino shoes from Italy are just two

El Ingenio.

examples. The shop also has a great range of hand-made and recycled toys and furniture, and it stages workshops and activities for kids.

### Prénatal

*Gran Via de les Corts Catalanes 611, Eixample (93 302 05 25/www.prenatal.es). Metro Passeig de Gràcia.* **Open** 10am-8.30pm Mon-Sat. **Credit** AmEx, DC, MC, V. **Map** p342 G8.

This ubiquitous but pricey chain has slightly frumpy maternity wear, clothes for under-eights, buggies, car seats, cots, feeding bottles and toys.

**Other locations**: Diagonal Mar, Avda Diagonal 3, Poblenou (93 356 04 03); throughout the city.

## Toys

### Almacen Marabi

*C/Flassaders 30, Born (no phone/www.almacen marabi.com). Metro Jaume I.* **Open** noon-2.30pm, 5-8.30pm Tue-Fri; 5-8.30pm Sat. **No credit cards. Map** p345 E6.

Mariela Marabi has created a felt funland with just a sewing machine and her imagination. Although she says she makes toys for adults, kids will love her finger puppets and stuffed animals, and they'll be intrigued by her anatomically correct fabric dolls.

### Drap

*C/Pi 14, Barri Gòtic (93 318 14 87/www.ample24.com/drap). Metro Liceu.* **Open** *early Jan-mid Dec* 9.30am-1.30pm, 4.30-8.30pm Mon-Fri; 10am-1.30pm, 5-8.30pm Sat. *Mid Dec-early Jan* 9.30am-8.30pm Mon-Fri; 10am-8.30pm Sat. **Credit** MC, V. **Map** p344 C4.

If you've ever wanted to feel like a giant, visit this fascinating store. Enthusiastic staff are happy to show you the astonishingly artistic Lilliputian wares on offer: tiny versions of everything to fully furnish the world's best-equipped doll's houses: mini saucepans bubbling on mini ovens, even mini dogs in mini dog baskets.

### El Ingenio

*C/Rauric 6, Barri Gòtic (93 317 71 38/www.el-ingenio.com). Metro Liceu.* **Open** 10am-1.30pm, 4.15-8pm Mon-Fri; 11am-2pm, 5-8.30pm Sat. **Credit** MC, V. **Map** p345 B5.

At once enchanting and disturbing, El Ingenio's handcrafted toys, tricks and costumes are reminders of a pre-digital world where people made their own entertainment. Its cabinets are full of practical jokes and curious toys; its fascinating workshop produces the oversized heads and garish costumes used in Barcelona's traditional festivities during carnival and the Mercé festival in September.

### Joguines Monforte

*Plaça Sant Josep Oriol 3, Barri Gòtic (93 318 22 85). Metro Liceu.* **Open** 9.30am-1.30pm, 4-8pm Mon-Fri; 10am-2pm, 4.30-8.30pm Sat. **Credit** MC, V. **Map** p345 B5.

Make sure you try the Spanish version of snakes and ladders (*el juego de la oca*, or the 'goose game') and ludo (*parchís*) at this old-school toy shop, which is dedicated to traditional board games. Other items for quiet pursuits sold here include chess boards, jigsaw puzzles, wooden solitaire sets, croquet sets and kites.

## Cleaning & repairs

Any shop marked '*rapid*' or '*rápido*' does shoe repairs and key cutting; **El Corte Inglés** (*see p189*) has both in the basement.

Ici et Là.

## La Hermosa

*C/Formatgeria 3, Born (93 319 97 26). Metro Jaume I.* **Open** 10am-9pm Mon-Sat. **No credit cards**. **Map** p345 E6.

A funky washing and dry-cleaning facility complete with sofas, magazines and free internet access for those who have to wash and wait. Opt for self-service washing and drying (€3.50 for a standard load) or go for the drop-off service (€11 for 8kg, €17 for 14kg). Dry-cleaning takes two to three days.

## LavaXpres

*C/Ferlandina 34, Raval (no phone). Metro Sant Antoni or Universitat.* **Open** 8am-11pm daily. **No credit cards**. **Map** p342 E9.

This completely self-service, American-owned launderette is open all day, 365 days a year. There are special machines big enough to wash a rucksack-full of dirty clothes and still have room for more. Smaller 9kg loads cost €3.50.

## Tintorería Ferran

*C/Ferran 11, Barri Gòtic (93 301 87 30). Metro Liceu.* **Open** 9am-2pm, 4.30-8pm Mon-Fri. **Credit** V. **Map** p345 B5.

A small, smart front of house operation reflects the professionalism and courtesy at this reasonably priced dry-cleaners. Services include cleaning of large items like duvets and rugs (which they will also store for you over the winter months), mending (which can be pricey), service washes and delivery. Look out for offers.

# Design & homeware

## Gotham

*C/Cervantes 7, Barri Gòtic (93 412 46 47/www.gotham-bcn.com). Metro Jaume I.* **Open** *Sept-July* 11am-2pm, 5-8pm Mon-Fri; 11am-2pm Sat. *Aug* 11am-2pm, 5-8pm Mon-Fri. Closed 2wks end Aug. **Credit** V. **Map** p345 C6.

Fab 1950s ashtrays in avocado green, bubble TV sets, teak sideboards, coat stands that look like molecular models… Take a trip down nostalgia lane with Gotham's classic retro furniture from the 1930s, '50s, '60s and '70s in warm cartoon colours. Be warned, however, that the prices will have you wishing you'd never given that fluted glass lampshade to the local jumble sale.

## Ici et Là

*Plaça Santa Maria del Mar 2, Born (93 268 11 67/www.icietla.com). Metro Jaume I.* **Open** 4.30-8.30pm Mon; 10.30am-8.30pm Tue-Sat. **Credit** AmEx, MC, V. **Map** p345 E7.

Colourful and quirky, the furniture and home accessories sold here are all limited editions by mainly young designers, handpicked by the French-Spanish duo who runs this shop-cum-gallery in the centre of the Born. The style of the pieces can vary widely, from curvaceous, almost organically carved tables to spiky, impossible-looking chairs; delicate hand-blown glass sits next to chunky, earthy ceramics. Each piece is intriguing and original.

## Recdi8

*C/Espaseria 20, Born (93 268 02 57/www.recdi8.com). Metro Jaume I.* **Open** 11.30am-2.30pm, 5-8.30pm Mon-Fri; noon-2pm, 5-9pm Sat. Closed 1wk Aug. **Credit** AmEx, DC, MC, V. **Map** p345 E7.

At first glance this may seem like yet another shop selling studenty knick-knacks – plastic flower garlands, jokey welcome mats and the like. But, while Recdi8 does score high on the quirkometer, it also has a fairly healthy showing in taste tests. All the products are made by top design houses using quality materials and have some serious design thought behind them – even the cutesy cuckoo clocks.

## Vinçon

*Passeig de Gràcia 96, Eixample (93 215 60 50/www.vincon.com). Metro Diagonal.* **Open** 10am-8.30pm Mon-Sat. **Credit** AmEx, DC, MC, V. **Map** p338 D4.

This is one of the vital organs that keeps Barcelona's reputation as a city of cutting-edge design alive. The building itself is a monument to the history of local design: its upstairs furniture showroom is surrounded by Modernista glory (and you get a peak at Gaudí's La Pedrera); downstairs in the kitchen, bathroom, garden and other departments, everything is black, minimalist and hip. Although not cheap, almost everything you buy here is, or will be, a design classic, whether it's a Bonet armchair or the so-called 'perfect' corkscrew.

**Other locations**: TincÇon, C/Rosselló 246, Eixample (93 215 60 50).

# Fashion

## Boutiques

### La Gauche Divine

*Passatge de la Pau 7, Barri Gòtic (93 301 61 25/www.lagauchedivine.com). Metro Drassanes.* **Open** 5-8.30pm Mon; 11am-2.30pm, 5-8.30pm Tue-Sat. **Credit** AmEx, DC, MC, V. **Map** p345 B7.

Tucked away in the sidestreets running off C/Ample, La Gauche Divine enlivens the clothes shopping experience with art exhibitions, video projections and DJ sets. It has a laid-back friendly vibe that belies the serious quality of its collections: this includes elegant tailoring from Ailanto, and complex, ambitiously constructed pieces from the young and talented Txell Miras.

### Jean-Pierre Bua

*Avda Diagonal 469, Eixample (93 439 71 00/ www.jeanpierrebua.com). Bus 6, 7, 15, 33, 34, 67, 68.* **Open** 10am-2pm, 4.30-8.30pm Mon-Sat. **Credit** AmEx, DC, MC, V. **Map** p338 E5.

The clothes are the highest of high-end fashion, the assistants are model-beautiful, and the shop itself has the air of a runway at a Paris catwalk show. No inferiority complexes are allowed: if you have the money, figure and label knowledge (and only if), come to worship at the altar of Miu Miu, Dries van Noten, Alexander McQueen, Matthew Williamson and many more.

### On Land

*C/Princesa 25, Born (93 310 02 11/www.on-land.com). Metro Jaume I.* **Open** *Sept-July* 5-8.30pm Mon; 11am-2pm, 5-8.30pm Tue-Fri; 11am-8.30pm Sat. *Aug* 11am-2pm, 5-8.30pm Tue-Sat. **Credit** AmEx, DC, MC, V. **Map** p345 C3.

On Land's two shops show a refreshing lack of pretension, with simple decor and a hint of playfulness echoed in the fashions they stock: local boy Josep Font's girly frocks are made for fun rather than flouncing, Petit Bateau's cute T-shirts are perfect for playing sailor girl, and Divinas Palabras' cartoony T-shirts put a smile on your face.

**Other locations**: C/València 273, Eixample (93 215 56 25).

### Suite

*C/Verdi 3-5, Gràcia (93 210 02 47/www.marta rgustems.com). Metro Fontana.* **Open** *Mar-July* 5-9pm Mon; 11am-2pm, 5-9pm Tue-Sat. *Aug* 5-9pm Mon-Thur; 11am-2pm, 5-9pm Fri, Sat. *Sept-Feb* 5-8.30pm Mon; 10.30am-2pm, 5-8.30pm Tue-Sat. Closed 2wks end Aug, 1wk Sept. **Credit** AmEx, V. **Map** p339 H5.

The designers showcased in this Gràcia boutique tend towards the sober rather than the showy in their pieces. But it doesn't mean school marms only need apply. P-Pi's bags combine prim tweed with pretty ribbons in avant-garde shapes. And La Casita de Wendy's fairy-tale inspired designs are a favourite with Björk.

## Budget

### Mango

*Passeig de Gràcia 65, Eixample (93 215 75 30/ www.mango.es). Metro Passeig de Gràcia.* **Open** 10am-9pm Mon-Sat. **Credit** AmEx, DC, MC, V. **Map** p338 G7.

A small step up from Zara in quality and price, Mango's womenswear is less chameleon-like but still victim to the catwalks. Strong points include funky winter coats, tailored trouser suits and skirts, knitwear and stretchy tops. Unsold items end up at the Mango Outlet (*see p196*), which is packed with frenzied girls on a mission.

**Other locations**: Passeig de Gràcia 8-10, Eixample (93 412 15 99); Portal de l'Àngel, Barri Gòtic (93 317 69 85); and throughout the city.

### Zara

*Portal de l'Àngel 32-34, Barri Gòtic (93 301 08 98/www.zara.com). Metro Catalunya.* **Open** 10am-9pm Mon-Sat. **Credit** AmEx, DC, MC, V. **Map** p344 C3.

Zara's recipe for success has won over the world, but items are cheaper on its home turf. Well-executed, affordable copies of catwalk fashions appear on the rails in a fashion heartbeat; while the women's section is the front-runner, the men's and kids' sections cover good ground. The introduction of the Zara Home department has also been a success. The price you pay (for the price you pay) becomes apparent in the despair-inducing queues at peak times.

**Other locations**: Rambla de Catalunya 67, Eixample (93 487 08 18); Passeig de Gràcia 16, Eixample (93 318 76 75); and throughout the city.

## Designer

### Antonio Miró

*C/Consell de Cent 349, Eixample (93 487 06 70/ www.antoniomiro.es). Metro Passeig de Gràcia.* **Open** 10.30am-8.30pm Mon-Sat. **Credit** AmEx, DC, MC, V. **Map** p338 G8.

Catalan designer Miró caused a bit of a stir when he showed his collection in a Barcelona men's prison last year, mingling prisoners on the catwalk with professional models. It was perhaps somewhat appropriate – Miró creates sober, almost uniform-like clothes for men and women in muted tones and androgynous shapes. His diffusion line, Miró jeans, is a bit more relaxed and playful.

**Other locations** (Miró Jeans): C/València 272, Eixample (93 272 24 91); C/Vidrieria 5, Born (93 268 82 03).

### Giménez y Zuazo

*C/Elisabets 20, Raval (93 412 33 81/www.boba.es). Metro Catalunya.* **Open** 10.30am-3pm, 5-8.30pm Mon-Sat. **Credit** AmEx, DC, MC, V. **Map** p344 A3.

This effortlessly cool designer duo has always been quirky. Previously, they've let themselves go when it comes to colour and print, although they have been quite restrained with the silhouette of their

Giménez y Zuazo. See p195.

women's clothing line. However, lately, they seem to have thrown the A-line shape rule book out of the window and have started playing with layers and asymmetric cuts.
**Other locations**: C/Rec 42, Born (93 310 67 43).

### Lydia Delgado

*C/Minerva 21, Gràcia (93 415 99 98/www.lydiadelgado.es). Metro Diagonal.* **Open** *Sept-July* 10am-2pm, 4.30-8.30pm Mon-Sat. *Aug* 10.30am-2pm, 5-8.30pm Mon-Fri; 10.30am-2pm Sat. **Credit** AmEx, DC, MC, V. **Map** p338 G6.
Lydia often claims Gothic influences on her womenswear collections, and there's certainly something vampish about her penchant for clinging silhouettes and a palette of black, charcoal and scarlet. Yet there's also a masculine touch in her clothes: one can imagine that the feisty yet feminine stars of the studio era, like Katharine Hepburn, would have loved being pretty but powerful in her designs.

### Purificación García

*Passeig de Gràcia 21, Eixample (93 487 72 92/www.purificaciongarcia.es). Metro Passeig de Gràcia.* **Open** 10am-8.30pm Mon-Sat. **Credit** AmEx, DC, MC, V. **Map** p342 G8.
Spanish-Uruguayan designer Purificación's sleek, sophisticated creations have appeared in many film and theatre productions. Indeed, there is something dramatic about her use of flashes of colour and tactile fabrics in otherwise conservative designs. García creates clothes for those who want to make an subtle statement in the office or at the dinner party.
**Other locations**: L'Illa, Avda Diagonal 545-557, Eixample (93 444 02 53).

## Designer bargains

One of Barcelona's hotspots for bargain clothes shopping is C/Girona. The two blocks between C/Ausiàs Marc and Gran Via de les Corts Catalanes are lined with remainder stores and factory outlets of fluctuating quality. **Mango Outlet**, crammed with last season's unsold stock, far outshines the rest: the C/Girona branch (No.37, 93 412 29 35) is larger and more frantic, while the uptown branch (C/Pau Casals 12, 93 209 07 73) offers a more select choice.

If you're a dedicated designer bargain-hunter, make the 30-minute pilgrimage just outside the city to **La Roca Village** (93 842 39 39, www.larocavillage.com), where more than 50 discount outlets will tempt you with designer apparel from popular brands such as Antonio Miró, Versace, Diesel and Camper.

### Contribuciones y Moda

*C/Riera Sant Miquel 30, Gràcia (93 218 71 40). Metro Diagonal.* **Open** 11am-2pm, 5-9pm Mon-Fri; 11am-2pm Sat. Closed 2wks Aug. **Credit** AmEx, DC, MC, V. **Map** p338 G6.
Unlike many discount stores, Contribuciones y Moda's decor doesn't make you feel like a discounted customer: it has the feel of an elegant apartment, with spiral staircases and cosy sofas. The raised ground floor houses the women's department, with a wide range of stock from jogging tops to evening gowns. Downstairs, the men's section is smaller, with a focus on designer jeans and clubby shirts.

### Stockland

*C/Comtal 22, Barri Gòtic (93 318 03 31). Metro Urquinaona.* **Open** 10am-8.30pm Mon-Sat. **Credit** AmEx, DC, MC, V. **Map** p344 D3.

A far cry from the elbow-deep frenzy of many remainder stores, this elegant boutique specialises in end-of-line clothing for women designed by respected Spanish names such as Josep Font, Jesús del Pozo and Purificación García at discount prices. Smart styles predominate; eveningwear is upstairs.

## Lingerie & underwear

Rambla de Catalunya is a mecca for underwear shoppers: boutiques brimming with lingerie, such as **La Perla** (No.88, 93 467 71 49), sit beside traditional retailers, among them **La Perla Gris** (No.220, 93 215 29 91). And then there's inexpensive swimwear and underwear at high-street chains such as **Oysho** (No.77, 93 488 36 01, www.oysho.com), from the same stable as Zara. **Vanity Fair** (No.11, 93 317 65 45) strikes a happy medium with reasonably priced Spanish labels as well as its own range. **El Corte Inglés** (*see p189*) has men's and women's underwear for all ages.

### Janina

*Rambla de Catalunya 94, Eixample (93 215 04 84). Metro Diagonal/FGC Provença.* **Open** *Sept-July* 10am-8.30pm Mon-Sat. *Aug* 10am-2pm, 5-8.30pm Mon-Sat. **Credit** AmEx, MC, V. **Map** p338 G7.

Good-quality women's underwear and nightwear by Calvin Klein, Christian Dior, La Perla and others. Some larger sizes are stocked; alternatively, bras can be sent to a seamstress to be altered overnight.

**Other locations**: Avda Pau Casals 8, Eixample (93 202 06 93).

### Le Boudoir

*C/Canuda 21, Barri Gòtic (93 302 52 81/www.leboudoir.net). Metro Catalunya.* **Open** *Sept-July* 10am-8.30pm Mon-Fri; 10.30am-9pm Sat. *Aug* 11am-9pm Mon-Sat. **Credit** AmEx, DC, MC, V. **Map** p344 C3.

Sensuality abounds in Barcelona's classy answer to Agent Provocateur. Sexy lingerie comes with designer labels (and prices), swimwear is not intended for shrinking violets, and fluffy kitten-heeled mules are not made with practicality in mind. Erotic books, sex toys, essential oils and other seductive stuff nestles discreetly on satin chaises longues and velvet cushions.

**Other locations**: Pedralbes Centre, Avda Diagonal 609, Pedralbes (93 321 05 39).

### Women's Secret

*C/Portaferrissa 7-9, Barri Gòtic (93 318 92 42/www.womensecret.com). Metro Liceu.* **Open** 10am-9pm Mon-Sat. **Credit** AmEx, DC, MC, V. **Map** p344 B4.

What's the secret? It seems to be that women would rather wear underwear that's cute, colourful and comfortable than some fussy, itchy pieces of black nylon string. There are some sexy pieces here, but mostly it's versatile strap bras, cool cotton Japanesey wraparound PJs and a funky line of under/outerwear in cartoonish stylings: skimpy shorts, miniskirts and vest tops. A great stop for cheap staples that can be worn to death on hols and chucked away at the airport.

**Other locations**: Portal de l'Àngel, Barri Gòtic (93 318 70 55); and throughout the city.

## Mid range

### Adolfo Domínguez

*C/Ribera 16, Born (93 319 21 59/www.adolfodominguez.com). Metro Barceloneta.* **Open** 11am-9pm Mon-Sat. **Credit** AmEx, DC, MC, V. **Map** p345 F7.

Men's tailoring remains Domínguez's forte, with his elegantly cut suits and shirts. The women's line reciprocates with tame, immaculately refined outfits, also squarely aimed at the 30- to 45-year-old market. The more casual U de Adolfo Domínguez line courts younger traditionalists, but doesn't quite attain the effortless panache of its grown-up precursor. This undervisited two-storey flagship store is supplemented by several others around the city.

**Other locations**: Avda Diagonal 490, Gràcia (93 416 17 16); Passeig de Gràcia 32, Eixample (93 487 41 70); Passeig de Gràcia 89, Eixample (93 215 13 39).

### Cortefiel

*Portal de l'Àngel 38, Barri Gòtic (93 301 07 00/www.cortefiel.com). Metro Catalunya.* **Open** 10am-8.30pm Mon-Sat. **Credit** AmEx, DC, MC, V. **Map** p344 C3.

This popular chain casts a wider net than Mango or Zara, its fine tailored jackets and elegant, mature renditions of current trends appealing to a variety of women, from conservative students to fashion-conscious fiftysomethings. If you like a bit of glitz in your wardrobe, take a peek at the swankier Pedro del Hierro collection downstairs. Both labels have less prominent, but successful, menswear lines.

**Other locations**: L'Illa, Avda Diagonal 545-557, Eixample (93 405 35 44).

### Custo Barcelona

*Plaça de les Olles 7, Born (93 268 78 93/www.custo-barcelona.com). Metro Jaume I.* **Open** 10am-10pm Mon-Sat. **Credit** AmEx, DC, MC, V. **Map** p345 E7.

The Catalan Dalmau brothers had to make it in LA before bringing their garish cut-and-paste style T-shirts back home, but now the Custo look is synonymous with Barcelona style, and has spawned a thousand imitations. The collections have now expanded and Custo's signature prints can be found on everything from coats to jeans to swimwear for both men and women, but a T-shirt is still the most highly prized (and highly priced) souvenir for any visiting fashionista.

**Other locations**: C/Ferran 36, Barri Gòtic (93 342 66 98).

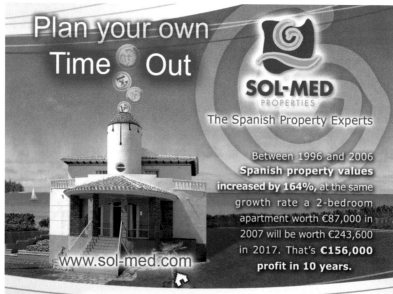

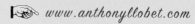

## Shoes

In summer, people of all ages wear *abarcas*, sloppy, peep-toe leather shoes from Menorca, or the traditional Catalan *espardenyes*, espadrilles of hemp and canvas. Footwear outlets line the main shopping strips, such as Portal de l'Àngel or C/Pelai; chains include **Casas**, **Mar Bessas**, **Royalty**, **Querol**, **Tascón** and **Vogue**, which have huge but almost identical collections.

### Camper

*C/Pelai 13-37, Eixample (93 302 41 24/www.camper.com). Metro Catalunya.* **Open** 10am-10pm Mon-Sat. **Credit** AmEx, DC, MC, V. **Map** p344 B2.

Mallorca-based eco shoe company Camper has sexed up its ladies' line recently. Each year it seems to flirt more with high heels (albeit rubbery wedgy ones) and girly straps. Of course, it still has its classic round-toed and clod-heeled classics, and the guys still have their iconic bowling shoes, but take another look if you've previously dismissed this lot.

**Other locations**: Plaça del Àngels 6, Raval (93 342 41 41); Rambla de Catalunya 122, Eixample (93 217 23 84); C/València 249, Eixample (93 215 63 90); and throughout the city.

### Czar

*Passeig del Born 20, Born (93 310 72 22). Metro Jaume I.* **Open** 5-9.30pm Mon; noon-2pm, 5-9.30pm Tue-Sat. **Credit** MC, V. **Map** p345 E6.

The hippest trainers are presented here like valuable pieces in a museum. You should be able to find an Adidas Originals or Vision Streetwear pair to suit even the most demanding of street feet. The collection is mainly aimed at men, but girls have a small and sassy range at the back.

### La Manual Alpargatera

*C/Avinyó 7, Barri Gòtic (93 301 01 72/www.lamanual.net). Metro Liceu.* **Open** 9.30am-1.30pm, 4.30-8pm Mon-Fri; 10am-1.30pm Sat. **Credit** AmEx, DC, MC, V. **Map** p345 C6.

The catwalk-blessed revival of the espadrille may not have convinced everyone, but a stop at handmade espadrille emporium La Manual Alpargatera, open since 1910, is a must for any Barcelona visitor. The store has shod such luminaries as Pope John Paul II and Jack Nicholson during its years of service.

### Muxart

*C/Rosselló 230, Eixample (93 488 10 64/www.muxart.com). Metro Diagonal.* **Open** 10am-2pm, 4.30-8.30pm Mon-Fri; 10am-2pm, 5-8.30pm Sat. **Credit** AmEx, DC, MC, V. **Map** p338 G6/7.

Muxart sells shoes around which to build an outfit. Materials are refined, styles are sharp, avant-garde and blatantly not intended to hide under a pair of baggy beige slacks. Lines for men and women are complemented by equally creative and attractive bags and accessories.

**Other locations**: Rambla de Catalunya 47, Eixample (93 467 74 23).

### U-Casas

*C/Espaseria 4, Born (93 310 00 46/www.casasclub.com). Metro Jaume I.* **Open** 10.30am-9pm Mon-Thur; 10.30am-9.30pm Fri, Sat. **Credit** MC, V. **Map** p345 E7.

The pared-down, post-industrial decor so beloved of this neighbourhood provides the perfect backdrop for bright and quirky shoes. Strange heels and toes are out in force this season, and after trying on all those snub-nosed winklepickers and rubber wedgies from the likes of Helmut Lang, Fly, Fornarina and Irregular Choice, you can rest your weary pins on the giant, shoe-shaped chaise longue.

**Other locations**: C/Tallers 2, Raval (93 318 3405); L'Illa, Avda Diagonal 345-557, Eixample (93 419 14 85); Barcelona Glòries, Avda Diagonal 208, Eixample (93 486 0145).

## Street

### Dirty Dawg

*C/Duc de la Victòria 13, Barri Gòtic (no phone). Metro Catalunya.* **Open** *Oct-June* 10am-2.30pm, 4.30-8.30pm Mon-Sat. *July-Sept* 11.30am-2.30pm, 4.30-9.30pm Mon-Sat. **No credit cards**. **Map** p344 C4.

Hip-hop garb for guys and girls that focuses mainly on US labels: plenty of Ecko, South Pole and Sir Benni Miles. Chilled staff hang among the hoodies.

### Free

*C/Ramelleres 5, Raval (93 301 61 15). Metro Catalunya.* **Open** *Sept-June* 10am-2pm, 4.30-8.30pm Mon-Sat. *July, Aug* 10am-8.30pm Mon-Sat. **Credit** V. **Map** p344 B3.

This skate emporium has grown exponentially to cater for Barcelona's expanding population of enthusiasts. For boys, there's casual wear from Stüssy, Carhartt, Fresh Jive et al; girls get plenty of Compobella and Loreak Mendian. The requisite chunky or retro footwear comes courtesy of Vans, Vision and Etnies.

**Other locations**: C/Rec 16, Born (93 295 50 36).

### Kwatra

*C/Antic de Sant Joan 1, Born (93 268 08 04/www.kwatra.com). Metro Barceloneta or Jaume I.* **Open** *Sept-June* 11am-2pm, 4-8pm Mon-Sat. *July, Aug* 1-9pm Mon-Sat. **Credit** MC, V. **Map** p345 F6.

The ex-Nike employee in charge of Kwatra still has the connections to get hold of the most limited of limited editions. Other labels are not left out: Diesel, Adidas and Puma shoes, bags and clothes make up the rest of the urban sportswear stock, with accessories by City Knife, Waffle and Speedsweep.

**Other locations**: Bulevard Rosa, Passeig de Gràcia 55, Eixample (93 488 04 27).

### Red Market

*C/Verdi 20, Gràcia (93 218 63 33). Metro Fontana.* **Open** *Sept-July* 5-9.30pm Mon; 11.30am-2pm, 5-9.30pm Tue-Sat. *Aug* 5-9.30pm Mon-Sat. **Credit** AmEx, MC, V. **Map** p339 H5.

A choice selection of streetwear includes the very latest in girls' and boys' urban outfitting by aemkei, Zoo York, Lambretta, Punk Royal, Diesel 55,

Franklin & Marshall and others, as well as a rare crop of seriously good-looking trainers by Gola, Puma, Nike and Adidas.

### Tribu

*C/Avinyó 12, Barri Gòtic (93 318 65 10). Metro Jaume I or Liceu.* **Open** 11am-2.30pm, 4.30-8.30pm Mon-Fri; 11am-8.30pm Sat. **Credit** MC, V. **Map** p345 C6.

One of the countless clued-up fashion platforms in town for international and home-grown casual labels such as Jocomomola, Nolita, Diesel and Freesoul. Don't miss the designer trainers at the back.

## Vintage & second-hand

The narrow C/Riera Baixa in the Raval is where most of Barcelona's second-hand clothes retailers cluster. **Holala! Ibiza** at No.11 (93 441 99 94) has affordable thrift-store staples, while at No.7, **Smart And Clean**'s 1960s and '70s second-hand gear is largely made up of mod essentials, with a decent range of leather jackets and vintage trainers (93 441 87 64, www.smartandclean.com).

### Lailo

*C/Riera Baixa 20, Raval (93 441 37 49). Metro Liceu or Sant Antoni.* **Open** 11am-2pm, 5-8pm Mon-Sat. Closed 1wk end Aug. **Credit** AmEx, DC, MC, V. **Map** p342 E10.

Lailo stands out from the second-hand crowd by the quality of its stock. Designers are known to come for inspiration to this cornucopia of vintage clothing. It even has a 'museum' of old costumes from the Liceu theatre, some dating back to the 18th century. If you want something for a one-off occasion, you can hire everything from the tuxedos to the coming-out gowns.

### Le Swing

*C/Riera Baixa 13, Raval (93 324 84 02). Metro Liceu or Sant Antoni.* **Open** 10.30am-2.30pm, 4.30-8.30pm Mon-Sat. **Credit** AmEx, DC, MC, V. **Map** p342 E10.

Today's second-hand is known as vintage, and thrift is not on the agenda. Fervent worshippers of Pierre Cardin, YSL, Dior, Kenzo and other fashion deities scour all corners of the sartorial stratosphere and deliver their booty back to this little powder puff of a boutique. The odd Zara number and other mere mortal brands creep in as well.

### Produit National Brut

*C/Avinyó 29, Barri Gòtic (93 268 27 55). Metro Jaume I or Liceu.* **Open** 11am-9pm Mon-Sat. **Credit** MC, V. **Map** p345 C7.

Wear your *barri* on your chest with PNB's sweat tops emblazoned with the names of Barcelona's hipster neighbourhoods, such as Barrio Chino. This store also stocks a good supply of second-hand fashions: the usual range of ironic US high-school ties, '60s-styled shirts, smock dresses, denim, corduroy and leather. If that doesn't tempt you, perhaps a kitsch knick-knack or piece of grafittiesque artwork will.

# Fashion accessories

## Jewellery

The Born's C/Argenteria takes its name from the numerous silversmiths who established themselves there in the 15th century. Even today, this street and the surrounding area are home to a number of shops selling silver jewellery, such as **Platamundi** (Plaça Santa Maria 7, 93 310 10 87, www.platamundi.com), part of a successful chain that has pretty, affordable pieces in its shops throughout Barcelona. Nearby, boutiques such as **Ad Láter** (C/Ases 1, 93 310 66 00, www.prudencisanchez.com) exhibit pieces by innovative local jewellery designers. Upmarket jewellers naturally gravitate towards the glamorous shopping districts, such as Passeig de Gràcia and Avda Diagonal.

### Alea Majoral Galería de Joyas

*C/Argenteria 66, Born (93 310 13 73/www.majoral.com). Metro Jaume I.* **Open** *Sept-July* 10.30am-8.30pm Mon-Fri; 11am-8.30pm Sat. *Aug* 11am-8.30pm Mon-Sat. Closed 1wk Aug. **Credit** AmEx, DC, MC, V. **Map** p345 E6.

This elegant jewellery gallery dedicates its street-front space to Enric Majoral's structural silver and gold pieces. A small back room plays host to a changing exhibition of works by various young artists. Many of the creations are more artworks than accessories.

**Other locations**: Majoral, C/Consell de Cent 308, Eixample (93 467 72 09); Majoral Pedralbes Centre, Avda Diagonal 609, Zona Alta (93 363 12 91).

### Bagués

*Passeig de Gràcia 41, Eixample (93 216 01 73/www.bagues.es). Metro Passeig de Gràcia.* **Open** *Sept-July* 10am-8.30pm Mon-Fri; 10am-1.30pm, 5-8.30pm Sat. *Aug* 10am-1.30pm, 4.30-8.30pm Mon-Fri; 10am-1.30pm Sat. **Credit** AmEx, DC, MC, V. **Map** p338 G8.

Housed in a jewel of a building – the Modernista palace Casa Amatller – Bagués is, perhaps, Barcelona's most prestigious and historic jeweller. The original master jeweller of the house, Lluis Masriera, created revolutionary pieces using a 'translucid enamel' technique in the early 1900s. His signature motifs, the art nouveau favourites of flowers, nymphs, insects and birds, are still reflected in today's designs.

**Other locations**: Rambla de les Flors 105, Raval (93 481 70 50).

### Freya

*C/Verdi 17, Gràcia (93 237 36 89). Metro Fontana.* **Open** 5-9pm Mon; 11am-2pm, 5-9pm Tue-Sat. **Credit** AmEx, MC, V. **Map** p339 H5.

Freya's owner likes to trick customers into her shop by creating kooky and confusing window displays, arranging bright baubles with a caramel sheen to look like jars of sweeties. There's no need for deception, though. Teresa hand-picks fun and funky designs by local makers to suit all pockets and all tastes (except for shy and retiring ones). The pieces, from bright plastic beads to felt rings and faux rocks, all share a quirky, attention-seeking sense of fun.

### Hipotesi

*C/Provença 237, Eixample (93 215 02 98).* **Open** *Sept-July* 10am-1.30pm, 5-8.30pm Mon, Sat; 10am-8.30pm Tue-Fri. *Aug* 10.30am-2pm, 5-8.30pm Mon-Fri. **Credit** AmEx, DC, MC, V. **Map** p338 F7.

The friendly owner of Hipotesi loves jewellery and is as happy for fellow fans to browse in this gallery/shop and ask about the artists whose work she sells as for them to buy. Both local artisans, such as Ramon Puig Cuyàs, head of Barcelona's Massana jewellery school, and international jewellers, like Briton Kathryn Marchbank, are represented. Styles vary considerably, and materials can range from the finest spun gold to plastic, felt or ribbon.

## Leather & luggage

### Casa Antich SCP

*C/Consolat del Mar 27-31, Born (93 310 43 91/ www.casaantich.com). Metro Jaume I.* **Open** 9am-8.30pm Mon-Fri; 9.30am-8.30pm Sat. **Credit** AmEx, DC, MC, V. **Map** p345 D7.

Under the arches at the back end of the Born you'll find a luggage wares shop that in levels of service and size of stock recalls the golden age of travel. Here you can still purchase trunks for a steam across the Atlantic and ladies' vanity cases that would be perfect for a sojourn on the Orient Express. But you'll also find cutting-edge computer cases and slouchy shoulder bags from the likes of Mandarina Duck and Kipling.

### Loewe

*Passeig de Gràcia 35, Eixample (93 216 04 00/ www.loewe.com). Metro Passeig de Gràcia.* **Open** 10am-8.30pm Mon-Sat. **Credit** AmEx, DC, MC, V. **Map** p342 G8.

The price tags are bigger than the handbags at this couturier, where the Daddy Warbucks prices go well into the thousands. With a decadent setting on two floors of Domènech i Montaner's Casa Morera, the store's products, from crocodile-skin demi bags to men's sheepskin coats, are of superb quality.

**Other locations**: Avda Diagonal 570, Eixample (93 200 09 20); Hotel Arts, C/Marina 19-21, Barceloneta (93 225 99 27).

## Scarves & textiles

Textiles were once one of Barcelona's main industries. It's a legacy visible in many of the street names of the Born, where the highest concentration of textile shops and workshops is to be found. Contact tourist offices (*see p323*) for information about taking a tour of the official Textile Itinerary.

### Almacenes del Pilar

*C/Boqueria 43, Barri Gòtic (93 317 79 84/www. almacenesdelpilar.com). Metro Liceu.* **Open** 9.30am-2pm, 4-8pm Mon-Sat. Closed 2wks Aug. **Credit** AmEx, MC, DC, V. **Map** p345 B5.

An array of fabrics and accessories for traditional Spanish costumes is on display in this colourful, shambolic interior dating back to 1886. Making your way through bolts of material, you'll find bolts of the richly hued brocades used for Valencian *fallera* outfits and other rudiments of folkloric dress from various parts of the country. Lace *mantillas*, and the high combs over which they are worn, are stocked, along with fringed, hand-embroidered pure silk *mantones de manila* (shawls) and colourful wooden fans.

### Alonso

*C/Santa Ana 27, Barri Gòtic (93 317 60 85/ www.tiendacenter.com). Metro Liceu.* **Open** 10am-8pm Mon-Sat. Closed 1wk Aug. **Credit** AmEx, DC, MC, V. **Map** p344 C3.

Elegant Catalan ladies have come here for those important finishing touches for their outfit for more than 100 years. Behind the Modernista façade lie soft gloves in leather and lace, intricate fans, both traditional and modern, and floating scarves in mohair or painted silk.

### Rafa Teja Atelier

*C/Santa Maria 18, Born (93 310 27 85). Metro Jaume I.* **Open** 11am-9pm Mon-Sat. Closed 1wk Aug. **Credit** AmEx, DC, MC, V. **Map** p345 E6.

Few Spanish women would dream of attending a wedding without a shawl, and this is something of a mecca for them. Apart from elegant pashminas, fringed silk numbers, practical classic or quirky woollen scarves and sheer evening wraps, stock also includes some pretty silk jackets.

**Other locations**: Conde de Salvatierra 10, Eixample (93 237 70 59).

## Flowers

The 18 flower stalls ranged along the Rambla de les Flors originated from the old custom of Boqueria market traders giving a free flower to their customers. There are also flower stands at the **Mercat de la Concepció** (C/Aragó 311, Eixample, 93 457 53 29, www.laconcepcio.com), on the corner of C/València and C/Bruc (map p339 H7), some of which are open all night. Many florists around town offer the Interflora delivery service.

### Flors Navarro

*C/València 320, Eixample (93 457 40 99/www. floresnavarro.com). Metro Verdaguer.* **Open** 24hrs daily. **Credit** AmEx, MC, V. **Map** p338 H7.

At Flors Navarro, fresh-cut blooms, pretty house plants and stunning bouquets are available to buy 24 hours a day. A dozen red roses can be delivered anywhere in the city, day or night, for €30.

# Food & drink

## Food specialities

### La Botifarreria de Santa Maria

*C/Santa Maria 4, Born (93 319 97 84). Metro Barceloneta or Jaume I.* **Open** 8.30am-2.30pm, 5-8.30pm Mon-Fri; 8.30am-3pm Sat. Closed Aug. **Credit** MC, V. **Map** p345 E7.

Coarse farmhouse pâtés, hand-cut smoked salmon, fine melting chèvre cheeses and free-range chickens are not why this shop is always so crowded. The main draw is the sausage that gives the Botifarreria its name. This traditional Catalan pork sausage is almost worshipped here, and curious versions (squid, chocolate) are made up fresh in the back room to be sold each day.

### Cafés El Magnífico/Sans & Sans

*C/Argenteria 64/59, Born (93 310 33 61/www.cafeselmagnifico.com). Metro Jaume I.* **Open** 10am-2pm, 4-8pm Mon-Sat. Closed 2wks Aug. **Credit** AmEx, MC, V. **Map** p345 E6.

For the finest coffees roasted on the premises and the widest range of teas in elegant lacquer boxes, visit this pair of shops that sit opposite each other on C/Argenteria. As well as the various infusions, you can also purchase all the paraphernalia necessary to enjoy them at their best.

**Other locations**: Avda Diagonal 520, Eixample (93 414 56 23).

### Casa Gispert

*C/Sombrerers 23, Born (93 319 75 35/www.casagispert.com). Metro Jaume I.* **Open** *Jan-Sept* 9.30am-2pm, 4-7.30pm Tue-Fri; 10am-2pm, 5-8pm Sat. *Oct-Dec* 9.30am-2pm, 4-7.30pm Mon-Fri; 10am-2pm, 5-8pm Sat. **Credit** MC, V. **Map** p345 E6.

Casa Gispert radiates a warmth that has something to do with more than its original wood-fired nut and coffee roaster. Like a stage-set version of an olde schoole shoppe, its wooden cabinets and shelves groan with the finest and most fragrant nuts, herbs, spices, preserves, sauces, oils, seasonings and, most importantly, huge hand-made chocolate truffles. The pre-packed kits for making local specialities such as *panellets* (Hallowe'en bonbons) make great gifts.

### Formatgeria La Seu

*C/Dagueria 16, Barri Gòtic (93 412 65 48/www.formatgerialaseu.com). Metro Jaume I.* **Open** 10am-2pm, 5-8pm Tue-Fri; 10am-3pm, 5-8pm Sat. Closed Aug. **No credit cards. Map** p345 D6.

Spain has long neglected its cheese heritage, which perhaps explains why this is the only shop in the whole country to specialise in Spanish-only farmhouse cheeses. Scottish owner Katherine hand-picks her wares, such as the fruity blue Valdeón and the melting, bittersweet Torta de la Serena. Her *tast* of three cheeses and a glass of wine for just a few euro is a great way to explore what's on offer. *See also p205* **A little of what you fancy**.

### Jamonísimo

*C/Provença 85, Eixample (93 439 0847/www.jamonisimo.com). Metro Hospital Clínic.* **Open** *Sept-July* 1.30-9pm Mon; 9.30am-2.30pm, 5-9pm Tue-Fri; 9.30am-2.30pm, 5.30-9pm Sat. *Aug* 9.30am-2.30pm, 5-9pm Mon-Fri; 9.30am-2.30pm Sat. **Credit** AmEx, DC, MC, V. **Map** p338 D7.

If you really want to know what all the fuss with regard to *jamón iberico* is about, you have to come to Jamonísimo and try its plate of 'the three textures' of *jamón*. It will spoil you for ham sandwiches at the local bar, but it's worth it.

### Papabubble

*C/Ample 28, Barri Gòtic (93 268 86 25/www.papabubble.com). Metro Barceloneta or Drassanes.* **Open** 10am-2pm, 4-8pm Tue-Sat; 11am-7pm Sun. Closed Aug. **Credit** AmEx, MC, V. **Map** p345 C7.

Crowds of kids are lured by the sugary wafts floating out of this cute shop at sweet-making time. You can watch the Aussie owners create their kaleidescope-coloured humbugs before your eyes in flavours both usual (orange, mint) and unusual (lavender, passion fruit). The adults are served by a recent venture into obscene lolly territory.

## General food stores

The supermarket in the basement of **El Corte Inglés** (*see p189*) in Plaça Catalunya has a gourmet section of local and foreign specialities.

### Champion

*La Rambla 113, Barri Gòtic (93 302 48 24). Metro Catalunya.* **Open** 10am-10pm Mon-Sat. **Credit** MC, V. **Map** p344 B3.

Not the best of the supermarket sweep, but the opening hours and unbeatable location more than make up for its slight shabbiness, confusing layout and agonisingly slow checkout lines.

### Colmado Quilez

*Rambla Catalunya 63, Eixample (93 215 23 56). Metro Passeig de Gràcia.* **Open** *Jan-mid Oct* 9am-2pm, 4.30-8.30pm Mon-Fri; 9am-2pm Sat. *Mid Oct-Dec* 9am-2pm, 4.30-8.30pm Mon-Sat. **Credit** MC, V. **Map** p338 F/8.

*Colmados* – old-school grocery stores – are relics of the old way of shopping before the invasion of the supermarkets. This is one of the few surviving examples in the Modernista Eixample, with floor-to-ceiling shelves stacked full of gourmet treats, such as local preserved fungi in cute mushroom-shaped bottles (Delicias del Bosque), and the store's own-label caviar, cava, saffron and anchovies.

## Pâtisseries & chocolate

### Caelum

*C/Palla 8, Barri Gòtic (93 302 69 93). Metro Liceu.* **Open** 5-8.30pm Mon; 10.30am-8.30pm Tue-Thur; 10.30am-midnight Fri, Sat; 11.30am-9pm Sun. Closed 2wks Aug. **Credit** AmEx, DC, MC, V. **Map** p344 C4.

Enric Rovira Shop.

If you feel guilty eating sweet treats, Caelum is the place to come. All the sweety goodness sold here is made by nuns in cloistered orders, to recipes handed down by the Lord himself (so they say). The shop's pre-packed biccies and cakes make lovely gifts, or the more selfish can sample them themselves in the café.

### Enric Rovira Shop

*Avda Josep Tarradellas 113, Les Corts (93 419 25 47/www.enricrovira.com). Metro Entença.* **Open** 10am-2.30pm, 5-8pm Tue-Fri; 10am-2.30pm Sat. Closed Aug. **Credit** MC, V. **Map** p337 D6.

Perhaps the best place in town for designer chocolates, this is where substance actually keeps up with style. Rovira's Gaudí-esque chocolate tile is an iconic gift for any choc lover, and his pink peppercorn truffles make great after-dinner conversation pieces.

### Escribà

*Gran Via de les Corts Catalanes 546, Eixample (93 454 75 35/www.escriba.es). Metro Urgell.* **Open** *Sept-July* 8am-3pm, 5-9pm Mon-Fri; 8am-9pm Sat, Sun. *Aug* 9am-3pm daily. **Credit** DC, MC, V. **Map** p342 E8.

Antoni Escribà, the 'Mozart of Chocolate', died in 2004, but his legacy lives on. His team produces jaw-dropping creations for Easter, from a hulking chocolate Grand Canyon to a life-size model of Michelangelo's *David*. Smaller miracles include cherry liqueur encased in red chocolate lips. The Rambla branch is particularly worth visiting as it's situated in a pretty Modernista building.

**Other locations**: La Rambla 83, Raval (93 301 60 27).

### Planelles Donat

*Portal de l'Àngel 7, Barri Gòtic (93 317 29 26). Metro Catalunya.* **Open** *Apr-mid Oct, Nov, Dec* 10am-10pm Mon-Sat. **Credit** V. **Map** p344 C4.

*Turrón* is Catalunya's traditional sweet treat eaten at Christmas. It comes in two types: the nougat-like *turrón de Alicante* and the grainy marzipan-ish *turrón de Jijona*. You can try both, along with dusty '*polvorones*' (marzipan-like sweets similar to *turrón*), ice-cream and refreshing *horchata* (tiger nut milk) here and at its nearby ice-cream parlour (Portal de l'Àngel 25).

## Wine

Craft shop **Art Escudellers** (*see p206*) has a good selection of wines in its cellar.

### Lavinia

*Avda Diagonal 605, Eixample (93 363 44 45/www.lavinia.es). Metro Maria Cristina.* **Open** 10am-9pm Mon-Sat. **Credit** AmEx, DC, MC, V. **Map** p338 D5.

This ultra-slick store houses the largest selection of wines in Europe. Knowledgeable, polyglot staff happily talk customers through the thousands of horizontally displayed Spanish and international wines, including exceptional vintages and special editions at good prices. They'll also help you put together cases to send home and let you try before you buy.

### Torres

*C/Nou de la Rambla 25, Barri Gòtic (93 317 32 34/www.vinosencasa.com). Metro Drassanes or Liceu.* **Open** 9am-2pm, 4-9pm Mon-Sat. **Credit** MC, V. **Map** p345 A6.

After moving from its old and dusty grocery store across the road, Torres' shiny new shop is a bit out of place in the run-down end of the Raval. Now it stocks a good range of Spanish wines (with a particularly good cava section) and interesting international beers and spirits, including black Mallorcan absinthe. Handily, the shop's competitive prices weren't also revamped during the move.

# A little of what you fancy

Barcelona is currently basking in the glow of top-rank, Ferran Adrià-anointed gastro fame so many visitors will be wanting to take some tastes of Catalonia home with them. But, purchasing unfamiliar products may make you nervous about making the right choice. A chance to try before you buy is the ideal and, thankfully, there are plenty of emporiums in Barcelona where you can do just that, some for free (if you're genuinely buying, please), some for a minimal charge, others witha bar-like service but at shop-like prices.

Wines from Spain are growing in prestige (and price), but are still fairly unknown outside the country, so you might like to head for the smart **Vila Viniteca** (*see p206; photo right*), where you can sample various of its wines, along with cheese, sausage and ham from its deli across the road, at almost-shop prices.

If you buy wine, you won't be able to resist the cheese to accompany. The best place to find out about artisanal Spanish cheeses is at **Formatgeria La Seu** (*see p202; photo above*). This tiny shop manages to stock a great variety of rare national cheeses. It's not a bewildering experience as the sociable Scottish owner, Katherine, offers a '*tast*' of three slices of cheese (one cow's, one goat's and one sheep's milk) on crackers with a glass of young Rioja for just a few euro. Check out her special own-designed '*tast*' plates – they're also for sale and would be perfect for cheese and wine parties at home.

Perhaps Spain's most emblematic and lauded gastro star (apart from Adrià) is its *jamón iberico* – cured ham made from the native Iberian black pig. Barcelona's cathedral for worshippers of this heavenly product is **Jamonísimo** (*see p202*), which roughly translates as something like 'Really really ham!'. Good ham should cost, and it certainly does here, so it's expected you'll want to try before you buy. It's interesting to compare ham from the three different DOs (regulated production areas) the store sells, and also to taste slices from the three different parts of the leg – they taste completely different. There is a small tasting room at the back of the shop where you can have more leisurely plates of ham and a glass of wine at (reasonably pricey) shop prices.

What about dessert? If Jamonísimo's cleaned you out, try the free humbugs on the counter of handmade sweetshop **Papabubble** (*see p202*), or if you're in town the first or third weekend of the month, pass by the artisan food market in Plaça del Pi, where you can sample honey, cheese, cakes, biscuits, jam and, most deliciously, El Vall D'Or's intriguing range of chocs.

Eat, Drink, Shop

### Vila Viniteca

*C/Agullers 7, Born (93 268 32 27/www.vila viniteca.es). Metro Jaume I.* **Open** *Sept-June* 8.30am-2.30pm, 4.30-8.30pm Mon-Sat. *July, Aug* 8.30am-2.30pm, 4.30-8.30pm Mon-Fri; 8.30am-2.30pm Sat. **Credit** DC, MC, V. **Map** p345 D7.

Newly renovated and expanded, this family-run business has built up a stock of more than 6,000 wines and spirits since 1932. With everything from a 1953 Damoiseau rum, which costs as much as €500, through to €6 bottles of table wine, the selection here is mostly Spanish and Catalan, but it also takes in international favourites. The new food shop situated next door at No.9 stocks fine cheeses, cured meats and oils. The perfect stop for upmarket foodie gifts.

**Other locations**: Vinacoteca, València 595, Eixample (93 232 58 35).

### Vinus & Brindis

*Torrent de l'Olla 147, Gràcia (93 218 30 37/ www.vinusbrindis.com). Metro Fontana.* **Open** *June-Oct* 11am-2.15pm, 5-9.15pm Mon-Sat. *Nov-May* 10.30am-2pm, 5-9pm Mon-Sat. **Credit** DC, MC, V. **Map** p338 G5.

This franchise of approachable wine shops has a young, funky feel, both in its staff and its wines. It specialises in young and upcoming wine areas, winemakers and wines. Staff are always more than eager to advise, and it always has a good range of easy-drinking wines for under six euro, as well as special monthly offers.

**Other locations**: Avda Diagonal 381 (93 217 64 27); Centre Comercial L'Illa, Avda Diagonal 557, Eixample (93 512 17 13); and throughout the city.

## Gifts

The city's museums have some good gift shops. The Espai Gaudí at **La Pedrera** (*see p127*) is the mother of all Gaudíana purveyors, while the **MACBA** (*see p107*) and **CaixaForum** (*see p117*) shops are excellent sources of games, gifts, designer gizmos and kooky postcards. The **Fundació Joan Miró** (*see p118*) has plenty of boldly designed espresso cups, coasters and so on, while the **Museu Tèxtil** (*see p101*) has a good supply of creative scarves, ties, shirts, bags and quirky jewellery.

### Art Escudellers

*C/Escudellers 23-25, Barri Gòtic (93 412 68 01/www.escudellers-art.com). Metro Drassanes.* **Open** 11am-11pm daily. **Credit** AmEx, DC, MC, V. **Map** p345 C6.

Art Escudellers sells an extravaganza of stunning clay and glassware that's mostly handmade by Spanish artists and labelled by region. Decorative and practical items include sturdy kitchenware, traditional *azulejos* (tiles) and Gaudí-themed coffee cups. Downstairs is a wine cellar and diminutive café, while the nearby branch (at No.12) specialises in some unusual glassware: a kitsch-fest of lurid Swarovski crystal bonsais, to be precise.

### Caixa de Fang

*C/Freneria 1, Barri Gòtic (93 315 17 04). Metro Jaume I.* **Open** 10am-8pm Mon-Sat. **Credit** AmEx, DC, MC, V. **Map** p345 D5.

Nothing to do with vampires – *fang* means clay, and the 'Box of Clay' sells colourful local ceramics that would be a good gift for a kitchen-friendly pal. Ideas include an olive-wood pestle and traditional yellow mortar, or a rough-hewn casserole dish.

### Xilografies

*C/Freneria 1, Barri Gòtic (93 315 07 58). Metro Jaume I.* **Open** *Jan-July, Sept, Oct* 10am-2pm Mon-Sat. *Nov, Dec* 10am-2pm, 4.30-7.30pm Mon-Sat. Closed Aug. **No credit cards. Map** p345 D5.

Using painstakingly detailed 18th-century carved boxwood blocks that have been passed down in her family for generations (some of which you will see displayed in a glass cabinet in this tiny shop), Maria creates *ex libris* stickers for books, bookmarks, notepaper, address books and prints. She also sells prints of 18th-century maps, pens, birthday cards and reproduction pocket sundials.

## Hair & beauty

## Beauty treatments

### Bienestar Augusta Natural

*Via Augusta 217, Zona Alta (93 241 69 00/ www.augustanatural.com). FGC Bonanova.* **Open** 8.30am-9pm Mon-Sat. **Credit** AmEx, DC, MC, V. **Map** p338 D3.

This flash, health and beauty complex for both sexes in the Zona Alta is complete with minimalist decor, Japanese garden, restaurant and vitamin shop. As well as manicures and facials, there's a hairdresser (with private booths), new techniques such as colour therapy, and an impressive array of shiatsu, Thai and Ayurvedic massage.

### Instituto Francis

*Ronda de Sant Pere 18, Eixample (93 317 78 08). Metro Catalunya.* **Open** 9.30am-8pm Mon-Fri; 9am-4pm Sat. **Credit** DC, MC, V. **Map** p344 D2.

Instituto Francis is Europe's largest women's beauty centre. It has seven floors and more than 50 members of staff all dedicated to making you beautiful – inside and out. As well as offering all the usual facials, massages, anti-cellulite treatments and manicures, the institute specialises in depilation, homeopathic therapies and non-surgical procedures such as teeth whitening and micropigmentation. Spend a day here and you'll leave a different person.

### Masajes a 1000

*C/Mallorca 233, Eixample (93 215 85 85/ www.masajesa1000.com). Metro Diagonal/FGC Provença.* **Open** 8am-midnight daily. **Credit** MC, V. **Map** p338 F7.

An efficient and economic beauty centre in the Eixample, operating via a voucher system. You can try a half-hour massage and siesta in an ergonomic

chair, or a luxurious 90-minute 'four-hand' massage. There are also pedicures, manicures, hair and skin care and tanning, with no need to book ahead.
**Other locations**: Travessera de les Corts 178, Les Corts (93 490 92 90); C/Numancia 76, Les Corts (93 410 87 82).

## Cosmetics & perfumes

The ground floor of **El Corte Inglés** (*see p189*) also has a good range of toiletries.

### Regia

*Passeig de Gràcia 39, Eixample (93 216 01 21/ www.regia.es). Metro Passeig de Gràcia.* **Open** 10am-8.30pm Mon-Sat. **Credit** AmEx, DC, MC, V. **Map** p338 G8.

Regia was founded in 1928, and all six of its Barcelona branches have a good selection of upmarket perfumes and cosmetics on sale, as well as its own house line of skin and hair products. What makes this particular outlet special is the outstanding perfume museum (*see p127*) hidden at the back of the shop, past the offices.
**Other locations**: Bulevard Rosa, Passeig de Gràcia 55, Eixample (93 215 73 48); C/Muntaner 242, Sant Gervasi (93 200 63 48); and throughout the city.

### Sephora

*El Triangle, C/Pelai 13-37, Eixample (93 306 39 00/ www.sephora.es). Metro Catalunya.* **Open** 10am-10pm Mon-Sat. **Credit** AmEx, DC, MC, V. **Map** p344 B2.

With no Boots or Superdrug around, Sephora is your best bet for unfettered playing around with scents and make-up if you suddenly catch yourself having a dowdy moment in town. Another French chain (like Decathlon and FNAC), this chi-chi scent superstore lines its perfumes up in alphabetical order, men's on one side, women's on the other, so you know exactly how to get from Aramis to Zoa. Make-up and toiletries include most of the usual mid- to high-end brands, plus there are handy beauty tools, such as eye-brow tweezers and pencil sharpeners, at throwaway prices.
**Other locations**: La Maquinista, C/Potosí s/n, Sant Andreu (93 360 87 21); Diagonal Mar, Avda Diagonal 3, Poblenou (93 356 23 19).

## Hairdressers

### Llongueras

*Passeig de Gràcia 78, Eixample (93 215 41 75/ www.llongueras.com). Metro Passeig de Gràcia.* **Open** *Sept-July* 9am-7pm Mon-Sat. *Aug* 9am-6pm Mon-Fri; 9am-2pm Sat. **Credit** AmEx, DC, MC, V. **Map** p338 G7.

A safe bet for all ages, this reassuringly pricey Catalan chain of hairdressers also has well-trained stylists, who take the time to give a proper consultation, wash and massage. The cuts themselves are up to the minute but generally as natural as possible and free of the excesses of the trendier salons.
**Other locations**: throughout the city.

### Rock & Roll

*C/Palma de Sant Just 12, Barri Gòtic (93 268 74 75). Metro Jaume I.* **Open** 10.30am-8pm Tue-Fri; 10am-4pm Sat. **Credit** AmEx, MC, V. **Map** p345 C6.

Blinding white decor and bleeping electronica usually indicate a traumatic regime of enforced mullets and badger streaks, but the friendly and very experienced stylists, Laura and Christian, don't insist on the latest fashion foibles: if you demand a tiny trim, that's what you'll get. A basic cut and blow-dry is €35 for women and €23 for men.

### La Tijereta

*C/Vidrieria 13, Born (93 319 70 01). Metro Barceloneta or Jaume I.* **Open** *Sept-July* 3-7pm Mon; 10am-7pm Tue-Fri; 9am-2pm Sat. *Aug* 10am-7pm Mon-Fri. **Credit** MC, V. **Map** p345 E7.

As long as you don't mind passers-by gawking at you through the goldfish-bowl windows, tiny La Tijereta is a little more than half the price of the rest of the Born crop of hi-design hairdressers with no discernible drop in quality. A wash, cut and blow-dry is €22 for women and €13 for men.

## Opticians

### Grand Optical

*El Triangle, Plaça Catalunya 4, Eixample (93 304 16 40/www.grandoptical.com). Metro Catalunya.* **Open** 10am-10pm Mon-Sat. **Credit** AmEx, DC, MC, V. **Map** p344 B2.

When summer comes, it's traditional to swarm to this gleaming, air-conditioned spectacle superstore to try on sunglasses and make faces at yourself in the mirror. Of course, there's a more serious side to Grand Optical's services, with top-class eye testing, thousands of designer frames and a super-efficient lab that will prepare your specs in an hour.

## Markets

For details of the 40 permanent neighbourhood food markets in Barcelona, check www.bcn.es/ mercatsmunicipals. **Mercat Santa Caterina** (93 319 57 40, www.mercatsantacaterina.net) reopened on its original site on Avda Francesc Cambó in May 2005,and is especially worthy of note, in a stunning Gaudíesque new building designed by the late Enric Miralles.

Other markets to look out for include the **stamp and coin market** on Plaça Reial (9am-2.30pm Sun) and the **Fira de Santa Llúcia** on Plaça Nova (*see p222*). Of the city's various **artisan food fairs**, the most central is usually held on picturesque Plaça del Pi on the first and third Friday, Saturday and Sunday of every month, as well as during local fiestas.

### Antiques Market

*Plaça Nova, Barri Gòtic (93 302 70 45). Metro Jaume I.* **Open** 10am-9pm Thur. Closed Aug. **No credit cards**. **Map** p344 C4.

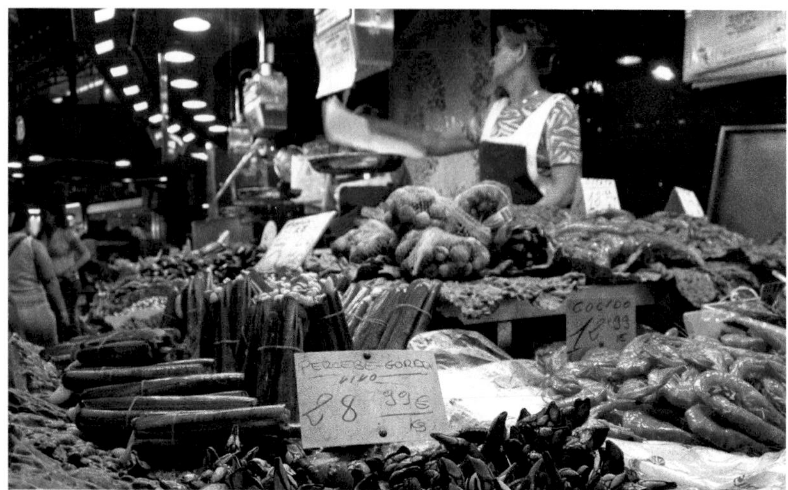


Piles of seasonal food at **La Boqueria**, the city's renowned market.

With its location in front of the cathedral, this market charges prices that are targeted at tourists, so be prepared to haggle. The market dates from the Middle Ages, but antiques generally consist of small items such as sepia postcards, *manila* shawls, pocket watches, typewriters, lace, cameras and jewellery among bibelots and bric-a-brac. In the first week of August and for all of December, the market is held at Portal de l'Àngel.

## Book & Coin Market

*Mercat de Sant Antoni, C/Comte d'Urgell 1, Eixample (93 423 42 87). Metro Sant Antoni.* **Open** 8am-2pm (approx) Sun. **No credit cards. Map** p342 D/E9.

If you're winding your way home down C/Hospital early on Sunday morning after a bit of a Saturday night, you're likely to see Dickensian scenes of urchin-like chaps pushing old wooden barrows up to the Sant Antoni market. They're preparing one of the most important Sunday rituals in town – the Book and Coin Market, as it's officially known. It should, more accurately, be called the ancient porn and Pogs (or whatever the kids are collecting these days) market. Of course, most stalls are selling second-hand books of all kinds and old Hollywood blockbusters on VHS, but its main audience is drawn by these two genres. Like Els Encants, this market is as much about people-watching as browsing and purchasing.

## La Boqueria

*La Rambla 89, Raval (93 318 25 84/www.boqueria.info). Metro Liceu.* **Open** 8am-8.30pm Mon-Sat. **Map** p344 A/B4.

Riding the current wave of fascination with all things gastronomic in Barcelona, the city's most famous food market is now a must-stop for any visitor. It has its fair share of celebrities: you may see bow-tied Juanito of the Pinotxo bar or rotund Llorenç Petras at his mushroom stall at the rear being filmed by TV crews from across the globe. But the real stars are the sheep's heads with eyeballs intact, fragrant seasonal fruits, glistening hanging hams, and fresh fish and seafood on the stalls. Prices are inflated by the gaggle of tourists at the market's front and outer limits: penetrate to the centre and rear for better deals. If you visit in the morning, you'll see the best produce, including the smallholders' fruit and veg stalls in the little square attached to the C/Carme side of the market. If you do come to ogle, remember this is where locals come to shop, so don't touch what you don't want to buy, ask before taking photos and watch out for vicious old ladies with ankle-destroying shopping trolleys.

## Els Encants

*C/Dos de Maig 177-187, Plaça de la Glòries, Eixample (93 246 30 30). Metro Glòries.* **Open** 9am-6pm Mon, Wed, Fri, Sat. *Auctions* 7.30-9am Mon, Wed, Fri. **No credit cards. Map** p343 L8.

Unfortunately, it's increasingly hard to find a bargain at Barcelona's old fleamarket. Still, it's a diverting way to pass the time strolling around this suntrap: the buyers and sellers are as varied and curious as the bric-a-brac, big pants, Barça memorabilia, cheap electrical gadgets, religious relics and ancient Spanish school books that make up the majority of the stalls' booty. If you want to buy furniture at a decent price come to the auctions at 7am with the commercial buyers or at noon, when unsold stuff drops in price. Don't forget to check out the cavernous warehouses on the market's outskirts, where you may find a bargain

– even if you have to dig your way through an Everest of junk to find it. Avoid Saturdays, when prices shoot up (except in the early morning) and the crowds move in, and be on your guard for pick-pockets and short-changing.

## Music

C/Tallers, C/Bonsuccès and C/Riera Baixa in the Raval are dotted with speciality music shops catering to all tastes and formats, with plenty of instruments and sheet music. Mainstream music selections are found in the huge Portal de l'Àngel branch of **El Corte Inglés** (*see p189*) and, more cheaply, at **FNAC** (*see p189*), which also has world music and acres of classical.

### Casa Beethoven

*La Rambla 97, Raval (93 301 48 26/www.casa beethoven.com). Metro Liceu.* **Open** 9am-2pm, 4-8pm Mon-Fri; 9am-1.30pm, 5-8pm Sat. Closed 3wks Aug. **Credit** MC, V. **Map** p344 B4.

The metronome seems to have stopped in this dark and dusty sheet music emporium. You could even imagine Beethoven himself popping in to drop off his 5th Symphony. Its range hasn't stopped in time, though, with songbooks offering arrangements of tracks by the White Stripes for the thoroughly modern busker. There are even new-fangled CDs, mostly Spanish classical titles. **Photo** *p211.*

### CD Drome

*C/Valldonzella 3, Raval (93 317 46 46/www.cd drome.com). Metro Catalunya or Universitat.* **Open** *Sept-July* 10.30am-8.30pm Mon-Fri; 10.30am-2pm, 4.30-8.30pm Sat. *Aug* 10.30am-2pm, 5-9pm Mon-Fri. **Credit** DC, MC, V. **Map** p344 A2.

Budding DJs come to CD Drome just to absorb the hipness in the air. Genres are precisely delineated into groups such as minimal beats and hands-up vinyl. Once you've decided what your particular flavour is, you can listen to your selections on the professional-looking decks. It's also good for picking up flyers, listings magazines and for buying tickets.

### Discos Castelló

*C/Tallers 3, 7, 9 & 79, Raval (93 302 59 46/ www.discoscastello.es). Metro Catalunya.* **Open** 10am-8.30pm Mon-Sat. **Credit** AmEx, DC, MC, V. **Map** p344 B2.

Discos Castelló is a homegrown cluster of small shops, each with a different speciality: No.3 is devoted to classical; the largest, No.7, covers pretty much everything; No.9 does hip hop, rock and alternative pop plus T-shirts and accessories; and No.79 is best for jazz and '70s pop. The branch at No.79 is good for ethnic music and electronica.

**Other locations**: throughout the city.

### Gong

*C/Consell de Cent 343, Eixample (93 215 3431/www.gongdiscos.com). Metro Passeig de Gràcia.* **Open** 10am-9pm Mon-Sat. **Credit** AmEx, MC, V. **Map** p338 G8.

An unglamorous but serious record shop chain with a wide range of stock in its stacks. A Top Ten is displayed for each genre so you can follow the crowds if you can't decide what to buy for yourself. The poor can flick through the always-extensive bargain rack: a compilation of old Spanish pop will probably be good for a laugh and may even unearth some gems. Gong is also a good source of concert tickets and information.

### New Phono

*C/Ample 35-37, Barri Gòtic (93 315 13 61/ www.newphono.com). Metro Jaume I.* **Open** 10am-2pm, 4.30-8pm Mon-Fri; 10am-2pm Sat. **Credit** AmEx, DC, MC, V. **Map** p345 C7.

Budding Segovias will splurge on a fine Ramírez classical guitar; others will just want a dirt-cheap Admira to strum on the beach. New Phono's cluster of display rooms holds a range of wind, string and percussion instruments and accessories, while keyboards and recording equipment reside over the road (Nos.39-40). Check the noticeboard for musical contacts.

### Verdes

*C/Duc de la Victòria 5, Barri Gòtic (93 301 91 77).* **Open** *Sept-Jun* 11am-8pm Mon-Fri; *July, Aug* 5pm-8pm Mon-Fri. **Credit** MC, V. **Map** p344 C4.

The best vinyl shop in town for soul, breakbeat, funk, jazz and nu jazz also comes with its own label, Verdes Records. It's a subterranean hangout complete with private listening booths that's great for imports, flyers, club chat and DJ spotting.

## Photography

If Casanova Foto doesn't have what you need, try **ARPI** (La Rambla 38-40, Barri Gòtic, 93 301 74 04), which has a wide range too but scores more poorly on service and digital equipment.

### Casanova Foto

*C/Pelai 18, Raval (93 302 73 63/www.casanova foto.com). Metro Universitat.* **Open** 10am-2pm, 4.30-8.30pm Mon-Fri; 10am-2pm, 5-8.30pm Sat. **Credit** MC, V. **Map** p344 B1.

One for the pros and enthusiastic amateurs (they'll take two days to process your snaps). It's not the most user-friendly of establishments, either, but if you know what you want and what you're talking about, you should be able to find it among the extensive stock of new and second-hand digital and film equipment: camera bodies, lenses, tripods, darkroom gear, bags and more. There's also a slow but thorough repair lab.

**Other locations**: Casanova Professional, C/Tallers 68, Raval (93 301 61 12); Casanova Col·lecció, C/Pelai 9, Raval (93 317 28 69).

### Fotoprix

*C/Pelai 6, Raval (93 318 20 36/www.fotoprix.es). Metro Universitat.* **Open** 9.30am-8.30pm Mon-Fri; 10am-8.30pm Sat. **Credit** MC, V. **Map** p344 A1.

All 45 branches offer one-hour APS and standard film development and copies from negatives. Other

The **Casa Beethoven**, a music-lover's delight. *See p209.*

services are also on offer, such as passport photos, slide processing, printing from CDs and memory cards, and converting Super 8 film to video or DVD.
**Other locations**: C/Ferran 33, Barri Gòtic (93 317 02 13); and throughout the city.

## Speciality shops

### Arlequí Mascares

*C/Princesa 7, Born (93 268 27 52/www.arlequi mask.com). Metro Jaume I.* **Open** 10.30am-8.30pm Mon-Sat; 10.30am-4.30pm Sun. **Credit** MC, V. **Map** p345 D5.

The walls here are dripping with masks, crafted from papier mâché and leather. Whether gilt-laden or in feathered commedia dell'arte style, simple Greek tragicomedy styles or traditional Japanese or Catalan varieties, they make striking fancy dress or decorative staples. Other trinkets and toys include finger puppets, mirrors and ornamental boxes.
**Other locations**: Plaça Sant Josep Oriol 7, Barri Gòtic (93 317 24 29); C/Caballeros 10, Poble Espanyol (93 426 21 69).

### Cereria Mas

*C/Carme 3, Raval (93 317 04 38/www.cereriamas. com).* **Open** 10am-2pm, 4.30-8pm Mon-Thur; 10am-2pm, 4.30-8.30pm Fri; 10.30am-2pm, 5-8.30pm Sat. Closed last 2wks Aug. **Credit** MC, V. **Map** p344 B4.

The Mas candle-makers have been making award-winning bundles of wax for more than a century. The shop specialises in extremely realistic representations of fruit and other objects, as well as the usual range of tapered dinner-table candles, votive candles, scented floating candles and candles for every occasion, from birthdays to Christmas to Hallowe'en.

### Flora Albaicín

*C/Canuda 3, Barri Gòtic (93 302 10 35). Metro Catalunya.* **Open** 10.30am-1pm, 5-8pm Mon-Sat. **Credit** AmEx, MC, V. **Map** p344 B3.

If you're even mildly tempted by the frilly flamenco dresses hanging forlornly in the tourist traps lining La Rambla, make a beeline for this haven of ruffles and polka dots. The tiny store is bursting to the seams with brightly coloured flamenco frocks, shoes, head combs, bangles, shawls and so on.

### Herboristeria del Rei

*C/Vidre 1, Barri Gòtic (93 318 05 12). Metro Liceu.* **Open** 10am-2pm, 5-8pm Tue-Sat. Closed 1-2wks Aug. **Credit** MC, V. **Map** p345 B6.

Designed by a theatre set designer in the 1860s, the shop's intricate wooden shelving hides myriad herbs and infusions, ointments and unguents for health and beauty. Its more up-to-date stock includes vegetarian foods, organic olive oils and organic mueslis.

### El Rei de la Màgia

*C/Princesa 11, Born (93 319 39 20/www.elreidela magia.com). Metro Jaume I.* **Open** *Sept-July* 10am-2pm, 5-8pm Mon-Fri; 11am-2pm Sat. *Aug* 11am-2pm, 5-8pm Mon-Fri. **Credit** MC, V. **Map** p345 E5.

# Oh, what a picture!

Herboristeria del Rei.

Barcelona's loyalty to the old ways of retail are reflected in more than just quaintly longwinded service. Just as many shops have stayed in the same familial hands for generations, so many have also maintained their original façades and fittings. All this means that time-strapped tourists can shop and sightsee all at once.

Starting in the Born, **Casa Gispert** (*see p202*) has kept its 150-year-old elegant mirror, glass and wood frontage, dark wood fittings and ancient roasting oven. Crossing the Via Laietana into the Barri Gòtic, the slightly younger **Herboristeria del Rei** (*see p211*) conserves a stunning interior of marble, mahogany and painted glass dating from 1860. It's worth getting the camera out for nearby **El Ingenio**'s (*see p193*) – its wood and gilt frontage and the word sculpture *Gymnastic Letters* by local artist Joan Brossa, are worthy of some photographic action.

Although there are some Modernista jewels worth seeking out among the tacky souvenir shops of La Rambla, the Antigua Casa Figueras, now home to the **Escribà** patisserie (*see p203*), is the product of a whole team of Modernista artists, from sculptor Lambert Escaler to mosaic artist Mario Maragliano. This is just down the street from the **Boqueria** (*see p208*), which has recently renovated some of its Modernista wrought iron and stained glass in a bid to boost its landmark status even further. Pop through the market up to C/Carme and you'll find one of the Raval's few Modernista treasures – the **El Indio** textile store (No.24), with a stunning flourish-laden theatrical frontage of marble and Modernista motifs.

But the Eixample, as the cradle of Modernista architecture, is where you'll find the most preened and preserved frontages. **Forn Sarret**'s (C/Girona 73) extravagantly crafted, graceful wooden door frames seem to herald the entrance to a fairy world rather than the place to buy your daily loaf. And **Queviures Murria**'s (C/Roger de Llúria 85, 93 215 57 89) shopfront is a veritable art gallery, featuring original handpainted adverts for local booze Anis del Mono by Modernista artist Ramon Casas.

Pharmacies, however, are the cream of the crop when it comes to retaining original Modernista splendours. One of the most stunning is **Farmacia Nordbeck** (C/Ausias Marc 31), which dates from around 1905. Its façade is divided by three wood-panelled pillars carved with ornate floral motifs – patterns that are repeated in the stained-glass doors and original wooden interior. But there are plenty more with intriguing interiors: look for the stained glass orange tree welcoming you to **Farmacia Bolos** (Rambla de Catalunya 77), the painted bandstand on the ceiling of **Farmacia Ferrer Argelaguet** (C/Roger de Lluria 74) and **Farmacia Puigoriol**'s (C/Mallorca 312) pretty, stone-encrusted glass doors.

Farmacia Nordbeck.

Harry Potter-syndrome has no doubt lured many a young visitor to the 'King of Magic'. Although it's a serious set-up that prepares stage-ready illusions for pros, it also welcomes the amateur magician, curious fan and even prank-obsessed schoolboy, who may levitate with joy on seeing its fine range of fake turds, itching powder and the like.

### Sombreria Obach

*C/Call 2, Barri Gòtic (93 318 40 94). Metro Jaume I or Liceu.* **Open** *Oct-July* 9.30am-1.30pm, 4-8pm Mon-Fri; 10am-2pm, 4.30-8.30pm Sat. *Aug, Sept* 9.30am-1.30pm, 4-8pm Mon-Fri; 10am-2pm Sat. **Credit** MC, V. **Map** p345 C5.

Sombreria Obach's old-fashioned display windows are like a United Nations of hats holding a general assembly: Kangol's mohair berets share space with fedoras, while stetsons nod to trilbies and matador's caps (like Mickey Mouse ears) face off with traditional red Catalan beanies.

## Sport

The tourist shops on La Rambla stock a huge range of football strips.

### La Botiga del Barça

*Maremàgnum, Moll d'Espanya, Port Vell (93 225 80 45). Metro Drassanes.* **Open** 10am-10pm daily. **Credit** AmEx, DC, MC, V. **Map** p342 F12/13.

Everything for the well-dressed Barça fan, from the standard blue and burgundy strips to scarves, hats, crested ties, aftershave and even underpants. The myriad souvenirs and gifts also include calendars, shirts printed with your name, shield-embossed ashtrays, beach towels and so on.

**Other locations**: Museu del FC Barcelona, Nou Camp (93 409 02 71).

### Decathlon

*C/Canuda 20, Barri Gòtic (93 342 61 61/ www.decathlon.es). Metro Catalunya.* **Open** 9.30am-9.30pm Mon-Sat. **Credit** AmEx, DC, MC, V. **Map** p344 C3.

This multi-storey French chain is a handy all-in-one sportsgear department store. It's a good place to stock up on the necessaries if you're going hiking in the hills or chilling on the beach. As well as the usual clothing and equipment, it has some interesting peripherals such as first-aid kits, a small selection of hiking maps, sporting kites and energy drinks. Services include bike repair and hire and team kit stamping.

**Other locations**: L'Illa, Avda Diagonal 545-557, Eixample (93 444 01 65); Gran Via 2, Gran Via de les Corts Catalanes 75-97, Hospitalet de Llobregat (93 259 15 92).

## Ticket agents

**FNAC** (*see p189*) has a very efficient ticket desk situated on its ground floor: it sells tickets to theme parks and sights, but it's especially good for contemporary music concerts and events (it's also one of the main outlets for tickets to music festival Sónar; *see p219*). Concert tickets for smaller venues are often sold in record shops and at the venues themselves; check street posters for further details. For Barça tickets, *see p270 and below.*

### Servi-Caixa – La Caixa

*902 332 211/www.servicaixa.com.* **Credit** AmEx, DC, MC, V.

Use the special Servi-Caixa ATMs (you'll find them in most larger branches of La Caixa), dial 902 332 211 or check the website above to purchase tickets for cinemas, concerts, plays, museums, amusement parks and Barça games. You'll need to show the card with which you made the payment when you collect the tickets; but be sure to check the pick-up deadline so that you don't risk being too late.

### Tel-entrada – Caixa Catalunya

*902 101 212/www.telentrada.com.* **Credit** MC, V.

Through the Tel-entrada agency you can purchase tickets for theatre performances, cinemas (including shows at the IMAX), concerts, museums and sights over the phone, online from the website above, or even over the counter at any branch of the Caixa Catalunya savings bank. Tickets can be collected from either Caixa Catalunya ATMs or the tourist office at Plaça Catalunya (*see p323*).

## Travel services

**FNAC** (*see p189*) and **El Corte Inglés** (*see p189*) also have travel agencies. Alternatively, one very worthwhile Spanish travel website can be found at www.rumbo.es.

### Halcón Viajes

*C/Aribau 34, Eixample (93 454 59 95/902 300 600/www.halconviajes.com). Metro Universitat.* **Open** 9.30am-1.30pm, 4.30-8pm Mon-Fri; 10am-1pm Sat. **Credit** AmEx, DC, MC, V. **Map** p338 F8.

This mammoth chain has exclusive deals with Air Europa and Globalia, among others, and can offer highly competitive rates in most areas. Service tends to be quite brisk but efficient.

**Other locations**: throughout the city.

### Viajes Zeppelin

*C/Villarroel 49, Eixample (93 412 00 13/www.viajeszeppelin.com). Metro Urgell.* **Open** 9am-8pm Mon-Fri; 10am-1pm Sat. **Credit** AmEx, DC, MC, V. **Map** p342 E9.

The friendly staff at this agency speak some English and offer all the usual travel services, from flight, bus, train and hotel bookings to car rental and travel insurance (which is available even if you haven't booked the travel itself with this company). Viajes Zeppelin also provides international student identity cards (ISIC) and youth discount cards for those aged under 25. Be sure to check online at the above website for any special offers going.

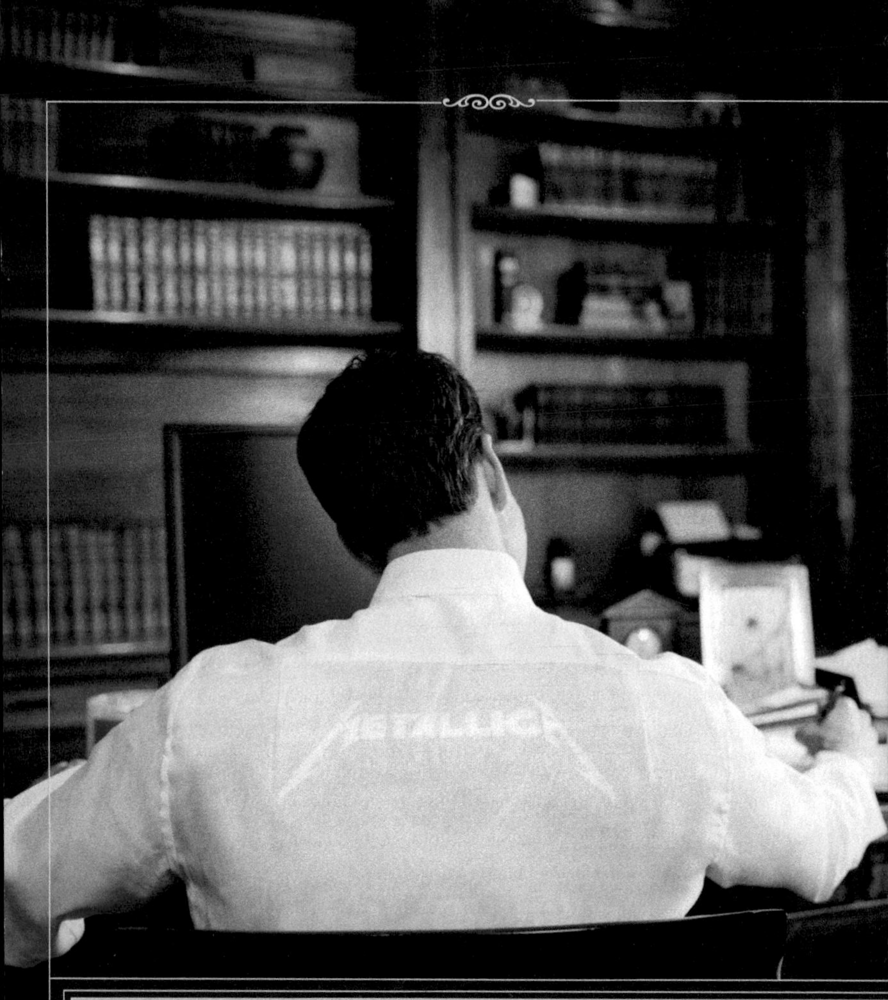

Hard Rock
CAFE

# Arts & Entertainment



## Features



**Zoo de Barcelona**. *See p226.*

# Festivals & Events

You dancin'?

Barcelona needs more festivals like it needs more designer architecture, but still they keep on coming. Just as you thought the market for, say, music festivals was saturated, along comes a whole raft of newbies, from indie-kid Summercase to the De Cajón! flamenco festival, rhythm and soul at B-estival or even a local edition of Creamfields. Another fast-growing area is the Barcelona speciality of small multimedia art festivals, with a seemingly huge subculture of young cyber sculptors, DJs and graffiti artists rising up to fill events such as Loop, BAC and Artfutura.

It's not all bleeps and knob-twiddling, though: Barcelona's great strength has always been its traditional street festivals. The most fertile time of year is undoubtedly September, when the Festes de la Mercè, Barcelona's main city celebrations, inspire entertainment ranging from wine-tasting fairs to street art competitions and free music concerts. The Mercè and the other 30 or so neighbourhood *festes* share many traditional ingredients; among them are the *correfoc* and the *sardana*, dwarves, *castellers* (human castles) and *gegants* (16-foot/five-metre-high papier-mâché/fibreglass giants dressed as princesses, fishermen, swarthy sultans and even topless chorus girls). The *correfoc* ('fire run') is a nocturnal frenzy of pyromania, when groups of horned devils dance through the streets, brandishing tridents that spout fireworks, and generally flouting just about every safety rule in the book. The more daring onlookers, protected by cotton caps and long sleeves, try to stop the devils and touch the giant, fire-breathing dragons being dragged along in their wake.

The orderly antidote to this pandemonium is the *sardana*, Catalonia's folk dance. Watching the dancers executing their fussy little hops and steps in a large circle, it's hard to believe that *sardanes* were once banned as a vestige of pagan witchcraft. The music is similarly restrained, a reedy noise played by an 11-piece *cobla* band. The *sardana* is much harder than it looks, and the joy lies in taking part rather than watching. To try your luck, check out the *sardanes populars* held in front of the cathedral (noon-2pm Sun, plus 6.30-8.30pm Sat from March to November) or www.fed.sardanista.com for monthly programmes around the city.

### INFORMATION

Organisers are prone to change dates. For more information, try tourist offices, the city's information line on 010, or the cultural agenda section at www.bcn.es. Newspapers also carry details, especially in their Friday or Saturday supplements. Events listed below that include public holidays (when many shops will be closed for the day) are marked *.

## Spring

### Festes de Sant Medir de Gràcia

*Information www.santmedir.org. Gràcia to Sant Cugat & back, usually via Plaça Lesseps, Avda República Argentina & Ctra de l'Arrabassada.* **Starting point** Metro Fontana. **Date** early Mar. **Map** p338 G4/5 & p339 H4/5.

Since 1830, decorated horses and carts have gathered bright and early around the Plaça Rius i Taulet to ride up to the hermitage of Sant Medir in the Collserola hills. Mass is celebrated, *sardanes* are danced and barbecued *botifarres* are eaten with beans. At mid morning and again in the evening, neighbourhood societies drive horse-drawn carts around the main streets of Gràcia and shower the crowd with more than 100 tons of blessed boiled sweets.

### Nous Sons – Músiques Contemporànies NC

*L'Auditori (see p260) & CCCB (see p107). Metro Catalunya or Marina.* **Date** Mar-Apr. **Map** p343 K9 & p344 A4.

Previously known as the Festival of Contemporary Music, the New Sounds festival is an interesting burst of new music of all types, featuring national and international ensembles.

### Festival Guitarra

*Various venues (93 481 70 40/www.the-project.net/festival_guitarra).* **Date** Mar-June.

This prestigious guitar festival is a classic on the Barcelona music scene and has the ability to attract world-class players, from Jackson Browne to John Williams. Styles span everything from flamenco to Latin sounds, classical guitar and gypsy jazz.

### Setmana Santa* (Holy Week)

**Date** 2-9 Apr 2007.

The main Easter event in Barcelona is the blessing of the palms on *diumenge de rams* (Palm Sunday). Crowds surge into the cathedral clutching bleached palm fronds bought from the stalls along Rambla de Catalunya and outside the Sagrada Família. On Good Friday a series of small processions and

Mystery Jets and Keane who rock out at **Summercase**. *See p220.*

blessings takes place in front of the cathedral; a procession sets out from the church of Sant Agustí on C/Hospital at around 5pm and arrives at the cathedral a couple of hours later. On Easter Sunday, godparents dole out the *mones*: originally, marzipan cakes decorated with boiled eggs, but these days more likely to be a chocolate cartoon character.

## Sant Jordi

*La Rambla & all over Barcelona.* **Date** 23 Apr.
On the feast day of Sant Jordi (St George), the patron saint of Catalonia, nearly every building bears the red and gold Catalan flag, while bakeries sell Sant Jordi bread streaked with red *sobrassada* pâté. Red roses decorate the Palau de la Generalitat and the city's many statues and paintings of George in all his dragon-slaying glory. It's said that as the drops of the dragon's blood fell, they turned into red flowers; for more than five centuries, this has been the Catalan version of St Valentine's Day.

Men traditionally give women a rose tied to an ear of wheat, and women reciprocate with a book, many now give both. This is also the 'Day of the Book', thanks to the coincidence that both Cervantes and Shakespeare died on 23 April 1616. The day accounts for an amazing 10% of Catalonia's annual book sales; street stalls and bookshops give good discounts.

### Festival de Música Antiga

*L'Auditori (see p260).* **Concerts** €4-€10.
**Date** Apr/May. **Map** p343 K9.

In 2007 a special edition will celebrate the 30th anniversary of the Festival of Early Music. It will feature some 14 concerts from performers from all over the globe, with plenty of side activities including workshops, conferences and interactive family concerts. The accompanying El Fringe festival is held over three days around the Barri Gòtic and offers young performers an opportunity to perform alongside more established musicians.

### Feria de Abril de Catalunya

*Fòrum area (information Federación de Entidades Culturales Andaluces en Cataluña www.fecac.com). Metro El Maresme-Fòrum.* **Date** end Apr/May.

The move to its new site at the seaside Fòrum area means a greatly improved venue for this enormous and joyously tacky event, but a sad goodbye to the entrances on horseback. The city's Andalucian population parties furiously and, unlike elitist Seville's equivalent, the Barcelona version is a free-for-all, with more than 60 open *casetas* (decorated marquees) offering manzanilla sherry, free flamenco shows, throbbing speakers and heaving dancefloors.

### Dia del Treball* (May Day)

*Various venues.* **Date** 1 May.

A day of mass demonstrations led by trade unionists representing an alphabet soup of organisations, including the communist CCOO, the socialist UGT and anarcho-syndicalist CGT. The main routes cover Plaça da la Universitat, Via Laietana, Passeig de Gràcia, Passeig Sant Joan and Plaça Sant Jaume, as well as the Sants neighbourhood.

### Sant Ponç

*C/Hospital. Metro Liceu.* **Date** 11 May.
**Map** p344 A4.

In honour of the patron saint of beekeepers and herbalists, C/Hospital becomes a charming outdoor market for the day, full of fresh herbs, home-produced honey, natural infusions and candied fruit, most of it straight off the farmer's cart.

### Festa Major de Nou Barris

*All over Nou Barris (www.bcn.es). Metro Poblenou.*
**Date** May.

Nou Barris has a very lively *festa major*, which is particularly strong on music, attracting top-notch local acts such as Ojos de Brujo. The music also incorporates the Nou Barris flamenco festival, with stars such as Farruquito or Chocolate attracting huge crowds. Music aside, the festivities include a medieval market and all the usual ingredients of street theatre, fireworks, parades and *castellers*.

### Barcelona Poesia & Festival Internacional de Poesia

*All over Barcelona (information Institut de Cultura 93 316 10 00/www.bcn.es/barcelonapoesia).*
**Date** May.

# Party animals

What's a party without a giant fire-breathing tortoise or a topless female dragon to get things going with a bang? Barcelona's official historic *bestiari* dates from the early 15th century and is regularly trotted out for festivals such as the Mercè and solemn occasions, including Corpus Christi. Originally made of wooden frames and papier mâché, many figures had either disappeared or fallen into disrepair by the 1840s, but seven of them were rebuilt in fibreglass at around the time of the Olympics in 1992. The crowned eagle represents the city and is a symbol of solemnity and nobility; the lion is a more cheery creature, roaring and ringing its bell when people throw money; there's also a mule, a gentle bull and a prehistoric-looking tortoise that sprays fireworks, water or sweets. The two dragons are the baddies of Catalan folklore – the *víbria* is a terrifying female dragon with bared breasts who, like the male *drac*, has a split personality; for the *correfoc* (fire run, *see p216*) they become moving fireballs, emitting flames and fireworks from their mouths, wings and tails, surrounded by a diabolic retinue of prancing devils; for ceremonial parades their mouths are filled with red roses and they perform a positively coquettish dance. In addition to the *bestiari* are the charming *cavallets cotoners*, eight little horses worn in the manner of Bernie Clifton's ostrich. Originally made for the powerful cotton guilds, they have a repertoire of synchronised dance routines for official events.

On Ash Wednesday the humble sardine takes centre stage. Marking the end of carnival, a huge papier mâché sardine is paraded along the streets by a mock funeral cortège of transvestite widows in saucy black garters and corsets. In the Barceloneta district the procession is followed by children carrying sardines on tiny fishing rods to be buried on the beach. No one is sure of the origins of the Burial of the Sardine, but it's thought the fish might symbolise the penis (and meat in general) and thus the end of all animal pleasures for Lent.

This poetry festival started in 1393 as the courtly *Jocs Florals* (Floral Games), which were named after the prizes: a silver violet for third prize; a golden rose as second; and, naturally, a real flower for the winner. The games died out in the 15th century but were resuscitated in 1859 as a vehicle for the promotion of the Catalan language. Prizes went to the most suitably florid paeans to the motherland; these days, however, Spanish is also permitted, as are Basque and Gallego; many foreign languages can also be heard at the International Poetry Festival.

### Festival de Flamenco de Ciutat Vella

*Information (93 443 43 46/www.tallerdemusics.com). Metro Catalunya.* **Date** May. **Map** p344 A2.

Although there are plenty of traditional performers, old-school purists should be warned that the 14th Old City flamenco festival is just as likely to include DJs fusing flamenco with anything from electronica to jazz and rock.

### Primavera Sound

*Fòrum (information www.primaverasound.com).* **Tickets** €65 until Mar; €75 Apr; €100 May. **Date** May.

Fast stealing Sónar's thunder, this three-day, six-stage music festival is one of the best in Spain. Credit for its success is due to its range of genres. There are rafts of electronica acts, DJs and local bands, plus a record fair and the Soundtrack Film Festival.

## Summer

### Festa dels Cors de la Barceloneta

*Barceloneta.* **Date** 2-4 June. **Map** p343 H12/13.

In a tradition dating back 150 years, some 24 choirs of workers and regulars from Barceloneta's restaurants and bars sing traditional *caramelles* and march in carnival parades around the district. Singers wear costumes garlanded with objects typical of their profession – nets and oars for a fisherman, cereal boxes and sausage for a grocer – and carry long, decorated hatchets, oars or pitchforks bearing their choir's symbol. The more sober parade is on Saturday morning; at midday, the choirs take off for an overnight jolly on the coast, returning rather the worse for wear on Monday afternoon for song, dance, drink and fireworks.

### L'Ou Com Balla

*Ateneu Barcelonès, C/Canuda 6; Casa de l'Ardiaca, C/Santa Llúcia 1; Cathedral cloisters; Museu Frederic Marès; all in Barri Gòtic (information Institut de Cultura 93 301 77 75/www.bcn.es/icub).* **Date** wk of 7 June 2007.

L'Ou Com Balla (the 'dancing egg') is a local Corpus Christi tradition dating from 1637: a hollowed-out eggshell in spinning and bobbing *perpetuum mobile* on the spout of a fountain garlanded with flowers and cherry blossom. The Sunday Corpus procession leaves from the cathedral in the early evening; on the Saturday there's free entrance to the Ajuntament, the Palau Centelles behind it and the Museu d'Història de la Ciutat, along with *sardanes* at 7pm outside the cathedral.

### Sónar

*Information www.sonar.es.* **Tickets** approx €30-€130. **Date** 14-16 June 2007.

The three-day International Festival of Advanced Music and Multimedia Art is still a must for anyone into electronic music, contemporary urban art and media technologies. The event is divided into two parts: SónarDay comprises multimedia art, record fairs, conferences, exhibitions and sound labs around the CCCB, while DJs play. SónarNight means a scramble for the desperately overcrowded shuttle bus from the bottom of La Rambla out to the vast hangars of the site in Hospitalet (tip: share a cab between four – it'll cost you the same – and get there by midnight to avoid the queues), where concerts and DJs are spread out over SónarClub, SónarPark and SónarPub. Advance tickets are available online or from the Palau de la Virreina.

### Sant Joan*

*All over Barcelona.* **Date** night of 23 June.

The beach is the place to be for an orgy of all-night pyromania on the eve of Sant Joan (St John the Baptist). Being summer solstice, it's traditional to stay up 'til dawn, munching *coca de Sant Joan* – flat, crispy bread topped with candied fruit – and drinking endless bottles of cava while partying by the light of huge bonfires. The biggest fireworks displays are at Montjuïc, Tibidabo and L'Estació del Nord. Don't miss Barceloneta's Nit del Foc (Night of Fire), where devils incite the crowds to dance around the bonfires before everyone drunkenly heads down to the beach to watch the sunrise. Special metro and FGC trains run all night.

### Festa de la Música

*All over Barcelona (information Institut de Cultura 93 316 10 00/www.bcn.es/icub or www.festadela musica.info).* **Date** late June.

Started in France in 1982 and now celebrated in more than 100 countries, the three-day Festival of Music sees amateur musicians from 100 countries take to the streets. All events are free, and you're as likely to see a kid slapping a bongo as a first-rate blues band, symphonic orchestra or choir.

### Gran Trobada d'Havaneres

*Passeig Joan de Borbó, Barceloneta (information Institut de Cultura 93 316 10 00/www.bcn.es/icub).* **Date** last Sat in June. **Map** p345 E7/8.

The barnacled legacy of Catalonia's old trade links with Cuba, *havaneres* are melancholy 19th-century sea shanties accompanied by accordions and guitars. The main event is at the port town of Calella de Palafrugells, but the Barcelona satellite is no less fun. Performances by groups dressed in stripy shirts, with salty sea-dog names such as Peix Fregit (fried fish) and Xarxa (fishing net), are followed by *cremat* (flaming spiced rum) and fireworks.

### Dies de Dansa

*Information Associació Marató de l'Espectacle (93 268 18 68/www.marato.com).* **Date** June/July.

This three-day Festival of Dance aims to create what insiders like to call a 'dialogue' between public spaces and individual expression. All the shows are free, and most of them centre around the terraces of the CCCB (Centre de Cultura Contemporània de Barcelona), MACBA (Museu d'Art Contemporani de Barcelona), CaixaForum and Fundació Miró, including popular events such as dance-offs and the Spanish-Portuguese breakdancing championships.

### Festival del Grec

*Information Institut de Cultura (93 316 10 00/ www.bcn.es/grec).* **Date** June-Aug.

An integral part of summer in the city, El Grec began in 1976 as a series of plays in the eponymous Greek-style amphitheatre on Montjuïc and three decades on has grown into a two-month spree of dance, music and theatre all over the city.

### De Cajón!

*Various venues (www.deflamenco.com).* **Date** July.

This high-quality new mini festival has snagged some of Barcelona's top venues to showcase spectacular flamenco talents such as *cantaor* Antonio Vargas 'Potito', flamenco pianist Diego Amador, singer Estrella Morente and the world-famous guitarist Paco de Lucía.

### Clàssics als Parcs

*Information Parcs i Jardins (93 413 24 00/ www.bcn.es/parcsijardins).* **Date** July.

What nicer way can there be to spend a balmy summer evening than listening to classical music in one of Barcelona's most beautiful parks? Throughout July, young musicians perform a varied concert programme, alfresco and for free. On Thursdays, concerts are held at the secluded Jardins de la Tamarita and the pretty Turó Park, on Fridays at the futuristic Diagonal Mar and the Jardins de Ca n'Altimira, and on Saturdays at the Parc de la Ciutadella.

### B-estival

*Poble Espanyol, Avda Marquès de Comillas s/n (www.b-estival.com). Metro Espanya.* **Date** 11 nights mid July. **Map** p341 A9.

Defining itself as Barcelona's 'festival of rhythms', B-estival was born in 2006, and the impressive programming covers blues, soul, R&B, Brazilian music and plenty of flamenco and rai to fill in the gaps.

### Summercase

*Parc del Fòrum (www.summercase.com). Metro El Maresme-Fòrum.* **Date** two days mid July.

This new two-day festival is the sunny partner to Wintercase (*see p222*), with a healthy line-up of indie rock and some big-name dance acts. The event has a retro, definitively British feel (2006's acts included Primal Scream and Massive Attack). **Photos** *p217.*

## Rave rivals

Don't get us wrong, Sónar (*see p219*) rocks – 90,000 people hitting town for some of the most forward-thinking electronic music in the world is never going to be a bad thing. But, as if choosing who to see at festivals of this calibre wasn't difficult enough, for a good few years a rival Sónar movement has been in full swing, and it's not to be sniffed at.

Residents, claiming the festival is too snobby, too expensive or too druggy, have led to the inevitable, and somewhat smug cries of 'it's not what it used to be', and an alternative party itinerary has established itself during the week of the festival. The movement takes a couple of guises, the first being the fairly ramshackle Anti-Sónar; patronised mainly by the city's vast troop of dreadlocked anarcho-bohemians (and their dogs on strings, naturellement), these outdoor free parties provide ear bleeding psy-trance for all from around 5am.

Then there's the more organised club nights. From record label showcases to super sought-after DJ appearances, the line-up in almost every one of the city's clubs during Sónar week could be a festival in itself, and while clubbing lacks the stylistic flair of Sónar proper, it is kinder on the wallet.

2006 saw Razzmatazz (*see p259*) rammed every night, featuring everyone from 2 many Djs and Felix da Housecat to Vitalic and Klaxons. Meanwhile, Tomas Anderson joined the Swedish showcase that took over Nitsa (*see p255*), Ivan Smagghe and Chloé brought Paris's Kill the DJ soirée to La Paloma (*see p252*, and London's Secret Sundaze threw a party at Shôko (*see p253*) down on the beach.

The beachfront, incidentally, is worth checking out, as its *xiringuitos* host some of the best parties. While the sound lacks bass oomph and can be temperamental, it's an opportunity to hear world-class DJs for free. Most record labels worth their salt will try and get a slot at one of the bars on Marbella beach, and in 2006 Ellen Allien, Miss Kittin and James Holden among many others had the crowds, Estrella in hand, digging themselves into the sand.

### Mas i Mas Festival

*Information (93 319 17 89/www.masimas.com). Various venues.* **Date** late July-early Sept.

This impeccably tasteful music festival stretches over the summer months and has gone from concentrating on Latin sounds to providing a little bit of everything. Concerts take place at various venues, including the Palau de la Música (*see p261*) and Jamboree (*see p247*).

### Festa de Sant Roc

*(Information 010/www.bcn.es). Various venues around Plaça Nova, Barri Gòtic. Metro Jaume I.* **Date** 11-15 Aug. **Map** p344 C4.

The Festa de Sant Roc, celebrated every year since 1589, is the Barri Gòtic's street party. It's hard to beat for lovers of Catalan traditions: there are parades with the giants and fat heads, *sardana* dancing and 19th-century street games. The festivities, which centre around the Plaça Nova in front of the cathedral, conclude with a *correfoc* and fireworks. **Photo** *p222.*

### Festa Major de Gràcia

*All over Gràcia (information 93 459 30 80/www.festamajordegracia.org). Metro Fontana.* **Date** 3rd wk in Aug. **Map** p338 G4/5 & p339 H4/5.

Gràcia's extravagant *festa major* is most distinctive for its best-dressed street competition, where residents transform some 25 streets into pirate ships, rainforests and even a giant strawberry gâteau. The festival opens with giants and castles in Plaça Rius i Taulet, and climaxes with a *correfoc* and a *castell de focs* (castle of fireworks). In between, 600 activities, from concerts to *sardanes* and kids' bouncy castles, are centred around Plaça Rius i Taulet, Plaça de la Revolució, Plaça del Sol and Plaça de la Virreina.

### Festa Major de Sants

*All over Sants (information Federació Festa Major de Sants 93 490 62 14/www.festamajordesants.org). Metro Plaça de Sants or Sants Estació.* **Date** last wk in Aug.

One of the lesser-known *festes majors*, Sants has a traditional flavour, with floral offerings to images of St Bartholomew at the local church and the market. Major events, such as the *correfoc* on the night of the 24th, are held in the Parc de l'Espanya Industrial; others are held at Plaça del Centre, C/SantAntoni, Plaça de la Farga and Plaça Joan Peiro, behind Sants station.

## Autumn

### Diada Nacional de Catalunya*

*All over Barcelona.* **Date** 11 Sept.

Catalan National Day commemorates Barcelona's capitulation to the Bourbon army in the 1714 War of the Spanish Succession, a bitter defeat that led to the repression of many Catalan institutions. It's lost some of its vigour but is still a day for national re-affirmation, with the Catalan flag flying on buses and balconies. There are several marches throughout the city, the epicentre being the statue of Rafael Casanova (who directed the resistance) on the Ronda Sant Pere. Many make a pilgrimage to the monastery at Montserrat, the spiritual heart of the region and an important guardian of Catalan language and culture during the dictatorship.

### Festes de la Mercè*

*All over Barcelona (information tourist offices or www.bcn.es).* **Date** 18-24 Sept 2007.

What was once a small religious parade in honour of the patron saint of the city, Our Lady of Mercy, has gradually swollen to a week-long party with all things bright and Catalan hitched to its wagon. The event opens with *castellers* in the Plaça de la Mercè followed by more than 400 events including *gegants*, *capgrosses* (little scampering dwarves with large fibreglass heads), *sardanes* and the biggest and boldest *correfoc* of them all on the Saturday night. The highlights of this immense event include dazzling fireworks displays along the city beaches, a seafront air show and the solidarity festival, now returned to its original location on the Passeig de Gràcia. Free concerts fill the squares, while sporting events include a swim across the port and a regatta. Add to that exhibitions, children's activities, street entertainers and free entrance to many museums on 24 September, and it's a full, full week.

### Barcelona Acció Musical (BAM)

*Various venues (information 93 427 42 49/ www.bam.es).* **Date** 20-23 Sept 2007.

BAM stages a good number of free concerts on Plaça del Rei, La Rambla del Raval, outside the cathedral and at the Fòrum site. The prime mover of what has become known as So Barcelona (Barcelona Sound), BAM largely promotes left-field *mestissa* (vaguely, ethnic fusion) in its mission to provide 'music without frontiers'. The line-up of around 40 bands usually includes several international headliners, although 2006 offered mostly local fare.

### Mostra de Vins i Caves de Catalunya

*Moll d'Espanya, Port Vell. Metro Drassanes.* **Date** 21-23 Sept 2007. **Map** p342 F12.

This outdoor wine and cava fair has been running since 1980 and now showcases more than 400 labels from around 50 Catalan bodegas. Big names include Torres, Freixenet, Codorníu, Pinord and Mont Marçal; also on show are fine cheeses, charcuterie and related oenophilia. Ten wine or cava tastings with a commemorative glass cost €6; four food tastings cost €5.

### Festa Major de la Barceloneta

*All over Barceloneta (information 93 221 72 44/ www.cascantic.net). Metro Barceloneta.* **Date** last wk Sept. **Map** p343 H12/13.

This tight-knit maritime community throws itself into the local *festes* with incredible gusto. The fun kicks off with fireworks on the beach, a 24-hour football tournament, *sardana* dancing, falcons (acrobatic

Arts & Entertainment

City giants at a city neighbourhood *festa.*

groups) and a free tasting of traditional crispy coca bread washed down with muscatel, and finishes with more of the same ten days later. In between, expect parades, music, fire-breathing dragons, open-air cinema and bouncy castles. Look out, too, for a character called General Bum Bum, who parades with a wooden cannon but stops periodically to fire sweets into crowds of scrabbling children.

### Festival de Músiques del Món

*L'Auditori (see p260). Metro Marina.* **Tickets** €10; €8 concessions. **Date** Oct. **Map** p343 K9.

This World Music Festival has moved to the Auditori from the CaixaForum, but the format remains almost identical: around 20 concerts, along with related exhibitions, films and workshops. Concerts might include anything from Mongolian throat-singing to Turkish whirling dervishes alongside home-grown talent such as flamenco singer Miguel Poveda, a regular at this event.

### Festival de Tardor Ribermúsica

*Various venues, Born (information www.ribermusica.org). Metro Barceloneta or Jaume I.*
**Date** 17-21 Oct. **Map** p345 E6/7.

This lively autumn music festival boasts more than 100 free performances around the Born, and fills the squares, bars, galleries, shops, churches and clubs with concerts of all stripes. Wander down the narrow streets of the Passeig del Born to see baroque quartets, Celtic rockers or the flamenco flautists playing at Santa María del Mar church, the Picasso Museum, in open squares and among the clothes hangers of a number of boutiques.

### Artfutura

*Mercat de les Flors, C/Lleida 59, Poble Sec (www.artfutura.org). Metro Espanya or Poble Sec.*
**Date** last weekend in Oct. **Map** p341 C10.

This pioneer festival in the field of cyber-art is a great place to check out the latest progeny of the union between mind and machine, and a chance to find the next Warhol of the web or the future console Kandinsky.

### La Castanyada*

*All over Barcelona.* **Date** 31 Oct-1 Nov.

All Saints' Day and the evening before are known as the Castanyada after the traditional treats of *castanyes* (roast chestnuts) along with *moniatos* (roast sweet potatoes) and *panellets* (small almond balls covered in pine nuts). The imported tradition of Hallowe'en has rocketed in popularity of late, and there are now several celebrations around town. The largest is in Poble Espanyol, with music and a monsters' ball late into the witching hours. Tots Sants (All Saints') is also known as the Dia dels Difunts (Day of the Dead); the snacks switch to white, bone-shaped *ossos de sant* cakes. Thousands visit local cemeteries over the weekend to sprinkle the graves with holy water, leave flowers and hold vigils.

### Wintercase Barcelona

*Sala Razzmatazz 1, C/Almogàvers 122, Poblenou. Information www.wintercase.com). Metro Marina.*
**Tickets** from €18. **Date** late Nov. **Map** p343 L10.

This music festival showcases some of the finest indie bands over four nights. The Barcelona leg takes place in Razzmatazz (*see p259*), with past players including the likes of Ian Brown, Mercury Rev and Teenage Fanclub.

### Festival Internacional de Jazz de Barcelona

*(Information The Project 93 481 70 40/ www.the-project.net).* **Date** late Nov/early Dec.

One of Europe's most well-respected jazz festivals has grown to embrace everything from bebop to gospel to tribute bands around a core of mainstream performers that have recently included Chick Corea, Bebo Valdés and Caetano Veloso. Venues range from the Palau de la Música, Luz de Gas and Razzmatazz to L'Auditori, and there are big-band concerts and swing dancing in the Ciutadella park.

## Winter

### Fira de Santa Llúcia

*Pla de la Seu & Avda de la Catedral (93 402 70 00/ www.bcn.es/nadal). Metro Jaume I.* **Dates** 2-23 Dec. **Map** p344-345 D4/5.

Dating from 1786, this traditional Christmas fair has expanded to more than 300 stalls selling all manner of handcrafted Christmas decorations and gifts, along with mistletoe, poinsettias and Christmas trees. The most popular figure on sale for nativity scenes is the curious Catalan figure of the *caganer* (shitter), a small figure crouching over a steaming turd with his trousers around his ankles. Kids line up for a go on the giant *caga tió*, a huge, smiley-faced 'shit log' that poops out pressies upon being beaten viciously by a stick; smaller versions are on sale in the stalls. There's also a nativity scene contest, musical parades and exhibitions, including the popular life-size nativity scene in Plaça Sant Jaume.

### Resfest

*Various venues, mainly El Mercat de les Flors (www.resfest.com).* **Date** Dec.

Coolhunters unite. This travelling event celebrates the convergence of innovative film, music, art, design, fashion and technology and is the first global event to do so. Expect a celebration of creativity manifested through screenings, seminars, live music performances, parties and interactive entertainment.

### Nadal* & Sant Esteve* (Christmas Day & Boxing Day)

**Dates** 25 & 26 Dec.

The Catalan equivalent of the Christmas midnight mass is the *missa del gall* (cockerel's mass), held at dawn. Later, the whole family enjoys a traditional Christmas feast of *escudella i carn d'olla* (a meaty stew), seafood and roast truffled turkey, finishing off with great ingots of *turrón*. The *caga tió* (*see above* Fira de Santa Llúcia) gives small gifts but the real booty doesn't arrive until the night of 5 January.

### Cap d'Any (New Year's Eve)*

**Date** 31 Dec & 1 Jan.

During the day, look out for L'Home dels Nassos, the man who has as many noses as days of the year – it being the last day, the sly old fox has only one – who parades and throws sweets to the children. At night, bars and discos charge hiked-up prices, but free public celebrations are held around the city, mainly on La Rambla and Plaça Catalunya. At midnight everyone stops swilling cava and starts stuffing 12 grapes into their mouths, one for every chime of the bell. Wear red underwear for good luck.

### Cavalcada dels Reis

*Kings usually arrive at Parc Ciutadella then parade along C/Marquès de l'Argentera up Via Laietana to Plaça Catalunya & continue to Montjuïc. The detailed route changes each year (information Centre d'Informació de la Virreina 010/www.bcn.es/nadal).* **Date** 5 Jan, 5-9pm. **Map** p343 J11, p345 D6, p344 C2 & p341 B9.

Melchior, Gaspar and Balthasar arrive aboard the Santa Eulàlia boat at the bottom of La Rambla before beginning a grand parade around town with a retinue of acrobats, circus clowns and pages. The televised route is published in the newspapers, but the biggest crowds are on C/Marquès de l'Argentera. Later that night, children leave their shoes out on the balcony stuffed with hay for the kings' camels; in the morning, they're either full of presents or edible coal (lumps of coloured sugar) depending on their behaviour.

### Festa dels Tres Tombs

*Sant Antoni. Metro Sant Antoni.* **Date** 17 Jan. **Map** Map p342 E10.

St Anthony's day also marks the *festa major* of the district; all the usual ingredients of music and *gegants* here include a monstrous, symbolic fire-breathing pig. The devil is meant to have tempted the saint by taking the form of a pig; indeed, Sant Antoni is often depicted with a porker by his side. However, he is in fact the patron saint of all domestic animals and on his feast day it's still the custom to bring animals to the church of St Anthony to be blessed. Afterwards, horsemen ride three circuits (*tres tombs*) in a formal procession from Ronda Sant Antoni, through Plaça Catalunya, down La Rambla and along C/Nou de la Rambla.

### Santa Eulàlia

*All over Barcelona.* **Date** wk of 12 Feb.

The city's blowout winter festival is in honour of Santa Eulàlia (Laia), Barcelona's co-patron saint and a special favourite of children. In the fourth century, 13-year-old Laia spoke out against the Romans' persecution of the Christians and was promptly arrested, locked in a box of fleas and whipped with flaming scourges before being crucified naked (a miraculous snow fell to save her modesty). Her feast day on 12 February kicks off with a ceremony in Plaça Sant Jaume, followed by music, *sardanes* and parades, with masses and children's choral concerts held in the churches and cathedral. In the evening, the female giants gather in Plaça Sant Josep Oriol, then go to throw flowers on the Baixada de Santa Eulàlia (where the Romans rolled Laia down the hill in a barrel of broken glass) before a final boogie in the Plaça Sant Jaume. The Ajuntament and the cathedral crypt (where she's buried) are free and open to the public, as are more than 30 museums. The festival closes on Sunday evening with *correfocs* (for adults and children) centred around the cathedral.

### Carnestoltes (Carnival)

*All over Barcelona.* **Date** Shrove Tuesday/ Ash Wednesday (20 Feb & 21 Feb 2007).

The city drops everything for a last hurrah of overeating, overdrinking and underdressing prior to Lent. You'll have to hop on a Tuesday-night train to Sitges for the best carnival, but there's still plenty going on in Barcelona. The celebrations begin on Dijous Gras (Mardi Gras) with the appearance of potbellied King Carnestoltes – the masked personification of the carnival spirit – followed by the grand weekend parade, masked balls, *fartaneres* (neighbourhood feasts, typically with lots of pork), food fights and a giant *botifarrada* (sausage barbecue) on La Rambla, with most of the kids and market traders in fancy dress. It's over on Ash Wednesday, when the effigy of Carnestoltes goes up in flames and revellers celebrate the mock Burial of the Sardine on the beach (*see p218*).

# Children

Family fortunes.

Child-specific facilities are few in Barcelona, but over the last decade play parks, workshops, summer programmes and story sessions have cropped up all over the place.

The centre is compact, and a well-planned itinerary can easily include plenty of traffic-free squares, play parks and outdoor terraces for frequent refreshment stops. Pester power will ensure endless stops along **La Rambla** (*see p94*) for the entertainers, artists and animals, not to mention visits to the **zoo** (*see p226*) and the **Font Màgica de Montjuïc** (*see p117*) or trips on the **cable car** (*see p121*). Even the local museums are feeling the pull of small, sticky hands on the purse strings and provide an ever-growing choice of extra kids' activities, from making chocolate figurines at the **Museu de la Xocolata** (*see p225*) to blowing giant paint bubbles at **CosmoCaixa** (*see p225*).

In stereotypical Mediterranean manner, Catalans find it very natural to touch and coo over other people's children; don't be surprised if your waiter whips away your wee one for a quick cuddle between courses, or an old lady comes over to pull up your child's droopy socks. However, the nuts and bolts of childcare, such as nappy-changing rooms and special breastfeeding areas, are not generally provided. There are mother-and-baby facilities in El Corte Inglés (third floor) department store, the larger children's shops such as Prenatal, the airport, the large shopping malls and Poble Espanyol, but be warned that most nappy changes occur in the car or the pram; breastfeeding is totally accepted in public as long as you are discreet.

Public transport is only free for children under four, and only stations on line 2 and some on line 4 have lifts. Officially, pushchairs are supposed to be folded up on the metro, but in practice most people just grapple gamely with the obstacle course and the guards don't interfere. All but the oldest buses are low enough to wheel prams straight on.

## Entertainment

### Attractions

In the summer, it's hard to drag the kids away from the city's **beaches**. These have plenty of lifeguards, play areas, showers and ice-cream kiosks and an ever-increasing number of public toilets. Go early and bear in mind that the beaches on far side of the Port Olímpic tend to be cleaner and less crowded than Barceloneta. Those further out of town towards the south, such as Castelldefels or Sitges, have shallower waters and fine, pale sands.

The pedestrianised streets and squares of the Barri Gòtic and the Born are especially kid-friendly areas, as is the **Poble Espanyol** (*see p120*). The nearby music-and-light show of the **Font Màgica de Montjuïc** makes for a good evening activity.

From a child's-eye view, **La Rambla** is half theatre and half petting zoo; the animal stalls, Boqueria market, entertainers and caricature artists can easily fill an afternoon. At the bottom end, the **Maremàgnum** (*see p190*) centre attracts families with ice-creams, a summer funfair and sea views. Many museums run children's activities for the Estiu als Museus summer programme from June to September (ask for the leaflet at the tourist office), but there's also a spectrum of year-round children's options. The **CaixaForum** (*see p225*) runs 'Playing With Art', for children aged three and above, every Saturday and Sunday (11am-2pm, 4-8pm). **MACBA** (*see p107*) has various free Sunday morning workshops for children aged up to 14, and the **Museu d'Història de Catalunya** (*see p111*) runs tours for kids aged three to eight at noon on Saturdays. A must-see for junior footie fiends is the **Museu del FC Barcelona** (*see p135*), where the guided tour includes a walk from the dressing rooms through the tunnel, a few steps on the pitch and a spell on the bench.

#### L'Aquàrium

*Moll d'Espanya, Port Vell (93 221 74 74/www.aquariumbcn.com). Metro Barceloneta or Drassanes.* **Open** *Oct-May* 9.30am-9pm Mon-Fri; 9.30am-9.30pm Sat, Sun. *June, Sept* 9.30am-9.30pm daily. *July, Aug* 9.30am-11pm daily. **Admission** €15; €10 concessions; free under-4s. **Credit** AmEx, DC, MC, V. **Map** p342 G13.

Barcelona's modest aquarium houses an important collection of Mediterranean marine life with more than 450 species on display. The information panels are child-friendly and in English. Miniaquària is devoted to the smaller animals such as sea cucumbers, anenomes and the ever-popular seahorses, all displayed at tot's-eye level, but the main draw here is the Oceanari, a giant shark-infested tank traversed via a glass tunnel on a wooden conveyor belt.

The upstairs section is devoted to children: for pre-schoolers, Explora! has 50 knobs-and-whistles style activities, such as turning a crank to see how ducks' feet move underwater or climbing inside a deep-sea diver's suit. Older children should head to Planet Aqua – a quite extraordinary, split-level circular space with Humboldt penguins and a walk through model of a sperm whale.

## CosmoCaixa

*C/Teodor Roviralta 47-51 (93 212 60 50/ www.cosmocaixa.com). Bus 17, 22, 58/FGC Avda Tibidabo then Tramvia Blau (see p139).* **Open** 10am-8pm Tue-Sun. **Admission** €3; €2 concessions; free under-3s. *Planetarium* €2; €1.50 concessions; free under-3s. **Credit** AmEx, DC, MC, V.

Permanent exhibitions at the new science museum include the interactive Material Room, explaining everything from hormones to fire; the 90-ton geological wall of Iberian rocks; and the Flooded Forest, the world's first living, breathing bit of Amazonian rainforest inside a museum. Outside, the enormous Archimedes Gardens hold a number of games illustrating his principles and a scale model T-rex. Other attractions include the Bubble Planetarium (a digital 3D simulation of the universe); the Toca Toca! space where supervisors guide the exploration of natural phenomena such as tarantula and snakes and the candy-bright Javier Mariscal-designed spaces of Clik (for three- to six-year-olds) and Flash (for seven-to nine-year-olds), where children learn how to make electricity and how a kaleidoscope works.

## Museu de Cera

*Ptge de la Banca 7, Barri Gòtic (93 317 26 49/ www.museocerabcn.com). Metro Drassanes.* **Open** *Mid July-mid Sept* 10am-10pm daily. *Mid Sept-mid July* 10am-1.30pm, 4-7.30pm Mon-Fri; 11am-2pm, 4.30-8.30pm Sat, Sun. **Admission** €7.50; €4.50 children; free under-5s. **No credit cards. Map** p345 B7.

The Museu de Cera offers more of a giggle than an essential educational visit. This is a wax museum that belongs to the so-bad-it's-good school of entertainment. Expect the savvy PlayStation generation to be underwhelmed by clumsy renderings of Gaudí and Princess Di jumbled in with Frankenstein and ET. Recover with a cool drink at the museum's interesting enchanted-forest-cum-café.

## Museu de la Màgia

*C/Oli 6, Born (93 319 73 93/www.elreydelamagia. com). Metro Jaume I.* **Open** 6-8pm Thur. *Show* 6pm Sat; noon Sun. Closed Aug. **Admission** €7. Free Thur. **No credit cards. Map** p345 B3.

This collector's gallery of 19th- and 20th-century tricks and posters from the magic shop El Rei de la Màgia will enchant any budding Paul Daniels. To see some live sleight of hand, book for the shows; places are limited. They're not in English, but they are fairly accessible regardless.

## Museu de la Xocolata

*C/Comerç 36, Born (93 268 78 78/www.museu delaxocolata.com). Metro Arc de Triomf or Jaume I.* **Open** 10am-7pm Mon, Wed-Sat; 10am-3pm Sun. **Admission** €3.80; €3.20 concessions; free under-7s. **Credit** MC, V. **Map** p345 F7.

This delicious collection of chocolate sculptures includes characters from *Finding Nemo*, *Chicken Run*, *Ben-Hur* and so on, along with painstaking reproductions of Gaudí's buildings. Audio-visual shows and touch-screen computers help children make their way through what would otherwise be the rather dry history of the cocoa bean. Reserve in advance for weekend chocolate figurine-making courses and lessons in cooking desserts.

### Tibidabo Funfair

*Plaça del Tibidabo, Tibidabo (93 211 79 42/www.tibidabo.es). FGC Avda Tibidabo.* **Open** *Nov-mid Dec, mid Jan-Feb* noon-6pm Sat, Sun. *Mar, Apr* noon-7pm Sat, Sun. *May, June* noon-8pm Sat, Sun. *July* noon-8pm Wed-Fri; noon-11pm Sat; noon-10pm Sun. *Aug* noon-10pm Mon-Thur; noon-11pm Fri-Sun. *1st 2wks Sept* noon-8pm Wed-Fri; noon-9pm Sat, Sun. *last 2wks Sept* noon-9pm Sat, Sun. *Oct* noon-7pm Sat, Sun. Closed mid Dec-mid Jan. **Admission** *individual rides* €11. *Unlimited rides* €22; €17 concessions; €9 children under 1.2m (3ft11in); free children under 90cm (2ft11in). **Credit** MC, V.

It may date from 1889 but this mountain-top fairground is investing millions in getting itself bang up to date. After years of falling profits, the fair has boomed in popularity again with a terrifying new free-fall ride called the Pendulum and a new hot-air balloon style ride for smaller children. The raft of other attractions includes a house of horrors and bumper cars to the emblematic Avió, the world's first popular flight simulator when it was built in 1928. Don't miss the antique mechanical puppets and contraptions at the Museu d'Autòmats or the hourly puppet shows at the Marionetàrium (from 1pm). At the weekends, there are circus parades at the end of the day and, in the summer, *correfocs* (fire runs) and street theatre. **Photo** *p225*.

### Zoo de Barcelona

*Parc de la Ciutadella, Born (93 225 67 80/www.zoobarcelona.com). Metro Barceloneta or Ciutadella-Vila Olímpica.* **Open** *Mar, Oct* 10am-6pm daily. *Apr-Sept* 10am-7pm daily. *Nov-Feb* 10am-5pm daily. **Admission** €14.50; €8.75 3-12s. **Credit** MC, V. **Map** p343 J11/12.

The live dolphin shows (hourly at weekends) are the big draw now that Snowflake the albino gorilla has gone to the great swinging tyre in the sky. Other favourites include the hippos, sea lions, elephants and wide-open monkey houses, although there's barely enough room to move in some of the enclosures. Child-friendly features include a farmyard zoo, pony rides and plenty of restaurants, picnic areas and a brand-new adventure playground. If all that walking is too much, there's a zoo 'train', or you can rent electric cars from the C/Wellington entrance. Bear in mind that on hot days many of the animals are sleeping and out of sight.

## Festivals

The **Festes de Santa Eulàlia** in February are specially geared towards children, with hands-on activities and even a mini *correfoc*. **La Mercè** and the local *festes majors* of each neighbourhood also have plenty of parades, *gegants* and music; the decorated streets of **Festa Mejor de Gràcia** are especially popular with younger children, and there's a raft of bouncy castles, circus performers and story telling in many of the district's squares. Older kids will enjoy the late-night pyromania of the **Sant Joan** festival and music festivals such as **Primavera Sound**, while younger ones will go for the carnival parades of **Carnestoltes** or gathering sweeties from the streets at the **Festes de Sant Medir de Gràcia**. Christmas traditions are also particularly child-centred, with racks of pooping *caganers* (*see p223*) and shitting logs at the **Santa Llúcia market**. The **Three Kings'** procession on 5 January is also a guaranteed hit. For all, *see pp217-223*.

Zoo de Barcelona.

## Music, film & theatre

At weekends from September to May the **Auditori** (*see p260*) runs a cycle of 55-minute family concerts centred around various themes, such as metal instruments, and with audience participation. The **Teatre Principal** (Ramblas 27, 93 301 47 50) often puts on Spanish-language theatre shows based on familiar children's television programmes such as the Tweenies, and in the summer months the **Parc del Fòrum** (*see p227*) lays on theatre, circus and music acts, some of them free. English-language children's theatre is rare, with the exception of the Christmas pantomime; check *Metropolitan* magazine for details. To catch a film in English, the best bet is the huge **Yelmo Icària Cineplex** (*see p230*) for mainstream blockbusters, while the **FilmoTeca** (*see p230*) shows original-language children's films on Sundays at 5pm. On a rainy day, a good but pricey standby can be the **IMAX Port Vell** (*see p230*), although the films here are only shown in Spanish and Catalan, and tend to be rather dreary nature or sport documentaries. For all, *see pp229-232 and pp260-268*.

## Parks & playgrounds

The **Parc del Fòrum** (*see p227*) is working hard to establish itself as an all-day family destination and has a specially designed new area entirely devoted to children that includes plenty of free activities. The **Parc de la Ciutadella** (*see p102*) has shady gardens, giant mammoth sculpture, play parks, picnic areas, rowing boats and a zoo which make for a relaxing day out. At the **Ludoteca**, in the Ciutadella's main play park (by the lake), young children can make free use of the many toys.

Gaudí's quirky **Park Güell** (*see p132*) makes up for its lack of grass with bright gingerbread houses and winding coloured benches. High above the city, the **Parc de la Creueta del Coll** (*see p138*) has a large playground, ping-pong tables, a picnic area and great views, and the large artificial lake is filled up in the summertime for use as an outdoor public swimming pool. The delightful **Parc del Laberint** (*see p141*) has hidden benches and elfin tables, picnic areas and a deceptively difficult maze, while the **Jardins de la Tamarita** (*see p137*) form a tranquil dog-free enclave of swings and slides hidden away next to the stop for the Tramvia Blau. The largest of them all is the **Parc de Collserola** (*see p136*), perfect for young nature lovers.

The best areas for bike riding and roller skating are the beachfront esplanades and the Arc de Triomf boulevard.

### Jardíns de la Torre de les Aigües

*C/Roger de Llúria 56 interior (93 291 62 60/637 40 28 66). Metro Girona.* **Admission** €1.30; free under-1s. **Open** *Last wk June-July* 10am-8pm Mon-Sat; 10am-3pm Sun. *Aug* 10am-8pm Mon-Fri; 10am-3pm Sat, Sun. **No credit cards. Map** p338 G8.

In the summer months, this leafy inner patio becomes the 'beach of the Eixample', an oasis for under-sevens. There's a huge knee-high wading pool, plenty of clean sand with buckets and spades provided, trees for shade and the eponymous water tower in the centre along with outdoor showers, old-school changing tents and toilets.

### Parc del Castell de l'Oreneta

*Camí de Can Caralleu & Ptge Blada, Zona Alta (93 413 24 80/www.bcn.es/parcsijardins). By car Ronda de Dalt exit 9/bus 22, 34, 64, 66, 75.* **Open** *May-Aug* 10am-9pm daily. *Apr, Sept, Oct* 10am-8pm daily. *Mar* 10am-7pm daily. *Nov-Feb* 10am-6pm daily.

The castle (*castell*) may be long gone, but the old grounds remain a wonderful place to roam through forest glades and flowery meadows. There are two signposted walks with great views, plus picnic areas, supervised pony rides for three- to 12-year-olds on Saturdays and Sundays (Sept-July 10.30am-2pm, €5), ping-pong tables and adventure playgrounds. On Sundays, hop aboard the miniature train.

### Parc del Fòrum

*Rambla Prim, Sant Martí (93 356 10 50/www.bcn.es/parcdelforum). Metro El Maresme Forum.* **Open** *Zona de Banys* May-Oct 11am-7pm daily. *Àrea Lúdica Infantil i Familiar* June-Oct 11.30-2pm, 5.30-8.30pm Sat, Sun. **Admission** Free.

The Àrea Lúdica Infantil i Familiar offers free children's activities, including bouncy castles, arts and crafts workshops and performances, an area for playing traditional games, and music concerts. Paying activities in the same enormous area include two skating rinks, a minature train, go karts, PlayStation, minigolf and the like. To top off what can only be called a nipper nirvana, the vast Zona de Banys swimming area is just next door, with free pools and plenty of extra paying activities such as kayaking, canoeing and snorkelling.

## Out of town

As well as the water parks mentioned below, Catalonia has four others: **Aqua Brava** (in Roses), **Aquadiver** (Platja d'Aro), **Water World** (Lloret de Mar) along the Costa Brava and **Marineland** (Palafolls). For the endlessly popular **Port Aventura** theme park (*see p285*).

### Catalunya en Miniatura

*Can Balasch de Baix, Torrelles de Llobregat, Outer Limits (93 689 09 60/www.catalunyaenminiatura.com). By car A2 south to Sant Vicens dels Horts then left to Torrelles de Llobregat (5km/3 miles)/by bus 62 Soler i Sauret (info 93 632 51 33) from Travessera de les Corts.* **Open** *Mar-Sept* 10am-7pm daily. *Oct-Feb* 10am-6pm Tue-Sun. **Admission** €9.50; €6.50 4-12s; free under-4s. **Credit** MC, V.

Imagine Gulliver as you stroll around tiny renderings of 170 of Catalonia's most emblematic buildings and sights. Highlights include a miniature Montserrat, Girona cathedral and everything Gaudí ever laid a finger on. For the kiddies, an appropriately munchkin-sized train circles part of the complex, and clowns perform at 1pm on Sundays in the amphitheatre.

### Illa de Fantasia

*Finca Mas Brassó, Vilassar de Dalt (93 751 45 53/www.illafantasia.com). By car NII north to Premiàde Mar then left (24km/15 miles).* **Open** *Mid June-1st wk Sept* 10am-7pm daily. **Admission** €15.50; €12 2-10s; free under-2s. **Credit** AmEx, DC, MC, V.

Port Aventura on a budget, this water park has foam slides, kamikaze-style rides and rubber-dinghy chutes, along with pools, a restaurant, supermarket and a range of activities. There's also a picnic/barbecue area in a pine grove.

## Eating & drinking

It's rare to find a children's menu in Barcelona, but many restaurants will provide smaller portions on request. That said, there's little need to do so when children and tapas were so clearly made for each other – Basque pintxo bars such as **Euskal Etxea** (*see p176*) are an even better option, as children can simply serve themselves from the food that is laid out, waiting for hungry young mouths, on the bar. An important point to remember for families with early eating children is that most restaurants in Barcelona don't serve lunch before 1.30pm or dinner before 9pm, so play it like the locals and encourage a siesta followed by tea at 5pm so the kids can hold out for a late dinner. However, if the children are desperate for a snack, there are plenty of options available: **Bar Mendizábal** (*see p177*) and **Juicy Jones** (*see p160*) are good for fresh juices and healthy sandwiches, and there's all-day pizza at **Al Passatore** (Pla de Palau 8, Born, 93 319 78 51). For kicking back and relaxing in the sun (near a playground), you could try the outdoor terraces at **Bar Kasparo** (*see p177*), **Iposa** (*see p177*) or **Filferro** (C/ Sant Carles 29, Barceloneta, *93 22198 36*). There's also lots of safe open space around the beachfront terraces of **Bar Colombo**, (*see p180*) and **Bar Daguiri** (*see p180*).

Museum cafés are often child-friendly spots, and you don't always have to buy a ticket for the museum itself to enjoy them. **La Miranda del Museu** (*see p180*), at the Catalan history museum, has fantastic views and plenty of terrace space on which to play. The café of the **Fundació Joan Miró** (*see p181*) is an oasis of sustenance on Montjuïc, while next to the wax museum, the **Bosc de les Fades** is gussied up like a fairy grotto.

## Babysitting & childcare

### Canguro Gigante

*Passeig de Sant Gervasi 16-20, Sant Gervasi (93 211 69 61). FGC Avda Tibidabo.* **Open** 9am-9pm Mon-Fri. Closed Aug. **Rates** From €6/hr. **No credit cards.**

A day care centre for kids aged from one to ten. Meals are available. Some English is spoken.

### Cinc Serveis

*C/Pelai 50, 3° 1ª, Eixample (93 412 56 76/24hr mobile 639 361 111/609 803 080/www.5serveis.com). Metro Catalunya.* **Open** 9.30am-1.30pm, 4.30-8.30pm Mon-Fri. **No credit cards. Map** p344 B2.

The basic rate after 8pm is €11 per hour, plus the cost of the sitter's taxi home. Long-term rates are cheaper and vary according to the age of the child.

### Happy Parc

*C/Pau Claris 97, Eixample (93 317 86 60/www.happyparc.com). Metro Passeig de Gràcia.* **Open** *Aug* 5-9pm daily; *Sept-July* 5-9pm Mon-Fri; 11am-9pm Sat, Sun. **Rates** €4/hr; €1 each subsequent 15mins. **No credit cards. Map** p342 G8.

Ball pools, twister slides and more at this giant indoor fun park and drop-in day care centre for kids up to 11 years old (maximum height 1.45m/4ft 7in).

### Tender Loving Canguros

**Information** *Mobile 647 605 989/www.tlcanguros.com.* **Open** 9am-9pm Mon-Sat. **No credit cards.**

English residents Julie Stephenson and Julia Fossi provide short- and long-term nannies and babysitters for Barcelona and surrounds. All babysitters and nannies speak fluent English. Prices start at €7 an hour; the agency fee is €15 per session.

## On the box

*Els Teletubbies*, *En Bob el manetes* (Bob the Builder) and *En Pat el carter* (Postman Pat) are all familiar faces on Catalan kids' TV, along with the usual Japanese cartoons.

However, it's the home-grown programmes that are the best loved, and one of the biggest successe stories is *Les Tres Bessones* (The Triplets), which is now the longest-running animated series in Europe. It all started in 1983, when illustrator Roser Capdevila i Valls created three curly-headed characters based on her own triplets: Ana, Teresa and Elena. In their adventures with *la Bruixa Avorrida* (the Bored Witch), the mischievous girls are sent into traditional stories, legends or literary works from *Don Quixote* to *Ali Baba*. An immediate success, the stories were made into a TV series in 1994, produced in Barcelona by the public Catalan Television channel TV3.

A newer show is *Lacets*, set in the prehistoric world of Catalan tribalism. This animated 3D adaptation of the book *Journey to the Land of the Lacets* by Sebastià Sorribas is, again, produced by TV3. The story starts when Bora, an 11-year-old girl, is banished from her tribe, the Laïtes, for a day after cutting off her hair – one of the great tribal taboos. On her wanderings, she meets the Lacets and begins a series of adventures during which she discovers that the Lacets and the Laïtes are not so different after all.

A little more fluffy is *Rovelló* (known as Scruff in the English version), a cartoon about a friendly mongrel puppy. Lost by a family of tourists, he is adopted by a boy called Llisot and taken to live in a family of country-dwelling Catalans who christen him Rovelló after his habit of digging up the eponymous local species of wild mushrooms.

# Film

High reels.

Business is booming in the Spanish film industry. Film production has more than doubled in under a decade and, despite an overall decline in audience numbers in the last year or two – due in large part to the onslaught of DVDs both authorised and pirated – the audience for Spanish films has actually increased. Hollywood blockbusters still account for the lion's share of revenue, but one or two Spanish films manage to infiltrate the top ten each year.

The iconic figure of Spanish cinema, both at home and abroad, continues to be Pedro Almodóvar, whose place in the pantheon of Spanish cinema is assured, sitting at the right hand of Luis Buñuel, from whence he shall judge the quick and the dull. Showing no signs of slowing down, the histrionics of his early style have been replaced by a more mature, slightly less melodramatic approach to human drama, and his films invariably shoot to the top of the charts. In fact they are so popular, he almost seems to have claimed the Spanish Oscar nomination for Best Foreign Film as his by right, causing the Spanish Film Academy a major headache when other, more deserving but less idiosyncratic, films come along – although when *Hable Con Ella* was passed over in favour of Fernando León de Aranoa's *Los Lunes al Sol* as the official choice in 2002, Almodóvar's influence in Hollywood ensured he was nominated for the far more prestigious Oscars for best original screenplay (which he won) and best director (which he didn't).

As a key member of the next generation of filmmakers, Fernando León de Aranoa (*Barrio*, *Princesas*) has built up an impressive body of work as a social realist in the vein of Ken Loach, though with greater doses of well-observed naturalist comedy. Equally distinctive are the ethereal dreamscapes of Julio Medem, including *Cows*, *The Lovers of the Artic Circle*, and *Sex and Lucia*. His latest film, *Chaotic Ana*, is due for release in 2007, a welcome return to fiction after the controversial but highly praised documentary *The Basque Ball*. Also due for release in 2007 is *Mataharis*, by actor-turned-director Icíar Bollaín, following her acclaimed 2003 feature *Te Doy Mis Ojos*. But perhaps the two best-known filmmakers of this generation, at least internationally, are Alejandro Amenábar (*The Others*, *The Sea Inside*) and Isabel Coixet (*My Life Without Me*, *The Secret Life of Words*), who cunningly produce Hollywood-friendly films, generally in English, and starring Hollywood-friendly actors. Given the complete acceptance of Americana at Spanish cinemas, this has increased their audience internationally, while doing nothing to harm it domestically. Even irreverent, genre-hopping wildchild Álex de la Iglesia (*The Day of the Beast*, *Ferpect Crime*) is returning to the language of Shakespeare and Joel Silver for his next film, *Oxford Crimes,* also due out in 2007. Meanwhile, his regular collaborator Santiago Seguro continues to break all records as writer, director and star of the detective comedy franchise *Torrente*, currently on two sequels and counting, which is as Spanish as Manchego, and no less cheesy.

## SEEING FILMS

Where once Barcelona boasted a fine array of cinemas screening subtitled foreign films, there has been a gradual 'consolidation'. In other words, all the small, charming venues have been forced to close down by the sterile, voracious multi-screens, leading to a corresponding reduction in choice. Hollywood blockbusters predominate, with mainstream Asian and European independents fighting it out for the remaining screen space. Release dates vary widely: blockbusters are usually released more or less simultaneously worldwide, while smaller productions can sometimes take up to three years to hit cinemas, long after they are available on DVD.

Newspapers carry full details of all cinema screenings, as does the weekly *Guía del Ocio* and its online version at www.guiadelocio.com/barcelona/cine/. Subtitled films are marked VO or VOSE (for '*versió original subtitulado en espanyol*'). Some of the larger cinemas open at 11am, though most have their first screenings around 4pm. Early evening showings start between 7.30pm and 8.30pm; later screenings begin between 10.15pm and 10.45pm. Weekend evenings can be very crowded, especially for recent releases, so turn up early. On Fridays and Saturdays, many cinemas have a late-night session starting around 1am. All cinemas have a cheap night: usually Monday, occasionally Wednesday. You can buy tickets for an increasing number of cinemas online at www.entradas.com or via **Servi-Caixa** (*see p213*).

## Original-language cinemas

### Casablanca-Kaplan

*Passeig de Gràcia 115, Eixample (93 218 43 45). Metro Diagonal.* **Tickets** *Mon* €4.50. *Tue-Sun* €6. **No credit cards. Map** p338 G6.

This centrally located cinema is the smallest in Barcelona, with two screens offering independent Spanish and European films.

**Other locations**: Casablanca-Gràcia, C/Girona 173-175, Eixample (93 459 34 56).

### Méliès Cinemes

*C/Villarroel 102, Eixample (93 451 00 51/ www.cinesmelies.net). Metro Urgell.* **Tickets** *Mon* €2.70. *Tue-Sun* €4. **No credit cards. Map** p338 E8.

A small, two-screen cinema that is the nearest the city comes to arthouse, with a familiar idiosyncratic roster of accessible classics alongside more recent films that aren't quite commercial enough for general release. This is the place to bone up on your Billy Wilder, Antonioni, Hitchcock and others, with up to eight films per week and regular cycles based around a director, star or theme.

### Renoir-Floridablanca

*C/Floridablanca 135, Eixample (93 228 93 93/ www.cinesrenoir.com). Metro Sant Antoni.* **Tickets** *Mon* €4.50. *Tue-Fri* €6; €4.50 1st screening. *Sat, Sun* €6.20. *Late show Fri & Sat* €4.50. **Credit** MC, V. **Map** p342 E9.

The closest first-run original-version cinema to the centre of town, this four-screen branch of the Renoir chain screens up to eight independent, offbeat American, British and Spanish films per day, though note that programming tends towards the worthy rather than the exciting.

**Other locations**: Renoir-Les Corts, C/Eugeni d'Ors 12, Les Corts (93 490 43 05).

### Verdi

*C/Verdi 32, Gràcia (93 238 79 90/www.cines-verdi.com). Metro Fontana.* **Tickets** *Mon* €4.50. *Tue-Fri* €6; €4.50 1st screening daily. *Sat, Sun* €6. **Credit** MC, V. **Map** p339 H5.

The five-screen Verdi and its four-screen annexe Verdi Park on the next street have transformed this corner of Gràcia, bringing with them vibrant bars and cheap eats for the crowds that flock to their diverse programme of independent, mainly European and Asian cinema. At peak times, chaos reigns; arrive early and make sure you don't mistake the line to enter for the ticket queue.

**Other locations**: Verdi Park, C/Torrijos 49, Gràcia (93 238 79 90).

### Yelmo Icària Cineplex

*C/Salvador Espriú 61, Vila Olímpica (information 93 221 75 85/tickets 902 22 09 22/www.yelmo cineplex.es). Metro Ciutadella-Vila Olímpica.* **Tickets** *Mon* €5. *Tue-Sun* €6.50; €5 before 3pm & concessions. **No credit cards. Map** p343 K12.

The Icària has all the atmosphere of the empty shopping mall that surrounds it, but what it lacks in charm, it makes up in choice, with 15 screens offering a very commercial roster of films, particularly Hollywood blockbusters, but also mainstream English and Spanish releases. Weekends are seat-specific, so queues tend to be slow-moving; it's worth booking your seat on the internet before you go.

## Specialist cinemas

An increasing number of bars are showing films. **Planeta Rai** (C/Carders 12, principal, 93 268 13 21, Born, www.pangea.org/rai) runs mainly classic movies twice a week on Tuesdays and Thursdays (€2).

### Cine Ambigú

*Casablanca-Gràcia, C/Girona 173-175, Eixample (93 459 34 56/www.retinas.org). Metro Verdaguer.* **Shows** 8pm, 10pm Tue. Closed July-Sept. **Tickets** €5. **No credit cards. Map** p339 H6.

After nine years and more than 200 screenings in a charming 1930s music hall, the Cine Ambigú has moved home to C/Girona. The cinema screens a couple of accessible but alternative arthouse films from around Europe each week. The website provides details of forthcoming shows.

### FilmoTeca de la Generalitat de Catalunya

*Cinema Aquitania, Avda Sarrià 31-33, Eixample (93 410 75 90/http://cultura.gencat.net/filmo). Metro Hospital Clínic.* **Open** Three screenings daily. Closed Aug. **Tickets** €2.70; €2 concessions; €18 for 10 films. **Credit** (block tickets only) AmEx, MC, V. **Map** p338 D5.

Funded by the Catalan government, the Filmoteca is a little dry for some tastes, offering comprehensive seasons of cinema's more recondite auteurs, alongside better-known classics, plus screenings each spring of all films nominated in the Goya Awards. Overlapping cycles last two or three weeks, with each film screened at least twice at different times. Books of 20 and 100 tickets bring down the price per film to a negligible amount. The 'Filmo' also runs an excellent library of film-related books, videos and magazines at Portal Santa Madrona 6-8 (93 316 27 80), just off La Rambla. **Photo** *p231*.

### IMAX Port Vell

*Moll d'Espanya, Port Vell (93 225 11 11/ www.imaxportvell.com). Metro Barceloneta or Drassanes.* **Tickets** €7-€10. **Credit** MC, V. **Map** p342 G12.

A squat white hulk in the middle of the marina, the IMAX has yet to persuade many that it's anything more than a gimmick. Its predictable programming, recognisable from similar enterprises the world over, covers fish, birds, ghosts and adventure sports, possibly in 3D. (If it's fish in 3D you want, the Aquarium next door is excellent; *see p224*.)

**Filmoteca de la Generalitat de Catalunya.** *See p230.*

## Festivals

Barcelona is home to an increasing number of film festivals. Though none is as big or brash as **Sitges** (*see below*), they all show interesting work unlikely to feature elsewhere. New events pop up every year, but regular festivals include the following: **Asian** (April/May), **Women's** (June), **Animation** (June), **Jewish** (July), **Gay and Lesbian** (July and October), **Open-Air Shorts** (September), **Documentaries** (October), **Human Rights** (October), **African** (November) and **Alternative Film** (November). **OVNI**, a well-established alternative video festival, takes place every 18 months, in early spring and late autumn; the next is scheduled for autumn 2007.

### Festival Internacional de Cinema de Catalunya, Sitges

*93 894 99 90/www.cinemasitges.com.* **Advance tickets** available from Tel-entrada (mobile 902 101 212/www.telentrada.com). **Date** Oct.

Despite suffering occasional identity crises, the Sitges Film Festival is widely recognised as the leading European festival for gore, horror, sci-fi and fantasy, offering dozens of screenings, as well as conferences, retrospectives, premieres and appearances from leading figures in the rarefied world of genre filmmaking. Like the genre as a whole, the festival would like to be taken more seriously by the mainstream, and has experimented with different times of year, although now it's back to its traditional slot in early October. A special late-night train service returns to Barcelona after the final screening of the evening.

## Open-air cinema

Stranded at the drive-in...?

OK, it's not quite a drive-in, but **Sala Montjuïc** (www.salamontjuic.com, admission €4) has transformed the grassy moat of the castle on Montjuïc into Barcelona's main outdoor cinema, making it a wonderful way to spend a balmy evening. Bring a picnic, a rug and a bottle of wine, turn up early for the jazz band, then lie back and think of Ingrid. A blend of classics and recent independent cinema is shown every Wednesday and Friday throughout the season, from July to early August.

A special free bus service from Metro Espanya runs before and after the film (8.30 and 9.30pm going up, returning after the 10.15pm screening), though as screenings regularly attract several hundred people, you're usually faced with a scrum, a wait or a rather long (though pleasant) walk.

Every August, the **CCCB** takes over (C/Montalegre 5, Raval, 93 306 41 00, www.cccb.org, admission free) with **Gandules** (or 'Slackers'), offering free screenings of experimental/arthouse cinema every Tuesday, Wednesday and Thursday at 10pm, complete with bar. Space is limited, though, and the courtyard tends to get fairly full.

Other outdoor film cycles tend to come and go, depending on short-lived initiatives and the granting of official licences; check the *Guía del Ocio* or www.bcn.es for the latest information.

# Barcelona woos Bollywood

Masala.

Twins separated at birth, moustache-twirling villains, star-crossed lovers and a rousing dance number or six: it can only be Bollywood. An average running time of three hours makes these extravaganzas difficult to slot into conventional cinema schedules, but Bolly has found an unlikely home at one of Barcelona's iconic old cinemas. The much-loved **Cine Maldà** (C/Pi 5, Barri Gòtic, mobile 605 271 379), due to reopen in December 2006 after extensive remodelling, has become the first cinema in Spain to offer a permanent programme of Indian cinema. The project is run by long-term Indian resident, Shankar Kishnani Lal, who offers the city's South Asian population and growing legions of local Bolly fans the latest releases from Mumbai alongside some classics of the genre, thus continuing the tradition of rereleases for which the Maldà has always been famous.

Offering an alternative to the glitzy Bolly blockbusters, the **BAFF** (Barcelona Asian Film Festival) is the largest of its kind in Europe. India was the featured country in 2006 and famous Bollytotty featured alongside independent projects by little-known directors and respected veterans such as Satyajit Ray. The Bollywood Party has become a highlight of the BAFF Lounge section of the festival.

Another place to catch independent and more offbeat subcontinental cinema is the enormous Asian cultural centre, **Casa Àsia** (Avda Diagonal 373, 93 238 73 37; *see p126*), which hosts themed double features every Saturday in its Tagore Auditorium, along with myriad classes, exhibitions and conferences; it also runs the Orient Express section of the prestigious Sitges Film Festival (*see p231*); in August and September, it also organises Festival Asia (held at venues across the city), which is devoted to all aspects of Asian culture, including an adventurous cinema programme.

Meanwhile, the South Asian Cultural Association, **Masala** (www.club-masala.com) organises popular monthly Bollywood Lounge parties at the Sweet Café club (C/Casanova 75, www.sweetcafebcn.blogspot.com), with music, dancing and Indian snacks. Masala also runs a Sunday movie club, along with classes in dancing, cookery and Urdu.

On the other end of the deal, the growing clout of the rupee has attracted the attentions of the city council, which is trying to woo the South Asian tourist market by promoting Barcelona as Bollywood backdrop. Over the last two years, city officials have made several trips to India to try and close a deal for the shooting of a Bollywood blockbuster in Barcelona, even offering partial financing. Barcelona also put in a bid to host the 2007 International Indian Film Academy Awards, India's equivalent of the Oscars. Maybe the *sardana* in a sari is not too far off.

# Galleries

Creatively resourceful.

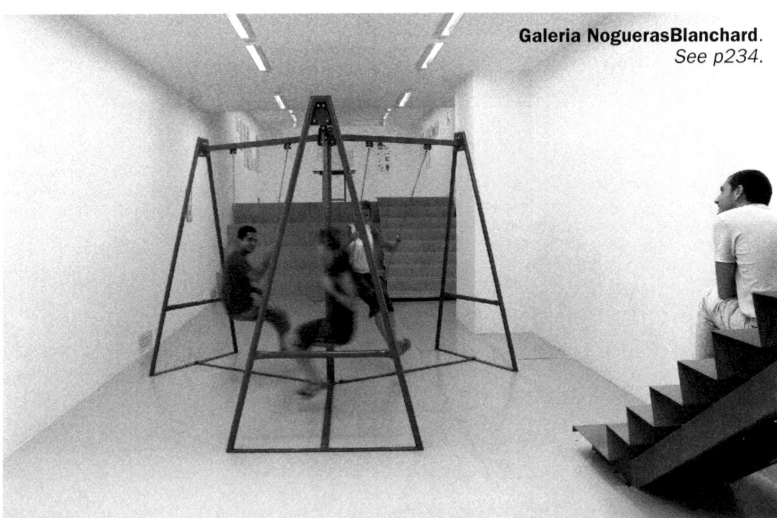

Galeria NoguerasBlanchard. *See p234.*

Madrid makes the hard cash with big art shows that have international clout, such as Arco and PhotoEspaña, while Barcelona plays the social butterfly with its flamboyant architecture, sharp interior design, sparkling international reputation and joie de vivre.

The Barcelona contemporary art world, however, is in financial strife. With public cash and private sponsors better persuaded by massive money-making ventures, such as monster music fest Sónar, visual arts projects are left fending for themselves.

Commendably, however, no one seems in the least bit put off. Insularism has been beaten by enthusiasm: locally based artists and patrons in the commercial gallery sector are exploring mutually beneficial and cost-effective ways of making art work; and the Barcelona arts world is doing a pretty good job of promoting itself.

Galleries, formerly huddled together in a small, pricey part of the Eixample, are now scattered about town and reflect the distinct character of their neighbourhoods.

Tàpies, Dalí, Picasso and Miró personify Barcelona's artistic heritage and hold fort in the Barri Gòtic and the Born. In the Eixample, you can see exhibitions by local and national contemporary artists of international repute, including Tere Recarens, Frederic Amat and Carlos Pazos. It is the more prestigious galleries, such as **Galeria Llucià Homs** (*see p235*), that nudge at non-convention, showing the darkly provocative work of artists such as Enrique Marty. Downtown, in the Raval, chic and cheeky are all the rage, with approachable, hands-on exhibitions that play about the feet of the MACBA. Hip youngsters, Jaume Pitarch or Ester Partegàs exhibit here. The lower, seedier bit of the Barri Gòtic is a hub for the city's international artists, many of whom dwell and/or work in the area. Galleries blend with the cool bars kitted out in kitsch.

Within the arts world there is tentative networking between what were once well-defined ranks of prestige. A good example of this is May's spirited commercial video arts event **Loop** (www.loop-barcelona.com). Commercial fairs feature a melange of locals and internationals, newcomers and stars, with big galleries like Llucià Homs and **Joan Prats** (*see p235*) taking bets on lesser-known artists; meanwhile, the events unearths the intrigues of the audio-visual arts scene, promoted by galleries such as **NIU** (*see p236*), previously tagged to Barcelona's experimental music scene. The **CCCB** (www.cccb.org; *see p107*) plays host to a number of mini-fests, particularly in digital art and film: **OFFF** (www.offf.ws), also in May, is particularly interesting to the technologically savvy.

Gallery listings appear in the weekly *Guía del Ocio*, sold in most kiosks. The information office at Palau de la Virreina (La Rambla 99, Barri Gòtic, 93 316 10 00, www.bcn.es/cultura) has a plethora of publicity materials.

## Commercial galleries

### Barri Gòtic

Bohemia meets bourgeois: the atmospheric Barri Gòtic has a few surprises up its sleeve. The narrow C/Peritxol is home to Parés and Trama (for both, *see below*), and it is marked by colourful wall tiles with tips for those travelling by horse and carriage. For antiques, C/Palla winds from the cathedral's Plaça Nova to Plaça Sant Josep Oriol and sprouts various outlets of local dealer **Artur Ramón** (C/Palla 10, 23 & 25, 93 302 59 70, www.arturamon.com), including some lovely lithographs by Picasso, Mariano Fortuny and Joan Serrà at No.23.

#### Galeria Loft

*C/Ample 5 (93 301 11 12/www.espace-ample.com). Metro Drassanes or Jaume I.* **Open** *July, Aug* 5-8.30pm Tue-Sat. *Sept-June* 11am-2pm, 5-8.30pm Tue-Sat. **Credit** AmEx, MC, V. **Map** p345 B7.

French-owned galleries have mushroomed in the lower Barri Gòtic in recent years, and they are brought together by the Ruta del Arte: a thrice-yearly multiple inauguration project, spearheaded by Loft gallery. Specialising in the Chinese avant-garde, Loft's exhibitions blend into the designer-kitsch decor. Coming up for 2007 are the bubblegum colours of Chen Wenbo and the ashy images of innocence lost captured by Guo Wei. The Yves Klein, fiercely blue, is easy to spot.

#### Galeria Trama

*C/Petritxol 8 (93 317 48 77/www.galeriatrama.com). Metro Liceu.* **Open** 10.30am-2pm, 4.30-8.30pm Mon-Sat. Closed Aug. **Credit** AmEx, MC, V. **Map** p344 B4.

This unassuming space opposite Parès shows some of the best contemporary photography and video exhibitions, in town. Jordi Fulla, Matías Quetglas in the spring; Gonzalo Sicre shows in early summer.

#### Sala Parés

*C/Petritxol 5 (93 318 70 08/www.salapares.com). Metro Liceu.* **Open** *June-Sept* 10.30am-2pm, 4.30-8.30pm Mon-Sat. *Oct-May* 10.30am-2pm, 4.30-8.30pm Mon-Sat; 11.30am-2pm Sun. Closed 3wks Aug. **Credit** AmEx, MC, V. **Map** p344 B4.

A bastion of bourgeois taste, Sala Parés (c1840), is watched over by an image of Barcelona's patron saint La Mercè outside. Inside, it's a spacious haven of timeless tranquillity. Figurative and historical works from Laura Piñel, Raimon Sunyer and Miquel Vila will be shown in spring 2007; in September, Parès will host the Young Painters Prize.

### Raval

Hip gallery/bookshop **Ras** (C/Doctor Dou 10, 93 412 71 99, www.actar.es) is good for a browse.

#### Galeria dels Àngels

*C/Àngels 16 (93 412 54 54/www.galeriadelsangels.com). Metro Catalunya.* **Open** noon-2pm, 5-8.30pm Tue-Sat. Closed Aug. **No credit cards. Map** p344 A3.

Charm and confidence abound: the multidisciplinary shows at the Àngels gallery resonate the personality of its owner, energetic entrepreneur, Emilio Álvarez. Look out for local artists Jaume Pitarch and Mayte Vieta in 2007, backed by young internationals. Àngels has two other spaces nearby, in C/Pintor Fortuny and C/Joaquin Costa, that open for specific events and are worth a look.

#### Galeria NoguerasBlanchard

*C/Xuclà 7 (93 224 71 60/www.noguerasblanchard.com). Metro Liceu.* **Open** *Sept-June* 10.30am-2pm, 4-8pm Tue-Sat. *July* 10.30am-2pm, 4-8pm Tue-Fri. Closed Aug. **No credit cards. Map** p342 B3.

Bright young gallery NoguerasBlanchard, tucked behind a bar terrace on the winding C/Xuclà, has smart, fun and often interactive exhibitions, incorporating installation, video and performance. Bright, brazen images from local Ester Partegàs and Taiwanese artist Michael Lin coming up in 2007. Look for the sketchily drawn cats on the wall outside. **Photo** *p233*.

## Born

### Galeria Maeght

*C/Montcada 25 (93 310 42 45/www.maeght.com). Metro Jaume I.* **Open** 10am-2pm, 4-7pm Tue-Fri; 10am-3pm Sat. Closed 3wks Aug. **Credit** AmEx, DC, MC, V. **Map** p345 E6.

This gallery, housed in what was once a Renaissance palace, features a gorgeous courtyard with winding stone steps. One of the few galleries that can survive the soaring prices of this atmospheric barrio, Paris-based Maeght pays homage to the sombre Spanish greats: Antoni Tàpies, Eduardo Arroyo and Pablo Palazuelo, among others.

## Eixample

Galleries jostle for space on C/Consell de Cent, between Rambla de Catalunya and Balmes, once the *cuadre d'or* of the Barcelona art scene. **Galeria Toni Tàpies** (C/Consell de Cent 282, 93 487 64 02, www.tonitapies.com), owned by the son of the prestigious painter, or the two branches of **Galeria Joan Prats** (Rambla Catalunya 54, 93 216 02 84 and C/Balmes 54, 93 488 13 98, www.galeriajoanprats.com), which are located in the pretty Passatge Mercader (between C/Provença and C/Mallorca).

### Galeria Carles Taché

*C/Consell de Cent 290 (93 487 88 36/www.carles tache.com). Metro Passeig de Gràcia.* **Open** *Sept-May* 10am-2pm, 4-8.30pm Tue-Sat. *June, July* 10am-2pm, 4-8.30pm Tue-Fri. Closed Aug. **No credit cards**. **Map** p342 F8.

Struggle with the enormous door and you'll be well rewarded. Taché offers solo shows, from the imposing abstracts of Sean Scully to the wriggly personable rocks of the brilliant Tony Cragg, and from the juicy scrawlings of local star Frederic Amat to the fiendishly clever pop of Carlos Pazos.

### Galeria Estrany de la Mota

*Ptge Mercader 18 (93 215 70 51/www.estrany delamota.com). FGC Provença.* **Open** *Sept-June* 10.30am-1.30pm, 4.30-8.30pm Tue-Sat. *July* 10.30am-1.30pm, 4.30-8.30pm Mon-Fri. Closed Aug. **No credit cards**. **Map** p338 F7.

A cavernous basement space plays host to consistently excellent contemporary exhibitions, particularly in photography. The atypical picturesque photos of Jean-Marc Bustamante feature in 2007.

### Galeria Llucià Homs

*C/Consell de Cent 315 (93 467 71 62/www.galeria lluciahoms.es). Metro Passeig de Gràcia.* **Open** 10am-2pm, 4.30-8pm Tue-Fri. Closed Aug. **No credit cards**. **Map** p342 F8.

An ingenious use of space, established dealer Llucià Homs swerves to the ultra-contemprary.

### Galeria Senda

*C/Consell de Cent 337 (93 487 67 59/www. galeriasenda.com). Metro Passeig de Gràcia.* **Open** 10.30am-2pm, 4-8pm Tue-Sat. Closed Aug. **Credit** V. **Map** p342 F8.

Languishing on the best spot on the street, Senda makes good use of its ample space with large-scale photographic exhibitions, abstract art and sculpture shows. The gallery has opened a smaller space just opposite, Espai 2nou2 (C/Consell de Cent 292, 93 487 57 11), which showcases local work.

**NIU**. *See p236.*

### ProjecteSD

*Ptge Mercader 8 (93 488 13 60/www.projectesd.com). FGC Provença.* **Open** *Sept-June* 11.30am-8.30pm Tue-Sat. *July* 11.30am-8.30pm Tue-Fri. Closed Aug. **No credit cards. Map** p338 F7.

This is more than just a project: Silvia Dauder's penchant for new photography and film is sculpted into subtle, provocative and highly original shows. Limited-edition artists' texts, detailed explanations in English and Silvia's own bilingual talents complement the exhibitions. Look out for Jochen Lempert, Pieter Vermeersch and Raimond Chaves, who all show in the spring.

## Gràcia & Other Districts

### Galeria Alejandro Sales

*C/Julián Romea 16, Gràcia (93 415 20 54/www.alejandrosales.com). FGC Gràcia.* **Open** *Oct-June* 11am-2pm, 5-8.30pm Tue-Sat. *July, Sept* 11am-2pm, 5-8.30pm Tue-Fri. Closed Aug. **No credit cards. Map** p338 F5.

Crossing Diagonal into Gràcia, Alejandro Sales's contemplative, sophisticated shows are given the space and tranquillity they deserve. High-profile artists Steve Afif, Marina Núñez and Eduard Arbós are coming up in 2007. The Fundació Foto Colectània (*see p132*) is on the same street.

### Galeria $H_2O$

*C/Verdi 152, Gràcia (93 415 18 01/www.h2o.es). Metro Lesseps.* **Open** 4-8pm Tue-Fri; 11am-1pm Sat. Closed Aug. **Credit** V. **Map** p339 H4.

Local architect Joaquim Ruiz Millet and writer Ana Planella founded this gorgeous Gràcia gallery in 1989. Diverse design and photography shows, book publications and spontaneous musical performances fuel the liveliest inaugurations in town.

### NIU

*C/Almogàvers 208, Poble Nou (93 356 88 11/www.niubcn.com). Metro Glòries or Llacuna/bus 40, 42.* **Open** 4-10pm Mon-Sat. Closed 2wks Aug. **Credit** MC, V. **Map** p343 off L10.

NIU is a buzzing centre for audio-visual and media art, incorporating a small exhibition space, live music, conferences, workshops and information on a range of musical and art events. Check the website for a comprehensive list. **Photos** *p234 and p235.*

## The fringe

Barcelona's visual arts fringe dangles on a shoestring. In the Barri Gòtic many gallery spaces moonlight as bars (or vice versa), with the corresponding degree of respect for their exhibits and a rather liberal selection process. Still, it can be enormous fun. Try **KBB** (C/Joaquim Costa 24, Raval, 93 442 06 95, www.kbb.org.es, 93 442 06 95) or **Miscelänea** (C/Guardia 10, Raval, 93 317 93 98, www.miscelanea.info), both of which incorporate exhibition spaces and cinema. Or, up in Gràcia, **Saladestar** (C/Martinez de la Rosa 40, www.saladestar.com, 93 218 39 20). Many artists take part in **Tallers Oberts** (www.tallersoberts.org, 93 443 75 20), opening their studios, or flats, to the curious public for two weekends in late May. The event is administered by **FAD** (Convent dels Àngels, Plaça dels Àngels 5-6, www.digiteca.com/tallersoberts), which has regular exhibitions of its own.

In Poble Nou the spacious **Centre Civic Can Felipa** (C/Pallars 277, 93 266 44 41) hosts regular shows. The aloof production centre **Hangar** (Passatge del Marqués de Santa Isabel 40, Poblenou, 93 308 40 41, www.hangar.org), runs workshops.

### La Xina A.R.T.

*C/Doctor Dou 4 (93 301 67 03/www.laxinaart.org). Metro Catalunya.* **Open** 5.30-8.30pm Mon-Fri; 11am-2pm, 5.30-8.30pm Sat. Closed Aug. **No credit cards. Map** p344 A3.

A collective of artists runs this tiny space near the MACBA. Topical exhibitions from artists such as Benxamín Álvarez and Tito Inchaurralde.

## Art in the time of virtual reality

As the cost of real space soars, the net is where it's at. The past year has spawned two privately run websites with the aid of cash from the Ajuntament and the Generalitat.

**www.barcelonacreativa.info**, which is run by FUSIC Fundació Societat i Cultura, aims to encourage 'creative tourism' and promote local talent by means of an electronic classified ads page.

**www.terminalb.org**, run by FAD (*see above*), is a slick database aimed at visual artists, designers and filmmakers in the city.

Graphic designers No-domain, **www.no-domain.com**, are a tour de force in the city, and were the group behind the visuals for the 2006 edition of the mammoth music fest Sónar (*see p219*), a hugely popular event held over three days in June.

**www.famousfor15mb.com** runs a monthly competition in which an international snowfall of audio and/or visual contributions is sifted into an eclectic, inventive and unfailingly entertaining top 15. Downloads are free, and there are links to artists' own websites.

# Gay & Lesbian

Seen to preen.

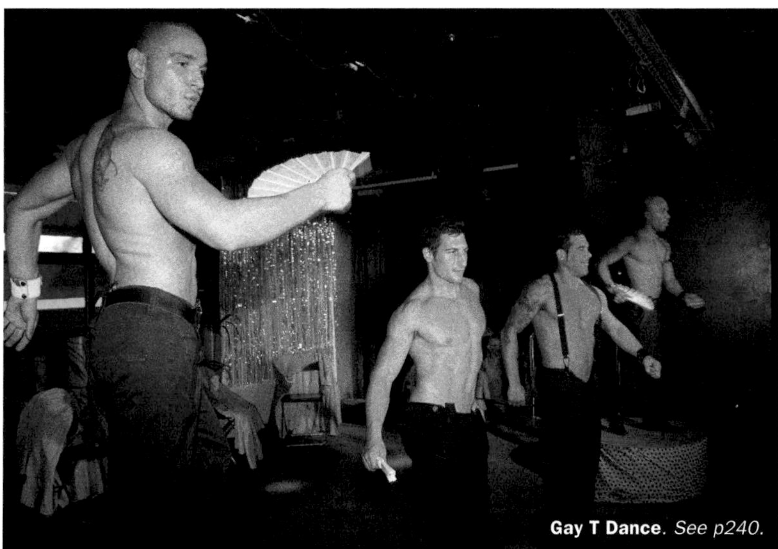

**Gay T Dance**. *See p240.*

Let's be honest, folks: claims that Barcelona is Europe's new gay capital are a tad premature. The clubbing scene, for a start, could do with a little more musical variety and a little less hair gel. But still, considering that homosexuality was illegal in Spain until 1978, there's no doubt that an enormous amount has changed; gay marriage, gay adoption, even great big gay hotels – queer Catalonia's certainly never had it so good.

The gay scene, or *el ambiente* as it's known in Spanish, is roughly centred around an area in the Eixample bordered by the streets Diputació, Villarroel, Aragó and Balmes, delightfully/dizzily nicknamed the Gaixample. But there are also shops and bars dotted throughout the Old City, or if it's alfresco entertainment you're after, head up to the leafy shadows of Montjuïc, behind Plaça d'Espanya.

It is worth noting that, as most of the city's nightlife is pretty mixed, there's a lot of fun to be had off the official scene; a keen ear to the ground and the occasional flyer will often deliver an embarrassment of riches when it comes to partying in Barcelona. The summer's fiestas at shacks on gay-friendly Marbella beach are a particularly fine example of minimum advertising, maximum raving.

For more information, pick up free copies of *Shanguide*, *Nois* and *Gay Barcelona* in bars and gay shops around town. Alternatively, for online info check out www.mensual.com, www.naciongay.com, www.barcelonagay.com and www.guiagay.com.

## Bars

### Gaixample

In addition, bars worth checking out include **Mi Madre!** (C/Consell de Cent 223, no phone) and **Oui Café** (C/Consell de Cent 247, no phone).

#### Átame

*C/Consell de Cent 257 (93 454 92 73). Metro Universitat.* **Open** 6.30pm-2.30am Mon-Thur, Sun; 6.30pm-3am Fri, Sat. **Credit** MC, V. **Map** p342 E8.

Endless diva nonsense on the TV screens keeps the largely older local crowd grinning along. On Tuesdays, Thursdays and Sundays there's a drag show, which varies from run-of-the-mill sing-song to hilarious (Hispanic) bitch-fest. On Tuesdays there's free tapas and a happy hour until 10pm.

Arena. See p239.

### Col·lectiu Gai de Barcelona

*Ptge Valeri Serra 23 (93 453 41 25/ www.colectiugai.org). Metro Universitat or Urgell.* **Open** 7-9.30pm Mon-Thur; 7-9.30pm, 11pm-3am Fri; 11pm-3am Sat. **No credit cards. Map** p342 E8.

The headquarters of this gay association has an easygoing, quiet and unpretentious bar, with cheap drinks and few tourists. It's a long, narrow space, where strangers have little choice but to talk to each other.

### Dietrich

*C/Consell de Cent 255 (93 451 77 07). Metro Universitat.* **Open** 10.30pm-2.30am Mon-Thur, Sun; 10.30pm-3am Fri, Sat. **Admission** (incl drink) €6 Fri, Sat in July & Aug. **Credit** AmEx, MC, V. **Map** p342 E8.

Dietrich is a classic club, although now rather care-worn, that attracts a mixed lively crowd. Drag shows and acrobats perform on the dancefloor, and the friendly international bar crew all speak English.

### Punto BCN

*C/Muntaner 63-65 (93 453 61 23/www.arenadisco.com). Metro Universitat.* **Open** 6pm-2.30am Mon-Thur, Sun; 6pm-3am Fri, Sat. **No credit cards. Map** p342 E8.

A large, bright and airy (read: slightly freezing) place popular with all sorts that's been around for many years in the Gaixample. Snag a table on the mezzanine and get gawping at the variety of fine-looking chaps that pre-party here before heading elsewhere. Free passes to the Arena clubs are available behind the bar.

### Sweet

*C/Casanova 75 (no phone). Metro Universitat.* **Open** 8pm-2.30am Tue-Thur; 8pm-3am Fri, Sat. **No credit cards. Map** p345 E8.

A slick affair, that, like many of the city's bars, makes you feel like you're in a hip vodka ad. An illusion somewhat shattered upon checking out the punters; everyone from mouthy local trannies to gaggles of merry Swedish queens, who descend for the films, exhibitions and eye candy. Toni, the owner, is always good for advice on where to go next.

### Z:eltas Club

*C/Casanova 75 (93 451 84 69/www.zeltas.net). Metro Universitat.* **Open** 10.30pm-3am daily. **Credit** MC, V. **Map** p342 E8.

Z:eltas is one of the more stylish of the Gaixample's bars. Although open every day, it only really comes into its own later on in the week, when the trendy young *guapos* show their appreciation for the DJ's tunes (mainly funky house) by squashing each other on the mini dancefloor.

## The rest of the city

### La Bata de Boatiné

*C/Robadors 23, Raval (no phone). Metro Liceu.* **Open** 10pm-3am Tue-Sat; 10pm-2.30am Sun. **No credit cards. Map** p345 A5.

Without doubt the most alternative gay bar in Barcelona, this squat-like former brothel is popular with all shapes and forms. It's not huge to start with, but cheap drinks and a no-attitude atmosphere mean it can be packed at weekends.

### Burdel 74

*C/Carme 74, Raval (mobile 678 464 515). Metro Liceu.* **Open** 7pm-3am Tue-Sun. **No credit cards. Map** p342 E10.

A bit of a Raval staple, Burdel's louche, intimate interior has more than a touch of Almodóvar's high-camp chic about it. Deep reds and hallowed divas on the walls make it ideal for taking a date, or swing by for the bingo on Sunday nights.

### Eagle

*Passeig de Sant Joan 152, Eixample (93 207 58 56/ www.eaglespain.com). Metro Verdaguer.* **Open** 10pm-2.30am Mon-Thur, Sun; 10pm-3am Fri, Sat. **Admission** (incl drink) €7-€10 (party nights only) .**No credit cards. Map** p339 H6.

Don't be intimidated by the dress code (jeans or leathers and no open shoes): the Eagle has a friendly clientele, generally over 30. It has a variety of theme nights; for details, check the website. A small bar gives off to a back room with all manner of contraptions, including a bathtub for watersports.

### New Chaps

*Avda Diagonal 365, Eixample (93 215 53 65/ www.newchaps.com). Metro Diagonal or Verdaguer.* **Open** 9pm-3am Mon-Sat; 7pm-3am Sun. **No credit cards. Map** p338 G6.

The more mature clientele who frequents this sex bar avoids studying the rather bizarre collection of objects hung around the place and instead heads for the busy darkroom downstairs. If you are tempted, make sure you check in your valuables first.

### La Penúltima

*Riera Alta 40 (mobile 675 246 262). Metro Sant Antoni, Raval.* **Open** *June-Sept* 5pm-2am Mon, Wed, Thur, Sun; 5pm-3am Fri, Sat. *Oct-May* 7pm-2am Mon-Thur; Fri, Sat 7pm 3am. **No credit cards. Map** p342 E9.

Away from the tight T-shirts and high prices of the Gaixample is this relaxed and friendly bar. Converted from a former bodega, it retains the large barrels in the entrance and has plenty of tables at the back. A good place to start the evening.

## Clubs

## Gaixample

### Arena

**Classic & Madre** *C/Diputació 233 (93 487 83 42). Metro Universitat.* **Open** 12.30-5am Tue-Sat; 7.30pm-5am Sun. **Admission** (incl 1 drink) €5 Fri; €10 Sat. **No credit cards. Map** p338 F8. **VIP & Dandy** *Gran Via de les Corts Catalanes 593 (93 487 83 42/www.arenadisco.com). Metro Universitat.* **Open** 1-6am Fri, Sat. **Admission** (incl 1 drink) €5 Fri; €10 Sat. **No credit cards. Map** p342 F8.

Ten years on, and the four Arena clubs are still packed to the rafters every week with a huge variety of punters. The USP is that you pay once, get your hand stamped and can then switch between all four clubs as well as lesbian club Aire (*see p241*). Madre is the biggest and most full-on, with thumping house and a darkroom; there are shows and strippers at the beginning of the week but Wednesday's semi-riotous foam party is where it's really at. VIP doesn't take itself too seriously and is popular with everyone from mixed gangs of Erasmus students to parties of thirtysomethings down from Sabadell, all getting busy to Snoop Dogg and vintage Mariah. Classic is similarly mixed, if even cheesier, playing only '80s and '90s chart hits and, finally, Dandy bangs away with somewhat unimaginative house. **Photo** *p238*.

### Bear Factory

*Ptge Domingo 3 (no phone/www.bearfactory barcelona.com). Metro Passeig de Gràcia.* **Open** 11pm-3am Wed, Thur, Sun; 11pm-5am Fri, Sat. **Admission** €5 Fri; (incl 1 drink) €6 Sat. **No credit cards. Map** p338 G7.

This spacious and well-designed bar has become very popular and not just with bears. There is, however, bearaphernalia everywhere and, on closer examination, even the bar has hair! The good-sized dancefloor is open for hard house on Fridays and Saturdays, while the small darkroom never closes.

### Kiut

*C/Consell de Cent 280 (no phone). Metro Passeig de Gracia.* **Open** midnight-5.30am daily. **Admission** free Mon-Thur, Sun; €10 Fri, Sat. **Credit** (Bar only) Amex, MC, V. **Map** p342 F8.

Kiut, pronounced 'cute', is the latest addition to the gay scene, brought to you by the owner of Z:eltas (*see p238*). Lots of shiny black marble and mirrors mean queens can preen wherever they go. The resident DJs play happy house to liven up the smallish dancefloor, while the smokers take refuge in the back bar.

### Martins

*Passeig de Gràcia 130 (93 218 71 67). Metro Diagonal.* **Open** midnight-5am Tue-Sun. **Admission** (incl 1 drink) €10. **Credit** MC, V. **Map** p338 G6.

Metro's temporary closure for refurbishment breathed new life into this old favourite. While still lacking some TLC, even with three bars, porno lounge and decent dancefloor, it can still be packed at the weekends.

### Metro

*C/Sepúlveda 185 (93 323 52 27/metro disco.bcn). Metro Universitat.* **Open** 1-5am Mon; midnight-5am Tue-Sun. **Admission** (incl 1 drink) €13. **Credit** MC, V. **Map** p342 C5.

Fully refurbished and with a redesigned bar, Metro's dingier corners now have a better shine. With stiffer competition around, it's to be seen if this will be enough to sustain it as the pre-eminent gay club in town. Latin beats prevail on the smaller dancefloor, with house on the main one to keep the boys entertained (when they're not entertaining each other).

# Wedding belles

On 30 June 2005, in accordance with the pre-electoral promises of the Socialist Party, Spain became the fourth country in the world to legalise gay marriage, after Belgium, Holland and Canada.

However, the measure, which was approved by an overwhelming majority of MPs from all parties (apart from the opposition People's Party), broke new ground. Spain became the first country in the world to give full and equal rights, including the right of adoption, to gay couples.

This may seem a barely credible event bearing in mind Spain's recent past under the Franco dictatorship, when homosexuality was not tolerated at all. Gay people were regularly harassed, firstly under the more general Law of Vagrancy, and later, under the more specific Law of Danger and Social Rehabilitation – it's estimated that between 1970 and 1979, more than 1,000 gay people, the majority men, were imprisoned under this act. Even as recently as 1986, the public expression of homosexuality remained a crime on the statute books, although it was rarely enforced.

The timing of the passing of the law, despite the desperate attempts by the Popular Party and the Roman Catholic Church to delay it by organising large rallies in support of 'traditional family values', coincided with Gay Pride marches all over Spain – turning them into the largest explosions of gay outness ever seen.

Although the first of the new wave of gay marriages occurred in July 2005, it may not in fact have been the first gay marriage in Spain. This honour reportedly goes to a lesbian couple, Marcela Gracia Ibeas and Elisa Sánchez from La Coruña who, in 1901, confounded the authorities by marrying in church. Marcela and Elisa originally met and fell in love at teacher training college but lost contact for some years until, by chance, they both became teachers at the same school. Desperate to wed, Elisa disguised herself as a man – using the name Mario – and the couple then fooled the hapless parish priest into marrying them. Sadly, things did not end happily for the pair. Once the news got out, they were hounded by the judiciary and abused by local people, losing their jobs in the process and eventually emigrating to Argentina.

These days gay couples can expect to get slightly better treatment ,with opinion polls showing the majority of the population approve the new law. In July 2006 an estimated 4,500 couples, most of them in long-term relationships, took advantage of the new law and tied the knot, including TV presenter Jesús Vázquez to his partner of ten years Roberto Cortés and two members of the Spanish Air Force.



## The rest of the city

### Gay T Dance

*Space Barcelona, C/Tarragona 141-147, Sants (93 426 84 44/www.gaytdance.com). Metro Tarragona.* **Open** 7.30pm-1.30am Sun. **Admission** (incl 1 drink) €15. **No credit cards. Map** p341 C7.

Sunday is the new Saturday at Space where modern design and plenty of bar space allow you to choose who you rub shoulders with. The new afterclub Tio Vivo at LaFira (C/Provença 17, mobile 650 855 384) is free for those who want to carry on. **Photo** p237.

### La Luna

*Avda Diagonal 323, Eixample (no phone). Metro Verdaguer.* **Open** 5am-8.30am Mon; 5am-8.30am, 11pm-3am Thur, Fri; 5am-10.30am, 11pm-3am Sat, Sun. **Admission** (incl 1 drink) €20 . Free before 3am. **No credit cards. Map** p339 J7.

As the Spanish saying goes, 'never the last drink, always the penultimate', and so it is for La Luna, the only genuine 'after hours' in the centre of Barcelona. While a friendly kind of place, the faces of those still clinging on by their fingertips or other body parts speak for themselves.

### Salvation

*Ronda Sant Pere 19-21, Eixample (93 318 06 86/ www.matineegroup.com). Metro Urquinaona.* **Open** midnight-5am Thur-Sat. **Admission** (incl 1 drink) €15. **No credit cards. Map** p342 E2.

It's been said of Salvation – one of the city's enduringly popular gay clubs – that 'everyone you see naked on Gaydar…you can see them in here with their clothes on'. One room is full of said tanned, buff torsos lurching around to house; in the other sprightly young things bounce about to pop. Hot staff lean towards the God-complex side of approachable.

## Lesbian bars & nightclubs

Sadly, Barcelona's lesbian scene doesn't seem to have much consistency, with bars struggling to survive amid constant changes of ownership. On the other hand. there are several thriving groups that organise regular parties, including **Nextown Ladys** (www.nextownladys.com) and **Silk** (www.silkbcn.com). Check online for details. You'll also find lesbians in some spots favoured by gay men, such as **Arena** (*see p239*) or **La Bata de Boatiné** (*see p238*). Other events are organised by a variety of groups: **Casal Lambda** (C/Verdaguer i Callís 10, Barri Gòtic (93 319 55 50/ www.lambdaweb.org). Metro Urquinaona. Open 5-9pm Mon-Fri. Closed 2wks Aug) is a reliable source of information, as is Complices (see p242). Admission to the bars listed below is free unless stated.

### Aire

*C/València 236, Eixample (93 454 63 94/ www.arenadisco.com). Metro Passeig de Gràcia.* **Open** 11pm-3am Thur-Sat. **Admission** (incl 1 drink) €5 Fri, Sat. **No credit cards. Map** p338 F7.

The girly outpost of the Arena group is the city's largest lesbian club and as such sees a decent variety of girls (and their boyfriends, by invitation) head down to shoot pool and dance to pop, house and '80s classics. On the first Sunday of the month there's a women-only strip show. **Photo** *p242.*

### La Femme

*C/Plató 13, Sant Gervasi (no phone). Metro Lesseps/FGC Muntaner.* **Open** midnight-3am Fri, Sat. **No credit cards. Map** p338 E3.

Hip dance music, comfortable seating, red and green neon lighting and pretty people on both sides of the bar. Lots of trendy young things and fortysomethings. This is not a place for boys.

### Via

*María Cubí 4 (mobile 605 099 942), Gràcia. Metro Fontana/FGC Gracia.* **Open** 11.30pm-5.30am Fri, Sat. **No credit cards. Map** p338 F5.

This is the newest name for one of the longest-running lesbian haunts in Barcelona. A friendly atmosphere and small dancefloor means that it fills up after the others close their doors.

## Restaurants

In addition to those listed here, plenty of mixed restaurants in Barcelona have thriving gay followings. Among the most popular are the Barri Gòtic's **La Verònica** (C/Avinyó 30, 93 412 11 22 and **Venus Delicatessen** (C/Avinyó 25, 93 301 15 85) and the Eixample's **Café Miranda** (C/Casanova 30, 93 453 52 49).

### Castro

*C/Casanova 85, Eixample (93 323 67 84/ www.castrorestaurant.com). Metro Universitat.* **Open** 1-4pm, 9pm-midnight Mon-Fri; 9pm-midnight Sat. **Main courses** €10-€18. **Set lunch** €8.30 Mon-Fri. **Credit** MC, V. **Map** p342 C5.

Still ahead of the crowd as far as gay restaurants go, Castro continues to provide imaginative dishes such as duck breast with wild strawberries or deer in balsamic vinegar, all served up by the cutest of staff.

### Cubaneo

*C/Casanova 70, Eixample (93 454 83 94). Metro Universitat.* **Open** *Oct-June* 1-4pm, 8.30pm-1am Mon-Sat. *July-Sept* 8.30pm-1am Tue-Sun. **Main courses** €8.50-€11.80. **Set lunch** €7. **Credit** MC, V. **Map** p342 E8.

Cuban soul food, invigorating Mojitos and handsome muscled waiters, not to mention an unholy mix of Cuban personalities and gay icons on the walls. The set meals start with salads, followed by a choice of mains, and include a bottle of wine or cava.

### Iurantia

*C/Casanova 42, Eixample (93 454 78 87/www. iurantia.com). Metro Universitat* **Open** 1.30-4pm, 9pm-midnight Mon-Fri; 9pm-midnight Sat. **Main courses** €7.50-€17. **Credit** MC, V. **Map** p342 E8.

Though not a gay eaterie per se, Iurantia's Gaixample location assures it's frequented by a stylish crowd keen on the slick red paint job, downbeat tunes and the menu, which varies from imaginative fusion – octopus carpaccio – to popular and fairly priced pasta and pizzas. Leave room for the home-made bitter chocolate truffles with a touch of mint.

## Shops & services

### General shops

### Antinous Libreria Café

*C/Josep Anselm Clavé 6, Barri Gòtic (93 301 90 70/ www.antinouslibros.com). Metro Drassanes.* **Open** 10.30am-2pm, 5-8.30pm Mon-Fri; noon-2pm, 5-8.30pm Sat. **Credit** AmEx, DC, MC, V. **Map** p345 B7.

A large bright bookshop with an appealing café at the back. Ideal for checking out your purchases, from DVDs to postcards, poetry to magazines, art to comics all with a queer twist; they also have a great selection of nude photobooks. Its website lists the top 10 best-selling items so you know what's popular; it also features online reviews.

### Complices

*C/Cervantes 2, Barri Gòtic (93 412 72 83/ www.libreriacomplices.com). Metro Jaume I.* **Open** 10.30am-8pm Mon-Fri; noon-8pm Sat. **Credit** AmEx, MC, V. **Map** p345 C6.

Barna's oldest gay bookshop is run by a helpful lesbian duo who stock a variety of literature and films – everything from highbrow paperback classics (some in English) and *Queer As Folk* box sets to porn mags and DVDs.

### D'Arness

*C/Casanova 63, Eixample (mobile 639 959 224). Metro Universitat.* **Open** 5-9pm Mon-Fri. **Credit** MC, V. **Map** p342 E8.

This small specialist leather shop has all the gear you could need. The fully kitted-out room at the back is available for hire by the hour.

### Ovlas

*Via Laietana 33, Barri Gòtic (93 268 76 91). Metro Jaume I.* **Open** 10.15am-8.30pm Mon-Fri; 10.15am-9pm Sat. **Credit** AmEx, MC, V. **Map** p345 D4.

A large space that keeps Barcelona's boys in lurid briefs, singlets and other assorted revealing garments – thus making it a perfect one-stop shop for a weekend in Sitges.

### La Tienda de Ken

*C/Casanova 56, Eixample (93 534 67 70/ www.latiendadeken.com). Metro Universitat.* **Open** 5-9pm Mon; 11am-2pm, 5-9pm Tue-Fri; 5-9pm Sat. Closed 1wk Aug. **Credit** MC, V. **Map** p342 E8.

This tiny shop sells a variety of gay clothing and accessories. Male Barbie fans can buy anything from Tarzan-like swimwear in rags to chains and kinky leather bracelets. But the best are some original badges, portraying everyone from *Sesame Street* characters to Camilla Parker-Bowles.

## Hairdressers

### Fashion Chaning

*C/Diputació 159, Eixample (93 454 24 10). Metro Urgell.* **Open** 4-9pm Mon; 11am-8.30pm Tue-Sat. **Credit** V. **Map** p342 E8.

A gay hairdressing salon for boys and girls, and one place where men ask for manicures, pedicures and facials without getting odd looks. You can get your eyebrows, eyelashes and even your body hair dyed.

## Saunas

At all of the establishments listed below, you'll find enough showers, steam rooms and dry saunas to justify the name, along with bars and colourful porn lounges. On arrival, you'll be supplied with locker key, towel and flip-flops.

### Corinto

*C/Pelai 62, Eixample (93 318 64 22). Metro Catalunya.* **Open** noon-5am Mon-Thur; 24hrs Fri-Sun. **Admission** €13.50 Mon, Wed, Thur, Sat, Sun; €11 Tue, Fri. **Credit** MC, V. **Map** p342 B2.

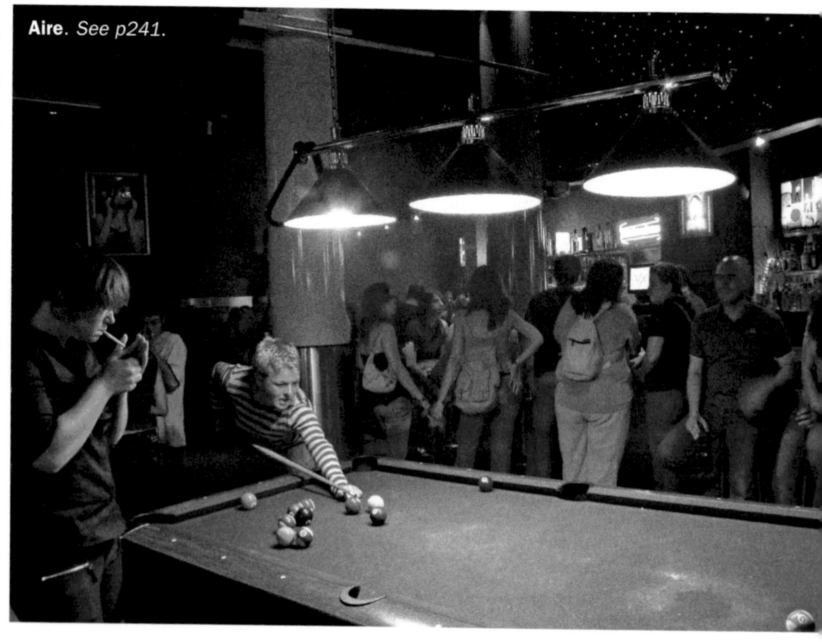

**Aire**. *See p241.*

Nothing really changes at the Corinto, smack in the centre, on perhaps the busiest corner in town, and it still remains the most popular place for tourists to go get busy, aided by some fine vistas of Plaça Catalunya and the Ramblas.

### Sauna Casanova

*C/Casanova 57, Eixample (93 323 78 60). Metro Urgell.* **Open** 24hrs daily. **Admission** €13.50 Mon, Wed, Fri-Sun; €11 Tue, Thur. **Credit** MC, V. **Map** p342 E8

Recently refurbished, Casanova is the city's most popular sauna, attracting plenty of well-muscled eye candy for the visitor. It's at its busiest on Tuesday and Thursday evenings, every night after the clubs close and all day Sunday.

## Sex shops

The following gay-oriented sex shops have viewing cabins for videos.

### Nostromo

*C/Diputació 208, Eixample (93 451 33 23). Metro Universitat.* **Open** 11am-11pm Mon-Fri; 3-11pm Sat, Sun. **No credit cards**. **Map** p342 E8.

### Zeus

*C/Riera Alta 20, Raval (93 442 97 95). Metro Sant Antoni.* **Open** 10am-9pm Mon-Sat. **Credit** MC, V. **Map** p342 E10.

# Sitges

Just a short (30min) train ride down the coast is Sitges, the internationally renowned gay capital of Spain. For nine months of the year, this pretty little town is the bolt-hole for city-weary Barcelonans, but in the summer months the streets heave with muscled flesh and the party atmosphere goes on and on. There is a small (and packed) gay beach in the centre of town, but for the more adventurous, the nudist beach, which has a small, but pricey *xiringuito*, is about another hour's walk (plenty of water and comfortable shoes advisable).

## Accommodation

Be aware that finding somewhere in August is a nightmare and book at least three months in advance for anything decent. This goes in particular for **El Xalet** (C/Illa de Cuba 35, 93 894 55 79, www.elxalet.com, rates €75-€102 incl breakfast) and its sister **Hotel Noucentista** (C/Illa de Cuba 21, 93 894 85 53, rates €75-€102 incl breakfast, closed Nov-Feb) , both of which occupy Modernista palaces and are furnished with period furniture. Almost next door is **Hotel Liberty** (C/Illa de Cuba 45, 93 811 08 72, www.libertyhotelsitges.com, rates €76-€126 incl breakfast), with spacious rooms, a lush garden and, if you feel like splashing out, a luxury penthouse with two terraces overlooking the town. The owners also have 41 apartments for rent – see www.staysitges.com. The follow-the-herd choice is the **Hotel Romàntic**, a beautifully restored 19th-century house with a secluded palm-filled garden (C/Sant Isidre 33, 93 894 83 75, www.hotelromantic.com, rates €87.50-€102.45 incl breakfast, closed Nov-Mar). In a quieter residential area is the friendly French-run **Hotel Los Globos** (Avda Nuestra Señora de Montserrat s/n, 93 894 93 74, www.hotellosglobos.com, rates €60-€95 incl breakfast), in need of slight redecoration but with a balcony or private garden for each room. Peter and Rico at **RAS** (mobile 607 14 94 51, www.raservice.com) may be able to help you out if you're stuck.

## Bars & nightclubs

For a night out in Sitges, first squeeze your way through the sweating herd at the beginning of C/Primer de Maig, aka Sin Street, and take a seat at one of the numerous pavement cafés to watch the world go by. Later, head round the corner to **Privilege** (C/Bonaire 24, no phone) with its friendly atmosphere and small but packed dancefloor, passing **Mari Pili** (C/Joan Tarrida Ferratges 14, mobile 653 771 071), the local lesbian hangout on the way. Two minutes from there is the much larger but rammed **Mediteraneo** (C/Sant Bonaventura 6, no phone) frequented by a slightly older but equally lively crowd; beware of the rather intimate toilets. If you feel the urge to keep going, there is the eternal **Organic** (C/Bonaire 15, no phone) or **Trailer** (C/Angel Vidal 36, 93 894 04 01) in the centre of town. On Tuesdays from June to September head for the gay beach party at **L'Atlantida** (Platja les Coves, no phone), a short taxi ride from the centre.

## Restaurants

Finding good food in Sitges can be a problem, but if you're looking for a particularly gay experience try **Parrots Restaurant** (C/Joan Tarrida Ferratges 18, 93 811 12 19, mains €13, closed Nov-Mar), where the food is decent, the portions large and the staff delicious. Also worth a mention is **Monroe's** (C/Sant Pau 36, 93 894 16 12, mains €12.50), dedicated to Marilyn and serving a range of international cuisine. If it's charm you're after try **Flamboyant** (C/Pau Barrabeitg s/n 16, 93 894 58 11, mains €16, closed Oct-May). The food is fairly average, but served in a magical leafy courtyard.

# Music & Nightlife

Dance with me...

**Fonfone**. *See p247.*



It's a curiosity that Barcelona's popularity as a tourist destination (now Europe's third most visited city after London and Paris) has, in large part, been driven by its reputation as a party city. Yes, you can party, but if you want to step out 24 hours, seven days a week, you're much more likely to find this party heaven in Madrid and Ibiza in summer. That being said, there is a distinct qualitative difference in Barcelona's nightlife – there's an energy and creativity in Barcelona that's been missing from Madrid ever since La Movida petered out in the late '80s. That difference is reflected primarily in the mix of people in bars, a willingness to experiment with sound and art, and a proud resolve to continue the city's fine devotion to excellence in interior bar design.

But, and it's a big but, the present government's acquiescence over growing, and quite often irrational, neighbourhood protests about noise pollution has transformed, and will continue to transform, the nightlife landscape. Two areas have fallen victim already – the Born and Gràcia. Both have been issued with indefinite bans on new bar licences. It was certainly a sign of the times that 2005 saw the closure (after noise complaints) of the city's best-loved club, La Terrrazza, up on Montjuïc. It managed to reopen and in summer 2006 the venue made a bigger and better return than ever.

Clampdowns on premises aside, Barcelona has it all – from superclubs hosting famed international celebrity DJs to tiny little clubs specialising in the latest electro, drum 'n' bass and techno. There are lounge clubs and gilded ballrooms, *salsatecas* and Brazilian samba bars, seductive tango emporiums and alternative club nights offering anything from northern soul to Bollywood bhangra and crooning drag queens. There are even bars with beds (**Sugar Club**, *see p253* and **CDLC**, *see p253*), so why would you ever go home?

Going out in Barcelona happens late, but that's mainly Thursday until Saturday. Barcelona on a Monday evening is a dead city. Tuesday and Wednesday things pick up slightly. People rarely meet for a drink much before 11pm – if they do, it's a pre-dinner thing. Downtown bars don't shut until 3am (in Gràcia it's 2am during the week), and it's not until they kick people out that the clubs (cutesily still known as *discotecas*) really get going. If you're still raring to go at 6am, there's a good chance you'll find an after-party party for even more hedonism. Afters, some better known than others litter the city at sunrise. Just ask a regular at any major nightclub. Traditionally, you had to head uptown to hit the posh clubs, but the Port Olímpic is putting on some serious competition with places like **Club Catwalk** (*see p253*) and **CDLC** luring the *pijos* (snobs) downtown. There are also nightly beach parties running up and down the coast from Bogatell. Meanwhile, you'll find smaller venues pulsating with life in the Barri Gòtic, particularly around the Plaza Reial and C/Escudellers. Across La Rambla, in the Raval, you can skulk the grittier, grungier places, though in the last year or so many have fallen prey to the Ajuntament's drive to wipe out late-night noise. If hippie chic, joints and chill-ums are your thing, Gràcia is good for hanging with the artsy crowd, though in truth it's a far better place for drinking than it is for dancing.

In the end, if it's beautiful people you want to see and you don't mind the try-hard pretension and steep prices, then the clubs are worth a go. But the cute local bar has always been the city's strength, and it offers a more genuine experience.

## LIVE MUSIC

The term 'live music' has been threatening to become a bit of a misnomer in Barcelona over the last few years. The closure of grown-up venues La Boîte and Jazzroom and the threatened closure of **Harlem Jazz Club** (*see p247*) were seen by some as a worrying symptom of the music scene's sickly state, particularly as these venues were run by long-time champions of live music in Barcelona. But perhaps the rumours of the death of music in the city are exaggerated. There is still plenty of variety, with a healthy dose of genres and bands from northern Europe and America – good news for visitors, who often get to see their favourite bands in venues half the size they'd normally play at home. But rocketing ticket prices (perhaps to support seemingly ever-growing guest lists – blaggers, take note!) mean you pay for such privilege.

For a city that's hardly booming with smaller live-music venues, over the past five or so years Barcelonahas, incredibly, managed to garner somewhat of a reputation for a burgeoning local music movement that is claiming considerable international recognition. *Mestizaje* (basically meaning 'mix') performers generally draw from a blend of influences including rock, flamenco, rai, hip hop and various South American, Asian and African styles. The top *mestizaje* draws at the moment are Ojos de Brujo and the Raval's 08001.

## Nights

### To make jazz cool again

The What the Fuck night at jazz cave **Jamboree** (*see p247*) offers the bizarre vision of baggy-panted b-boys won over to the jazz thang by the hot, hard, funk-tinged playing on stage and a young, up-for-it crowd getting down on the floor.

### To come dancing

La Gardenia Blanca orchestra at **La Paloma** (*see p252*) is a classic, with moustachioed, fedora-ed guys crooning the cruise-ship favourites, and well-endowed ladies squeezed into sequin-laden, thigh-split gowns. Watch them rumba and cha cha cha from 6pm till 9.30pm Thursday to Saturday.

### For summer lovin'

Soak it up at the **Teatre Grec** (*see p264*) in summer. On a blissful night, with drink in hand and the likes of Gotan Project entertaining outdoors, there can be nothing more pleasurable.

### To hang with big ballers

Claim to be on the Australian water polo team and hang out with affluent and glamorous athletes, and their entourage of fabulous friends and bewitching beauties dripping in bling. The best places to get away with it include **CDLC** (*see p253*) and nearby **Club Catwalk** (*see p253*). **Shôko** (*see p253*) gives them a run for their money too.

### To blag it

Don't miss the monthly residencies of Barcelona's favourite international superstars: Miss Kittin at **Razzmatazz** (*see p259*) attracts electro-cuties by way of her hard-hitting Berlinesque sound; Powder Room at **Sala Apolo** (*see p255*) sets the stage for Keb Darge's impossible-to-find soul tunes; and sexy Swedes come out in droves when Scandinavian chart-topper Jay Jay Johanson mixes up his blend of disco-pop at **Mond Club** (*see p251*).

### To get spiritual

New Year's Eve at the majestically volcanic **Cap de Creus** (*see p295*) peak near Cadaqués. Now a legendary sojourn for many to see sunrise, recover or continue on partying.

As well as the venues listed below, you can catch the occasional visits of pop-rock superstars in one of Montjuïc's sports stadiums, one of which has become the **Barcelona Teatre Musical** (C/Joaquim Blume s/n, 93 423 15 41), and Vall d'Hebron, or even way out in Badalona's Palau Olímpic. The other main music venues for seeing international names (as well as hotly tipped unknowns and local musicians) are the multifaceted industrial space **Razzmatazz** (*see p259*) and the old dance halls **La Paloma** (*see p252*) and **Sala Apolo** (*see p255),* the former hosting both cutting-edge live and electronic music, the latter specialising in feel-happy DJs and special theme nights. The mall-like **Bikini** (*see p258*), which has revived the quality of its programming with an impressively eclectic roster of recent acts including Radio 4, Terry Callier, Marianne Faithfull and Everlast, is the grand old survivor of the Barcelona scene.

### INFORMATION AND TICKETS

For concert information, buy the weekly listings guide *Guía del Ocio* (out on Thursday) or the Friday papers, which usually include listings supplements. Look in bars and music shops for free magazines such as *Go, AB, Mondo Sonoro* (all mostly independent pop/rock/electronica) and *Batonga!* (which covers world music). *Punto H* and *Suite* are good for keeping up to date on the club scene.

Try web listings sites www.lecool.com, ww.atiza.com,www.salirenbarcelona.com,www.barcelonarocks.com, and ww.clubbing spain.com. For festivals, try www.festivales.com and

## Sounds of the city

BBC music guru Charlie Gillett recently wrote that if the 1990s belonged to Paris in terms of new musical output, then the period from 2000 onwards was very much Barcelona's. The lack of quality small-scale live-music venues in the city, compared to, say, Madrid, doesn't seem to have hindered a remarkable energy that is turning out some of the most exciting music in Europe. Never one to lose a marketing opportunity, the city' has already come up with a label for the new wave of groups – Barcelona Sound, a nod to the *mestizaje,* or mix of styles, that immigration from both abroad and within the country has thrown up over the last ten years. Musically, it's meant the virtual disappearance of the inward-looking *rock català* that was so pervasive in the 1980s and early '90s.

Ex-Mano Negra frontman, sometime Barcelona resident and now global superstar Manu Chao first rang in the changes with his million-dollar-selling album *Clandestino,* and his influence is still being felt – ex-members of his Radio Bemba collective now play in myriad groups around town. Hip-hop flamenco outfit **Ojos de Brujo** probably carries the city's greatest weight of expectations. Closely aligned with a range of social movements and fronted by the extraordinarily talented Marina Abad, Ojos have come from nowhere to comfortably selling out venues like Razzmatazz and beginning to enjoy success in places like the UK, where they've already sold more than 20,000 discs on the back of a gig or two, something unheard of from a Spanish act in that market. Hopes are high that the US and Japanese visits will take them still further.

Label mates **08001** haven't enjoyed the same level of success, but a couple of years ago they produced the stunning *Raval Ta Joie* and give an extraordinary live show that incorporates recorded footage of the lead singer – who was expelled to his home country of Algeria for immigration reasons. 08001 are more of a collective than a group, and they have never played together as a complete outfit, in fact – the album was recorded with all 17 members individually and then mastered in the studio. The very size of the group, together with the technical elements of the live show, are proving an unfortunate hindrance to touring.

The newest darling of the scene is **Muchachito Bombo Infierno**, a rumba-swing outfit with a punk aesthetic that packs a mean live show that includes a stage artist recording all the gig's details. Muchachito's success is also being carefully guided outside Spain. It joins the power-ska, hip-hop rock combo Kinky Beat and the Arabic rock/jazz fusionist Cheb Balowski as the latest group to try its hand at steady overseas touring.

Well worth seeing too is **Pastora**'s sweet and streetwise electro pop, the hugely respected flamenco rap originals **Solo Los Solo** and ex- Ojos de Brujo frontman **Macaco** and his global sound. If you're into a hardcore rock sound, **Standstill** are being touted as the next big thing here, but many also punt for **Unfinished Sympathy**.

www.whatsonwhen.com. You can also get information and tickets from Tel-entrada and Servi-Caixa, and FNAC. Specialist record shops, such as those on C/Tallers in the Raval, are good for info and club flyers.

## Barri Gòtic

### Barcelona Pipa Club

*Plaça Reial 3, pral (93 302 47 32/www.bpipa club.com). Metro Liceu.* **Open** 11pm-4am daily. **Admission** free. **No credit cards**. **Map** p345 B6.

Once up some stairs and through a door, the chaos of the Plaça Reial below couldn't seem further away. Indeed, it feels less Barcelona, more Baker Street boozer circa 1900. Dusty wood, heavy curtains and cabinets full of antique pipes preserve a sedate atmosphere and, when it's not sectioned off for members' use, a small pool table sees a fair bit of action.

### Fonfone

*C/Escudellers 24 (93 317 14 24/www.fonfone.com). Metro Drassanes or Liceu.* **Open** 11pm-2.30am Mon-Thur, Sun; 11pm-3am Fri, Sat. **Admission** free. **Credit** MC, V. **Map** p345 B6.

A refreshingly spacious bar on a seedy backstreet, Fonfone stands out by virtue of its green-and-orange glowing decor. It pulls a mixed crowd of locals and lost tourists of a studenty bent. Pop, electronica, house and breakbeats attempt to distract the punters from their conversation. **Photo** *p244*.

### Harlem Jazz Club

*C/Comtessa de Sobradiel 8 (93 310 07 55). Metro Jaume I.* **Open** 8pm-4am Tue-Thur, Sun; 8pm-5am Fri, Sat. *Gigs* 10.30pm, midnight Tue-Thur, Sun; 11.30pm, 1am Fri, Sat. Closed 2wks Aug. **Admission** free Mon-Thur; (incl 1 drink) €6 Fri-Sun. **No credit cards**. **Map** p345 C6.

For a time, the gig looked over for this Barcelona institution. To cut a long story short, it's managed to come back bigger and stronger than ever, remodelled and, as a nod to the times, with a DJ booth. But live music is still what it does best, and it's for this reason that it's a regular hangout for not-so-cashed up musicians, serious music buffs and students. A lot of history's gone down at Harlem – some of the city's most promising talent and the occasional special international artist have played here. Jazz, klezmer and flamenco fusion all get a run in a venue that holds no musical prejudices.

### Jamboree/Los Tarantos

*Plaça Reial 17 (93 319 17 89 /www.masimas.com). Metro Liceu.* **Open** 8pm-11am daily. *Gigs* 8.30pm, 9.30pm, 10.30pm daily. **Admission** €5. **Credit** V. **Map** p345 B6.

Every night Jamboree hosts jazz, Latin or blues gigs by mainly Spanish groups; when they're over the beatbox comes out. On Mondays, particularly, the outrageously popular What the Fuck (WTF) jazz jam session is crammed with a young local crowd waiting for the funk/hip-hop night that follows.

Harlem Jazz Club.

Upstairs, sister venue Los Tarantos stages flamenco performances, then joins forces with Jamboree as a smooth-grooves chill-out space.

### La Macarena

*C/Nou de Sant Francesc 5 (no phone/www.macarena club.com). Metro Drassanes.* **Open** 11.30pm-4.30am Mon-Thur, Sun; 11.30pm-5.30am Fri, Sat. **Admission** free before 1.30am; €5 afterwards. **No credit cards**. **Map** p345 B7.

This is not a centre for embarrassing synchronised arm movements performed to cheesy pop tunes, but a completely soundproofed cosy little dance space/bar with a kicking sound system that will pound away electro, minimal and house beats until the early hours. Guest house DJs Brett Johnson and Vincenzo have shared the decks with local talent, usually a day before or after a bigger gig elsewhere.

### New York

*C/Escudellers 5 (93 318 87 30). Metro Drassanes or Liceu.* **Open** midnight-5am Thur-Sat. **Admission** (incl 1 drink) €5 with flyer and before 2am, €10 without flyer & after 2am. **No credit cards**. **Map** p345 B6.

After a facelift and a change of management, this ancient former brothel-turned-rock-club is now indulging Spain's obsession for Depeche Mode and other newly trendy '80s sounds, alongside the typical floppy-haired party fare from the likes of Franz Ferdinand, The Strokes et al. A long hallway

No self-respecting clubber will miss the **Fellini**. *See p251.*

bar leads on to the main dancefloor, where fairground figures leer from the stage and wallflowers gaze from the mezzanine. In its previous incarnation, such well-known figures as Gilles Peterson, King Britt and Norman Jay all played here.

### Sidecar Factory Club

*Plaça Reial 7 (93 302 15 86/www.sidecarfactoryclub.com). Metro Liceu.* **Open** 6pm-4.30am Tue-Thur, Sun; 6pm-5am Fri, Sat. **Admission** (incl 1 drink) €4-€6 before 2am Tue-Thur, Sun; €5-€7 before 2am Fri, Sat. *Gigs* €5-€15. **No credit cards. Map** p345 B6.

Sidecar still has all the ballsy attitude of the spit 'n' sawdust rock club that it once was and, while the gigs and weekend's rock-pop extravaganza continue to pack in the local indie kids and Interrailers, the programming has thankfully diversified considerably to include breakbeat on Wednesdays and Brazilian tunes on Tuesdays. Monday night's anti-karaoke is a particularly genius example of the club's rock take on a pop theme.

## Born & Sant Pere

### Dr Astin

*C/Abaixadors 9 (mobile 676 220 736). Metro Jaume I.* **Open** 11pm-2.30am Mon-Thur; 11pm-3am Fri, Sat. **Admission** free. **No credit cards. Map** p345 D6.

Minute and slightly grungy, this spot has been hammering out house and techno beats for years, in spite of a recent change of management. The Born's cool hipsters come here to get their groove before heading out to the bigger venues. Free and completely soundproofed, it's a good place to start the night.

### Drop Bar

*Via Laietana 20 (93 310 75 04). Metro Jaume I.* **Open** *Sept-July* 8am-10pm Mon-Wed; 8am-3am Thur-Fri; 11pm-3am Sat. *Aug* 8am-5pm Mon-Sat. **Admission** free. **Credit** Amex, MC, V. **Map** p345 D6.

Drop Bar stood ignored for a long time on its corner of Via Laietana with C/Argenteria. One reason for this neglect may be the fact that it sports unpromising 1980s-style curved windows overlooking the street. But never mind the outside, within you'll find three different spaces, including an open-air area and a daytime café. Cool, cutting-edge programming includes EBM, IDM and ICBM nights (whatever the vogue of the week is). Dance music for the head-bobbers and the unprententious.

## Raval

### Aurora

*C/Aurora 7 (93 442 30 44/mobile 680 518 250). Metro Paral·lel.* **Open** 8pm-2.30am Mon-Thur; 9.30pm-3am Fri, Sat. **Admission** free. **No credit cards. Map** p342 E10.

Aurora used to be an unkempt ramshackle place, but it was given a makeover a few years ago and now has a considerably smarter look. It's today inhabited by arty types who remain here well into the small hours, and its mini dancefloor appeals to students and Raval locals, who cram on to it for weekends of varied DJ sounds. During the week, the cocktails and the conversation forthcoming from the party-hungry bar staff will keep you sustained at the bar till the clock strikes 'close'.

## Bar Pastis

*C/Santa Mònica 4 (93 318 79 80). Metro Drassanes.* **Open** 7.30pm-2.30am Tue-Thur, Sun; 7.30pm-3.30am Fri, Sat. **Credit** AmEx, MC, V. **Map** p345 A7.

This quintessentially Gallic bar once served pastis to the visiting sailors and the denizens of the Barrio Chino underworld. It has since moved on, but, thankfully, not much: it still has a louche Marseilles feel, floor-to-ceiling indecipherable oil paintings (painted by the original owner when drunk, apparently), Edith Piaf gracing the stereo, and latter-day troubadours on Tuesdays, Wednesdays and Sundays. It's kind of touristy these days, but if your Spanish is up for it there are enough regular locals here who can tell you what the Raval was really like pre-Olympic Games.

## Benidorm

*C/Joaquín Costa 39 (no phone). Metro Universitat.* **Open** *Apr-mid Oct* 8pm-2.30am Mon-Thur, Sun; 8pm-3am Fri, Sat. *Mid Oct-Mar* 7pm-2.30am Mon-Thur, Sun; 7pm-3am Fri, Sat. Closed Aug. **Admission** free. **No credit cards**. **Map** p342 E9.

This lively, smoky little place is a kitsch paradise of brothel-red walls, crystal lanterns and 1980s disco paraphernalia, boasting the world's smallest toilet, dancefloor and chill-out room. The sounds being absorbed by the mass of humanity packed in here on weekends (watch your wallet) range from hip hop to '70s stuff, although mostly they are variations on the same electronica theme.

## Big Bang

*C/Botella 7 (93 443 28 13/www.bigbangbcn.net). Metro Liceu or Sant Antoni.* **Open** *Bar* 9.30pm-2.30am Wed, Thur, Sun; 10.15pm-3am Fri, Sat. *Gigs* around 10.30pm-1am Fri, Sat. *Jam sessions* 11pm-1am Wed, Thur, Sun. **Admission** *Bar & jam sessions* free. *Gigs* prices vary. **No credit cards**. **Map** p342 E10.

Brothers Jesus, Robert and Ran of heavy rock group DE KALLE run Big Bang, one of the few ungentrified bars in the Raval and one of the few hosting free rock jam sessions. Sure, it's shabby, but hey, that's the way rock jam sessions are supposed to be and that's the way they they want it here. On top of the gigs, throw in film nights on Thursdays, a cruddy table football machine and straight-down-the-line bar staff, and it's no surprise that it attracts all sorts – crusty types, ageing rockers, boyz from the 'hood and some slightly confused-looking backpackers. Bang on the shutters if you're thirsty and wandering the streets after everything else has closed to try your luck at getting a drink.

## El Cangrejo

*C/Montserrat 9 (93 301 29 78). Metro Drassanes.* **Open** 10pm-3am Thur; 10pm-3.30am Fri-Sun. **Admission** free. **Credit** MC, V. **Map** p345 A7.

The original Barcelona drag cabaret, El Cangrejo attracts a mixed bag of old-timers, honeymooners, gay couples and revellers. Tuesday and Wednesday evenings feature DJ sessions, but otherwise the acts consist largely of drag performers lip-synching to the usual golden-oldie Spanish ballads interspersed with raconteurs whose outrageous get-ups combine early Divine, Prince and the Jolly Green Giant to extraordinary effect. You'd have to go a long, long way to find a more sequin-spangled line-up. As for the decor: imagine being sandwiched between a lemon meringue pie and a paella.



# Midweek mayhem

It's barely dark on a school night, and the queue trails down three blocks. At its head, the hand-wringing ambassadors of various groups (generally the most attractive females) insist to bouncers they must be on the guest list. Others, in line, edge forward by spotting 'friends' 50 metres ahead. Itinerant beer-sellers do a roaring trade.

At the end of all this, through the red velvet curtains and into the hallowed belle époque hall of La Paloma, you might expect a star-studded glamourfest, something as exclusive as, say, the *Vanity Fair* post-Oscars bash. But, no – what lies ahead is one of the most unpretentious club nights in the city, combining the colours, sounds, smells and feel-good vibe of a world-music festival with the buzz of a private party where everybody knows everybody.

Hippies, lounge lizards, Ibiza throwbacks and even Goths throw their differences and ages aside as they wander the stalls selling jewellery, samosas and mint tea, stop for an Ayurvedic massage and gaze open-mouthed at the bikini-clad maidens doing the rounds entwined with two-metre pythons. From the ceiling, acrobats twirl down bands of crimson fabric, while on stage an improbably bendy doe-eyed Indian goddess gives a warm-up yoga class to the blissed-out group stretched across cushions in front of her.

Once the tone of the evening has been established, things start to warm up with 'Bollywood vs Bhangra', where, like rival flocks of birds of paradise, the two groups go head to head in a head-spinning kaleidoscope of colour to an ecstatic reception from the crowd, before the club night proper begins, with DJs and live acts from around the world.

If this sounds like your bag, head to La Paloma (*see p252*) on the second Wednesday of the month – not long after lunch.

## La Concha

*C/Guàrdia 14 (93 302 41 18). Metro Drassanes.* **Open** 5pm-2.30am Mon-Thur, Sun; 5pm-3am Fri, Sat. **Admission** free. **No credit cards**. **Map** p345 A6.

Local complaints that La Concha ain't as gay as it used to be under its new management seem a little harsh: the homo-to-hetero ratio of the crowd that packs it every night remains one of the highest for blocks. As does the camp factor, with Sara Montiel, Queen of the Spanish silver screen, watching over her loyal subjects from hundreds of faded photographs as they sip cocktails and dance to anything from Moroccan pop to salsa.

## Dos Trece

*C/ Carme 40 (93 301 73 06/www.dostrece.net). Metro Liceu.* **Open** 7pm-3am Mon, Sun; Tue-Sat 1pm-3am. *DJs* 10pm-3am Thur-Sun. *Live music* from 10pm Wed. **Admission** free. **Credit** Amex, DC, MC, V. **Map** p344 A4.

Dos Trece makes a welcome return with the re-opening of its downstairs lounge, which had been closed for a few years. The newly remodelled basement lounge has a Moroccan feel to it, but it's the programming of live music and DJs that's most anticipated. Funk, soul and Afrobeat sessions launched the new space in August, and live jazz, bossa nova and bolero feature on Wednesdays. One of the Raval's most popular spots at all times of the day – brunch, lunch, dinner or late night.

## Fellini

*C/La Rambla 27 (93 272 49 80/www.clubfellini.com). Metro Liceu.* **Open** midnight-5am Mon-Sat. **Admission** *Mon-Thur* free before 1.30am, €6 before 3am, €9 afterwards. *Fri, Sat* €9-€12. **No credit cards**. **Map** p345 A6.

Due to its location on the Rambla, Fellini, with its themed club spaces, has had to work pretty hard to earn kudos but, with its manic flyering and some good programming, it's managed to establish itself as the most talked-about new club in town. The monthly polysexual Puticlub parties are quite mixed and lots of fun, and the last Thursday of the month is the semi-legendary Mond Club, with everyone from The Glimmers to Freelance Hellraiser playing dancey rock and rocky dance for a muso crowd. **Photo** *p248*.

## Guru

*C/Nou de la Rambla 22 (93 318 08 40/www.guru barcelona.com) Metro Liceu.* **Open** 8pm-2.30am daily. **Admission** €3. **No credit cards**. **Map** p345 A6.

Guru has its eyes set on becoming the latest addition to the Raval bar scene's sleekification, but, palm trees and mood lighting aside, you can't help thinking that, with its white padded walls, it looks rather like a loony bin. As a newcomer in tourist central, it hasn't yet achieved the exclusive status it's aiming for and, as such, Cosmo-sipping, black-clad Parisians are still having to deal with gangs of tipsy Scousers hopping about to live salsa. For the moment.

The swanky **CDLC**. *See p253.*

## Jazz Sí Club

*C/Requesens 2 (93 329 00 20/www.tallerdemusics.com). Metro Sant Antoni.* **Open** 5pm-2.30am Mon-Thur, Sun; 5pm-3am Fri, Sat. **Admission** free. **No credit cards**. **Map** p342 E10.

This tiny music-school auditorium-cum-bar is a space where students, teachers and music lovers can meet, perform and listen: heaven or hell depending on your preference. Each night is dedicated to a different musical genre: trad jazz on Mondays, pop/rock/blues jams on Tuesdays, jazz jams on Wednesdays, Cuban music on Thursdays, flamenco on Fridays, rock on Saturdays and Sundays. A place for people who are serious about their music.

## Moog

*C/Arc del Teatre 3 (93 301 72 82/www.masimas.com). Metro Drassanes.* **Open** midnight-5am daily. **Admission** €9. **Credit** DC, MC, V. **Map** p345 A7.

Moog's an odd club; almost like partying on an aeroplane: it's long, narrow and enclosed, with full-blast air-conditioning and service with a smile. Some fine techno and house keep everything ticking along just right; Angel Molina, Laurent Garnier and Jeff Mills, among countless others, have all played here, with Wednesday nights being especially popular. Upstairs there's a tiny concession to those not feeling the bleeps – an even smaller dancefloor that plays R&B and 1970s tunes into the night.

**La Paloma**, from the eclectic to the curious.

## La Paloma

*C/Tigre 27 (93 301 68 97/www.lapaloma-bcn.com). Metro Universitat.* **Open** 6-9.30pm, 11.30pm-5am Thur; 6-9.30pm, 11.30pm-2am; 2.30-5am Fri, Sat; 5.45-9.45pm Sun. **Admission** (incl 1 drink) €3-€8. **Credit** (bar only) MC, V. **Map** p342 E9.

If the Addams family ran a club, it'd be something like La Paloma: refined, steeped in history and a little bit nuts. The chandeliers, velvet curtains and dancers create a burlesque vibe oddly complemented by the varied range of nights. There's Swasthya Yoga on Tuesdays; Thursday's Bongo Lounge continues to pump out Latin tunes and funk, while the weekend's So Rebel Club!, depending on who's on the decks (from Justice to Jon Carter), can be anything from techno to pop and rock. The second Wednesday of every month is the eclectic mini-festival of sorts, Rawal Launch, which brings together international dance, food and DJs.

## Zentraus

*Rambla del Raval 41 (93 443 80 78/www.zentraus.com). Metro Liceu.* **Open** 9pm-2.30am Tue-Wed; 9pm-3am Thur-Sat. Closed mid Aug-mid Sept. **Admission** free. **No credit cards**. **Map** p342 E10.

Stepping into this minimalist black, grey and red setting, you could forget that you're smack in the middle of the Raval and not in some uptown dig. The uplit bar, black-clad bartenders and completely soundproofed dancefloor make this a prime hotspot for beat-seekers in the area, bringing in a diverse and unpredictable crowd. The harder side of techno, electro, drum 'n' bass, breakbeats and minimal house normally take control of the dancefloor.

# Port Vell & Port Olímpic

Around the right-angled quayside of the Port Olímpic, you'll find dance bars interspersed with seafood restaurants, fast-food outlets, ice-cream parlours, coffee shops and mock-Irish pubs; with video screens, glittery lights and go-go girls and boys in abundance, it makes little difference which one you choose.

## Baja Beach

*Passeig Marítim 34 (93 225 91 00/www.bajabeach.es). Metro Ciutadella-Vila Olímpica.* **Open** *June-Oct* 11am-midnight Mon-Wed, Sun; 11am-6am Thur-Sat. *Nov-May* 11am-6am Thur-Sat; 11am-midnight Sun. **Admission** (incl 1 drink) €12 Thur, Sun; €14 Fri; €18 Sat. **Credit** AmEx, MC, V. **Map** p343 J13.

Baja Beach, the epitome of the Port Olímpic's brashness, is like one endless wedding disco, student night and Planet Hollywood extravaganza rolled into one but, providing you've got euro to spend, there's loads of fun to be had. Nearly nude barstaff play on espaneesh holiday-romance fantasies, blowing whistles and serving up body-shots to everyone from fresh-faced school leavers (turning green) to business-trippers (turning 50). Meanwhile, the DJ commands from his speedboat overlooking the dancefloor,

giving the masses what they want: cheeeese. Those who can still stand come closing are often found, faces pressed into the sand, come sunrise.

### CDLC

*Passeig Marítim 32 (93 224 0470/www.cdlcbarcelona.com). Metro Ciutadella-Vila Olímpica.* **Open** 10pm-2.30am Mon-Wed; noon-3am Thur-Sun. **Admission** free. **Credit** AmEx, MC, V. **Map** p343 J13.
Carpe Diem Lounge Club remains at the forefront of Barcelona's splash-the-cash, see-and-be-seen celeb circuit – the white beds flanking the dancefloor, guarded by a clipboarded hostess, are perfect for showing everyone who's the daddy. Or, for those not celebrating six-figure record deals, funky house and a busy terrace provide an opportunity for mere mortals (and models) to mingle and discuss, firstly, who's going to finance their next drink and, secondly, how to get chatting to whichever member of the Barça team that has just walked in.

### Club Catwalk

*C/Ramon Trias Fargas s/n (93 221 61 61/www.club catwalk.net). Metro Ciutadella-Vila Olímpica.* **Open** midnight-5.30am Wed-Sun. **Admission** €15-€18. **Credit** DC, MC, V. **Map** p343 K12.
Maybe it's the name or maybe it's the location (slap bang under the celeb-tastic Hotel Arts), but most of the Catwalk queue seems to think they're headed for the VIP room – that's crisp white collars and gold for the boys and short, short skirts for the girls. Inside it's suitably snazzy; upstairs there's R&B and hip hop, but the main house room is where most of the action is, with regular appearances from the likes of Erick Morillo and Roger Sanchez keeping the club's prestige firmly intact.

### Le Kasbah

*Plaça Pau Vilà (Palau del Mar) (93 238 07 22/ www.ottozutz.com). Metro Barceloneta.* **Open** 11pm-3am daily. **Admission** free. **Credit** AmEx, MC, V. **Map** p345 E8.
A white awning over terrace tables heralds the entrance to this louche bar behind the Palau de Mar. Inside, a North African harem look seduces a young and up-for-it mix of tourists and students on to its plush cushions for a cocktail or two before going out. As the night progresses, so does the music, from chill-out early on to full-on boogie after midnight.

### Shôko

*Passeig Marítim 36 (93 225 92 03/www.shoko.biz). Metro Ciutadella-Vila Olímpica.* **Open** 11.30pm-3am daily. **Admission** free. **Credit** AmEx, MC, V. **Map** p343 J13.
Another restaurant-club and another semi-exclusive joint in the Port Olímpic. The tried and tested formula continues to go down a treat with Sàrria's pseudo-fashionistas – all Britney hats, spray-on jeans and little wiggles – as they strut their stuff on the dancefloor, gutted they couldn't get into CDLC. Meanwhile, outside on the terrace, civilised sets of chino-clad tourists recline on the comfy beds sipping cocktails.

### Sugar Club

*World Trade Center, Moll de Barcelona (93 508 83 25/www.sugarclub-barcelona.com). Metro Drassanes.* **Open** 8pm-4am Wed-Sat. **Admission** free. **Credit** MC, V. **Map** p342 F13.
Grupo Salsitas continues its quest to rule all that's cool with this latest addition to the stable of Danzatoria, Danzarama et al. Beautiful people and a twinkling view across the marina provide the decoration in this otherwise minimal couple of spaces, one small and intimate with a splash of smooth and soulful vocal house, the other a large dancefloor with sofas. DJs blend tribal, electro and tech house beats with the odd remixed 1980s classic thrown in.

## Montjuïc & Poble Sec

### Barcelona Rouge

*C/Poeta Cabanyes 21 (93 442 49 85). Metro Paral·lel.* **Open** 11pm-4am Tue-Sat. **Admission** free. **No credit cards. Map** p342 D11.
A hidey hole of a place in one of Barcelona's unsung barris. It's small enough to get packed even though it's little known, hard to get into and hard on the wallet. Once inside, there's ambient music, good cocktails and battered sofas draped with foreign and local thirtysomethings – those with a bit of money and a bit of class who want to avoid the more obvious nightspots. Occasionally, there's a performance or two. Ring the buzzer to get in.

### Discothèque

*Poble Espanyol, Avda Marquès de Comillas (no phone). Metro Espanya.* **Open** midnight-6am Fri, Sat. **Admission** (incl 1 drink) €15 without flyer, €12 with flyer. **Credit** MC, V. **Map** p341 A9/B9.

Clubs rise and clubs fall, but new promoters have taken on the arduous task of keeping Discothèque, which was formerly La Terrrazza's winter gig, at the forefront of the A-list of nightspots. The snaking queues of the young and the beautiful using looks and attitude to blag their way in suggest success. Nights with names like 'Ken loves you' or 'Fuck me, I'm famous' mix up house and techno in the main room, while hip hop and R&B fill the smaller room. Projections, drag queens, podium dancers and a VIP bar re-create the Ibiza-when-it-was-still-hot vibe.

### Maumau

*C/Fontrodona 33 (93 441 80 15/www.maumaunderground.com). Metro Paral·lel.* **Open** 11pm-2.30am Thur; 11pm-3am Fri, Sat; 7pm-midnight Sun. **Admission** (membership) €5. **No credit cards**. **Map** p342 D11.

Recently renovated to include, among other things, a wheelchair ramp and better lavatories, Maumau is the long-time favourite of the Poble Sec haunts. Behind the anonymous grey door (ring the bell), first timers to this likeable little chill-out club pay €5 to become members. In practice it rarely charges out-of-towners. Inside, a large warehouse space is humanised with colourful projections, IKEA sofas and scatter cushions, and a friendly, laid-back crowd. DJ Wakanda schools us in the finer points of deep house, jazz, funk or whatever takes his fancy.

## Sex in the city

Any visitor to Barcelona who buys a newspaper at one of La Rambla's kiosks can't fail to notice the plethora of hardcore pornographic magazines and DVDs that sit alongside the latest editions of Spanish *Marie Claire* and *¡Hola!*

Port cities and sex are pretty happy bedmates. The novelist Jean Genet wrote at length from his Sant Pau bedsit of his encounters with sailors in the sleazy backstreets of the Raval and, up until the great clean-up in the late 1980s and '90s ahead of the 1992 Olympics, prostitution was very much a part of the landscape in and around La Rambla. Live sex shows, like the ones that exist in the grand old palace of sin called the Bagdad, still exist but the net, TV and other forms of sexual participation have turned them almost into tourist kitsch.

Today, Barcelona's community TV stations all run second-rate porn fests in the wee hours of the morning. The city is now host to one of Europe's biggest erotic film festivals (read porn), FICEB, in October, and this year, a Catalan erotic expo was held.

### Sala Apolo

*C/Nou de la Rambla 113 (93 441 40 01/www.sala-apolo.com). Metro Paral·lel.* **Open** midnight-5am Wed, Thur; midnight-7am Fri, Sat; 10.30pm-3am Sun. **Admission** varies. **No credit cards.** **Map** p342 E11.

Who'd have thought that one of the most popular clubs in this most stylish city would be a poorly lit 1940s dancehall. A smaller space downstairs features intimate relaxed gigs from up-and-coming talent, while upstairs on Wednesdays and Thursdays is a more upbeat affair, with an international crowd of music buffs, from hipster geeks to hip-hop gals, trekking across the Raval for funk and Latin grooves from the likes of Kid Koala and Gotan Project. And, ten years on, there's still epic queues for the weekend's bleeping techno extravaganza, Nitsa.

### La Terrrazza

*Poble Espanyol, Avda Marquès de Comillas s/n (93 272 49 80/www.laterrrazza.com) Metro Espanya.* **Open** *May-mid October* midnight-6am Thur-Sat. **Admission** (incl 1 drink) €18 without flyer, €15 with flyer. **Credit** MC, V. **Map** p341 A9/B9.

La Terrrazza re-opened in May 2006 after noise complaints closed it down in 2005. Driven by resident DJ Sergio Patricio, the club packs them in on its huge outdoor space that moves to a tech house beat. Compilation albums, international guest DJs and partner club Fellini in La Rambla (*see p251*) make it one energetic enterprise. If you get to go to only one nightclub in Barcelona, or Spain for that matter, make it this one. A long cold drink on a balmy night checking out the eye candy prancing, preening and boogieing is pretty hard to beat.

Not so well known is the fact that Barcelona is the swinging capital of Spain – some say, in all of Europe. There are some 150 or so official establishments throughout the country, and around a quarter do business, in Barcelona. Widely known as *clubs liberales*, these venues provide the opportunity for liberal-minded couples to both observe and participate in consensual sex with other like-minded people. Many include bars and dancefloors with contracted 'animators' and, depending on a couple's whims on any given night, they can move into sofa rooms, darkrooms, French passages (!) and private rooms for orgies. Some establishments are more reputable than others, others have websites and others still invite well-known pornstars to special nights. One in particular, Club 6 y 9, plies its trade at FICEB each year.

If you're male, interested and not in a relationship, don't despair. Providing you've got a 'good presence' and the doormen like the look of you and feel good about your intentions, you might be one of the lucky handful allowed each night to participate in the proceedings. But be warned: there's a strict code of ethics in most of these venues, the backbone of which is that no one is obliged to do anything they don't want to.

Another growing industry in the city is the renting of apartmentos discretos, of which La Casita Blanca is the best known. The idea here is for people looking for a clandestine quickie or a neutral place to enjoy the services of a prostitute. Apartments can be rented on an hourly basis or longer and feature a luxury pad with the works – jacuzzi, spa, sauna and, of course the inevitable huge double bed. Starting rates are approximately €30 an hour.

Barcelona is, ahem, your oyster, so to speak.

## Apartments for rent/ *Apartmentos discretos*

### Luxtal 177

*Tarragona 177, 1°, Eixample (92 423 99 55/ www.luxtal.es). Metro Sants or Tarragona.*

## Live sex shows

### Bagdad

*Avda Paral·lel 58, Poblesec, (93 442 07 77/www.bagdad.com). Metro Paral·lel.*

## Swinging clubs/ *Clubs liberales*

### Club 6 y 9

*Avda Príncep de Astúries 18, Gràcia (93 217 12 58/www.6y9.net). Metro Fontana or Plaça de Lesseps.*

### Limousine

*Teodora La Madrid 32, near Plaça Bonanova (93 417 88 57/www.enjoy-club.com/ limousine). FGC El Putxet.*

### Patty Club

*Josep Estivell 32, bajos, Navas, (93 349 92 45/www.pattyclub.com). Metro Navas.*

### Tinta Roja

*C/Creu dels Molers 17 (93 443 32 43/www.tinta roja.net). Metro Poble Sec.* **Open** *Bar* 8pm-2am Wed, Thur; 8pm-3am Fri, Sat; 7pm-1am Sun. *Shows* 10pm-midnight Wed-Sat. Closed 2wks Aug. **Admission** *Bar* free. *Shows* (incl 1 drink) €8-€10. **No credit cards. Map** p341 D10.

Word has it that this ace was once a former dairy farm. Push through the depths of the bar to be transported to a Buenos Aires bordello/theatre/circus/cabaret by plush red velvet sofas, smoochy niches and ancient ticket booth. It's an atmospheric place for a late-ish drink, and a distinctly different entertainment experience from Friday to Sunday when there are live performances of tango, jazz and flamenco in a small theatre at the back. Tango classes are also offered.

## Eixample

### Antilla BCN Latin Club

*C/Aragó 141 (93 451 45 64/www.antillasalsa.com). Metro Urgell.* **Open** 11pm-3.30am Mon-Wed, Sun; 11pm-4.30am Fri, Sat. *Gigs* around 1am. **Admission** (incl 1 drink) €10. **No credit cards. Map** p338 E8.

The Antilla prides itself on being a 'Caribbean cultural centre', hosting exhibitions and publishing its magazine *Antilla News*. But, its true calling lies in being the self-claimed best *salsateca* in town, offering dance classes (including acrobatic salsa and Afro-Cuban styles) and a solid programme of live music, which covers all Latin flavours from son to merengue and Latin jazz.

### Astoria

*C/París 193 (93 200 98 25/www.grupocostaeste.com/astoria). Metro Diagonal.* **Open** 11.30pm-3.30am Tue-Sat. Closed Aug. **Admission** free. **Credit** AmEx, MC, V. **Map** p338 F6.

From the same people who brought you Bucaro and the Sutton Club, Astoria offers a break from the norm. For a start, the club is housed in a converted 1950s cinema, which means the projections are big and actually watchable. There are three bars, so you're spared endless queues; there's plenty of comfortable seating along with a small dancefloor; and if you're very wonderful, you may get to sit on a heart-shaped cushion in the tiny VIP area. With all this going for it, it has inevitably become the domain of Barcelona's moneyed classes.

### Bucaro

*C/Aribau 195 (93 209 65 62/www.grupocostaeste.com/bucaro). FGC Provença.* **Open** 11.30pm-3.30am Mon-Thur; 11pm-4.30am Fri, Sat. **Admission** free. **Credit** AmEx, MC, V. **Map** p338 F5.

Looking a tad jaded, Bucaro's worn leather sofas and grubby pouffes still manage to pull a crowd of glamour pusses. With the giant skylight looming above the dancefloor like a portal to another world, and a mezzanine from where you can stalk your prey, this is a place that knows class when it sees it. Drinks are a couple of euro more expensive if you're sitting at a table. A list of dress code dos and don'ts and a friendly but firm bouncer to enforce them, greet you at the entrance.

### Buda Restaurante

*C/Pau Claris 92 (93 318 42 52/www.buda restaurante.com). Metro Catalunya.* **Open** 9pm-3am daily. **Admission** free. **Credit** MC, V. **Map** p344 D1.

The centre of Barcelona is strangely devoid of glamorous nightspots, or at least it was until Buda came along. The place has lots of throne-style furniture and gilded wallpaper, topped off with a colossal chandelier. The laid-back nature of the staff (dancing on the bar seems completely acceptable) and upbeat house music make it excellent for drinks and an ogle. Tuesday is 'Model's night', Wednesday is flamenco night, every second Thursday is Asian night (complete with geishas) Friday's is well, Friday Night Fever, Saturday is Indian Bollywood…you get the drift.

### City Hall

*Rambla Catalunya 2-4 (93 317 21 77/www.grupo-ottozutz.com). Metro Catalunya.* **Open** midnight-6am Tue-Sun. **Admission** (incl 1 drink) €12 . **Credit** (door only) MC, V. **Map** p344 C1.

Delusions of grandeur or a misnomer, whatever you want to call it, City Hall ain't that big, but it is surprisingly popular. In particular, Soul City on Thursdays has made a name for itself among the local NY-capped, billowing trouser-wearing posses by bringing acts like Killa Kela and the Scratch Perverts to town. The rest of the week it's a little more mixed, with music from deep house to electro

Sleek **Danzatoria** for the moneyed and glamorous. *See p259.*

rock, and an older post-(pre-?) work crowd joining the young, tanned and skinny to show the dancefloors some love. Outside, the terrace is a veritable (and in summer, literal) melting pot of tourists and locals, who rub shoulders under the watchful (anti-pot-smoking) eye of the bouncer.

### Danzarama

*Gran Via de les Corts Catalanes 604 (93 301 97 43/ reservations 93 342 5070/www.gruposalsitas.com). Metro Universitat.* **Open** 7am-3am Mon-Sat. **Admission** free. **Credit** AmEx, DC, MC, V. **Map** p342 F8.

Make your way past the flash restaurant upstairs – we're talking white sofas swinging from the ceiling – and down on to the brick-walled, loud dancefloor. With no entry charge and lots of tables, Danzarama has become a popular pre-party venue for Pacha (on Thursdays; *see p259*) and Catwalk (on Sundays; *see p253*), with a free shuttle bus and thumping tunes making up for the club-priced drinks.

### Distrito Diagonal

*Avda Diagonal 442 (mobile 607 113 602/www.distrito diagonal.com). Metro Diagonal.* **Open** midnight-6am Fri, Sat. **Admission** free before 4am, (incl 1 drink) €15 after. **No credit cards. Map** p338 G6.

Distrito Diagonal attracts a slightly older crowd with an easygoing atmosphere. The venue's bathed in red light, there are sounds from nu jazz to deep house and plenty of chairs to sink into. It's become a sought-after place for small promoters and one-off parties, which means the music can veer anywhere from Bollywood to hip hop. Thursday nights, Cabaret Club educates listeners with the latest indietronica.

### Luz de Gas

*C/Muntaner 246 (93 209 77 11/www.luzdegas.com). FGC Muntaner.* **Open** *Club* 11.30pm-5am daily. *Gigs* 12.30am daily. **Admission** (incl 1 drink) €15. **Credit** AmEx, DC, MC, V. **Map** p338 E5.

This lovingly converted old music hall, garnished with chandeliers and classical friezes, is a real stayer. It occasionally hosts classic MOR acts: Kool and the Gang or Bill Wyman's Rhythm Kings. In between the visits from international 'names' like Monica Green, you'll find nightly residencies: blues on Mondays, Dixieland jazz on Tuesdays, cover bands on Wednesdays, Saturdays and Sundays, soul on Thursdays and rock on Fridays.

### Raum

*Gran Via 593 (mobile 600 422 318/www.raum.es). Metro Universitat.* **Open** midnight-5am Thur. **Admission** €10. **No credit cards. Map** p338 F8.

Raum's cold industrial decor lends itself well to this weekly electronic night, where the tunes run the gamut from minimal to hard techno to the occasional chunk of deep electro-house. The Thursday slot ensures the crowd – a chatty bunch of expats and locals – come for the tunes rather than to pose among the steel pillars and lunar-style projections.

### Santa Locura

*C/Consell de Cent 294 (93 200 14 66). Metro Passeig de Gràcia.* **Open** midnight-5.30am Thur-Sat. **Admission** (incl 1 drink) €10. **Credit** V. **Map** p342 F8.

Perhaps Barcelona's most extraordinary (if that's the right word) clubbing experience, Santa Locura has three floors filled with weird and wonderful nocturnal pleasures: get married at the bar; watch a Chippendale-style show; plead guilty at the confessional box; and hit the dancefloor to the music of Kylie and Sophie Ellis-Bextor.

### Space Barcelona

*C/Tarragona 141-147 (93 426 84 44/ www.spacebarcelona.com). Metro Tarragona.* **Open** midnight-6am Fri, Sat; 9pm-3am Sun. **Admission** (incl 1 drink) €12 without flyer; €10 with flyer. **No credit cards**. **Map** p341 C7.

Like its superclub rival Pacha, Space tries desperately to cash in on Barcelona's Balearic party aspirations and with equally limited success. A young crowd of pseudo-fashionistas and wannabe diehard clubbers descends en masse to strike poses under the deep lights and pounding bass, or to lean against one of the four bars. Occasional appearances from the likes of Carl Cox keep the brand's reputation safe, or Sunday night's Gay T Dance is great if you're into ripped abs and man-boobs.

## Gràcia

### El Dorado

*Plaça del Sol 4 (93 237 36 96/mobile 607 548 273). Metro Fontana.* **Open** *May-Sept* 7pm-2.30am Mon-Thur; 7pm-3am Fri, Sat. *Oct-Apr* 10pm-2.30am Tue-Thur; 10pm-3am Fri, Sat. **Admission** free. **Credit** MC, V. **Map** p338 G5.

OK, it's not CDLC nor is it La Terrrazza. No, El Dorado is the nightclub equivalent of your disco night at the local pub in some English village. A place for local Gràciencs, it's as unpretentious as they come – a cosy, (sometimes too cosy) bar/dancefloor that doesn't charge a fortune for drinks and unashamedly plays the hits, from local heroes Estopa through to Michael Jackson. Friendly and simple, it's the place you'd go to if you wanted dinner or drinks in Gràcia and followed by an uncomplicated boogie.

### Gusto

*C/Francisco Giner 24 (no phone/www.fatproducts.com com). Metro Diagonal.* **Open** 10pm-2.30am Tue-Thur; 10pm-3am Fri, Sat. **Admission** free. **No credit cards**. **Map** p338 G6.

Gusto gets full to bursting on weekend nights, seemingly due to one rather bizarre feature – past the normal but attractive red-painted front bar, where a DJ plays chilled electronica, a quirky back room lures a young crowd with a floor covered in sand. Actually, the fact that it's Gràcia's funkiest space by a long shot might be another reason.

### KGB

*C/Alegre de Dalt 55 (93 210 59 06/www.salakgb.net). Metro Joanic.* **Open** 3-7am Thur; 1-7am Fri, Sat; 7pm-midnight Sun. **Admission** free before 3am with flyer; (incl 1 drink) €9 after 3am or without flyer. **No credit cards**. **Map** p339 J4.

This aptly named place looks much like it sounds – hardcore. A dark, intimidating space, it was, in its heyday, the rock 'n' roll disco barn capital of the city and the 'after' where Sidecar heads would bolt to at 6am on the weekend. It still remains loud and these days pumps out ear-bleed-inducing techno. It also re-visits its roots somewhat with a wider music policy that includes ska and reggae. Mostly, though, the promoters stick to the tried and tested recipe of any music that makes kids think they're hard: hip hop, punk, hardcore and nu metal.

### Otto Zutz

*C/Lincoln 15 (93 238 07 22/www.grupo-ottozutz. com). FGC Gràcia.* **Open** midnight-5am Tue, Wed; midnight-5.30am Thur-Sat. **Admission** (incl 1 drink) €15. **Credit** AmEx, DC, MC, V. **Map** p338 F4.

Run by the same people as City Hall, Otto Zutz was once *the* nightclub in Barcelona, the place where models, film people and posers used to hang and tread the Bolivian powder marching line. The space hasn't changed much, but the models have moved on elswewhere. It has a similar feel to its more central sister club, but would do well to be a little less wrapped up in *pija* (snobbish) pretentions and a little more concerned with the music. Three floors of an old textile factory feature R&B, hip hop and some electro, but the main focus is on same old not-so-funky house. Not that the uptown boys and girls, who arrive by the Audi-load, seem to care – it's constantly rammed. The monthly Poker Flat parties are the exception to the uninspiring rule.

### Vinilo

*C/Matilde 2 (mobile 626 464 759/http://vinilus.blog spot.com). Metro Fontana.* **Open** 8pm-2.30am Mon-Thur, Sun; 7pm-3am Fri, Sat. **Admission** free. **No credit cards**. **Map** p338 G5.

A venue for grown-ups like this was long overdue in Gràcia, indeed in Barcelona. Local musician Jordi opened this cosy red-velveted bar/café almost a year ago and he's having rip-roaring success. Doubling up as a casual eating place that serves up damn fine savoury and sweet crêpes, Vinilo gets a mention in this section simply because of its immaculate music selection – Sparklehorse, Rufus Wainwright, Antony and the Johnsons, Coco Rosie and the Sleepy Jackson all get good runs here, so too do the Beatles and Pink Floyd. No chill-out in sight and it's a good bet that most of his clients come in for that reason. Some great Japanese animation projections too. A place that comes into its own during the colder months.

## Other areas

### Bikini

*C/Déu i Mata 105, Les Corts (93 322 08 00/ www.bikinibcn.com). Metro Les Corts or Maria Cristina.* **Open** *Club* midnight-5am Wed-Sat; 8.30pm-5am Sun. **Admission** (incl 1 drink) €15. **Credit** MC, V. **Map** p337 C5.

A legendary Barcelona venue, Bikini is hard to find in the soulless streets behind the L'Illa shopping centre, but it's worth seeking out for top-flight gigs by serious musicians of any stripe, from Femi Kuti to the Thievery Corporation, Marianne Faithfull and Amp Fiddler. After the gigs, stay for club nights with house, funk and hip hop on the turntables. On Sunday watch Barça football matches on the big screen from 8.30pm, then party on to the latest dance sounds from 10.30pm.

### Danzatoria

*Avda Tibidabo 61 (93 211 62 61/www.danzatoria-barcelona.com). FGC Avda Tibidabo then 10min walk.* **Open** *Club* 11pm-2.30pm Tue, Wed; 11.30pm-3am Thur-Sat. *Restaurant* 9-11.30pm Tue-Sat. **Admission** free. **Credit** AmEx, DC, MC, V.

The uptown location attracts an upscale crowd to this spectacular converted manor house on a hill overlooking Barcelona. The top floor was recently converted to a restaurant. The hipness factor goes up as you climb the club's glamour-glutted storeys. Preened *pija* flesh is shaken on hothouse dance-floors, or laid across sofas hanging from the ceiling in the chill-out lounges. We've had reports of snotty staff, but who cares when you're lounging in one of the layers of palm-filled gardens, accompanied by some gorgeous creature and some (very expensive) champagne. **Photos** *p256 and p257.*

### Elephant

*Passeig dels Til·lers 1 (93 334 02 58/www.elephantbcn.com). Metro Palau Reial.* **Open** 11.30pm-4am Wed, Thur; 11.30pm-5am Fri, Sat. **Admission** free Wed, Thur; €12 Fri, Sat. **Credit** MC, V. **Map** 337 A2.

If you have a Porsche and a model girlfriend, this is where you meet your peers. Housed in a converted mansion, Elephant is as elegant and hi-design as its customers. The big attraction is the outdoor bar and terrace dancefloor – though the low-key, low-volume (due to neighbours' complaints) house music doesn't inspire much hands-in-the-air action.

### Mirablau

*Plaça Doctor Andreu 1, Tibidabo (93 418 58 79). FGC Avda Tibidabo then Tramvia Blau.* **Open** 11am-4.30am Mon-Thur; 11am-5.30am Fri-Sun. **Admission** free. **Credit** V.

It doesn't get any more uptown than this, geographically and socially. Located at the top of Tibidabo, this small bar is packed with the high rollers of Barcelona, from local footballers living on the hill to international businessmen on the company card, as well as young *pijos* stopping by for a drink before heading off to nearby Danzatoria on daddy's ride. Apart from the blaring cheesy Spanish pop, its only attraction is the breathtaking view.

### Universal

*C/Marià Cubí 182 bis-184 (93 201 35 96/www.grupocostaeste.com). FGC Muntaner.* **Open** 11pm-3.30am Mon-Thur; 11pm-5am Fri, Sat. **Credit** AmEx, MC, V. **Admission** free. **Map** p338 E5.

One of a very few clubs in the city that caters to an older, well-dressed crowd, Universal doesn't charge admission, but the drink prices are steep as a result. Recent renovations by the designer of the Salsitas chain have brought slide projections in the upstairs chill-out area, along with a sharper look downstairs. Later, the music moves from downtempo to soft house, which works the crowd up to a gentle shimmy.

## Poblenou

### Razzmatazz

*C/Almogàvers 122 (93 320 82 00/www.salarazzmatazz.com). Metro Bogatell or Marina.* **Open** 1-5am Fri, Sat. **Admission** (incl 1 drink) €12. **Credit** V. **Map** p343 L10.

Skinny jeans, battered Converse and a heavy dose of party-rock dominate this warehouse superclub, and while some of the punters are a bit young and the toilets a bit vile, line-ups are on the ball, diverse and international. As it's essentially five clubs in one, if you're tired of 2 ManyDjs or Miss Kittin in the main Razz Room, you can head upstairs to check out Queens of Noize, Four Tet or Tiga playing The Loft. It's also one of the city's best venues for live music, with acts from Arctic Monkeys to Queens of the Stone Age to, no word of a lie, Bananarama, producing awesome crowd-surfing mayhem.

## Outer limits

### Pacha

*Avda Doctor Marañon 17 (93 334 32 33/www.clubpachabcn.com). Metro Zona Universitaria.* **Open** 11.30pm-4.30am Mon-Sat; 9pm-3am Sun. **Admission** (incl 1 drink) €15. **Credit** MC, V.

When Pacha was set to open in Barcelona a few years back, the queues of potential barstaff were so long that they made the evening news. Such is the power of the global clubbing giant that armies of tourists, out-of-towners and locals, many deluded about their party-animal status, continue rolling up for fair sound quality, a so-so venue and heaps of attitude. Regular sets from David Guetta, Paul Oakenfold and Jeff Mills etc are more worthwhile.

### Sala Salamandra

*Avda Carrilet 301, L'Hospitalet (93 337 06 02/www.salamandra.cat). Metro A.Carrilet.* **Open** Midnight-5am Fri-Sat. **Admission** *Gigs* Prices vary, see website for details. *Club* €7 after 2am. **No credit cards**.

It's often lamented that some of Barcelona's best home-grown acts are hard to see live in Barcelona outside of festivals. But that's not strictly true. If you're happy to travel 30 minutes on the metro's red line to L'Hospitalet, you'll find a 500-person venue, which doubles as a nightclub, that regularly hosts the cream of local artists, such as Macaco, Muchachito Bombo Infierno, Kinky Beat, as well as Spanish acts like Canteca de Macao and Amparanoia. Local and visiting DJs take over afterwards. It also actively promotes emerging Catalan musicians, so you may well discover the next big thing too. Drawing mainly a local crowd, the atmosphere's unprententious and the drinks cheaper than elsewhere.

# Performing Arts

Music, maestro.

## Classical Music & Opera

Casals, Caballé, Carreras – Barcelona has produced its fair share of musical maestros over the years, but, until recently, places to actually go and see concerts were scarce. This all changed with the addition of the uncompromisingly modern concert hall L'Auditori and the appearance of a number of smaller venues, including the Auditori Winterthur, a small, charming outpost in the otherwise-soulless business and university district. Barcelona's two most venerable institutions are also experiencing something of a renaissance: the Liceu, impressively reconstructed after the disastrous blaze of 1992, has begun to take more risks with its previously conservative programming policy, and the stunning Palau de la Música is undergoing a facelift that will soon see the addition of a subterranean 500-seat auditorium. These venue changes have been supplemented by a subtle switch in repertoire. The canon still reigns, of course. But, as a younger generation of cultural programmers takes charge, newer work has also found an audience. You no longer have to be dead to get your music heard.

The last few years have seen the deaths of two leading Catalan composers – Joaquim Homs and Xavier Montsalvatge – leaving Joan Guinjoan as Catalonia's most important living composer. Another local, manic genius, Carles Santos, composes, directs and performs in surreal operatic-theatrical performances that combine sex, psychology and sopranos (*see p262* **Carles Santos**).

The main musical season runs September to June. During this time the city orchestra, the **OBC**, plays weekly at the **Auditori**, while the **Liceu** hosts a different opera every three or four weeks. Both the Auditori and the **Palau de la Música** hold several concert cycles of various genres, either programmed by the venues or by independent promoters (Ibercamera and Euroconcert are the most important). Several festivals are also staged, the foremost of which are the **Festival de Música Antiga** (*see p218*) and the **Nous Sons** festival of contemporary music (*see p216*).

In summer, the focus moves. Various museums, among them the **Museu Marítim** (*see p112*), the **Fundació Miró** (*see p118*), the **Museu Barbier-Mueller** (*see p99*) and **La Pedrera** (*see p127*), hold small outdoor concerts, and there are weekly events in several of the city's parks (*see p220* **Clàssics als Parcs**). More serious musical activity, though, follows its audience and heads up the coast, to major festivals in the towns of Perelada, Cadaqués, Toroella de Montgrí and Vilabertrán.

### INFORMATION AND TICKETS

The monthly *Informatiu Musical*, published by Amics de la Música (93 268 01 22, www.amicsmusica.org), lists concerts in all genres. Pick up a copy at tourist offices and record shops. Weekly entertainment guide *Guía del Ocio* has a music section; both *El País* and *La Vanguardia* list forthcoming concerts. The council website, www.bcn.es, also has details. Tickets for most major venues can be bought by phone or online from venues, or from **Tel-entrada** or **Servi-Caixa** (*see p214*).

## Venues

In addition to the venues below, several churches also hold concerts. The most spectacular is **Santa Maria del Mar** (*see p103*) in the Born, whose tall, ghostly interior exemplifies the Gothic intertwining of music, light and spirituality. Concerts include everything from Renaissance music to gospel. There's a monthly free organ concert at the cathedral, usually (but not always) held on the second Wednesday of the month. Other churches with regular programmes include **Santa Maria del Pi**, **Sant Felip Neri**, **Santa Anna** and the monastery in **Pedralbes**.

### L'Auditori

*C/Lepant 150, Eixample (93 247 93 00/ www.auditori.org). Metro Marina.* **Open** *Information* 8am-10pm daily. *Box office* noon-9pm Mon-Sat; 1hr before performance Sun. Closed Aug. **Tickets** vary. **Credit** MC, V. **Map** p343 K9.

Serious music lovers in Barcelona prefer to see concerts at Rafael Moneo's sleek L'Auditori: what it lacks in architectural warmth, it more than makes up for in acoustics and facilities. The 2,400-seat hall has provided the city with a world-class music venue and a home to its orchestra, the OBC, now under the baton of conductor Ernest Martínez

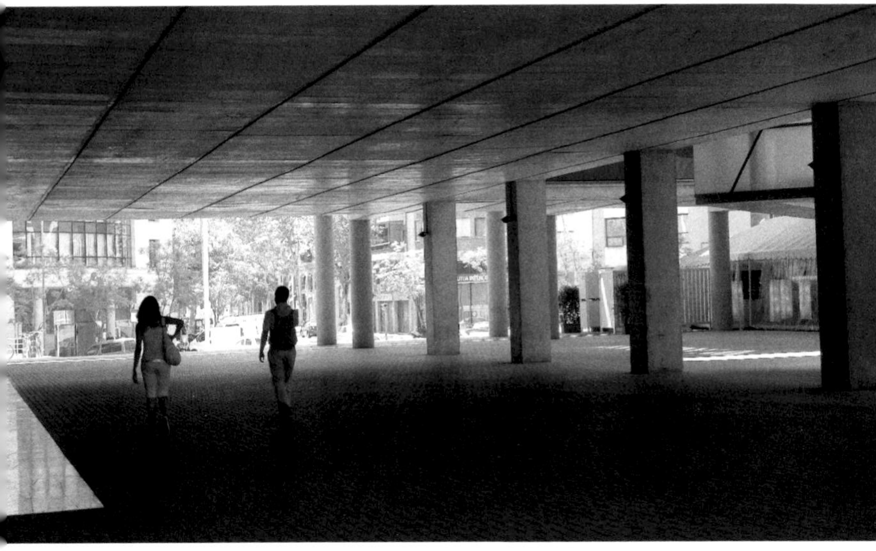

**L'Auditori**, the world-class music venue. *See p260.*

Izquierdo. Highlights for 2007 include Bach's *Passion in March* and a season of Russian music in May. The Museu de la Música is expected to open here soon, as is a new 600-seat auditorium, which will add more variety to an already-impressive programme that covers not just classical music, but jazz, contemporary and world music. A late-night bus service connects the Auditori with Plaça Catalunya after evening performances.

### Auditori Winterthur

*L'Illa, Avda Diagonal 547, Les Corts (93 290 11 02/www.winterthur.es). Metro Maria Cristina.*
**Open** *Information* 8.30am-1.30pm, 3-5.30pm Mon-Fri. Closed Aug. **Tickets** vary. **Credit** varies. **Map** p337 C4.

A charming, intimate venue in the unlikely setting of L'Illa, a monolithic shopping centre. Though it hosts few concerts, they're generally of a high quality; the Schubert cycle and series of song recitals, both annual events, are well worth catching.

### Gran Teatre del Liceu

*La Rambla 51-59, Barri Gòtic (93 485 99 13/tickets 902 53 33 53/www.liceubarcelona.com). Metro Liceu.*
**Open** *Information* 11am-2pm, 3-8pm Mon-Fri. *Box office* 2-8pm Mon-Fri; 1hr before performance Sat, Sun. Closed 2wks Aug. **Tickets** vary. **Credit** AmEx, MC, V. **Map** p345 A/B5.

The impressive speed with which the Liceu was resurrected after a fire, as well as the meticulous recreation of the original 1847 design, is indicative of the central importance the city's opera house has in the cultural life of Barcelona. Compared with the restrained façade, the 2,292-seat auditorium is an elegant, classical affair of red plush, gold leaf and ornate carvings, but with mod cons that include seat-back subtitles in various languages that complement the Catalan surtitles above the stage. Under the stewardship of artistic director Joan Matabosch and musical director Sebastian Wiegle, the Liceu has consolidated its programming policy, which mixes in-house productions (with occasional forays into the cutting-edge with productions directed by the likes of Calixto Bieito and the Fura dels Baus) with co-productions with leading opera houses in Europe, as well as major international dance companies. The large basement bar hosts pre-performance talks, recitals, children's shows and other musical events; the Espai Liceu is a 50-seat auditorium with a regular programme of screenings of past operas.

### Palau de la Música Catalana

*C/Sant Francesc de Paula 2, Sant Pere (93 295 72 00/www.palaumusica.org). Metro Urquinaona.*
**Open** *Box office* 10am-9pm Mon-Sat; 1hr before performance Sun. Closed Aug for concerts.
**Tickets** vary. **Credit** MC, V. **Map** p344 D/E3.

This visual explosion of Modernista architectural flights of fancy is on the UNESCO list of World Heritage sites. Built in 1908 by Lluís Domènech i Montaner, it is certainly one of the most spectacular music venues anywhere in the world. A recent extension, adding a terrace, a restaurant and a subterranean hall, has been controversial: concert-goers approve, but architecture critics have been less sure. The palau has seen some of the best international performers over the years, including the likes of Leonard Bernstein and Daniel Barenboim.

# The piano man

Although, in many respects, Carles Santos typifies the Catalan preference for spectacle over text, his work is much more subtle and expressive than many of his contemporaries whose flamboyance all too often serves to dazzle and distract the audience lest they question what the show is actually about.

Invariably described as 'eclectic' or 'impossible to classify', Santos, who hails from Vinaròs, just south of the Catalan border, was born in 1940 and trained as a pianist at the Liceu conservatory in Barcelona and later in Paris and the United States where he developed a taste for modern composers such as John Cage and Stockhausen. But his career, in what might be termed 'musical spectacles', began in the 1960s when he worked with Joan Brossa on the Concert Irregular to commemorate the 75th anniversary of the birth of Joan Miró which was performed in Saint Paul de Vence, Barcelona and in New York. Around the same time he began working in film as a director, screenwriter and composer making short and feature-length films as well as documentaries.

Since the 1970s he has dedicated himself almost exclusively to performing his own music which, in its use of repetitive figures, is sometimes reminiscent of Philip Glass. He has always emphasised live performance over recording and has sought ways of making modern music more accessible to a non-specialised audience. With his heightened visual sense, over the years he has developed a distinctive, though distinctly Catalan, theatrical style of his own. Whacky and surrealist, he mixes motifs of food and sex and presents his audience with extra-ordinary stage sets and fantastical costumes designed by his long-time professional partner Mariaelena Roqué. It is spectacular, but it has the depth and nuance so often absent from this type of theatre. In Santos's case the spectacle always has a point and the point is the music, and what happens on stage is at the service of the music and not the other way round. In *La Pantera Imperial*, for example, his homage to Bach, Santos plays a Bach concerto accompanied by two other pianists and a pianola. In one passage the tenor Antoni Comas sings an aria while a dominatrix holds him by the collar and repeatedly plunges his head into a vat of water. Comas emerges each time, dripping but still singing: a triumph of the human spirit over brutality.

## Orchestras & ensembles

### La Capella Reial de Catalunya, Le Concert des Nations & Hespèrion XXI

*Information 93 580 60 69/www.alia-vox.com.*

The popularity of Catalonia's rich heritage in early music is due in large part to the indefatigable Jordi Savall, the driving force behind these three interlinked groups which, between them, play around 300 concerts a year worldwide. La Capella Reial specialises in Catalan and Spanish Renaissance and baroque music; Le Concert des Nations is a period-instrument ensemble playing orchestral and symphonic work from 1600 to 1850; and Hespèrion XXI plays pre-1800 European music.

### Orfeó Català

*Information 93 295 72 00/www.palaumusica.org.*

The Orfeó Català, which began life as one of 150 choral groups that sprang up as part of the patriotic and social movements at the end of the 19th century, was banned by Franco as a focus of Catalan nationalism. While it's no longer as pre-eminent as it once was, the group still stages around 25 performances a year, giving a cappella concerts, as well as providing a choir for the Orquestra Simfònica and other Catalan orchestras. The largely amateur group also includes a small professional nucleus, the Cor de Cambra del Palau de la Música, which gives 50 performances a year.

### Orquestra Simfònica de Barcelona Nacional de Catalunya (OBC)

*Information 93 247 93 00/www.obc.es.*

Representing both Barcelona and Catalonia, the awkwardly named Orquestra Simfònica de Barcelona is the busiest orchestra in the city, performing at the Auditori almost every weekend of the season. Under the right baton, the Simfònica can excel, though it's difficult to know who wields it, with many different conductors performing in a single season. The orchestra provides a fairly standard gallop through the symphonic repertoire, though the artistic director (and principal conductor) Ernest Martínez Izquierdo has brought in a more adventurous programme. The orchestra is also committed to new Catalan composers, commissioning two works a year and giving a handful of others their first performance.

### Orquestra Simfònica i Cor del Gran Teatre del Liceu

*Information 93 485 99 13/www.liceubarcelona.com.*

Upcoming operatic productions for the 2007 season include Richard Wagner's *Der Fliegender Holländer* in April and Vincenzo Bellini's *Norma* in July. There's also a programme of concerts and recitals, including sessions linked to the current opera, and half a dozen mini operas for children; in 2007 these include *The Magic Flute* and *The Superbarber of Seville*.

### Orquestra Simfònica del Vallès

*Information 93 727 03 00/www.osvalles.com.*

This run-of-the-mill provincial orchestra, based in the nearby town of Sabadell, performs regularly in Barcelona, often at the Palau de la Música, where it plays a dozen symphonic concerts each season.

## Contemporary music

### AvuiMúsica

*Associació Catalana de Compositors, Passeig Colom 6, space 4, Barri Gòtic (93 268 37 19/ www.accompositors.com). Metro Jaume I.* **Open** *Information* 9.30am-1.30pm Mon-Fri. **Tickets** €9; €4.50 concessions. **No credit cards**. **Map** p345 D7.

A season of small-scale contemporary concerts run by the Association of Catalan Composers at various venues around the city. Members of the association are well represented, and around half the works each year have not been played in public before.

### Barcelona 216

*Information 93 487 87 81.*

A small ensemble with a strong commitment to contemporary music of all types, including written compositions and more experimental works.

### CAT

*Travessia de Sant Antoni 6-8, Gràcia (93 218 44 85/ www.tradicionarius.com). Metro Fontana.* **Open** *Gigs* about 10pm Thur, Fri. Closed Aug. **Admission** €8-€10. **No credit cards**. **Map** p338 G5.

The Centre Artesà Tradicionàrius promotes traditional Catalan music and culture and hosts a number of festivals, including a showcase of folk music and dance staged between January and April. The centre's concerts and workshops also cover indigenous music from Spain as well as other countries.

### Diapasón

*Information 60 508 10 60/telungc@hotmail.com.*

A septet specialising in Satie and more playful works of contemporary classical music led by composer/performer Domènec González de la Rubia.

### Festival d'Òpera de Butxaca i Noves Creacions

*Information 93 301 84 85/mobile 659 454 879/www.festivaloperabutxaca.org.* **Date** Nov.

A successful series of small-scale chamber operas performed in various venues, including the former anatomy theatre of the Royal Academy of Medicine.

### Fundació Joan Miró

*Parc de Montjuïc, Montjuïc (93 443 94 70/www.bcn.fjmiro.es). Metro Paral·lel then Funicular de Montjuïc/bus 50, 55.* **Open** Mid June-July *Box office* 1hr before performance Thur. **Tickets** €6; €15 for 3 concerts. **Credit** MC, V. **Map** p341 C11.

**Gran Teatre del Liceu.** *See P261.*

Arts & Entertainment

When the rest of the city gets too hot, head up to the Fundació Miró for its annual festival of jazz, improv and other performance-based music. It's not the greatest venue in the city, but the electric performances soon dispel any discomfort. Some concerts take place on the roof terrace.

### Gràcia Territori Sonor

*Information 93 237 37 37/www.gracia-territori.com.*
The main focus of this dynamic, tirelessly creative collective is the month-long LEM festival in autumn: held in various venues in Gràcia, it's a rambling, eclectic series of musical happenings, much of them experimental, improvised and electronic, and most of them free. The concerts are supplemented by dance performances, sound installations and poetry readings. The larger, more formal events are held at MACBA, La Pedrera and CaixaForum.

### Nous Sons – Músiques Contemporànies

*Information 93 247 93 00/www.auditori.org.*
**Date** 10-29 Mar 2007.
Previously known as the festival of contemporary music, New Sounds is an interesting burst of new music that continues to evolve yearly, and features national and international ensembles. The 12 or so concerts range from symphonic and chamber music to experimental, improvisation and free jazz.

### Trio Kandinsky

*Information 93 301 98 97/www.triokandinsky.com.*
Formed in 1999, the Trio Kandinsky has an excellent reputation, performing contemporary repertoire.

# Theatre & Dance

Catalan theatre thrives on spectacle, often at the expense of text. The big names such as La Fura dels Baus, Els Comediants and Tricicle, for all their undoubted talents, are starting to look past their sell-by date, although all are in receipt of what appear to be subsidies for life from the Generalitat. Physical theatre grew out of the Franco years, when Catalan was banned, and the lack of text has aided these companies' international success as it removes the language barrier. Calixto Bieito, renowned for his wildly polemical interpretations of *Hamlet* and *Don Giovanni*, thrives on controversy. Theatre is cliquish everywhere, but in Catalonia it often seems that the same coterie of directors and performers get all the work, whether at the Teatre Nacional or in the latest TV soap.

Although Barcelona has many thriving contemporary dance companies, there are few major dance venues, and most companies spend a large amount of their time touring. Performers such as Pina Bausch and the Compañía Nacional de Danza (directed by the revered Nacho Duato) have played to sell-out crowds in the Teatre Nacional and the Liceu, while the Teatre Nacional has a resident company led by Sol Picó, and the Teatre Lliure hosts quite a lot of new work. However, it's generally difficult for companies to find big audiences.

Innovative companies such as Sol Picó and Mar Gómez usually run a new show every year, as do emblematic, influential companies such as Metros, Mudances and Gelabert-Azzopardi.

### SEASONS AND FESTIVALS

The **Grec Festival** (*see p220*) brings in major international acts, although of late there has been more emphasis on local acts. It is held at venues all over the city but the open-air Grec amphitheatre is magical on a summer night. New companies have a chance to launch their work at the **Mostra de Teatre** (93 436 32 62, www.mostradeteatredebarcelona.com) in October and November, when they're assigned two nights apiece and judged by a panel of directors. The **Marató de l'Espectacle** at the Mercat de les Flors, C/Llieda 59, Poble (information Associació Marató de l'Espectacle 93 268 18 68/www.marato.com) runs from June to July and is a showcase for new talent on nights of non-stop five-minute performances. **Dies de Dansa** (*see p220*) offers three days of national and international dance in public sites such as the Port, the CCCB or the MACBA.

### TICKETS AND TIMES

Main shows start around 9-10.30pm, although many theatres have earlier (and cheaper) shows at 6-7pm on Saturdays. On Sundays there are morning matinées aimed at family audiences; most theatres are dark on Mondays. Advance bookings are best made through Servi-Caixa or Tel-entrada (*see p214*). The best places to find information are *Guía del Ocio* and the *cartelera* (listings) pages of the newspapers. Online, check www.teatral.net and www.teatrebcn.com; for dance, try www.dancespain.com. You can also visit Canal Cultura in the pull-down menu on www.bcn.es.

## Major venues

Large-scale commercial productions are shown in the vast **Teatre Condal** (Avda Paral·lel 91, Poble Sec, 93 442 31 32), home to the popular Tricicle mime group; the **Borràs** (Plaça Urquinaona 9, Eixample, 93 412 15 82), and the **Tívoli** (C/Casp 10-12, Eixample, 93 412 20 63), which hosts giant productions such as the musical *Fame*. For more information on these two venues, see www.grupbalana.com.
The **Monumental** bullring (*see p116*) and the **Barcelona Teatre Musical** (C/Guàrdia Urbana s/n, Montjuïc, 93 423 64 63) are used

for mega-shows in the off season. Ballet and modern-dance troupes occasionally appear at the **Liceu** and the **Teatre Nacional**, while cultural centres such as the **CCCB** (*see p107*) are often used for contemporary dance, as is the Grec theatre. The Liceu also stages children's shows and mini-operas both in the main house and in the Auditori de Cornellà.

### Mercat de les Flors

*Plaça Margarida Xirgú, C/Lleida 59, Poble Sec (93 426 18 75/www.mercatflors.org). Metro Poble Sec.* **Box office** 1hr before show. Advance tickets also available from Palau de la Virreina. **Tickets** vary. **No credit cards. Map** p341 C10.

The former flower market has been converted into a theatre city (Ciutat de Teatre) housing three performance spaces, making the Mercat one of the most innovative venues in town. Performances here experiment with unusual formats and mix new technologies, pop culture and performing arts, as well as staging more conventional theatre and providing a venue for jazz.

### Teatre Lliure

*Plaça Margarida Xirgú, Montjuïc (93 289 27 70/ www.teatrelliure.com). Metro Poble Sec.* **Box office** 11am-3pm, 4.30-8pm Mon-Fri; 2hrs before show Sat, Sun. **Tickets** €12-€16 Tue, Wed; €16-€22 Thur-Sun; concessions 25% discount. **Credit** MC, V. **Map** p341 C10.

One of the most prestigious venues for serious theatre. Under director Àlex Rigola the Lliure has tended towards the attention-seeking (*Hamlet* with no text) or the clichéd (*Richard III* in a mafia setting). Bigger shows are subtitled in English on Wednesdays.

### Teatre Nacional de Catalunya (TNC)

*Plaça de les Arts 1, Eixample (93 306 57 00/www.tnc.es). Metro Glòries.* **Box office** 3-9pm Tue-Sun. **Tickets** €15-€25; €10-€15 concessions. **Credit** AmEx, DC, MC, V. **Map** p343 K9.

The Generalitat-funded theatre designed by Ricardo Bofill boasts three superb performance spaces. Its main stage promotes large-scale Catalan and Spanish classical theatre, while more contemporary European theatre and works by new writers are normally staged in the more experimental Sala Tallers. New director Sergi Belbel opened the 2006-07 season with the Catalan classic *En Pólvora* by Àngel Guimerà and a visit from Sweden's Cullberg Ballet. The Projecte Tdansa gives young dancers their first professional experience; Sol Picó's excellent troupe is the resident dance company.

### Teatre Poliorama

*La Rambla 115, Barri Gòtic (93 317 75 99/ www.teatrepoliorama.com). Metro Catalunya.* **Box office** 5-8pm Tue; 5-8.30pm Wed-Sat; 5-7pm Sun. Open till 9.30pm Wed-Sat for same day purchase. Closed 2wks Aug. **Tickets** varies. **Credit** MC, V. **Map** p344 B3.

Run by private producers 3xtr3s, this once adventurous theatre now stages mainly mainstream comedies and musicals, plus the odd piece of serious theatre. It also stages shows for children.

### Teatre Romea

*C/Hospital 51, Raval (information 93 301 55 04/tickets 902 10 12 12/www.fundacioromea.org). Metro Liceu.* **Box office** 5-8pm Tue-Sat. **Performances** 9pm Tue-Fri; 6.30pm, 10pm Sat; 6.30pm Sun. **Tickets** €16-€24. **Credit** (phone bookings only) AmEx, DC, MC, V. **Map** p344 A4.

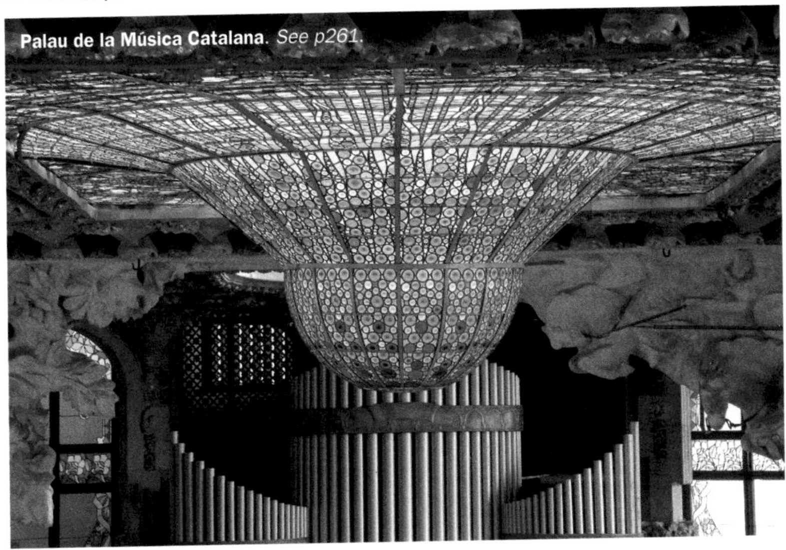
**Palau de la Música Catalana**. *See p261.*

# Classical Catalans

## Montserrat Caballé (1933-)

**Make mine a treble** Caballé is Barcelona's world-famous soprano and reputedly the highest-paid female operatic singer of all time. Also known as *La Superba*.

**Key signature** Her trademark is an exquisite floating pianissimo.

**Claim to fame** In 1965 she filled in for a pregnant Marilyn Horne in the title role of Donizetti's *Lucrezia Borgia* at Carnegie Hall. The next day's front-page headline of the *New York Times* read: CALLAS + TEBALDI = CABALLÉ.

**Another one bites the dust** Her duet *Barcelona* with Freddie Mercury was a chart hit but rejected at the last minute as the theme song for the 1992 Olympics.

**Hold it** During her morning breathing exercises she measures how long it takes her to exhale completely. Two minutes is not unusual.

## José Carreras (1946-)

**Who** The smallest of the Three Tenors. Also known as the 'Anti-Divo' for his mild demeanour.

**High note** This local lad from Sants sang at the Liceu opera house even before his voice broke.

**Spotted** His first tenor role in *Norma* was tiny but enough to convince fellow *barcelonina*, Caballé, to take him on as her leading man.

**Fast start** By the age of 28 he had sung the tenor lead in 24 different operas and had made his debut at the world's greatest opera houses.

**Diminished interval** Diagnosed with leukaemia in 1987 and given a one-in-ten chance of survival.

**Crescendo** The 1990 World Cup concert in Rome with Plácido Domingo and Luciano Pavarotti was originally conceived to raise money for the José Carreras International Leukaemia Foundation. The Three Tenors went on to sing operatic footie songs for three more World Cups and made a mint.

## Pau Casals (1876-1973)

**Who** The king of string. Casals single-handedly lifted the cello from mere accompaniment to expressive solo instrument.

**Gestation of a genius** Legend has it that Casals was conceived when Brahms began composing his *Quartet in B-flat major* and that he was born when it was completed.

**Opening movement** An infant prodigy, Casals played the piano, flute and violin by the time he was four years old.

**Unstrung** Casal's first cello was made from a dried gourd, a broomstick and some cat gut.

**Strung out** At the age of 95 Casals famously continued to practice six hours a day because he thought he was still 'making progress'.

**Coda** Fiercely opposed to the Franco regime in Spain, Casals died in exile in Puerto Rico at the age of 96. He commented: "The love of one's country is a splendid thing. But why should love stop at the border?"

## Enric Granados (1867-1916)

**Who** Composer, virtuoso pianist and founder of 19th-century Spain's romantic piano movement.

**Also known as** The Spanish Chopin.

**High note** Granados' crowning achievement was his piano suite *Goyescas*, inspired by the paintings of Francisco Goya. They were so popular he expanded them to form an opera of the same title, produced in New York in 1916.

**Low note** The opera's *Nightingale* aria was the inspiration for slushy crooner hit, *Bésame Mucho*.

**Coda** On a return trip from New York, his ship was torpedoed by a German U-boat while crossing the English Channel. Granados made it on to a raft, but leapt back in the water to save his wife. He drowned in the attempt, aged 49.

The notorious Calixto Bieito is the artistic director of the Teatre Romea. The theatre looks to contemporary European theatre for inspiration; the 2007 programme includes a stage production of Javier Cercas' *Soldados de Salamina* and Michel Houellebecq's *Plataforma*.

## Alternative theatres

Things are not looking good for smaller venues; a few have had to close lately, tired of fighting for funding and audiences. However, theatres such as the **Nou Tantarantana** (C/Flors 22, Raval, 93 441 70 22, www.tantarantana.com), the **Espai Escènic Joan Brossa** (C/Allada-Vermell 13, Born, 93 310 13 64, www.espaibrossa.com), **L'Antic Teatre** (C/Verdaguer i Callis 12, Barri Gòtic, 93 315 23 54, www.lanticteatre.com) and the **Versus Teatre** (C/Castillejos 179, Eixample, 93 232 31 84, www.versusteatre.com) often produce interesting work. The **Teatre de la Riereta** (C/Reina Amalia 3, Raval, 93 442 98 44, www.lariereta.es) hosts a few English works, as does the **Teatre Llantiol** (C/Riereta 7, Raval, 93 329 90 09, www.llantiol.com).

### Sala Beckett

*C/Alegre de Dalt 55 bis, Gràcia (93 284 53 12/ www.salabeckett.com). Metro Joanic.* **Box office** from 8pm Wed-Sat; from 5pm Sun. Closed Aug. **Tickets** €6-€16; €4-€12 concessions. **No credit cards**. **Map** p339 J4.

This small venue was founded by the Samuel Beckett-inspired Teatro Fronterizo group, run by playwright José Sanchis Sinisterra. He's no longer based at the theatre, but his influence prevails. The theatre also hosts the annual Opera de Butxaca (pocket opera) festival.

## Theatre companies

As well as those reviewed below, companies to check include the satirical, camp **Chanclettes**, and the **Compañia Nacional Clásica** for versions of the Spanish masters. For English-language theatre, look out for the **Jocular** company and **Black Custard Theatre**.

### Els Comediants

*www.comediants.com.*

Now a national institution, Els Comediants has its roots in commedia dell'arte and street performance; its mix of mime, circus, music, storytelling and fireworks is as likely to appear on the street to celebrate a national holiday as at any major theatre festival.

### Compañia Mar Gómez

*www.danzamargomez.com.*

A wonderful mix of contemporary dance and theatre with a wicked sense of humour, fun images and good music.

### La Cubana

*www.lacubana.es.*

One of the best, although its recent attempt to stage a show in English fell flat. Both satirical and spectacular, La Cubana's shows have a cartoonish quality, using multimedia effects, camp music and audience participation.

### La Fura dels Baus

*www.lafura.com.*

Never mind the plot, just get your kit off, seems to be the motto at La Fura. Barcelona's bad boy company has been going for 27 years and has toured the world with polemical and stimulating shows such as the infamous *XXX*, a porn cabaret inspired by the Marquis de Sade.

### Els Joglars

*www.elsjoglars.com.*

Darkly satirical, Els Joglars has been at the forefront of political theatre for 30-odd years. Albert Boadella, the company's founder and leader, was imprisoned under the Franco regime for his political stance, and he was recently among the founders of an anti-nationalist Catalan political party.

### Tricicle

*www.tricicle.com.*

Local boys Carles Sans, Paco Mir and Joan Gràcia founded this mime trio 25 years ago. The goofy, clean-cut humour appeals to the Spanish taste for slapstick; they're not above the odd Benny Hill moment of cross-dressing or chase sequences.

## Dance companies

In addition to those listed below, groups worth seeing include popular and established company **Metros**, the collective **La Caldera**, newer group **Búbulus** (www.bubulus.net) and Toni Mira's company **Nats Nus** (www.natsnus.com). Its highly successful offshoot **Nats Nens** produces contemporary dance shows for children.

### Compañia Metros

*www.metrosdansa.com.*

Metros got rave reviews when it put on its version of *Carmen* at London's Sadlers Wells in 2006.

### Erre que erre

*www.errequeerredanza.net.*

Completely dedicated to its art, this company of younger dancers gives fresh, original performances, with well-measured doses of excellent theatre. It tours regularly, and gives workshops.

### Gelabert-Azzopardi

*www.gelabertazzopardi.com.*

The duo of Barcelona's Cesc Gelabert and Londoner Lydia Azzopardi is at its peak and displays an extraordinary emotional range and versatility. Its new production *Orion* opens at the Lliure early in 2007.

### Mal Pelo

*www.malpelo.com.*

Mal Pelo has a particular Catalan sensibility, creating expressive, earthy and somewhat-surreal choreographies.

### Marta Carrasco

*www.martacarrasco.com.*

Carrasco has choreographed many plays and musicals, and is regarded as one of Catalonia's finest dancers.

### Mudances

*www.margarit-mudances.com.*

Director Àngels Margarit has been growing in stature as a choreographer for the past decade, producing highly structured work with creative use of video. Mudances often holds children's shows.

### Raravis-Andrés Corchero-Rosa Muñoz

*http://raravisdanza.com.*

This is the dancers' dance company, but its experimental and intimate style can make it a little difficult for the uninitiated.

### Sol Picó

*www.solpico.com.*

Through perserverance, charisma, hard work and lots of energy, Sol Picó and her company are probably the best known outside Catalonia.

Teatre Nacional de Catalunya. *See p265.*

## Flamenco

Bar-restaurant **TiriTiTran** (C/Buenos Aires 28, Gràcia, 93 410 86 77, www.tiritittran.com) is a favourite with flamenco aficionados; impromptu performances often happen at weekends, with concerts every Wednesday. The Friday night flamenco shows at the restaurant **Nervion** (C/Princesa 2, Born, 93 315 21 03) seem to be aimed at tourists, but it is a lot cheaper than the established *tablaos*: if you don't eat, entry is €12, which includes a drink. **Flamenco Barcelona** (C/Marquès de Barberà 6, Raval, 93 443 66 80) is a shop specialising in flamenco paraphernalia and music, with exhibitions and occasional concerts. It also offers flamenco guitar, singing and dance courses.

### El Tablao de Carmen

*Poble Espanyol, Avda Marquès de Comillas, Montjuïc (93 325 68 95/www.tablaodecarmen.com). Metro Espanya.* **Open** 7pm-2am Tue-Sun. **Shows** 7.45pm, 10pm Tue-Sun. Closed 2wks Jan. **Admission** *show & 1 drink* €31; *show & dinner* €59. **Credit** AmEx, DC, MC, V. **Map** p341 A/B9.

This rather sanitised version of the traditional flamenco *tablao* sits in faux-Andalucían surroundings in the Poble Espanyol. You'll find both established stars and new young talent, displaying the various styles of flamenco singing, dancing and music. The emphasis is on panache rather than passion, so you might prefer your flamenco with a bit more spit and a little less polish. You must reserve in advance (up to a week ahead in summer), which will allow you to enter the Poble Espanyol free after 7pm.

### Los Tarantos

*Plaça Reial 17, Barri Gòtic (93 319 17 89/ www.masimas.com). Metro Liceu.* **Open** *Flamenco show* 8.30pm, 9.30pm, 10.30pm daily. **Admission** €5. **Credit** MC, V. **Map** p342 B6.

This flamenco *tablao* has presented many top stars over the years, as well as offering some rumba catalana. It now caters mainly to the tourist trade.

## Dance schools & workshops

Many of the major companies allow you to join their own classes for short periods, but call to check first. Some, like **Mudances** and **Lanónima Imperial**, also run special workshops. The **Institut del Teatre** runs summer classes, but they're often expensive. Two good spots for contemporary dance classes are **Area Espai de Dansa i Creació** (C/Alegre de Dalt 55, Gràcia, 93 210 78 50, www.areadansa.com) and its neighbour **Company & Company** (C/Alegre de Dalt 57, Gràcia, 93 210 59 72, www.companyscp.com). A more complete list of dance schools in Barcelona can be found at www.dancespain.com/schools.html.

# Sport & Fitness

More than just a Barça.

Take a stroll through any square, park or beach in Barcelona and you'll soon find yourself surrounded by suntanned rollerblading yuppies, flying skateboards owned by spotty teens and venerable 'third-agers', packed tightly into their pink lycra cycling shorts as they happily relive the previous day's Tour de France stage. The Catalans love their sport, and it is a passion that transcends social class, age and background. Of course, football reigns supreme, and every *barri* in town has its own local team and most (nearly always male) *barcelonins* like a run-out at weekends, either in six-a-side matches at the numerous indoor gyms around town, or on the dusty wastelands that pass for football pitches in this grass-challenged city.

Since the Olympics, the city has become a popular venue for international events: the Champions League Final in 1999 and the World Swimming Championship in 2003, to name just two. The racetrack, at Montmeló, a few kilometres outside Barcelona is the location for the Spanish Grand Prix and a host of other motorsport events, and the sporting legacy of the Olympics can still be found at spectacular venues like the Estadi Olímpic and the Palau Sant Jordi.

The ultimate symbol of the Catalan love of sport, however, is FC Barcelona. The fetishistic love of the *blaugrana* (burgundy and red) shirt, still 'untainted' by commercial sponsorship, and pride in the Camp Nou, Europe's biggest football stadium, make membership of the club de rigueur for any self-respecting football fan (unless they are one of those stick-in-the muds who prefer to support Espanyol).

## Spectator sports

Tickets can often be purchased by credit card with **Servi-Caixa** or **Tel-entrada** (*see p214*). Check www.agendabcn.com or newspapers such as *El Mundo Deportivo* for event details.

### Basketball

*Baloncesta* or, simply, 'basket', is easily Spain's second most popular sport, and the country hosts Europe's most competitive league, the ACB. **FC Winterthur Barcelona** are among the most powerful sides, fielding top-drawer European players; the other top local club is **DKV Joventut**, from nearby Badalona. The season runs September to early June; league matches are on weekend evenings, with European matches played midweek.

#### FC Winterthur Barcelona

*Palau Blaugrana, Avda Arístides Maillol, Les Corts (93 496 36 00/www.fcbarcelona.com). Metro Collblanc or Palau Reial.* **Ticket office** *Sept-June* 9am-1.30pm, 3.30-6pm Mon-Thur; 9am-2.30pm Fri. *Aug* 8.30am-2.30pm Mon-Fri; also 2hrs before a game. Advance tickets available from day before match; if match is Sun, tickets available from Fri. **Tickets** €5-€30. **No credit cards**.

Barcelona are an ambitious side and, after a highly disappointing 2005/6 season, they have injected some serious cash into the team, signing players like Mario Kasun, Jaka Lakovic and Roko Ukic, who, alongside local star Javi Navarro, have given the team arguably the strongest squad in Europe. Barça are also rumoured to be on the lookout for an NBA star to complete the line-up for this year.

**Bowling Pedralbes.** *See p272.*

## Bullfighting

### Plaza de Toros Monumental

*Gran Via de les Corts Catalanes 749, Eixample (93 245 58 04/93 215 95 70). Metro Monumental.* **Open** *Bullfights* Apr-Sept 6.30-7pm Sun. *Museum* Apr-Sept 11am-2pm, 4-8pm Mon-Sat; 10.30am-1pm Sun. **Admission** *Bullfights* €20-€97. Advance tickets available from Servi-Caixa. *Museum* €4; €3 concessions. **No credit cards. Map** p343 K8.

In April 2004 the council voted the city to be *anti-taurino* (anti-bullfighting), though this was largely a symbolic gesture: 100 bulls are still killed every year at the city's one remaining bullring. *Corridas* take place on Sundays in summer, largely in front of tourists and immigrant Andalusians.

## Football

Barcelona boasts two Primera (top flight) teams, **FC Barcelona** and **Espanyol**. Every weekend from mid August to May, one or the other will be playing, usually on Saturday or Sunday evening; check the press for details, and keep checking as kick-off times can change. **Europa** (based in Gràcia) and **Júpiter** (in Poblenou) are worthwhile semi-pro teams.

### FC Barcelona

*Nou Camp, Avda Arístides Maillol, Les Corts (93 496 36 00/www.fcbarcelona.com). Metro Collblanc or Palau Reial.* **Ticket office** *Sept-June* 9am-1.30pm, 3.30-6pm Mon-Thur; 9am-2.30pm Fri. *Aug* 8.30am-2.30pm Mon-Fri; from 11am match days. Tickets available from 2wks before each match. **Tickets** €19-€125. Advance tickets for league games available from Servi-Caixa. **Credit** AmEx, DC, MC, V. **Map** p337 A4.

Everyone agreed (even, grudgingly, at Real Madrid) that Barça deserved to pick up the Champions League trophy last year. Barça's mixture of flair and professionalism managed to combine the brawn of the likes of Puyol and Márquez with the outstanding creativity of players like Xavi and Messi. Of course, having the best footballer in the world

# Champion of the world

He's not as handsome as David Beckham, nor does he sport as many tattoos. He doesn't go out with famous B-grade celebrities nor make the headlines in international gossip mags as often as the former England captain. But Barcelona FC's Ronaldo de Assis Moreira, known to fans as Ronaldinho Gaucho, is pure marketing gold, simply because he's the best.

Now acknowledged as the world's greatest player and the world's most highly paid, Ronaldinho has become part of the Barcelona landscape – literally – his huge buck-tooth smile can be seen on billboards everywhere, flogging yoghurt, chips and Nike.

Catapulted from his modest family home in Porto Alegre, Brazil, to stardom, Ronaldinho, at the age of 26, has won just about everything there is to win at football's elite level: a World Cup with Brazil and La Liga and the Champions League with Barcelona.

No one's laughing more loudly than Barcelona FC who fought off a pack of bidders to buy the Brazilian in 2003, when the player decided to leave French Paris St-Germain. Then he cost around €26 million; these days if any club wants a look in, they'll have to cook up a cool €125 million just to start talking.

Since Ronaldinho's arrival in Barcelona, the football club has enjoyed unending success. Beautiful to watch in full flight and loaded with a bag of tricks that impress even the most hardened critics, Ronaldinho's prowess and sportsmanship on the field, combined with that unmistakeable buck-toothed grin, have won him adulation with the dads, the mums, the sons and the daughters.

But, aside from the football, what does Ronaldinho think about...

**Barcelona**: 'Barcelona is a beautiful city. The people are similar to the people in Brazil. Paris was more distinct than Porto Alegre but here in Barcelona things are closer in feel to

playing at the top of his game didn't do any harm, either. But Ronaldinho (*see p270* **Champion of the world**) remains very much a team player and, unlike a certain other club, Barça's *galácticos* enjoyed their football and kept themselves focused on common goals. The credit for this can largely be given to the laid-back Rikjaard, who has built a solid block to which he has only chosen to add three new signings this season (Thuram, Zambrotta and Gudjohnsen). Barça won the double last year, but with success comes the pressure to keep up the momentum. Barça fans seem to have overcome their natural pessimism, but it has not escaped their notice that Real Madrid has significantly strengthened its side and looks like it'll be mounting a stronger challenge this year. An exciting season looms.

Getting tickets can be something of a lottery, especially for the big games. Around 4,000 tickets usually go on sale on the day of the match: phone to find out when, and join the queue an hour or so beforehand at the intersection of Travessera de les Corts and Avenida Arístides Maillol. 'Rented out' seats go on sale from these offices and can also be bought through Servi-Caixa. If there are none left, buy a *reventa* ticket from touts at the gates. The 'B' team, a couple of divisions down the league system, plays in the mini-stadium over the road.

Porto Alegre so my adaptation to life in Barcelona was easier.'

**Learning Catalan**: 'It has been a little complicated. I can understand it very well, but it's harder to speak it.'

**Football**: 'I play for my team and for the love I have for football. I try to be as happy as I can. I have the luck to be doing what I love and have the opportunity to make 100,000 people happy too. There is nothing better.'

**Girlfriend(s)**: '*La pelota*! (the ball)'

**Fans**: 'In my case it's easy because everybody treats me with so much affection.'

**Fame**: 'I'm living the dream I've had since I was a young boy, so I'm enjoying and taking advantage of it as much as I can. I don't stop doing things that I want to do,but I'm conscious of the fact there will always be people wanting autographs, taking photos.'

**The future**: 'I'm very happy here...I can say now that I'm certain that I chose well. I had an opportunity to join Manchester and three other clubs, but I decided to come here so I could have friends who were working in the club. I wanted to continue the line of Romario, Rivaldo and Ronaldo who've played here, and now that I'm here, I'm very happy and hope to stay for a long time.'

### RCD Espanyol

*Estadi Olímpic de Montjuïc, Passeig Olímpic 17-19, Montjuïc (93 292 77 00/www.rcdespanyol.com). Metro Espanya then free bus or Paral·lel then Funicular de Montjuïc.* **Ticket office** (matchdays only). Opening times vary so check website first. **Tickets** €25-€55. **Credit** V. **Map** p341 A/B11.

Espanyol escaped relegation by the skins of their teeth last year and seem to have recovered their status as perennial underachievers after a brief blip of success two years ago. New manager Ernesto Valverde is hoping to prove that Espanyol deserve a place in the increasingly competitive Primera Liga. To do so, he will be putting faith in a talented crop of young Catalan players (Espanyol have always been regarded as a good *cantera* – mine – of footballing talent), alongside their two veterans: 'the little Buddha' Ivan de la Peña and their faithful top scorer and captain, Raúl Tamudo. Espanyol currently play their home games in the Estadi Olímpic on the side of Montjuïc. Free buses ferry ticket-holders from Plaça Espanya from 90 minutes before kick-off. The club is scheduled to move to a new, 42,000-capacity, ground in Cornellà in 2008.

## Other team sports

Catalonia's best **rugby** team, UE Santboiana (93 640 07 26 ,www.uesantboiana.com), from the suburb of Sant Boi, is now in the new 2,000-capacity Baldiri Aleu stadium (C/Baldiri Aleu 1-7), a short walk from the Sant Boi FGC station. Tickets cost €6.

**Handball** and **roller hockey** are also well represented in the region (Catalunya even has its own roller-hockey national team, something that many would love to see happen in football too); FC Barcelona's teams (www.fcbarcelona.com) have done well of late in both these sports. Both Terrassa Hockey, a top-level **hockey** team based in Terrassa (93 787 03 51, www.athc.es) and Viladecans, Spain's main baseball team (93 637 25 88/www.viladecans.net/jsp/WEBVILA/HOME.html), welcome spectators.

## Special events

### La Cursa del Corte Inglés

**Information & entry forms** *El Corte Inglés (93 270 17 30/www.elcorteingles.com).* **Date** May.

Barcelona's biggest fun run in May is sponsored by the city's favourite department store.

### Motorsports

*Circuit de Catalunya, Ctra de Parets del Vallès a Granollers, Montmeló, Outer Limits (93 571 97 00/*

*www.circuitcat.com). By car: C17 north to Parets del Vallès exit (20km/13 miles).* **Times & tickets** vary by competition; available from Servi-Caixa. **Credit** MC, V.

Until 1975, Barcelona's Formula One track used to be a death-defying race through the roads of Montjuïc. Now, the city boasts one of the world's best racing circuits at Montmeló. Last year the calculating, passionless Spaniard Fernando Alonso won the World Championship, and since then, tickets are a lot harder to come by. Make sure you book well in advance if you want to see the race.

### Tennis

*Reial Club de Tennis Barcelona-1899, C/Bosch i Gimpera 5, Les Corts (93 203 78 52/www.rctb 1899.es). FGC Reina Elisenda/bus 63, 78.* **Ticket office** *During competitions* 8.30am-1.30pm, 3.30-6.30pm Mon-Fri; 9am-1pm Sat. **Tickets** €20-€64; available from Servi-Caixa. **Credit** AmEx, MC, V. **Map** p337 B2.

The annual Open Seat Comte de Godó tournament in Pedralbes, is considered one of the ATP circuit's most important clay-court tournaments. Consequently, all the top players usually attend, including the amazing new Majorcan wunderkind, Rafael Nadal, who has already won the competition twice. The 2007 tournament takes place in April.

## Active sports & fitness

The 237 municipally run facilities include a network of *poliesportius* (sports centres). One-day entry tickets are usually available. Still, you can just head to the beach: there's a free outdoor gym and ping-pong table at Barceloneta, and the sea can be swum in from May to October. All beaches have wheelchair ramps, and most of the city's pools are fully equipped for disabled people. See **Servei d'Informació Esportiva** below for details.

### Servei d'Informació Esportiva

*Avda de l'Estadi 30-40, Montjuïc (93 402 30 00). Metro Espanya then escalators or Paral·lel then Funicular de Montjuïc/bus 50.* **Open** *Oct-June* 8am-2pm, 3.45-6pm Mon-Thur; 8am-2.30pm Fri. *July-Sept* 8am-2.30pm Mon-Fri. **Map** p341 B10/11.

The Ajuntament's sports' information service is based at the Piscina Bernat Picornell. Call for information (although not all the staff speak English), or consult the Ajuntament's very thorough listings on the Esports section of its website: www.bcn.es.

## Bowling

### Bowling Pedralbes

*Avda Dr Marañón 11, Les Corts (93 333 03 52/ www.bowlingpedralbes.com). Metro Collblanc or Zona Universitaria.* **Open** 10am-2am Mon-Thur; 10am-4am Fri, Sat; 10am-midnight Sun. *Aug* open only from 5pm daily. **Rates** €2-€6/ person. **Credit** MC, V.

Fourteen lanes to try for that perfect 300, in an alley that hosts international tournaments. Early afternoons are quiet; otherwise, sit at the bar and wait to be paged. Shoe hire is available (€1), as are pool, snooker and *futbolín* (table football).

## Cycling

Tourist offices have maps detailing cycle routes. These make cycling just about viable as a mode of transport, though major roads in the Eixample can get a bit hairy. The seafront is a good bet for leisure cycling; otherwise, try the spectacular **Carretera de les Aigües**, a flat gravel road that skirts along the side of Collserola mountain. To avoid a killer climb, take your bike on the FGC to Peu del Funicular station, then take the Funicular de Vallvidrera to the midway stop. For serious mountain biking, check http://amicsbici.pangea.org, which also has information on when you can take your bike on public transport. A really good lock is a must; bicycle theft is big business.

### Probike

*C/Villarroel 184, Eixample (93 419 78 89/www.pro bike.es). Metro Hospital Clínic.* **Open** 10am-8.30pm Mon-Sat. **Credit** AmEx, MC, V. **Map** p338 E6.

The Probike club organises regular excursions, from day trips to a summertime cross-Pyrenees run. Its centre, which has a broad range of equipment and excellent service, plus maps and information on all manner of routes, is a magnet for mountain bikers.

**Piscines Bernat Picornell.** *See p274.*



Arts & Entertainment

## Football

### Barcelona International Football League

*Info 93 415 01 67/649 261 328/ nicksimonsbcn@yahoo.co.uk.*
Matches, of Sunday League standard, are generally played at weekends from September to June among teams of expats and locals. New players are welcome.

## Golf

Catalonia is currently *a la moda* as a golfing-holiday destination. Visitors should book in advance; courses can be full at weekends.

### Club de Golf Sant Cugat

*C/Villa, Sant Cugat del Vallès, Outer Limits (93 674 39 58/www.golfsantcugat.com). By car Túnel de Vallvidrera (C16) to Valldoreix/by train FGC from Plaça Catalunya to Sant Cugat.* **Open** 8am-8pm Mon; 7.30am-8.30pm Tue-Fri; 7am-9pm Sat, Sun. **Rates** *Non-members* €65 Mon-Thur; €150 Fri-Sun. Club hire €36. **Credit** MC, V.
Designed by Harry S Colt back in 1917 and built by British railway workers, the oldest golf course in Catalonia is a tight, varied 18-hole set-up, making the most of natural obstacles, that's challenging enough to host the Ladies' World Matchplay Tour. There's a restaurant and swimming pool on site. You may be asked to pay a membership fee depending on the time of year: call ahead.

## Gyms & fitness centres

Sports centres run by the city council are cheaper and generally more user-friendly than most private clubs. Phone the **Servei d'Informació Esportiva** (*see p272*) for more information.

### Centres de Fitness DiR

*C/Casp 34, Eixample (902 10 19 79/93 301 62 09/ www.dir.es). Metro Urquinaona.* **Open** 7am-10.45pm Mon-Fri; 9am-3pm Sat, Sun. **Rates** vary. **Credit** MC, V. **Map** p344 D1.
This plush, well-organised private chain has ten fitness centres. Additional installations vary from a huge outdoor pool (at DiR Diagonal) to a squash centre (DiR Campus). **Other locations**: DiR Campus, Avda Dr Marañón 17, Les Corts (93 448 41 41); DiR Diagonal, C/Ganduxer 25-27, Eixample (93 202 22 02); and throughout the city.

### Europolis

*Travessera de les Corts 252-254, Les Corts (93 363 29 92/www.europolis.es). Metro Les Corts.* **Open** 7am-11pm Mon-Fri; 8am-8pm Sat; 9am-3pm Sun. **Rates** *Non-members* €9.50/day. *Membership* approx €46/mth, plus €79 joining fee. **Credit** MC, V. **Map** p337 B5.
Europolis centres, as large and well equipped as any private gym in town, are municipally owned but run by the British chain Holmes Place. They provide exercise machines for every conceivable muscle, as well as pools, classes, trainers and weight-lifting gear. **Other locations**: C/Sardenya 549-553, Gràcia (93 210 07 66).

## Ice skating

### FC Barcelona Pista de Gel

*Nou Camp, entrance 7 or 9, Avda Joan XXIII, Les Corts (93 496 36 30/www.fcbarcelona.com). Metro Collblanc or Maria Cristina.* **Open** *Sept-June* 10am-2pm, 4-6pm Mon, Tue, Thur; 10am-2pm, 4-8pm Wed, Fri; 10.30am-2pm, 5.15-8.30pm Sat, Sun. *July* 10am-1.45pm, 5-7.45pm Mon-Fri; 5.15-8.30pm Sat, Sun. Closed Aug. **Rates** (incl skates) €9.80. **No credit cards**. **Map** p337 A4.
Functional rink next to the Nou Camp complex, also used for ice-hockey matches. It's perfect for the non-football fans in the family to kill 90 minutes or so. Gloves are obligatory, and on sale at €1.80 a pair.

### Skating Roger de Flor

*C/Roger de Flor 168, Eixample (93 245 28 00/www.skatingclub.cat). Metro Tetuan.* **Open** *July-mid Sept* 10.30am-1.30pm, 5-9pm Mon-Fri, Sun; 10.30am-1.30pm, 5-10pm Sat. *Mid Sept-June* 10.30am-1.30pm Mon, Tue; 10.30am-1.30pm, 5-9pm Wed-Fri, Sun; 10.30am-1.30pm, 5-10pm Sat. **Rates** (incl skates) €12. **Credit** MC, V. **Map** p339 J8.
A family-oriented ice rink in the Eixample. Gloves are compulsory and on sale for €2.80. Any non-skaters in a group get in free and can use the café.

## Jogging & running

The seafront is a good location for an enjoyable jog. If you can handle the initial climb, or use other transport for the ascent, there are scenic runs on Montjuïc, especially around the castle and Olympic stadium, the Park Güell/Carmel hills and Collserola.

## Rollerblading

The **APB** (Asociacion de Patinadores de Barcelona, www.patinar-bcn.com) organises skating convoys: beginners meet at the Forum at 10.15pm on Fridays. Better skaters hook up at the Plaça Catalunya at 10.30pm on Thursday and follow an 'unofficial' route. See www.sat.org.es/bcnskates for details. The APB also offers classes (free for beginners, €7 for equipment) at 10pm on Tuesdays in Parc Clot. **RODATS** (635 629 948/www.rodats.com/ tours) organises skating convoys and classes (€7 plus €7 for equipment; tours for €15)

Going it alone, you're not officially allowed on roads or cycle paths, and the speed limit is 10 km/h. The pedestrian broadways of Rambla de Catalunya, Avda Diagonal and Passeig Marítim are popular haunts.

## Sailing

### Base Nàutica de la Mar Bella

*Avda Litoral, between Platja Bogatell & Platja de Mar Bella (93 221 04 32/www.basenautica.org). Metro Poblenou.* **Open** *Apr-Aug* 10am-8pm daily. *Sept-Oct* 10am-7pm daily. *Nov-Dec* 10am-6pm daily. *Jan-Mar* 10am-5.30pm daily. **Rates** *Windsurfing* €163.20/10hr course; €20/hr equipment hire. *Catamaran* €191.24/16hr course; €26-€60/hr equipment hire. *Kayak* €110/10hr course; €15-€25/hr equipment hire. **Credit** MC, V.

Situated next to Barcelona's official nudist beach, the Base Nàutica hires out catamarans and windsurf gear to those with experience. There's a proficiency test when you first get on the water (€20 fee if you fail); unofficial registered 'friends', who will join your catamaran team for a fee, are usually available for beginners. You can hire a kayak without a test. There are also different options available for intensive or longer-term sailing proficiency courses.

## Skiing

If you sicken of the urban bustle, within three hours you can be in the Pyrenees. The best bet for a skiing day trip is the resort of **La Molina** (972 89 20 31/www.lamolina.cat). A RENFE train from Plaça Catalunya at 7.05am or 9.22am (€7.90 single, €14.30 return) takes you to the train station (get off at La Molina) and a bus takes you up to the resort. A day's ski pass (known as the *forfait*) will set you back around €35. Trains return at 4.58pm and 7.16pm (check the timetable in the station or www.renfe.com). There are runs to suit all comers, from green for relative beginners to black for speed freaks. More information is available at the La Molina office in El Triangle (C/Pelai, 93 205 15 15).

## Swimming

The city has dozens of municipal pools, many of them open air. It also has more than three miles of beach, patrolled by lifeguards in summer. For a list of pools, contact the **Servei d'Informació Esportiva** (*see p272*). Flip-flops and swimming caps are generally obligatory.

### Club de Natació Atlètic Barceloneta

*Plaça del Mar, Barceloneta (93 221 00 10/ www.cnab.org). Metro Barceloneta then bus 17, 39, 64.* **Open** *Oct-Apr* 6.30am-11pm Mon-Fri; 7am-11pm Sat; 8am-5pm Sun. *May-Sept* 6.30am-11pm Mon-Fri; 7am-11pm Sat; 8am-8pm Sun. **Admission** *Non-members* €9.50/day. *Membership* €31/mth, plus €64 joining fee. **Credit** AmEx, DC, MC, V. **Map** p342 G13.

This historic beachside centre, which celebrates its centenary in 2007, has an indoor pool and two outdoor pools (one heated), as well as sauna and gym facilities. There's a *frontón* (Spanish ball sports venue) if you fancy a go at the world's fastest sport: jai alai, a fierce Basque game somewhere between squash and handball.

### Piscines Bernat Picornell

*Avda de l'Estadi 30-40, Montjuïc (93 423 40 41/ www.picornell.com). Metro Espanya then escalators, or Paral·lel then Funicular de Montjuïc/bus 50.* **Open** *June-Sept* Outdoor pool only 9am-9pm Mon-Sat; 9am-8pm Sun. *Oct-May* Outdoor pool 10am-7pm Mon-Sat; 10am-4pm Sun. Covered pool & rest of complex 7am-midnight Mon-Fri; 7am-9pm Sat; 7.30am-4pm Sun. **Admission** *June-Sept* €4.70; €3.30 concessions; free under-6s. *Oct-May* €8.50; €5.40-€5.30 concessions; free under-6s. **Credit** MC, V. **Map** p341 A10.

The 50m (164ft) indoor pool here was the main venue for the Olympics; there's also a 50m outdoor pool, a climbing wall and a gym. There are also regular sessions for nudists (9-11pm Saturday all year, 4.15-6pm Sundays from October to May). Daredevils can risk taking a jump from the city's highest diving board.

### Poliesportiu Marítim

*Passeig Marítim 33-35 (93 224 04 40/www.claror.org). Metro Ciutadella-Vila Olímpica.* **Open** *Sept-July* 7am-midnight Mon-Fri; 8am-9pm Sat; 8am-4pm Sun. *Aug* 7am-8.30pm Mon-Fri; 8am-3pm Sat, Sun. **Admission** *Non-members* €13.50 Mon-Fri; €16 Sat, Sun; 5-visit pass €56; 10-visit pass €99. **Credit** AmEx, DC, MC, V. **Map** p343 K12.

This spa centre specialises in thalassotherapy, a popular hydrotherapy treatment using seawater. There are eight saltwater pools of differing temperatures, including a vast whirlpool with waterfalls to massage your shoulders. There's also an icy plunge-pool, a sauna and a steam room. Other services include a bigger freshwater pool, a gym, bike hire, and some well-priced classes. The centre has access to Barceloneta beach; in the summer, leave your belongings safe in a locker while you're on the beach.

## Tennis

### Barcelona Tenís Olímpic

*Passeig de la Vall d'Hebron 178-196, Vall d'Hebron (93 427 65 00/www.fctennis.org). Metro Montbau.* **Open** *Dec-Apr* 8am-11pm Mon-Fri; 8am-7pm Sat, Sun. *May-Nov* 8am-11pm Mon-Fri; 8am-9pm Sat, Sun. **Rates** *Non-members* courts €13.60-€18/hr; floodlights €5. **No credit cards**.

Originally built for the Olympics, these tennis courts are a little way from the city centre, but there's a good metro connection. There are 24, mostly clay, courts, as well as paddle courts and racket hire (€3.50).

### Club Tennis Pompeia

*C/Foixarda, Montjuïc (93 325 13 48). Bus 13, 50.* **Open** 8am-10pm daily. **Rates** *Non-members* €12/hr; €4.40 floodlights. €141/3mths. **No credit cards**.

There are good rates for non-members at this pleasant club above the Poble Espanyol, with a wonderful view of Barcelona to distract your smashes. There are seven clay courts; racket hire is €3.

# Trips Out of Town



**Tossa del Mar**. *See p292.*

# Getting Started

Discover Catalonia.

Catalonia boasts one of the most diverse landscapes in Spain: sea, mountains, islands, virtual deserts and wetlands. It's an outdoors person's paradise, but that's not to say there isn't plenty to entertain culture vultures. There's Ferran Adrià's celebrated El Bulli restaurant (*see p171*), little boutique wineries, honeypot villages, art and architecturally rich medieval cities, weird and wonderful festivals and daredevil sporting events.

For information on roads and public transport, see the Generalitat's www.mobilitat.org. The Palau Robert tourist centre (*see p323*) is a hub of useful information about the region.

Catalonia has a network of *casa de pagès* – country houses or old farmhouses – where you can rent a room or a whole house. For details, see the Generalitat's widely available guide *Residències – Casa de pagès*. For holiday cottages, try the Rural Tourism Association, online at www.ecoturismocatalunyarural.com.

## On foot

Catalonia's hills and low mountain ranges make it hugely popular for walking. In many places this is made easier by GR (*gran recorregut*) long-distance footpaths, indicated with red-and-white signs. Good places for walking within easy reach of the city include the **Parc de Collserola** (*see p136*), **Montserrat** (*see p280*) and **La Garrotxa** (*see p301*). Another excellent Generalitat website, **www.gencat.net** (click on 'Catalonia', and then 'Touring routes in Catalonia'), has particularly good information on walks. For detailed walking maps, try **Altaïr** (*see p191*) or **Llibreria Quera** (C/Petritxol 2, 93 31 807 43).

## By bus

Transport around the region is reliable and reasonably priced. It's a good way to get to main hubs, though a rental car is better for exploring more out-of-the-way areas. The **Estació d'Autobusos Barcelona-Nord** (C/Alí Bei 80, map p343 J9) is the principal bus station for coach services around Catalonia. General information and timetables for all the different private companies are on 902 26 06 06/ www.barcelonanord.com. The Costa Brava is better served by buses than trains.

## By road

Be warned that over the last few years Spain's roads have undergone a gradual process of renaming, and many locally bought maps are still out of date. Road signs generally post both the new and the old name, but signage often doesn't make itself clear until you're right on top of your junction. Plan your route in advance.

Roads beginning C1 run north–south; C2 runs east–west; C3 run parallel to the coast. Driving in or out of Barcelona, you will come across either the **Ronda de Dalt**, running along the edge of Tibidabo, or the **Ronda Litoral** along the coast, meeting north and south of the city. They intersect with several motorways (*autopistes*): the C31 (heading up the coast from Mataró); the C33/A7 (to Girona and France) and the C58 (Sabadell, Manresa), which both run into Avda Meridiana; the A2 (Lleida, Madrid), a continuation of Avda Diagonal that connects with the A7 south (Tarragona, Valencia); and the C32 to Sitges, reached from the Gran Via.

All are toll roads, which in Catalonia tend to be quite expensive; where possible, we've given toll-free alternatives. Avoid the automatic ticket dispensers if on a motorbike: you'll pay less in the 'Manual' lanes. The **Túnel de Vallvidrera**, the continuation of Via Augusta that leads out of Barcelona under Collserola to Sant Cugat and Terrassa, also has a high toll, as does the **Túnel de Cadí**, running through the mountains just south of Puigcerdà. For more information on tolls, call 902 20 03 20 or see www.autopistas.com.

## By train

All **RENFE** (902 24 02 02, www.renfe.es) trains stop at **Sants** station, and some at **Passeig de Gràcia** (Girona, Figueres, the south coast), **Estació de França** (the south coast) or **Plaça Catalunya** (Montseny, Vic, Puigcerdà). RENFE's local and suburban trains (*rodalies/ cercanías*) are integrated into the metro and bus fares system (*see p305*). Tickets for these are sold at separate windows. Catalan Government Railways (**FGC**) serves destinations from **Plaça d'Espanya** (including Montserrat) and **Plaça Catalunya** (Tibidabo, Collserola, Sant Cugat and Terrassa). FGC information is available on 93 205 15 15 and at www.fgc.net.

# Around Barcelona

Day trips for carnival queens, water babies and miracle seekers.

For a leisurely bathe hop off the train at **Garraf**.

## South along the coast

Often compared to the cities of California, which enjoy both sea and mountains, Barcelona really does have the best of both worlds, and all within a short train ride from the centre. About 30 minutes south is the broad strand at **Castelldefels**, popular among both sun worshippers and water sports fanatics. It's also become something of a mecca for kite-surfers, and although the sport is banned in the summer months, it is fun to watch the multicoloured kites perform when the sea gets too cold for swimming. **Escola Náutica Garbí** (mobile 609 752 175/www.escolagarbi.com) can teach you how. The town also has a large recreational port, where kayaks and catamarans can be hired from the **Catamaran Center** (Port Ginesta, local 324, 93 665 22 11, www.catamaran-center.com). If traditional surfing is more your scene, then it's a good idea to keep an eye on the swell in Sitges.

For bathing of a more lackadaisical nature, stay on the train a while longer, and get off at the tiny port of **Garraf**, with its small curved beach backed by green-and-white striped bathing huts. Miraculously, it is still relatively undiscovered, and the steep-sided mountains that surround it mean that development is not something to worry about. It's worth taking a stroll to the **Celler de Garraf** at the northern tip of the bay, a magical Modernista creation built by Gaudí for the Güell family in 1895, and now housing a restaurant. Behind the village stretches the **Parc del Garraf** nature reserve, with hiking and biking opportunities on trails marked out on maps available from the tourist office in Sitges. More adventurous souls can also go spelunking here in its intricate network of caves and grottoes. Contact the **Oficina i Centre d'Informació del Parc del Garraf** (935 971 819, www.diba.es).

The pretty, whitewashed streets of **Sitges** burst with party-goers in the summertime, while providing a relaxing getaway in the winter. Sitges was 'discovered' by Modernista artist Santiago Rusiñol in the 1890s: this legendary figure threw massive parties for the

Trips Out of Town

great and the good of Barcelona's cultural heyday, among them a teenage Pablo Picasso. It has remained a magnet for artists, writers and assorted leisure-lovers, and since the 1960s it has become Spain's principal gay resort, served by a hotchpotch of gay bars and discos (*see p243*). The *madre* of all Sitges's parties, in the week leading up to Shrove Tuesday, is the camp-as-they-come carnival, a riot of floats, fancy dress and men in high heels.

In the 19th century, Sitges became the fashionable retirement spot for the merchants, known as *'los americanos'*, who made fortunes in the Caribbean and spent them on increasingly lavish mansions until beyond the turn of the 20th. There are more than 100 of these palaces dotted around the centre of town: in the tourist office you can pick up an excellent booklet that takes you round the most important. Alternatively, **Agis Sitges** (C/Lope de Vega 9, 2º-2ª, mobile 619 793 199) offers guided tours of these houses the first three Sundays of the month, plus a Modernista route on the first Sunday (€9).

Sitges's highest building, topping a rocky promontory overlooking the sea, is the pretty 17th-century **Església Sant Bartomeu i Santa Tecla**, offering wonderful views of the Mediterranean. Behind the church is the **Museu Cau Ferrat** (C/Fonollar, 938 940 364, www.diba.es/museus/sitges.asp, admission €3.50, €1.75 concessions, closed Mon). Rusiñol set up his home here: the building houses his collection of paintings (including works by El Greco, Picasso and Ramon Casas, as well as his own) and wrought-iron sculptures, all on view. Over the road is the **Palau Maricel** (C/Fonollar, 93 811 33 11, guided tours €10, 8pm Tue & 10pm Thur, book beforehand, closed Oct-June), an old hospital that's been converted into a Modernista palace and is now used as a concert hall on summer nights. The building contains medieval and baroque paintings and sensuous marble sculptures.

Also worth visiting is the **Museu Romàntic** in the Casa Llopis (C/Sant Gaudenci 1, 93 894 29 69, admission €3.50, concessions €1.75, closed Mon), which portrays the lifestyle of the aristocratic 19th-century family that once lived there. The original furnishings and decorations haven't been changed; you can wander from room to room among grandfather clocks, music boxes and antique dolls. Those who prefer messing about in boats are served well at the Port Esportiu Aiguadolç. The **Centro Náutico Aiguadolç-Vela** (938 113 105, www.advela.net) rents sailing boats and organises sailing excursions; a private hour-long session costs €40 (closed Mon & Dec-Feb). The **Yahoo Motor Centre** rents jet skis with guides (938 113 061, €40 for 15min ride). And for those who prefer to paddle, the **Adventure Factory Sea Kayak Centre** (C/Josep de Coroleu 85, Vilanova I la Geltrú, 938 101 125) runs courses and excursions.

But Sitges is most famous for its more hedonistic pleasures. At mealtimes, tourists throng the Passeig de la Ribera, a beachside promenade lined with restaurants and bars, and at night they head up the hill into the town's narrow streets, especially C/Primer de Maig – known to locals as 'Carrer de Pecat' (Sin Street) – the epicentre of Sitges's mainly gay nightlife. The partying and street life in this charming town is at its fiercest during carnival and in the town's noisy and colourful *festa major* at the end of August. Sitges also hosts an annual international film festival in autumn (*see p231*).

Beyond this, **Vilanova i la Geltrú** is an actual working fishing port. From here you can walk along the cliff tops all the way back to Sitges (about two hours).

## Where to eat & stay

When it comes to long, lazy lunches looking out to sea, nothing beats commandeering one of the terraces at **La Cúpula** (936 320 015, mains €15) in Garraf. Booking is essential and note that if you specify the *xiringuito* as opposed to the higher-elevated restaurant, it's a little bit cheaper.

In Sitges, a fisherman's lunch of steamed mussels, clams and razor clams, and *arroz negre* doesn't come better than from friendly **El Tambucho** (Port Alegre 49, Platja Sant Sebastià, 938 947 912, mains €12). For something a little more upmarket **Maricel** (Passeig de la Ribera 6, 938 942 054, www.maricel.es, tasting menu €66.50) gives local produce an elegant twist along the lines of foie with curried plums and mango, and red mullet with anchovy parmentier. For classics, such as rabbit with snails and *xató* (a local salad of salt cod, tuna and escarole lettuce), head to **La Masia** (Passeig de Vilanova 164, 938 941 076, mains €14). The restaurant in **El Xalet** (C/Illa de Cuba 35, 938 945 579, www.elxalet.com, mains €22, €64.20-€99.50) is on the pricey side but worth it for the Modernista decor in the dining room. Don't leave town without stopping for a cava cocktail on the terrace at the delightful **Hotel Romàntic** (C/Sant Isidre 33, 938 948 372, www.hotelromantic.com, closed Nov-Mar, €84-€99).

It's possible to get superb fish and seafood in Vilanova and generally it's less pricey than in Sitges. Those in the know go to **La Fitorra** (C/Isaac Peral 8, 938 151 125, www.hotelcesar.net, set menu €17.50) where, despite a rather uninspiring façade, the accomplished cooking offers superbly fresh fish from the local market. **Can Pagès** (C/Sant Pere 24, 938 941 195, closed Mon & 2 wks Nov, set menu €16.85, tasting menu €38.25) has grilled meat, and **Peixerot** (Passeig Marítim 56, 938 150 625, closed Sun dinner, mains €25) fish.

## Tourist information

### Oficina de Turisme de Castelldefels

*C/Pintor Serrasanta 4 (93 635 27 27/www.turismocastelldefels.com).* **Open** *June-Sept* 9am-8pm Mon-Fri; 9am-2pm, 4-8pm Sat; 10am-8pm Sun. *Oct-May* 4-6.30pm Mon; 9am-2pm, 4-6.30pm Tue-Fri; 9am-2pm Sat.

### Oficina de Turisme de Sitges

*C/Sinia Morera 1 (93 894 42 51/www.sitgestur.com).* **Open** *July-Sept* 9am-8pm daily. *Oct-June* 9am-2pm, 4-6.30pm daily.

## Getting there

### By bus

Mon-Bus (93 893 70 60) runs a frequent service from 5.55am to 9.55pm to Sitges, and an hourly night service between 12.10am and 3.10am to Ronda Universitat in Barcelona.

### By car

C32 toll road to Castelldefels, Garraf and Sitges (41km/25 miles), or C31 via a slow, winding drive around the Garraf mountains.

### By train

Frequent trains leave from Passeig de Gràcia for Platja de Castelldefels (20min journey) and Sitges (30mins); not all stop at Castelldefels and Garraf.

# North along the coast

The beaches of the Maresme fringe; the coast immediately north of Barcelona – **Montgat**, **Montgat Nord**, **El Masnou** and **Ocata** – are all far better options than any of the city beaches, with trains every 30 minutes from Plaça Catalunya. If you walk back towards Barcelona from Montgat Nord, you'll come across a clutch of white fishermen's cottages with blue shutters on the beach and a good *xiringuito* that gets rammed at the weekends for its sumptuous paella and mussels. Go a little further afield, and the sand and sea are better still, such as at **Caldes d'Estrac** (popularly known as **Caldetes**), **Sant Pol de Mar** and **Calella**, which boast atmospheric towns to boot. Caldetes (45 minutes away) was the playground of the Barcelona bourgeoisie at the turn of the 20th century, and a string of ostentatious Modernista mansions lines the seafront. Pretty Sant Pol is a few kilometres further. Calella is more touristy, but its lush Parc Dalmau is worth a visit and there are several interesting Gothic buildings. Thanks to massively improved cycle paths, it's now possible to cycle all the way from Barcelona to Blanes along the seafront.

## Where to eat

In Caldes d'Estrac, the **Fonda Manau Can Raimón** (C/Sant Josep 11, 93 791 04 59, closed Tue & dinner Sun-Thur Oct-May, mains €11) is a small *pensión* with great food, while **Hispania** (Ctra Real 54, Arenys de Mar-Caldetes, 93 791 03 06, mains €35) is revered for the staunchly traditional dishes turned out by the hands of sisters Francisca and Dolores Rexach, who've been pleasing punters since 1952. In Sant Pol, **La Casa** (C/Riera 13, 93 760 23 73, closed Mon, mains €12) serves simple food in a pretty dining room, while Carme Ruscalleda at **Sant Pau** (C/Nou 10, 93 760 06 62, www.ruscalleda.com, closed all Mon, Thur lunch & Sun dinner, 3wks May & all Nov, mains €38) now boasts three Michelin stars.

## Getting there

### By car

NII to El Masnou (10km/6 miles), Caldes d'Estrac (36km/22 miles), Sant Pol (48km/30 miles) and Calella (52km/32 miles).

### By train

RENFE trains leave every 30mins from Sants or Plaça Catalunya for El Masnou, Caldes d'Estrac, Sant Pol and Calella. Journey approx 1hr.

# Montserrat & Colònia Güell

Religious visitors to Montserrat (saw-toothed mountain) come to pay homage to La Moreneta, the Black Virgin, discovered in a nearby cave in the 12th century, while others come to enjoy the view or listen to the all-boy choir that fills the air of the basilica with angelic singing every Sunday at noon. Take the funicular to the top and, if you're hardy enough, hike the three-hour circular route along the top ridge to the peak of **Sant Jeroni**, at 1,235 metres (4,053 feet), which offers 360-degree views from a vertigo-inducing platform, before heading back down the gorge to the monastery. From here the views of the strange and wonderful formations of the mountain – often with climbers dangling aloft – are at their most spectacular, with the plains of Catalonia spread out far below. Take a picnic, perhaps stocking up on the monk-made chocolate at the monastery shop before you go, for the food up here is far from godly.

## Spider man

Trevor ap Simon is the brains behind one of Barcelona's wackiest excursions: his Follow the Baldie's walks, all within an hour of the city, follow a number of themes ranging from 'Poultry Freakout' to more genteel village bar-hopping. You can follow in the footsteps of the first Catalan Modernista novel, absorb the dust and detritus of the Industrial Revolution, and gape at forgotten churches hiding disturbing torture frescoes.

The Baldie's most popular tour is the 'Night of the Tarantula', which takes people into the cave-riddled Garraf national park. It starts with a few fortifying drinks before trekking off into the mountains under a full moon in search of a mythical man-eating spider. *Lycosa,* otherwise known as the wolf spider, is endemic to the area and can be found lurking around deserted farmhouses and down old wells. It's about half the size of a hand and not poisonous.

Combined with the eerie squawk of the eagle owl and bats fluttering above, this walk can be spooky stuff. It only takes place on a full moon, leaving around 11pm and getting into Sitges around 4am; walkers then either wait for the first train or hit the clubs until dawn. Walks cost €25 per person not including drinks or travel, with progressive discounts for larger groups.

**Follow the Baldie** (mobile 617 039 956/ http://oreneta.com/baldie).

The monastery's **museum** (10am-7pm, admission €5.50) is unexpectedly good, stocked with fine art, including paintings by Picasso, Dalí, El Greco, Monet and Caravaggio, as well as a collection of liturgical gold and silverware, archaeological finds and gifts for the Virgin. From here there are a number of shorter walks to various caves, among them **Santa Cova**, where La Moreneta statue was discovered, a 20-minute hike from the monastery or a funicular ride (10am-1pm, 2-5.30pm daily, €2.50). The most accessible hermitage is **Sant Joan**, also 20 minutes away or a funicular ride (€6.30, 10am-7.15pm daily).

Closer to Barcelona, on the western outskirts of Santa Coloma de Cervelló, is the **Colònia Güell** (936 305 807, open daily, €4, guided tours €5-€8), which was commissioned by the textile baron Eusebi Güell, designed by Antoni Gaudí and, like so many of the projects started by the great architect, never actually completed. The utopian idea was to build a garden city for the textile workers around the factory where they worked. Gaudí did, however, manage to complete the crypt of the church, which, with its ribbed ceiling and twisted pillars, is an extraordinary achievement.

## Tourist information

### Oficina de Turisme de Montserrat

*Plaça de la Creu, Montserrat (938 777 777/www. montserratvisita.com).* **Open** *June-Sept* 9am-8pm daily. *Oct-May* 9am-6pm daily.

## Getting there

### By bus

**Montserrat** A Julià-Via (93 490 40 00) bus leaves at 9.15am from Sants bus station and returns at 5pm (6pm July-Sept) daily; journey time is approx 80mins.

### By car

**Montserrat** Take the NII to exit km 59, or the A2 to the Martorell exit, then the C55 towards Monistrol (60km/37 miles).
**Colònia Güell** A2 to Sant Boi exit, then turn towards Sant Vicenç dels Horts (5km/3 miles).

### By train

**Montserrat** FGC trains from Plaça d'Espanya hourly from 8.36am to Montserrat-Aeri (1hr) for the cable car (every 15mins); or to Monistrol de Montserrat for the rack train (every hour) to the monastery. Last cable car and rack train 6pm.
**Colònia Güell** FGC trains from Plaça d'Espanya.

# Tarragona & the Costa Daurada

Roman temples, paddy fields and some of the best wine in Spain.

## Tarragona

Tárraco, as Tarragona was known back then, was the first Roman city to be built outside Italy and dates back to the year 218 BC. It outranked Barcelona economically and strategically for centuries. Nowadays, Tarragona can feel rather staid; but what it lacks in pzazz, it more than makes up for in ancient architecture. Start with the Roman walls that once ringed the city. The path along them is known as the **Passeig Arqueològic** (Avda Catalunya, 977 24 57 96) and has its entrance at **Portal del Roser**, one of three remaining towers, two of which are medieval. Inside the walls, the superb Roman remains include the ancient **Pretori**, or 'praetorium' (977 22 17 36), used as both palace and government office and reputed to have been the birthplace of Pontius Pilate. From here, walk to the ruins of the **Circ Romans** (977 23 01 71), the first-century Roman circus where chariot races were held. The **Museu Nacional Arqueològic**, home to an important collection of Roman artefacts and mosaics, is nearby.

To see all of the **Catedral de Santa Maria**, not to mention some wonderful religious art and archaeological finds, you'll need a ticket for the **Museu Diocesà** (Pla de la Seu, 977 23 86 85, closed Mon). The majestic cathedral was built on the site of a Roman temple to Jupiter, and is Catalonia's largest. The cloister, built in the 12th and 13th centuries, is glorious, and the carvings alone are worth the trip.

Leading from the Old Town towards the sea, the **Passeig de las Palmeres** runs to the **Balcó del Mediterrani** overlooking the Roman **amphitheatre** (Parc del Miracle, 977 24 25 79). The same street also leads to the bustling, pedestrianised **Rambla Nova**, from where you can follow C/Canyelles to the **Fòrum** (C/Lleida, 977 24 25 01) to the remains of the juridical basilica and Roman houses. A couple of miles north of the city (but an unpleasant walk along a busy main road; take bus No.5 from the top of the Rambla Nova) is the spectacular **Pont del Diable** (Devil's Bridge), a Roman aqueduct built in the first century AD.

Entry to the Passeig Arqueològic, the circus and praetorium, the amphitheatre and the Fòrum costs €2.10 (€1 concessions, free under-16s); entry is free to holders of **Port Aventura** tickets (*see p285*). An all-in ticket for the city's five main museums is €8.30 (€4.10 concessions). All are closed on Mondays. If you're interested in the treasures of more recent times, there's a decent **antiques market** on Sunday mornings next to the cathedral.

### Museu Nacional Arqueològic de Tarragona

*Plaça del Rei 5 (977 23 62 09/www.mnat.es).* **Open** *June-Sept* 9.30am-8.30pm Tue-Sat; 10am-2pm Sun. *Oct-May* 9.30am-1.30pm, 3.30-7pm Tue-Sat; 10am-2pm Sun. **Admission** (incl entrance to Museu i Necròpolis Paleocristians) €2.40; €1.20 concessions; free under-18s, over-65s. **No credit cards**.

### Where to eat

In the old city **Les Coques** (C/Sant Llorenc 15, 977 228 300, closed Sun, mains €16) serves traditional roast kid and cod dishes. The neighbourhood of El Serrallo is the place to head for fish and seafood. Try the paella at **Cal Martí** (C/Sant Pere 12, 977 21 23 84, closed dinner Sun & Mon and Sept, mains €22.50) or the super-fresh fish at **La Puda** (Moll Pescadors 25, 977 211 511, closed dinner Sun and Oct-May, mains €25). Alternatively, head out of the centre to the west to **Sol-Ric** (Via Augusta 227, 977 23 20 32, closed Mon, dinner Sun and Jan, mains €22.50).

Those on a budget can fall back on **Bufet el Tiberi** (C/Martí d'Ardenya 5, 977 23 54 03, www.eltiberi.com, closed Mon & dinner Sun, buffet €11.35), while below the cathedral is **La Cuca Fera** (Plaça Santiago Rusiñol 5, 977 24 20 07, closed Tue, set lunch €13.90), which has great fish *suquet* (stew).

### Where to stay

In town the smartest hotel is the towering **Imperial Tarraco** (Passeig de les Palmeres, 977 23 30 40, www.husa.es, €123-€289). The **Lauria** (Rambla Nova 20, 977 23 67 12,

The Catedral de Santa Maria at **Tarragona.**

www.hlauria.es, €63-€75) has a swimming pool and offers large discounts to visitors if they arrive for weekends out of season. Some other mid-range hotels include the **Astari** (Via Augusta 95, 977 23 69 00, €71-€96), which also has a swimming pool, and the central **Hotel Urbis** (C/Reding 20 bis, 977 24 01 16, www.urbis.com, €66-€100). **Alexandra Aparthotel** (Rambla Nova 71, 977 248 701, www.ah-alexandra.com, €70) is a good option for those who want a little more independence. You'll find cheaper accommodation on the Plaça de la Font at the **Pensión Forum** (No.37, 977 23 17 18, closed Nov, €38-€42) and the nearby **Pensión La Noria** (No.53, 977 23 87 17, €38-€44); there's little to choose between them in either price or amenities.

## Tourist information

### Tarragona

*C/Fortuny 4 (977 23 34 15/www.tarragona turisme.es).* **Open** 9am-2pm, 4-6.30pm Mon-Fri; 9am-2pm Sat.

## Getting there

### By bus

Alsa (902 42 22 42/www.alsa.es) runs 12 buses daily from Barcelona Nord station.

### By train

RENFE from Sants or Passeig de Gràcia. Trains depart hourly (journey time 1hr 6mins).

## The Wine Country

Just south-west of Barcelona you'll find prime wine terrain, where the majority of Catalan wines are produced. Various of the region's many *denominaciones de origen* are found here, but the main suppliers are found in the **Penedès**, with vineyards dating back to Roman times. **Vilafranca** is the winemaking capital of this region, and a handsome medieval town in its own right, presided over by the elegant 14th-century **Basílica de Santa Maria**. The town's wine museum, the **Museu del Vi** (Plaça Jaume I 1-3, 938 900 582, www.museudelvi.org, closed Mon) has old wooden presses and wine jugs, some dating to the fourth century. The Saturday morning market here is the region's best, and a great place to stock up on local produce.

The two main wineries in the area are both owned by the Torres family. **Torres** (Finca El Maset, Pacs del Penedès, 938 177 487, www.torres.es) itself, is Penedès' largest winemaker and runs tours at its cellars outside town. More interesting for serious wine-lovers is **Jean León** (Pago Jean León, 938 995 512, www.jeanleon.com, admission €3), a pioneering brand credited with introducing cabernet sauvignon and chardonnay to Spain. Nearby **Albet i Noya** (Can Vendrell de la Codina, Sant Pau d'Ordal, 938 994 812, www.albetinoya.com, tours €5.50, min 4 people, closed Sun) was Spain's first organic winery and now leads the way in restoring traditional, pre-phylloxera varietals to the area.

Just north of here is **Sant Sadurní d'Anoia**, the capital of the Penedès cava industry. It's not a pretty town, but it's much easier to visit by public transport than the more remote wine producers. More than 90 per cent of Spain's cava is made here. **Codorníu** (Avda Codorníu, 938 183 232, www.grupo codorniu.com, admission €2), one of the largest producers, offers a wonderful tour of its Modernista headquarters, designed by Puig i Cadafalch. A train takes visitors through parts of the 26 kilometres (16 miles) of underground cellars, finishing, of course, with a tasting. **Freixenet** (C/Joan Sala 2, 938 917 000, www.freixenet.es), another mega wine producer, is opposite Sant Sadurní station and offers free tours and tastings.

**Alatafulla**. See *p285*.

The **Priorat** area is renowned for its full-bodied (and full-priced) red wines. Monks were producing wine here as long ago as the 11th century, but the area had been all but abandoned as a centre of viticulture when young winemaker **Alvaro Palacios** set up a tiny vineyard here in the late 1980s. He battled steep hills and a sceptical wine industry, but within a few years he won global acclaim, and the region is now one of Spain's most popular among wine buyers. *Bodegas* to look out for in and around the town of Gratallops include **Clos l'Obac** (Costers del Siurana, C/Manyetes, s/n, 977 839 276), **Mas Igneus** (Ctra Falset a La Vilella Baixa km 11.1, 977 262 259) and **Clos Mogador** (Camí Manyetes, 977 839 171). The Priorat wineries are less accessible to casual visitors and it pays to call ahead to let them know you're coming if you want to visit.

The small **Alella** district, east of Barcelona, is best known for light, dry whites, but more important is **Terra Alta**: near the Priorat in Tarragona, with Gandesa as its capital, this area is renowned for its heavy reds. **Montsant**, a newly created DO, is also growing in popularity. Montsant's **Celler Capçanes** makes one of the world's top kosher wines and is also visitor-friendly.

## Where to stay & eat

To try excellent local wines in Vilafranca, head to the **Inzolia** wine bar and store (C/Palma 21, 938 181 938, www.inzolia.com). **El Purgatori** (Plaça Campanar 5, 938 921 263, dinner only, mains €9) serves *pa amb tomàquet* with charcuterie and cheese in a tiny square. **Cal Ton** (C/Casal 8, 938 903 741, closed Mon, mains €20) offers Catalan dishes like salt-cod tripe salad, and *mató* (fresh cheese) mousse with tomato jam. In Sant Sadurní, **Cal Blay** (C/Josep Rovira, 11, 938 910 022, www. calblay.com, mains €13.50) is also of the new wave and serves a good fixed lunch.

The three-star **Hotel Pere III** (Plaça del Penedès 2, 938 903 100, www.hotelpedro tercero.com, €58-€63), in the centre of Vilafranca is good if you're travelling here by train as there are several wineries within walking distance; ask at the museum. In Torrelavit is **Masia Can Cardús** (938 995 018, www.masiasdelpenedes.com, €47), a farm and vineyard with rooms to rent. In the Priorat, the dreamy **Mas Ardèvol** (Ctra Falset a Porrera km 5.3, 630 324 578, www. masardevol.net, €85-€130, dinner €22) has cheerful decor and gardens of fruit trees and flowers. For updated regional cooking, try **El Cairat** (C/Nou 3, 977 830 481, closed Mon, mains €14.50) in Falset.

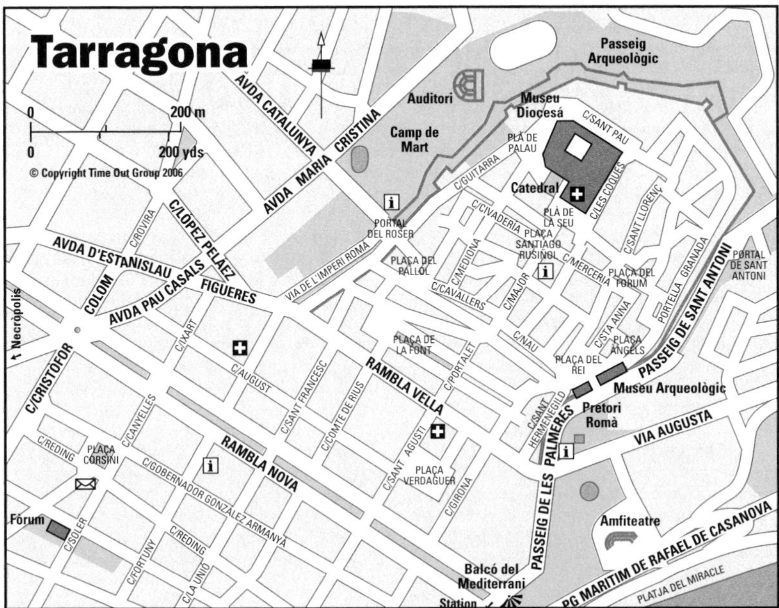


## Tourist information

### Falset

*C/Sant Marcel 2 (977 831 023/www.priorat.org).* **Open** 10am-2pm, 4-7pm Mon-Fri; 10am-2pm Sat; 11am-2pm Sun.

### Sant Sadurní d'Anoia

*C/Hospital 26 (938 913 188).* **Open** *Sept-July* 10am-2pm, 4.30-6.30pm Mon-Fri; 10am-2pm Sat, Sun. *Aug* 10am-2pm Tue-Sun.

### Vilafranca del Penedès

*C/Cort 14 (938 181 254).* **Open** 4-7pm Mon; 9am-1pm, 4-7pm Tue-Sat.

## Getting there

### By bus

**Alella** Sagales Barcelona Bus (902 130 014/ www.sagales.es) from Plaça Urquinaona.
**Alt Penedès** Hispano Igualadina (938 04 44 51) provides 15 buses daily from Sants.
**Falset & Gandesa** Hispano Igualadina (938 04 44 51). There are two buses daily from Sants.

### By train

**Alt Penedès** RENFE from Sants or Plaça Catalunya; trains hourly 6am-10pm (journey 45mins), then taxi for Torres, Jean León and Codorníu.
**Falset & Gandesa** RENFE from Sants or Passeig de Gràcia to Marcà-Falset. Six trains daily (2hrs). For Gandesa go to Mora d'Ebre (20mins) and catch a bus.

## Costa Daurada

Known as the Costa Daurada, or 'Gold Coast', the area beyond Sitges and Vilanova boasts long strands of sand, backed by alluvial plains. Development has been rife, however, and most of it is lined by concrete apartment blocks. Before you hit Tarragona, the seaside town of **Calafell** is popular with yachties, and its Iberian citadel is worth a mooch.

Continuing along the coast, the town of **Altafulla** hugs the sea with an esplanade of low-rise houses. Altafulla Pueblo, meanwhile, is a jumble of cobbled streets with a medieval feel; it's a ten-minute walk inland. Further south along the coast, towards the unlovely resort of **Salou**, is the **Port Aventura** theme park.

### Universal Mediterránea Port Aventura

*977 779 090/www.portaventura.es. By car A2, then A7 or N340 (108km/67 miles)/by train from Passeig de Gràcia (1hr 15mins).* **Open** *Mid Mar-mid June, mid Sept-Oct* 10am-7pm daily. *Mid June-mid Sept* 10am-midnight daily. *Nov, Dec* 10am-6pm Fri; 10am-7pm Sat, Sun. **Admission** *Port Aventura* €35; €28 concessions; night ticket €24; €19.50 concession. Free under-4s. *Costa Caribe* (mid June-mid Sept) €19; €15.50 concessions. *3-day combined ticket* €65; €52 concessions. **Credit** AmEx, DC, MC, V.
Port Aventura theme park is the main attraction of this beach resort, but there are also two hotels and

## Double, double toil and trouble

Catalonia isn't a place associated with witchcraft and paganism, and yet, in the countryside especially, witches hold powerful associations. An hour inland, due south-west of Barcelona, Cervera is a handsome, and quite sizeable, medieval town, perched on a hilltop amid the orchards and olive groves of Lleida. The hollow outer walls of the city act as beamed tunnels; dark and narrow, with occasional alleyways running off them down to gardens and courtyards and up steep, stone steps to the heart of the town. Known as the Carrers de les Bruixes ('Streets of Witches'), to walk them by night evokes an air that is not so much sinister as magical – it was here that the so-called witches of Cervera were said to have practised the dark arts.

The Aquelarre was revived nearly 30 years ago. A sort of Catalan Hallowe'en, complete with pointy black hats and the worship of a central character known as El Macho Cabrón, its purpose is two-fold: as a means of celebrating the harvest and granting favours with the harvest gods for the following year, and as a way of commemorating the life of Bruja Magdalena – a young witch who lived in Cervera in the 17th century and who was persecuted and eventually executed by the Inquisition in 1640. Thus, when the sun sets, devils and witches congregate all over the city, dancing and screeching and performing mystical acts long into the night.

The festivities kick off with the *correfoc* (fire run) on the Friday evening of the last weekend in August, in which more than 200 young devils and witches dance through the street streaming fireworks in their wake. But it's not until Saturday night, with the arrival of El Macho Cabrón – a sinister-looking creature sporting sackcloth, ashes and a pair of horns – that things really get going, with a series of rock and classical concerts, *gigant* (papier-mâché giants) processions and fire-dancing. For more information, see www.aquelarre.org.

the tropically landscaped Costa Caribe water park. Port Aventura has 90 rides spread across five internationally themed areas (Mexico, the Far West, China, Polynesia and the Mediterranean), while Popeye and the Pink Panther roam the time-space continuum and hug your kids. The truly stomach-curdling Dragon Khan rollercoaster is one of the highlights; for the little ones, there's the usual slew of carousels and spinning teacups. There are also 100 daily live shows and a spectacular lakeside Fiesta Aventura with lights, music and fireworks.

### Where to stay & eat

Located in Calafell, the **Hotel Ra** is a sleek spa and thalassotherapy centre on the site of an old sanatorium (Avda Sanatori 1, 977 694 200, www.hotelra.com, €241-€385). For great breakfasts and artisan pastries by the sea try **Calafell 66** (San Juan de Dios 83, 977 622 918). For a blowout head to **Giorgio** (C/Àngel Guimerà 4, 977 691 159) and sample the dishes of eccentric chef-painter Giorgio Serafíni.

Altafulla has the elegant **Hotel Gran Claustre** (C/Cup 2, 977 651 557, www.granclaustre.com, €144-€177), housed in an old convent with a central patio and swimming pool. The **Hotel San Martín** (C/Mar 7, 977 650 307, www.hotelsanmartin.com, €54-€86) is basic, but has a pool. The **Faristol** (C/Sant Martí 5, 977 650 077, closed lunch June-Sept, closed Mon-Thur Oct-May, €64-€75, mains €11), in the Old Town, is a hotel, bar and particularly good restaurant in an 18th-century house run by an Anglo-Catalan couple. For seafood tapas on the seafront, try **El Braser** (C/Botigues de Mar 15, 977 651 162, closed Wed, mains €10) and for cheap eats, **La Chunga** (C/Mar 13, 977 652 281, mains €8).

### Tourist information

#### Altafulla

*Plaça dels Vents (977 650 752/www.altafulla.org).* **Open** *June-Sept* 11am-1pm, 5-9pm daily.

### Getting there

#### By bus

Autobuses Plana (977 214 475) runs one bus each day to Altafulla from Passeig Sant Juan. Hispano Igualadina (938 044 451) runs one bus a day (Mon-Fri) to El Vendrell from Sants.

#### By train

RENFE from Sants or Passeig de Gràcia to Altafulla (1hr 15mins). Trains run hourly, approx 6am-9.20pm.

## The Cistercian Route

The three architectural gems of the area inland from Tarragona are the extraordinary Cistercian monasteries in **Poblet**, **Santes Creus** and **Vallbona de les Monges**.

A signposted path, the GR175, runs between them; the trail, more than 100 kilometres (62 miles) long, is known as **La Ruta del Cister** (the Cistercian Route). There are plenty of places to stay en route, though, and all three monasteries are easily accessible by car from **Montblanc**, 112 kilometres (70 miles) west of Barcelona and a beautiful town in its own right. In the Middle Ages, it was one of Catalonia's most powerful centres, with an important Jewish community. Its past is today reflected in its narrow medieval streets, magnificent 13th-century town walls, its churches, the **Palau Reial** and the **Palau del Castlà** (Chamberlain's Palace).

**Poblet**, a few kilometres west, was founded in 1151 as a royal residence and monastery. The remarkable complex includes a 14th-century **Gothic royal palace**, the 15th-century chapel of **Sant Jordi** and the main **church**, which houses the tombs of most of the count-kings of Barcelona. **Santes Creus**, founded in 1158, grew into a small village when families moved into the old monks' residences in the 1800s. Fortified walls shelter the **Palau de l'Abat** (Abbot's Palace), a monumental fountain, a 12th-century church and a superb Gothic cloister and chapterhouse.

**Santa Maria de Vallbona**, the third of these Cistercian houses was, unlike the others, a convent of nuns. It has a fine part-Romanesque cloister but is less grand than the other two. Like them, it still houses a religious community.

### Monestir de Poblet

*977 870 254/www.abadía-poblet.org.* **Open** *Mar-Sept* 10am-12.45pm, 3-6pm daily. *Oct-Feb* 10am-12.30pm, 3-5.30pm daily. **Admission** €4.50; €2.50 concessions. **No credit cards**.

### Monestir de Santa Maria de Vallbona

*973 33 02 66/www.vallbona.com.* **Open** *Mar-Oct* 10.30am-1.30pm, 4.30-6.30pm Mon-Sat; noon-1.30pm, 4.30-6.30pm Sun. *Nov-Feb* 10.30am-1.30pm, 4.30-5.30pm Mon-Sat; noon-1.30pm, 4.30-5.30pm Sun. **Admission** €3; €2 concessions. **No credit cards**.

### Monestir de Santes Creus

*977 638 329.* **Open** *Mid Mar-mid Sept* 10am-1pm, 3-6.30pm Tue-Sun. *Mid Sept-mid Jan* 10am-1.30pm, 3-5.30pm Tue-Sun. *Mid Jan-mid Mar* 10am-1.30pm, 3-6pm Tue-Sun. **Admission** €3.60; €2.40 concessions. Free Tue. **No credit cards**.

## Where to stay & eat

In Montblanc, you'll need to book in advance in order to secure a room at the popular **Fonda dels Àngels** (Plaça dels Àngels 1, 977 860 173, closed Sun and 3wks Sept, €37, set menu €15 & €20), which also has a great restaurant. The **Fonda Colom** is a friendly old restaurant located behind the Plaça Major (C/Civaderia 5, 977 860 153, closed Mon, 2 wks Sept & 2 wks Dec, mains €13.50).

In L'Espluga de Francolí, along the route to Poblet, the **Hostal del Senglar** (Plaça Montserrat Canals 1, 977 870 121, ww.hostal

The town and Cistercian monastery at **Santes Creus**.

Trips Out of Town

delsenglar.com, €60-€67) is a great-value country hotel with lovely gardens, a swimming pool and an atmospheric, if slightly pricey, restaurant (mains €12). In Santes Creus the **Hotel La Plana del Molí** (Avda Plana del Molí 21, 977 638 309, €48) is set in extensive gardens. Try the delicious partridge broth or wild-boar stew at its restaurant (mains €9). The **Hostal Grau** (C/Pere El Gran 3, 977 638 311, www.pensiongrau.com, closed mid Oct-June, €41, restaurant closed Mon and mid Dec-mid Jan, mains €17) is another very reasonable option, with good Catalan food, as is the **Restaurant Catalunya** (C/Arbreda 2, 977 63 84 32, closed Wed, mains €9).

## Tourist information

### Montblanc

*Antiga Església de Sant Francesc (977 861 733/ www.montblancmedieval.org).* **Open** 10am-1.30pm, 3-6.30pm Mon-Sat; 10am-2pm Sun.

## Getting there

### By bus

Hispano Igualadina (938 044 451) runs a service to Montblanc from Sants station leaving at 3.30pm Mon-Fri. There are more buses running from Valls and Tarragona.

### By train

RENFE trains leave from Sants or Passeig de Gràcia to Montblanc. There are five trains a day. The journey takes about 2hrs.

# Tortosa & the Ebre Delta

About an hour further down the coast from Tarragona is **Tortosa**, a little-visited town with a rich history evident in the fabric of its buildings. A magnificent Gothic cathedral, built on the site of a Roman temple, is surrounded by narrow medieval alleyways, and traces of the town's Jewish and Arab quarters can still be seen (and are clearly signposted). Interesting Modernista buildings around the town include the colourful, Mudéjar-inspired pavilions of the former slaughterhouse (Escorxador), on the banks of the Ebre river.

East of here is the astonishing **Parc Natural del Delta de l'Ebre**, an ecologically remarkable protected area. The towns of the delta are themselves nothing special, but the immense, flat, green expanses of wetlands, channels, dunes and still-productive rice fields are eerily beautiful. It's this variety of habitat, so attractive to birds, that makes the area such a popular birdwatching destination, since birders can hope to tick off nearly half the 600 bird species that are found in Europe at this one site. The flocks of flamingos make a spectacular sight as they shuffle around filter feeding, and the wetlands are full of herons, great crested grebes, spoonbills and marsh harriers.

The town of **Deltebre** is the base for most park services; from here, it's easy to make day trips to the bird sanctuaries, especially the remote headland of **Punta de la Banya**. The delta's flatness makes it an ideal place for walking or cycling; for bicycle hire, check at the tourist office in Deltebre. Small boats offer trips along the river from the north bank about eight kilometres (five miles) east of Deltebre.

## Where to stay & eat

Tortosa has a wonderful parador, **Castell de la Suda** (977 44 44 50, €117-€161), built on the site of a Moorish fortress with panoramic views of the countryside. See www.paradors.es for occasional offers. On the eastern edge of the Ebre delta is a wide, sweeping beach, Platja dels Eucaliptus, where you'll find the **Camping Eucaliptus** (977 479 046, www.campingeucaliptus.com, closed mid Oct-mid Mar, €3.65/€5.20/person; €4.50/€5.60/tent; €3.25/€3.85/car). The **Hotel Rull** in Deltebre is friendly and organises occasional 'safaris' (Avda Esportiva 155, 977 487 728, www.hotelrull.com, €68-€95, mains €18). You can also stay and eat at the ecologically friendly **Delta Hotel** (Avda del Canal, Camí de la Illeta, 977 480 046, www.deltahotel.net, €73-€81). Local specialities include dishes made with delta rice, duck, frogs' legs and the curious *chapadillo* (sun-dried eels): try them all at **Galatxo**, at the mouth of the river (Desembocadura Riu Ebre, 977 26 75 03, mains €15).

## Tourist information

### Delta de l'Ebre

*C/Doctor Martí Buera 22, Deltebre (977 489 679/ www.parcsdecatalunya.net).* **Open** *Oct-Apr* 10am-2pm, 3-6pm Mon-Sat; 10am-2pm Sun. *May-Sept* 10am-2pm, 3-7pm Mon-Sat; 10am-2pm Sun.

### Tortosa

*Plaça Carrilet 1 (977 449 648/www.turisme tortosa.com).* **Open** *Oct-Mar* 10am-1.30pm, 3.30-6.30pm Tue-Sat; 10.30am-1.30pm Sun. *Apr-Sept* 10am-1.30pm, 4.30-7.30pm Tue-Sat; 10.30am-1.30pm Sun.

## Getting there

### By train & bus

RENFE from Sants or Passeig de Gràcia every 2hrs to Tortosa (journey time 2hrs) or L'Aldea (journey time 2hrs 30mins), then three buses daily (HIFE 977 440 300) to Deltebre.

# Girona & the Costa Brava

Golden triangles, crazy artists, Kabbalah and the wildest coast in Spain.

Girona.

## Girona

Smart, peaceful and solidly middle class, Girona is a city far more staunchly Catalan than its cosmopolitan cousin Barcelona, and increasingly it is becoming almost as much a destination thanks to Ryanair's monopoly on the airport. Time spent in Girona rewards with a carefully restored Jewish quarter dominating the handsome medieval heart, a stunning cathedral and a handful of interesting museums. These include the one-off **Museu del Cinema** (C/Sequia 1, 972 412 777, www.museudel cinema.org, closed Mon) – a fascinating collection of early animation techniques right through to the present day.

The **River Onyar**, which is lined by buildings in red and ochre, divides the Old City from the new, and connects one to the other by the impressive Eiffel-designed bridge, the **Pont de les Peixateries**. A walk up the lively riverside **Rambla de la Llibertat** takes you towards the city's core and major landmark, the magnificent **cathedral**. Its 1680 baroque façade conceals a graceful Romanesque cloister and understated Gothic interior, which happens to boast the widest nave in Christendom. In the cathedral museum is the stunning 12th-century **Tapestry of Creation** and the **Beatus**, an illuminated tenth-century set of manuscripts.

Before its expulsion in 1492, the city's sizeable Jewish population had its own district, the **Call**, whose labyrinthine streets running off and around the C/Força are among the most beautifully preserved in Europe. The story of this community is told in the Jewish museum in the **Centre Bonastruc ça Porta** (C/Força 8, 972 216 761, www.ajuntament.gi/call/cat/index.php), built on the site of a 15th-century synagogue. Nearby is the **Museu d'Història de la Ciutat** (C/Força 27, 972 222 229, www.ajuntament.gi/museu_ciutat, closed Mon), set in an 18th-century monastery. Look out for the alcoves with ventilated seating on the ground floor: this is where the deceased monks were placed to dry out for two years, before their mummified corpses were put on display.

Heading north from here, the **Mudéjar Banys Àrabs** (C/Ferran el Catòlic, 972 190 797) is actually a Christian creation, a 12th-century bathhouse with a blend of Romanesque and Moorish architecture. The nearby monastery of **Sant Pere de Galligants** is a fine example of Romanesque architecture, its beautiful 12th-century cloister rich with intricate carvings. The monastery also houses the **Museu Arqueològic** (Plaça Santa Llúcia 1, 972 202 632, www.mac.es, closed Mon), showing day-to-day objects from the Paleolithic to the Visigothic periods. Continuing from here, the **Passeig Arqueològic** runs along what's left of the old city walls, intact until 1892.

For those of a more active disposition, the **carrilet** (an old steam-rail route dating back to 1892) has been reincarnated as a cycle path running from Girona to Sant Feliu de Guíxols. It starts at the Plaça dels Països Catalans and continues along a lovely route of ancient Iberian villages, iron bridges and long-dry river beds. It takes about three hours going at a gentle pace.

## Where to stay & eat

The **AC Palau de Bellavista** (C/Pujada Polvorins 1, 872 080 670, www.ac-hotels.com, €140-€190) is the business option in the New Town. It has a terrace with wonderful views of the city and the gourmet restaurant **Numun**, headed by the Roca brothers. The **Hotel Ciutat de Girona** (C/Nord 2, 972 483 038, www.hotel-ciutatdegirona.com, €123-€144.50) is similar, with the odd designer touch. In the Old Town, the **Hotel Històric** (C/Bellmirall 6, 972 223 583, www.hotelhistoric.com, €122-€321) is a shade cheaper. The owners also rent fully equipped apartments for two or three people (€96) in the adjacent building. **Pensión Bellmirall** (C/Bellmirall 3, 972 204 009, closed Jan & Feb, €60-€70) is in a pretty 14th-century building with a shady breakfast courtyard. The **Hotel Peninsular** (C/Nou 3 & Avda Sant Francesc 6, 972 203 800, www.novarhotels.com, €64-€70) is good value.

The best restaurant in town, and one of the best in Spain, is the **Celler de Can Roca** (C/Taialà 40, 972 22 21 57, www.cellercanroca.com, closed Mon & Sun, mains €30). Located in an unprepossessing suburb just north of the city, it's an essential trip for food-lovers, though you'll need to book ahead. If the coffers won't quite stretch to this, the affordable tasting menu at **Massana** (C/Bonastruc de Porta 10, 972 213 820, closed Sun & dinner Tue, tasting menu €52.30) offers yet more creativity.

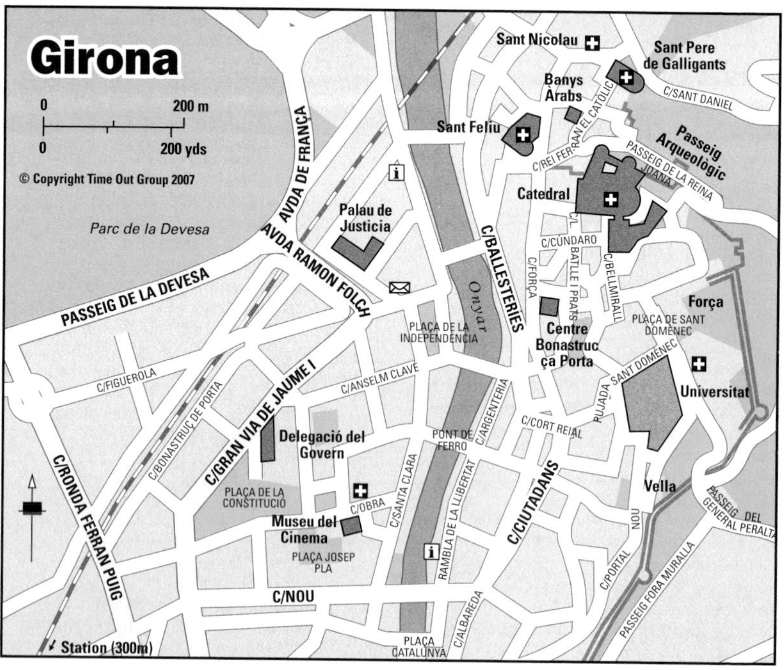

Over the river from the Old Town, you'll find Girona's oldest and possibly best-value restaurant, **Casa Marieta** (Plaça de la Independència 5-6, 972 201 016, www.casamarieta.com, closed Mon, mains €12), while the old Modernista flour factory houses **La Farinera** (Ptge Farinera Teixidor 4, 972 220 220, menu €9), which has good tapas. Halfway up a medieval flight of steps nearby is a Francophile's delight, **Le Bistrot** (Pujada Sant Domènec 4, 972 218 803, mains €12), with a cheap (and good) set lunch in a pretty setting.

## Tourist information

### Girona

*Rambla de la Llibertat 1 (972 22 65 75/www.ajuntament.gi).* **Open** 8am-8pm Mon-Fri; 8am-2pm, 4-8pm Sat; 9am-2pm Sun.

## Getting there

### By bus

Sagales Barcelona Bus (902 260 606/www.sagales.com) runs approximately five buses daily from Estació del Nord.

### By train

RENFE from Sants or Passeig de Gràcia (1hr 15mins). Trains leave hourly from 6am-9.15pm.

## From Girona to the coast

The C66 takes you from Girona to the coast through the Baix (Lower) Empordà, coined the 'Golden Triangle' by locals, and the 'Tuscany of Spain' by foreigners. Both amount to much the same thing: a postcard-perfect patchwork of corn fields, oak copses and sunflowers and a seriously moneyed, part-time population. The region's strategic importance in medieval times is demonstrated by a legacy of castles and walled, honey-coloured towns and villages. The road splits in dignified **La Bisbal**, where you can buy no end of ceramic goods and visit the **Museu de Terracotta** (C/Sis d'Octubre de 1869, 972 642 067, open July-Sept). Nearby **Verges** is most famous for its grotesque 'dance of death' procession on Maundy Thursday. Up the road is the 12th-century **Castell de Púbol**, bought by Salvador Dalí to house (and eventually bury) his wife-muse Gala in her later years. Relations were strained by then: Dalí had to book appointments to see her, and the tomb that he prepared for himself next to hers lies empty (he changed his mind), guarded by a stuffed giraffe.

A few miles east lies the walled, moated town of **Peratallada**. Dominated by an 11th-century castle, it is famous for its indigo-painted arcades and for its excellent restaurants. Nearby **Ullastret** takes you further back in time, with extensive ruins from a third-century BC Iberian settlement, explained in the small **Museu d'Arqueològic** (Puig de Sant Andreu, 972 179 058/www.mac.es, closed Mon). The medieval town of **Pals**, with its imposing **Torre de les Hores**, has great views of the coast, as does **Begur**, a 14th-century town built around its castle. The latter acts as a gateway to the Costa Brava, and is a steep three-kilometre (two-mile) walk from the sea.

Castell de Púbol.

### Castell de Púbol

*Information Teatre-Museu Dalí (972 67 75 00/www.salvador-dali.org).* **Open** *15 Mar-14 June, 16 Sept-1 Nov* 10.30am-5.15pm Tue-Sun. *15 June-15 Sept* 10.30am-7.15pm daily. *2 Nov-31 Dec* 10.30am-4.15pm. Closed 1 Jan-14 Mar. **Admission** €6; €4 concessions. **No credit cards**.

## Where to stay & eat

In Peratallada, the **Hostal Miralluna** (Plaça de l'Oli 2, 972 634 304, www.hostalmiralluna.com, €150-€180) is a tranquil 14th-century place to stay, and filled with antiques. **El Cau del Papibou** (C/Major 10, 972 634 018, www.hotelcau.net, €107-€128) is a pleasant, eight-room hotel with all the technological advances of the 21st century. The charming **Ca l'Aliu** (C/Roca 6, 972 634 061, www.calaliu.

com, €55-€60) is probably the best value accommodation in town. In Ullastret the **Hotel Restaurant El Fort** (C/Presó 2, 972 757 773, www.hotelelfort.com, €128-€161) has four comfortable studio apartments, and offers a range of packages. In Pals, the **Hotel Mas Salvi** (C/Carmany 13, 972 636 478, www.mas salvi.com, closed mid Jan-mid Feb, €202-€360) is located down a long, gravel lane, in the middle of pristine countryside. A sprawling, converted farmhouse, it has immense rooms, landscaped gardens, indoor and outdoor pools, tennis courts and a good, avant-garde restaurant. At the other end of the scale is the **Barris** (C/Enginyer Algarra 51, 972 636 702, €40). If you're staying in Begur, try the **Hotel Rosa** (C/Pi i Ralló 19, 972 623 015, www.hotel-rosa.com, closed Nov-Feb, €72-€93).

Locals travel from far and wide to eat in Peratallada's restaurants; try the famous *galtes de porc a l'empordanesa* (pigs' cheeks with artichoke and carrots) at the **Restaurant Bonay** (Plaça de les Voltes 13, 972 634 034, www.bonay.com, closed Jan & Dec, mains €14). Also making a name for itself in the centre of town is **La Païssa d'en Cardina** (C/Jaume II 10, 972 634 708, www.lapaissa.net, mains €15, closed dinner Tue & all day Wed), which has superb Empordan and Italian fare, with a wood-fired pizza oven and dishes such as home-made ravioli stuffed with anis-flavoured carrots. The €10 set lunch is fantastic. In Begur, **Els Patis de Begur** (C/Pi i Rallo 9, 972 623 741, mains €14) specialises in paellas; in Pals, **Restaurant Sa Punta** (Urbanizació Sa Punta, 972 667 376, mains €25) serves excellent Mediterranean dishes by a pool. In Ullastret, head to **Restaurant Ibèric** (C/Valls 11, 972 757 108, mains €15) for truly great regional fare including snails, *suquet* and wild-boar stew, with home-grown vegetables. Another superb-value little eaterie is **Sa Torre** (Plaça de la Mota 6, Palau-sator, 972 634 118, closed Wed, mains €12) serving exceptional grilled meats. It is also famed for its *arròs a la cassola* (a dark stew made with Pals rice, baked in terracotta and beefed out with *botifarra*, calamares and pork). Make like a local and take it to the beach.

## Tourist information

### Begur

*Avda 11 de Setembre 5 (972 624 520/www.begur.es).* **Open** *June-Sept* 9am-2pm, 4-9pm daily. *Oct-May* 9am-2pm, 4-7pm Mon-Sat; 10am-2pm Sun.

### Pals

*Plaça Major 7 (972 637 380/www.pals.es).* **Open** *mid June-mid Sept* 10am-2pm, 5-8pm Mon-Sat; 10am-2pm Sun. *Mid Sept-mid June* 10am-5pm Mon-Sat; 10am-2pm Sun.

## Getting there

### By bus

Sarfa (902 302 025/www.sarfa.com) runs nine daily buses from Estació del Nord to Palafrugell (some continue to Begur), and regular buses to La Bisbal, which stop at Púbol.

# Costa Brava

In its heyday, before the arrival of the bulldozers, high-rises and masses of pink-fleshed tourists, the Costa Brava (meaning 'wild' or 'rugged' coast) was the most exclusive resort area in Spain, attracting legions of film stars, artists and writers. Today, despite the concrete resorts that have swamped towns like **Calella**, **Blanes** and **Lloret de Mar**, it's still possible to find pockets of prettiness along the coast thanks to the soaring cliffs and rocky, sea-buffeted coves that prevent overdevelopment. A train will get you as far as Blanes, beyond which, the road spins into a series of cliff-hugging hairpin bends that mark the start of the Costa Brava proper, with **Tossa del Mar** as its gateway. While the new town has been constructed with little thought, Tossa still has one of the loveliest medieval quarters in Spain, crowning a hill jutting into the sea. It used to be a favourite haunt of Ava Gardner – a bronze statue of her marks the entry to the Old Town – harking back to the days when it looked like Tossa might be the new Capri. **Cala Bona** and **Cala Pola** are both lovely and relatively isolated beaches a short walk from here.

The tortuous 20-kilometre (12-mile) drive through coastal pine forests from here to **Sant Feliu de Guíxols** offers brief, but unforgettable, views of the sea. Sant Feliu itself has some fine Modernista buildings along the dignified Passeig Marítim, and the town museum has a fine collection of local ceramics. **Sant Pol** beach is three kilometres (two miles) north of the crowded town sands, and offers more towel room. Just north of Sant Pol the GR92 path, or 'Camino de Ronda', starts out from below the Hostal de la Gavina in S'Agaró and continues on along many secluded coves and rocky outlets for swimming. The sandy bay of **Sa Conca** – considered to be one of the most beautiful beaches on the Costa Brava – has a couple of good *xiringuitos* for a sardine lunch. Continue on at a leisurely pace all the way to Torre Valentina, from where you can catch a bus back. The only tedious stretch is the one that traverses **Platja d'Aro**. This and **Palamós** are worth avoiding generally; the latter has never recovered from an attack by the infamous pirate Barba Roja (Redbeard) in 1543. Instead, continue to **Palafrugell**, which has a great Sunday market and offers access to a number of picturesque villages built into the rocky coves. The **Fundació Vila Casas** (Plaça Can Mario 7, 972 306 246, www.fundaciovilacasas.com, closed Tue) houses a surprisingly good collection of works by local artists and sculptures, and gives an idea of the kind of creativity the environment inspires. **Calella de Palafrugell**, not to be confused with its ugly near-namesake down the coast, is a quiet, charming town, even during its annual Cantada d'Havaneres song festival in July. A scenic 20-minute walk away, **Llafranc** offers a long curved beach where you can swim between fishing boats at anchor in the bay. The cliff-top botanical gardens at **Cap Roig** (972 614 582) host a wonderful music and arts festival every July and August, attracting names such as Bob Dylan and Roberta Flack.

**Tamariu**, known for its good seafood, is the perfect base for waterskiing and fishing. Giro Náutic (www.gironautic.com) is a useful portal for all things aquatic in the area. Next up is **Aiguablava**, with its modern parador and white sandy beach, and **Fornells** – both are accessible from **Begur**, as is the small **Aiguafreda**, a cove that's sheltered by pines. Nearby **Sa Riera**, the northernmost cove, shelters two beaches: **La Platja del Raco**, where bathing costumes must be worn, and **Illa Roja**, where they mustn't.

Beyond the Ter estuary and the Montgri hills, which divide the Baix and Alt Empordà, is **L'Estartit**. This small resort town caters for tourists interested in exploring the **Illes Medes**, a group of rocky limestone outcrops. The biggest housed a British prison in the 19th century, but Les Illes are now home only to a unique ecosystem, an underwater paradise where divers can contemplate colourful coral and hundreds of different species of sea life. For a view of the islands, it's worth the climb up to the 12th-century **Castell de Montgrí**.

**Tossa del Mar.** *See p292.*

## Where to eat

In Tossa, **Santa Marta** (C/Francesc Aromir 2, 972 340 472, mains €18) has a pretty terrace in the Old Town and specialises in Catalan cuisine. **Da Nino** (C/Pola 9, 972 341 126, mains €8) is a friendly pizzeria in the centre. In Sant Feliu de Guíxols, try the **Nàutic** (Port Esportiu, 972 320 663, closed dinner Sun & all day Mon mid Sept-May, set lunch €15, set dinner €30) in the Club Nàutic sailing club, for great views and superb seafood. In Mont-ras, just outside Palafrugell, **La Cuina de Can Pipes** (Barri Canyelles s/n, Mont-ras, 972 306 677, www.canpipes.com, closed Mon, Tue & lunch Wed, Thur, mains €30) is one of the finest restaurants in the area, with tables on a large lawn. Calella has the excellent **Tragamar** (Platja de Canadell s/n, 972 614 336, www.grupotragaluz.com, mains €14.50), a branch of the restaurant Tragaluz in Barcelona. For something really special though, head for **El Didal** (Plaça de Port Bo, 972 615 776, closed Mon, Tue, mains €40) located in a tiny boathouse on the front. It serves only fresh, locally caught fish and shellfish. In Tamariu, there's more good seafood at the **Royal** on the beachfront (Passeig de Mar 9, 972 620 041, closed Jan & Dec, mains €17); while in Aiguablava, the **Hotel Aiguablava** (Platja de Fornells, 972 622 058, www.aiguablava.com, closed Nov-Feb, mains €24.50, set lunch/dinner €37.50) has an excellent beachfront restaurant.

## Where to stay

In Tossa, the **Hotel Diana** (Plaça España 6, 972 341 886, www.diana-hotel.com, €66-€137) is situated in a Modernista building with a

## Chick flit

With such a range of terrains (wetland, mountains, coasts and so on) and more than 3,200 species of breeding birds in the region, Catalonia is twitchers' heaven. Flying into Barcelona via El Prat, you don't have to venture far to start birding, since the **Llobregat delta**, at the edge of the airport, has some great hides and attracts a decent selection of migrant birds: more than 300 species make a visit every year.

At nearly 5,000 hectares (57,950 acres), one of the top all-round spots is the **Parc Natural dels Aiguamolls de l'Empordà** (PNAE). Local environmental groups were successful in their battle against developers who wanted to turn the area into a concrete jungle in the early 1980s, and it became a park in 1983. Today it's one of the most important homes for aquatic birds in the country. One of the reasons for its popularity is the wide range of habitats, including dunes, salt marshes, paddy fields and pasture. Another is that it is excellently managed, with easy-to-follow trails leading to carefully placed hides. The result is that it's extremely popular – especially the two artificial habitats, Estany de Cortalet and Estanys d'Europa – with both homegrown and foreign twitchers.

It's hard to pinpoint what you'll see and when, but among the highlights of Catalan birding are the **Delta de l'Ebre** wetlands (*see p288*) – the best place for seeing gulls and terns, especially the rare Audouin's gull and Caspian tern, as well as herons and flamingos; the **Cap de Creus** (*see p295*), **Garraf** (*see p278*) and other rocky headlands, are home to Bonelli's eagle, Ortolan bunting, black wheatear and Yelkouan shearwaters, while in the Pyrenean **Vall d'Aran** black woodpeckers, wallcreeper and lammergeier can be seen.

For more information, the non-profit-making Institut Català d'Ornitologia publishes winter and breeding bird atlases and runs long-term monitoring and ringing schemes (www.ornitologia.org/admin/english.htm), while the Spanish equivalent of the RSPB is the Sociedad Española Ornitología (www.seo.org). There are also various operators specialising in birdwatching tours. Try **Catalan Bird Tours** (www.catalanbirdtours.com) or **Audouin Birding Tours** (www.audouinbirding.com).

beautifully preserved marble staircase and tiled floors. Bargain rooms are to be had at **Fonda Lluna** (C/Roqueta 20, 972 340 365, www.fondalluna.com, €36-€44). In Sant Feliu de Guíxols, try the small, friendly **Hotel Plaça** (Plaça Mercat 22, 972 325 155, www.hotelplaza.org, €75-€107), close to the beach. North of Sant Feliu, in **S'Agaró**, is the nearest luxury option, the **Hostal de la Gavina** (Plaça de la Rosaleda, 972 32 11 00, www.lagavina.com, closed Nov-Easter, €198-€417), a five-star in the European grand-hotel tradition. Near the Platja d'Aro, **Mas Torrellas** (Ctra de Santa Cristina a Platja d'Aro km2, 972 837 526, €64-€90) is removed from the madness somewhat. It is an 18th-century farmhouse with bags of charm and a pretty garden pool.

Llafranc has the **Hotel Llafranch** (Passeig de Cipsela 16, 972 300 208, www.hllafranch.com, €94-€148), which is run by two brothers, and was a favourite haunt of Salvador Dalí and various of his cronies back in the 1960s. Alternatively, the friendly **Hotel Casamar** (C/Nero 3-11, 972 30 01 04, closed Jan-mid Mar, €55-€130) is a good budget option.

Tamariu is home to the relaxed **Hotel Tamariu** (Passeig de Mar 2, 972 62 00 31, www.tamariu.com, closed Nov-Mar, €87-€122), while in Aiguablava, there's the pleasant parador, **Platja d'Aiguablava** (972 62 21 62, www.parador.es, €140-€171) or the stately, family-run **Hotel Aiguablava** (*see above* **Where to eat**, €158-€224). In Begur, try **AiguaClara** (972 622 905, www.aigua

clara.com, €87-€130), a colonial-style palace dating back to 1876. Light, airy rooms, original tiles and colourful paintwork give it a chilled-out, funky edge. There's live jazz in the restaurant on Friday evenings. Nearby, in Sa Tuna, the **Hostal Sa Tuna** (Platja Sa Tuna, 972 62 21 98, www.hostalsatuna.com, closed mid Oct-mid Mar, €107-€128) has five rooms and enjoys a perfect position by the sea. L'Estartit has the **Santa Clara** (Passeig Marítim 18, 972 75 17 67, €50-€58).

## Tourist information

### L'Estartit

*Passeig Maritim (972 75 19 10/www.torroella.org).* **Open** *June, Sept* 9.30am-2pm, 4-8pm daily. *July, Aug* 9.30am-2pm, 4-9pm daily. *Oct-May* 9am-1pm, 3-6pm daily.

### Palafrugell

*C/Carrilet 2 (972 30 02 28/www.palafrugell.net).* **Open** *May-June, Sept* 10am-1pm, 5-8pm Mon-Sat; 10am-1pm Sun. *July, Aug* 9am-9pm Mon-Sat; 10am-1pm Sun. *Oct-Apr* 10am-1pm, 4-7pm Mon-Sat; 10am-1pm Sun.

### Sant Feliu de Guíxols

*Plaça del Mercat 28 (972 82 00 51/www.guixols.net).* **Open** *Mid June-mid Sept* 10am-2pm, 4-8pm daily. *Mid Sept-mid June* 10am-1pm, 4-7pm Mon-Sat; 10am-2pm Sun.

## Getting there

### By bus

Sarfa (902 302 025/www.sarfa.com) runs 13 buses daily to Sant Feliu from Estació del Nord (journey time 1hr 20mins), and nine to Palafrugell (2hrs); some continue to Begur. Change in Palafrugell or Torroella for L'Estartit.

## North to France

The port town of **L'Escala** is best known for its anchovies, best enjoyed from one of its seafront terraces. A mere 15-minute walk away, in **Empúries**, you'll find the remains of an ancient city that dates back to 600 BC, when it was founded by the Phoenicians, before being recolonised by the Greeks and finally the Romans. Today, ruins from all three periods – including a stunning mosaic of Medusa, as well as the layout of the original Greek harbour – are clearly visible.

On the other side of the huge Golf de Roses is the overcrowded tourist resort of **Roses**, which has little to recommend it apart from a 16th-century citadel and the nearby legendary restaurant **El Bulli** (*see p171*) in Cala Montjoi. From Roses, the road coils over the hills that form the **Cap de Creus** nature reserve, before dropping spectacularly down to **Cadaqués**. The town's relative isolation has made it the chosen destination for the discerning: Picasso painted much of his early cubist work here, but it was Salvador Dalí who really put the place on the map. The artist spent his childhood summers here, brought his surrealist circle to see it, and ended up building his home in **Port Lligat**, a short walk away. Cadaqués later became the preferred resort among the Catalan cultural elite. It has kept its charm primarily thanks to a ban on the high-rise buildings that have blighted the rest of coastal Spain. Dalí's house, with much of its zany furniture, peculiar fittings and stuffed animals, is now a museum, that offers extraordinary insight into the eccentric genius's strange lifestyle. Note that you should book some days before you visit, as only eight people are allowed in at a time.

On the north side of the cape, you'll find **Port de la Selva**, which looks towards France. Less touristy than Cadaqués, it's also within hiking distance of the remarkable **Sant Pere de Rodes** fortified abbey (972 38 75 59, closed Mon, admission €3.60; €2.40 concessions, free Tue), the area's most accomplished example of Romanesque architecture. A further climb takes you up to the imposing **Castell de Sant Salvador**, an imposing tenth-century castle that seems to grow out of the rock, with unparalleled views out over the Pyrenees to France, and back into Catalonia.

The capital of the Alt Empordà region is **Figueres**, where Dalí was born and is buried in his own museum in the city's old theatre, the **Teatre-Museu Dalí**. The artist donated many of his works to the museum and also redesigned the place, putting thousands of yellow loaves on the external walls and huge eggs on its towers. The highlight inside is the three-dimensional room-sized Mae West face, a collection of furniture arranged to look like the star when viewed from a certain angle, with a plump red sofa for her famous pout. All of this somewhat overshadows the city's other two (rather good) museums: the **Museu de l'Empordà** (Rambla 2, 972 50 23 05, www.museuemporda.org, closed Mon), which gives an overview of the history of the area, and the **Museu del Joguet** (C/Sant Pere 1, 972 50 45 85, closed Mon), full of 19th- and early 20th-century toys, some of which belonged to Dalí and Miró.

Between Figueres and the sea sits the **Parc Natural dels Aiguamolls de l'Empordà**, which is a haven for rare species of birds that flock to the marshy lowlands at the mouth of the Fluvia river in spring and autumn. As well as flamingos, bee-eaters and moustached warblers, this nature reserve is home to turtles, salamanders and otters.

### Casa-Museu de Port Lligat

*972 25 10 15/www.dali-estate.org.* **Open** *Mid Mar-mid June, mid Sept-Dec* 10.30am-5.10pm Tue-Sun. *Mid June-mid Sept* 10.30am-8.10pm Tue-Sun. Closed Jan-mid Mar. **Admission** €8; €6 concessions. **No credit cards**. Advisable to book ahead.

### Teatre-Museu Dalí

*Plaça Gala-Salvador Dalí 5, Figueres (972 67 75 00/www.dali-estate.org).* **Open** *July-Sept* 9am-7.15pm daily. *Oct-June* 10.30am-5.15pm Tue-Sun. **Admission** €10; €7 concessions. **No credit cards**.

## Where to stay & eat

Next to the ruins in Empúries, the **Hostal Empúries** (Platja Portitxol, 972 77 02 07, www.hostalempuries.com, €93-€140, set menu €21.40-€27.80) offers sparse but clean rooms in a fantastic setting in front of the rocky beach. It also does good Mediterranean food all year round. Fifteen minutes' walk away, in the pretty village of Sant Martí d'Empúries, is the comfortable **Riomar** (Platja del Riuet, 972 77 03 62, www.riumarhotel.com, closed late Oct-Easter, €70-€120). Over the bay, a twisting seven-kilometre (four-and-a-half-mile) drive from Roses, is the extraordinary and world-famous **El Bulli** (*see p171*).

Perched on a cliff-top between Roses and Cadaqués, the **Hotel Cala Jóncols** (Ctra Vella de Roses a Cadaqués, 972 253 970, www.calajoncols.com, closed Dec-Mar, €56-€77 full board) is completely isolated and basic; a blissful hideaway for those who can do without luxuries, it makes for a great romantic weekend, especially out of season.

Cadaqués has few hotels, and most are closed in winter, so always call first. The **Hotel Rocamar** (C/Virgen del Carment s/n, 972 258 150, www.rocamar.com, €73-€171) is the finest hotel in Cadaqués and set away from the rest of the town, looking back over the bay. Alternatively, **Playa Sol** (Platja Pianc 3, 972 25 81 00, www.playasol.com, closed Jan & Dec, €105-€166) puts you in the thick of things and also has lovely sea views. Over the hill in Port Lligat, the two-star **Hotel Port Lligat** (972 258 162, €64-€99) is right next door to the Dalí museum and has a boutiquey feel to it, while the **Hotel Calina** (Avda Salvador Dalí, 33, 972 258 851, www.hotelcalina.com, incl breakfast €68-€126) is more modern, more comfortable and has a good-sized swimming pool overlooking the beach. Restaurants, too, have a habit of closing in winter, so it pays to call ahead. **Restaurant Can Rafa** (C/Passeig Marítim 7, 972 159 401, www.restaurantcanrafa.com, closed Wed and Dec, mains €22) specialises in local lobster, while the pretty **Es Balconet** (C/Sant Antoni 2, 972 258 814, closed Tue and Jan, Feb, Nov, mains €15), up a winding street back from the bay, is good for paella. **Casa Anita** (C/Miguel Roset, 972 258 471, www.casa-anita.com, closed Mon and Nov, mains €18) is a popular, friendly and family-owned place with excellent fresh seafood and long queues. Dalí used to eat here. At Cap de Creus, the **Restaurant Cap de Creus** (972 199 005, www.cbrava.com/restcapc.es.htm, closed 2 wks Nov, mains €16.50) serves an eclectic range of dishes from seafood to curry, all in a stunning setting on a headland jutting out to sea. Rooms are also available here (€85).

In Figueres, the **Hotel Duran** (C/Lasauca 5, 972 501 250, www.hotelduran.com, €86-€107, set menu €18) was an old haunt of Dalí and exudes comfortable, battered elegance. The restaurant serves fine game and seafood. For clean and simple rooms, head for **La Barretina** (C/Lasauca 13, 972 673 425, www.hostallabarretina.com, closed Nov, €45). **President** (Ronda Firal 33, 972 501 700, set lunch €16) offers good, solid Catalan fare and excellent seafood. C/Jonquera is the main drag for cheap *menús del dia*, with alfresco tables. A couple of kilometres west, **Mas Pau** (Ctra de Figueres a Besalú, Avinyonet de Puigventós, 972 546 154, www.maspau.com, closed Sun dinner, all day Mon and Tue lunch, mains €25) is an excellent and creative restaurant.

## Tourist information

### Cadaqués

*C/Cotxe 2A (972 25 83 15/www.cadaques.org).* **Open** *June-Sept* 9am-9pm Mon-Sat; 10.30am-1pm Sun. *Oct-May* 9am-1pm, 4-7pm Mon-Sat.

### L'Escala

*Plaça de les Escoles 1 (972 770 603/www.lescala.org).* **Open** *Mid June-mid Sept* 9am-8.30pm daily. *Mid Sept-mid June* 9am-1pm, 4-7pm Mon-Fri; 10am-4pm Sat; 10am-1pm Sun.

### Figueres

*Plaça del Sol (972 50 31 55).* **Open** *Mar-June, Oct* 9am-2pm, 4-7pm Mon-Fri; 9.30am-2pm, 3.30-6.30pm Sat. *July-Sept* 9am-8pm Mon-Sat; 10am-3pm Sun. *Feb* 9am-2pm Mon-Fri. Closed Nov-Jan.

## Getting there

### By bus

Sagales (902 260 606/www.sagales.com) runs several buses daily to Figueres from Estació del Nord (2hrs 30mins). Sarfa (902 302 025) runs two buses daily to Roses and Cadaqués (2hrs 15mins).

### By train

RENFE from Sants or Passeig de Gràcia to Figueres (journey 2hrs). Trains leave every hour.

# Vic to the Pyrenees

Beech forests, white-water rafting and the best snow this side of the Alps.

## Vic & around

Vic reveals its magic slowly, offering a good deal more than one might expect on first impressions. The capital of the verdant Osona region has at its heart the impressive arcaded Plaça Major, home to a famous market that is nearly as old as the town itself (Tuesday and Saturday mornings). In one corner of the market square is the Modernista Casa Comella. Sgraffiti designed by Gaietà Buïgas depict the four seasons. Buïgas was also responsible for the Monument a Colom in Barcelona. Of Vic's many churches, the **Catedral de Sant Pere** contains Romanesque, Gothic and neo-classical elements, along with a set of dramatic 20th-century murals by Josep Lluís Sert, who is buried here. The **Temple Romà** was only discovered in 1882, when the 12th-century walls that surrounded it were knocked down. It's since been well restored, and now houses an art gallery that shows some of Sert's work. The **Museu Episcopal** (Plaça del Bisbe Oliva 3, 93 886 93 60, www.museuepiscopalvic.com, closed Mon, admission €4) is worth visiting for its magnificent 12th-century murals and a superb collection of Romanesque and Gothic art.

The beech forests, medieval villages, gorges and Romanesque hermitages make this area rewarding to explore by foot but it is also a centre of both parapenting and hot air ballooning (Osona Globus, 609 832 974, www.osonaglobus.com). Following the C153 road towards Olot, **Rupit** makes a remarkably beautiful stop. An ancient village built on the side of a medieval castle, it has a precarious hanging bridge across the Ter gorge. Later building has been done so sympathetically to the style that it's difficult to tell the old from the new. Almost as lovely, and not quite as touristy, is nearby **Tavertet**.

### Where to stay & eat

In **Vic** itself, there's very little in the way of accommodation; its only *pensión* is **Hostal Osona** (C/Remei 3, 938 832 845, €28). It does, however, have some great restaurants. **Cardona 7** (C/Cardona 7, 938 863 815, tapas €6.50, closed Sun dinner and all day Mon) serves new-wave tapas such as pig's trotter salad and salt cod in rosemary. **La Taula** (C/Sant Marius 8, 934 172 848, closed lunch Sat, all day Sun and Aug, mains €14.50) offers a range of excellent-value set menus.

If you have transport, the nicest places to stay are outside Vic. The **Hotel Torre Martí** (C/Ramon Llull 11, St. Julià de Vilatorta, 938 888 372, www.hoteltorremarti.com, €120-€150) is one of the loveliest in the area. Painted fire-red with blue galleries, it was built in 1945 by local architect Riera Clariana. It's now an enclave of music and art, fine wine and gastronomy. The **Parador de Vic** (Paraje el Bac de Sau, 938 122 323, www.parador.es, €118) is modern and comfortable, and sits in a fabulous location overlooking the Ter gorge; take the C153 north of Vic and follow the signs (around 14km/10 miles). Just before Tavèrnoles, **Mas Banús** (938 122 091, www.elbanus.com) is a giant old farmhouse, with self-contained cottages costing from €250 for four people for a weekend. In Tavèrnoles is the **Fussimanya** (Ctra del Parador km 7, 938 122 188, closed dinner Wed

The arcaded Plaça Major in **Vic**.

& all day Thur, mains €12), a rambling old restaurant famous for its sausages; it is popular at weekends. In Rupit, **Hostal Estrella** (Plaça Bisbe Font 1, 938 522 005, www.hostalestrella.com, €96, set lunch €13) is a *pensión* with a huge and popular restaurant. For something truly memorable, head the 28 kilometres (17 miles) out of town to **Lluçanès** (C/Major 1, Prat de Lluçanés, 938 508 050, www.restaurantllucanes.com, mains €19-€21). Superbly creative dishes include mackerel marinated in rice water and roast apples with thyme liquor.

## Tourist information

### Vic

*C/Ciutat 4 (938 862 091/http://victurisme.ajvic.net).*
**Open** 10am-2pm, 4-8pm Mon-Fri; 9.30am-2pm, 4-7pm Sat; 10am-1.30pm Sun.

## Getting there

### By bus

Empresa Sagalès (902 130 014) from the Fabra i Puig bus station (near the metro of the same name) to Vic. For Rupit, take a local bus from Vic.

### By train

RENFE from Sants or Plaça Catalunya to Vic. Trains leave about every 90mins. Journey time is 1hr 20mins.

## Berga to Puigcerdà

To the west, on the most popular approach to the Pyrenees from Barcelona, is **Berga**, famous for the frenzied festival of La Patum, held each May. Just north from there, the giant cliffs of the **Serra del Cadí**, one of the ranges of the Pre-Pyrenees, or Pyrenees foothills, loom above the town. Berga has **Sant Ferran**, a medieval castle with a suitably storybook air, but the blight of endless holiday apartment blocks has taken its toll on the charm of its old centre.

Far prettier is the little town of **Bagà**, north of here along the C17. With its partially preserved medieval walls around an atmospheric old quarter, Bagà marks the beginning of the **Parc Natural del Cadí-Moixeró**, a gigantic mountain park containing wildlife and forest reserves, and some 20 or so ancient villages. All retain some medieval architecture, and many offer stunning views. Picasso stayed and painted in the village of **Gósol** in 1906. Rising above this are the twin peaks of **Pedraforça**, practically a pilgrimage for hiking enthusiasts and well worth the effort (allow a full day to get up there and back).

Above Bagà, the C16 road enters the Túnel del Cadí to emerge into the wide, fertile plateau of the **Cerdanya**. Described by writer Josep Pla as a 'huge casserole', the area has an obvious geographical unity, but the French/Spanish border runs through its middle. **Puigcerdà**, the capital of the area (on the Spanish side), is a lively ski-resort town, and while not particularly interesting in its own right, it does make a good base (and a memorable train journey from Barcelona) for exploring the area on foot: the tourist office has a decent selection of maps and itineraries. Head over the border a few miles from here and you'll stumble across the charming and quirky town of **Llívia**. When 33 villages were ceded to the French under the treaty of the Pyrenees in 1659, it was pointed out that Llívia was technically a town, and therefore exempt from inclusion. It remains Catalan to this day, despite being geographically part of France.

One of the more charming places to stay in the area is **Bellver de Cerdanya**, a lovely hilltop village with a lively market and Gothic church. There is an information centre and all over town noticeboards list hikes of varying degrees of difficulty.

## Where to stay & eat

On the the C26 outside Berga, the tiny village of Les Llosses has a couple of rustic *cases rurales* tucked away in the pine forests. **Domus de Maçanós** (mobile 645 403 337, www.elripolles.com/masmacanos, €96 half-board) is open year-round and has pretty stone arches, beams, log fires and fabulous views. In Bagà, the **Hotel Ca L'Amagat** (C/Clota 4, 938 244 160, www.hotelcalamagat.com, €51) has rooms with large balconies, and a restaurant serving dishes such as trout with almonds or veal with redcurrants (mains €11, closed Mon Oct-May).

Puigcerdà has no shortage of hotels in the town centre, including the small and charming **Avet Blau** (Plaça Santa Maria 14, 972 882 552, €70-€100). The **Hotel Rita-Belvedere** (C/Carmelites 6-8, 972 880 356, closed May to mid July, €39-€53) has a small garden and terrace. The **Hotel del Lago** (Avda Doctor Piguillem 7, 972 881 000, www.hotellago.com, €97), with its terracotta paintwork and green shutters, is not quite so pretty inside, but both the staff and the atmosphere are friendly, and there's a heated pool, a sauna and a jacuzzi. For modern French-Mediterranean food, try **La Col d'Hivern** (C/Baronia 7, 972 141 204, closed Mon-Wed, mains €17).

A little further, out in Bolvir, the sumptuous **Torre del Remei** (C/Camí Reial, 972 140 182, www.torredelremei.com, €214-€621) also has one of the best (and the most expensive) restaurants in the area (mains €22.50).
In Bellver, the **Fonda Bianya** (C/Sant Roc 11,

**Berga**: site of one of the wildest festivals in Spain. *See p298.*

973 510 475, €80) is utterly charming, with its sweet cornflower-blue woodwork, a sunny bar and a lively feel. The rooms are simple but clean.

In Llívia the **Hostal Rusó** (Pujada de l'Església 2, 972 146 264, €70) is a small, fairly basic village house and one of the best deals for accommodation locally. For eats, check out **Can Ventura** (Plaça Major 1, Llívia, 972 896 178, mains €18) for regional cooking in an 18th-century stone house. The **Xalet de la Formatgeria** (Pla de Ro, Gorguja-Llívia, 972 146 279, mains €20) is an old dairy that now does good, hearty country fare.

## Tourist information

### Berga

*C/Angels 7 (938 221 500/www.elbergueda.cat).* **Open** 9am-1pm, 3-6pm Mon-Sat; 9am-2pm Sun.

### Puigcerdà

*C/Querol (972 880 542).* **Open** 9am-1pm, 4.30-7pm Mon-Fri; 10am-1.30pm, 4.30-7.30pm Sat; 10am-1pm Sun.

## Getting there

### By bus

Alsina-Graëlls (932 656 866) runs five buses daily to Berga from the corner of C/Balmes and Ronda de Universitat 11-13; journey time is about 2hrs. The same company has daily buses to Puigcerdà from Estació del Nord; journey time is 3hrs.

### By train

RENFE from Sants or Plaça Catalunya to Puigcerdà. About one train every 2hrs, and the journey generally takes about 3hrs.

## Ripoll to the Vall de Núria

**Ripoll** is best known for its extraordinary monastery, **Santa Maria de Ripoll**, founded in 879 by Wilfred the Hairy, one of the founding fathers of Catalonia, who is buried here. The church has a superb 12th-century stone portal, its carvings among the finest examples of Romanesque art in Catalonia. Wilfred also founded the monastery and town of **Sant Joan de les Abadesses**, ten kilometres (six miles) east up the C26, which is worth a visit for its Gothic bridge as well as the 12th-century monastery buildings. Neither town holds much charm outside its monastery.

**Ribes de Freser**, the next town on the C17 north of Ripoll, is an attractive base from which to travel to the pretty, if slightly gentrified, villages of **Campelles** and **Queralbs**. Ribes is also the starting point for the *cremallera*, or 'zipper train', a narrow-gauge cog railway that runs via Queralbs along the Freser river up to the sanctuary of **Núria**, affording incredible views. Many choose to walk back to Queralbs (around two hours), following the path through dramatic rock formations, crumbling scree, pine-wooded slopes and dramatic, crashing waterfalls.

Núria itself nestles by a lake on a plateau at over 2,000 metres (6,500 feet), and was the first ski resort on this side of the border. Home to the second most famous of Catalonia's patron virgins, a 12th-century wooden statue of the Madonna, Núria was a refuge and a place of pilgrimage long before then. The mostly 19th-century monastery that surrounds the shrine is nothing special, but its location is spectacular. You can bury your head in a pot to gain fertility or ring a bell to cure headaches, but most choose to hike, ski, row boats or ride horses. Get maps and information from the tourist office.

## Where to stay & eat

In Ribes de Freser, the family-run **Hotel Els Caçadors** (C/Balandrau 24-26, 972 727 722, closed Nov, €54-€88) is the first eco-hotel in the Pyrenees and has good food and comfortable rooms. If it's full, try **Hostal Porta de Núria** (C/Nostra Senyora de Gràcia 3, 972 727 137, closed May, €58-€68). In Queralbs, there's **Calamari Hostal l'Avet** (C/Major 17-19, 972 727 377, closed Mon-Thur Oct-May, €80 half-board). **La Perdiu Blanca** (C/Puigcerdà 5, 972 727 150, closed Wed, mains €12) in Ribes, is a village classic and good value. The one good place to eat in Queralbs is **De La Plaça** (Plaça de la Vila 2, 972 727 037, closed Tue, closed 2wks July-Oct, mains €8.50), especially for regional specialities. **Reccapolis** (Ctra de Sant Joan 68, 972 702 106, www.reccapolis.com, mains €15.50) is intimate and romantic, offering unusual twists on regional specialities. In Núria is the **Hotel Vall de Núria** (Estació de Muntanya Vall de Núria, 972 732 020, www.valldenuria.com, closed mid Oct-Nov, €107-€157 half-board), with a two-night minimum stay. This is your only option for food up here.

## Tourist information

### Núria

*Estació de Muntanya del Vall de Núria (972 73 20 20/www.valldenuria.cat).* **Open** *Mid July-mid Sept* 8.30am-5.45pm daily. *Mid Sept-mid July* 8.30am-6.30pm daily.

### Ribes de Freser

*Plaça del Ajuntament 3 (972 72 77 28).* **Open** *Sept-June* 10am-2pm, 5-8pm Tue-Sat; 11am-1pm Sun. *July, Aug* 10am-2pm, 5-8pm Mon-Sat; 11am-1pm Sun.

## Getting there

### By bus

TEISA (932 15 35 66) runs one bus a day from the corner of C/Pau Claris and C/Consell de Cent to Ripoll, Sant Joan de les Abadesses and Camprodon.

Pretty **Santa Pau**, at the heart of La Garrotxa's beech forest. *See p301.*

### By train

RENFE from Sants or Plaça Catalunya (journey time to Ripoll 2hrs). For Queralbs and Núria, change to the *cremallera* train in Ribes de Freser.

## Besalú & Olot

The medieval fortified town of **Besalú** is one of the loveliest in Catalonia, its impressive 12th-century fortified bridge spanning the Fluvià river marking its entrance. Once home to a sizeable Jewish community, it boasts the only remaining Jewish baths (*mikveh*) in Spain. These extraordinary structures date back to the 13th century but were only discovered in the 1960s. Charmingly, if the doors are locked when you arrive, the tourist office will give you a key so that you can let yourself in. Also worth visiting are the Romanesque church of Sant Pere and the arcaded Plaça de la Llibertat.

West from here the N260 runs to **Olot**, past a spectacular view of **Castellfollit de la Roca**, a village perched on the edge of a precipitous crag. The town is prettier from below than it is once you really get inside, but the old section still makes for an interesting stroll. **Olot** was destroyed in an earthquake in 1427, and so lost much of its oldest architecture, but it has some impressive 18th-century and Modernista buildings. In the last century it was home to a school of landscape painters: the local **Museu de la Garrotxa** has works by them, along with Ramon Casas, Santiago Rusiñol and other Modernista artists (C/Hospice 8, 972 27 91 30, closed Tue). The town is not especially interesting, however, and is mainly worth visiting because of its position amid the 30-odd inactive volcanoes and numerous lava flows of the volcanic region of **La Garrotxa**. Just south of town, on the road to Vic, is elegant **Casal dels Volcans** (Ctra Santa Coloma 43, 972 26 67 62, closed Tue Sept-June), an information centre and museum where you can pick up maps detailing hikes.

Off the G1524 toward Banyoles is a vast beech forest, the **Fageda d'en Jordà**, immortalised by Catalan poet Joan Maragall, and the pretty, if touristy, village **Santa Pau**, with an impressive castle and arcaded squares.

### Where to stay & eat

In Besalú a 19th-century riverside inn, **Fonda Siqués** (Avda Lluís Companys 6-8, 972 59 01 10, €63-€72), offers clean if drab rooms and is located above a charming restaurant (set meal €9). For nicer, though still simple, rooms, try **Els Jardins de la Martana** (C/Pont 2, 972 590 009, www.lamartana.com, €90-€103). Restaurants in Besalú include the **Pont Vell** (C/Pont Vell 24, 972 591 027, mains €14.50), which offers magnificent views of the bridge and an interesting menu including sweet and sour rabbit, pigs' trotters stuffed with wild mushrooms and foie gras, and a good vegetarian selection. The terrace of the **Cúria Reial** (Plaça de la Llibertat 8-9, 972 590 263, closed dinner Mon & all day Tue, Feb, mains €14) is very popular, with good traditional cooking. A couple of miles north of the town in Beuda, is a pretty *masia* (farmhouse) with a pool, **Mas Salvanera** (972 59 09 75, www.salvanera.com, €125). If you stop to explore Castellfollit de la Roca, **Can Bundacia** (Ctra de Castellfollit de la Roca a Oix, 972 294 481, closed Mon & Tue, mains €9) is good for regional fare in hearty portions.

In Olot, **La Perla** (Avda Santa Coloma 97, 972 262 326, www.laperlahotels.com, €51-€77) is a large hotel with a good restaurant, or **Pensión La Vila** (C/Sant Roc 1, 972 26 98 07, €44-€55) is modern and very central. **Can Guix** (C/Mulleres 3-5, 972 261 040, closed dinner Wed & all day Sun, mains €5) has great, cheap local dishes. **La Deu** (Ctra de la Deu s/n, 972 261 001, closed Thur, mains €14) specialises in '*cocina volcánica*', including beef stewed in onions and beer, and duck breast stuffed with foie gras. North of the town is the **Restaurant Les Cols** (Crta de la Canya, 972 269 209, closed Sun & dinner Mon & Tue, mains €23), which is famed as much for the design as the food, a work of architectural brilliance that seamlessly combines a modernist steel-and-glass dining room with an 18th-century farmhouse. South of Olot, in La Pinya, is **Mas Garganta** (972 271 289, www.masgarganta.com, closed Jan & Feb, €68), an 18th-century *masia* with magnificent views that has walking tours in conjunction with two *masies* nearby, so you can stay in one place and walk without bags to the next.

In Banyoles, try the red mullet with tomato confit at the **Restaurant Fonda La Paz**, which also has rooms (C/Ponent 18, 972 570 432, closed Mon, dinner Sun, Jan & 2wks Sept, €40, mains €13).

### Tourist information

#### Olot

*C/Hospici 8 (972 26 01 41/www.olot.org).* **Open** *Mid Sept-June* 9am-2pm, 5-7pm Mon-Fri; 11am-2pm Sun. *July-mid Sept* 10am-8pm Mon-Sat; 11am-2pm Sun.

### Getting there

#### By bus

TEISA (932 15 35 66) to Besalú and Olot from the corner of C/Pau Claris and C/Consell de Cent.

# Directory



## Features



**La Pedrera**. *See p127*.

# Directory

## Getting Around

Barcelona's centre is compact and easily explored on foot. Bicycles are good for the Old City and port: there is a decent network of bike lanes across the city. The cheap, efficient metro and bus systems are best for longer journeys. Cars can be a hindrance: there's little parking space, and most of the city is subject to one-way systems. For transport outside Barcelona, see *p277*.

## Arriving & leaving

### By air

#### Aeroport de Barcelona

*902 40 47 04/www.aena.es.*
Barcelona's airport is at El Prat, south-west of the city. Each airline works from one of three main terminals (A, B or C) for all arrivals and departures. There are tourist information desks and currency exchanges in terminals A and B.

#### Aerobús

The airport bus (information 93 415 60 20) runs from each terminal to Plaça Catalunya, with stops at Plaça d'Espanya, C/Urgell and Plaça Universitat. Buses to the airport go from Plaça Catalunya (in front of El Corte Inglés), stopping at Sants station and Plaça d'Espanya. Buses run every 8-10mins, leaving the airport 6am-1am Mon-Fri and 6.30am-1am on weekends, returning from Plaça Catalunya 5.30am-12.15am Mon-Fri and 6am-12.15am at weekends. The trip takes 35-45mins; a single is €3.75, a return (valid one week) €6.45.

At night the N17 runs every hour, on the hour, between the airport (from 10pm) and Plaça Catalunya (from 11pm), with several stops on the way, including Plaça d'Espanya and Plaça Universitat. Last departures are at 5am. Journey time is 45 mins; the cost is a single metro fare.

#### Airport trains

By train: the long overhead walkway between terminals A and B leads to the train station. The Cercanías train (C10) leaves the airport at 29mins and 59mins past the hour, 6am-10.59pm, with an extra train at 11.44pm daily, stopping at Barcelona Sants, Passeig de Gràcia and Estaçio França. Trains to the airport leave Barcelona Sants at 25mins and 55mins past the hour, 5.25am-10.55pm daily (13mins earlier from Estaçio França and 5mins earlier from Passeig de Gràcia). The journey takes 20-30mins and costs €2.40 one way (there are no return tickets). Be aware that tickets are valid only for 2hrs after purchase. A little-publicised fact is that the T-10 metro pass (*see p305*) can also be used, (information 902 24 02 02/www.renfe.es/cercanias).

#### Taxis from the airport

The basic taxi fare to central Barcelona should be €14-€26, including a €3 airport supplement. Fares are about 15 per cent higher after 9pm and at weekends. There is a 90¢ supplement for each large piece of luggage placed in the car boot. All licensed cab drivers use the ranks outside the terminals.

#### Airlines

Terminals are shown in brackets.
**Aer Lingus** (A) 902 502 737/www.aerlingus.com.
**Air Europa** (B) 93 478 47 63/www.air-europa.com.
**British Airways** (B) 902 111 333/www.british-airways.com.
**easyJet** (A) 902 299 992/www.easyjet.com.
**Iberia** (B or C) 902 400 500/www.iberia.com.
**Monarch Airlines** (A) 902 502 737/www.flymonarch.com.
**Ryanair** (from Girona or Reus) 807 220 220/www.ryanair.com.
**Spanair** (B) 902 131 415/www.spanair.com.
**Virgin Express** (A) 902 888 459/www.virgin-express.com.
**Vueling** (B) 902 333 933/www.vueling.com.

### By bus

Most long-distance coaches (national and international) stop or terminate at **Estació d'Autobusos Barcelona-Nord** (C/Alí Bei 80, 902 26 06 06, www.barcelonanord.com, map p343 J9). The **Estació d'Autobusos Barcelona-Sants** at C/Viriat, between Sants rail station and Sants-Estació metro stop, is only a secondary stop for many coaches, though some international **Eurolines** services (information 93 490 40 00, www.eurolines.es) both begin and end their journeys at Sants.

### By car

The easiest way to central Barcelona from almost all directions is the Ronda Litoral, the coastal half of the ring road. Take exit 21 (Paral·lel) if you're coming from the south, or exit 22 (Via Laietana) from the north. Motorways also feed into Avda Diagonal, Avda Meridiana and Gran Via, which all lead to the city centre. Tolls are charged on most of the main approach routes, payable in cash (the lane marked 'manual'; motorbikes are charged half) or by credit card ('automatic'). For more on driving in Barcelona, *see p307*.

### By sea

Balearic Islands ferries dock at the **Moll de Barcelona** quay, at the bottom of Avda Paral·lel; **Trasmediterránea** (902 45 46 45, www.trasmediterranea.es) is the main operator. **Grimaldi Lines** runs a ferry a day, except Sundays, between Barcelona and Civitavecchia (Rome) from the **Moll Sant Bertran** (information and reservations 93 508 88 50, www.grimaldi-ferries.com); or to Genoa three times a week from the **Moll de Ponent**, a few hundred metres south (902 40 12 00). Cruise ships use several berths around the harbour. The **PortBus** shuttle service (information 93 415 60 20) runs between them and the bottom of La Rambla when ships are in port.

## By train

Most long-distance services operated by the Spanish state railway company **RENFE** run from **Barcelona-Sants** station, easily reached by metro. A few services from the French border or south to Tarragona stop at the **Estació de França** in the Born, near the Barceloneta metro which is otherwise sparsely served. Many trains stop at **Passeig de Gràcia**, which can be the handiest for the city centre and also has a metro stop.

### RENFE

*National 902 24 02 02/international 902 24 34 02/www.renfe.es.* **Open** *National* 5am-10pm daily. *International* 7am-midnight daily. **Credit** AmEx, DC, MC, V.
Some English-speaking operators. RENFE tickets can be bought at train stations or travel agents, or reserved over the phone and delivered to an address or hotel for a small extra fee.

## Maps

For street, local train and metro maps, see *pp337-50*. Tourist offices provide a reasonable free street map, or a better-quality map for €1. Metro maps (ask for *una guía del metro*) are available free at all metro stations; bus maps can be obtained from city transport information offices (*see below*). There is an excellent interactive street map at www.bcn.es/guia.

## Public transport

Although it's run by different organisations, Barcelona's public transport is now highly integrated, with the same tickets valid for up to four changes of transport (within 75 minutes) on bus, tram, local train and metro lines. The metro is generally the quickest and easiest way of getting around the city. All metro lines operate from 5am to midnight Monday to Thursday, Sunday and public holidays; 5am to 2am Friday and Saturday. Buses run throughout the night and to areas not covered by the metro system. Local buses and the metro are run by the city transport authority (TMB). Two underground train lines connect with the metro, run by Catalan government railways, the FGC. One runs north from Plaça Catalunya; the other runs west from Plaça d'Espanya to Cornellà. Two tram lines are of limited use to visitors.

### FGC information

*Vestibule, Plaça Catalunya FGC station (93 205 15 15/www.fgc.net).* **Open** 7am-9pm Mon-Fri. **Map** p344 C1. **Other locations**: FGC Provença (open 9am-7pm Mon-Fri, closed Aug); FGC Plaça d'Espanya (open 9am-2pm, 4-7pm Mon-Fri).

### TMB information

*Main vestibule, Metro Universitat, Eixample (93 318 70 74/www.tmb.net).* **Open** 8am-8pm Mon-Fri. **Map** p344 A1. **Branches**: vestibule, Metro Sants Estació and Sagrada Família (both open7am-9pm Mon-Fri; Sants also open 9am-7pm Sat, 9am-2pm Sun); vestibule, Metro Diagonal (8am-8pm Mon-Fri).

## Buses

Many bus routes (*see p319* **Bussing it**) originate in or pass through Plaça Catalunya, Plaça Universitat and Plaça Urquinaona. However, they often run along parallel streets, due to the city's one-way system. Not all stops are labelled, and street signs are not always easy to locate.

Most routes run 6am-10.30pm daily except Sundays; some begin earlier and finish later. There's usually a bus every 10-15mins, but they're less frequent before 8am, after 9pm and on Saturdays. On Sundays, buses are less frequent still; a few do not run at all.

Only single tickets can be bought from the driver; if you have a *targeta (see below)*, insert it into the machine behind the driver as you board.

### Useful routes

The following services connect Plaça Catalunya with popular places:
**22** via Gràcia to the Tramvia Blau up to Tibidabo and the Pedralbes monastery.
**24** goes up Passeig de Gràcia and to Park Güell.
**39** connects Gràcia, the town centre and the beach.
**41** also goes to Ciutadella and the Vila Olímpica.
**41**, **59**, **67** and **68** go to the Plaça Francesc Macià area, which is not served by the metro.
**45** stops in Plaça Urquinaona and goes to the beach near Port Olímpic.

Three good cross-town routes:
**7** runs the length of Avda Diagonal, from the Zona Universitària to Diagonal Mar and along Passeig de Gràcia and Gran Via to Glòries.
**50** goes from north-east Barcelona past Sagrada Família, along Gran Via and then climbs Montjuïc from Plaça d'Espanya to Miramar.
**64** goes from Barceloneta beach, past Colom, Avda Paral·lel, Plaça Universitat to Sarrià and Pedralbes.

### Night buses

There are 16 urban night bus (Nitbus) routes (information 902 02 33 93), most of which run from around 10.30-11.30pm to 4.30-6am nightly, with buses every 20-30mins, plus an hourly bus to the airport; *see p304*. Most pass through Plaça Catalunya. Fares and *targetes* are as for daytime buses. Plaça Catalunya is also the terminus for all-night bus services linking Barcelona with more distant parts of its metropolitan area.

## Fares & tickets

Travel in the Barcelona urban area has a flat fare of €1.20 per journey, but multi-journey tickets or *targetes* are better value. The basic ten-trip *targeta* is the **T-10** (Te-Deu in Catalan, Te-Diez in Spanish), which can be shared by any number of people travelling simultaneously; the ticket is validated in the machines on the metro, train or bus once per person per journey.

Along with the other integrated *targetes* listed below, the T-10 offers access to all five of the city's main transport systems (local RENFE and FGC trains within the main metropolitan area, the metro, the tram and buses). To transfer, insert your card into a machine a second time; unless 75 minutes have elapsed since your last journey, no other unit will be deducted. Single tickets do not allow free transfers.

You can buy T-10s in newsagents and Servi-Caixa cashpoints, as well

as on the metro and train systems (from machines or the ticket office), but not on buses. More expensive versions of all *targetes* take you to the outer zones of the metropolitan region, but the prices listed below will get you anywhere in central Barcelona, and to the key sights on the outskirts of the city itself.

### Integrated *targetes*

**T-10** Valid for ten trips; can be shared by two or more people. €6.65.
**T-Familiar** Gives 70 trips in any 30-day period; can be shared. €40.45.
**T-50/30** Gives 50 trips in any 30-day period; but can only be used by one person. €27.55.
**T-Dia** A one-day travelcard. €5.
**T-Mes** Valid for any 30-day period. €42.75.
**T-Trimestre** Valid for three months. €118.
**T-Jove** Valid for three months; for under-21s only. €100.

### Other *targetes*

**2, 3, 4 & 5 Dies** Two-, three-, four- and five-day travelcards on the metro, buses and FGC trains. Also sold at tourist offices. €9.20, €13.20, €16.80 and €20.
**Barcelona Card** A tourist discount scheme offering unlimited use of public transport for up to five days. *See p83.*

## Local trains

Regional trains to Sabadell, Terrassa and other towns beyond Tibidabo depart from FGC Plaça Catalunya, and those for Montserrat from FGC Plaça d'Espanya.

All trains on the RENFE local network ('Rodalies/Cercanías') stop at Sants but can also be caught at either Plaça Catalunya and Arc de Triomf (for Vic and the Pyrenees, Manresa, the Penedès and Costa del Maresme) or Passeig de Gràcia (for the southern coastal line to Sitges and the Girona-Figueres line north).

## Trams

Lines **T1**, **T2** and **T3** go from Plaça Francesc Macià, Zona Alta, to the outskirts of the city. T1 goes to Cornellà via Hospitalet and Esplugues de Llobregat; T2 goes the same way but contines further to Sant Joan Despí; and T3 runs to Sant Just Desvern. The fourth line runs from Ciutadella-Vila Olímpica (also a metro stop), via Glòries and the Fòrum, on to Sant Adrià (also a RENFE train station) and the new fifth line follows the same route, splitting off at Glòries to go on to Badalona.

All trams are fully accessible for wheelchair-users and are part of the integrated TMB *targeta* system: simply insert the ticket into the machine as you board. You can buy integrated tickets and single tickets from the machines at tram stops.

### Tram information

*Trambaix (902 19 32 75/www.trambcn.com).* **Open** 9am-2pm, 4-7pm Mon-Thur; 9am-2pm Fri.

## Taxis

It's usually easy to find one of the 10,300 black-and-yellow taxis. There are ranks at railway and bus stations, in main squares and throughout the city, but taxis can also be hailed on the street when they show a green light on the roof and a sign saying *lliure/libre* ('free') behind the windscreen. Information on taxi fares, ranks and regulations can be found at www.emt-amb.com.

## Fares

Current rates and supplements are shown inside cabs on a sticker on the rear side window (in English). The basic fare for a taxi hailed in the street is €1.30 (or €1.40 at nights, weekends and holidays), which is what the meter should register when you set off. The basic rates (74¢/km) apply 7am-9pm Mon-Fri; at other times, including public holidays, the rate is 20-30 per cent higher. There are supplements for luggage (90¢), for the airport (€3) and the port (€2), and for nights such as New Year's Eve (€3), as well as a waiting charge. Taxi drivers are not required to carry more than €20 in change; few accept credit cards.

## Radio cabs

These companies take bookings 24 hours daily. Phone cabs start the meter when a call is answered but, by the time it picks you up, it should not display more than €2.93 during weekdays and €3.66 at night, at weekends or public holidays.
**Autotaxi Mercedes Barcelona** 93 307 07 07.
**Barnataxi** 93 357 77 55.
**Fono-Taxi** 93 300 11 00.
**Ràdio Taxi '033'** 93 303 30 33.
**Servi-Taxi** 93 330 03 00.
**Taxi Groc** 93 322 22 22.
**Taxi Miramar** 93 433 10 20.

## Receipts & complaints

To get a receipt, ask for *un rebut/ un recibo*. It should include the fare, the taxi number, the driver's NIF (tax) number, the licence plate, the driver's signature and the date; if you have a complaint about a driver, insist on all these, and the more details (time, route) the better . Complaints must be filed in writing to the Institut Metropolità del Taxi (93 223 51 51, www.taxibarcelona.com).

## Driving

For information (only in Catalan or Spanish) on driving in Catalonia, call the **Servei Catalá de Trànsit** (93 567 40 00); the local government's general information line (012), which has a more extended timetable and English speakers, or see www.gencat.net/transit. Driving in the city can be intimidating and time-consuming. If you do drive, bear these points in mind:

- Keep your driving licence, vehicle registration and insurance documents with you at all times.
- Do not leave anything of value, including car radios, in your car. Foreign plates can attract thieves.
- Be on your guard at motorway service areas, and take care to avoid thieves in the city who may try to make you stop, perhaps by indicating you have a flat tyre.

## Breakdown services

If you're planning to take a car, join a motoring organisation such as the AA (www.theaa.co.uk) or the RAC (www.rac.co.uk) in the UK, which usually have reciprocal agreements.

### RACE (Real Automóvil Club de España)

*Information 902 40 45 45/24hr assistance 902 30 05 05/www.race.es.*
The RACE has English-speaking staff and offers 24-hour breakdown assistance throughout Spain. Repairs are carried out on the spot if it's possible; if not, your vehicle will be towed to a nearby garage. Members of affiliated organisations abroad are not charged for call-outs, but non-members will have to pay a fee (which is usually in cash).

## Car & motorbike hire

Car hire is relatively pricey, but it's a competitive market, so shop around. Ideally, you want unlimited mileage, 16 per cent VAT (*IVA*) included and full insurance cover (*seguro todo riesgo*) rather than the third-party minimum (*seguro obligatorio*). You'll need a credit card as a guarantee. Most companies require you to have had a licence for at least a year; many also enforce a minimum age limit.

### Europcar

*Plaça dels Països Catalans, Sants (93 491 48 22/reservations 902 10 50 30/www.europcar.com). Metro Sants Estació.* **Open** 7am-11pm Mon-Fri; 8am-8pm Sat; 8am-10pm Sun. **Credit** AmEx, DC, MC, V. **Map** p341 B7.

A large international agency. Prices change daily: phone for details. **Other locations**: Airport, terminals B & C (93 298 33 00); Gran Via de les Corts Catalanes 680, Eixample (93 302 05 43); C/Viladomat 214, Eixample (93 439 84 01).

### Motissimo

*C/Portbou 14-28, Sants (93 490 84 01/www.motissimo.es). Metro Badal.* **Open** *Oct-June* 9am-1.30pm, 4-8pm Mon-Fri; 10am-1pm Sat. *July-Sept* 9am-1.30pm, 4-8pm Mon-Fri. **Credit** AmEx, DC, DC, V.

Bike rental, from 50cc Honda mopeds to Suzuki and Honda motorbikes, as well as sale and repair of new and old models. To rent bigger bikes, you must have had the A-class licence for at least two years. You'll need to call to reserve a bike; you can't drop by.

### Pepecar

*C/Rivadeneyra, underground car park (807 41 42 43/www.pepecar.com). Metro Catalunya.* **Open** 8am-8pm daily. **Credit** AmEx, MC, V. **Map** p344 C2/C3.

Basic rates can be absurdly low (for example, Smart cars for €5 per day), but check conditions – in this case you cannot leave the Barcelona area. Look out too for limited mileage, credit-card supplements and insurance. There are branches at Sants railway station (8am-8pm) and the Tryp Hotel near Barcelona airport (7am-11pm). Minimum rental age is 23.

### Vanguard

*C/Viladomat 297, Eixample (93 439 38 80/www.vanguardrent.com). Metro Hospital Clínic.* **Open** 8am-1.30pm, 4-7.30pm Mon-Fri; 9am-1pm Sat, Sun. **Credit** AmEx, DC, MC, V. **Map** p337 D6.

Bike prices start at €32/day for a 50cc Honda; a small car costs €58/day. You must be 21 to hire a small bike and have had a licence for a year; for cars, the age limit is 23, and the minimum licence requirement is two years. *Time Out* readers are promised a 15 per cent discount.

## Legal requirements

For full details of driving laws and regulations (in Spanish), see the Ministry of Interior's website (www.dgt.es).

- Tourists can drive with a valid driving licence from many other countries. EU licences are valid, though Spanish age restrictions prevail; older all-green UK licences are valid, but may cause confusion.
- For bikes over 125cc, you need to be over 18 and have a bike licence.
- Helmets are compulsory on motorbikes and scooters.
- You must wear seatbelts in the front seats and the back if fitted, and carry warning triangles, spares and tools to fit them. If you wear glasses, you must carry a spare pair.
- The speed limit is 50km/h (31mph) in built-up areas, 120km/h (75mph) on motorways and other major roads, and 90km/h (55mph) or 100km/h (62.5mph) on other roads. Most drivers ignore these limits.
- Children aged from three to 12 (and anyone measuring less than 150cm/5ft) cannot travel in the front, unless a restraint system is fitted. Under-threes must be in a child's car seat.
- Severe penalties may be enforced if the level of alcohol in your blood is found to be 0.05% or above.

## Parking

Parking is fiendishly complicated, and municipal police are quick to hand out tickets or tow away cars. In some parts of the Old City, access is limited to residents for much of the day. In some Old City streets, time-controlled bollards pop up, meaning your car may get stuck. Wherever you are, don't park in front of doors marked '*Gual Permanent*', indicating an entry with 24-hour right of access.

### Pay & display areas

The Àrea Verda contains zones exclusively for residents' use (most of the Old City), and 'partial zones' (found in Gràcia, Barceloneta and the Eixample), where non-residents pay €2.75/hr with a 1hr or 2hr maximum stay, as indicated on the meter.

If you overstay by no more than an hour, you can cancel the fine by paying an extra €6; to do so, press *Anul·lar denúncia* on the machine, insert €6, then press Ticket. Some machines accept credit cards (AmEx, MC, V); none accepts notes or gives change. For information, check www.bcn.es/areaverda or call 010. There's a drop-in centre for queries on the ground floor of the Ajuntament building on Plaça Carles Pi i Sunyer 8-10, open 8.30am-5.30pm Mon-Fri.

### Car parks

Car parks (*parkings*) are signalled by a white 'P' on a blue sign. Those run by **SABA** (Plaça Catalunya, Plaça Urquinaona, Rambla de Catalunya, Avda Catedral, airport and elsewhere; 902 28 30 80, www.saba.es) cost around €2.30/hr, while **SMASSA** car parks (Plaça Catalunya 23, C/Hospital 25-29, Avda Francesc Cambó 10, Passeig de Gràcia 60 and elsewhere; 93 409 20 21, www.bsmsa.es/mobilitat) cost €1.95-€2.35/hr. The €5 fare at the **Metro-Park** park-and-ride (Plaça de les Glòries, Eixample, 93 265 10 47, open 4.30am-12.30am Mon-Sat) includes a day's unlimited travel on the metro and buses.

### Towed vehicles

If the police have towed your car, they should leave a triangular sticker on the pavement where it was. The sticker should let you know to which pound it's been taken. If not, call 902 36 41 16; staff generally don't speak English. Recovering your vehicle within 4hrs costs €137.50, with each extra hour costing €1.80, or €18/day. On top of this, you'll have to pay a fine to the police. You'll need your passport and documentation, or rental contract, to prove ownership.

## Petrol

Most *gasolineres* (petrol stations) have unleaded (*sense plom/sin plomo*), regular (*super*) and diesel (*gas-oil*).

# Cycling

There's a network of bike lanes (*carrils bici*) along major avenues and alongside the seafront; local authorities are very keen to promote cycling. However, weekday traffic can be risky, despite legislation that states drivers must slow down when they are near cyclists. No more than two bikes are allowed to ride side by side. Be warned too that bike theft is rife: always carry a good lock. SMASSA underground car parks (*see above*) rent spaces by the day for €1.20. For information on cycling in Barcelona, log on to: www.bcn.es/bicicleta.

### Al punt de trobada (bicycle hire)

*C/Badajoz 24, Poblenou (93 225 05 85/bicipuntrobada@hotmail.com). Metro Llacuna.* **Open** 9am-2pm, 4-8pm Mon-Fri; 9am-2pm Sat; 10am-3pm Sun. **Credit** MC, V.

# Resources A-Z

## Addresses

Most apartment addresses consist of a street name followed by a street number, floor level and flat number, in that order. So, to go to C/València 246, 2º 3ª, find No.246, go to the second floor and find the door marked 3 or 3ª. Ground-floor flats are usually called *baixos* or *bajos* (often abbreviated *bxs/bjos*); one floor up, the *entresol/ entresuelo* (*entl*), and the next is often the *principal* (*pral*). Confusingly, numbered floors start here: first, second, up to the *àtic/ático* at the top.

## Age restrictions

The minimum legal age for drinking alcohol or smoking is 18. The age of consent is just 13, one of the lowest in Europe. In Spain, you must be 18 to drive a car.

## Business

Anyone wanting to set up shop in Barcelona needs to know the intricacies of local, Spanish and EU regulations. A visit to the **Cambra de Comerç** (*see p310*) is a must; some consulates can refer you to professionals, and a *gestoria* (*see below*) will save you time and energy.

### Admin services

The *gestoria* is a very Spanish institution, the main function of which is to lighten the weight of local bureaucracy by dealing with it for you. A combination of bookkeeper, lawyer and business adviser, a good *gestor* can be helpful in handling all of the paperwork and advising on various short cuts, although *gestoria* employees rarely speak English.

#### Martin Howard Associates

*C/Aribau 177, entl 1ª, Eixample (93 240 52 75/mobile 607 401 184/617 966 689/www.mhasoc.com).* **Open** *Sept-July* 9am-6pm Mon-Thur; 9am-2pm Fri. *Aug* 8am-3pm Mon-Fri. **Map** p338 F6.

British accountant Alex Martin and his Spanish associate offer consultancy, accounting, tax services and advice on buying property for English-speaking expats in Spain.

#### Tutzo Assessors

*C/Aribau 226, pral 2ª, Eixample (93 209 67 88/www.tutzo-assessors.com). Metro Diagonal/FGC Gràcia.* **Open** *Sept-June* 8.30am-2pm, 4-7pm Mon-Fri; *July, Aug* 9am-2pm Mon-Fri. Closed 2wks Aug, Fri pm July, Aug. **Map** p338 F5.

Lawyers and economists as well as a *gestoria*. Some English speakers.

### Conventions & conferences

#### Barcelona Convention Bureau

*Rambla Catalunya 123, pral, Eixample (93 368 97 00/www.barcelonaturisme.com). Metro Diagonal.* **Open** *Sept-mid June* 9am-2.30pm, 3.30-6.30pm Mon-Thur; 9am-3pm Fri. *Mid June-Aug* 8am-3pm Mon-Fri. **Map** p338 F6.

Specialist arm of the city tourist authority that assists organisations with conferences.

#### Fira de Barcelona

*Avda Reina Maria Cristina, Montjuïc (93 233 20 00/www.firabcn.es). Metro Espanya.* **Open** *Mid Sept-mid June* 9am-1.30pm, 3.30-5.30pm Mon-Fri. *Mid June-mid Sept* 9am-2pm Mon-Fri. **Map** p341 B9.

The Barcelona Trade Fair is one of the largest exhibition complexes in Europe. In addition to the main area, it includes a huge site, Montjuïc-2, towards the airport, and administers the Palau de Congressos conference hall in the Plaça d'Espanya site, which can be let separately.

#### World Trade Center

*Moll de Barcelona, Port Vell (93 508 88 88/www.wtcbarcelona.com). Metro Drassanes.* **Open** *Sept-June* 9am-2pm, 4-7pm Mon-Thur; 9am-3pm Fri. *July, Aug* 9am-3pm Mon-Fri. **Map** p342 F13.

The WTC rents 130,000sqm (72,624 sq ft) of office space in a modern complex in the old port. Conferences can be arranged.

### Courier services

#### Estació d'Autobusos Barcelona-Nord

*C/Alí Bei 80, Eixample (93 232 43 29). Metro Arc de Triomf.* **Open** 7am-9.30pm Mon-Fri; 7am-1.30pm Sat. **No credit cards. Map** p343 J9.

An inexpensive service available at the bus station for sending parcels on scheduled buses within Spain.

#### Missatgers Trèvol

*C/Antonio Ricardos 14, La Sagrera (93 498 80 70/www.trevol.com). Metro Sagrera.* **Open** *Sept-July* 8am-7.30pm Mon-Fri. *Aug* 8am-3pm Mon-Fri. **No credit cards.**

Courier firm serving central Barcelona. Check online for rates.

#### Seur

*902 10 10 10/www.seur.es.* **Open** 8am-8pm Mon-Fri; 9am-2pm Sat. **No credit cards.**

## Travel advice

For current information on travel to a specific country – including the latest news on health issues, safety and security, local laws and customs – contact your home country's government department of foreign affairs. Most have websites with useful advice for would-be travellers.

**Australia**
www.smartraveller.gov.au

**Canada**
www.voyage.gc.ca

**New Zealand**
www.safetravel.govt.nz

**Republic of Ireland**
http://foreignaffairs.gov.ie

**UK**
www.fco.gov.uk/travel

**USA**
http://travel.state.gov

An efficient (though not always cheap) service for national and international deliveries. Call by 6pm for same-day pick-up.

### UPS

*902 88 88 20/www.ups.com.* **Open** 8am-8pm Mon-Fri. **Credit** AmEx, MC, V.
Next-day delivery to both Spanish and international destinations. There are some English-speaking operators.

## Office & computer services

The area round Ronda Sant Antoni (map p342 E9) is your best bet for PC hardware. **Life Informática** (C/Sepúlveda 173, Sant Antoni, 902 90 15 32, www.lifeinformatica.com) is good for components; **PC City** (C/Casanova 2, Eixample, 902 10 03 02, www.pccity.es) is a reliable option for branded equipment.

### Centro de Negocios

*C/Pau Claris 97, 4º 1ª, Eixample (93 304 38 58/www.centro-negocios.com). Metro Passeig de Gràcia.* **Open** *Sept-July* 8am-9pm Mon-Fri. *Aug* 9am-3pm Mon-Fri. **No credit cards. Map** p342 G8.
Desks in shared offices, mailboxes, meeting rooms, secretarial services and administrative services.

### GeoMac

*Mobile 606 30 89 32/geomac@ya.com.* **Open** by appointment. **No credit cards.**
Apple-certified US technician George Cowdery offers maintenance, trouble-shooting and tuition for Mac users.

### K-Tuin

*C/Muntaner 537, (93 418 02 03/ www.k-tuin.es). FGC El Putxet.* **Open** 10am-2pm, 4.30-8.30pm Mon-Fri; 10am-2.30pm Sat. **Credit** DC, MC, V.
Mac repairs, equipment and accessories are all available here.

### Microrent

*C/Rosselló 35, Eixample (93 363 32 50/www.microrent.es). Metro Entença.* **Open** *Sept-June* 9am-6pm Mon-Fri. *July, Aug* 8am-3pm Mon-Fri. **No credit cards. Map** p341 C6.
Computer equipment for rent: PCs, Macs, laptops, printers, projectors.

## Translators

For more translators, see www.act.es.

### DUUAL

*C/Ciutat 7, 2º 4ª, Barri Gòtic (93 302 29 85/www.duual.com). Metro Jaume I or Liceu.* **Open** *Sept-June* 9am-2pm, 4-7pm Mon-Thur; 9am-2pm Fri. *July* 8.30am-3pm Mon-Fri. Closed 3wks Aug. **No credit cards. Map** p345 C6.

### Traduit

*C/Ribeira 6, 1º 2ª, Born (93 268 74 95/www.traduit.com). Metro Jaume I.* **Open** 9am-2pm, 4-6.30pm Mon-Fri. **Credit** MC, V. **Map** p345 F7.

## Useful organisations

### Ajuntament de Barcelona

*Plaça Sant Miquel 4-5, Barri Gòtic (93 402 70 00/www.bcn.es). Metro Jaume I.* **Open** *Sept-June* 8.30am-5.30pm Mon-Fri. *July, Aug* 8.15am-2.15pm Mon-Fri. **Map** p345 C6.
The city council. Permits for new businesses are issued by the ten municipal districts.

### Borsa de Valors de Barcelona

*Passeig de Gràcia 19, Eixample (93 401 35 55/www.borsabcn.es). Metro Passeig de Gràcia.* **Open** *Reception* 9am-5.30pm Mon-Fri. *Library* 9am-noon Mon-Fri. **Map** p344 C1.
The stock exchange.

### Cambra de Comerç de Barcelona

*Avda Diagonal 452-454, Eixample (902 448 448/www.cambrabcn.es). Metro Diagonal/FGC Provença.* **Open** 9am-5pm Mon-Thur; 9am-2pm Fri. **Map** p338 G6.
The Chamber of Commerce.

### Generalitat de Catalunya

*Information 012/new businesses 902 20 15 20/www.gencat.net.*
The Catalan government provides a range of consultancy services.

## Complaints

Ask for a complaint form (*full de reclamació/hoja de reclamación*), which many businesses and all shops, bars and restaurants are required to keep. Leave one completed copy with the business. Take the other forms to the consumer office.

### Oficina Municipal d'Informació al Consumidor

*Ronda de Sant Pau 43-45, Barri Gòtic (93 402 78 41/www.omic.bcn.es). Metro Paral·lel or Sant Antoni.* **Open** 9am-1pm Mon-Fri. **Map** p342 E10.
The official centre for consumer advice and complaints follow-up. You can file complaints in English through the website.

### Telèfon de Consulta del Consumidor

*012.* **Open** 9am-6pm Mon-Fri.
A phone line run by the Generalitat for consumer advice.

## Consulates

**Australian Consulate** *Plaça Gal.la Placidia 1-3, 1º, Gràcia (93 490 90 13/fax 93 411 09 04/www.spain.embassy.gov.au). FCG Gràcia.* **Open** 10am-noon Mon-Fri. Closed Aug. **Map** p338 F5.
**British Consulate** *Avda Diagonal 477, 13º, Eixample (93 366 62 00/fax 93 366 62 21/www.ukinspain.com). Metro Hospital Clínic.* **Open** *Mid Sept-mid June* 9.30am-2pm Mon-Fri. *Mid June-mid Sept* 8.30am-1.30pm Mon-Fri. **Map** p338 E5.
**Canadian Consulate** *C/Elisenda de Pinós 10, Zona Alta (93 204 27 00/fax 93 204 27 01/ www.canada-es.org). FGC Reina Elisenda.* **Open** 10am-1pm Mon-Fri.
**Irish Consulate** *Gran Via Carles III 94, 10º, Zona Alta (93 491 50 21/fax 93 490 09 86). Metro Maria Cristina.* **Open** 10am-1pm Mon-Fri. **Map** p337 B4.
**New Zealand Consulate** *Travessera de Gràcia 64, 2º, Gràcia (93 209 03 99/fax 93 202 08 90). Metro Diagonal.* **Open** 9am-2pm, 4-7pm Mon-Fri. **Map** p338 F5.
**South African Consulate** *Travessera de Gràcia 43, Zona Alta (93 366 10 25/93 366 10 26). FGC Gràcia/bus 14, 27, 32, 58, 64.* **Open** 9am-noon Mon-Fri. **Map** p338 E5.
**US Consulate** *Passeig Reina Elisenda 23, Zona Alta (93 280 22 27/fax 93 205 52 06/ www.embusa.es). FGC Reina Elisenda.* **Open** 9am-1pm Mon-Fri. **Map** p337 B1.

## Customs

Custom declarations are not usually necessary if you arrive from another EU country and are carrying legal goods for personal use. The amounts given below are guidelines: if you approach these maximums in several categories, you may still have to explain your personal habits.

- 800 cigarettes, 400 small cigars, 200 cigars or 1kg loose tobacco

● 10 litres of spirits (more than 22% alcohol), 90 litres of wine (less than 22% alcohol) or 110 litres of beer

Coming from a non-EU country or the Canary Islands, you can bring:

● 200 cigarettes, 100 small cigars, 50 regular cigars or 250g (8.82oz) of tobacco.

● 1 litre of spirits (more than 22% alcohol) or 2 litres of wine or beer (more than 22% alcohol).

● 50g (1.76oz) of perfume.

● 500g coffee; 100g tea.

Visitors can also carry up to €6,000 in cash without having to declare it. Non-EU residents can reclaim VAT (*IVA*) on some large purchases when they leave. For details, *see p188.*

## Disabled

**www.accessiblebarcelona.com**, run by a British expat wheelchair-user living in Barcelona, is a useful resource.

### Institut Municipal de Persones amb Disminució

*Avda Diagonal 233, Eixample (93 413 27 75/www.bcn.es/accessible). Metro Glòries or Monumental/bus 56, 62.* **Open** 9am-2pm Mon-Fri. **Map** p343 K8.

The city's organisation for the disabled has information on access to venues and transport, and can provide a map with wheelchair-friendly itineraries. It's best to call in advance to make an appointment. English speakers are available.

## Access to sights

Although many sites claim to be accessible, you may still need assistance. Phoning ahead to check is always a good idea.

Newer museums such as the **Museu Egipci de Barcelona** (*see p127*) have good accessibility (and, occasionally, adapted toilets), but others, such as the **MACBA** (*see p107*), despite appearances, are impractical. The process of converting older buildings is slow. Wheelchair-friendly museums and galleries include the following: CCCB; Espai Gaudí – La Pedrera; Fundació Joan Miró; Fundacío Antoni Tàpies; MNAC; Museu Barbier-Mueller d'Art Precolombi; Museu d'Arqueologia de Catalunya; Museu de les Arts Decoratives; Museu del Calçat; Museu de Cera de Barcelona; Museu del Temple Expiatori de la Sagrada Família; Museu d'Història de Catalunya; Museu d'Història de la Ciutat; Museu de la Ciència – CosmoCaixa; Museu de la Xocolata; Museu Frederic Marès; Museu Picasso; Museu Tèxtil i d'Indumentaria; Palau de la Música; Palau de la Virreina.

## Transport

Access for disabled people to local transport is improving but still leaves quite a lot to be desired. For wheelchair-users, buses and taxis are usually the best bets. For transport information, call **TMB** (93 318 70 74) or 010. Transport maps, which can be picked up from transport information offices (*see below*) and some metro stations, indicate wheelchair access points and adapted bus routes. For a list of accessible metro stations and bus lines, check **www.tmb.net** and click on Transport for Everyone.

### Buses

All the Aerobús airport buses, night buses and the open-topped tourist buses are fully accessible, though you may need assistance with the steep ramps. Adapted buses also alternate with standard buses on many daytime routes. Press the blue button with the wheelchair symbol to alert the driver before your stop.

### Metro & FGC

Only L2 has lifts and ramps at all stations. On L1 and L3, some stations have lifts. There is usually a step on to the train, the size of which varies; some assistance may be required. The Montjuïc funicular railway is fully wheelchair-adapted. Accessible FGC stations include Provença, Muntaner and Avda Tibidabo. The FGC infrastructures at Catalunya and Espanya stations are accessible, but interchanges with metro lines are not.

### RENFE trains

Sants and Plaça Catalunya stations are wheelchair-accessible, but trains are not. If you go to the Atenció al Viajero office ahead of time, help on the platform can be arranged.

### Taxis

All taxi drivers are officially required to transport wheelchairs and guide dogs for no extra charge, but cars can be small, and the willingness of drivers to co-operate varies widely. Special minibus taxis adapted for wheelchairs can be ordered from the Taxi Amic service, as well as from some general taxi services such as Servi-Taxi (93 330 03 00). You need to book at least 24-48 hours ahead.

### Taxi Amic

*93 420 80 88/www.terra.es/personal/taxiamic.* **Open** 7am-11pm Mon-Fri; 9am-10pm Sat, Sun.

Fares are the same as for regular cabs, but there is a minimum fare of €9.50 for Barcelona city (€10.50 at weekends), and more for surrounding areas. Numbers are limited, so call well in advance (two days if possible) to request a specific time.

### Trams

All tram lines throughout Barcelona are fully accessible for wheelchair-users, with ramps that can access all platforms. A symbol on each platform indicates where the accessible doors will be situated.

## Drugs

Many people smoke cannabis openly in Spain, but possession or consumption in public is illegal. In private, the law is contradictory: smoking is OK, but you can be nabbed for possession or distribution. Enforcement is often not the highest of police priorities, but you could theoretically receive a fine. Larger amounts entail a fine and, in extreme cases, prison. Smoking in bars is also prohibited; most proprietors are strict on this issue because it could cost them their licences. Having said that, it's not unheard of to catch a whiff of spliff on some terraces in summer. If caught in possession of any other drugs, you are looking at hefty fines and a prison sentence.

## Electricity

The standard current in Spain is 220V. Plugs are of the two-round-pin type. You'll need a plug adaptor to use British-bought electrical devices.

If you have US (110V) equipment, you will need a current transformer as well as an adaptor.

## Emergencies

The following are available 24 hours a day.

**Emergency services** 112. Police, fire or ambulance.

**Ambulance/*Ambulància*** 061. For hospitals and other health services, *see pp312-13.*

**Fire/*Bombers/Bomberos*** 080.

**Policía Nacional** (first choice in a police emergency) 091.

**Guàrdia Urbana** 092. The city police; for traffic but also general law and order. For more information on police forces, *see p317*.
**Mossos d'Esquadra** 088.
**Electricity/*Fecsa-Endesa*** 900 77 00 77.
**Gas/*Gas Natural*** 900 75 07 50.
**Water/*Aigües de Barcelona*** 900 70 07 20.

## Etiquette

The Catalans are less guarded about personal space than people in the UK or US. The common greeting between members of the opposite sex and between two women, even if it is the first time the two parties meet, is a kiss on both cheeks. Men usually greet each other by shaking hands. Don't be surprised if people bump into you on the street, or crowd or push past you on the bus or metro without saying sorry: it's not considered rude.

## Gay & lesbian

### Casal Lambda

*C/Verdaguer i Callís 10, Barri Gòtic (93 319 55 50/www.lambdaweb.org). Metro Urquinaona.* **Open** 5-9pm Mon-Fri. Closed 2wks Aug. **Map** p344 D4/E4.
Gay cultural organisation that is the focus for a wide range of activities and publishes the magazine Lambda.

### Coordinadora Gai-Lesbiana

*C/Finlàndia 45, Sants (93 298 00 29/www.cogailes.org). Metro Plaça de Sants.* **Open** 7-9pm Mon-Fri. **Map** p341 A7.
This gay umbrella group works with the Ajuntament on concerns for the gay, bisexual and transsexual communities. Its Telèfon Rosa service (900 601 601, open 6-10pm daily) gives help or advice.

### Front d'Alliberament Gai de Catalunya

*C/Verdi 88, Gràcia (93 217 26 69/ www.fagc.org). Metro Fontana.* **Open** 7-9pm Mon-Thur. Map p339 H4.
A vocal group that produces the Debat Gai information bulletin.

## Health

Visitors can obtain emergency care through the public health service, **Servei Catalá de la Salut**. EU nationals are entitled to free basic medical attention if they have the European Emergency Health Card, also known as the Health Insurance Card. This recently replaced the E111 form and is valid for one year. Contact the health service in your country of residence for details. If you don't have one but can get one sent or faxed within a few days, you will likely be exempt from charges. Citizens of certain other countries that have a special agreement with Spain, among them several Latin American states, can also have access to free care. For general details, check the website www.gencat.net/ temes/eng/salut.htm, or call the Catalan government's 24-hour health information line on 902 11 14 44 or the Instituto Nacional de Seguridad Social on 900 16 65 65.

For non-emergencies, it's usually quicker to use private travel insurance rather than the state system. Similarly, non-EU nationals with private medical insurance can also make use of state health services on a paying basis, but it will usually be simpler to use a private clinic.

### Accident & emergency

In a medical emergency, go to the casualty department (*Urgències*) of any of the main public hospitals in the city. All are open 24 hours daily. The most central are the **Clínic**, which also has a first-aid centre for less serious emergencies two blocks away (C/València 184, 93 227 93 00, open 9am-9pm Mon-Fri, 9am-1pm Sat) and the **Perecamps**. If necessary, call 061 for an ambulance.
**Centre d'Urgències Perecamps** *Avda Drassanes 13-15, Raval (93 441 06 00). Metro Drassanes or Paral·lel.* **Map** p342 E11.
**Hospital Clínic** *C/Villarroel 170, Eixample (93 227 54 00). Metro Hospital Clínic.* **Map** p338 E6/E7.
**Hospital Dos de Maig** *C/Dos de Maig 301, Eixample (93 507 27 00). Metro Hospital de Sant Pau.* **Map** p339 L6.
**Hospital del Mar** *Passeig Marítim 25-29, Barceloneta (93 248 30 00). Metro Ciutadella-Vila Olímpica.* **Map** p343 J12.
**Hospital de Sant Pau** *C/Sant Antoni Maria Claret 167, Eixample (93 291 90 00). Metro Hospital de Sant Pau.* **Map** p339 L5.

### AIDS/HIV

Spain's high death rate from AIDS is falling, but the HIV virus continues to spread in many groups, such as drug-users and, particularly, heterosexuals. Local chemists take part in a needle-exchange and condom-distribution programme for intravenous drug-users. Anti-retroviral drugs for HIV treatment are covered by social security in Spain. Free, anonymous blood tests for HIV and other STDs are given at the **Unidad de Infección de Transmisión Sexual** (93 441 46 12, open by appointment 8.30am-1pm, 2.30-7pm Mon-Fri) at **CAP Drassanes** (*see p313*). HIV tests are also available at the **Coordinadora Gai-Lesbiana** (*see above*), at the **Asociació Ciutadana Antisida de Catalunya** (C/Junta de Comerç 23, Raval, 93 317 05 05, www.acasc.info, open 10am-2pm, 4-7pm Mon-Thur, 10am-2pm Fri) and at **Projecte dels Noms** (C/Comte Borrell 164 izq, 93 318 20 56, www.hispanosida.com, open by appointment 10am-2pm, 3-7pm Mon-Thur, 10am-2pm Fri).

#### Actua

*C/Gomis 38, Zona Alta (93 418 50 00/www.actua.org.es). Metro Vallcarca/bus 22, 27, 28, 73.* **Open** (by appointment) 10am-2pm, 4-7pm Mon-Thur; 10am-2pm Fri.
Support group for people with HIV. There are some English speakers.

#### AIDS Information Line

*Freephone 900 21 22 22.* **Open** *Mid Sept-May* 8am-5.30pm Mon-Thur; 8am-3pm Fri. *June-mid Sept* 8am-3pm Mon-Fri.

### Complementary medicine

#### Integral: Centre Mèdic i de Salut

*C/Diputació 321, 1° 1ª, Eixample (93 467 74 20/www.integralcentre mecic.com). Metro Girona.* **Open** (by appointment) 9am-9pm Mon-Fri. Closed Aug. **Map** p339 H8.
Acupuncture, homeopathy and other forms of complementary medicine are offered at this well-established clinic. A few practioners speak English, including the osteopath.

## Contraception & abortion

All pharmacies sell condoms (*condons/preservativos*) and other forms of contraception including pills (*la píndola/la píldora*), which can be bought without a prescription. You'll generally need a prescription to get the morning-after pill (*la píndola del dia seguent/la píldora del día siguiente*) but some CAP health centres (*see below*) will dispense it free themselves. Many bars and clubs have condom-vending machines.

While abortion is decriminalised (the law is ambiguous in not using the term 'legal'), during the first 11 weeks of pregnancy, procedures usually take place in private clinics; doctors can normally recommend one. Under-18s must have parental consent. The only time when abortions might be carried out in public hospitals is when there is foetal abnormality, in which case it's legal up to 22 weeks.

### Centre Jove d'Anticoncepció i Sexualitat

*C/La Granja 19-21, Gràcia (93 415 10 00/www.centrejove.org). Metro Lesseps.* **Open** *Sept-mid June* noon-7pm Mon-Thur; 10am-2pm Fri. *Mid June-July* 10am-5pm Mon-Fri. *1st and last wk in Aug* 10am-2pm Mon-Fri. **Map** p339 H4.
A family-planning centre aimed at young people (under 25s). It can provide information on the morning-after pill; free HIV tests are given to people under 30. There's a small fee for pregnancy tests.

## Dentists

Most dentistry is not covered by the Spanish public health service (to which EU citizens have access; *see above*). Check the classified ads in *Barcelona Metropolitan* (*see p315*) for English-speaking dentists.

### Institut Odontològic Calàbria

*Avda Madrid 141-145, Eixample (93 439 45 00/www.ioa.es). Metro Entença.* **Open** 9am-1pm, 3-8pm Mon-Fri. **Credit** DC, MC, V. **Map** p341 C6.
These well-equipped clinics provide a complete range of dental services. Several of the staff speak English.
**Other locations**: Institut Odontològic Sagrada Família, C/Sardenya 319, Eixample (93 457 04 53); Institut Odontològic, C/Diputació 238, Eixample (93 342 64 00).

## Doctors

A **Centre d'Assistència Primària** (CAP) is a local health centre (aka *ambulatorio*), where you should be seen fairly quickly by a doctor, but you may need an appointment. There are around 40 in town, including:
**CAP Casc Antic** *C/Rec Comtal 24, Sant Pere (93 310 14 21). Metro Arc de Triomf.* **Open** 9am-8pm Mon-Fri; (emergencies only) 9am-5pm Sat. **Map** p344 F4.
**CAP Doctor Lluís Sayé** *C/Torres i Amat 8, Raval (93 301 25 32). Metro Universitat.* **Open** 9am-8pm Mon-Fri; (emergencies only) 9am-5pm Sat. **Map** p344 A1.
**CAP Drassanes** *Avda Drassanes 17-21, Raval (93 329 44 95). Metro Drassanes.* **Open** 8am-8pm Mon-Fri. **Map** p342 E11.
**CAP Vila Olímpica** *C/Joan Miró 17, Vila Olímpica (93 221 37 85). Metro Ciutadella-Vila Olímpica or Marina.* **Open** 8am-8.30pm Mon-Fri. **Map** p343 K11.

### Centre Mèdic Assistencial Catalonia

*C/Provença 281, Eixample (93 215 37 93). Metro Diagonal.* **Open** 8am-9pm Mon-Fri. **Map** p338 G7.
Dr Lynd is a British doctor. She can be seen at this surgery 3.50-7.10pm every Wednesday, but it is best to call beforehand.

### Dr Mary McCarthy

*C/Aribau 215, pral 1ª, Eixample (93 200 29 24/mobile 607 220 040). FGC Gràcia/bus 14, 58, 64.* **Open** by appointment. **Credit** MC, V. **Map** p338 F5.
Dr McCarthy is an internal medicine specialist from the US. She will also treat general patients at American health-care rates.

## Opticians

*See p207.*

## Pharmacies

Pharmacies (*farmàcies/farmacias*) are signalled by large green-and-red neon crosses. Most are open 9am-1.30pm and 4.30-8pm weekdays, and 9am-1.30pm on Saturdays. About a dozen operate around the clock, while more have late opening hours; some of the most central are listed below. The full list of chemists that stay open late (usually until 10pm) and overnight on any given night is posted daily outside every pharmacy door and given in the day's newspapers. You can also call the 010 and 098 information lines. At night, duty pharmacies often appear to be closed, but knock on the shutters and you will be attended to.

The Spanish attitude to dispensing drugs is relaxed. You can legally obtain many things that are more tightly regulated in other countries, including contraceptive pills and some antibiotics, without a prescription. This state of affairs, coupled with the fact that they tend to be quite knowledgeable, means that pharmacists' advice is often sought in order to avoid a trip to the doctor. Some have even been known to dispense drugs that do require prescriptions over the counter. Those with the EU Health Insurance Card will pay the same for prescriptions as residents: 40 per cent less than full price.

**Farmàcia Alvarez** *Passeig de Gràcia 26, Eixample (93 302 11 24). Metro Passeig de Gràcia.* **Open** 8am-10.30pm Mon-Thur; 8am-midnight Fri; 9am-midnight Sat. **Credit** MC, V. **Map** p342 G8.
**Farmàcia Cervera** *C/Muntaner 254, Eixample (93 200 09 96). Metro Diagonal/FGC Gràcia.* **Open** 24hrs daily. **Credit** AmEx, MC, V. **Map** p338 E5.
**Farmàcia Clapés** *La Rambla 98, Barri Gòtic (93 301 28 43). Metro Liceu.* **Open** 24hrs daily. **Credit** AmEx, MC, V. **Map** p344 B4.
**Farmàcia Vilar** *Vestibule, Estació de Sants, Sants (93 490 92 07). Metro Sants Estació.* **Open** 7am-10.30pm Mon-Fri; 8am-10.30pm Sat, Sun. **Credit** AmEx, MC, V. **Map** p341 B7.

## Helplines

### Alcoholics Anonymous

*93 317 77 77/www.alcoholicos-anonimos.org.* **Open** 10am-1pm, 5-8pm Mon-Fri.
Among the local AA groups, several have dedicated English-speaking sections. Call for details.

### Narcotics Anonymous

*902 11 41 47/www.na-esp.org.* **Open** hours vary.
Check the website for details of twice-weekly meetings in English.

### Telèfon de l'Esperança

*93 414 48 48/ www.telefono-esperanza.com.* **Open** 24hrs daily.
Apart from 24-hour counselling, the staff at this local helpline run by a private foundation can put you in contact with other specialist help groups, from psychiatric to legal. English is occasionally spoken by the staff, but is not always guaranteed.

## ID

From the age of 14, Spaniards are legally obliged to carry their **DNI** (identity card). Foreigners are also meant to carry an ID card or passport, and are in theory subject to a fine – in practice, you're more likely to get a warning. If you don't want to carry it around with you (wisely, given the prevalence of petty crime), it's a good idea to carry a photocopy or a driver's licence instead: technically, it's not legal, but usually acceptable. ID is needed to check into a hotel, hire a car, pay with a card in shops and exchange or pay with travellers' cheques.

## Insurance

For health-care and EU nationals, *see P312*. Some non-EU countries have reciprocal health-care agreements with Spain, but for most travellers it's usually more convenient to have private travel insurance, which will also, of course, cover you in case of theft and flight problems.

## Internet

Broadband (ADSL), now more affordable than ever, is fast taking over from basic dial-up offered by ISPs such as **Wanadoo** (902 012 220, www.wanadoo.es). Ex-monopoly **Telefónica** (902 35 70 00, www.telefonicaonline.es) controls most of the infrastructure, but is obliged to rent its lines to other firms. Telefónica (Terra), Wanadoo, **Ya** (902 90 29 02, www.ya.com) and **Auna** (ONO) (902 50 00 60, www.auna.es) all offer high-speed Router or Wi-Fi connection with 24-hour access for a flat monthly rate. Many firms also offer discount 'package' deals for phone lines and high-speed internet (and, increasingly, cable TV). Initial connection times can vary. Be aware that rock-bottom price deals may slow down the process considerably, and/or be applicable for a short time.

### Internet access

There are internet centres all over Barcelona. Some libraries (*see below*) have internet points and Wi-Fi for public use.

#### Bornet Internet Cafè

*C/Barra de Ferro 3, Born (93 268 15 07/fax 901 02 07 16/www.bornet-bcn.com). Metro Jaume I.* **Open** 10am-10pm Mon-Fri; 3-10pm Sat, Sun. **No credit cards. Map** p345 E6.

There are ten terminals in this small café and six more for laptops. One hour is €2.60; but you're really paying for the atmosphere.

#### easyEverything

*La Rambla 31, Barri Gòtic (93 301 75 07/www.easyeverything.com). Metro Drassanes or Liceu.* **Open** 8am-2am daily. **No credit cards. Map** p345 A6.

There are 330 terminals here and 240 at Ronda Universitat 35 (open 8am-2am daily). Buy credit from the machines; price then increases with demand. Alternatively, buy passes that allow unlimited access during a set period (from 24 hours to 30 days).

## Left luggage

Look for signs to the *consigna*.

**Aeroport del Prat** *Terminal B.* **Open** 24hrs daily. **Rates** €4/day.

**Estació d'Autobusos Barcelona-Nord** *C/Alí Bei 80, Eixample. Metro Arc de Triomf.* **Open** 24hrs daily. **Rates** €3-€4.50/day. **Map** p343 J9.

**Train stations** Sants-Estació & Estació de França, Born. **Open** 6am-11.45pm daily. **Rates** €3-€4.50/day. **Map** p341 B7 & p343 H11. Some smaller stations have lockers.

## Legal help

Consulates (*see p310*) help tourists in emergencies, and recommend lawyers.

#### Marti & Associats

*Avda Diagonal 584, pral 1ª, Eixample (93 201 62 66/www.martilawyers.com). Bus 6, 7, 15, 33, 34.* **Open** *Sept-July* 9am-2pm, 4-8pm Mon-Fri; *Aug* 9am-2pm Mon-Fri. **Map** p338 E5.

Australian John Rocklin is one of the lawyers at this Catalan firm that also has native speakers of other languages on staff. The firm can help with work and residency permits.

## Libraries

There is a network of public libraries around the city thatoffers free internet access, some English novels and information on cultural activities. Membership is free. Opening times are generally 10am-2pm, 3.30-8.30pm Monday-Saturday and 10am-2pm Sunday. See www.bcn.es/icub/biblioteques/ or call 93 316 10 00 for details. Private libraries (*see below*) are better stocked but generally require paid membership to use their facilities.

#### Ateneu Barcelonès

*C/Canuda 6, Barri Gòtic (93 343 61 21/www.ateneubcn.org). Metro Catalunya.* **Open** 9am-11pm daily. **Map** p344 C3.

This venerable cultural and philosophical society has the city's best private library, plus a peaceful interior garden patio and a quiet bar. It also organises cultural events. Membership is €20 a month.

#### Biblioteca de Catalunya

*C/Hospital 56, Raval (93 270 23 00/www.bnc.es). Metro Liceu.* **Open** 9am-8pm Mon-Fri; 9am-2pm Sat. **Map** p344 A4.

The Catalan national collection is housed in the medieval Hospital de la Santa Creu and has a wonderful stock reaching back centuries. Readers' cards are required, but free one-day research visits are allowed for over-18s (take your passport).

#### British Council/ Institut Britànic

*C/Amigó 83, Zona Alta (93 241 97 11/www.britishcouncil.es). FGC Muntaner.* **Open** *Oct-mid June* 9.30am-12.30pm, 3.30-9pm Mon-Fri; 10.30am-2pm Sat. *Mid June-July, Sept* 9.30am-12.30pm, 4-8.30pm Mon-Fri. *Aug* 9.30-12.30pm Mon-Fri. **Map** p338 E4.

The British Council has the UK press, English books, satellite TV, internet access and a multimedia section oriented towards learning English. Membership is obligatory for use of the library and borrowing materials .
The charge is €58 a year.

### Mediateca

*CaixaForum, Avda Marquès de Comillas 6-8, Montjuïc (902 22 30 40/93 476 86 51/www.mediatecaonline.net). Metro Espanya.* **Open** *Sept-July* 10am-8pm Tue-Fri; 10am-2pm, 4-8pm Sat. *Aug* 4-8pm Tue, Thur-Sun; 4pm-midnight Wed. **Map** p341 B9.

A high-tech art, music and media library in the arts centre of Fundació la Caixa. Most materials are open-access; though use of the internet is limited to Mediateca-related subjects. You can borrow books, magazines, CDs, etc. Membership is €6 (€3 concessions). The lending desk is open 10am-7.30pm Tue-Fri and 10am-2pm Sat (closed Sat in Aug).

## Lost property

If you lose something at the airport, report it to the lost property centre (*Oficina d'objectes perduts/Oficina de objetos perdidos*, Bloque Técnico building, between terminals B and C, 93 298 33 49). If you have mislaid anything on a train, look for the *Atenció al Passatger/Atención al Viajero* desk or *Cap d'Estació* office at the nearest station to where your property went astray. Call ahead to the destination station, or call station information and ask for *objetos perdidos*.

### Municipal Lost Property Office

*Oficina de Troballes, Plaça Carles Pi i Sunyer 8-10, Barri Gòtic (lost property enquiries 010). Metro Catalunya or Jaume I.* **Open** 9am-2pm Mon-Fri. **Map** p344 C4.

All items found on city public transport and taxis, or picked up by the police in the street, should eventually find their way to this Ajuntament office, just off Avda Portal de l'Àngel, within a few days. Call 010 for information. Within 24 hours of the loss, you can also try ringing the city transport authority on 93 318 70 74, or, for taxis, the Institut Metropolità del Taxi lost property office on 902 10 15 64.

## Media

Spanish and Catalan newspapers tend to favour serious political commentary. There are no sensationalist tabloids in Spain: for scandal, the *prensa rosa* ('pink press', or gossip magazines) is the place to look. Television channels, though, go straight for the mass market, with junk television (*telebasura)* prevalent. Catalan is the dominant language on both radio and TV, less so in print.

### Daily newspapers

Free daily papers of reasonable quality, such as *20 Minutes* and *Metro*, are handed out in the city centre every morning. Articles in these papers jump between Spanish and Catalan for no apparent reason.

#### ABC

Heavyweight, reactionary reading (www.abc.es).

#### Avui

A conservative, nationalist Catalan-language newspaper.

#### El Mundo

A decent centrist option (www.elmundo.es).

#### El País

This serious, socialist-leaning paper is the most extensively read, with the best foreign coverage and all-round political commentary (www.elpais.es).

#### El Periódico

Of the local press, this is the most akin to the British tabloid in terms of format, with bright colours and bold headlines, but it has serious content. There are two editions: one in Catalan and the other in Spanish (www.elperiodico.com).

#### La Vanguardia

The city's top-selling daily newspaper is conservative in tone, with a daily Barcelona supplement. Written in Spanish, it often includes the work of syndicated correspondents from around the world (www.lavanguardia.es).

### English language

Foreign newspapers are available at most kiosks on La Rambla, Barri Gòtic, and Passeig de Gràcia, Eixample and there is an international newsstand at FNAC (*see p189*).

#### Barcelona Connect

A small free magazine with tips for travellers to the city (www.barcelonaconnect.com).

#### Barcelona Metropolitan

A free monthly general-interest magazine for English-speaking locals, distributed in bars, embassies and other anglophone hangouts (www.barcelona-metropolitan.com).

#### b-guided

Quarterly style magazine in Spanish and English for bars, clubs, shops, restaurants and exhibitions (www.b-guided.com).

#### Catalonia Today

English-language weekly paper run by the publisher of Catalan-language daily *El Punt*; available from newsstands throughout the city (www.cataloniatoday.cat).

### Listings & classifieds

The main papers have daily 'what's on' listings, with entertainment supplements on Fridays (most run TV schedules on Saturdays). For monthly listings, see *Metropolitan* or the handy *Butxaca*, which can be picked up in cultural information centres, such as Palau de la Virreina (*see p323*) on the Rambla; and freebies such as *Mondo Sonoro* (www.mondo-sonoro.com) or *GO* (www.go-mag.com), found in bars and music shops. Of the dailies, *La Vanguardia* has the best classifieds; you can also consult it at www.los-clasificados.com. www.infojobs.net is a popular resource for job vacancies.

#### Primeramà

The largest classified-ad publication, is available on Mondays, Wednesdays and Fridays. (www.anuntis.es)

#### Guía del Ocio

This weekly listings magazine, published Fridays, is available at any kiosk for €1 (www.guiadelociobcn.es).

### Radio

There are vast numbers of local, regional and national stations, with Catalan having a high profile. **Catalunya Música** (101.5 FM) is mainly classical and jazz, while **Flaix** FM (105.7 FM) provides news and music. For something a little more alternative, try **Radio Bronka** (99 FM) or **Radio 3** (98.7 FM), which has a wonderfully eclectic music policy. You can listen to the **BBC World Service** on shortwave on 15485, 9410, 12095 and 6195 KHz, depending on the time of day.

# Lost and found

You were so relaxed sitting on the park bench that you left behind your prized digital camera when you got up to leave. You return ten minutes later to look for it but it's gone. It's very likely someone laid claim to it without giving it a second thought and is now busily shooting pictures of his girlfriend and golden retriever. But there's always a chance, slim as it might be, that an understanding soul found it and promptly turned it into the municipal lost and found office.

Not only is the city lost and found office central (Plaça Carles Pi i Sunyer 8-10, Barri Gòtic, to be exact; call the city helpline 010 for information), but it's located near the trendy pedestrian shopping strip of Portal de l'Àngel, making for easy shopping to replace the bag or clothes you don't happen to recover. It usually takes a few days for found objects to be officially entered into the office's books; once there, the office holds on to them for three months. Money and valuable jewels, however, can remain on the premises for up to two years. Unclaimed objects either go to a local charity, the Fundació Engrunes, where they are sold, or the person who originally turned the object into the office can claim them. Apparently, taxi drivers have a reputation for coming back after three months to claim sunglasses found in their cabs.

Objects and documentation that may have been stolen and then recovered by the police are also sent to the office. Documents such as passports and IDs belonging to foreigners are sent on to local consulates, but any objects associated with these remain at the lost and found. To recover your property, you must thoroughly identify it, preferably by its serial number in the case of a camera or mobile phone. You can also visit the city's website, www.bcn.es, and go to its lost and found section to check for found documents or objects.

If the office statistics are any indication, people are losing more objects every year. In 2005, some 49,000 objects were found (and a remarkable 47,000 returned), up from 40,000 in 2004 and 33,000 in 2003. The vast majority of these objects are bags, purses and wallets.

Among the more unusual items found have been various surfboards, a church bell, laptops and a bag containing some 50 passports belonging to a group of Italian school children. Significant sums of money have also been turned in and so far remain unclaimed.

A quick glance at the list of objects found and returned makes it clear that umbrellas and gloves are the least loved of all. Less than one per cent of these are ever reclaimed. Mobile phones and digital cameras, surprisingly, don't rate much higher, with only six per cent ever getting picked up by their owners.

## Television

The inauguration of two free new channels in 2006, Cuatro and La Sexta, has added a couple of decent American series to TV schedules The emphasis is on mass entertainment, with tedious variety shows, lame comedians, gossip shows, home-grown sitcoms and trashy American films, peppered with ad breaks. Programme times are unreliable and films are mainly dubbed; undubbed films are shown by 'VO' in listings or, on 'dual' by TVs, the dual symbol on screen – press the audio monitor button on the remote.

### TVE1

Spanish state broadcaster 'La Primera' is controlled by the government. Do not expect cutting-edge TV.

### TVE2

Also state-run, TVE2, 'La Dos' offers more highbrow fare with some good late-night movies and documentaries.

### TV3

Programmes are entirely in Catalan with generally mainstream subject matter. TV3 often has good films in original version or 'dual'.

### Canal 33

Also regional and in Catalan, with documentaries, sports programmes and round-table discussions.

### Antena 3

A private channel providing a mixture of chat and American films, as well as popular US programmes such as *The Simpsons* or *South Park*.

### Cuatro

Owned by pay-TV giant Sogecable, Cuatro shows US and Spanish soaps, such as *House* and *Married with Children*, some sports and the excellent *Las Noticias del Guiñol* (a daily news spoof using puppets).

### La Sexta

La Sexta boasts big sporting events and some decent US shows, such as *The Sopranos*. Yet it competes for frequency in the overcrowded Spanish market, and the picture can be fuzzy; many can't tune in at all.

### Tele 5

Also private and part-owned by Silvio Berlusconi. Its main recent attraction has been *Gran Hermano* (Big Brother), as well as various celebrity gossip programmes.

### Digital+

The predominant subscription channel fuses the defunct Canal + and Via Digital, showing films, sport and US series.

### BTV

The young staff of the Ajuntament's city channel produce Barcelona's most groundbreaking TV.

### City TV

A private Catalan channel, cloned from a Toronto city station. The schedules are filled with magazine-style programmes and soft porn.

### Satellite & cable

Satellite and cable are becoming increasingly popular in Barcelona. The leader is Digital+ (see above).

## Money

Spain's currency is the euro. Each euro (€) is divided into 100 cents (¢), known as *céntims/céntimos*. Notes come in denominations of €500, €200, €100, €50, €20, €10 and €5. Due to the increasing circulation of counterfeit notes, smaller businesses may be reluctant to accept denominations larger than €50.

### Banks & currency exchanges

Banks (*bancos*) and savings banks (*caixes d'estalvis/cajas de ahorros*) usually accept euro travellers' cheques for a commission, but they tend to refuse any kind of personal cheque except one issued by that bank. Some bureaux de change (*cambios*) don't charge commission, but rates are worse. Obtaining money through an ATM (which are everywhere) with a debit or credit card is the easiest option, despite the fees often charged.

### Bank hours

Banks are normally open 8.30am-2pm Mon-Fri. From October to April, most branches also open 8.30am-1pm on Saturdays. Hours vary a little between banks. Savings banks offer the same exchange facilities as banks and open the same hours; from October to May many are also open late on Thursdays, 4.30-7.45pm.

### Out-of-hours banking

Foreign exchange offices at the airport (terminals A and B) are open 7am-11pm daily. Others in the centre open late: some on La Rambla open until midnight, later between July and September. At Sants, change money at La Caixa (8am-8pm daily). At the airport and outside some banks are automatic exchange machines that accept notes in major currencies. The American Express shop offers full AmEx card services, plus currency exchange, money transfers and a travel agency; Western Union is the quickest (but not the cheapest) way of sending money abroad.

**American Express** *La Rambla 74, Barri Gòtic (93 342 73 11). Metro Liceu.* **Open** 9am-9pm Mon-Sat. **Map** p345 B5.
**Western Union Money Transfer** *Loterías Manuel Martín, La Rambla 41, Barri Gòtic (93 412 70 41/ www.westernunion.com). Metro Liceu.* **Open** 9.30am-10pm daily. **Map** p345 A6.
**Other locations**: Mail Boxes, C/València 214, Eixample (900 63 36 33); and throughout the city.

### Credit & debit cards

Major credit cards are accepted in hotels, shops, restaurants and other places (including metro ticket machines and pay-and-display on-street parking machines). American Express and Diners Club cards are less accepted than MasterCard and Visa. Many debit cards from other European countries can also be used: check with your bank beforehand. You can withdraw cash with major cards from ATMs, and banks will also advance cash against a credit card.

Note: you need photo ID (passport, driving licence or similar) when using a credit or debit card in a shop, but usually not in a restaurant.

### Lost/stolen cards

All lines have English-speaking staff and are open 24 hours daily. Maestro do not have a Spanish helpline.
**American Express** 902 11 11 35.
**Diners Club** 901 10 10 11.
**MasterCard** 900 97 12 31.
**Visa** 900 99 11 24.

### Tax

The standard rate for sales tax (*IVA*) is 16 per cent; this drops to 7 per cent in hotels and restaurants, and 4 per cent on some books. IVA may or may not be included in listed prices at restaurants, and it usually isn't included in rates quoted at hotels. If it's not, the expression *IVA no inclòs/incluido* (sales tax not included) should appear after the price. Beware of this when getting quotes on expensive items. In shops displaying a 'Tax-Free Shopping' sticker, non-EU residents can reclaim tax on large purchases when leaving the country.

## Opening times

Most shops open from 9am or 10am to 1pm or 2pm, and then 4pm or 5pm to 8pm or 9pm, Monday to Saturday. Many smaller businesses don't reopen on Saturday afternoons. All-day opening (10am to 8pm or 9pm) is becoming increasingly common, especially for larger and more central establishments.

Markets open at 7am or 8am; most stalls are shut by 2pm, although many open on Fridays until 8pm. The Ajuntament encourages stallholders at each municipal market to remain open in the afternoons during the rest of the week in an effort to compete with supermarkets. Larger shops are allowed to open on Sundays and on a few holidays, mostly near Christmas.

In summer, many shops and restaurants shut for all or part of August. Some businesses work a shortened day from June to September, from 8am or 9am until 3pm. Most museums close one day each week, usually Mondays.

## Police

Barcelona has several police forces. The **Guàrdia Urbana** (municipal police) wear navy and pale blue, and are concerned with traffic and local regulations, but also law and order, and noise complaints. The **Policía Nacional**, in darker blue uniforms and white shirts (or blue, combat-style gear), patrol the streets, and are responsible for dealing with more serious crime, as well as paperwork concerning ID and passports.

The **Mossos d'Esquadra** (in a uniform of navy and light blue with red trim), the Catalan government's police work alongside the Guàrdia Urbana and Policía Nacional patrolling the streets, particularly in more touristy areas; they take a leading role in dealing with lower-level crime and security.

The **Guàrdia Civil** is a paramilitary force with green uniforms, policing highways, customs posts, government buildings and rural areas.

### Reporting a crime

If you're robbed or attacked, report the incident as soon as possible at the nearest police station (*comisaría*), or dial 112. In the centre, the most convenient is the 24hr **Guàrdia Urbana** station (La Rambla 43, Barri Gòtic, 092/93 256 24 30), which often has English-speaking officers on duty; they may transfer you to the **Mossos d'Esquadra** (C/Nou de la Rambla 76, Raval, 088/93 306 23 00) to formally report the crime. To do this, you'll need to make an official statement (*denuncia*). It's highly improbable that you will recover your property, but you need the *denuncia* to make an insurance claim. You can also make this statement over the phone or online (902 10 21 12, www.policia.es); except for crimes involving physical violence, or if the author has been identified. You'll still have to go to the *comisaría* within 72 hours to sign the *denuncia*, but you'll be able to skip some queues.

## Postal services

Letters and postcards weighing up to 20g cost 28¢ within Spain; 53¢ to the rest of Europe; 78¢ to the rest of the world – though prices normally rise on 1 January. It's usually easiest to buy stamps at *estancs* (*see below*). Mail sent abroad is slow: 5-6 working days in Europe, 8-10 to the USA. Postboxes in the street are yellow, sometimes with a white or blue horn insignia. Postal information (902 197 197 or at www.correos.es).

### Correu Central

*Plaça Antonio López, Barri Gòtic (93 486 80 50). Metro Barceloneta or Jaume I.* **Open** 8.30am-9.30pm Mon-Fri; 8.30am-2pm Sat. **Map** p345 D7.

Take a ticket from the machine as you enter and wait your turn. Apart from the typical services, fax-sending and receiving is offered (with the option of courier delivery in Spain, using the Burofax option). To send something express, ask for *urgente*. Some post offices close in August. Many have painfully slow queues. **Other locations**: Ronda Universitat 23 and C/Aragó 282, Eixample (both 8.30am-8.30pm Mon-Fri, 9.30am-1pm Sat); and throughout the city.

### Estancs/estancos

Government-run tobacco shops, known as an *estanc/estanco* (at times, just *tabac*) and identified by a brown-and-yellow sign, are important institutions. As well as tobacco, they supply postage stamps, public transport *targetes* and phonecards.

### Post boxes

A PO box (*apartado postal*) address costs €46.10 annually.

### Postal Transfer

*C/Ausiàs Marc 13-17, Eixample (93 301 27 32). Metro Urquinaona.* **Open** 8.30am-8.30pm Mon-Fri; 9.30am-1pm Sat.

Apart from postal services, there's Western Union money transfer, internet access, cheap international calls, fax, photocopying and banking.

### Poste restante

Poste restante letters should be sent to Lista de Correos, 08080 Barcelona, Spain. Pick-up is from the main post office (*see above*); you'll need your passport.

## Queueing

Contrary to appearances, Catalans have an advanced queuing culture. They may not stand in an orderly line, but they're normally very aware of when it's their turn, particularly at market stalls. The standard drill is to ask when you arrive, *¿Qui es l'últim/la última?* ('Who's last?') and say *jo* ('me') to the next person who asks.

## Religion

### Anglican: St George's Church

*C/Horaci 38, Zona Alta (93 417 88 67/www.st-georges-church.com). FGC Avda Tibidabo.* **Main service** 11am Sun.

An Anglican/Episcopalian church with a multicultural congregation. Activities include the Alpha course (directed at faith-seekers), a weekly women's club, bridge and Sunday school. See website for details.

### Catholic mass in English: Parròquia Maria Reina

*Carretera d'Esplugues 103, Zona Alta (93 203 41 15). Metro Maria Cristina/bus 22, 63, 75.* **Mass** 10.30pm Sun. **Map** p337 A1.

### Jewish Orthodox: Sinagoga de Barcelona & Comunitat Israelita de Barcelona

*C/Avenir 24, Zona Alta (93 209 31 47/www.cibonline.org). FGC Gràcia.* **Prayers** call for times. **Map** p338 F5.

### Jewish Reform: Comunitat Jueva Atid de Catalunya

*Call for address (tel/fax 93 417 37 04/www.atid.es). FGC El Putxet.* **Prayers** call for times.

You must give notice that you'll be attending this organisation: make sure to email or fax the above number with your passport details by 2pm Friday.

### Muslim: Mosque Tarik Bin Ziad

*C/Hospital 91, Raval (93 441 91 49). Metro Liceu.* **Prayers** 2pm Fri. Phone the above number for other times. **Map** p342 F10.

Follow the corridor to the end and turn left; the mosque is on the top floor.

## Renting a flat

Rental accommodation in Barcelona is pricier than ever. A room in a shared flat costs €300/month plus, while a one- to two-bed apartment in the centre goes for €600/month or more. Standards vary a great deal, so do shop around. Rental agreements generally cover a five-year period, within which the landlord can only raise the rent in line with inflation. Landlords usually ask for a month's rent as a *fiança/fianza* (deposit) and a month's rent in advance; some may also require an employment contract as proof of income. Details of contracts vary wildly: don't sign unless you're confident of your Spanish or Catalan and/or a local lawyer or *gestor* has seen it.

Classified ads in *La Vanguardia* and *Barcelona Metropolitan* (*see p316*) carry apartment ads. Also useful are *administradores de fincas*: these companies run buildings and sometimes have to find tenants for vacant apartments. Check www.coleadministradors.com for a list, but bear in mind that its classified ads are often out of date. Try calling instead. Also, while walking, look out for *Es lloga/Se alquila* or *En lloguer/En alquiler* (for rent) signs: you do get lucky. Be cautious of agencies that ask for cash upfront for finding you a flat. If you decide to pay, go by recommendation.

## Safety

Pickpocketing and bag-snatching are epidemic in Barcelona, with tourists a prime target. Be especially careful around the Old City, particularly La Rambla, as well as at stations and on public transport, the airport train being a favourite. However, thieves go anywhere tourists go, including parks, beaches and – the latest hotspot – internet cafés. Most street crime is aimed at the inattentive, and can be avoided by taking a few simple common-sense precautions:

- Avoid giving invitations: don't keep wallets in accessible pockets, keep your bags closed and in front of you. When you stop, put your bags down beside you (or hold them on your lap), where you can see them.
- Don't flash about wads of cash or fancy cameras.
- In busy streets or crowded places, keep an eye on what is happening around you. If you're suspicious of someone, move somewhere else.
- As a rule, Barcelona street thieves tend to use stealth and surprise rather than violence. However,

## Bussing it

The tourist bus whisks you to the top sights, but there is nothing like a leisurely meander on the public bus to get a sense of the city. For the price of a stamp on a T10, TMB buses may not be the fastest way to get around Barcelona, but they are cool, comfortable and cost-effective.

Roads are quieter on weekends and in the lunchtime lull (2.30-4.30pm). There's a comprehensive map detailing routes posted on the back of bigger bus stops, and a small version can be picked up at tourist offices. The routes, below, also connect up.

**PM (Parc Montjuïc)**
If you don't like to linger, or are down to your last *céntims*, opt for the PM, which whips you round the mountain in about half an hour. Get on at the smaller stop through the Plaça d'Espanya pillars (Avda Reina Maria Cristina). Jump off at the Fundació Miró, where the PM connects with the 55.

**55** (**Parc de Montjuïc-Plç Catalana**).
The 55 zigzags through Poble Sec; as it crosses Avda Paral.lel, look out for the snail-encrusted Casa dels Cargols (C/Entença 2, C/Tamarit 89) on the corner: a flamboyant ode to the creeping delicacy, this building dates from 1896. The route takes you past the university, through the centre of town, then up Passeig San Joan. The ornate wrought-iron and coloured-glass lamp at No.26 protrudes from the first public library in the city, the Biblioteca Arús, built in 1894. The lamp was fashioned by local illustrator Josep Lluís Pellicer. Puig i Cadafalch's Casa Macaya (*see p42*) is at No.108. The 55 carries on up to Parc de les Aigües (*see p141*), connecting with the 92.

**92** (**Pg Marítim-Gràcia**).
Best caught on the beachfront outside the Hospital del Mar, the 92 makes a sweeping ascent via Poble Nou, through the humbler, right-hand side of the Eixample, to Carmel. In Poble Nou, look out for the neo-classical Cementiri de l'Est (Av Icaria-C/Taulat). Initially built outside the city walls in 1775, it reached its heyday in 1821, when some 6,000 Barcelonins were struck down by yellow fever. Passing the Hospital de la Santa Creu i Sant Pau (*see p125*), the 92 lumbers into Carmel, where ancient folk, with legs like iron, stagger up steep inclines with their shopping. Promoted in the late 19th century as a place of refuge, Carmel has a lofty, villagey feel to it. Look out for the tiny church on the left, on the winding C/Santuari.

Crossing the viaduct into Vallcarca, the Modernista gem Casa Comas d'Argemí, with its peaked blue turret, perches on C/Bolivar. Descending to Lesseps, you'll see the cool curves of the new Biblioteca Jaume Fuster (2003), designed by architect Josep Llinás. Across the junction, the enormous yellow-and-orange leaf-printed façade of Cases Ramos, built by Jaume Torres i Grau in 1906, heralds the end of the journey in Gràcia.

If you're feeling particularly adventurous, however, you could always do the whole route again, and be back to the beach for sunset.

muggings and knife threats do sometimes occur. Avoid deserted streets in the city centre if you're on your own at night, and offer no resistance when threatened.
● Despite precautions, sometimes you can just be unlucky. Don't carry more money and valuables than you need: use your hotel's safe deposit facilities, and take outtravel insurance.

## Smoking

For the visitor to Barcelona, it may seem that smoking when and where you want is a given right and, in fact, one effect of the recent tightening of the tobacco law is that there are as many signs telling you that you can smoke, as there are telling you that you can't.

Smoking is banned in banks, shops and offices; while in hotels, and restaurants larger than 100 square metres (1076 square feet), non-smoking zones are required by law. Yet while tobacco is still relatively cheap and socially acceptable, it's common to see small crowds of undeterred employees puffing away on the pavement on their lunch breaks; and few cafés and even fewer bars have opted for a strict no-smoking policy, for fear of losing business. In Catalonia, the smoking law applying to the physical separation of smoking and non-smoking areas in larger restaurants has already been relaxed, as many complain of the cost and unfeasibility of restructuring their interiors.

Most hotels have non-smoking rooms or floors; although if you ask for a non-smoking room, some hotels may just give you a room that has had the ashtray removed. Some restaurants and a few, but growing number of hotels, however, are completely smoke-free. Smoking bans in such places as cinemas, theatres and on public transport are generally respected.

## Study

Catalonia is pro-European, and the vast majority of foreign students in Spain under the EU's Erasmus scheme are studying at Catalan universities or colleges. Catalan is usually spoken in these universities, although some lecturers are relaxed about the use of Castilian in class for the first few months.

### Accommodation & advice

#### Barcelona Allotjament

*C/Pelai 12, pral B, Eixample (93 268 43 57/www.barcelona-allotjament.com). Metro Catalunya or Universitat.* **Open** 10am-2pm, 5-7pm Mon-Thur; 10am-2pm Fri. Closed Aug. **No credit cards. Map** p344 A1.
Rooms with local families, in shared student flats and in B&Bs can be booked through this agency, aimed mainly at students. Rooms in shared apartments cost €300 and up per month, plus a €120 agency fee. It can also rent whole flats.

#### Centre d'Informació i Assessorament per a Joves (CIAJ)

*C/Sant Oleguer 6-8, Raval (93 442 29 39/www.bcn.es/ciaj). Metro Liceu or Paral·lel.* **Open** *Sept-July* 10am-2pm, 4-8pm Mon-Fri. *Aug* 10am-3pm Mon-Fri. **Map** p342 E11.
Youth information centre run by the city council, with information on work, study, accommodation (classifieds are online, not in the centre itself) and more.

#### Secretaria General de Joventut – Punt d'Informació Juvenil

*C/Calabria 147-C/Rocafort 116, Eixample (reception 93 483 83 83/ information 93 483 83 84/ www.gencat.net/joventut). Metro Rocafort.* **Open** *Oct-May* 10am-2pm, 4-8pm Mon-Fri. *June-Sept* 10am-3pm Mon-Fri. **Map** p341 D8.
Generalitat-run centre with a number of services: information for young people on travel, work and study. Other Secretaria General de Joventut services include Borsa Jove d'Habitatge (93 483 83 92, www.habitatge jove.com), an accommodation service for 18-35s; it's mostly for whole flats, but there are some single rooms available.

### Language classes

If you plan to stay in bilingual Barcelona for a while, you may want (or need) to learn some Catalan. The city is also a popular location for studying Spanish. For full course lists, try the youth information centres above. See www.cervantes.es for schools recommended by Spain's official language institute, the Instituto Cervantes.

#### Babylon Idiomas

*C/Bruc 65, pral 1ª, Eixample (93 488 15 85/www.babylon-idiomas.com). Metro Girona.*
**Open** 9am-8pm Mon-Fri.
**Credit** MC, V. **Map** p339 H8.
Small groups (up to eight people) run at all levels of Spanish in this school, which also has business courses. Staff can arrange accommodation.

#### Consorci per a la Normalització Lingüística

*C/Quintana 11, 1° 1ª, Barri Gòtic (93 412 72 24/www.cpnl.cat). Metro Liceu.* **Open** *mid Sept-mid June* 9am-2pm Mon-Fri. *Mid June-mid Sept* 9am-1pm, 4-5.30pm Mon-Thur; 9am-2pm Fri. **No credit cards. Map** p345 B5.
The Generalitat organisation for the promotion of the Catalan language has centres around the city offering Catalan courses for non-Spanish speakers at very low prices or for free (level one). Courses start in September and February; classes are very big and the queues to enrol long. There are also free monthly intensive courses and multimedia classes for beginners all year. The CPNL in Plaça Catalunya 9, 2º 1ª (902 07 50 60) specialises in beginners' courses and has a wider timetable. Places are limited to around 23 students per class; call or arrive early when it's time to sign up.
**Other locations**: C/Mallorca 115, entl 1ª, Eixample (93 451 24 45); and throughout the city.

#### Escola Oficial d'Idiomes de Barcelona – Drassanes

*Avda Drassanes, Raval (93 324 93 30/www.eoibd.es). Metro Drassanes.* **Open** *Sept-June* 8.30am-9pm Mon-Fri. **Map** p342 E11.
This state-run school has semi-intensive four-month courses, starting in October and February (enrollment tends to be in September and January, check the website for details), at all levels in Spanish; and longer courses, usually starting in October, in Catalan, French, German,

English and ten other languages. It's cheap and has a good reputation; demand is high and classes are big. There's also a self-study centre and a good library. There are several other Escolas Oficials in Barcelona where it may be easier to get a place, although they do not offer such a wide range as Drassanes. Call 012 or see www.gencat.net/educacio for details.
**Other locations**: Escola Oficial, Avda del Jordà 18, Vall d'Hebrón (93 418 74 85/93 418 68 33); and throughout the city.

### Estudios Hispánicos de la Universitat de Barcelona

*Gran Via de les Corts Catalanes 585, Eixample (information 93 403 55 19/www.eh.ub.es). Metro Universitat.* **Open** *Information* (Pati de Ciències entrance) *mid June-Aug* 9am-2pm Mon-Fri. *Sept-mid June* 9am-2pm, 4-5.30pm Mon-Thur; 9am-2pm Fri. **Credit** AmEx, DC, MC, V. **Map** p342 F8.
Intensive three-month and year-long Spanish language and culture courses. Enrolment runs year-round.

### International House

*C/Trafalgar 14, Eixample (93 268 45 11/www.ihes.com/bcn). Metro Urquinaona.* **Open** 8am-9pm Mon-Fri; 10am-1.30pm Sat. **Map** p344 E3.
Intensive Spanish courses all year round. IH is also a leading TEFL teacher training centre, and offers additional courses in Spanish-English translation.

## Universities

The Erasmus student-exchange scheme is part of the EU's Socrates programme to help students move between member states. Interested students should contact the Erasmus co-ordinator at their home college. Information is available in Britain from the UK Socrates-Erasmus Council, Rothford, Giles Lane, Canterbury, Kent CT2 7LR (01227 762712/fax 01227 762711/www.erasmus.ac.uk). See also europa.eu.int for an overview.

### Universitat Autònoma de Barcelona

*Campus de Bellaterra (93 581 10 00/information 93 581 11 11/www.uab.es). FGC or RENFE Universidad Autonoma/ by car A58 to Cerdanyola del Valles.* **Open** *Information* Sept-July 10am-1.30pm, 3.30-4.30pm Mon-Fri. Aug 10am-1.30pm Mon-Fri.
A 1960s campus outside the city at Bellaterra, near Sabadell. Frequent FGC train connections to the centre.

### Universitat de Barcelona

*Gran Via de les Corts Catalanes 585, Eixample (information 93 403 54 17/www.ub.es). Metro Universitat.* **Open** *Information* 9am-2pm Mon-Fri. Closed 1wk Aug. **Map** p342 F8.
Barcelona's oldest and biggest university has faculties in the main building on Plaça Universitat, and elsewhere. For Spanish courses, *see p319*.

### Universitat Pompeu Fabra

*Information 93 542 22 28/ www.upf.edu. Information points: La Rambla 30-32, Barri Gòtic; C/Ramon Trias Fargas 25-27, Vila Olímpica; Passeig Circumval·lació 8, Born.* **Open** *mid June-mid Sept* 9am-8pm Mon-Fri. *Mid Sept-mid June* 9am-9pm Mon-Fri.
There are faculties in various parts of central Barcelona, many of which are in the Old City.

### Universitat Ramon Llull

*Main offices: C/Claravall 1-3, Zona Alta (902 50 20 50/93 602 22 00/www.url.es). FGC Avda Tibidabo.* **Open** *Information* 9am-2pm, 4-6.30pm Mon-Fri. Closed 2wks Aug.
A private university bringing together a number of once-separate institutions, including the prestigious ESADE business school (93 280 61 62/93 280 29 95, www.esade.edu).

# Telephones

The recent liberalisation of the phone market has led to the dissolution of former state operator Telefónica's monopoly. However, while several new operators have emerged, the market is still very dependent on Telefónica's infrastructure, and rates remain high compared to other European countries.

One of the outcomes of diversification has been the confusion among users, exemplified by the profusion of numbers for directory enquiries. There are now more than 20 numbers (which are operated by various companies) for information; their cost fluctuates wildly. Telefónica itself has several, and is severely criticised for its massive advertising of the more expensive ones. It is, however, forced to offer a cheap number (which is free from payphones); *see below*. Phonecards, and the phone centres that sell them, generally give cheaper call rates, especially for international calls.

## Dialling & codes

Normal Spanish phone numbers have nine digits; the area code (93 in the province of Barcelona) must be dialled with all calls, both local and long-distance. Spanish mobile numbers always begin with 6. Numbers starting 900 are freephone lines, while other 90 numbers are special-rate services.

### International & long-distance calls

To make an international call, dial 00 and then the country code, followed by the area code (omitting the first zero in UK numbers), and then the number. Country codes are as follows:

**Australia** 61.
**Canada** 1.
**Irish Republic** 353.
**New Zealand** 64.
**South Africa** 27.
**United Kingdom** 44.
**USA** 1.
To phone Spain from abroad, dial 00, followed by 34, followed by the number.

## Mobile phones

The mobile phone, or *móvil*, is omnipresent in Spain. Calls are paid for either through direct debit or by using prepaid phones, topped up with vouchers. Most mobiles from other European countries can be used in Spain, but you may need to set this up before you leave. You may be charged international roaming rates even when making a local call, and you will be charged for incoming calls. Not all US handsets are GSM-compatible; check with your service provider before you leave.
If you're staying more than a few weeks, it may work out cheaper to buy a pay-as-you-go package when you arrive, from places such as FNAC (*see p89*), or buy a local SIM card for your own phone. Handsets usually include a little credit, which you can then top up (from newsagents, cash machines and *estancs*). Firms include Amena (1474, www.amena.com), Movistar (1485, www.movistar.es) and Vodafone (607 123 000, www.vodafone.es).

## Average climate

| | Max temp (C°/F°) | Min temp (C°/F°) | Rainfall (mm/in) |
|---|---|---|---|
| **Jan** | 13/56 | 6/43 | 44/1.7 |
| **Feb** | 15/59 | 7/45 | 36/1.4 |
| **Mar** | 16/61 | 8/47 | 48/1.9 |
| **Apr** | 18/64 | 10/50 | 51/2 |
| **May** | 21/70 | 14/57 | 57/2.2 |
| **June** | 24/76 | 17/63 | 38/1.5 |
| **July** | 27/81 | 20/67 | 22/0.9 |
| **Aug** | 29/84 | 20/67 | 66/2.6 |
| **Sept** | 25/78 | 18/64 | 79/3.1 |
| **Oct** | 22/71 | 14/57 | 94/3.7 |
| **Nov** | 17/63 | 9/49 | 74/2.9 |
| **Dec** | 15/59 | 7/45 | 50/2.5 |

## Operator services & useful phone numbers

Operators normally speak Catalan and Spanish only, except for international operators, most of whom speak English.

**General information (Barcelona)** 010 (8am-10pm Mon-Sat).
**International directory enquiries** 11825.
**International operator for reverse charge calls** Europe 1008; rest of world 1005.
**National directory enquiries** 11818 (Telefónica, the cheapest) or 11888 (*Yellow Pages*, more expensive, or free on www.paginas amarillas.com), among others.
**National operator for reverse charge calls** 1009. After the recorded message, press the asterisk key twice, and then 4.
**Pharmacies, postcodes, lottery** 098.
**Telephone faults service** (Telefónica) 1002.
**Time** 093.
**Wake-up calls** 096. After the message, key in the time at which you wish to be woken, in the 24hr clock, in four figures: for example, 0830 for 8.30am, 2030 for 8.30pm.
**Weather** 807 170 365.

## Phone centres

Phone centres (*locutorios*) are full of small booths where you can sit down and pay at the end. They offer cheap calls and avoid the need for change. Concentrated particularly in streets such as C/Sant Pau and C/Hospital in the Raval, and along C/Carders-C/Corders in Sant Pere, they generally offer other services too, including international money transfer, currency exchange and internet access.

**Locutorio** *C/Hospital 17, Raval (93 318 97 39). Metro Liceu.* **Open** 10am-10pm daily. **No credit cards. Map** p345 A5.
**Oftelcom** *C/Canuda 7, Barri Gòtic (93 342 73 71). Metro Catalunya.* **Open** 9am-midnight daily. **No credit cards. Map** p344 B3.

## Public phones

The most common type of payphone in Barcelona accepts coins (5¢ and up), phonecards and credit cards. There is a multilingual digital display (press 'L' to change language) and written instructions in English and other languages. Take plenty of small coins with you. For the first minute of a daytime local call, you'll be charged around 8¢; to a mobile phone around 13¢; and to a 902 number around 20¢. Calls to directory enquiries on 11818 are free from payphones, but you'll usually have to insert a coin to make the call (it will be returned when you hang up). If you're still in credit at the end of your call, you can make further calls by pushing the 'R' button and dialling again. Bars and cafés often have payphones, but these can be more expensive than street booths.

Telefónica phonecards (*targetes telefònica/tarjetas telefónica*) are sold at newsstands and *estancs* (*see p318*). Other cards sold at phone centres, shops and news stands give cheaper rates on all but local calls. This latter type of card contains a toll-free number to call from any phone.

## Time

Local time is one hour ahead of GMT, six hours ahead of US Eastern Standard Time and nine ahead of Pacific Standard Time. Daylight saving time runs concurrently with the UK: clocks go back in October and forward in March.

## Tipping

There are no fixed rules for tipping in Barcelona, but locals generally don't tip much. It's fair to leave 5-10 per cent in restaurants, but if you think the service has been bad, don't feel you have to. People sometimes leave a little change in bars. In taxis, tipping is not standard, but if the fare works out at a few cents below a euro, many people will round up. It's usual to tip hotel porters.

## Toilets

The problem of people urinating outside in the Old City has pressed the Ajuntament into introducing more public toilets. There are 24 hour public toilets in Plaça del Teatre, just off La Rambla, and more at the top of C/dels Àngels, opposite the MACBA. Most of the main railway stations have clean toilets. Parks such as Ciutadella and Güell have a few dotted about, and you need a 20¢ coin to use them. The beach at Barceloneta has six (heavily in demand) Portaloos; there are five further up at the beach at Sant Sebastià, and in season there are also toilets open under the boardwalk, along the beach towards the Port Olímpic. Most bar and café owners do not mind if you use their toilets (you may have to ask for the key), although some in the centre and at the beach are less amenable. Fast-food restaurants are good standbys.

Toilets are known as *serveis*, *banys* or *lavabos* (in Catalan) or *servicios, aseos, baños* or *lavabos* (in Spanish).

In bars or restaurants, the ladies' is generally denoted by a D (*dones/damas*), and occasionally by an M (*mujeres*) or S (*señoras*) on the door; while the men's mostly say H (*homes/hombres*) or C (*caballeros*).

## Tourist information

The city council (Ajuntament) and Catalan government (Generalitat) both run tourist offices. Information about what's on can be found in local papers as well as listings magazines. See those listed under Media.

### 010 phoneline

**Open** 8am-10pm Mon-Sat.
This city-run information line is aimed mainly at locals, but it does an impeccable job of answering all kinds of queries. There are sometimes English-speaking operators available.

### Centre d'Informació de la Virreina

*Palau de la Virreina, La Rambla 99, Barri Gòtic (93 316 10 00/ www.bcn.es/cultura). Metro Liceu.* **Open** 10am-8pm Mon-Sat; 11am-3pm Sun. **Ticket sales** *Virreina exhibitions* 11am-8pm Tue-Sat; | 11am-3pm Sun; timetable varies for other events, generally 10am-7pm Tue-Sat. **Map** p344 B4.
The information office of the city's culture department has details of shows, exhibitions and special events. The good bookstore specialises in Barcelona-related items.

### Oficines d'Informació Turística

*Plaça Catalunya, Eixample (information 807 11 72 22/ from outside Spain +34 93 285 38 34/www.bcn.es/www.barcelona turisme.com). Metro Catalunya.*
**Open** *Office* 9am-9pm daily.
*Call centre* 9am-8pm Mon-Fri.
**Map** p344 C2.
The main office of the city tourist board is underground on the El Corte Inglés/south side of the square: look for big red signs with 'i' in white. It has information, money exchange, a shop and a hotel booking service, and sells phonecards and tickets for shows, sights and public transport.
**Other locations**: C/Ciutat 2 (ground floor of Ajuntament), Barri Gòtic; C/Sardenya (opposite the Sagrada Família), Eixample; Plaça Portal Pau (opposite Monument a Colom), Port Vell; Sants station; La Rambla 115, Barri Gòtic; corner of Plaça d'Espanya and Avda Maria Cristina, Exiample; airport.

### Palau Robert

*Passeig de Gràcia 107, Eixample (93 238 80 91/www.gencat.net/ probert). Metro Diagonal.* **Open** 10am-7pm Mon-Sat; 10am-2.30pm Sun. **Map** p338 G7.
The Generalitat's lavishly equipped centre is at the junction of Passeig de Gràcia and the Diagonal. It has maps and other essentials for Barcelona, but its speciality is a huge range of information in different media for elsewhere in Catalonia. It sometimes hosts interesting exhibitions on local art, culture, gastronomy and nature.
**Other locations**: Airport terminals A (93 478 47 04) and B (93 478 05 65), open 9am-9pm daily.

## Visas & immigration

Spain is one of the European Union countries that's covered by the Schengen Agreement, which led to common visa regulations and limited border controls among member states who were signatories in the agreement. However, neither the UK nor the Republic of Ireland are signatories in this agreement; nationals of those countries will need their passports. Most European Union citizens, as well as Norwegian and Icelandic nationals, only need a national identity card.

Visas are not required for United States, Canadian, Australian and New Zealand citizens for stays of up to 90 days not for work or study. Citizens of South Africa and other countries need visas to enter Spain; approach Spanish consulates and embassies in other countries for information on entry requirements. Visa regulations are subject to change; check before leaving home.

## Water

Tap water is drinkable in Barcelona, but it tastes of chlorine. Bottled water is what you will be served if you ask for *un aigua/agua* in a bar or restaurant, *fresca* is from the fridge, natural is at room temperature. *Agua con gas* is carbonated water.

## When to go

Barcelona is usually agreeable year-round, though the humidity in summer can be debilitating, particularly when it's overcast. Many shops, bars and restaurants close (especially during August). Public transport can over-compensate for the summer heat, with bracing air-conditioning.

### Climate

Spring in Barcelona is unpredictable: warm, sunny days can alternate, dramatically at times, with cold winds and showers. Temperatures in May and June are pretty much perfect; the city is especially lively around 23 June, when locals celebrate the beginning of summer with all kinds of fireworks and fiestas. July and August can be decidedly unpleasant, as the summer heat and humidity kick in and make many locals leave town. Autumn weather is generally warm and fresh, with heavy downpours common around October. Crisp, cool sunshine is normal from December to February. Snow is very rare.

### Public holidays

Almost all shops, banks and offices, and many bars and restaurants, close on public holidays (*festius/ festivos*), and public transport runs a limited service. Many locals take long weekends whenever a major holiday comes along. If the holiday coincides with, say, a Tuesday or a Thursday, many people will take the Monday or Friday off: this is what is known as a *pont/puente*. The city's official holidays are as follows:
**New Year's Day/*Any Nou*** 1 Jan
**Three Kings/*Reis Mags*** 6 Jan
**Good Friday/Divendres Sant**

**Easter Monday/*Dilluns de Pasqua***
**May (Labour) Day/*Festa del Treball*** 1 May
**Whitsun/*Segona Pascua*** 31 May
**Sant Joan** 24 June
**Verge de l'Assumpció** 15 Aug
**Diada de Catalunya** 11 Sept
**La Mercè** 24 Sept
**Dia de la Hispanitat** 12 Oct
**All Saints' Day/*Tots Sants*** 1 Nov
**Constitution Day/*Día de la Constitución*** 6 Dec
**La Immaculada** 8 Dec
**Christmas Day/*Nadal*** 25 Dec
Boxing Day/***Sant Esteve*** 26 Dec.

## Working & living

Common recourses for English speakers in Barcelona are to find work in the tourist sector (often seasonal and outside the city), work in a downtown bar or teach English in the numerous language schools. For the latter, it helps to have the TEFL (Teaching English as a Foreign Language) qualifications; these can be gained in reputable institutions in the city as well as in your home country. Bear in mind that teaching work dries up in June until the end of summer, usually September, although it's possible to find intensive teaching courses during July. The amount of jobs in call centres for English speakers and other foreigners has also rocketed of late.

Queries regarding residency and legal requirements for foreigners who are working in Spain can be addressed to the Ministry of Interior's helpline on 900 150 000 (where there are English-speaking operators). Its website (www.mir.es/SGACAVT/extranje/) lays out the regulations in force on these residency matters, but makes for dense reading.

### EU citizens

Most EU citizens living in Spain are exempt from the obligation to own a resident's card (*tarjeta de residencia*). Students, contracted workers, freelancers, business owners or retired people who have made Spanish social security contributions are entitled to live here and use their own country's ID card or passport for all dealings. However, in order to get a work contract or a resident's bank account, to make tax declarations or for other official bureaucracy, you will need a Número de Identificación del Extranjero (foreigner's identity number), otherwise known as NIE. To do this, head to the *Oficina de Comunitarias* (*see below*). To obtain a residency card, you may apply for one at the Delegación de Gobierno's Oficina de Extranjería (*see below*). First, though, you must get an NIE.

#### Oficina de Extranjería (EU citizens)

*Avda Marquès de l'Argentera 2, 2º, Born (93 482 05 44/appointments 93 520 95 30). Metro Barceloneta.* **Open** *June-mid Sept* 8am-3pm Mon-Fri. *Mid Sept-May* Phone lines 9am-2pm Mon-Fri. Office 9.30am-5.30pm Mon-Thur; 9am-2pm Fri. **Map** p345 E7.

You need an appointment before you can make your residency card application, and it can take up to three months for an available slot. You'll need three passport photos, your passport, NIE, two photocopies of each and a photocopy of the completed application form.

The application can be downloaded from ww.mir.es/SGACAVT/modelos/extranjeria/documentacion/ex16.pdf. To pick up the card, you may also be asked for an official proof of address (*volant d'empadronament*), which you can apply for at any Ajuntament office. You'll need the contract for your flat, or, if your name is not on it, the signature and a photocopy of the identity card of a registered person living there, or the owner. Call 010 for more information.

#### Oficina de Tarjetas Comunitarias

*Passeig Joan de Borbó 32, Barceloneta (93 224 06 02/www.mir.es).* **Open** 9am-2pm Mon-Fri. **Map** p342 G13.

Arrive early and queue here for your NIE application. Remember to bring your passport along with a photocopy of its main pages and two passport photos. You can download the form at www.mir.es/SGACAVT/modelos/extranjeria/documentacion/ex14.pdf, but you will still have to bring it with you in person. Once you've submitted the paperwork, staff will send your NIE by post within 30-40 days. It consists of an unimpressive-looking piece of paper with a number printed on it, but this is the legal document that backs up your identification number.

### Non-EU citizens

Thanks to the soaring levels of immigration, the legal situation is tougher than ever for people from the rest of the world. While in Spain on a tourist visa, you are not legally allowed to work. First-time applicants officially need a special visa, obtained from a Spanish consulate in their home country. Even if you are made a job offer while in Spain, you must still make the trip home to apply for this visa. The process can be lengthy, and not all applications are successful. Armed with this, you can begin the protracted application process for a resident's card and work permit (*permís de treball/permiso de trabajo*) at the Oficina de Extranjería (*see below*). Go prepared: queues can be extremely long. Getting good legal advice is important, given the length of the process and possible rule changes. Note that if you wish to renew or modify your work or residency permit, you can present your documentation at any city post office, rather than queue up again.

#### Oficina de Extranjería (Non-EU citizens)

*Avda Marquès de l'Argentera 4, sala A, Born (93 482 05 44/information and appointments 93 520 14 10). Metro Barceloneta.* **Open** *June-mid Sept* 8am-3pm Mon-Fri. *Mid Sept-May* Phone lines 9am-2pm Mon-Fri. Office 9.30am-5.30pm Mon-Thur; 9am-2pm Fri. **Map** p345 E7.

On making the application for your residency card and work permit, you will need to submit the following documents, along with the completed application form (available at www.mir.es/SGACAVT/modelos/extranjeria/documentacion/ex01.pdf): a photocopy of your passport; a police certificate from your home city stating you don't have a criminal record (translated into Spanish by a sworn translator; *see p310*); an official medical certificate (obtained on arrival in Spain); three identical passport photographs; where applicable, documents proving why you are more capable of performing the job than an EU citizen; and, where necessary, proof that you have the qualifications or training required for the job.

# Spanish Vocabulary

Spanish is generally referred to as *castellano* (Castilian) rather than *español*. Although many locals prefer to speak Catalan, everyone in the city can speak Spanish, and will switch to it if visitors show signs of linguistic jitters. The Spanish familiar form for 'you' – *tú* – is used very freely, but it's safer to use the more formal *usted* with older people and strangers (verbs below are given in the *usted* form).
For menu terms, *see p166-7*.

## Spanish pronunciation

**c** before an **i** or an **e** and **z** are like **th** in **th**in
**c** in all other cases is as in **c**at
**g** before an **i** or an **e** and **j** are pronounced with a guttural **h**-sound that doesn't exist in English – like **ch** in Scottish 'loch', but much harder;
**g** in all other cases is as in **g**et
**h** at the beginning of a word is normally silent
**ll** is pronounced almost like a **y**
**ñ** is like **ny** in ca**ny**on
a single **r** at the beginning of a word and **rr** elsewhere are heavily rolled

### Stress rules

In words ending with a vowel, **n** or **s**, the penultimate syllable is stressed: eg *barato, viven, habitaciones.*
In words ending with any other consonant, the last syllable is stressed: eg *exterior, universidad.*
An accent marks the stressed syllable in words that depart from these rules: eg *estación, tónica.*

## Useful expressions

**hello** *hola*; **hello** (when answering the phone) *hola, diga*
**good morning, good day** *buenos días*; **good afternoon, good evening** *buenas tardes*; **good evening** (after dark), **good night** *buenas noches*
**goodbye/see you later** *adiós/hasta luego*
**please** *por favor*; **thank you** (very much) *(muchas) gracias*; **you're welcome** *de nada*
**do you speak English?** *¿habla inglés?*; **I don't speak Spanish** *no hablo castellano*
**I don't understand** *no entiendo*
**can you say that to me in Catalan, please?** *¿me lo puede decir en catalán, por favor?*
**what's your name?** *¿cómo se llama?*
**speak more slowly, please** *hable más despacio, por favor*; **wait a moment** *espere un momento*
**Sir/Mr** *señor (sr)*; **Madam/Mrs** *señora (sra)*; **Miss** *señorita (srta)*
**excuse me/sorry** *perdón*;
**excuse me, please** *oiga* (the standard way to attract someone's attention, politely; literally, 'hear me')
**OK/fine/**(to a waiter) **that's enough** *vale*
**where is...?** *¿dónde está...?*
**why?** *¿porqué?*, **when?** *¿cuándo?*, **who?** *¿quién?*, **what?** *¿qué?*, **where?** *¿dónde?*, **how?** *¿cómo?*
**who is it?** *¿quién es?*, **is/are there any...?** *¿hay...?*
**very** *muy*; **and** *y*; **or** *o*; **with** *con*; **without** *sin*
**open** *abierto*; **closed** *cerrado*; **what time does it open/close?** *¿a qué hora abre/cierra?*
**pull** (on signs) *tirar*; **push** *empujar*
**I would like** *quiero*; **how many would you like?** *¿cuántos quiere?*,
**how much is it** *¿cuánto es?*
**I like** *me gusta*; **I don't like** *no me gusta*
**good** *bueno/a*; **bad** *malo/a*; **well/badly** *bien/mal*; **small** *pequeño/a*; **big** *gran, grande*; **expensive** *caro/a*; **cheap** *barato/a*; **hot** (food, drink) *caliente*; **cold** *frio/a*;
**something** *algo*; **nothing** *nada*
**more/less** *más/menos*; **more or less** *más o menos*
**do you have any change?** *¿tiene cambio?*
**price** *precio*; **free** *gratis*; **discount** *descuento*; **bank** *banco*; **to rent** *alquilar*; **(for) rent, rental** *(en) alquiler*; **post office** *correos*; **stamp** *sello*; **postcard** *postal*; **toilet** *los servicios*

## Getting around

**airport** *aeropuerto*; **railway station** *estación de ferrocarril/estación de RENFE* (Spanish railways); **metro station** *estación de metro*
**entrance** *entrada*; **exit** *salida*
**car** *coche*; **bus** *autobús*; **train** *tren*
**a ticket** *un billete*; **return** *de ida y vuelta*; **bus stop** *parada de autobus*;
**the next stop** *la próxima parada*
**excuse me, do you know the way to...?** *¿oiga, señor/señora/etc, sabe cómo llegar a...?*
**left** *izquierda*; **right** *derecha*
**here** *aquí*; **there** *allí*; **straight on** *recto*; **to the end of the street** *al final de la calle*; **as far as** *hasta*; **towards** *hacia*; **near** *cerca*; **far** *lejos*

## Accommodation

**do you have a double/single room for tonight/one week?** *¿tiene una habitación doble/para una persona/para esta noche/una semana?*
**we have a reservation** *tenemos reserva*; **an inside/outside room** *una habitación interior/exterior*
**with/without bathroom** *con/sin baño*; **shower** *ducha*; **double bed** *cama de matrimonio*; **with twin beds** *con dos camas*; **breakfast included** *desayuno incluído*; **air-conditioning** *aire acondicionado*; **lift** *ascensor*; **pool** *piscina*

## Time

**now** *ahora*; **later** *más tarde*; **yesterday** *ayer*; **today** *hoy*; **tomorrow** *mañana*; **tomorrow morning** *mañana por la mañana*
**morning** *la mañana*; **midday** *mediodía*; **afternoon/evening** *la tarde*; **night** *la noche*; **late night** (roughly 1-6am) *la madrugada*
**at what time...?** *¿a qué hora...?*, **at 2** *a las dos*; **at 8pm** *a las ocho de la tarde*; **at 1.30** *a la una y media*; **at 5.15** *a las cinco y cuarto*; **in an hour** *en una hora*

## Numbers

**0** *cero*; **1** *un, uno, una*; **2** *dos*; **3** *tres*; **4** *cuatro*; **5** *cinco*; **6** *seis*; **7** *siete*; **8** *ocho*; **9** *nueve*; **10** *diez*; **11** *once*; **12** *doce*; **13** *trece*; **14** *catorce*; **15** *quince*; **16** *dieciséis*; **17** *diecisiete*; **18** *dieciocho*; **19** *diecinueve*; **20** *veinte*; **21** *veintiuno*; **22** *veintidós*; **30** *treinta*; **40** *cuarenta*; **50** *cincuenta*; **60** *sesenta*; **70** *setenta*; **80** *ochenta*; **90** *noventa*; **100** *cien*; **200** *doscientos*; **1,000** *mil*; **1,000,000** *un millón*

## Dates & seasons

**Monday** *lunes*; **Tuesday** *martes*; **Wednesday** *miércoles*; **Thursday** *jueves*; **Friday** *viernes*; **Saturday** *sábado*; **Sunday** *domingo*
**January** *enero*; **February** *febrero*; **March** *marzo*; **April** *abril*; **May** *mayo*; **June** *junio*; **July** *julio*; **August** *agosto*; **September** *septiembre*; **October** *octubre*; **November** *noviembre*; **December** *diciembre* **spring** *primavera*; **summer** *verano*; **autumn/fall** *otoño*; **winter** *invierno*

# Catalan Vocabulary

Over a third of Barcelona residents use Catalan as their predominant everyday language, around 70 per cent speak it fluently, and more than 90 per cent understand it. If you take an interest and learn a few phrases, it is likely to be appreciated.

Catalan phonetics are significantly different from those of Spanish, with a wider range of vowel sounds and soft consonants. Catalans use the familiar (*tu*) rather than the polite (*vosté*) forms of the second person very freely, but for convenience, verbs are given here in the polite form. For menu terms, *see p166-7*.

## Pronunciation

In Catalan, as in French but unlike in Spanish, words are run together, so *si us plau* (please) is more like *sees-plow*.

**à** at the end of a word (as in Francesc Macià) is an open **a** rather like **ah**, but very clipped
**ç**, and **c** before an **i** or an **e**, are like a soft **s**, as in **s**it; **c** in all other cases is as in **c**at
**e**, when unstressed as in *cerves***e***s* (beers), or Jaum**e** I, is a weak sound like centr**e** or comfortabl**e**
**g** before i or e and **j** are pronounced like the **s** in plea**s**ure; **tg** and **tj** are similar to the **dg** in ba**dg**e
**g** after an **i** at the end of a word (Pui**g**) is a hard ch sound, as in wat**ch**; **g** in all other cases is as in **g**et
**h** is silent
**ll** is somewhere between the **y** in **y**es and the **lli** in mi**lli**on
**l·l**, the most unusual feature of Catalan spelling, has a slightly stronger stress on a single **l** sound, so paral·lel sounds similar to the English para**ll**el
**o** at the end of a word is like the **u** sound in fl**u**; **ó** at the end of a word is similar to the **o** in tomat**o**; **ò** is like the **o** in h**o**t
**r** beginning a word and **rr** are heavily rolled; but at the end of many words is almost silent, so *carrer* (street) sounds like carr-ay
**s** at the beginning and end of words and **ss** between vowels are soft, as in **s**it; a single **s** between two vowels is a **z** sound, as in la**z**y
**t** after **l** or **n** at the end of a word is almost silent
**x** at the beginning of a word, or after a consonant or the letter **i**, is like the **sh** in **sh**oe, at other times like the English e**x**pert
**y** after an **n** at the end of a word or in **nys** is not a vowel but adds a nasal stress and a y-sound to the n

## Basics

**please** *si us plau*; **very good/ great/OK** *molt bé*
**hello** *hola*; **goodbye** *adéu*
**open** *obert*; **closed** *tancat*
**entrance** *entrada*; **exit** *sortida*
**nothing at all** *zilch res de res* (said with both s silent)
**price** *preu*; **free** *gratuït/de franc*; **change, exchange** *canvi*
**to rent** *llogar*; **(for) rent, rental** *(de) lloguer*

## More expressions

**hello** (when answering the phone) *hola, digui'm*
**good morning, good day** *bon dia*; **good afternoon, good evening** *bona tarda*; **good night** *bona nit*
**thank you (very much)** *(moltes) gràcies*; **you're welcome** *de res*
**do you speak English?** *parla anglès?*; **I'm sorry, I don't speak Catalan** *ho sento, no parlo català*
**I don't understand** *no entenc*
**can you say it to me in Spanish, please?** *m'ho pot dir en castellà, si us plau?*
**how do you say that in Catalan?** *com se diu això en català?*
**what's your name?** *com se diu?*
**Sir/Mr** *senyor (sr)*; **Madam/Mrs** *senyora (sra)*; **Miss** *senyoreta (srta)*
**excuse me/sorry** *perdoni/disculpi*; **excuse me, please** *escolti* (literally, 'listen to me'); **OK/fine** *val/d'acord*
**how much is it?** *quant és?*
**why?** *perqué?*; **when?** *quan?*; **who?** *qui?*; **what?** *qué?*; **where?** *on?*; **how?** *com?*; **where is...?** *on és...?*; **who is it?** *qui és?*; **is/are there any...?** *hi ha...?/n'hi ha de...?*
**very** *molt*; **and** *i* or *o*; **with** *amb*; **without** *sense*; **enough** *prou*
**I would like...** *vull...* (literally, 'I want'); **how many would you like?** *quants en vol?*; **I don't want** *no vull*; **I like** *m'agrada*; **I don't like** *no m'agrada*
**good** *bo/bona*; **bad** *dolent/a*; **well/badly** *bé/malament*; **small** *petit/a*; **big** *gran*; **expensive** *car/a*; **cheap** *barat/a*; **hot** (food, drink) *calent/a*; **cold** *fred/a*
**something** *alguna cosa*; **nothing** *res*; **more** *més*; **less** *menys*; **more or less** *més o menys*
**toilet** *el bany/els serveis/el lavabo*

## Getting around

**a ticket** *un bitllet*; **return** *d'anada i tornada*; **card expired** (on metro) *títol esgotat*
**left** *esquerra*; **right** *dreta*; **here** *aquí*; **there** *allí*; **straight on** *recte*; **at the corner** *a la cantonada*; **as far as** *fins a*; **towards** *cap a*; **near** *a prop*; **far** *lluny*; **is it far?** *és lluny?*

## Time

In Catalan, quarter- and half-hours can be referred to as quarters of the next hour (so, 1.30 is two quarters of 2).

**now** *ara*; **later** *més tard*;
**yesterday** *ahir*; **today** *avui*; **tomorrow** *demà*; **tomorrow morning** *demà pel matí*;
**morning** *el matí*; **midday** *migdía*; **afternoon** *la tarda*; **evening** *el vespre*; **night** *la nit*; **late night** (roughly, 1-6am) *la matinada*
**at what time...?** *a quina hora...?*
**in an hour** *en una hora;*
**at 2** *a les dues*; **at 8pm** *a les vuit del vespre*; **at 1.30** *a dos quarts de dues/a la una i mitja*; **at 5.15** *a un quart de sis/a las cinc i quart*; **at 22.30** *a vint-i-dos-trenta*

## Numbers

**0** *zero*; **1** *u, un, una*; **2** *dos, dues*; **3** *tres*; **4** *quatre*; **5** *cinc*; **6** *sis*; **7** *set*; **8** *vuit*; **9** *nou*; **10** *deu*; **11** *onze*; **12** *dotze*; **13** *tretze*; **14** *catorze*; **15** *quinze*; **16** *setze*; **17** *disset*; **18** *divuit*; **19** *dinou*; **20** *vint*; **21** *vint-i-u*; **22** *vint-i-dos, vint-i-dues*; **30** *trenta*; **40** *quaranta*; **50** *cinquanta*; **60** *seixanta*; **70** *setanta*; **80** *vuitanta*; **90** *noranta*; **100** *cent*; **200** *dos-cents, dues-centes*; **1,000** *mil*; **1,000,000** *un milló*

## Dates & seasons

**Monday** *dilluns*; **Tuesday** *dimarts*; **Wednesday** *dimecres*; **Thursday** *dijous*; **Friday** *divendres*; **Saturday** *dissabte*; **Sunday** *diumenge*
**January** *gener*; **February** *febrer*; **March** *març*; **April** *abril*; **May** *maig*; **June** *juny*; **July** *juliol*; **August** *agost*; **September** *setembre*; **October** *octobre*; **November** *novembre*; **December** *desembre*
**spring** *primavera*; **summer** *estiu*; **autumn/fall** *tardor*; **winter** *hivern*

# Further Reference

## Books

### Food & drink

**Andrews, Colman** *Catalan Cuisine* A mine of information on food and much else (also with usable recipes).
**Davidson, Alan** *Tio Pepe Guide to the Seafood of Spain and Portugal* An excellent pocket-sized guide with illustrations of Spain's fishy delights.

### Guides & walks

**Amelang, J, Gil, X & McDonogh, GW** *Twelve Walks through Barcelona's Past* (Ajuntament de Barcelona) Well-thought-out walks by historical theme. Original, and better informed than many walking guides.
**Güell, Xavier** *Gaudí Guide* A handy guide, with good background on all the architect's work.
**Pomés Leiz, Juliet, & Feriche, Ricardo** *Barcelona Design Guide* An eccentrically wide-ranging but engaging listing of everything ever considered 'designer' in BCN.

### History, architecture, art & culture

**Burns, Jimmy** *Barça: A People's Passion* The first full-scale history in English of one of the world's most overblown football clubs.
**Elliott, JH** *The Revolt of the Catalans* Fascinating, detailed account of the Guerra dels Segadors and the Catalan revolt of the 1640s.
**Fernández Armesto, Felipe** *Barcelona: A Thousand Years of the City's Past* A solid history.
**Fraser, Ronald** *Blood of Spain* A vivid oral history of the Spanish Civil War and the tensions that preceded it. It is especially good on the events of July 1936 in Barcelona.
**Hooper, John** *The New Spaniards* An incisive and very readable survey of the changes in Spanish society since the death of Franco.
**Hughes, Robert** *Barcelona* The most comprehensive single book about Barcelona: tendentious at times, erratic, but beautifully written, and covering every aspect of the city up to the 1992 Olympics.
**Kaplan, Temma** *Red City, Blue Period: Social Movements in Picasso's Barcelona* An interesting book, tracing the interplay of avant-garde art and avant-garde politics in the 1900s.
**Orwell, George** *Homage to Catalonia* The classic account of Barcelona in revolution, as written by an often bewildered, but always perceptive observer.
**Paz, Abel** *Durruti, The People Armed* A biography of the most legendary of Barcelona's anarchists.
**Solà-Morales, Ignasi** *Fin de Siècle Architecture in Barcelona* Large-scale and wide-ranging description of the city's Modernista heritage.
**Tóibín, Colm** *Homage to Barcelona* Evocative and perceptive journey around the city: good on the booming Barcelona of the 1980s.
**van Hensbergen, Gijs** *Gaudí* A thorough account of the life of the Modernista architect.
**Vázquez Montalbán, Manuel** *Barcelonas* Idiosyncratic but insightful reflections on the city by one of its most prominent modern writers.
**Zerbst, Rainer** *Antoni Gaudí* Lavishly illustrated and comprehensive survey.

### Literature

**Calders, Pere** *The Virgin of the Railway and Other Stories* Ironic, engaging, quirky stories by a Catalan writer who spent many years in exile in Mexico.
**Català, Victor** *Solitude* This masterpiece by female novelist Caterina Albert shocked readers in 1905 with its open, modern treatment of female sexuality.
**Marsé, Juan** *The Fallen* Classic novel of survival in Barcelona during the long *posguerra* after the Civil War.
**Martorell, Joanot & Martí de Gualba, Joan** *Tirant lo Blanc* The first European prose novel, from 1490: a rambling, bawdy, shaggy-dog story of travels, romances and chivalric adventures.
**Mendoza, Eduardo** *City of Marvels*; *Year of the Flood* A sweeping saga of the city between its great Exhibitions in 1888 and 1929; and a more recent novel of passions in the city of the 1950s.
**Oliver, Maria-Antònia** *Antipodes*; *Study in Lilac* Two adventures of Barcelona's first feminist detective.
**Rodoreda, Mercè** *The Time of the Doves*; *My Cristina and Other Stories* A translation of *Plaça del Diamant*, the most widely read of all Catalan novels; plus a collection of similarly bittersweet short tales.
**Ruiz Zafón, Carlos** *Shadow of the Wind* Required beach reading of recent years; enjoyable neo-Gothic melodrama set in post-war Barcelona.
**Vázquez Montalbán, Manuel** *The Angst-Ridden Executive*; *An Olympic Death; Southern Seas* Three thrillers starring detective and gourmet Pepe Carvalho.

## Music

**Angel Molina** Leading Barcelona DJ with an international reputation and various remix albums released.
**Barcelona Raval Sessions** Dance/funk compilation of local artists, famous and unknown, conceived as a soundtrack to the city's most dynamic and multicultural *barri*.
**Lluís Llach** An icon of the 1960s and early '70s protest against the Fascist regime combines a melancholic tone with brilliant musicianship. One of the first to experiment with electronic music.
**Maria del Mar Bonet** Though from Mallorca, del Mar Bonet always sings in Catalan and specialises in her own compositions, North African music and traditional Mallorcan music.
**Ojos de Brujo** Current darlings of world-music awards everywhere and leading proponents of *rumba catalana* fused with flamenco.
**Pep Sala** Excellent musician and survivor of the extremely successful Catalan group Sau. Sala now produces his own music, much of which shows a rockabilly and country influence.

## Barcelona online

**www.barcelonareporter.com** Local news items in English.
**www.barcelonarocks.com** Music listings and news.
**www.barcelonaturisme.com** Official tourist authority information.
**www.bcn.es** The city council's information-packed website.
**www.catalanencyclopaedia.com** Comprehensive English-language reference work covering Catalan history, geography and 'who's who'.
**www.diaridebarcelona.com** Local online newspaper with good English content.
**www.lecool.com** Excellent weekly round-up of offbeat and interesting cultural events in the city.
**www.mobilitat.net** Generalitat's website about getting from A to B in Catalonia, by bus, car or train.
**www.renfe.es** Spanish railways.
**www.timeout.com/barcelona** The online city guide, with a select monthly agenda.
**www.vilaweb.com** Catalan web portal and links page; in Catalan.

# Index

Note: Page numbers in **bold** indicate section(s) giving key information on a topic; *italics* indicate photographs.

Index

## Accommodation



## Restaurants



## Cafés, Tapas & Bars

# Advertisers' Index

Please refer to the relevant pages for contact details

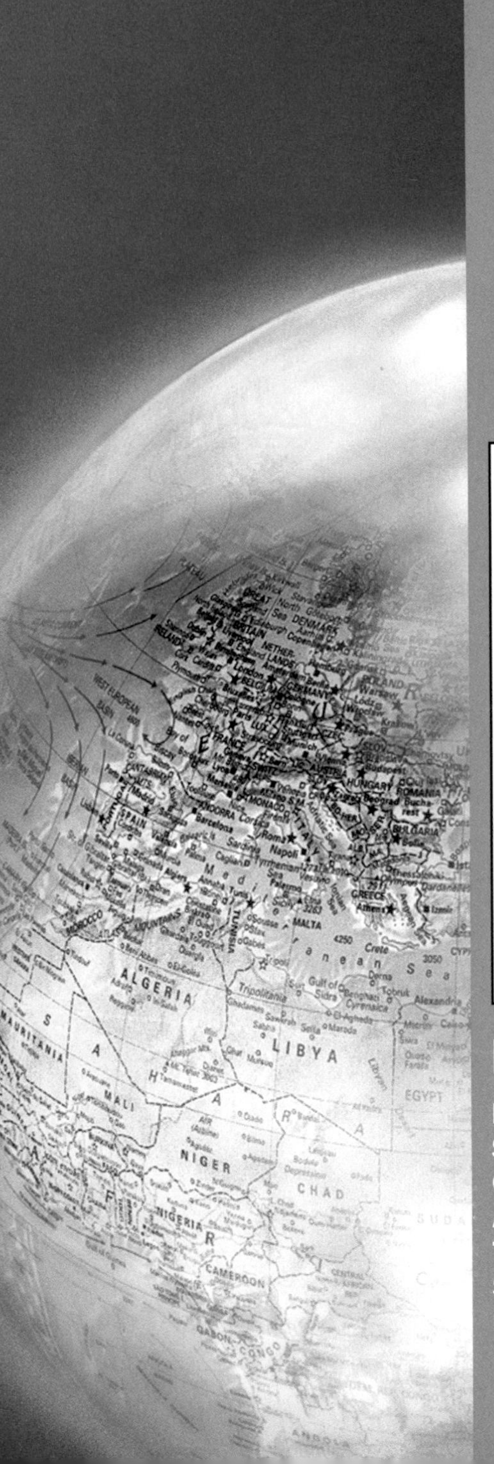

| | |
|---|---|
| Place of interest and/or entertainment | |
| Hospital or college | |
| Railway station | |
| Parks | |
| River | |
| Carretera | |
| Main road | |
| Main road tunnel | |
| Pedestrian road | |
| Airport | |
| Church | |
| Metro station, FGC station | |
| Area name | EIXAMPLE |
| Hotels | 1 |
| Restaurants | 1 |
| Cafés, Tapas & Bars | 1 |

# Maps

Barcelona Areas
Barri Gòtic (pp86-96)
Born & Sant Pere (pp97-103)
Raval (pp104-109)
Barceloneta & Ports (pp110-114)
Montjuïc (pp115-121)
The Eixample (pp122-130)
Gràcia & Other Districts (pp131-142)
Parc del Guinardó
Park Güell
RONDA GENERAL MITRE
SANT GERVASI
LES CORTS
GRÀCIA
GUINARDÓ
Hospital de Sant Pau
SANT ANDREU
AVDA DE LA MERIDIANA
Estació Barcelona-Sants
AVDA JOSEP TARRADELLAS
C/TARRAGONA
GRAN VIA CARLES III
SANTS
EIXAMPLE (ESQUERRA)
PASSEIG DE GRÀCIA
AVDA DIAGONAL
Sagrada Família
LA SAGRERA
C/ARAGÓ
C/GUIPÚSCOA
EIXAMPLE (DRETA)
CLOT
Plaça d'Espanya
GRAN VIA DE LES CORTS CATALANES
Plaça de les Glòries
Plaça Catalunya
POBLE SEC
AVDA PARAL.LEL
RAVAL
Catedral
SANT PERE
BORN
MONTJUÏC
LA RAMBLA
BARRI GÒTIC
Parc de la Ciutadella
POBLENOU
Estadi Olímpic
Estació de França
VILA OLÍMPICA
RONDA LITORAL
PORT VELL
PORT OLÍMPIC
BARCELONETA
0
2 km
1 mile
© Copyright Time Out Group 2007

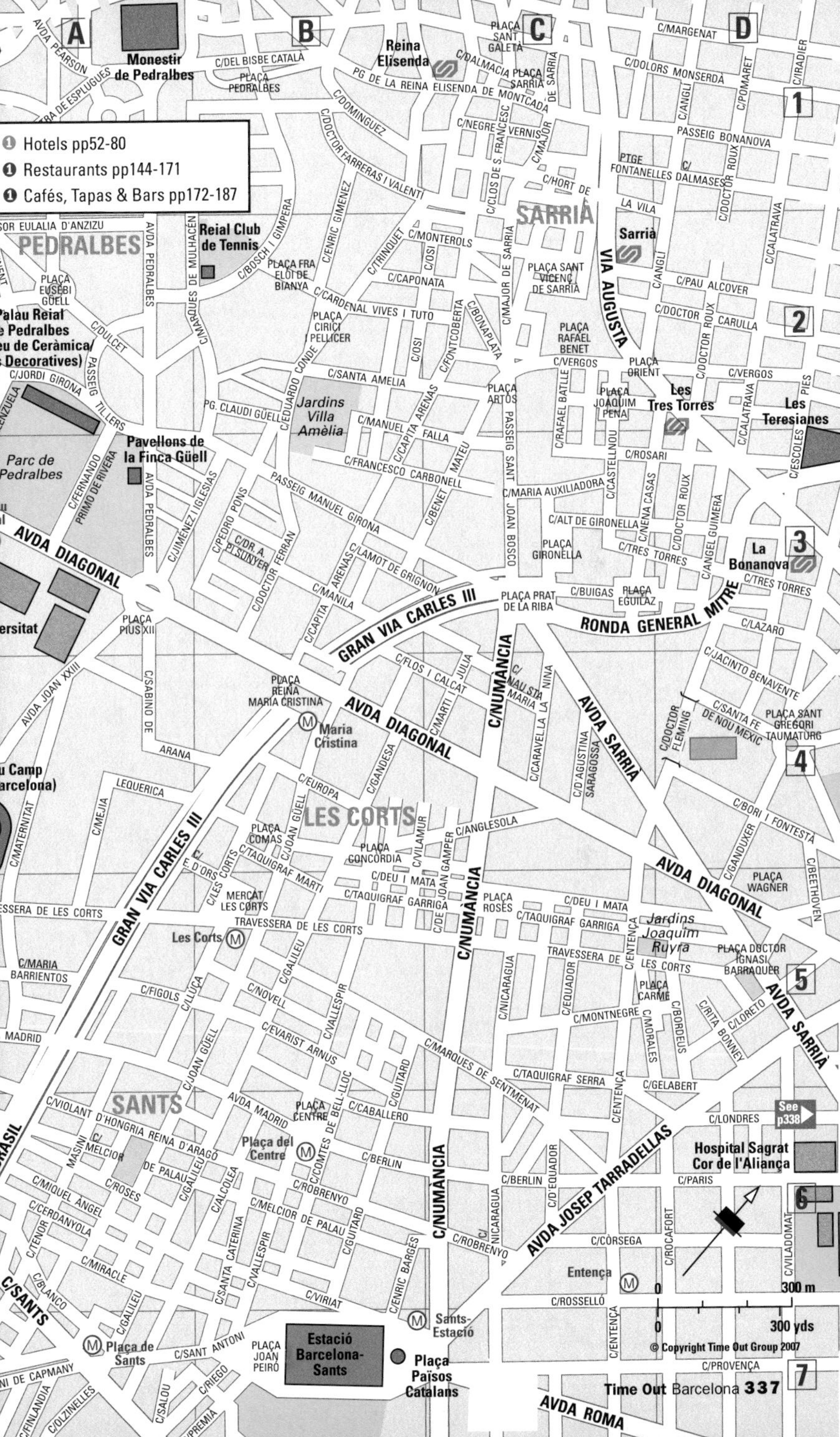
A
B
C
D
1
2
3
4
5
6
7
Monestir de Pedralbes
Reina Elisenda
Hotels pp52-80
Restaurants pp144-171
Cafés, Tapas & Bars pp172-187
PEDRALBES
SARRIÀ
Sarrià
Reial Club de Tennis
Palau Reial de Pedralbes
Jardins Villa Amèlia
Les Tres Torres
Les Teresianes
Pavellons de la Finca Güell
Parc de Pedralbes
La Bonanova
Maria Cristina
LES CORTS
Les Corts
Jardins Joaquim Ruyra
SANTS
Plaça del Centre
Hospital Sagrat Cor de l'Aliança
Entença
Sants-Estació
Estació Barcelona-Sants
Plaça Països Catalans
Plaça de Sants
AVDA DIAGONAL
GRAN VIA CARLES III
RONDA GENERAL MITRE
VIA AUGUSTA
AVDA SARRIÀ
C/NUMÀNCIA
AVDA JOSEP TARRADELLAS
AVDA ROMA
C/SANTS
TRAVESSERA DE LES CORTS
See p338
0 300 m
0 300 yds
© Copyright Time Out Group 2007

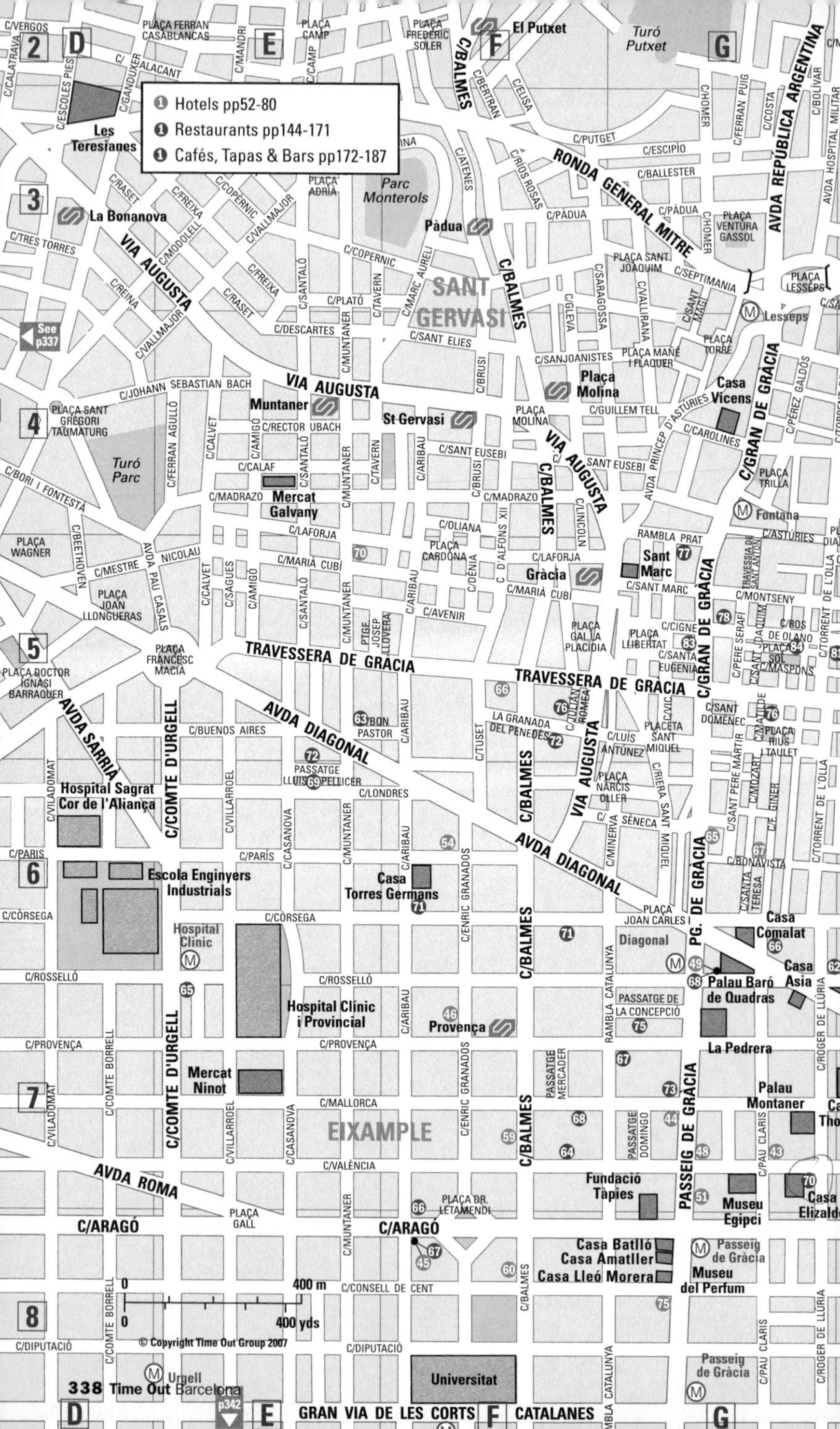

Hotels pp52-80
Restaurants pp144-171
Cafés, Tapas & Bars pp172-187
D
E
F
G
2
3
4
5
6
7
8
C/VERGOS
C/CALATRAVA
PLAÇA FERRAN CASABLANCAS
C/MANDRI
PLAÇA CAMP
C/CAMP
PLAÇA FREDERIC SOLER
El Putxet
Turó Putxet
C/BALMES
C/BERTRAN
C/ELISA
C/ALACANT
C/GANDUXER
C/ESCOLES PIES
Les Teresianes
C/HOMER
C/FERRAN PUIG
C/COSTA
C/BOLÍVAR
AVDA REPÚBLICA ARGENTINA
AVDA HOSPITAL MILITAR
C/PUTGET
C/ESCIPIÓ
C/BALLESTER
RONDA GENERAL MITRE
C/ATENES
C/RIOS ROSAS
Parc Monterols
PLAÇA ADRIÀ
C/RASET
C/FREIXA
C/COPÈRNIC
C/VALLMAJOR
La Bonanova
C/TRES TORRES
C/MODOLELL
Pàdua
C/PÀDUA
PLAÇA VENTURA GASSOL
VIA AUGUSTA
C/REINA
C/SANTALÓ
C/PLATÓ
C/TAVERN
C/MARC AURELI
SANT GERVASI
PLAÇA SANT JOAQUIM
C/SEPTIMANIA
PLAÇA LESSEPS
Lesseps
C/SARAGOSSA
C/GLEVA
C/VALLIRANA
C/SANT MAGÍ
See p337
C/DESCARTES
C/MUNTANER
C/SANT ELIES
C/SANJOANISTES
PLAÇA MANÉ I FLAQUER
PLAÇA TORRÉ
C/GRAN DE GRÀCIA
C/PÉREZ GALDÓS
C/JOHANN SEBASTIAN BACH
Muntaner
St Gervasi
C/BRUSI
Plaça Molina
C/GUILLEM TELL
AVDA PRÍNCEP D'ASTÚRIES
Casa Vicens
C/CAROLINES
PLAÇA SANT GREGORI TAUMATURG
Turó Parc
C/FERRAN AGULLÓ
C/CALVET
C/AMIGÓ
C/RECTOR UBACH
C/ARIBAU
C/SANT EUSEBI
PLAÇA MOLINA
C/TORRENT DE L'OLLA
PLAÇA TRILLA
C/BORI I FONTESTÀ
C/CALAF
Mercat Galvany
C/MADRAZO
C/LINCOLN
Fontana
C/BEETHOVEN
C/LAFORJA
C/OLIANA
C/ALFONS XII
RAMBLA PRAT
C/ASTÚRIES
PLAÇA WAGNER
C/MESTRE NICOLAU
AVDA PAU CASALS
C/SAGUES
C/MARIÀ CUBÍ
PLAÇA CARDONA
C/DÈNIA
Gràcia
Sant Marc
C/SANT MARC
TRAVESSIA DE SANT ANTONI
C/MONTSENY
PLAÇA JOAN LLONGUERAS
PTGE. JOSEP LLOVERA
C/AVENIR
PLAÇA GAL.LA PLACÍDIA
PLAÇA LLIBERTAT
C/CIGNE
C/ROS DE OLANO
C/SANTA EUGÈNIA
C/PERE SERAFÍ
PLAÇA SOL
C/MASPONS
PLAÇA DOCTOR IGNASI BARRAQUER
PLAÇA FRANCESC MACIÀ
TRAVESSERA DE GRÀCIA
C/JULIÁN ROMEA
C/SANT DOMÈNEC
C/MATILDE
PLAÇA RIUS I TAULET
AVDA SARRIÀ
C/COMTE D'URGELL
C/BUENOS AIRES
AVDA DIAGONAL
C/BON PASTOR
LA GRANADA DEL PENEDÈS
C/TUSET
C/LLUÍS ANTÚNEZ
PLACETA SANT MIQUEL
C/VIC
PASSATGE LLUÍS PELLICER
C/LONDRES
PLAÇA NARCÍS OLLER
C/RIERA SANT MIQUEL
C/SANT PERE MÀRTIR
C/MOZART
C/E. GINER
C/VILADOMAT
Hospital Sagrat Cor de l'Aliança
C/VILLARROEL
C/CASANOVA
C/SÈNECA
C/MINERVA
C/PARÍS
Escola Enginyers Industrials
Casa Torres Germans
C/ENRIC GRANADOS
C/BONAVISTA
C/SANTA TERESA
C/CÒRSEGA
Hospital Clínic
PLAÇA JOAN CARLES I
Diagonal
PG. DE GRÀCIA
Casa Comalat
Casa Asia
C/ROSSELLÓ
Palau Baró de Quadras
RAMBLA CATALUNYA
PASSATGE DE LA CONCEPCIÓ
C/ROGER DE LLÚRIA
Hospital Clínic i Provincial
Provença
C/PROVENÇA
La Pedrera
C/COMTE BORRELL
Mercat Ninot
PASSATGE MERCADER
Palau Montaner
C/MALLORCA
EIXAMPLE
PASSATGE DOMINGO
PASSEIG DE GRÀCIA
C/PAU CLARIS
C/VALÈNCIA
AVDA ROMA
Fundació Tàpies
Museu Egipci
Casa Elizalde
PLAÇA DR. LETAMENDI
PLAÇA GALL
C/ARAGÓ
Casa Batlló
Casa Amatller
Casa Lleó Morera
Passeig de Gràcia
Museu del Perfum
0
400 m
400 yds
C/CONSELL DE CENT
C/DIPUTACIÓ
© Copyright Time Out Group 2007
Urgell
Universitat
GRAN VIA DE LES CORTS CATALANES
p342

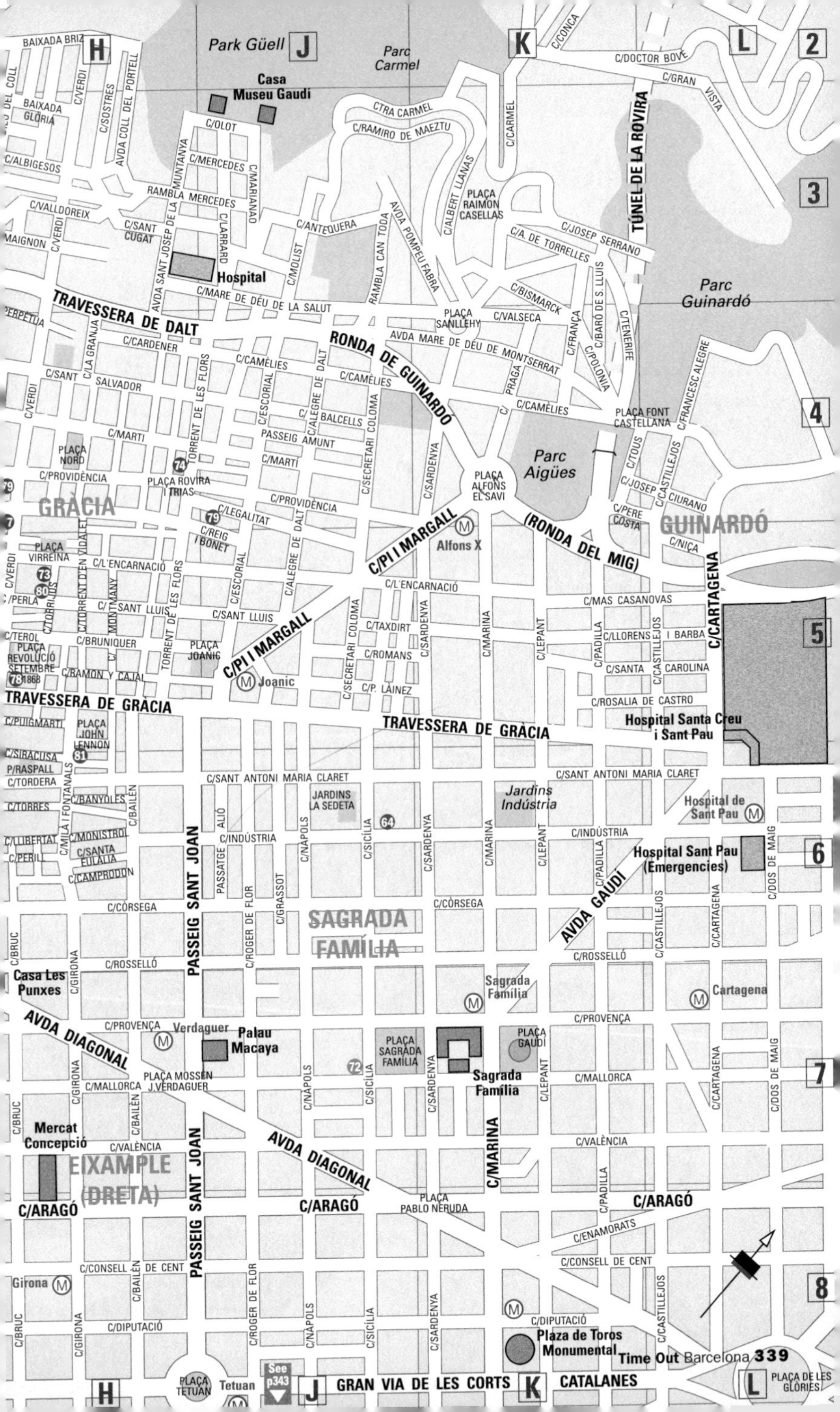
H
J
K
L
2
3
4
5
6
7
8
Park Güell
Parc Carmel
Casa Museu Gaudí
BAIXADA BRIZ
BAIXADA GLÒRIA
C/VERDI
C/SOSTRES
AVDA COLL DEL PORTELL
C/ALBIGESOS
C/VALLDOREIX
C/OLOT
C/MERCEDES
C/MARIANAO
RAMBLA MERCEDES
MUNTANYA
C/SANT CUGAT
AVDA SANT JOSEP DE LA
C/LARRARD
Hospital
C/MARE DE DÉU DE LA SALUT
CTRA CARMEL
C/RAMIRO DE MAEZTU
C/ANTEQUERA
C/MOLIST
RAMBLA CAN TODA
AVDA POMPEU FABRA
C/ALBERT LLANAS
PLAÇA RAIMON CASELLAS
C/CARMEL
C/CONCA
C/DOCTOR BOVÉ
C/GRAN VISTA
TÚNEL DE LA ROVIRA
C/JOSEP SERRANO
C/A. DE TORRELLES
C/BISMARCK
C/SANT LLUÍS
C/BARÓ DE S. LLUÍS
C/TENERIFE
C/FRANÇA
C/POLONIA
Parc Guinardó
TRAVESSERA DE DALT
PERPÈTUA
C/CARDENER
C/LA GRANJA
C/SANT SALVADOR
C/CAMÈLIES
RONDA DE GUINARDÓ
PLAÇA SANLLEHY
C/VALSECA
AVDA MARE DE DÉU DE MONTSERRAT
PRAGA
C/FRANCESC ALEGRE
PLAÇA FONT CASTELLANA
C/ESCORIAL
C/ALEGRE DE DALT
C/BALCELLS
PASSEIG AMUNT
C/SECRETARI COLOMA
TORRENT DE LES FLORS
C/MARTÍ
PLAÇA NORD
C/PROVIDÈNCIA
PLAÇA ROVIRA I TRIAS
C/SARDENYA
PLAÇA ALFONS EL SAVI
Parc Aigües
C/TOUS
C/CASTILLEJOS
C/JOSEP CIURANO
C/PERE COSTA
GRÀCIA
C/LEGALITAT
C/REIG I BONET
C/PI I MARGALL
Alfons X
(RONDA DEL MIG)
GUINARDÓ
C/NIÇA
C/CARTAGENA
PLAÇA VIRREINA
C/TORRENT D'EN VIDALET
C/L'ENCARNACIÓ
C/PERLA
C/TORRIJOS
MONTMANY
C/SANT LLUÍS
C/MAS CASANOVAS
C/TEROL
PLAÇA REVOLUCIÓ SETEMBRE 1868
C/BRUNIQUER
PLAÇA JOANIC
C/TAXDIRT
C/ROMANS
C/P. LAINEZ
C/MARINA
C/LEPANT
C/PADILLA
C/LLORENS I BARBA
C/SANTA CAROLINA
C/ROSALIA DE CASTRO
C/RAMON Y CAJAL
Joanic
TRAVESSERA DE GRÀCIA
Hospital Santa Creu i Sant Pau
C/PUIGMARTÍ
PLAÇA JOHN LENNON
C/SIRACUSA
P/RASPALL
C/TORDERA
C/TORRES
C/FONTANALS
C/BANYOLES
C/BAILÈN
C/SANT ANTONI MARIA CLARET
JARDINS LA SEDETA
Jardins Indústria
Hospital de Sant Pau
C/LLIBERTAT
C/MILÀ I FONTANALS
C/MONISTROL
C/SANTA EULÀLIA
C/PERILL
C/CAMPRODON
PASSEIG SANT JOAN
ALIÓ
C/INDÚSTRIA
PASSATGE
C/NÀPOLS
C/SICÍLIA
Hospital Sant Pau (Emergencies)
C/DOS DE MAIG
AVDA GAUDÍ
C/CÒRSEGA
C/ROGER DE FLOR
C/GRASSOT
SAGRADA FAMÍLIA
C/BRUC
C/GIRONA
C/ROSSELLÓ
Casa Les Punxes
Sagrada Família
Cartagena
AVDA DIAGONAL
C/PROVENÇA
Verdaguer
Palau Macaya
PLAÇA SAGRADA FAMÍLIA
PLAÇA GAUDÍ
PLAÇA MOSSÈN J. VERDAGUER
C/MALLORCA
Mercat Concepció
C/VALÈNCIA
EIXAMPLE (DRETA)
C/ARAGÓ
PLAÇA PABLO NERUDA
C/ENAMORATS
C/CONSELL DE CENT
Girona
C/DIPUTACIÓ
Plaza de Toros Monumental
PLAÇA TETUAN
Tetuan
See p343
GRAN VIA DE LES CORTS CATALANES
PLAÇA DE LES GLÒRIES

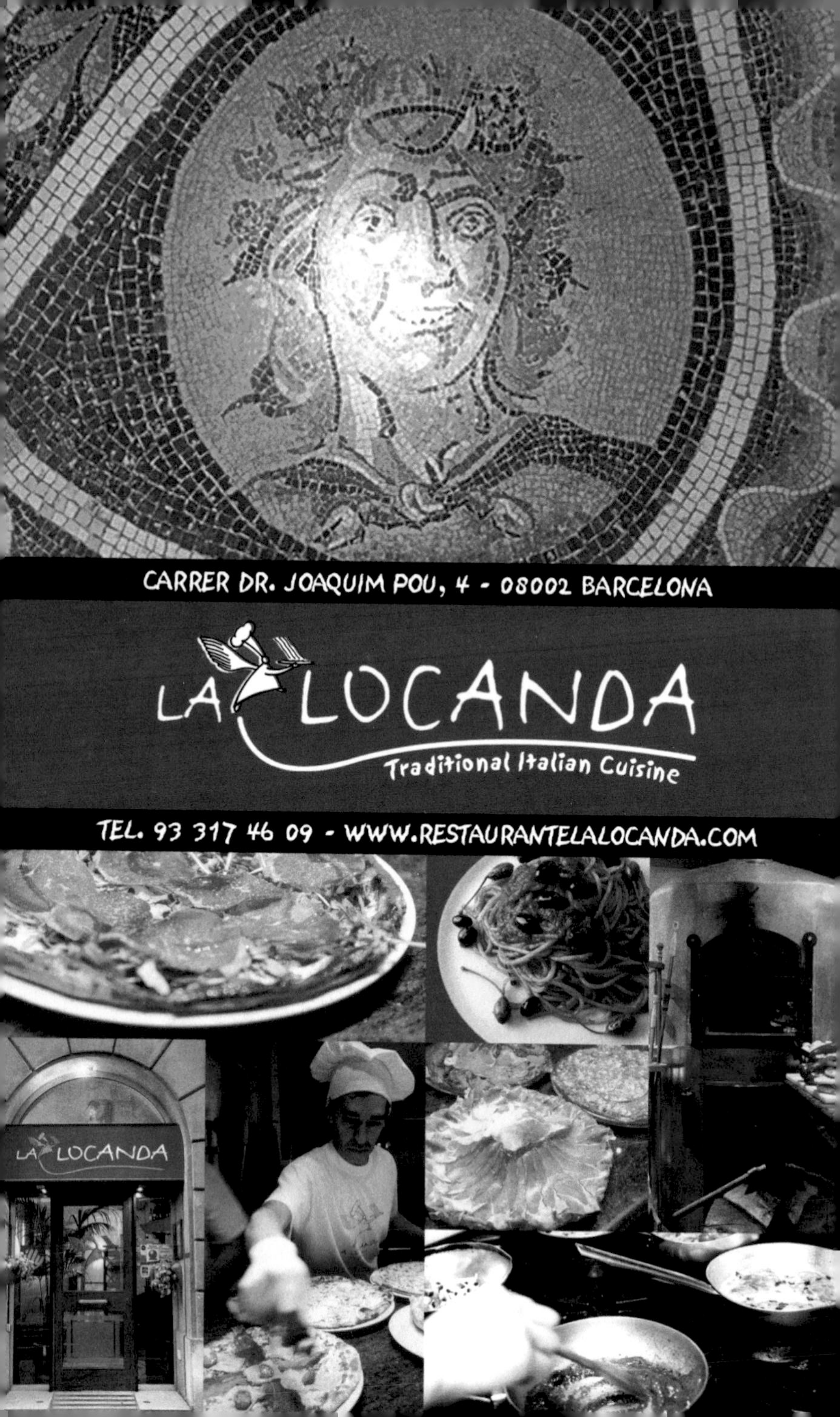
CARRER DR. JOAQUIM POU, 4 - 08002 BARCELONA
LA LOCANDA
Traditional Italian Cuisine
TEL. 93 317 46 09 - WWW.RESTAURANTELALOCANDA.COM
LA LOCANDA

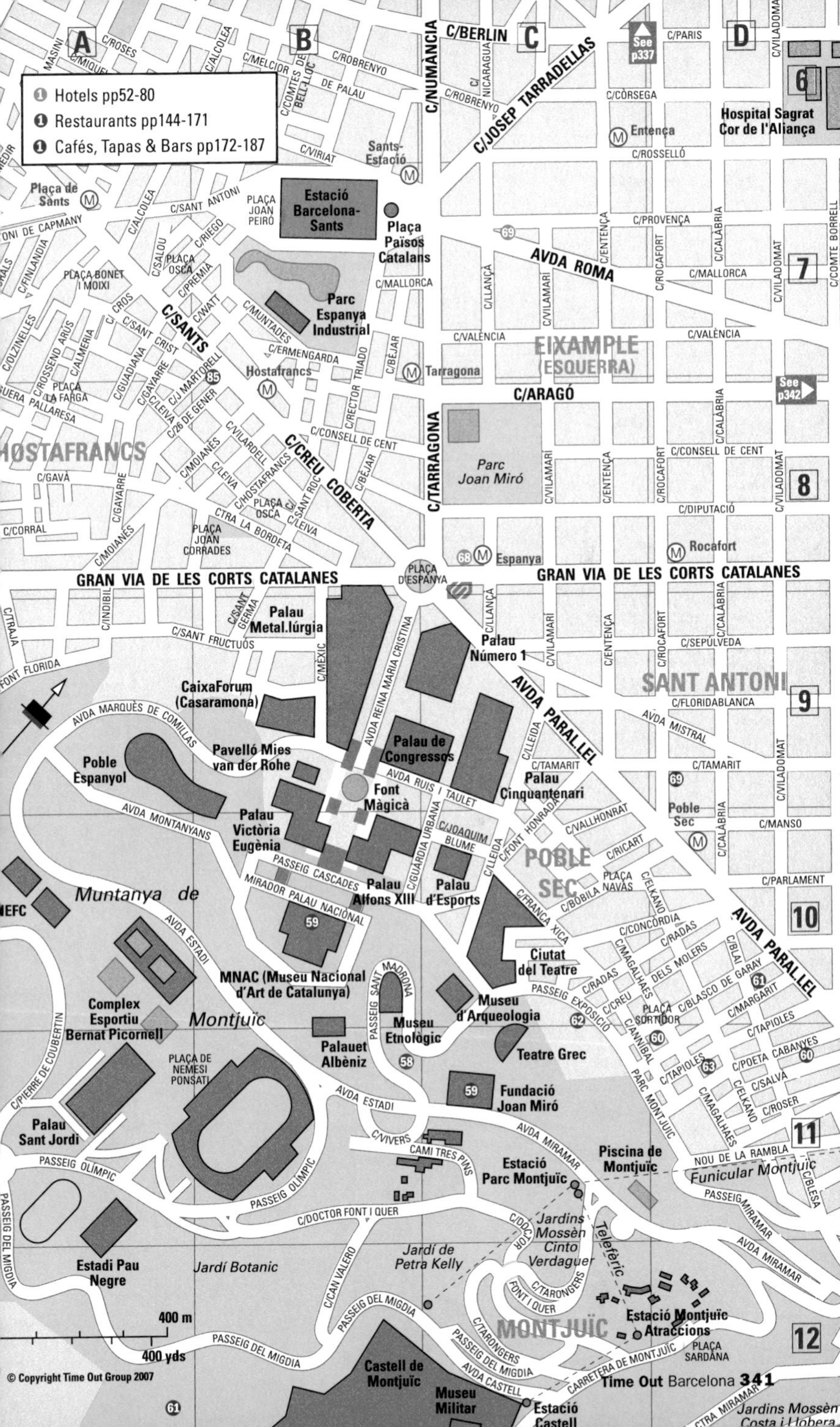

A
B
C
D
6
7
8
9
10
11
12
Hotels pp52-80
Restaurants pp144-171
Cafés, Tapas & Bars pp172-187
See p337
See p342
C/ROSES
C/ALCOLEA
C/MELCIOR DE PALAU
C/ROBRENYO
C/COMTES DE BELL-LLOC
C/NUMÀNCIA
C/BERLIN
C/NICARAGUA
C/JOSEP TARRADELLAS
C/PARIS
C/VILADOMAT
C/CÒRSEGA
Hospital Sagrat Cor de l'Aliança
Entença
C/ROSSELLÓ
C/VIRIAT
Sants-Estació
Plaça de Sants
C/SANT ANTONI
PLAÇA JOAN PEIRÓ
Estació Barcelona-Sants
Plaça Països Catalans
C/PROVENÇA
C/ENTENÇA
C/ROCAFORT
C/CALÀBRIA
C/COMTE BORRELL
AVDA ROMA
C/MALLORCA
C/LLANÇÀ
C/VILAMARÍ
C/RIEGO
C/SALOU
PLAÇA OSCA
PLAÇA BONET I MOIXÍ
C/PREMIÀ
C/FINLANDIA
C/CROS
C/WATT
C/SANTS
C/MUNTADES
Parc Espanya Industrial
C/SANT CRIST
C/ALMERIA
C/ROSSEND ARÚS
C/OLZINELLES
C/GUADIANA
C/ERMENGARDA
C/BÉJAR
C/VALÈNCIA
EIXAMPLE (ESQUERRA)
Hostafrancs
Tarragona
C/RECTOR TRIADÓ
C/J MARTORELL
PLAÇA LA FARGA
C/GAVARRE
C/LEIVA
C/26 DE GENER
C/ARAGÓ
C/TARRAGONA
C/CONSELL DE CENT
C/VILARDELL
C/CREU COBERTA
Parc Joan Miró
HOSTAFRANCS
C/MOIANÈS
C/GAVÀ
C/HOSTAFRANCS
C/SANT ROC
C/DIPUTACIÓ
C/CORRAL
PLAÇA JOAN CORRADES
CTRA LA BORDETA
Espanya
Rocafort
PLAÇA D'ESPANYA
GRAN VIA DE LES CORTS CATALANES
C/INDÍBIL
C/SANT GERMÀ
Palau Metal.lúrgia
C/TRAJÀ
C/SANT FRUCTUÓS
C/MÈXIC
AVDA REINA MARIA CRISTINA
Palau Número 1
C/SEPÚLVEDA
SANT ANTONI
FONT FLORIDA
CaixaForum (Casaramona)
AVDA PARAL.LEL
C/FLORIDABLANCA
AVDA MARQUÈS DE COMILLAS
AVDA MISTRAL
Poble Espanyol
Pavelló Mies van der Rohe
Palau de Congressos
C/TAMARIT
C/LLEIDA
AVDA RUIS I TAULET
Palau Cinquantenari
Font Màgica
Poble Sec
AVDA MONTANYANS
Palau Victòria Eugènia
C/GUÀRDIA URBANA
C/JOAQUIM BLUME
C/FONT HONRADA
C/VALLHONRAT
C/MANSO
POBLE SEC
C/RICART
PASSEIG CASCADES
MIRADOR PALAU NACIONAL
Palau Alfons XIII
Palau d'Esports
PLAÇA NAVAS
C/BÒBILA
C/ELKANO
C/PARLAMENT
Muntanya de Montjuïc
INEFC
AVDA ESTADI
C/FRANCA XICA
C/CONCÒRDIA
C/RADAS
C/BLAI
C/MAGALHAES
DELS MOLERS
MNAC (Museu Nacional d'Art de Catalunya)
Ciutat del Teatre
C/BLASCO DE GARAY
PASSEIG SANT MADRONA
C/MARGARIT
PASSEIG EXPOSICIÓ
Complex Esportiu Bernat Picornell
Museu d'Arqueologia
C/CREU
PLAÇA SORTIDOR
C/TAPIOLES
Museu Etnològic
C/ANNIBAL
C/POETA CABANYES
Palauet Albèniz
Teatre Grec
C/PIERRE DE COUBERTIN
PLAÇA DE NEMESI PONSATI
C/SALVÀ
Fundació Joan Miró
PARC MONTJUÏC
C/ROSER
Palau Sant Jordi
C/VIVERS
AVDA MIRAMAR
CAMI TRES PINS
Estació Parc Montjuïc
Piscina de Montjuïc
NOU DE LA RAMBLA
Funicular Montjuïc
PASSEIG OLÍMPIC
C/BLESA
PASSEIG MIRAMAR
C/DOCTOR FONT I QUER
Jardins Mossèn Cinto Verdaguer
Telefèric
PASSEIG DEL MIGDIA
Estadi Pau Negre
Jardí Botànic
Jardí de Petra Kelly
C/CAN VALERO
C/TARONGERS
Estació Montjuïc Atraccions
MONTJUÏC
400 m
400 yds
PLAÇA SARDANA
CARRETERA DE MONTJUÏC
Castell de Montjuïc
Museu Militar
AVDA CASTELL
Estació Castell
CTRA MIRAMAR
Jardins Mossèn Costa i Llobera

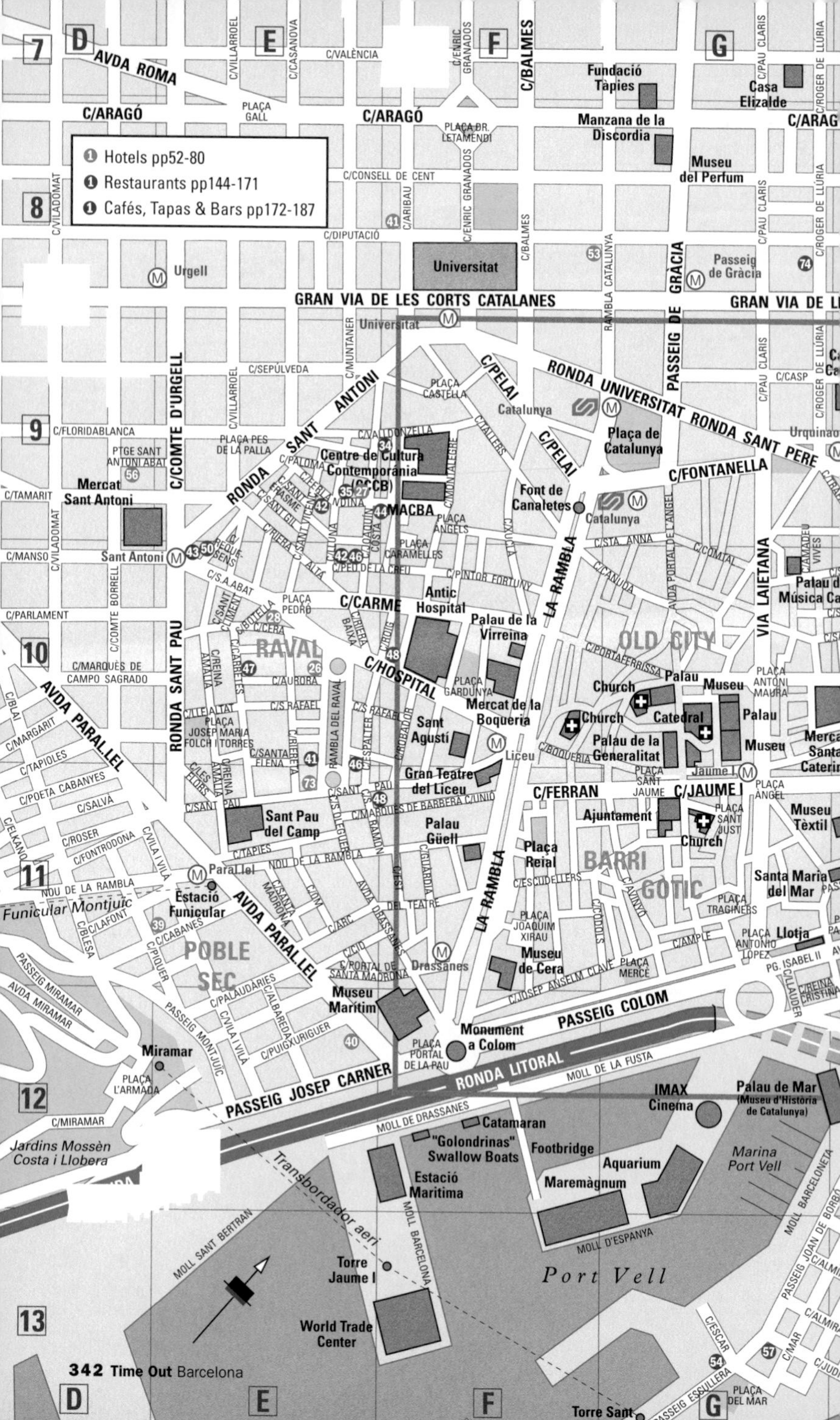

D
E
F
G
7
8
9
10
11
12
13
AVDA ROMA
C/ARAGÓ
C/VILLARROEL
C/CASANOVA
C/VALÈNCIA
C/ENRIC GRANADOS
C/BALMES
Fundació Tàpies
Casa Elizalde
C/PAU CLARIS
C/ROGER DE LLÚRIA
PLAÇA GALL
PLAÇA DR. LETAMENDI
Manzana de la Discordia
Museu del Perfum
Hotels pp52-80
Restaurants pp144-171
Cafés, Tapas & Bars pp172-187
C/CONSELL DE CENT
C/VILADOMAT
C/ARIBAU
C/DIPUTACIÓ
41
53
74
Universitat
Urgell
RAMBLA CATALUNYA
PASSEIG DE GRÀCIA
Passeig de Gràcia
GRAN VIA DE LES CORTS CATALANES
C/MUNTANER
C/SEPÚLVEDA
C/COMTE D'URGELL
RONDA SANT ANTONI
C/PELAI
PLAÇA CASTELLA
Catalunya
RONDA UNIVERSITAT
RONDA SANT PERE
C/CASP
Urquinaona
C/FLORIDABLANCA
PLAÇA PES DE LA PALLA
PTGE SANT ANTONI ABAT
56
C/VALLDONZELLA
34
Centre de Cultura Contemporània (CCCB)
C/MONTALEGRE
C/TALLERS
Plaça de Catalunya
C/FONTANELLA
Mercat Sant Antoni
C/TAMARIT
C/PALOMA
C/FERLANDINA
35
27
42
44
MACBA
Font de Canaletes
PLAÇA ANGELS
C/MANSO
Sant Antoni
43
50
46
PLAÇA CARAMELLES
C/PINTOR FORTUNY
C/XUCLA
LA RAMBLA
C/STA. ANNA
C/COMTAL
AVDA PORTAL DE L'ANGEL
VIA LAIETANA
C/AMADEU VIVES
Palau de la Música Catalana
C/S.A.ABAT
C/CANUDA
C/PARLAMENT
C/COMTE BORRELL
PLAÇA PEDRÓ
C/CARME
Antic Hospital
Palau de la Virreina
C/RIERA BAIXA
28
RAVAL
OLD CITY
C/PORTAFERRISSA
RONDA SANT PAU
C/MARQUÈS DE CAMPO SAGRADO
47
26
48
C/HOSPITAL
C/AURORA
PLAÇA GARDUNYA
Mercat de la Boqueria
Church
Palau
Museu
PLAÇA ANTONI MAURA
AVDA PARAL.LEL
C/BLAI
C/MARGARIT
C/TAPIOLES
C/POETA CABANYES
C/SALVÀ
C/ROSER
C/FONTRODONA
C/ELKANO
C/VILA I VILÀ
PLAÇA JOSEP MARIA FOLCH I TORRES
C/SANT RAFAEL
RAMBLA DEL RAVAL
Sant Agustí
Liceu
Catedral
Palau de la Generalitat
Mercat Santa Caterina
C/BOQUERIA
C/SANTA ELENA
41
73
46
Gran Teatre del Liceu
PLAÇA SANT JAUME
Jaume I
C/JAUME I
PLAÇA ANGEL
C/FERRAN
Sant Pau del Camp
C/MARQUÈS DE BARBERÀ
C/UNIÓ
Palau Güell
Ajuntament
PLAÇA SANT JUST
Church
Museu Tèxtil
C/TAPIES
NOU DE LA RAMBLA
Plaça Reial
BARRI GÒTIC
Paral.lel
Estació Funicular
Funicular Montjuïc
C/ESCUDELLERS
Santa Maria del Mar
C/AVINYÓ
C/CODOLS
PLAÇA TRAGINERS
C/LAFONT
C/BLESA
39
C/CABANES
POBLE SEC
C/ARC
DEL TEATRE
AVDA DRASSANES
PLAÇA JOAQUIM XIRAU
Museu de Cera
C/AMPLE
PLAÇA ANTONIO LOPEZ
Llotja
PG. ISABEL II
PASSEIG MIRAMAR
AVDA MIRAMAR
C/PIQUER
C/PORTAL DE SANTA MADRONA
Drassanes
PLAÇA MERCÈ
C/JOSEP ANSELM CLAVÉ
C/LLAUDER
C/REINA CRISTINA
C/PALAUDÀRIES
C/ALBAREDA
Museu Marítim
PASSEIG COLOM
PASSEIG MONTJUÏC
C/PUIGXURIGUER
40
Monument a Colom
Miramar
PLAÇA PORTAL DE LA PAU
RONDA LITORAL
MOLL DE LA FUSTA
PLAÇA L'ARMADA
PASSEIG JOSEP CARNER
IMAX Cinema
Palau de Mar (Museu d'Història de Catalunya)
C/MIRAMAR
MOLL DE DRASSANES
Catamaran
Jardins Mossèn Costa i Llobera
"Golondrinas" Swallow Boats
Footbridge
Aquarium
Marina Port Vell
Transbordador aeri
Estació Marítima
Maremàgnum
MOLL BARCELONETA
MOLL DE BARCELONA
MOLL D'ESPANYA
MOLL SANT BERTRAN
Torre Jaume I
Port Vell
PASSEIG JOAN DE BORBÓ
World Trade Center
C/ESCAR
54
57
C/MAR
C/ALMIRALL
PASSEIG ESCULLERA
PLAÇA DEL MAR
Torre Sant

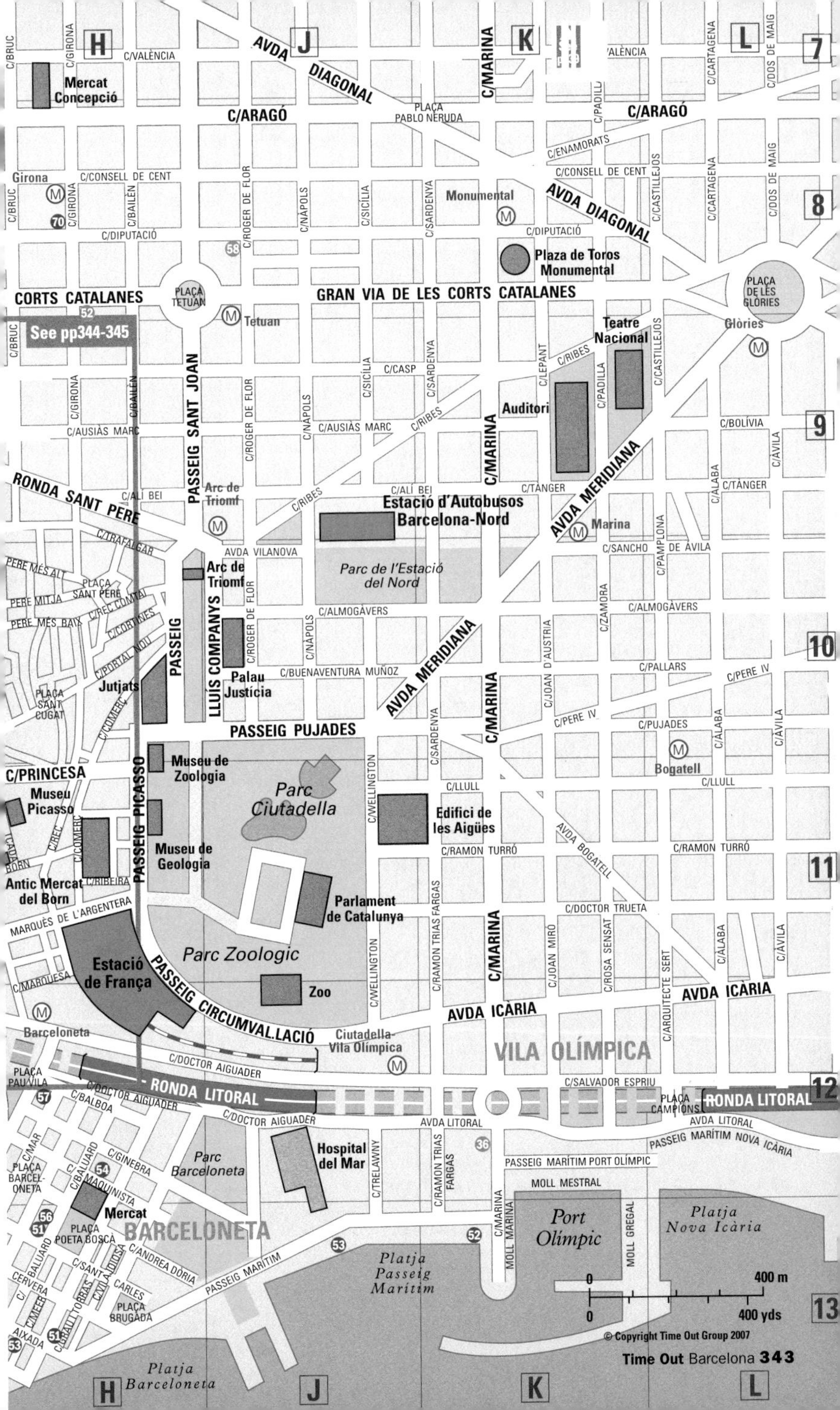
H
J
K
L
7
8
9
10
11
12
13
C/BRUC
C/GIRONA
C/VALÈNCIA
Mercat Concepció
AVDA DIAGONAL
C/MARINA
C/CARTAGENA
C/DOS DE MAIG
PLAÇA PABLO NERUDA
C/ARAGÓ
C/PADILLA
C/ENAMORATS
Girona
C/CONSELL DE CENT
C/BAILÈN
C/ROGER DE FLOR
C/NÀPOLS
C/SICÍLIA
C/SARDENYA
Monumental
C/CASTILLEJOS
C/DIPUTACIÓ
Plaza de Toros Monumental
CORTS CATALANES
PLAÇA TETUAN
GRAN VIA DE LES CORTS CATALANES
PLAÇA DE LES GLÒRIES
Tetuan
Glòries
Teatre Nacional
See pp344-345
PASSEIG SANT JOAN
C/CASP
C/RIBES
C/LEPANT
Auditori
C/AUSIÀS MARC
C/BOLÍVIA
C/ÀVILA
RONDA SANT PERE
C/ALÍ BEI
Arc de Triomf
C/TÀNGER
AVDA MERIDIANA
C/ÀLABA
Estació d'Autobusos Barcelona-Nord
Marina
C/TRAFALGAR
AVDA VILANOVA
C/SANCHO DE ÀVILA
C/PAMPLONA
PERE MÉS ALT
PLAÇA SANT PERE
Parc de l'Estació del Nord
PERE MITJÀ
C/REC COMTAL
C/CORTINES
C/ALMOGÀVERS
C/ZAMORA
PERE MÉS BAIX
LLUÍS COMPANYS
PASSEIG
C/PORTAL NOU
C/JOAN D'ÀUSTRIA
Palau Justícia
C/BUENAVENTURA MUÑOZ
C/PALLARS
C/PERE IV
Jutjats
PLAÇA SANT CUGAT
C/COMERÇ
PASSEIG PUJADES
C/PUJADES
C/PRINCESA
PASSEIG PICASSO
Museu de Zoologia
Parc Ciutadella
C/WELLINGTON
Bogatell
C/LLULL
Museu Picasso
Edifici de les Aigües
AVDA BOGATELL
C/REC
C/RAMON TURRÓ
BORN
Museu de Geologia
C/RIBEIRA
Antic Mercat del Born
Parlament de Catalunya
C/DOCTOR TRUETA
MARQUÈS DE L'ARGENTERA
Estació de França
PASSEIG CIRCUMVAL.LACIÓ
Parc Zoologic
C/RAMON TRIAS FARGAS
C/JOAN MIRÓ
C/ROSA SENSAT
C/ARQUITECTE SERT
C/MARQUESA
Zoo
AVDA ICÀRIA
Barceloneta
Ciutadella-Vila Olímpica
VILA OLÍMPICA
C/DOCTOR AIGUADER
PLAÇA PAU VILA
RONDA LITORAL
C/SALVADOR ESPRIU
PLAÇA CAMPIONS
C/BALBOA
AVDA LITORAL
PASSEIG MARÍTIM NOVA ICÀRIA
C/MAR
C/GINEBRA
Parc Barceloneta
Hospital del Mar
C/TRELAWNY
PASSEIG MARÍTIM PORT OLÍMPIC
PLAÇA BARCELONETA
C/BALUARD
C/MAQUINISTA
MOLL MESTRAL
Mercat
Port Olímpic
Platja Nova Icària
PLAÇA POETA BOSCÀ
BARCELONETA
MOLL MARINA
MOLL GREGAL
C/ANDREA DÒRIA
Platja Passeig Marítim
PASSEIG MARÍTIM
C/SANT CARLES
CERVERA
PLAÇA BRUGADA
C/MEER
C/GRAU I TORRAS
C/VILA I VILÀ
AIXADA
Platja Barceloneta
0
400 m
400 yds
36
51
52
53
54
56
57
58
70

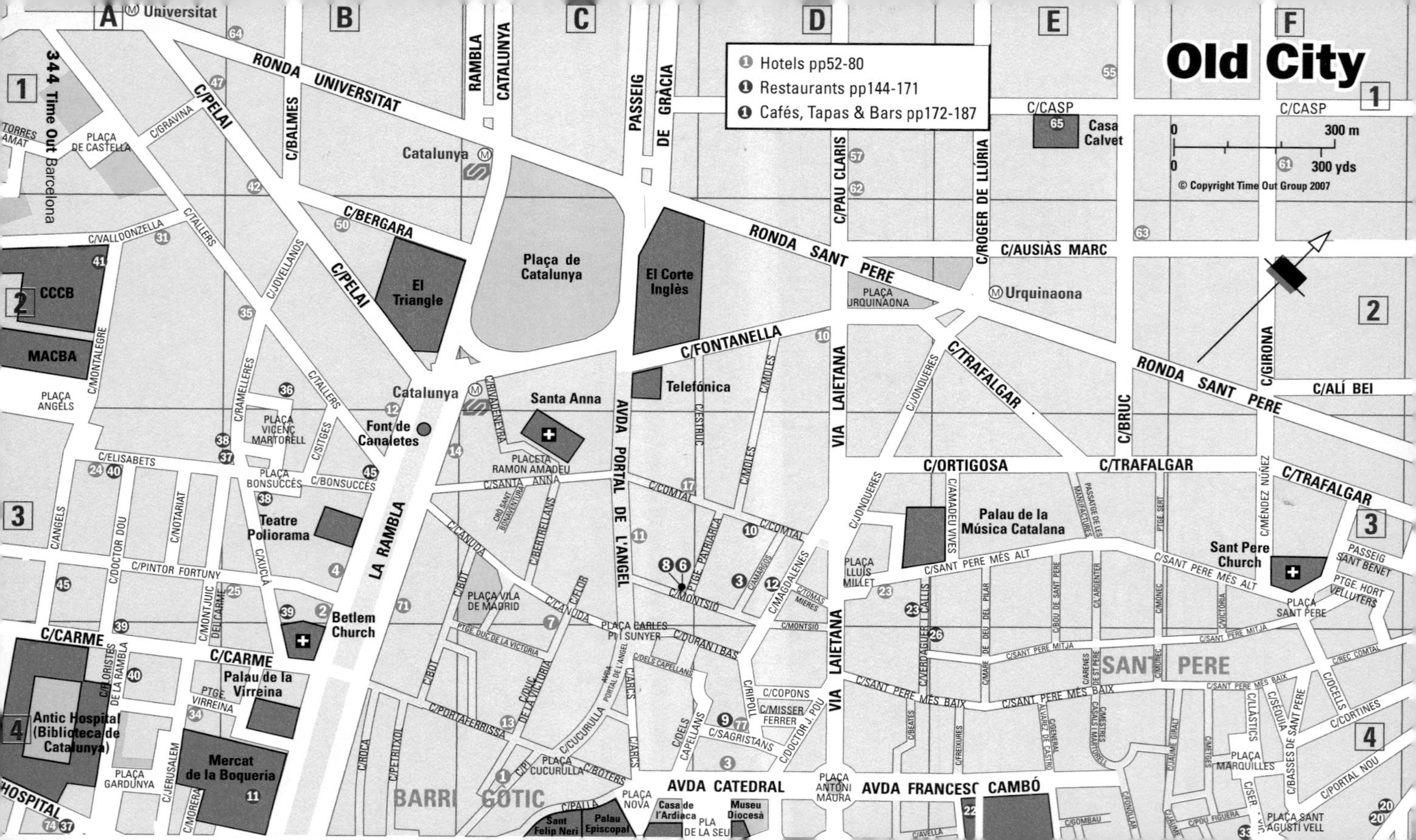
Old City
Hotels pp52-80
Restaurants pp144-171
Cafés, Tapas & Bars pp172-187
0 300 m
0 300 yds
© Copyright Time Out Group 2007
A B C D E F
1 2 3 4
Universitat
Catalunya
Urquinaona
RONDA UNIVERSITAT
C/PELAI
C/GRAVINA
PLAÇA DE CASTELLA
TORRES AMAT
C/BALMES
RAMBLA CATALUNYA
PASSEIG DE GRÀCIA
C/PAU CLARIS
C/ROGER DE LLÚRIA
C/CASP
Casa Calvet
C/BERGARA
C/VALLDONZELLA
C/TALLERS
C/JOVELLANOS
Plaça de Catalunya
El Triangle
El Corte Inglès
RONDA SANT PERE
C/AUSIÀS MARC
PLAÇA URQUINAONA
CCCB
MACBA
C/MONTALEGRE
PLAÇA ANGELS
C/RAMELLERES
PLAÇA VICENÇ MARTORELL
C/SITGES
Font de Canaletes
C/FONTANELLA
Telefónica
Santa Anna
C/RIVADENEYRA
PLACETA RAMON AMADEU
C/SANTA ANNA
C/ESTRUC
C/MOLES
VIA LAIETANA
C/JONQUERES
C/TRAFALGAR
C/BRUC
C/GIRONA
C/ALÍ BEI
C/ORTIGOSA
C/ELISABETS
PLAÇA BONSUCCÉS
C/BONSUCCÉS
C/NOTARIAT
Teatre Poliorama
LA RAMBLA
C/ANGELS
C/DOCTOR DOU
C/PINTOR FORTUNY
C/XUCLÀ
C/MONTJUIC DEL CARME
Betlem Church
C/CARME
Palau de la Virreina
PTGE. VIRREINA
C/FLORISTES DE LA RAMBLA
Antic Hospital (Biblioteca de Catalunya)
PLAÇA GARDUNYA
C/JERUSALEM
Mercat de la Boqueria
C/MORERA
HOSPITAL
C/CANUDA
CRÓ SANT BONAVENTURA
C/BERTRELLANS
PLAÇA VILA DE MADRID
C/BOT
PTGE. DUC DE LA VICTORIA
C/DUC DE LA VICTORIA
AVDA PORTAL DE L'ANGEL
C/COMTAL
PTGE. PATRIARCA
C/MONTSIÓ
C/CAMARGOS
C/MAGDALENES
C/TOMAS MIERES
PLAÇA CARLES PI I SUNYER
C/DURAN I BAS
C/FLOR
C/DELS CAPELLANS
C/ARCS
C/CUCURULLA
PLAÇA CUCURULLA
C/BOTERS
C/PORTAFERRISSA
C/PETRITXOL
C/ROCA
C/PALLA
BARRI GÒTIC
Sant Felip Neri
Palau Episcopal
PLAÇA NOVA
Casa de l'Ardiaca
PLA DE LA SEU
Museu Diocesà
AVDA CATEDRAL
C/RIPOLL
C/COPONS
C/MISSER FERRER
C/SAGRISTANS
C/DOCTOR J. POU
C/DELS CAPELLANS
PLAÇA ANTONI MAURA
AVDA FRANCESC CAMBÓ
PLAÇA LLUÍS MILLET
C/AMADEU VIVES
Palau de la Música Catalana
PASSATGE DE LES MANUFACTURES
PTGE SERT
C/MÉNDEZ NÚÑEZ
Sant Pere Church
PASSEIG SANT BENET
PTGE. HORT VELLUTERS
PLAÇA SANT PERE
C/SANT PERE MÉS ALT
C/SANT PERE MITJA
C/SANT PERE MÉS BAIX
C/VERDAGUER I CALLIS
C/MARE DE DEU DEL PILAR
C/BOU DE SANT PERE
C/L'ARGENTER
C/MONEC
C/VICTORIA
C/REC COMTAL
SANT PERE
C/BEATES
C/FREIXURES
C/GENERAL ALVAREZ DE CASTRO
C/MESTRES CASALS I MARTORELL
C/ARENES DE ST PERE
C/JAUME GIRALT
C/METGES
PLAÇA MARQUILLES
C/LLÀSTICS
C/SÉQUIA
C/BASSES DE SANT PERE
C/OCELLS
C/CORTINES
C/PORTAL NOU
C/FONOLLAR
C/GOMBAU
C/AVELLA
C/POU FIGUERA
C/SER.
PLAÇA SANT AGUSTÍ VELL
C/JAUME

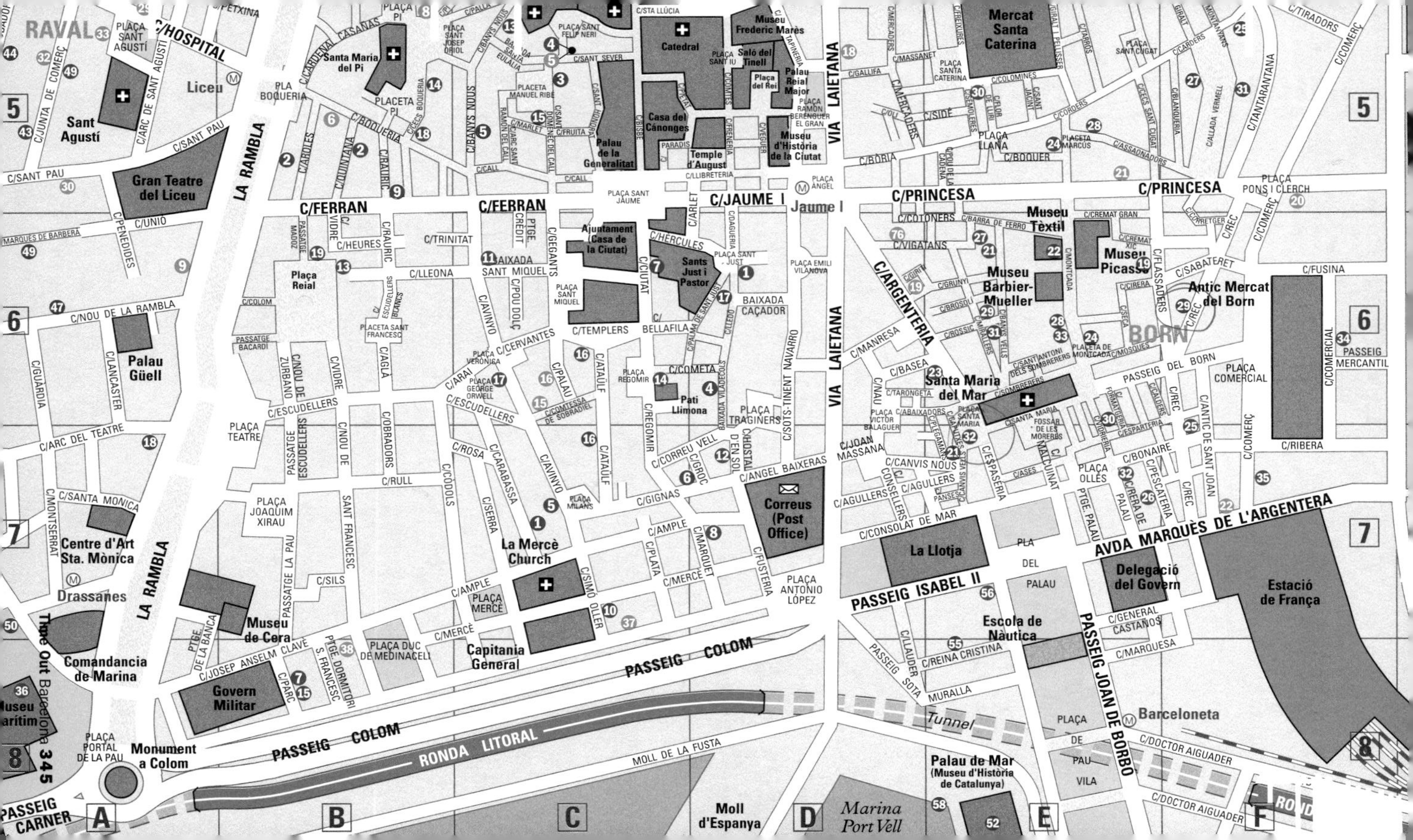

RAVAL
C/HOSPITAL
Liceu
Sant Agustí
Santa Maria del Pi
Catedral
Museu Frederic Marès
Saló del Tinell
Plaça del Rei
Palau Reial Major
Casa del Cànonges
Palau de la Generalitat
Temple d'August
Museu d'Història de la Ciutat
Mercat Santa Caterina
Gran Teatre del Liceu
LA RAMBLA
C/FERRAN
C/JAUME I
Jaume I
VIA LAIETANA
C/PRINCESA
Ajuntament (Casa de la Ciutat)
Sants Just i Pastor
Plaça Reial
Museu Tèxtil
Museu Picasso
Museu Barbier-Mueller
Antic Mercat del Born
BORN
C/ARGENTERIA
Santa Maria del Mar
PASSEIG DEL BORN
Palau Güell
Pati Llimona
Correus (Post Office)
La Mercè Church
Capitania General
Centre d'Art Sta. Mònica
Drassanes
Museu de Cera
Comandancia de Marina
Govern Militar
La Llotja
PASSEIG ISABEL II
AVDA MARQUÈS DE L'ARGENTERA
Delegació del Govern
Estació de França
Escola de Nàutica
PASSEIG JOAN DE BORBÓ
Barceloneta
PASSEIG COLOM
RONDA LITORAL
MOLL DE LA FUSTA
Monument a Colom
PASSEIG CARNER
Moll d'Espanya
Marina Port Vell
Palau de Mar (Museu d'Història de Catalunya)
Tunnel
A
B
C
D
E
F
5
6
7
8

# Around Barcelona

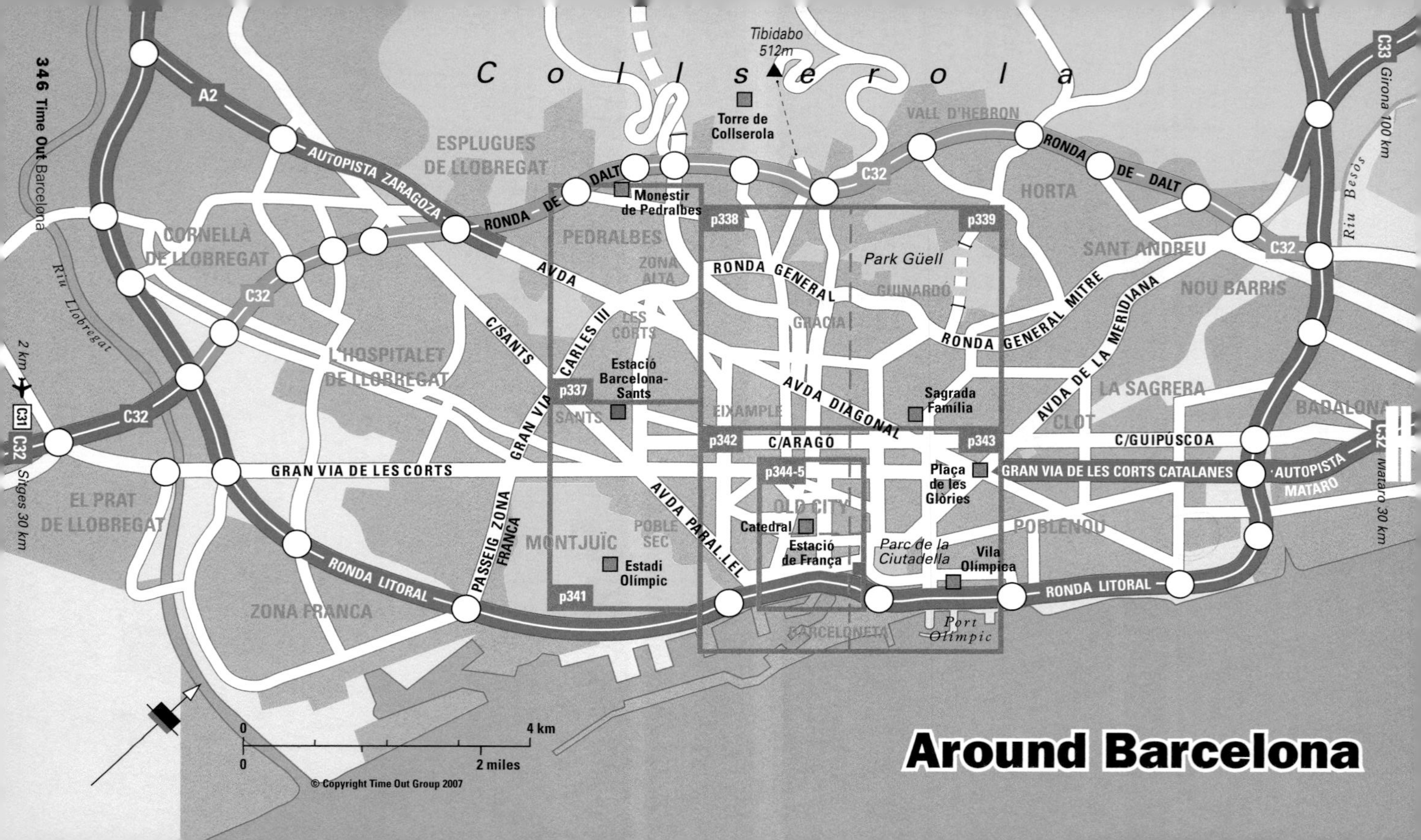

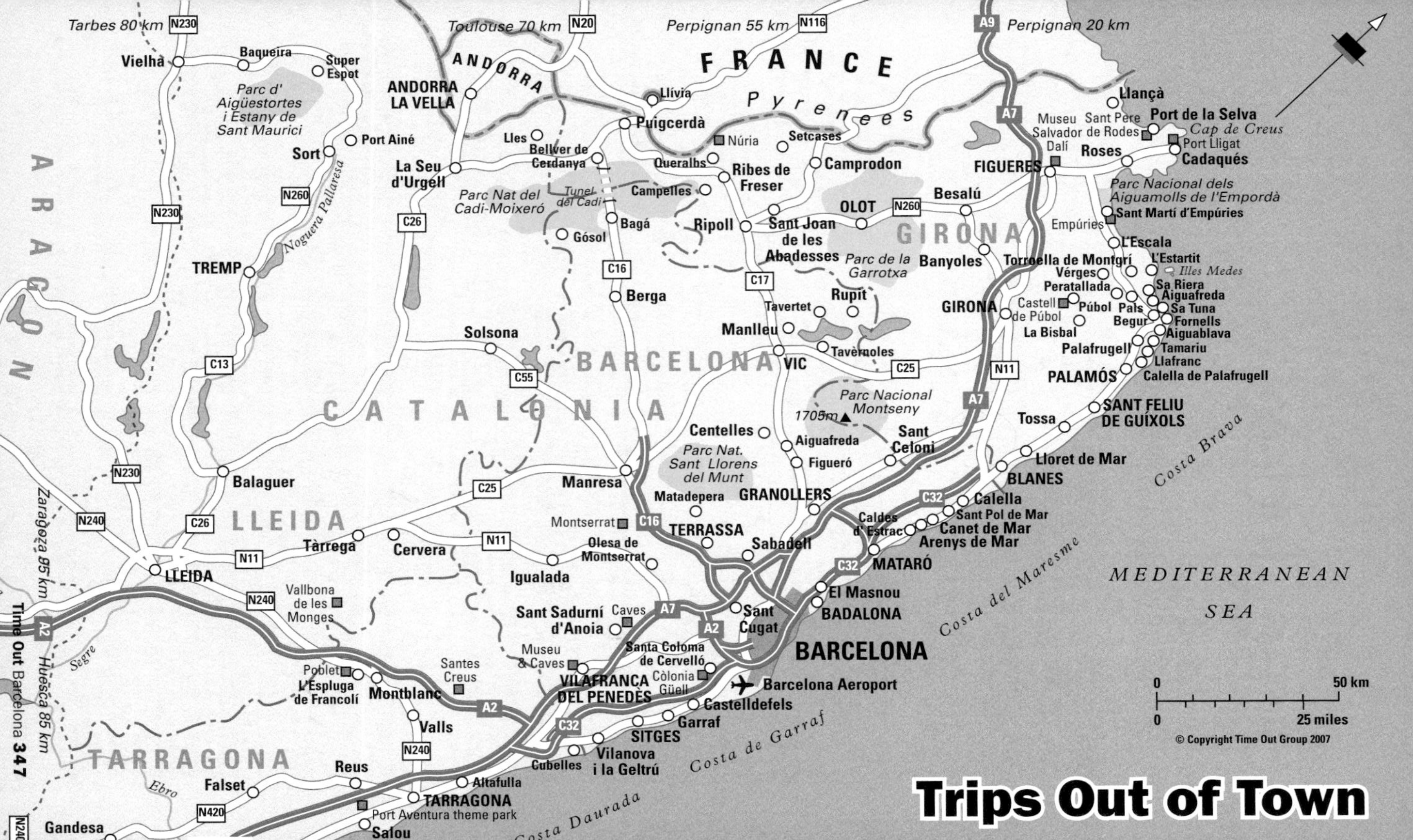

Trips Out of Town
FRANCE
ANDORRA
ARAGON
CATALONIA
GIRONA
BARCELONA
LLEIDA
TARRAGONA
Pyrenees
MEDITERRANEAN SEA
Costa Brava
Costa del Maresme
Costa de Garraf
Costa Daurada
Tarbes 80 km
Toulouse 70 km
Perpignan 55 km
Perpignan 20 km
Zaragoza 85 km
Huesca 85 km
Vielha
Baqueira
Super Espot
Parc d' Aigüestortes i Estany de Sant Maurici
Port Ainé
Sort
Noguera Pallaresa
TREMP
Balaguer
LLEIDA
Tàrrega
Cervera
ANDORRA LA VELLA
La Seu d'Urgell
Lles
Bellver de Cerdanya
Parc Nat del Cadí-Moixeró
Tunel del Cadí
Gósol
Bagá
Campelles
Puigcerdà
Llívia
Núria
Queralbs
Ribes de Freser
Setcases
Camprodon
Ripoll
Sant Joan de les Abadesses
OLOT
Parc de la Garrotxa
Besalú
Banyoles
Berga
Solsona
Manresa
Tavertet
Rupit
Manlleu
Tavèrnoles
VIC
Parc Nacional Montseny
1705m
Centelles
Aiguafreda
Figueró
Sant Celoni
Parc Nat. Sant Llorens del Munt
Matadepera
GRANOLLERS
TERRASSA
Sabadell
Montserrat
Olesa de Montserrat
Igualada
Sant Sadurní d'Anoia
Caves
Sant Cugat
BARCELONA
Barcelona Aeroport
Santa Coloma de Cervelló
Colònia Güell
Museu & Caves
VILAFRANCA DEL PENEDÈS
Castelldefels
Garraf
SITGES
Vilanova i la Geltrú
Cubelles
Vallbona de les Monges
Poblet
L'Espluga de Francolí
Santes Creus
Montblanc
Valls
Reus
Falset
Altafulla
TARRAGONA
Port Aventura theme park
Salou
Gandesa
Ebro
Segre
Cinca
FIGUERES
Museu Salvador Dalí
Sant Pere de Rodes
Llançà
Port de la Selva
Cap de Creus
Port Lligat
Cadaqués
Roses
Parc Nacional dels Aiguamolls de l'Empordà
Empúries
Sant Martí d'Empúries
L'Escala
L'Estartit
Illes Medes
Torroella de Montgrí
Vérges
Peratallada
Castell de Púbol
Púbol
Pals
Sa Riera
Aiguafreda
Sa Tuna
Fornells
Begur
Aiguablava
Tamariu
Llafranc
Calella de Palafrugell
GIRONA
La Bisbal
Palafrugell
PALAMÓS
SANT FELIU DE GUÍXOLS
Tossa
Lloret de Mar
BLANES
Calella
Sant Pol de Mar
Canet de Mar
Arenys de Mar
Caldes d'Estrac
MATARÓ
El Masnou
BADALONA
A9
A7
A2
C32
C16
C17
C25
C26
C13
C55
N11
N20
N116
N230
N240
N260
N420
0
50 km
0
25 miles
© Copyright Time Out Group 2007

# Street Index

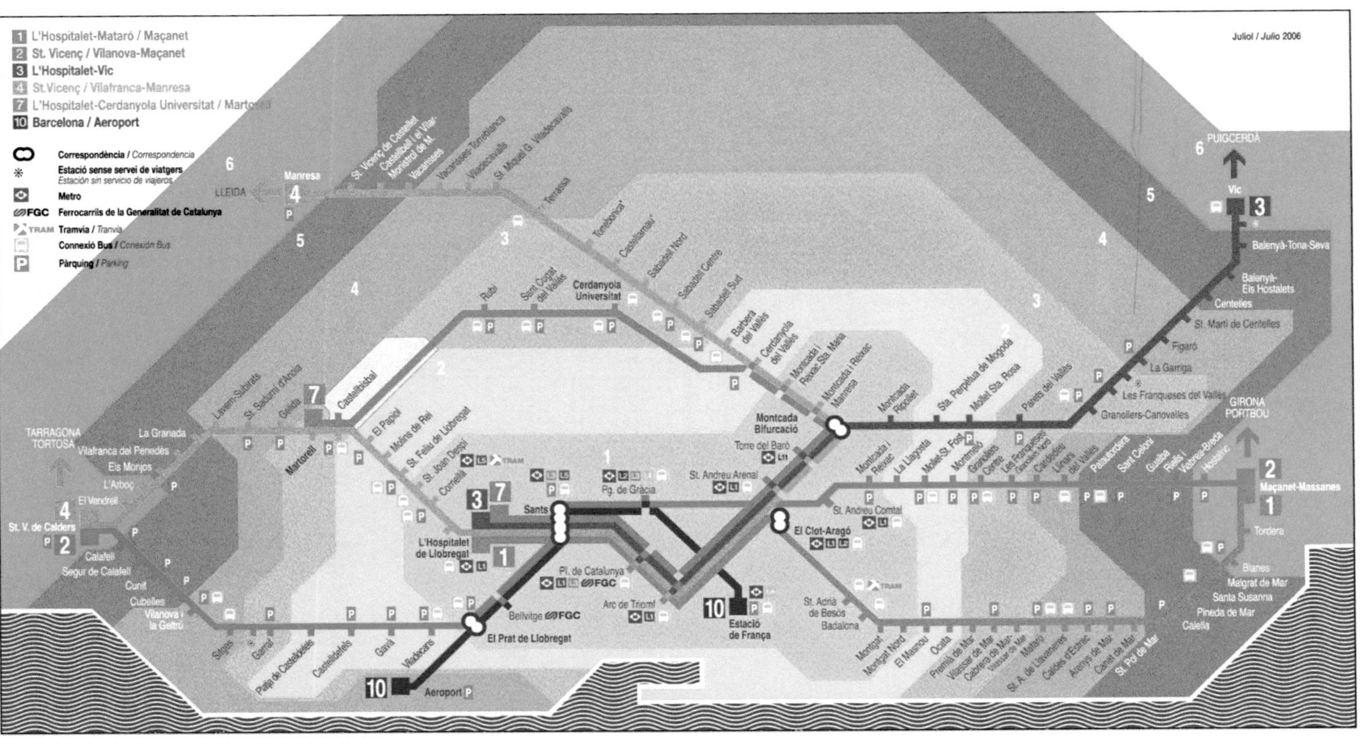
1 L'Hospitalet-Mataró / Maçanet
2 St. Vicenç / Vilanova-Maçanet
3 L'Hospitalet-Vic
4 St.Vicenç / Vilafranca-Manresa
7 L'Hospitalet-Cerdanyola Universitat / Martorell
10 Barcelona / Aeroport
Correspondència / Correspondencia
Estació sense servei de viatgers
Estación sin servicio de viajeros
Metro
FGC Ferrocarrils de la Generalitat de Catalunya
TRAM Tramvia / Tranvía
Connexió Bus / Conexión Bus
Pàrquing / Parking
Juliol / Julio 2006
PUIGCERDÀ
Vic
Balenyà-Tona-Seva
Balenyà-Els Hostalets
Centelles
St. Martí de Centelles
Figaró
La Garriga
Les Franqueses del Vallès
Granollers-Canovelles
GIRONA
PORTBOU
Maçanet-Massanes
Tordera
Blanes
Malgrat de Mar
Santa Susanna
Pineda de Mar
Calella
LLEIDA
Manresa
Terrassa
Sabadell Nord
Sabadell Centre
Sabadell Sud
Barberà del Vallès
Cerdanyola del Vallès
Cerdanyola Universitat
Rubí
Sant Cugat del Vallès
Montcada Bifurcació
Montcada Ripollet
Sta. Perpètua de Mogoda
Mollet Sta. Rosa
Parets del Vallès
Torre del Baró
St. Andreu Arenal
St. Andreu Comtal
El Clot-Aragó
Pg. de Gràcia
Pl. de Catalunya
Arc de Triomf
Sants
L'Hospitalet de Llobregat
Bellvitge
El Prat de Llobregat
Aeroport
Estació de França
St. Adrià de Besòs
Badalona
Montgat
Montgat Nord
El Masnou
Ocata
Premià de Mar
Vilassar de Mar
Cabrera de Mar-Vilassar de Mar
Mataró
St. A. de Llavaneres
Caldes d'Estrac
Arenys de Mar
Canet de Mar
St. Pol de Mar
Martorell
Castellbisbal
El Papiol
Molins de Rei
St. Feliu de Llobregat
St. Joan Despí
Cornellà
TARRAGONA
TORTOSA
La Granada
Vilafranca del Penedès
Els Monjos
L'Arboç
El Vendrell
St. V. de Calders
Calafell
Segur de Calafell
Cunit
Cubelles
Vilanova i la Geltrú
Sitges
Garraf
Platja de Castelldefels
Castelldefels
Gavà
Viladecans

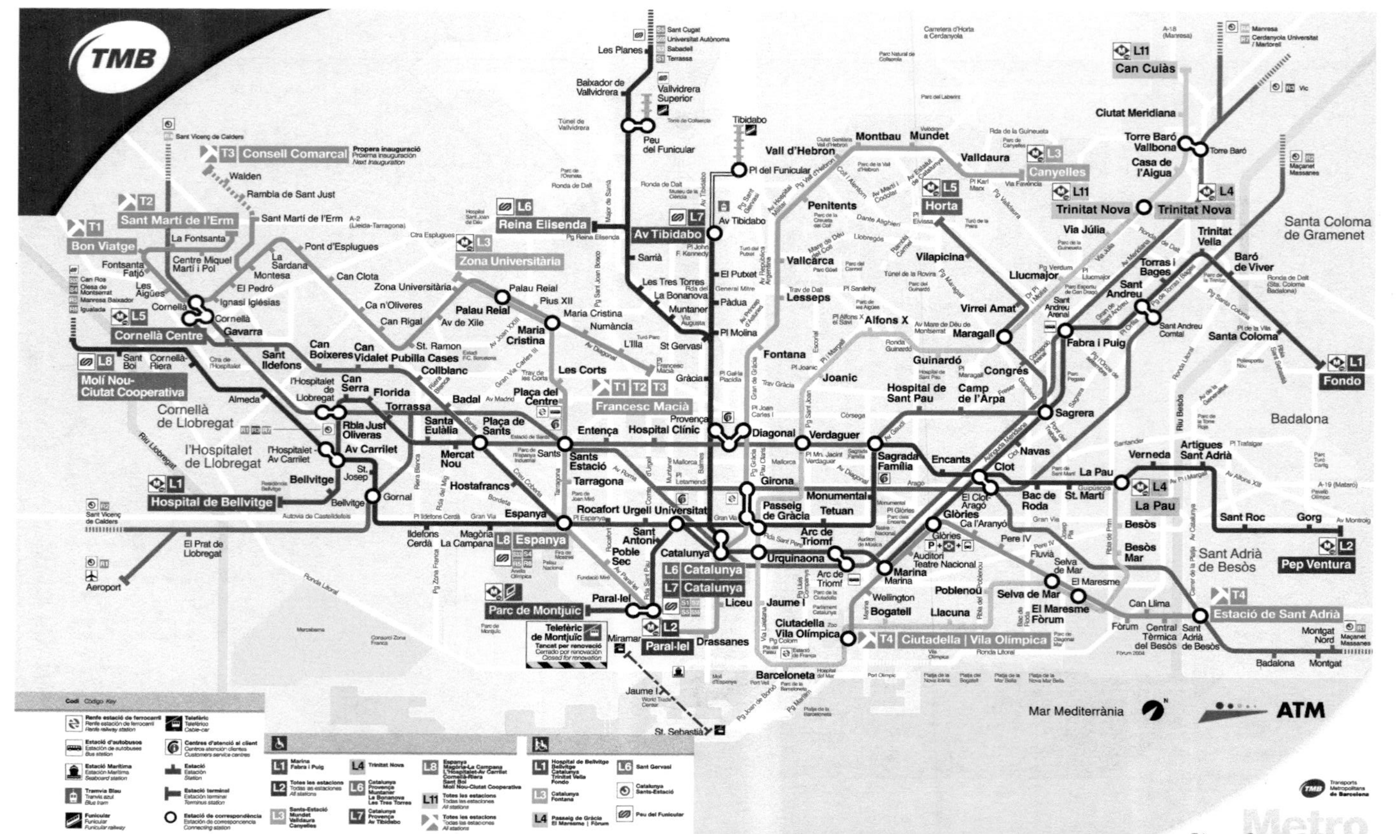
TMB
ATM
Metro
Mar Mediterrània
Badalona
Santa Coloma de Gramenet
Sant Adrià de Besòs
Cornellà de Llobregat
l'Hospitalet de Llobregat
Catalunya
Sagrada Família
Espanya
Sants Estació
Diagonal
Passeig de Gràcia
Parc de Montjuïc
Telefèric de Montjuïc
Tancat per renovació
Cerrado por renovación
Closed for renovation
Hospital de Bellvitge
Fondo
Trinitat Nova
Pep Ventura
Reina Elisenda
Av Tibidabo
Paral·lel
Estació de Sant Adrià
Ciutadella | Vila Olímpica
Francesc Macià
Zona Universitària
Molí Nou-Ciutat Cooperativa
Consell Comarcal
Propera inauguració
Próxima inauguración
Next inauguration
Codi Código Key